# America Today

## Political Theory and Practical Politics

First Edition

Edited by Antonio Campbell
*Towson University*

cognella®
academic publishing

Bassim Hamadeh, CEO and Publisher
Michael Simpson, Vice President of Acquisitions
Jamie Giganti, Managing Editor
Jess Busch, Graphic Design Supervisor
Amy Stone, Acquisitions Editor
Sarah Wheeler, Senior Project Editor/Interior Design
Alexa Lucido, Licensing Associate

Printed in the United States of America

ISBN: 978-1-63189-098-7 (pbk)/ 978-1-63189-099-4 (br)

www.cognella.com    800-200-3908

# Contents

# APPENDIX

# Preface

*Study the past if you would define the future.*
—*Confucius* (551 BC–479 BC)

The study of politics, in twenty-first-century America, is interpreted by the policies of governments and the actions of individual men. The experts of our time employ themselves in the guesswork of opinion and observation of the events of the day and who is winning and losing political skirmishes through broadcast media such as print and television and, yes, even at times through blogs on the Internet. In the era of the unending news cycle, these personalities have carved out a living (some of them very comfortable) by appearing to give answers as to what people in power are doing instead of asking the more important question of why are they doing it.

*America Today: Political Theory and Practical Politics* is written in an attempt to bridge the gap between small events and the big questions.

America, since the events of September 11, 2001, has changed significantly in terms of the obligations of what it means to be a citizen. From airport screenings performed by the Transportation Security Administration (TSA) to wiretaps of cellular communications by the National Security Administration (NSA), the relationship between the governed and the government has caused concern among liberals, libertarians, and, yes, even conservatives.

These concerns about the role of government are not a new phenomenon. Questions concerning the role and scope of government, as well as the balance between the safety of the community and the personal liberty of the individual, go all the way back to the philosopher Plato in ancient Greece. The seeds of democracy were planted in Greece and spread through history to connect a lineage of political thought that has culminated in the American political experience.

Citizens of the United States and most nation-states that have emerged from Western political thought have an emotional connection to the concepts identified as freedom, liberty, rights of the people, and self-determination. Many of these people will defend these concepts with their very lives. However, these concepts have existed in the relationship of the governed and the government for only the last four hundred years of human history.

It is important to mention this fact again—all the ideas we hold to be normal in the United States have existed in the world only for fewer than four hundred years. For most of human history, people were ruled by a king, a pharaoh, a caesar, or some other type of power structure where one person (or small group of people) held all the rights while the ordinary person had none. How did this change occur? What ideas were introduced to cause this significant shift in power? What lessons can we learn from these ideas in twenty-first-century America?

In the pages of this book, the writings of the greatest minds of Western political theory will be explored. The ideas of the past are crucial to take into account as we seek to ask the big questions of *why people make the decisions they do* instead of the easy question of *what is happening to us.*

The quote from Confucius at the beginning of this preface is a launching point into the convergence of political theory and practical politics: only by studying the important writings of the past can we clearly chart a path to a brighter future.

Antonio Campbell
Towson, Maryland

# Introduction

In the twenty-first century, in an age of the unending news cycle, a seemingly limitless number of cable television news networks have cropped up over the last twenty years, including one that calls itself "the place for politics." Politics in an age of pundits and experts has been reduced to who is doing what to whom. This warped idea of politics has reduced policymaking to a facsimile of an episode of a soap opera or, worse yet, a really bad reality show.

The purpose of this text, *America Today: Political Theory and Practical Politics*, is to return the discussion of politics and policymaking to a real conversation of *how and why* instead of just *what and whom.*

In the heated dialogue over the path that would be charted by the republic known as the United States of America, serious debates took place dealing with the relationship between the governed and the people who are enabled to make policy for them, meaning the government. In these public discussions, the Federalists and the anti-Federalists made their arguments for and against the proposed Constitution of the United States. These educated citizens were engaged in a serious discussion about the nature of politics in our society.

For the purpose of this text, *politics* has two meanings: (1) how people *should* live together in society and (2) the relationship between the governed and the government.

The first point is prescriptive—how people should live together in society. The Declaration of Independence states the following: "We hold these truths to be self-evident, *that all men are created equal,* that they are endowed by their Creator with certain unalienable Rights, that among these are Life, Liberty and the pursuit of Happiness" (italics added). It is the part that is italicized that is prescriptive. We cannot prove that all men are created equal; clearly, in the history of mankind, men and women have not been equal. It is the will of political decision making that we try to create a society in which all men are *treated equally.* It is a goal that through our political enterprise we will shape a society that will treat all men as equals.

The second point deals with the relationship between men. This relationship manifests itself through the concept of power. Simply put, one person or group has power; the rest do not. Power has always existed between individuals. Power goes all the way back to the alpha male with the biggest club back in the time of the caveman. Our focus, however, is power that is formalized in a form of government that places one person over another.

For most of human history, power has come from the gods or a deity. In Western political thought, the idea of the divine right of kings comes from the ordaining of human authority by God. This idea of the divine blessing of the Judeo-Christian God goes from King David in ancient Israel to "God Bless the Queen" in modern Great Britain.

From ancient times to the seventeenth century, the blessing of a human by the gods (or God) was the most important aspect of legitimacy that a ruler needed. In the seventeenth and eighteenth centuries, a dramatic shift occurred that redistributed the power balance to favor the people over the king. The writings of John Locke, and later those of Thomas Jefferson (who altered Locke's words of "life, liberty and estate" to "life, liberty and the pursuit of happiness"), were the spark that lit the flame to two civil wars that fundamentally changed the power relationship between the governed and their government.

Connected to the concept of power and its impact on political relationships is the question of rights. The thesis is that the person or group that holds the power in society generally also holds the rights within the society. For example, if the people are ruled by an emperor or pharaoh, the ruler would have all the rights, and his subjects would virtually have no rights. For most of human history, rulers had all the political rights in their realm. With the introduction of Aristotle's citizenship, the ancient Greeks and their Roman counterparts expanded the breadth of political rights to a type of nobility, including, in the Roman example, the Roman senate and its senators.

In 1215, the Magna Carta allowed the English nobility to begin the process of limiting the arbitrary authority of the king. The process would take another six centuries to complete the transfer of rights from the king to the people. The English Civil War (John Locke and Thomas Hobbes) and the French Revolution (Rousseau) were pivotal events in the movement of sovereignty from a ruler who is blessed by the Gods to a system that recognizes that the people should be trusted to rule themselves.

In the American experiment with representative democracy, the Federalist Papers were opinioned based editorials (op-eds) written by supporters and detractors of a centralized national government that would be equal with the thirteen states. This federal system of government, where the states and the national government hold equal levels of sovereignty, was brought into being by several compromises including the addition of the Bill of Rights as the first ten amendments to the Constitution of the United States.

The addition of the Bill of Rights to the Constitution was a major win for the anti-Federalists and was designed to protect the rights of the people and the states from an overbearing national government. For about 175 years, outside from national crises such as the Civil War and two World Wars, the balance of sovereignty between the people and the government maintained a comfortable equilibrium.

Over the past sixty years, a dramatic shift has taken place in the concept of political rights; the advent of placing the importance of individual rights over the will of the majority. In the case of Brown v. the Board of Education, the Supreme Court decided that segregation of educational resources was unconstitutional. It would be hard to prove that the majority of the American population in 1953 thought that mixing races in public schools was a good idea. In 1973, a similar scenario occurred with the landmark Supreme Court case, *Roe v. Wade*. Again, the decision dramatically moved to the pendulum of rights from the people to the individual.

The shift from majority rule to an emphasis on the rights of the individual is a dramatic change from the idea of political rights that has occurred only in the last century of human existence. Phrases that are part of our modern political dictionary, such as "civil rights," "equal opportunity," "affirmative action," and "universal suffrage" have been in place only for the last one hundred years. How has the change happened so quickly and without major disruptions to our country? The vehicle for this change is called the "social contract."

A *social contract*, according to *Merriam-Webster's Collegiate Dictionary*, means "an actual or hypothetical agreement among the members of an organized society or between a community and its ruler that defines and limits the rights and duties of each."[1] In short, individuals agree to give up part of their natural liberty to join a society. If the society feels inclined to change the parameters of rights to benefit a minority group (e.g., African Americans, women, gays, lesbians), as a member of that society, you will honor that change. In several states, marriage equality (or civil marriage) was passed by a majority of the voters. It is the legitimacy of the social contract that allows for the citizens to accept this change in political and legal rights, even though they may be personally opposed to the change.

Circling back to the initial conversation of the prescriptive nature of politics, as political scientists, one of the key questions of philosophy is *how men should organize their societies.*

---

1  http://www.merriam-webster.com/dictionary/social%20contract

It is a question of what *ought to be*, rather than what *is*. In America today, there are two major ideological points of view: liberal (Democrats) and conservative (Republicans). Through all of the talking-head shows on cable news networks, both sides are debating or making a case for their view of a question that has been around since the beginning of Western political philosophy in ancient Greece: *what should be the role of government in helping humans achieve their higher purpose?*

Throughout history, the writers of philosophical and political works have asked this question. Often, their writings exposed questions that bothered the status quo of political power in their society. Some of these philosophers paid for their ideas with persecution and the loss of their very lives. In these works, societal constructs such as gender, justice, and equality are examined as well as the fundamental nature of human beings.

It is a central question of human nature where this introduction will end to transition to the writings of the theorists contained within this text. In their writings, the philosophers were presenting their arguments for why their world should change and how they wanted it to change. In ancient Greece, Plato penned an indictment of democracy, the media, and pundits ("The Allegory of the Cave") that is as true today as it was more than two thousand years ago.

What should be the proper role of government? How should we organize it? Is a Congress with two houses, a presidency, and a Supreme Court the way to go, or should it be changed? What is the relationship of politics to other segments of our society—religion, education, economics, and so on?

These questions, along with ascertaining whether human beings are good or bad, are the tools used by political philosophers to go from the status quo of *what is* to the promised land of *what ought to be.*

All the works enclosed in this text have truths that resonate within our political structure today. Aristotle shares the importance of the expansion of the middle class and how the polis is strengthened if everyone can share in what has come to be known as the American Dream. Augustine lays the foundation of the separation of church and state when he introduces the concepts of the heavenly and earthly cities.

Machiavelli presents a guidebook for future leaders as they navigate the waters of politics by balancing their public perception versus their private ambitions. Martin Luther explains the proper role of faith and thereby sets the wheels in motion to break the hold of the papacy over secular human government in Western Europe. John Locke redefines sovereignty as coming from a legislative branch of government, with the executive branch being tasked to carry out those laws.

In studying the works of the writers mentioned above, as well as the other excerpts that are presented in this text, the reader will be able to see beyond the smokescreen curtain of what happened to whom in today's political skirmishes to consider the bigger questions of why and how the decisions are being made.

Welcome to *America Today: Political Theory and Practical Politics*. The path toward freedom and liberty has taken more than twenty centuries to get to us; the purpose of this academic journey is to help us understand the present by showing appreciation for the past.

# The Republic

By Plato

## Book I

### Justice as the Interest of the Stronger

Glaucon and the rest of the company joined in my request and Thrasymachus, as any one might see, was in reality eager to speak; for he thought that he had an excellent answer, and would distinguish himself. But at first he to insist on my answering; at length he consented to begin. Behold, he said, the wisdom of Socrates; he refuses to teach himself, and goes about learning of others, to whom he never even says thank you.

That I learn of others, I replied, is quite true; but that I am ungrateful I wholly deny. Money I have none, and therefore I pay in praise, which is all I have: and how ready I am to praise any one who appears to me to speak well you will very soon find out when you answer; for I expect that you will answer well.

Listen, then, he said; I proclaim that justice is nothing else than the interest of the stronger. And now why do you not me? But of course you won't.

Let me first understand you, I replied. justice, as you say, is the interest of the stronger. What, Thrasymachus, is the meaning of this? You cannot mean to say that because Polydamas, the pancratiast, is stronger than we are, and finds the eating of beef conducive to his bodily strength, that to eat beef is therefore equally for our good who are weaker than he is, and right and just for us?

That's abominable of you, Socrates; you take the words in the sense which is most damaging to the argument.

Not at all, my good sir, I said; I am trying to understand them; and I wish that you would be a little clearer.

Well, he said, have you never heard that forms of government differ; there are tyrannies, and there are democracies, and there are aristocracies?

Yes, I know.

And the government is the ruling power in each state?

Certainly.

And the different forms of government make laws democratical, aristocratical, tyrannical, with a view to their several interests; and these laws, which are made by them for their own interests, are the justice which they deliver to their subjects, and him who transgresses them they punish as a breaker of the law, and unjust. And that is what I mean when I say that in all states there is the same principle of justice, which is the interest of the government; and as the government must be supposed to have power, the only reasonable conclusion is, that everywhere there is one principle of justice, which is the interest of the stronger.

Now I understand you, I said; and whether you are right or not I will try to discover. But let me remark, that in defining justice you have yourself used the word 'interest' which you forbade me to use. It is true, however, that in your definition the words 'of the stronger' are added.

A small addition, you must allow, he said.

Great or small, never mind about that: we must first enquire whether what you are saying is the truth. Now we are both agreed that justice is interest of some sort, but you go on to say 'of the stronger'; about this addition I am not so sure, and must therefore consider further.

Proceed.

I will; and first tell me, Do you admit that it is just or subjects to obey their rulers?

I do.

But are the rulers of states absolutely infallible, or are they sometimes liable to err?

To be sure, he replied, they are liable to err.

Then in making their laws they may sometimes make them rightly, and sometimes not?

True.

When they make them rightly, they make them agreeably to their interest; when they are mistaken, contrary to their interest; you admit that?

Yes.

And the laws which they make must be obeyed by their subjects,—and that is what you call justice?

Doubtless.

Then justice, according to your argument, is not only obedience to the interest of the stronger but the reverse?

What is that you are saying? he asked.

I am only repeating what you are saying, I believe. But let us consider: Have we not admitted that the rulers may be mistaken about their own interest in what they command, and also that to obey them is justice? Has not that been admitted?

Yes.

Then you must also have acknowledged justice not to be for the interest of the stronger, when the rulers unintentionally command things to be done which are to their own injury. For if, as you say, justice is the obedience which the subject renders to their commands, in that case, O wisest of men, is there any escape from the conclusion that the weaker are commanded to do, not what is for the interest, but what is for the injury of the stronger?

Nothing can be clearer, Socrates, said Polemarchus.

### Socrates—CLEITOPHON— POLEMARCHUS —THRASYMACHUS

Yes, said Cleitophon, interposing, if you are allowed to be his witness.

But there is no need of any witness, said Polemarchus, for Thrasymachus himself acknowledges that rulers may sometimes command what is not for their own interest, and that for subjects to obey them is justice.

Yes, Polemarchus,—Thrasymachus said that for subjects to do what was commanded by their rulers is just.

Yes, Cleitophon, but he also said that justice is the interest of the stronger, and, while admitting both these propositions, he further acknowledged that the stronger may command the weaker who are his subjects to do what is not for his own interest; whence follows that justice is the injury quite as much as the interest of the stronger.

But, said Cleitophon, he meant by the interest of the stronger what the stronger thought to be his interest,—this was what the weaker had to do; and this was affirmed by him to be justice.

Those were not his words, rejoined Polemarchus.

*Socrates—THRASYMACHUS*

Never mind, I replied, if he now says that they are, let us accept his statement. Tell me, Thrasymachus, I said, did you mean by justice what the stronger thought to be his interest, whether really so or not?

Certainly not, he said. Do you suppose that I call him who is mistaken the stronger at the time when he is mistaken?

Yes, I said, my impression was that you did so, when you admitted that the ruler was not infallible but might be sometimes mistaken.

You argue like an informer, Socrates. Do you mean, for example, that he who is mistaken about the sick is a physician in that he is mistaken? or that he who errs in arithmetic or grammar is an arithmetician or grammarian at the me when he is making the mistake, in respect of the mistake? True, we say that the physician or arithmetician or grammarian has made a mistake, but this is only a way of speaking; for the fact is that neither the grammarian nor any other person of skill ever makes a mistake in so far as he is what his name implies; they none of them err unless their skill fails them, and then they cease to be skilled artists. No artist or sage or ruler errs at the time when he is what his name implies; though he is commonly said to err, and I adopted the common mode of speaking. But to be perfectly accurate, since you are such a lover of accuracy, we should say that the ruler, in so far as he is the ruler, is unerring, and, being unerring, always commands that which is for his own interest; and the subject is required to execute his commands; and therefore, as I said at first and now repeat, justice is the interest of the stronger.

# Book V

## Guardians in the Role of Women

Well, I replied, I suppose that I must retrace my steps and say what I perhaps ought to have said before in the proper place. The part of the men has been played out, and now properly enough comes the turn of the women. Of them I will proceed to speak, and the more readily since I am invited by you.

For men born and educated like our citizens, the only way, in my opinion, of arriving at a right conclusion about the possession and use of women and children is to follow the path on which we originally started, when we said that the men were to be the guardians and watchdogs of the herd.

True.

Let us further suppose the birth and education of our women to be subject to similar or nearly similar regulations; then we shall see whether the result accords with our design.

What do you mean?

What I mean may be put into the form of a question, I said: Are dogs divided into hes and shes, or do they both share equally in hunting and in keeping watch and in the other duties of dogs? or do we entrust to the males the entire and exclusive care of the flocks, while we leave the females at home, under the idea that the bearing and suckling their puppies is labour enough for them?

No, he said, they share alike; the only difference between them is that the males are stronger and the females weaker.

But can you use different animals for the same purpose, unless they are bred and fed in the same way?

You cannot.

Then, if women are to have the same duties as men, they must have the same nurture and education?

Yes.

The education which was assigned to the men was music and gymnastic. Yes.

Then women must be taught music and gymnastic and also the art of war, which they must practise like the men?

That is the inference, I suppose.

I should rather expect, I said, that several of our proposals, if they are carried out, being unusual, may appear ridiculous.

No doubt of it.

Yes, and the most ridiculous thing of all will be the sight of women naked in the palaestra, exercising with the men, especially when they are no longer young; they certainly will not be a vision of beauty, any more than the enthusiastic old men who in spite of wrinkles and ugliness continue to frequent the gymnasia.

Yes, indeed, he said: according to present notions the proposal would be thought ridiculous.

But then, I said, as we have determined to speak our minds, we must not fear the jests of the wits which will be directed against this sort of innovation; how they will talk of women's attainments both in music and gymnastic, and above all about their wearing armour and riding upon horseback!

Very true, he replied.

Yet having begun we must go forward to the rough places of the law; at the same time begging of these gentlemen for once in their life to be serious. Not long ago, as we shall remind them, the Hellenes were of the opinion, which is still generally received among the barbarians, that the sight of a naked man was ridiculous and improper; and when first the Cretans and then the Lacedaemonians introduced the custom, the wits of that day might equally have ridiculed the innovation.

No doubt.

But when experience showed that to let all things be uncovered was far better than to cover them up, and the ludicrous effect to the outward eye vanished before the better principle which reason asserted, then the man was perceived to be a fool who directs the shaft s of his ridicule at any other sight but that of folly and vice, or seriously inclines to weigh the beautiful by any other standard but that of the good.

Very true, he replied.

First, then, whether the question is to be put in jest or in earnest, let us come to an understanding about the nature of woman: Is she capable of sharing either wholly or partially in the actions of men, or not at all? And is the art of war one of those arts in which she can or can not share? That will be the best way of commencing the enquiry, and will probably lead to the fairest conclusion.

That will be much the best way.

Shall we take the other side first and begin by arguing against ourselves; in this manner the adversary's position will not be undefended.

Why not? he said.

Then let us put a speech into the mouths of our opponents. They will say: 'Socrates and Glaucon, no adversary need convict you, for you yourselves, at the first foundation of the State, admitted the principle that everybody was to do the one work suited to his own nature.' And certainly, if I am not mistaken, such an admission was made by us. 'And do not the natures of men and women differ very much indeed?' And we shall reply: Of course they do. Then we shall be asked, 'Whether the tasks assigned to men and to women should not be different, and such as are agreeable to their different natures?' Certainly they should. 'But if so, have you not fallen into a serious inconsistency in saying that men and women, whose natures are so entirely different, ought to perform the same actions?'—What defence will you make for us, my good Sir, against any one who offers these objections?

That is not an easy question to answer when asked suddenly; and I shall and I do beg of you to draw out the case on our side.

These are the objections, Glaucon, and there are many others of a like kind, which I foresaw long ago; they made me afraid and reluctant to take in hand any law about the possession and nurture of women and children.

By Zeus, he said, the problem to be solved is anything but easy.

Why yes, I said, but the fact is that when a man is out of his depth, whether he has fallen into a little swimming bath or into mid-ocean, he has to swim all the same.

Very true.

And must not we swim and try to reach the shore: we will hope that Arion's dolphin or some other miraculous help may save us?

I suppose so, he said.

Well then, let us see if any way of escape can be found. We acknowledged—did we not? that different natures ought to have different pursuits, and that men's and women's natures are different. And now what are we saying?— that different natures ought to have the same pursuits,—this is the inconsistency which is charged upon us.

Precisely.

Verily, Glaucon, I said, glorious is the power of the art of contradiction!

Why do you say so?

Because I think that many a man falls into the practice against his will. When he thinks that he is reasoning he is really disputing, just because he cannot define and divide, and so know that of which he is speaking; and he will pursue a merely verbal opposition in the spirit of contention and not of fair discussion.

Yes, he replied, such is very oft en the case; but what has that to do with us and our argument?

A great deal; for there is certainly a danger of our getting unintentionally into a verbal opposition.

In what way?

Why, we valiantly and pugnaciously insist upon the verbal truth, that different natures ought to have different pursuits, but we never considered at all what was the meaning of sameness or difference of nature, or why we distinguished them when we assigned different pursuits to different natures and the same to the same natures.

Why, no, he said, that was never considered by us.

I said: Suppose that by way of illustration we were to ask the question whether there is not an opposition in nature between bald men and hairy men; and if this is admitted by us, then, if bald men are cobblers, we should forbid the hairy men to be cobblers, and conversely?

That would be a jest, he said.

Yes, I said, a jest; and why? because we never meant when we constructed the State, that the opposition of natures should extend to every difference, but only to those differences which affected the pursuit in which the individual is engaged; we should have argued, for example, that a physician and one who is in mind a physician may be said to have the same nature.

True.

Whereas the physician and the carpenter have different natures?

Certainly.

And if, I said, the male and female sex appear to differ in their fitness for any art or pursuit, we should say that such pursuit or art ought to be assigned to one or the other of them; but if the difference consists only in women bearing and men begetting children, this does not amount to a proof that a woman differs from a man in respect of the sort of education she should receive; and we shall therefore continue to maintain that our guardians and their wives ought to have the same pursuits.

Very true, he said.

Next, we shall ask our opponent how, in reference to any of the pursuits or arts of civic life, the nature of a woman differs from that of a man?

That will be quite fair.

And perhaps he, like yourself, will reply that to give a sufficient answer on the instant is not easy; but after a little reflection there is no difficulty.

Yes, perhaps.

Suppose then that we invite him to accompany us in the argument, and then we may hope to show him that there is nothing peculiar in the constitution of women which would affect them in the administration of the State.

By all means.

Let us say to him: Come now, and we will ask you a question:—when you spoke of a nature gifted or not gifted in any respect, did you mean to say that one man will acquire a thing easily, another with difficulty; a little learning will lead the one to discover a great deal; whereas the other, after much study and application, no sooner learns than he forgets; or again, did you mean, that the one has a body which is a good servant to his mind, while the body of the other is a hindrance to him?—would not these be the sort of differences which distinguish the man gifted by nature from the one who is ungifted?

No one will deny that.

And can you mention any pursuit of mankind in which the male sex has not all these gift s and qualities in a higher degree than the female? Need I waste time in speaking of the art of weaving, and the management of pancakes and preserves, in which womankind does really appear to be great, and in which for her to be beaten by a man is of all things the most absurd?

You are quite right, he replied, in maintaining the general inferiority of the female sex: although many women are in many things superior to many men, yet on the whole what you say is true.

And if so, my friend, I said, there is no special faculty of administration in a state which a woman has because she is a woman, or which a man has by virtue of his sex, but the gift s of nature are alike diffused in both; all the pursuits of men are the pursuits of women also, but in all of them a woman is inferior to a man.

Very true.

Then are we to impose all our enactments on men and none of them on women?

That will never do.

One woman has a gift of healing, another not; one is a musician, and another has no music in her nature?

Very true.

And one woman has a turn for gymnastic and military exercises, and another is unwarlike and hates gymnastics?

Certainly.

And one woman is a philosopher, and another is an enemy of philosophy; one has spirit, and another is without spirit?

That is also true.

Then one woman will have the temper of a guardian, and another not. Was not the selection of the male guardians determined by differences of this sort?

Yes.

Men and women alike possess the qualities which make a guardian; they differ only in their comparative strength or weakness.

Obviously.

And those women who have such qualities are to be selected as the companions and colleagues of men who have similar qualities and whom they resemble in capacity and in character?

Very true.

And ought not the same natures to have the same pursuits?

They ought.

Then, as we were saying before, there is nothing unnatural in assigning music and gymnastic to the wives of the guardians—to that point we come round again.

Certainly not.

The law which we then enacted was agreeable to nature, and therefore not an impossibility or mere aspiration; and the contrary practice, which prevails at present, is in reality a violation of nature.

That appears to be true.

We had to consider, first, whether our proposals were possible, and secondly whether they were the most beneficial?

Yes.

And the possibility has been acknowledged?

Yes.

The very great benefit has next to be established?

Quite so.

You will admit that the same education which makes a man a good guardian will make a woman a good guardian; for their original nature is the same?

Yes.

I should like to ask you a question.

What is it?

Would you say that all men are equal in excellence, or is one man better than another?

The latter.

And in the commonwealth which we were founding do you conceive the guardians who have been brought up on our model system to be more perfect men, or the cobblers whose education has been cobbling?

What a ridiculous question!

You have answered me, I replied: Well, and may we not further say that our guardians are the best of our citizens?

By far the best.

And will not their wives be the best women?

Yes, by far the best.

And can there be anything better for the interests of the State than that the men and women of a State should be as good as possible?

There can be nothing better.

And this is what the arts of music and gymnastic, when present in such manner as we have described, will accomplish?

Certainly.

Then we have made an enactment not only possible but in the highest degree beneficial to the State?

True.

Then let the wives of our guardians strip, for their virtue will be their robe, and let them share in the toils of war and the defence of their country; only in the distribution of labours the lighter are to be assigned to the women, who are the weaker natures, but in other respects their duties are to be the same. And as for the man who laughs at naked women exercising their bodies from the best of motives, in his laughter he is plucking.

A fruit of unripe wisdom, and he himself is ignorant of what he is laughing at, or what he is about; for that is, and ever will be, the best of sayings, That the useful is the noble and the hurtful is the base.

Very true.

Here, then, is one difficulty in our law about women, which we may say that we have now escaped; the wave has not swallowed us up alive for enacting that the guardians of either sex should have all their pursuits in common; to the utility and also to the possibility of this arrangement the consistency of the argument with itself bears witness.

Yes, that was a mighty wave which you have escaped.

Yes, I said, but a greater is coming; you will of this when you see the next.

Go on; let me see.

The law, I said, which is the sequel of this and of all that has preceded, is to the following effect,—'that the wives of our guardians are to be common, and their children are to be common, and no parent is to know his own child, nor any child his parent.'

Yes, he said, that is a much greater wave than the other; and the possibility as well as the utility of such a law are far more questionable.

I do not think, I said, that there can be any dispute about the very great utility of having wives and children in common; the possibility is quite another matter, and will be very much disputed.

I think that a good many doubts may be raised about both.

You imply that the two questions must be combined, I replied. Now I meant that you should admit the utility; and in this way, as I thought; I should escape from one of them, and then there would remain only the possibility.

But that little attempt is detected, and therefore you will please to give a defence of both.

Well, I said, I submit to my fate. Yet grant me a little favour: let me feast my mind with the dream as day dreamers are in the habit of feasting themselves when they are walking alone; for before they have discovered any means of effecting their wishes—that is a matter which never troubles them—they would rather not tire themselves by thinking about possibilities; but assuming that what they desire is already granted to them, they proceed with their plan, and delight in detailing what they mean to do when their wish has come true—that is a way which they have of not doing much good to a capacity which was never good for much. Now I myself am beginning to lose heart, and I should like, with your permission, to pass over the question of possibility at present. Assuming therefore the possibility of the proposal, I shall now proceed to enquire how the rulers will carry out these arrangements, and I shall demonstrate that our plan, if executed, will be of the greatest benefit to the State and to the guardians. First of all, then, if you have no objection,

I will endeavour with your help to consider the advantages of the measure; and hereafter the question of possibility.

I have no objection; proceed.

First, I think that if our rulers and their auxiliaries are to be worthy of the name which they bear, there must be willingness to obey in the one and the power of command in the other; the guardians must themselves obey the laws, and they must also imitate the spirit of them in any details which are entrusted to their care.

That is right, he said.

You, I said, who are their legislator, having selected the men, will now select the women and give them to them;—they must be as far as possible of like natures with them; and they must live in common houses and meet at common meals, None of them will have anything specially his or her own; they will be together, and will be brought up together, and will associate at gymnastic exercises. And so they will be drawn by a necessity of their natures to have intercourse with each other—necessity is not too strong a word, I think?

Yes, he said;—necessity, not geometrical, but another sort of necessity which lovers know, and which is far more convincing and constraining to the mass of mankind.

True, I said; and this, Glaucon, like all the rest, must proceed after an orderly fashion; in a city of the blessed, licentiousness is an unholy thing which the rulers will forbid.

Yes, he said, and it ought not to be permitted.

Then clearly the next thing will be to make matrimony sacred in the highest degree, and what is most beneficial will be deemed sacred?

Exactly.

And how can marriages be made most beneficial?—that is a question which I put to you, because I see in your house dogs for hunting, and of the nobler sort of birds not a few. Now, I beseech you, do tell me, have you ever attended to their pairing and breeding?

In what particulars?

Why, in the first place, although they are all of a good sort, are not some better than others?

True.

And do you breed from them all indifferently, or do you take care to breed from the best only?

From the best.

And do you take the oldest or the youngest, or only those of ripe age?

I choose only those of ripe age.

And if care was not taken in the breeding, your dogs and birds would greatly deteriorate?

Certainly.

And the same of horses and animals in general?

Undoubtedly.

Good heavens! my dear friend, I said, what consummate skill will our rulers need if the same principle holds of the human species!

Certainly, the same principle holds; but why does this involve any particular skill?

Because, I said, our rulers will oft en have to practise upon the body corporate with medicines. Now you know that when patients do not require medicines, but have only to be put under a regimen, the inferior sort of practitioner is deemed to be good enough; but when medicine has to be given, then the doctor should be more of a man.

That is quite true, he said; but to what are you alluding?

I mean, I replied, that our rulers will find a considerable dose of falsehood and deceit necessary for the good of their subjects: we were saying that the use of all these things regarded as medicines might be of advantage.

And we were very right.

And this lawful use of them seems likely to be oft en needed in the regulations of marriages and births.

How so?

Why, I said, the principle has been already laid down that the best of either sex should be united with the best as oft en, and the inferior with the inferior, as seldom as possible; and that they should rear the offspring of the one sort of union, but not of the other, if the flock is to be maintained in first-rate condition. Now these goings on must be a secret which the rulers only know, or there will be a further danger of our herd, as the guardians may be termed, breaking out into rebellion.

Very true.

Had we not better appoint certain festivals at which we will bring together the brides and bridegrooms, and sacrifices will be offered and suitable hymeneal songs composed by our poets: the number of weddings is a matter which must be left to the discretion of the rulers, whose aim will be to preserve the average of population? There are many other things which they will have to consider, such as the effects of wars and diseases and any similar agencies, in order as far as this is possible to prevent the State from becoming either too large or too small.

Certainly, he replied.

We shall have to invent some ingenious kind of lots which the less worthy may draw on each occasion of our bringing them together, and then they will accuse their own ill-luck and not the rulers.

To be sure, he said.

And I think that our braver and better youth, besides their other honours and rewards, might have greater facilities of intercourse with women given them; their bravery will be a reason, and such fathers ought to have as many sons as possible.

True.

And the proper officers, whether male or female or both, for offices are to be held by women as well as by men—

Yes—

The proper officers will take the offspring of the good parents to the pen or fold, and there they will deposit them with certain nurses who dwell in a separate quarter; but the offspring of the inferior, or of the better when they chance to be deformed, will be put away in some mysterious, unknown place, as they should be.

Yes, he said, that must be done if the breed of the guardians is to be kept pure.

They will provide for their nurture, and will bring the mothers to the fold when they are full of milk, taking the greatest possible care that no mother recognizes her own child; and other wet-nurses may be engaged if more are required. Care will also be taken that the process of suckling shall not be protracted too long; and the mothers will have no getting up at night or other trouble, but will hand over all this sort of thing to the nurses and attendants.

You suppose the wives of our guardians to have a fine easy time of it when they are having children.

Why, said I, and so they ought. Let us, however, proceed with our scheme. We were saying that the parents should be in the prime of life?

Very true.

And what is the prime of life? May it not be defined as a period of about twenty years in a woman's life, and thirty in a man's?

Which years do you mean to include?

A woman, I said, at twenty years of age may begin to bear children to the State, and continue to bear them until forty; a man may begin at five-and-twenty, when he has passed the point at which the pulse of life beats quickest, and continue to beget children until he be fifty-five.

Certainly, he said, both in men and women those years are the prime of physical as well as of intellectual vigour.

Any one above or below the prescribed ages who takes part in the public hymeneals shall be said to have done an unholy and unrighteous thing; the child of which he is the father, if it steals into life, will have been conceived under auspices very unlike the sacrifices and prayers, which at each hymeneal priestesses and priest and the whole city will offer, that the new generation may be better and more useful than their good and useful parents, whereas his child will be the offspring of darkness and strange lust.

Very true, he replied.

And the same law will apply to any one of those within the prescribed age who forms a connection with any woman in the prime of life without the sanction of the rulers; for we shall say that he is raising up a bastard to the State, uncertified and unconsecrated.

Very true, he replied.

This applies, however, only to those who are within the specified age: after that we allow them to range at will, except that a man may not marry his daughter or his daughter's daughter, or his mother or his mother's mother; and women, on the other hand, are prohibited from marrying their sons or fathers, or son's son or father's father, and so on in either direction. And we grant all this, accompanying the permission with strict orders to prevent any embryo which may come into being from seeing the light; and if any force a way to the birth, the parents must understand that the offspring of such an union cannot be maintained, and arrange accordingly.

That also, he said, is a reasonable proposition. But how will they know who are fathers and daughters, and so on?

They will never know. The way will be this: —dating from the day of the hymeneal, the bridegroom who was then married will call all the male children who are born in the seventh and tenth month afterwards his sons, and the female children his daughters, and they will call him father, and he will call their children his grandchildren, and they will call the elder generation grandfathers and grandmothers. All who were begotten at the time when their fathers and mothers came together will be called their brothers and sisters, and these, as I was saying, will be forbidden to inter-marry. This, however, is not to be understood as an absolute prohibition of the marriage of brothers and sisters; if the lot favours them, and they receive the sanction of the Pythian oracle, the law will allow them.

Quite right, he replied.

Such is the scheme, Glaucon, according to which the guardians of our State are to have their wives and families in common. And now you would have the argument show that this community is consistent with the rest of our polity, and also that nothing can be better— would you not?

Yes, certainly.

Shall we try to find a common basis by asking of ourselves what ought to be the chief aim of the legislator in making laws and in the organization of a State,—what is the greatest I good, and what is the greatest evil, and then consider whether our previous description has the stamp of the good or of the evil?

By all means.

Can there be any greater evil than discord and distraction and plurality where unity ought to reign? or any greater good than the bond of unity?

There cannot.

And there is unity where there is community of pleasures and pains—where all the citizens are glad or grieved on the same occasions of joy and sorrow?

No doubt.

Yes; and where there is no common but only private feeling a State is disorganized—when you have one half of the world triumphing and the other plunged in grief at the same events happening to the city or the citizens?

Certainly.

Such differences commonly originate in a disagreement about the use of the terms 'mine' and 'not mine,' 'his' and 'not his.'

Exactly so.

And is not that the best-ordered State in which the greatest number of persons apply the terms 'mine' and 'not mine' in the same way to the same thing?

Quite true.

Or that again which most nearly approaches to the condition of the individual—as in the body, when but a finger of one of us is hurt, the whole frame, drawn towards the soul as a center and forming one kingdom under the ruling power therein, feels the hurt and sympathizes all together with the part affected, and we say that the man has a pain in his finger; and the same expression is used about any other part of the body, which has a sensation of pain at suffering or of pleasure at the alleviation of suffering.

Very true, he replied; and I agree with you that in the best-ordered State there is the nearest approach to this common feeling which you describe.

Then when any one of the citizens experiences any good or evil, the whole State will make his case their own, and will either rejoice or sorrow with him?

Yes, he said, that is what will happen in a well-ordered State.

It will now be time, I said, for us to return to our State and see whether this or some other form is most in accordance with these fundamental principles.

Very good.

Our State like every other has rulers and subjects?

True.

All of whom will call one another citizens?

Of course.

But is there not another name which people give to their rulers in other States?

Generally they call them masters, but in democratic States they simply call them rulers.

And in our State what other name besides that of citizens do the people give the rulers?

They are called saviours and helpers, he replied.

And what do the rulers call the people?

Their maintainers and foster-fathers.

And what do they call them in other States?

Slaves.

And what do the rulers call one another in other States?

Fellow-rulers.

And what in ours?

Fellow-guardians.

Did you ever know an example in any other State of a ruler who would speak of one of his colleagues as his friend and of another as not being his friend?

Yes, very oft en.

And the friend he regards and describes as one in whom he has an interest, and the other as a stranger in whom he has no interest?

Exactly.

But would any of your guardians think or speak of any other guardian as a stranger?

Certainly he would not; for every one whom they meet will be regarded by them either as a brother or sister, or father or mother, or son or daughter, or as the child or parent of those who are thus connected with him.

Capital, I said; but let me ask you once more: Shall they be a family in name only; or shall they in all their actions be true to the name? For example, in the use of the word 'father,' would the care of a father be implied and the filial reverence and duty and obedience to him which the law commands; and is the violator of these duties to be regarded as an impious and unrighteous person who is not likely to receive much good either at the hands of God or of man? Are these to be or not to be the strains which the children will hear repeated in their ears by all the citizens about those who are intimated to them to be their parents and the rest of their kinsfolk?

These, he said, and none other; for what can be more ridiculous than for them to utter the names of family ties with the lips only and not to act in the spirit of them?

Then in our city the language of harmony and concord will be more oft en beard than in any other. As I was describing before, when any one is well or ill, the universal word will be with me it is well' or 'it is ill.'

Most true.

And agreeably to this mode of thinking and speaking, were we not saying that they will have their pleasures and pains in common?

Yes, and so they will.

And they will have a common interest in the same thing which they will alike call 'my own,' and having this common interest they will have a common feeling of pleasure and pain?

Yes, far more so than in other States.

And the reason of this, over and above the general constitution of the State, will be that the guardians will have a community of women and children?

That will be the chief reason.

And this unity of feeling we admitted to be the greatest good, as was implied in our own comparison of a well-ordered State to the relation of the body and the members, when affected by pleasure or pain?

That we acknowledged, and very rightly.

Then the community of wives and children among our citizens is clearly the source of the greatest good to the State?

Certainly.

And this agrees with the other principle which we were affirming,—that the guardians were not to have houses or lands or any other property; their pay was to be their food, which they were to receive from the other citizens, and they were to have no private expenses; for we intended them to preserve their true character of guardians.

Right, he replied.

Both the community of property and the community of families, as I am saying, tend to make them more truly guardians; they will not tear the city in pieces by differing about 'mine' and 'not mine;' each man dragging any acquisition which he has made into a separate house of his own, where he has a separate wife and children and private pleasures and pains; but all will be affected as far as may be by the same pleasures and pains because they are all of one opinion about what is near and dear to them, and therefore they all tend towards a common end.

Certainly, he replied.

And as they have nothing but their persons which they can call their own, suits and complaints will have no existence among them; they will be delivered from all those quarrels of which money or children or relations are the occasion.

Of course they will.

Neither will trials for assault or insult ever be likely to occur among them. For that equals should defend themselves against equals we shall maintain to be honourable and right; we shall make the protection of the person a matter of necessity.

That is good, he said.

Yes; and there is a further good in the law; viz. that if a man has a quarrel with another he will satisfy his resentment then and there, and not proceed to more dangerous lengths.

Certainly.

To the elder shall be assigned the duty of ruling and chastising the younger.

Clearly.

Nor can there be a doubt that the younger will not strike or do any other violence to an elder, unless the magistrates command him; nor will he slight him in any way. For there are two guardians, shame and fear, mighty to prevent him: shame, which makes men refrain from laying hands on those who are to them in the relation of parents; fear, that the injured one will be succoured by the others who are his brothers, sons, one wi fathers.

That is true, he replied.

Then in every way the laws will help the citizens to keep the peace with one another?

Yes, there will be no want of peace.

And as the guardians will never quarrel among themselves there will be no danger of the rest of the city being divided either against them or against one another.

None whatever.

I hardly like even to mention the little mean-nesses of which they will be rid, for they are beneath notice: such, for example, as the flattery of the rich by the poor, and all the pains and pangs which men experience in bringing up a family, and in finding money to buy necessaries for their household, borrowing and then repudiating, getting how they can, and giving the money into the hands of women and slaves to keep—the many evils of so many kinds which people suffer in this way are mean enough and obvious enough, and not worth speaking of.

Yes, he said, a man has no need of eyes in order to perceive that.

And from all these evils they will be delivered, and their life will be blessed as the life of Olympic victors and yet more blessed.

How so?

The Olympic victor, I said, is deemed happy in receiving a part only of the blessedness which is secured to our citizens, who have won a more glorious victory and have a more complete maintenance at the public cost. For the victory which they have won is the salvation of the whole State; and the crown with which they and their children are crowned is the fulness of all that life needs; they receive rewards from the hands of their country while living, and after death have an honourable burial.

## Book IV

### The Just State and the Balanced Person

Nonsense, said Glaucon: did you not promise to search yourself, saying that for you not to help justice in her need would be an impiety?

I do not deny that I said so, and as you remind me, I will be as good as my word; but you must join.

We will, he replied.

Well, then, I hope to make the discovery in this way: I mean to begin with the assumption that our State, if rightly ordered, is perfect.

That is most certain.

And being perfect, is therefore wise and valiant and temperate and just.

That is likewise clear.

And whichever of these qualities we find in the State, the one which is not found will be the residue?

Very good.

If there were four things, and we were searching for one of them, wherever it might be, the one sought for might be known to us from the first, and there would be no further trouble; or we might know the other three first, and then the fourth would clearly be the one left .

Very true, he said.

And is not a similar method to be pursued about the virtues, which are also four in number?

Clearly.

First among the virtues found in the State, wisdom comes into view, and in this I detect a certain peculiarity.

What is that?

The State which we have been describing is said to be wise as being good in counsel?

Very true.

And good counsel is clearly a kind of knowledge, for not by ignorance, but by knowledge, do men counsel well?

Clearly.

And the kinds of knowledge in a State are many and diverse?

Of course.

There is the knowledge of the carpenter; but is that the sort of knowledge which gives a city the title of wise and good in counsel?

Certainly not; that would only give a city the reputation of skill in carpentering.

Then a city is not to be called wise because possessing a knowledge which counsels for the best about wooden implements?

Certainly not.

Nor by reason of a knowledge which advises about brazen pots, I said, nor as possessing any other similar knowledge?

Not by reason of any of them, he said.

Nor yet by reason of a knowledge which cultivates the earth; that would give the city the name of agricultural?

Yes.

Well, I said, and is there any knowledge in our recently founded State among any of the citizens which advises, not about any particular thing in the State, but about the whole, and considers how a State can best deal with itself and with other States?

There certainly is.

And what is knowledge, and among whom is it found? I asked.

It is the knowledge of the guardians, he replied, and found among those whom we were just now describing as perfect guardians.

And what is the name which the city derives from the possession of this sort of knowledge?

The name of good in counsel and truly wise.

And will there be in our city more of these true guardians or more smiths?

The smiths, he replied, will be far more numerous.

Will not the guardians be the smallest of all the classes who receive a name from the profession of some kind of knowledge?

Much the smallest.

And so by reason of the smallest part or class, and of the knowledge which resides in this presiding and ruling part of itself, the whole State, being thus constituted according to nature, will be wise; and this, which has the only knowledge worthy to be called wisdom, has been ordained by nature to be of all classes the least.

Most true.

Thus, then, I said, the nature and place in the State of one of the four virtues has somehow or other been discovered.

And, in my humble opinion, very satisfactorily discovered, he replied.

Again, I said, there is no difficulty in seeing the nature of courage; and in what part that quality resides which gives the name of courageous to the State.

How do you mean?

Why, I said, every one who calls any State courageous or cowardly, will be thinking of the part which fights and goes out to war on the State's behalf.

No one, he replied, would ever think of any other.

Certainly not.

The rest of the citizens may be courageous or may be cowardly but their courage or cowardice will not, as I conceive, have the effect of making the city either the one or the other.

The city will be courageous in virtue of a portion of herself which preserves under all circumstances that opinion about the nature of things to be feared and not to be feared in which our legislator educated them; and this is what you term courage.

I should like to hear what you are saying once more, for I do not think that I perfectly understand you.

I mean that courage is a kind of salvation.

Salvation of what?

Of the opinion respecting things to be feared, what they are and of what nature, which the law implants through education; and I mean by the words 'under all circumstances' to intimate that in pleasure or in pain, or under the influence of desire or fear, a man

preserves, and does not lose this opinion. Shall I give you an illustration?

If you please.

You know, I said, that dyers, when they want to dye wool for making the true sea-purple, begin by selecting their white colour first; this they prepare and dress with much care and pains, in order that the white ground may take the purple hue in full perfection. The dyeing then proceeds; and whatever is dyed in this manner becomes a fast colour, and no washing either with lyes or without them can take away the bloom. But, when the ground has not been duly prepared, you will have noticed how poor is the look either of purple or of any other colour.

Yes, he said; I know that they have a washed-out and ridiculous appearance.

Then now, I said, you will understand what our object was in selecting our soldiers, and educating them in music and gymnastic; we were contriving influences which would prepare them to take the dye of the laws in perfection, and the colour of their opinion about dangers and of every other opinion was to be indelibly fixed by their nurture and training, not to be washed away by such potent lyes as pleasure—mightier agent far in washing the soul than any soda or lye; or by sorrow, fear, and desire, the mightiest of all other solvents. And this sort of universal saving power of true opinion in conformity with law about real and false dangers I call and maintain to be courage, unless you disagree.

But I agree, he replied; for I suppose that you mean to exclude mere uninstructed courage, such as that of a wild beast or of a slave—this, in your opinion, is not the courage which the law ordains, and ought to have another name.

Most certainly.

Then I may infer courage to be such as you describe?

Why, yes, said I, you may, and if you add the words 'of a citizen,' you will not be far wrong;—hereafter, if you like, we will carry the examination further, but at present we are we w seeking not for courage but justice; and for the purpose of our enquiry we have said enough.

You are right, he replied.

Two virtues remain to be discovered in the State-first temperance, and then justice which is the end of our search.

Very true.

Now, can we find justice without troubling ourselves about temperance?

I do not know how that can be accomplished, he said, nor do I desire that justice should be brought to light and temperance lost sight of; and therefore I wish that you would do me the favour of considering temperance first.

Certainly, I replied, I should not be justified in refusing your request.

Then consider, he said.

Yes, I replied; I will; and as far as I can at present see, the virtue of temperance has more of the nature of harmony and symphony than the preceding.

How so? he asked.

Temperance, I replied, is the ordering or controlling of certain pleasures and desires; this is curiously enough implied in the saying of 'a man being his own master' and other traces of the same notion may be found in language.

No doubt, he said.

There is something ridiculous in the expression 'master of himself'; for the master is also the servant and the servant the master; and in all these modes of speaking the same person is denoted.

Certainly.

The meaning is, I believe, that in the human soul there is a better and also a worse principle; and when the better has the worse under control, then a man is said to be master of himself; and this is a term of praise: but when, owing to evil education or association, the better principle, which is also the smaller, is overwhelmed by the greater mass of the worse—in this case he is blamed and is called the slave of self and unprincipled.

Yes, there is reason in that.

And now, I said, look at our newly created State, and there you will find one of these two conditions realised; for the State, as you will acknowledge, may be justly called master of itself, if the words 'temperance' and 'self-mastery' truly express the rule of the better part over the worse.

Yes, he said, I see that what you say is true.

Let me further note that the manifold and complex pleasures and desires and pains are generally found in children and women and servants, and in the freemen so called who are of the lowest and more numerous class.

Certainly, he said.

Whereas the simple and moderate desires which follow reason, and are under the guidance of mind and true opinion, are to be found only in a few, and those the best born and best educated.

Very true. These two, as you may perceive, have a place in our State; and the meaner desires of the are held down by the virtuous desires and wisdom of the few.

That I perceive, he said.

Then if there be any city which may be described as master of its own pleasures and desires, and master of itself, ours may claim such a designation?

Certainly, he replied.

It may also be called temperate, and for the same reasons?

Yes.

And if there be any State in which rulers and subjects will be agreed as to the question who are to rule, that again will be our State?

Undoubtedly.

And the citizens being thus agreed among themselves, in which class will temperance be found—in the rulers or in the subjects?

In both, as I should imagine, he replied.

Do you observe that we were not far wrong in our guess that temperance was a sort of harmony?

Why so?

Why, because temperance is unlike courage and wisdom, each of which resides in a part only, the one making the State wise and the other valiant; not so temperance, which extends to the whole, and runs through all the notes of the scale, and produces a harmony of the weaker and the stronger and the middle class, whether you suppose them to be stronger or weaker in wisdom or power or numbers or wealth, or anything else. Most truly then may we deem temperance to be the agreement of the naturally superior and inferior, as to the right to rule of either, both in states and individuals.

I entirely agree with you.

And so, I said, we may consider three out of the four virtues to have been discovered in our State. The last of those qualities which make a state virtuous must be justice, if we only knew what that was.

The inference is obvious.

The time then has arrived, Glaucon, when, like huntsmen, we should surround the cover, and look sharp that justice does not steal away, and pass out of sight and escape us; for beyond a doubt she is somewhere in this country: watch therefore and strive to catch a sight of her, and if you see her first, let me know.

Would that I could! but you should regard me rather as a follower who has just eyes enough to, see what you show him—that is about as much as I am good for.

Offer up a prayer with me and follow.

I will, but you must show me the way.

Here is no path, I said, and the wood is dark and perplexing; still we must push on.

Let us push on.

Here I saw something: Halloo! I said, I begin to perceive a track, and I believe that the quarry will not escape.

Good news, he said.

Truly, I said, we are stupid fellows.

Why so?

Why, my good sir, at the beginning of our enquiry, ages ago, there was justice tumbling out at our feet, and we never saw her; nothing could be more ridiculous. Like people who go about looking for what they have in their hands—that was the way with us—we looked not at what we were seeking, but at what was far off in the distance; and therefore, I suppose, we missed her.

What do you mean?

I mean to say that in reality for a long time past we have been talking of justice, and have failed to recognise her.

I grow impatient at the length of your exordium.

Well then, tell me, I said, whether I am right or not: You remember the original principle which we were always laying down at the foundation of the State, that one man should practise one thing only, the thing to which his nature was best adapted;—now justice is this principle or a part of it.

Yes, we oft en said that one man should do one thing only.

Further, we affirmed that justice was doing one's own business, and not being a busybody; we said so again and again, and many others have said the same to us.

Yes, we said so.

Then to do one's own business in a certain way may be assumed to be justice. Can you tell me whence I derive this inference?

I cannot, but I should like to be told.

Because I think that this is the only virtue which remains in the State when the other virtues of temperance and courage and wisdom are abstracted; and, that this is the ultimate cause and condition of the existence of all of them, and while remaining in them is also their preservative; and we were saying that if the three were discovered by us, justice would be the fourth or remaining one.

That follows of necessity.

If we are asked to determine which of these four qualities by its presence contributes most to the excellence of the State, whether the agreement of rulers and subjects, or the preservation in the soldiers of the opinion which the law ordains about the true nature of dangers, or wisdom and watchfulness in the rulers, or whether this other which I am mentioning, and which is found in children and women, slave and freeman, artisan, ruler, subject,—the quality, I mean, of every one doing his own work, and not being a busybody, would claim the palm—the question is not so easily answered.

Certainly, he replied, there would be a difficulty in saying which.

Then the power of each individual in the State to do his own work appears to compete with the other political virtues, wisdom, temperance, courage.

Yes, he said.

And the virtue which enters into this competition is justice?

Exactly.

Let us look at the question from another point of view: Are not the rulers in a State those to whom you would entrust the office of determining suits at law?

Certainly.

And are suits decided on any other ground but that a man may neither take what is another's, nor be deprived of what is his own?

Yes; that is their principle.

Which is a just principle?

Yes.

Then on this view also justice will be admitted to be the having and doing what is a man's own, and belongs to him?

Very true.

Think, now, and say whether you agree with me or not. Suppose a carpenter to be doing the business of a cobbler, or a cobbler of a carpenter; and suppose them to exchange their implements or their duties, or the same person to be doing the work of both, or whatever be the change; do you think that any great harm would result to the State?

Not much.

But when the cobbler or any other man whom nature designed to be a trader, having his heart lifted up by wealth or strength or the number of his followers, or any like advantage, attempts to force his way into the class of warriors, or a warrior into that of legislators and guardians, for which he is unfitted, and either to take the implements or the duties of the other; or when one man is trader, legislator, and warrior all in one, then I think you will agree with me in saying that this interchange and this meddling of one with another is the ruin of the State.

Most true.

Seeing then, I said, that there are three distinct classes, any meddling of one with another, or the change of one into another, is the greatest harm to the State, and may be most justly termed evil-doing?

Precisely.

And the greatest degree of evil-doing to one's own city would be termed by you injustice?

Certainly.

This then is injustice; and on the other hand when the trader, the auxiliary, and the guardian each do their own business, that is justice, and will make the city just.

I agree with you.

We will not, I said, be over-positive as yet; but if, on trial, this conception of justice be verified in the individual as well as in the State, there will be no longer any room for doubt; if it be not verified, we must have a fresh enquiry. First let us complete the old investigation, which we began, as you remember, under the impression that, if we could previously examine justice on the larger scale, there would be less difficulty in discerning her in the individual. That larger example appeared to be the State, and accordingly we constructed as good a one as we could, knowing well that in the good State justice would be found. Let the discovery which we made be now applied to the individual—if they agree, we shall be satisfied; or, if there be a difference in the individual, we will come back to the State and have another trial of the theory. The friction of the two when rubbed together may possibly strike a light in which justice will shine forth, and the vision which is then revealed we will fix in our souls.

That will be in regular course; let us do as you say.

I proceeded to ask: When two things, a greater and less, are called by the same name, are they like or unlike in so far as they are called the same?

Like, he replied.

The just man then, if we regard the idea of justice only, will be like the just State?

He will.

And a State was thought by us to be just when the three classes in the State severally did their own business; and also thought to be temperate and valiant and wise by reason of certain other affections and qualities of these same classes?

True, he said.

And so of the individual; we may assume that he has the same three principles in his own soul which are found in the State; and he may be rightly described in the same terms, because he is affected in the same manner?

Certainly, he said.

Once more then, O my friend, we have alighted upon an easy question—whether the soul has these three principles or not?

An easy question! Nay, rather, Socrates, the proverb holds that hard is the good.

Very true, I said; and I do not think that the method which we are employing is at all adequate to the accurate solution of this question; the true method is another and a longer one. Still we may arrive at a solution not below the level of the previous enquiry.

May we not be satisfied with that? he said;—under the circumstances, I am quite content.

I too, I replied, shall be extremely well satisfied. Then faint not in pursuing the speculation, he said.

Must we not acknowledge, I said, that in each of us there are the same principles and habits which there are in the State; and that from the individual they pass into the State?—how else can they come there? Take the quality of passion or spirit;—it would be ridiculous to imagine that this quality, when found in States, is not derived from the individuals who are supposed to possess it, e.g.

the Thracians, Scythians, and in general the northern nations; and the same may be said of the love of knowledge, which is the special characteristic of our part of the world, or of the love of money, which may, with equal truth, be attributed to the Phoenicians and Egyptians.

Exactly so, he said.

There is no difficulty in understanding this.

None whatever.

But the question is not quite so easy when we proceed to ask whether these principles are three or one; whether, that is to say, we learn with one part of our nature, are angry with another, and with a third part desire the satisfaction of our natural appetites; or whether the whole soul comes into play in each sort of action—to determine that is the difficulty.

Yes, he said; there lies the difficulty.

Then let us now try and determine whether they are the same or different.

How can we? he asked.

I replied as follows: The same thing clearly cannot act or be acted upon in the same part or in relation to the same thing at the same time, in contrary ways; and therefore whenever this contradiction occurs in things apparently the same, we know that they are really not the same, but different.

Good.

For example, I said, can the same thing be at rest and in motion at the same time in the same part?

Impossible.

Still, I said, let us have a more precise statement of terms, lest we should hereafter fall out by the way. Imagine the case of a man who is standing and also moving his hands and his head, and suppose a person to say that one and the same person is in motion and at rest at the same moment—to such a mode of speech we should object, and should rather say that one part of him is in motion while another is at rest.

Very true.

And suppose the objector to refine still further, and to draw the nice distinction that not only parts of tops, but whole tops, when they spin round with their pegs fixed on the spot, are at rest and in motion at the same time (and he may say the same of anything which revolves in the same spot), his objection would not be admitted by us, because in such cases things are not at rest and in motion in the same parts of themselves; we should rather say that they have both an axis and a circumference, and that the axis stands still, for there is no deviation from the perpendicular; and that the circumference goes round. But if, while revolving, the axis inclines either to the right or left, forwards or backwards, then in no point of view can they be at rest.

That is the correct mode of describing them, he replied.

Then none of these objections will confuse us, or incline us to believe that the same thing at the same time, in the same part or in relation to the same thing, can act or be acted upon in contrary ways.

Certainly not, according to my way of thinking. Yet, I said, that we may not be compelled to examine all such objections, and prove at length that they are untrue, let us assume their absurdity, and go forward on the understanding that hereafter, if this assumption turn out to be untrue, all the consequences which follow shall be withdrawn.

Yes, he said, that will be the best way.

Well, I said, would you not allow that assent and dissent, desire and aversion, attraction and repulsion, are all of them opposites, whether they are regarded as active or passive (for that makes no difference in the fact of their opposition)?

Yes, he said, they are opposites.

Well, I said, and hunger and thirst, and the desires in general, and again willing and wishing,—all these you would refer to the classes already mentioned. You would say—would you not?—that the soul of him who desires is seeking after the object of his desires; or that he is drawing to himself the thing which he wishes to possess: or again, when a person wants anything to be given him, his mind, longing for the realisation of his desires, intimates his wish to have it by a nod of assent, as if he had been asked a question?

Very true.

And what would you say of unwillingness and dislike and the absence of desire; should not these be referred to the opposite class of repulsion and rejection?

Certainly.

Admitting this to be true of desire generally, let us suppose a particular class of desires, and out of these we will select hunger and thirst, as they are termed, which are the most obvious of them?

Let us take that class, he said.

The object of one is food, and of the other drink?

Yes.

And here comes the point: is not thirst the desire which the soul has of drink, and of drink only; not of drink qualified by anything else; for example, warm or cold, or much or little, or, in a word, drink of any particular sort: but if the thirst be accompanied by heat, then the desire is of cold drink; or, if accompanied by cold, then of warm drink; or, if the thirst be excessive, then the drink which is desired will be excessive; or, if not great, the quantity of drink will also be small: but thirst pure and simple will desire drink pure and simple, which

is the natural satisfaction of thirst, as food is of hunger?

Yes, he said; the simple desire is, as you say, in every case of the simple object, and the qualified desire of the qualified object.

But here a confusion may arise; and I should wish to guard against an opponent starting up and saying that no man desires drink only, but good drink, or food only, but good food; for good is the universal object of desire, and thirst being a desire, will necessarily be thirst after good drink; and the same is true of every other desire.

Yes, he replied, the opponent might have something to say.

Nevertheless I should still maintain, that of relatives some have a quality attached to either term of the relation; others are simple and have their correlatives simple.

I do not know what you mean.

Well, you know of course that the greater is relative to the less?

Certainly.

And the much greater to the much less?

Yes.

And the sometime greater to the sometime less, and the greater that is to be to the less that is to be?

Certainly, he said.

And so of more and less, and of other correlative terms, such as the double and the half, or again, the heavier and the lighter, the swifter and the slower; and of hot and cold, and of any other relatives;—is not this true of all of them?

Yes.

And does not the same principle hold in the sciences? The object of science is knowledge (assuming that to be the true definition), but the object of a particular science is a particular kind of knowledge; I mean, for example, that the science of house-building is a kind of knowledge which is defined and distinguished from other kinds and is therefore termed architecture.

Certainly.

Because it has a particular quality which no other has?

Yes.

And it has this particular quality because it has an object of a particular kind; and this is true of the other arts and sciences?

Yes.

Now, then, if I have made myself clear, you will understand my original meaning in what I said about relatives. My meaning was, that if one term of a relation is taken alone, the other is taken alone; if one term is qualified, the other is also qualified. I do not mean to say that relatives may not be disparate, or that the science of health is healthy, or of disease necessarily diseased, or that the sciences of good and evil are therefore good and evil; but only that, when the term science is no longer used absolutely, but has a qualified object which in this case is the nature of health and disease, it becomes defined, and is hence called not merely science, but the science of medicine.

I quite understand, and I think as you do.

Would you not say that thirst is one of these essentially relative terms, having clearly a relation—

Yes, thirst is relative to drink.

And a certain kind of thirst is relative to a certain kind of drink; but thirst taken alone is neither of much nor little, nor of good nor bad, nor of any particular kind of drink, but of drink only?

Certainly.

Then the soul of the thirsty one, in so far as he is thirsty, desires only drink; for this he yearns and tries to obtain it?

That is plain.

And if you suppose something which pulls a thirsty soul away from drink, that must be different from the thirsty principle which draws him like a beast to drink; for, as we were saying, the same thing cannot at the same time with the same part of itself act in contrary ways about the same.

Impossible.

No more than you can say that the hands of the archer push and pull the bow at the same time, but what you say is that one hand pushes and the other pulls.

Exactly so, he replied.

And might a man be thirsty, and yet unwilling to drink?

Yes, he said, it constantly happens.

And in such a case what is one to say? Would you not say that there was something in the soul bidding a man to drink, and something else forbidding him, which is other and stronger than the principle which bids him?

I should say so.

And the forbidding principle is derived from reason, and that which bids and attracts proceeds from passion and disease?

Clearly.

Then we may fairly assume that they are two, and that they differ from one another; the one with which man reasons, we may call the rational principle of the soul, the other, with which he loves and hungers and thirsts and feels the flutterings of any other desire, may be termed the irrational or appetitive, the ally of sundry pleasures and satisfactions?

Yes, he said, we may fairly assume them to be different.

Then let us finally determine that there are two principles existing in the soul. And what of passion, or spirit? Is it a third, or akin to one of the preceding?

I should be inclined to say—akin to desire.

Well, I said, there is a story which I remember to have heard, and in which I put faith. The story is, that Leontius, the son of Aglaion, coming up one day from the Piraeus, under the north wall on the outside, observed some dead bodies lying on the ground at the place of execution. He felt a desire to see them, and also a dread and abhorrence of them; for a time he struggled and covered his eyes, but at length the desire got the better of him; and forcing them open, he ran up to the dead bodies, saying, Look, ye wretches, take your fill of the fair sight.

I have heard the story myself, he said.

The moral of the tale is, that anger at times goes to war with desire, as though they were two distinct things.

Yes; that is the meaning, he said.

And are there not many other cases in which we observe that when a man's desires violently prevail over his reason, he reviles himself, and is angry at the violence within him, and that in this struggle, which is like the struggle of factions in a State, his spirit is on the side of his reason;—but for the passionate or spirited element to take part with the desires when reason that she should not be opposed, is a sort of thing which thing which I believe that you never observed occurring in yourself, nor, as I should imagine, in any one else?

Certainly not.

Suppose that a man thinks he has done a wrong to another, the nobler he is the less able is he to feel indignant at any suffering, such as hunger, or cold, or any other pain which the injured person may inflict upon him—these he deems to be just, and, as I say, his anger refuses to be excited by them.

True, he said.

But when he thinks that he is the sufferer of the wrong, then he boils and chafes, and is on the side of what he believes to be justice; and because he suffers hunger or cold or other pain he is only the more determined to persevere and conquer. His noble spirit will not be quelled until he either slays or is slain; or until he hears the voice of the shepherd, that is, reason, bidding his dog bark no more.

The illustration is perfect, he replied; and in our State, as we were saying, the auxiliaries were to be dogs, and to hear the voice of the rulers, who are their shepherds.

I perceive, I said, that you quite understand me; there is, however, a further point which I wish you to consider.

What point?

You remember that passion or spirit appeared at first sight to be a kind of desire, but now we should say quite the contrary; for in the conflict of the soul spirit is arrayed on the side of the rational principle.

Most assuredly.

But a further question arises: Is passion different from reason also, or only a kind of reason; in which latter case, instead of three principles in the soul, there will only be two, the rational and the concupiscent; or rather, as the State was composed of three classes, traders, auxiliaries, counsellors, so may there not be in the individual soul a third element which is passion or spirit, and when not corrupted by bad education is the natural auxiliary of reason

Yes, he said, there must be a third.

Yes, I replied, if passion, which has already been shown to be different from desire, turn out also to be different from reason.

But that is easily proved:—We may observe even in young children that they are full of spirit almost as soon as they are born, whereas some of them never seem to attain to the use of reason, and most of them late enough.

Book II

Excellent, I said, and you may see passion equally in brute animals, which is a further proof of the truth of what you are saying. And we may once more appeal to the words of Homer, which have been already quoted by us,

He smote his breast, and thus rebuked his soul, for in this verse Homer has clearly supposed the power which reasons about the better and worse to be different from the unreasoning anger which is rebuked by it.

Very true, he said.

And so, after much tossing, we have reached land, and are fairly agreed that the same principles which exist in the State exist also in the individual, and that they are three in number.

Exactly.

Must we not then infer that the individual is wise in the same way, and in virtue of the same quality which makes the State wise?

Certainly.

Also that the same quality which constitutes courage in the State constitutes courage in the individual, and that both the State and the individual bear the same relation to all the other virtues?

Assuredly.

And the individual will be acknowledged by us to be just in the same way in which the State is just?

That follows, of course.

We cannot but remember that the justice of the State consisted in each of the three classes doing the work of its own class?

We are not very likely to have forgotten, he said.

We must recollect that the individual in whom the several qualities of his nature do their own work will be just, and will do his own work?

Yes, he said, we must remember that too.

And ought not the rational principle, which is wise, and has the care of the whole soul, to rule, and the passionate or spirited principle to be the subject and ally?

Certainly.

# Book II

## Division of Labor and the Necessities of the State

I will tell you, I replied; justice, which is the subject of our enquiry, is, as you know, sometimes spoken of as the virtue of an individual, and sometimes as the virtue of a State.

True, he replied.

And is not a State larger than an individual?

It is.

Then in the larger the quantity of justice is likely to be larger and more easily discernible. I propose therefore that we enquire into the nature of justice and injustice, first as they appear in the State, and secondly in the individual, proceeding from the greater to the lesser and comparing them.

That, he said, is an excellent proposal.

And if we imagine the State in process of creation, we shall see the justice and injustice of the State in process of creation also.

I dare say.

When the State is completed there may be a hope that the object of our search will be more easily discovered.

Yes, far more easily.

But ought we to attempt to construct one? I said; for to do so, as I am inclined to think, will be a very serious task. Reflect therefore.

I have reflected, said Adeimantus, and am anxious that you should proceed.

A State, I said, arises, as I conceive, out of the needs of mankind; no one is self-sufficing, but all of us have many wants. Can any other origin of a State be imagined?

There can I be no other.

Then, as we have many wants, and many persons are needed to supply them, one takes a helper for one purpose and another for another; and when these partners and helpers are gathered together in one habitation the body of inhabitants is termed a State.

True, he said.

And they exchange with one another, and one gives, and another receives, under the idea that the exchange will be for their good.

Very true.

Then, I said, let us begin and create in idea a State; and yet the true creator is necessity, who is the mother of our invention.

Of course, he replied.

Now the first and greatest of necessities is food, which is the condition of life and existence.

Certainly.

The second is a dwelling, and the third clothing and the like.

True.

And now let us see how our city will be able to supply this great demand: We may suppose that one man is a husbandman, another a builder, some one else a weaver—shall we add to them a shoemaker, or perhaps some other purveyor to our bodily wants?

Quite right.

The barest notion of a State must include four or five men.

Clearly.

And how will they proceed? Will each bring the result of his labours into a common stock?—the individual husbandman, for example, producing for four, and labouring four times as long and as much as he need in the provision of food with which he supplies others as well as himself; or will he have nothing to do with others and not be at the trouble of producing for them, but provide for himself alone a fourth of the food in a fourth of the time, and in the remaining three-fourths of his time be employed in making a house or a coat or a pair of shoes, having no partnership with others, but supplying himself all his own wants?

Adeimantus thought that he should aim at producing food only and not at producing everything.

Probably, I replied, that would be the better way; and when I hear you say this, I am myself reminded that we are not all alike; there are diversities of natures among us which are adapted to different occupations.

Very true.

And will you have a work better done when the workman has many occupations, or when he has only one?

When he has only one.

Further, there can be no doubt that a work is spoilt when not done at the right time?

No doubt.

For business is not disposed to wait until the doer of the business is at leisure; but the doer must follow up what he is doing, and make the business his first object.

He must.

And if so, we must infer that all things are produced more plentifully and easily and of a better quality when one man does one thing which is natural to him and does it at the right time, and leaves other things.

Undoubtedly..

Then more than four citizens will be required; for the husbandman will not make his own plough or mattock, or other implements of agriculture, if they are to be good for any-thing. Neither will the builder make his tools—and he too needs many; and in like manner the weaver and shoemaker.

True.

Then carpenters, and smiths, and many other artisans, will be sharers in our little State, which is already beginning to grow?

True.

Yet even if we add neatherds, shepherds, and other herdsmen, in order that our husband-men may have oxen to plough with, and build-ers as well as husbandmen may have draught cattle, and curriers and weavers fleeces and hides,—still our State will not be very large.

That is true; yet neither will it be a very small State which contains all these.

Then, again, there is the situation of the city—to find a place where nothing need be imported is well-nigh impossible.

Impossible.

Then there must be another class of citi-zens who will bring the required supply from another city?

There must.

But if the trader goes empty-handed, having nothing which they require who would supply his need, he will come back empty-handed.

That is certain.

And therefore what they produce at home must be not only enough for themselves, but such both in quantity and quality as to accom-modate those from whom their wants are supplied.

Very true.

Then more husbandmen and more artisans will be required?

They will.

Not to mention the importers and export-ers, who are called merchants?

Yes.

Then we shall want merchants?

We shall.

And if merchandise is to be carried over the sea, skilful sailors will also be needed, and in considerable numbers?

Yes, in considerable numbers.

Then, again, within the city, how will they exchange their productions? To secure such an exchange was, as you will remember, one of our principal objects when we formed them into a society and constituted a State.

Clearly they will buy and sell.

Then they will need a market-place, and a money-token for purposes of exchange.

Certainly.

Suppose now that a husbandman, or an artisan, brings some production to market, and he comes at a time when there is no one to exchange with him,—is he to leave his call-ing and sit idle in the market-place?

Not at all; he will find people there who, seeing the want, undertake the office of sales-men. In well-ordered States they are com-monly those who are the weakest in bodily strength, and therefore of little use for any other purpose; their duty is to be in the mar-ket, and to give money in exchange for goods to those who desire to sell and to take money from those who desire to buy.

This want, then, creates a class of retail-traders in our State. Is not 'retailer' the term which is applied to those who sit in the mar-ket-place engaged in buying and selling, while those who wander from one city to another are called merchants?

Yes, he said.

And there is another class of servants, who are intellectually hardly on the level of companionship; still they have plenty of bodily strength for labour, which accordingly they sell, and are called, if I do not mistake, hirelings, hire being the name which is given to the price of their labour.

True.

Then hirelings will help to make up our population?

Yes.

And now, Adeimantus, is our State matured and perfected?

I think so.

Where, then, is justice, and where is injustice, and in what part of the State did they spring up?

Probably in the dealings of these citizens with one another. cannot imagine that they are more likely to be found anywhere else.

I dare say that you are right in your suggestion, I said; we had better think the matter out, and not shrink from the enquiry.

Let us then consider, first of all, what will be their way of life, now that we have thus established them. Will they not produce corn, and wine, and clothes, and shoes, and build houses for themselves? And when they are housed, they will work, in summer, commonly, stripped and barefoot, but in winter substantially clothed and shod. They will feed on barley-meal and flour of wheat, baking and kneading them, making noble cakes and loaves; these they will serve up on a mat of reeds or on clean leaves, themselves reclining the while upon beds strewn with yew or myrtle. And they and their children will feast, drinking of the wine which they have made, wearing garlands on their heads, and hymning the praises of the gods, in happy converse with one another. And they will take care that their families do not exceed their means; having an eye to poverty or war.

## Socrates—GLAUCON

But, said Glaucon, interposing, you have not given them a relish to their meal.

True, I replied, I had forgotten; of course they must have a relish-salt, and olives, and cheese, and they will boil roots and herbs such as country people prepare; for a dessert we shall give them figs, and peas, and beans; and they will roast myrtle-berries and acorns at the fire, drinking in moderation. And with such a diet they may be expected to live in peace and health to a good old age, and bequeath a similar life to their children after them.

Yes, Socrates, he said, and if you were providing for a city of pigs, how else would you feed the beasts?

But what would you have, Glaucon? I replied.

Why, he said, you should give them the ordinary conveniences of life. People who are to be comfortable are accustomed to lie on sofas, and dine off tables, and they should have sauces and sweets in the modern style.

Yes, I said, now I understand: the question which you would have me consider is, not only how a State, but how a luxurious State is created; and possibly there is no harm in this, for in such a State we shall be more likely to see how justice and injustice originate. In my opinion the true and healthy constitution of the State is the one which I have described. But if you wish also to see a State at fever heat, I have no objection. For I suspect that many will not be satisfied with the simpler way of way They will be for adding sofas, and tables, and other furniture; also dainties, and perfumes, and incense, and courtesans, and cakes, all these not of one sort only, but in every variety; we must go beyond the necessaries of which I was at first speaking, such as houses, and clothes, and shoes: the arts of the painter and the embroiderer will have to be set in motion, and gold and ivory and all sorts of materials must be procured.

True, he said.

Then we must enlarge our borders; for the original healthy State is no longer sufficient. Now will the city have to fill and swell with a multitude of callings which are not required by any natural want; such as the whole tribe of hunters and actors, of whom one large class have to do with forms and colours; another will be the votaries of music—poets and their attendant train of rhapsodists, players, dancers, contractors; also makers of divers kinds of articles, including women's dresses. And we shall want more servants. Will not tutors be also in request, and nurses wet and dry, tire-women and barbers, as well as confectioners and cooks; and swineherds, too, who were not needed and therefore had no place in the former edition of our State, but are needed now? They must not be forgotten: and there will be animals of many other kinds, if people eat them.

Certainly.

And living in this way we shall have much greater need of physicians than before?

Much greater.

And the country which was enough to support the original inhabitants will be too small now, and not enough?

Quite true.

Then a slice of our neighbours' land will be wanted by us for pasture and tillage, and they will want a slice of ours, if, like ourselves, they exceed the limit of necessity, and give themselves up to the unlimited accumulation of wealth?

That, Socrates, will be inevitable.

# Book II

## External Warriors and Internal Peacekeepers

And so we shall go to war, Glaucon. Shall we not?

Most certainly, he replied.

Then without determining as yet whether war does good or harm, thus much we may affirm, that now we have discovered war to be derived from causes which are also the causes of almost all the evils in States, private as well as public.

Undoubtedly.

And our State must once more enlarge; and this time the will be nothing short of a whole army, which will have to go out and fight with the invaders for all that we have, as well as for the things and persons whom we were describing above.

Why? he said; are they not capable of defending themselves?

No, I said; not if we were right in the principle which was acknowledged by all of us when we were framing the State: the principle, as you will remember, was that one man cannot practise many arts with success.

Very true, he said.

But is not war an art?

Certainly.

And an art requiring as much attention as shoemaking?

Quite true.

And the shoemaker was not allowed by us to be husbandman, or a weaver, a builder—in order that we might have our shoes well made; but to him and to every other worker was assigned one work for which he was by nature fitted, and at that he was to continue working all his life long and at no other; he was not to let opportunities slip, and then he would become a good workman. Now nothing can be more important than that the work of a soldier should be well done. But is war an art so easily acquired that a man may be a warrior who is also a husbandman, or shoemaker, or other artisan; although no one in the world would be a good dice or draught player who merely took up the game as a recreation, and had not from his earliest years devoted himself to this and nothing else?

No tools will make a man a skilled workman, or master of defence, nor be of any use to him who has not learned how to handle them, and has never bestowed any attention upon them. How then will he who takes up a shield or other implement of war become a good fighter all in a day, whether with heavy-armed or any other kind of troops?

Yes, he said, the tools which would teach men their own use would be beyond price.

And the higher the duties of the guardian, I said, the more time, and skill, and art, and application will be needed by him?

No doubt, he replied.

Will he not also require natural aptitude for his calling?

Certainly.

Then it will be our duty to select, if we can, natures which are fitted for the task of guarding the city?

It will.

And the selection will be no easy matter, I said; but we must be brave and do our best.

We must.

Is not the noble youth very like a well-bred dog in respect of guarding and watching?

What do you mean?

I mean that both of them ought to be quick to see, and swift to overtake the enemy when they see him; and strong too if, when they have caught him, they have to fight with him.

All these qualities, he replied, will certainly be required by them.

Well, and your guardian must be brave if he is to fight well?

Certainly.

And is he likely to be brave who has no spirit, whether horse or dog or any other animal? Have you never observed how invincible and unconquerable is spirit and how the presence of it makes the soul of any creature to be absolutely fearless and indomitable?

I have.

Then now we have a clear notion of the bodily qualities which are required in the guardian.

True.

And also of the mental ones; his soul is to be full of spirit?

Yes.

But are not these spirited natures apt to be savage with one another, and with everybody else?

A difficulty by no means easy to overcome, he replied.

Whereas, I said, they ought to be dangerous to their enemies, and gentle to their friends; if not, they will destroy themselves without waiting for their enemies to destroy them.

True, he said.

What is to be done then? I said; how shall we find a gentle nature which has also a great spirit, for the one is the contradiction of the other?

True.

He will not be a good guardian who is wanting in either of these two qualities; and yet the combination of them appears to be impossible; and hence we must infer that to be a good guardian is impossible.

I am afraid that what you say is true, he replied.

Here feeling perplexed I began to think over what had preceded. My friend, I said, no wonder that we are in a perplexity; for we have lost sight of the image which we had before us.

What do you mean? he said.

I mean to say that there do exist natures gifted with those opposite qualities.

And where do you find them?

Many animals, I replied, furnish examples of them; our friend the dog is a very good one: you know that well-bred dogs are perfectly gentle to their familiars and acquaintances, and the reverse to strangers.

Yes, I know.

Then there is nothing impossible or out of the order of nature in our finding a guardian who has a similar combination of qualities?

Certainly not.

Would not he who is fitted to be a guardian, besides the spirited nature, need to have the qualities of a philosopher?

I do not apprehend your meaning.

The trait of which I am speaking, I replied, may be also seen in the dog, and is remarkable in the animal.

What trait?

Why, a dog, whenever he sees a stranger, is angry; when an acquaintance, he welcomes him, although the one has never done him any harm, nor the other any good. Did this never strike you as curious?

The matter never struck me before; but I quite recognise the truth of your remark.

And surely this instinct of the dog is very charming;—your dog is a true philosopher.

Why?

Why, because he distinguishes the face of a friend and of an enemy only by the criterion of knowing and not knowing. And must not an animal be a lover of learning who determines what he likes and dislikes by the test of knowledge and ignorance?

Most assuredly.

And is not the love of learning the love of wisdom, which is philosophy?

They are the same, he replied.

And may we not say confidently of man also, that he who is likely to be gentle to his friends and acquaintances, must by nature be a lover of wisdom and knowledge?

That we may safely affirm.

Then he who is to be a really good and noble guardian of the State will require to unite in himself philosophy and spirit and swiftness and strength?

Undoubtedly.

Then we have found the desired natures; and now that we have found them, how are they to be reared and educated? Is not this enquiry which may be expected to throw light on the greater enquiry which is our final end—How do justice and injustice grow up in States? for we do not want either to omit what is to the point or to draw out the argument to an inconvenient length.

## Book II

### Education and Censorship

Adeimantus thought that the enquiry would be of great service to us.

Then, I said, my dear friend, the task must not be given up, even if somewhat long.

Certainly not.

Come then, and let us pass a leisure hour in story-telling, and our story shall be the education of our heroes.

By all means.

And what shall be their education? Can we find a better than the traditional sort?—and this has two divisions, gymnastic for the body, and music for the soul.

True.

Shall we begin education with music, and go on to gymnastic afterwards?

By all means.

And when you speak of music, do you include literature or not?

I do.

And literature may be either true or false?

Yes.

And the young should be trained in both kinds, and we begin with the false?

I do not understand your meaning, he said. You know, I said, that we begin by telling children stories which, though not wholly destitute of truth, are in the main fictitious; and these stories are told them when they are not of an age to learn gymnastics.

Very true.

That was my meaning when I said that we must teach music before gymnastics.

Quite right, he said.

You know also that the beginning is the most important part of any work, especially in the case of a young and tender thing; for that is the time at which the character is being formed and the desired impression is more readily taken.

Quite true.

And shall we just carelessly allow children to hear any casual tales which may be devised by casual persons, and to receive into their minds ideas for the most part the very opposite of those which we should wish them to have when they are grown up?

We cannot.

Then the first thing will be to establish a censorship of the writers of fiction, and let the censors receive any tale of fiction which is good, and reject the bad; and we will desire mothers and nurses to tell their children the authorised ones only. Let them fashion the mind with such tales, even more fondly than they mould the body with their hands; but most of those which are now in use must be discarded.

Of what tales are you speaking? he said.

You may find a model of the lesser in the greater, I said; for they are necessarily of the same type, and there is the same spirit in both of them.

Very likely, he replied; but I do not as yet know what you would term the greater.

Those, I said, which are narrated by Homer and Hesiod, and the rest of the poets, who have ever been the great story-tellers of mankind.

But which stories do you mean, he said; and what fault do you find with them?

A fault which is most serious, I said; the fault of telling a lie, and, what is more, a bad lie.

But when is this fault committed?

Whenever an erroneous representation is made of the nature of gods and heroes,—as when a painter paints a portrait not having the shadow of a likeness to the original.

Yes, he said, that sort of thing is certainly very blamable; but what are the stories which you mean?

First of all, I said, there was that greatest of all lies, in high places, which the poet told about Uranus, and which was a bad lie too,—I mean what Hesiod says that Uranus did, and how Cronus retaliated on him. The doings of Cronus, and the sufferings which in turn his son inflicted upon him, even if they were true, ought certainly not to be lightly told to young and thoughtless persons; if possible, they had better be buried in silence. But if there is an absolute necessity for their mention, a chosen few might hear them in a mystery, and they should sacrifice not a common [Eleusinian] pig, but some huge and unprocurable victim; and then the number of the hearers will be very few indeed.

Why, yes, said he, those stories are extremely objectionable.

Yes, Adeimantus, they are stories not to be repeated in our State; the young man should not be told that in committing the worst of crimes he is far from doing anything outrageous; and that even if he chastises his father when does wrong, in whatever manner, he will only be following the example of the first and greatest among the gods.

I entirely agree with you, he said; in my opinion those stories are quite unfit to be repeated.

Neither, if we mean our future guardians to regard the habit of quarrelling among themselves as of all things the basest, should any word be said to them of the wars in heaven, and of the plots and fightings of the gods against one another, for they are not true. No, we shall never mention the battles of the giants, or let them be embroidered on garments; and we shall be silent about the innumerable other quarrels of gods and heroes with their friends and relatives. If they would only believe us we would tell them that quarrelling is unholy, and that never up to this time has there been any, quarrel between citizens; this is what old men and old women should begin by telling children; and when they grow up, the poets also should be told to compose for them in a similar spirit. But the narrative of Hephaestus binding Here his mother, or how on another occasion Zeus sent him flying for taking her part when she was being beaten, and all the battles of the gods in Homer—these tales must not be admitted into our State, whether they are supposed to have an allegorical meaning or not. For a young person cannot judge what is allegorical and what is literal; anything that he receives into his mind at that age is likely to become indelible and unalterable; and therefore it is most important that the tales which the young first hear should be models of virtuous thoughts.

There you are right, he replied; but if any one asks where are such models to be found and of what tales are you speaking—how shall we answer him?

I said to him, You and I, Adeimantus, at this moment are not poets, but founders of a State: now the founders of a State ought to know the general forms in which poets should cast their tales, and the limits which must be observed by them, but to make the tales is not their business.

Very true, he said; but what are these forms of theology which you mean?

Something of this kind, I replied:—God is always to be represented as he truly is, whatever be the sort of poetry, epic, lyric or tragic, in which the representation is given.

Right.

And is he not truly good? and must he not be represented as such?

Certainly.

And no good thing is hurtful?

No, indeed.

And that which is not hurtful hurts not?

Certainly not.

And that which hurts not does no evil?

No.

And can that which does no evil be a cause of evil?

Impossible.

And the good is advantageous?

Yes.

And therefore the cause of well-being?

Yes.

It follows therefore that the good is not the cause of all things, but of the good only?

Assuredly.

Then God, if he be good, is not the author of all things, as the many assert, but he is the cause of a few things only, and not of most things that occur to men. For few are the goods of human life, and many are the evils, and the good is to be attributed to God alone; of the evils the causes are to be sought elsewhere, and not in him.

That appears to me to be most true, he said.

Then we must not listen to Homer or to any other poet who is guilty of the folly of saying that two casks Lie at the threshold of Zeus, full of lots, one of good, the other of evil lots, and that he to whom Zeus gives a mixture of the two Sometimes meets with evil fortune, at other times with good; but that he to whom is given the cup of unmingled ill, Him wild hunger drives o'er the beauteous earth. And again Zeus, who is the dispenser of good and evil to us. And if any one asserts that the violation of oaths and treaties, which was really the work of Pandarus, was brought about by Athene and Zeus, or that the strife and contention of the gods was instigated by Themis and Zeus, he shall not have our approval; neither will we allow our young men to hear the words of Aeschylus, that God plants guilt among men when he desires utterly to destroy a house. And if a poet writes of the sufferings of Niobe—the subject of the tragedy in which these iambic verses occur—or of the house of Pelops, or of the Trojan war or on any similar theme, either we must not permit him to say that these are the works of God, or if they are of God, he must devise some explanation of them such as we are seeking; he must say

that God did what was just and right, and they were the better for being punished; but that those who are punished are miserable, and that God is the author of their misery— the poet is not to be permitted to say; though he may say that the wicked are miserable because they require to be punished, and are benefited by receiving punishment from God; but that God being good is the author of evil to any one is to be strenuously denied, and not to be said or sung or heard in verse or prose by any one whether old or young in any well-ordered commonwealth. Such a fiction is suicidal, ruinous, impious.

I agree with you, he replied, and am ready to give my assent to the law.

Let this then be one of our rules and principles concerning the gods, to which our poets and reciters will be expected to conform—that God is not the author of all things, but of good only.

That will do, he said.

And what do you think of a second principle? Shall I ask you whether God is a magician, and of a nature to appear insidiously now in one shape, and now in another—sometimes himself changing and passing into many forms, sometimes deceiving us with the semblance of such transformations; or is he one and the same immutably fixed in his own proper image?

I cannot answer you, he said, without more thought.

Well, I said; but if we suppose a change in anything, that change must be effected either by the thing itself, or by some other thing?

Most certainly.

And things which are at their best are also least liable to be altered or discomposed; for example, when healthiest and strongest, the human frame is least liable to be affected by meats and drinks, and the plant which is in the fullest vigour also suffers least from winds or the heat of the sun or any similar causes.

Of course.

And will not the bravest and wisest soul be least confused or deranged by any external influence?

True.

And the same principle, as I should suppose, applies to all composite things—furniture, houses, garments; when good and well made, they are least altered by time and circumstances.

Very true.

Then everything which is good, whether made by art or nature, or both, is least liable to suffer change from without?

True.

But surely God and the things of God are in every way perfect?

Of course they are.

Then he can hardly be compelled by external influence to take many shapes?

He cannot.

But may he not change and transform himself? Clearly, he said, that must be the case if he is changed at all.

And will he then change himself for the better and fairer, or for the worse and more unsightly?

If he change at all he can only change for the worse, for we cannot suppose him to be deficient either in virtue or beauty.

Very true, Adeimantus; but then, would any one, whether God or man, desire to make himself worse?

Impossible.

Then it is impossible that God should ever be willing to change; being, as is supposed, the fairest and best that is conceivable, every god remains absolutely and for ever in his own form.

That necessarily follows, he said, in my judgment.

Then, I said, my dear friend, let none of the poets tell us that

The gods, taking the disguise of strangers from other lands, walk up and down cities in all sorts of forms; and let no one slander Proteus and Thetis, neither let any one, either in tragedy or in any other kind of poetry, introduce Here disguised in the likeness of a priestess asking an alms

For the life-giving daughters of Inachus the river of Argos;—let us have no more lies of that sort. Neither must we have mothers under the influence of the poets scaring their children with a bad version of these myths—telling how certain gods, as they say, 'Go about by night in the likeness of so many strangers and in divers forms'; but let them take heed lest they make cowards of their children, and at the same time speak blasphemy against the gods.

Heaven forbid, he said.

But although the gods are themselves unchangeable, still by witchcraft and deception they may make us think that they appear in various forms?

Perhaps, he replied.

Well, but can you imagine that God will be willing to lie, whether in word or deed, or to put forth a phantom of himself?

I cannot say, he replied.

Do you not know, I said, that the true lie, if such an expression may be allowed, is hated of gods and men?

What do you mean? he said.

I mean that no one is willingly deceived in that which is the truest and highest part of himself, or about the truest and highest matters; there, above all, he is most afraid of a lie having possession of him.

Still, he said, I do not comprehend you.

The reason is, I replied, that you attribute some profound meaning to my words; but I am only saying that deception, or being deceived or uninformed about the highest realities in the highest part of themselves, which is the soul, and in that part of them to have and to hold the lie, is what mankind least like;—that, I say, is what they utterly detest.

There is nothing more hateful to them.

And, as I was just now remarking, this ignorance in the soul of him who is deceived may be called the true lie; for the lie in words is only a kind of imitation and shadowy image of a previous affection of the soul, not pure unadulterated falsehood. Am I not right?

Perfectly right.

The true lie is hated not only by the gods, but also by men?

Yes.

Whereas the lie in words is in certain cases useful and not hateful; in dealing with enemies—that would be an instance; or again, when those whom we call our friends in a fit of madness or illusion are going to do some harm, then it is useful and is a sort of medicine or preventive; also in the tales of mythology, of which we were just now speaking—because we do not know the truth about ancient times, we make falsehood as much like truth as we can, and so turn it to account.

Very true, he said.

But can any of these reasons apply to God? Can we suppose that he is ignorant of antiquity, and therefore has recourse to invention?

That would be ridiculous, he said.

Then the lying poet has no place in our idea of God?

I should say not.

Or perhaps he may tell a lie because he is afraid of enemies?

That is inconceivable.

But he may have friends who are senseless or mad?

But no mad or senseless person can be a friend of God.

Then no motive can be imagined why God should lie?

None whatever.

Then the superhuman and divine is absolutely incapable of falsehood?

Yes.

Then is God perfectly simple and true both in word and deed; he changes not; he deceives not, either by sign or word, by dream or waking vision.

Your thoughts, he said, are the reflection of my own.

You agree with me then, I said, that this is the second type or form in which we should write and speak about divine things. The gods are not magicians who transform themselves, neither do they deceive mankind in any way.

I grant that.

Then, although we are admirers of Homer, we do not admire the lying dream which Zeus sends to Agamemnon; neither will we praise the verses of Aeschylus in which Thetis says that Apollo at her nuptials

Was celebrating in song her fair progeny whose days were to he long, and to know no sickness. And when he had spoken of my lot as in all things blessed of heaven he raised a note of triumph and cheered my soul. And I thought that the word of Phoebus being divine and full of prophecy, would not fail. And now he himself who uttered the strain, he who was present at the banquet, and who said this—he it is who has slain my son.

These are the kind of sentiments about the gods which will arouse our anger; and he who utters them shall be refused a chorus; neither shall we allow teachers to make use of them in the instruction of the young, meaning, as we do, that our guardians, as far as men can be, should be true worshippers of the gods and like them.

I entirely agree, be said, in these principles, and promise to make them my laws.

# Book V

## Philosophers Must Be Kings

Now then, I said, I go to meet that which I liken to the greatest of the waves; yet shall the word be spoken, even though the wave break and drown me in laughter and dishonour; and do you mark my words.

Proceed.

I said: Until philosophers are kings, or the kings and princes of this world have the spirit and power of philosophy, and political greatness and wisdom meet in one, and those commoner natures who pursue either to the exclusion of the other are compelled to stand aside, cities will never have rest from their evils,—nor the human race, as I believe,—and then only will this our State have a possibility of life and behold the light of day. Such was the thought, my dear Glaucon, which I would fain have uttered if it had not seemed too extravagant; for to be convinced that in no other State can there be happiness private or public is indeed a hard thing.

Socrates, what do you mean? I would have you consider that the word which you have uttered is one at which numerous persons, and very respectable persons too, in a figure pulling off their coats all in a moment, and seizing any weapon that comes to hand, will run at you might and main, before you know

where you are, intending to do heaven knows what; and if you don't prepare an answer, and put yourself in motion, you will be prepared by their fine wits,' and no mistake.

You got me into the scrape, I said.

And I was quite right; however, I will do all I can to get you out of it; but I can only give you good-will and good advice, and, perhaps, I may be able to fit answers to your questions better than another—that is all. And now, having such an auxiliary, you must do your best to show the unbelievers that you are right.

I ought to try, I said, since you offer me such invaluable assistance. And I think that, if there is to be a chance of our escaping, we must explain to them whom we mean when we say that philosophers are to rule in the State; then we shall be able to defend ourselves: There will be discovered to be some natures who ought to study philosophy and to be leaders in the State; and others who are not born to be philosophers, and are meant to be followers rather than leaders.

Then now for a definition, he said.

Follow me, I said, and I hope that I may in some way or other be able to give you a satisfactory explanation.

Proceed.

I dare say that you remember, and therefore I need not remind you, that a lover, if lie is worthy of the name, ought to show his love, not to some one part of that which he loves, but to the whole.

I really do not understand, and therefore beg of you to assist my memory.

Another person, I said, might fairly reply as you do; but a man of pleasure like yourself ought to know that all who are in the flower of youth do somehow or other raise a pang or emotion in a lover's breast, and are thought by him to be worthy of his affectionate regards. Is not this a way which you have with the fair: one has a snub nose, and you praise his charming face; the hook-nose of another has, you say, a royal look; while he who is neither snub nor hooked has the grace of regularity: the dark visage is manly, the fair are children of the gods; and as to the sweet 'honey pale,' as they are called, what is the very name but the invention of a lover who talks in diminutives, and is not adverse to paleness if appearing on the cheek of youth? In a word, there is no excuse which you will not make, and nothing which you will not say, in order not to lose a single flower that blooms in the spring-time of youth.

If you make me an authority in matters of love, for the sake of the argument, I assent.

And what do you say of lovers of wine? Do you not see them doing the same? They are glad of any pretext of drinking any wine.

Very good.

And the same is true of ambitious men; if they cannot command an army, they are willing to command a file; and if they cannot be honoured by really great and important persons, they are glad to be honoured by lesser and meaner people, but honour of some kind they must have.

Exactly.

Once more let me ask: Does he who desires any class of goods, desire the whole class or a part only?

The whole.

And may we not say of the philosopher that he is a lover, not of a part of wisdom only, but of the whole?

Yes, of the whole.

And he who dislikes learnings, especially in youth, when he has no power of judging what is good and what is not, such an one we maintain not to be a philosopher or a lover of knowledge, just as he who refuses his food is not hungry, and may be said to have a bad appetite and not a good one?

Very true, he said.

Whereas he who has a taste for every sort of knowledge and who is curious to learn and is never satisfied, may be justly termed a philosopher? Am I not right?

Glaucon said: If curiosity makes a philosopher, you will find many a strange being will have a title to the name. All the lovers of sights have a delight in learning, and must therefore be included. Musical amateurs, too, are a folk strangely out of place among philosophers, for they are the last persons in the world who would come to anything like a philosophical discussion, if they could help, while they run about at the Dionysiac festivals as if they had let out their ears to hear every chorus; whether the performance is in town or country—that makes no difference—they are there. Now are we to maintain that all these and any who have similar tastes, as well as the professors of quite minor arts, are philosophers?

Certainly not, I replied; they are only an imitation.

He said: Who then are the true philosophers?

Those, I said, who are lovers of the vision of truth.

That is also good, he said; but I should like to know what you mean?

To another, I replied, I might have a difficulty in explaining; but I am sure that you will admit a proposition which I am about to make.

What is the proposition?

That since beauty is the opposite of ugliness, they are two?

Certainly.

And inasmuch as they are two, each of them is one?

True again.

And of just and unjust, good and evil, and of every other class, the same remark holds: taken singly, each of them one; but from the various combinations of them with actions and things and with one another, they are seen in all sorts of lights and appear many? Very true.

And this is the distinction which I draw between the sight-loving, art-loving, practical class and those of whom I am speaking, and who are alone worthy of the name of philosophers.

How do you distinguish them? he said.

The lovers of sounds and sights, I replied, are, as I conceive, fond of fine tones and colours and forms and all the artificial products that are made out of them, but their mind is incapable of seeing or loving absolute beauty.

True, he replied.

Few are they who are able to attain to the sight of this.

Very true.

And he who, having a sense of beautiful things has no sense of absolute beauty, or who, if another lead him to a knowledge of that beauty is unable to follow—of such an one I ask, Is he awake or in a dream only? Reflect: is not the dreamer, sleeping or waking, one who likens dissimilar things, who puts the copy in the place of the real object?

I should certainly say that such an one was dreaming.

But take the case of the other, who recognises the existence of absolute beauty and is able to distinguish the idea from the objects which participate in the idea, neither putting the objects in the place of the idea nor the idea in the place of the objects—is he a dreamer, or is he awake?

He is wide awake.

And may we not say that the mind of the one who knows has knowledge, and that the mind of the other, who opines only, has opinion

Certainly.

But suppose that the latter should quarrel with us and dispute our statement, can we administer any soothing cordial or advice to him, without revealing to him that there is sad disorder in his wits?

We must certainly offer him some good advice, he replied.

Come, then, and let us think of something to say to him. Shall we begin by assuring him that he is welcome to any knowledge which he may have, and that we are rejoiced at his having it? But we should like to ask him a question: Does he who has knowledge know something or nothing? (You must answer for him.)

I answer that he knows something.

Something that is or is not?

Something that is; for how can that which is not ever be known?

And are we assured, after looking at the matter from many points of view, that absolute being is or may be absolutely known, but that the utterly non-existent is utterly unknown?

Nothing can be more certain.

Good. But if there be anything which is of such a nature as to be and not to be, that will have a place intermediate between pure being and the absolute negation of being?

Yes, between them.

And, as knowledge corresponded to being and ignorance of necessity to not-being, for that intermediate between being and not-being there has to be discovered a corresponding intermediate between ignorance and knowledge, if there be such?

Certainly.

Do we admit the existence of opinion?

Undoubtedly.

As being the same with knowledge, or another faculty?

Another faculty.

Then opinion and knowledge have to do with different kinds of matter corresponding to this difference of faculties?

Yes.

And knowledge is relative to being and knows being. But before I proceed further I will make a division.

What division?

I will begin by placing faculties in a class by themselves: they are powers in us, and in all other things, by which we do as we do. Sight and hearing, for example, I should call faculties. Have I clearly explained the class which I mean?

Yes, I quite understand.

Then let me tell you my view about them. I do not see them, and therefore the distinctions of fire, colour, and the like, which enable me to discern the differences of some things, do not apply to them. In speaking of a faculty I think only of its sphere and its result; and that which has the same sphere and the same result I call the same faculty, but that which has another sphere and another result I call different. Would that be your way of speaking?

Yes.

And will you be so very good as to answer one more question? Would you say that knowledge is a faculty, or in what class would you place it?

Certainly knowledge is a faculty, and the mightiest of all faculties.

# Book VII

## The Allegory of the Cave

And now, I said, let me show in a figure how far our nature is enlightened or unenlightened:—Behold! human beings living in a underground den, which has a mouth open towards the light and reaching all along the den; here they have been from their childhood, and have their legs and necks chained so that they cannot move, and can only see before them, being prevented by the chains from turning round their heads. Above and behind them a fire is blazing at a distance, and between the fire and the prisoners there is a raised way; and you will see, if you look, a low wall built along the way, like the screen which marionette players have in front of them, over which they show the puppets.

I see.

And do you see, I said, men passing along the wall carrying all sorts of vessels, and statues and figures of animals made of wood and stone and various materials, which appear over the wall? Some of them are talking, others silent.

You have shown me a strange image, and they are strange prisoners.

Like ourselves, I replied; and they see only their own shadows, or the shadows of one another, which the fire throws on the opposite wall of the cave?

True, he said; how could they see anything but the shadows if they were never allowed to move their heads?

And of the objects which are being carried in like manner they would only see the shadows?

Yes, he said.

And if they were able to converse with one another, would they not suppose that they were naming what was actually before them?

Very true.

And suppose further that the prison had an echo which came from the other side, would they not be sure to fancy when one of the passers-by spoke that the voice which they heard came from the passing shadow?

No question, he replied.

To them, I said, the truth would be literally nothing but the shadows of the images.

That is certain.

And now look again, and see what will naturally follow it' the prisoners are released and disabused of their error. At first, when any of them is liberated and compelled suddenly to stand up and turn his neck round and walk and look towards the light, he will suffer sharp pains; the glare will distress him, and he will be unable to see the realities of which in his former state he had seen the shadows; and then conceive some one saying to him, that what he saw before was an illusion, but that now, when he is approaching nearer to being and his eye is turned towards more real existence, he has a clearer vision,—what will be his reply? And you may further imagine that his instructor is pointing to the objects as they pass and requiring him to name them,—will he not be perplexed? Will he not fancy that the shadows which he formerly saw are truer than the objects which are now shown to him?

Far truer.

And if he is compelled to look straight at the light, will he not have a pain in his eyes which will make him turn away to take and take in the objects of vision which he can see, and which he will conceive to be in reality clearer than the things which are now being shown to him?

True, he now

And suppose once more, that he is reluctantly dragged up a steep and rugged ascent, and held fast until he 's forced into the presence of the sun himself, is he not likely to be pained and irritated? When he approaches the light his eyes will be dazzled, and he will not be able to see anything at all of what are now called realities.

Not all in a moment, he said.

He will require to grow accustomed to the sight of the upper world. And first he will see the shadows best, next the reflections of men and other objects in the water, and then the objects themselves; then he will gaze upon the light of the moon and the stars and the spangled heaven; and he will see the sky and the stars by night better than the sun or the light of the sun by day?

Certainly.

Last of he will be able to see the sun, and not mere reflections of him in the water, but he will see him in his own proper place, and not in another; and he will contemplate him as he is.

Certainly.

He will then proceed to argue that this is he who gives the season and the years, and is the guardian of all that is in the visible world, and in a certain way the cause of all things which he and his fellows have been accustomed to behold?

Clearly, he said, he would first see the sun and then reason about him.

And when he remembered his old habitation, and the wisdom of the den and his fellow-prisoners, do you not suppose that he would felicitate himself on the change, and pity them?

Certainly, he would.

And if they were in the habit of conferring honours among themselves on those who were quickest to observe the passing shadows and to remark which of them went before, and which followed after, and which were together; and who were therefore best able to draw conclusions as to the future, do you think that he would care for such honours and glories, or envy the possessors of them? Would he not say with Homer,

Better to be the poor servant of a poor master, and to endure anything, rather than think as they do and live after their manner?

Yes, he said, I think that he would rather suffer anything than entertain these false notions and live in this miserable manner.

Imagine once more, I said, such an one coming suddenly out of the sun to be replaced in his old situation; would he not be certain to have his eyes full of darkness?

To be sure, he said.

And if there were a contest, and he had to compete in measuring the shadows with the prisoners who had never moved out of the den, while his sight was still weak, and before his eyes had become steady (and the time which would be needed to acquire this new habit of sight might be very considerable) would he not be ridiculous? Men would say of him that up he went and down he came without his eyes; and that it was better not even to think of ascending; and if any one tried to loose another and lead him up to the light, let them only catch the offender, and they would put him to death.

No question, he said.

This entire allegory, I said, you may now append, dear Glaucon, to the previous argument; the prison-house is the world of sight, the light of the fire is the sun, and you will not misapprehend me if you interpret the journey upwards to be the ascent of the soul into the intellectual world according to my poor belief, which, at your desire, I have expressed whether rightly or wrongly God knows. But, whether true or false, my opinion is that in the world of knowledge the idea of good appears last of all, and is seen only with an effort; and, when seen, is also inferred to be the universal author of all things beautiful and right, parent of light and of the lord of light in this visible world, and the immediate source of reason and truth in the intellectual; and that this is the power upon which he who would act rationally, either in public or private life must have his eye fixed.

I agree, he said, as far as I am able to understand you.

Moreover, I said, you must not wonder that those who attain to this beatific vision are unwilling to descend to human affairs; for their souls are ever hastening into the upper world where they desire to dwell; which desire of theirs is very natural, if our allegory may be trusted.

Yes, very natural.

And is there anything surprising in one who passes from divine contemplations to the evil state of man, misbehaving himself in a ridiculous manner; if, while his eyes are blinking and before he has become accustomed to the surrounding darkness, he is compelled to fight in courts of law, or in other places, about the images or the shadows of images of justice, and is endeavouring to meet the conceptions of those who have never yet seen absolute justice?

Anything but surprising, he replied.

Any one who has common sense will remember that the bewilderments of the eyes are of two kinds, and arise from two causes, either from coming out of the light or from going into the light, which is true of the mind's eye, quite as much as of the bodily eye; and he who remembers this when he sees any one whose vision is perplexed and weak, will not be too ready to laugh; he will first ask whether that soul of man has come out of the brighter light, and is unable to see because unaccustomed to the dark, or having turned from darkness to the day is dazzled by excess of light. And he will count the one happy in his condition and state of being, and he will pity the other; or, if he have a mind to laugh at the soul which comes from below into the light, there will be more reason in this than in the laugh which greets him who returns from above out of the light into the den.

That, he said, is a very just distinction.

But then, if I am right, certain professors of education must be wrong when they say that they can put a knowledge into the soul which was not there before, like sight into blind eyes.

They undoubtedly say this, he replied. Whereas, our argument shows that the power and capacity of learning exists in the soul already; and that just as the eye was unable to turn from darkness to light without the whole body, so too the instrument of knowledge can only by the movement of the whole soul be turned from the world of becoming into that of being, and learn by degrees to endure the sight of being, and of the brightest and best of being, or in other words, of the good.

Very true.

And must there not be some art which will effect conversion in the easiest and quickest manner; not implanting the faculty of sight, for that exists already, but has been turned in the wrong direction, and is looking away from the truth?

Yes, he said, such an art may be presumed. And whereas the other so-called virtues of the soul seem to be akin to bodily qualities, for even when they are not originally innate they can be implanted later by habit and exercise, the of wisdom more than anything else contains a divine element which always remains, and by this conversion is rendered useful and profitable; or, on the other hand, hurtful and useless. Did you never observe the narrow intelligence flashing from the keen eye of a clever rogue—how eager he is, how clearly his paltry soul sees the way to his end; he is the reverse of blind, but his keen eyesight is forced into the service of evil,

and he is mischievous in proportion to his cleverness.

Very true, he said.

But what if there had been a circumcision of such natures in the days of their youth; and they had been severed from those sensual pleasures, such as eating and drinking, which, like leaden weights, were attached to them at their birth, and which drag them down and turn the vision of their souls upon the things that are below—if, I say, they had been released from these impediments and turned in the opposite direction, the very same faculty in them would have seen the truth as keenly as they see what their eyes are turned to now.

Very likely.

Yes, I said; and there is another thing which is likely. or rather a necessary inference from what has preceded, that neither the uneducated and uninformed of the truth, nor yet those who never make an end of their education, will be able ministers of State; not the former, because they have no single aim of duty which is the rule of all their actions, private as well as public; nor the latter, because they will not act at all except upon compulsion, fancying that they are already dwelling apart in the islands of the blest.

Very true, he replied.

Then, I said, the business of us who are the founders of the State will be to compel the best minds to attain that knowledge which we have already shown to be the greatest of all—they must continue to ascend until they arrive at the good; but when they have ascended and seen enough we must not allow them to do as they do now.

What do you mean?

I mean that they remain in the upper world: but this must not be allowed; they must be made to descend again among the prisoners in the den, and partake of their labours and honours, whether they are worth having or not.

But is not this unjust? he said; ought we to give them a worse life, when they might have a better?

You have again forgotten, my friend, I said, the intention of the legislator, who did not aim at making any one class in the State happy above the rest; the happiness was to be in the whole State, and he held the citizens together by persuasion and necessity, making them benefactors of the State, and therefore benefactors of one another; to this end he created them, not to please themselves, but to be his instruments in binding up the State.

True, he said, I had forgotten.

Observe, Glaucon, that there will be no injustice in compelling our philosophers to have a care and providence of others; we shall explain to them that in other States, men of their class are not obliged to share in the toils of politics: and this is reasonable, for they grow up at their own sweet will, and the government would rather not have them. Being self-taught, they cannot be expected to show any gratitude for a culture which they have never received. But we have brought you into the world to be rulers of the hive, kings of yourselves and of the other citizens, and have educated you far better and more perfectly than they have been educated, and you are better able to share in the double duty. Wherefore each of you, when his turn comes, must go down to the general underground abode, and get the habit of seeing in the dark. When you have acquired the habit, you will see ten thousand times better than the inhabitants of the den, and you will know what the several images are, and what they represent, because you have seen the beautiful and just and good in their truth. And thus our State which is also yours will be a reality, and not a dream only, and will be administered in a spirit unlike that of other States, in which men fight with one another about shadows only and are distracted in the struggle for power, which in their eyes is a great good. Whereas the truth is that the State in which the rulers are most reluctant to govern is always the best and most quietly governed, and the State in which they are most eager, the worst.

Quite true, he replied.

And will our pupils, when they hear this, refuse to take their turn at the toils of State, when they are allowed to spend the greater part of their time with one another in the heavenly light?

Impossible, he answered; for they are just men, and the commands which we impose upon them are just; there can be no doubt that every one of them will take office as a stern necessity, and not after the fashion of our present rulers of State.

Yes, my friend, I said; and there lies the point. You must contrive for your future rulers another and a better life than that of a ruler, and then you may have a well-ordered State; for only in the State which offers this, will they rule who are truly rich, not in silver and gold, but in virtue and wisdom, which are the true blessings of life. Whereas if they go to the administration of public affairs, poor and hungering after the' own private advantage, thinking that hence they are to snatch the chief good, order there can never be; for they will be fighting about office, and the civil and domestic broils which thus arise will be the ruin of the rulers themselves and of the whole State.

Most true, he replied.

And the only life which looks down upon the life of political ambition is that of true philosophy. Do you know of any other?

Indeed, I do not, he said.

And those who govern ought not to be lovers of the task? For, if they are, there will be rival lovers, and they will fight.

No question.

Who then are those whom we shall compel to be guardians? Surely they will be the men who are wisest about affairs of State, and by whom the State is best administered, and who at the same time have other honours and another and a better life than that of politics?

They are the men, and I will choose them, he replied.

And now shall we consider in what way such guardians will be produced, and how they are to be brought from darkness to light,—as some are said to have ascended from the world below to the gods?

By all means, he replied.

The process, I said, is not the turning over of an oyster-shell, but the turning round of a soul passing from a day which is little better than night to the true day of being, that is, the ascent from below, which we affirm to be true philosophy?

Quite so.

And should we not enquire what sort of knowledge has the power of effecting such a change?

Certainly.

What sort of knowledge is there which would draw the soul from becoming to being? And another consideration has just occurred to me: You will remember that our young men are to be warrior athletes

Yes, that was said.

Then this new kind of knowledge must have an additional quality?

What quality?

Usefulness in war.

Yes, if possible.

There were two parts in our former scheme of education, were there not?

Just so.

There was gymnastic which presided over the growth and decay of the body, and may therefore be regarded as having to do with generation and corruption?

True.

Then that is not the knowledge which we are seeking to discover? No.

But what do you say of music, which also entered to a certain extent into our former scheme?

Music, he said, as you will remember, was the counterpart of gymnastic, and trained the guardians by the influences of habit, by harmony making them harmonious, by rhythm rhythmical, but not giving them science; and the words, whether fabulous or possibly true, had kindred elements of rhythm and harmony in them. But in music there was nothing which tended to that good which you are now seeking.

You are most accurate, I said, in your recollection; in music there certainly was nothing of the kind. But what branch of knowledge is there, my dear Glaucon, which is of the desired nature; since all the useful arts were reckoned mean by us?

Undoubtedly; and yet if music and gymnastic are excluded, and the arts are also excluded, what remains?

Well, I said, there may be nothing left of our special subjects; and then we shall have to take something which is not special, but of universal application.

What may that be?

A something which all arts and sciences and intelligences use in common, and which every one first has to learn among the elements of education.

What is that?

The little matter of distinguishing one, two, and three—in a word, number and calculation:— do not all arts and sciences necessarily partake of them?

Yes.

Then the art of war partakes of them?

To the sure.

Then Palamedes, whenever he appears in tragedy, proves Agamemnon ridiculously unfit to be a general. Did you never remark how he declares that he had invented number, and had numbered the ships and set in array the ranks of the army at Troy; which implies that they had never been numbered before, and Agamemnon must be supposed literally to have been incapable of counting his own feet—how could he if he was ignorant of number? And if that is true, what sort of general must he have been?

I should say a very strange one, if this was as you say.

Can we deny that a warrior should have a knowledge of arithmetic?

Certainly he should, if he is to have the smallest understanding of military tactics, or indeed, I should rather say, if he is to be a man at all.

I should like to know whether you have the same notion which I have of this study?

What is your notion?

It appears to me to be a study of the kind which we are seeking, and which leads naturally to reflection, but never to have been rightly used; for the true use of it is simply to draw the soul towards being.

# Book VIII

## Democracy and the Democratic Man

And if there be any ally which aids the oligarchical principle within him, whether the influence of a father or of kindred, advising or rebuking him, then there arises in his soul a faction and an opposite faction, and he goes to war with himself.

It must be so.

And there are times when the democratical principle gives way to the oligarchical, and some of his desires die, and others are banished; a spirit of reverence enters into the young man's soul and order is restored.

Yes, he said, that sometimes happens.

And then, again, after the old desires have been driven out, fresh ones spring up, which are akin to them, and because he, their father, does not know how to educate them, wax fierce and numerous.

Yes, he said, that is apt to be the way.

They draw him to his old associates, and holding secret intercourse with them, breed and multiply in him.

Very true.

At length they seize upon the citadel of the young man's soul, which they perceive to be void of all accomplishments and fair pursuits and true words, which make their abode in the minds of men who are dear to the gods, and are their best guardians and sentinels.

None better.

False and boastful conceits and phrases mount upwards and take their place.

They are certain to do so.

And so the young man returns into the country of the lotus-eaters, and takes up his dwelling there in the face of all men; and if any help be sent by his friends to the oligarchical part of him, the aforesaid vain conceits shut the gate of the king's fastness; and they will neither allow the embassy itself to enter, private if private advisers offer the fatherly counsel of the aged will they listen to them or receive them. There is a battle and they gain the day, and then modesty, which they call silliness, is ignominiously thrust into exile by them, and temperance, which they nickname un-manliness, is trampled in the mire and cast forth; they persuade men that moderation and orderly expenditure are vulgarity and meanness, and so, by the help of a rabble of evil appetites, they drive them beyond the border.

Yes, with a will.

And when they have emptied and swept clean the soul of him who is now in their power and who is being initiated by them in great mysteries, the next thing is to bring back to their house insolence and anarchy and waste and impudence in bright array having garlands on their heads, and a great company with them, hymning their praises and calling them by sweet names; insolence they term breeding, and anarchy liberty, and waste magnificence, and impudence courage. And so the young man passes out of his original nature, which was trained in the school of necessity, into the freedom and libertinism of useless and unnecessary pleasures.

Yes, he said, the change in him is visible enough.

After this he lives on, spending his money and labour and time on unnecessary pleasures quite as much as on necessary ones; but if he be fortunate, and is not too much disordered in his wits, when years have elapsed, and the heyday of passion is over—supposing that he then re-admits into the city some part of the exiled virtues, and does not wholly give himself up to their successors—in that case he balances his pleasures and lives in a sort of equilibrium, putting the government of himself into the hands of the one which comes first and wins the turn; and when he has had enough of that, then into the hands of another; he despises none of them but encourages them all equally.

Very true, he said.

Neither does he receive or let pass into the fortress any true word of advice; if any one says to him that some pleasures are the satisfactions of good and noble desires, and others of evil desires, and that he ought to use and honour some and chastise and master the others—whenever this is repeated to him he shakes his head and says that they are all alike, and that one is as good as another.

Yes, he said; that is the way with him.

Yes, I said, he lives from day to day indulging the appetite of the hour; and sometimes he is lapped in drink and strains of the flute; then he becomes a water-drinker, and tries to get thin; then he takes a turn at gymnastics; sometimes idling and neglecting everything, then once more living the life of a philosopher; oft en he—is busy with politics, and starts to his feet and says and does whatever comes into his head; and, if he is emulous of any one who is a warrior, off he is in that direction, or of men of business, once more in that. His life has neither law nor order; and this distracted existence he terms joy and bliss and freedom; and so he goes on.

Yes, he replied, he is all liberty and equality.

Yes, I said; his life is motley and manifold and an epitome of the lives of many;—he answers to the State which we described as fair and spangled. And many a man and many a woman will take him for their pattern, and many a constitution and many an example of manners is contained in him.

Just so.

Let him then be set over against democracy; he may truly be called the democratic man.

Let that be his place, he said.

Last of all comes the most beautiful of all, man and State alike, tyranny and the tyrant; these we have now to consider.

Quite true, he said.

Say then, my friend, in what manner does tyranny arise?—that it has a democratic origin is evident.

Clearly.

And does not tyranny spring from democracy in the same manner as democracy from oligarchy—I mean, after a sort?

How?

The good which oligarchy proposed to itself and the means by which it was maintained was excess of wealth—am I not right?

Yes.

And the insatiable desire of wealth and the neglect of all other things for the sake of money-getting was also the ruin of oligarchy?

True.

And democracy has her own good, of which the insatiable desire brings her to dissolution?

What good?

Freedom, I replied; which, as they tell you in a democracy, is the glory of the State—and that therefore in a democracy alone will the freeman of nature deign to dwell.

Yes; the saying is in everybody's mouth.

I was going to observe, that the insatiable desire of this and the neglect of other things introduces the change in democracy, which occasions a demand for tyranny.

How so?

When a democracy which is thirsting for freedom has evil cupbearers presiding over the feast, and has drunk too deeply of the strong wine of freedom, then, unless her rulers are very amenable and give a plentiful draught, she calls them to account and punishes them, and says that they are cursed oligarchs.

Yes, he replied, a very common occurrence.

Yes, I said; and loyal citizens are insultingly termed by her slaves who hug their chains and men of naught; she would have subjects who are like rulers, and rulers who are like subjects: these are men after her own heart, whom she praises and honours both in private and public. Now, in such a State, can liberty have any limit?

Certainly not.

By degrees the anarchy finds a way into private houses, and ends by getting among the animals and infecting them.

How do you mean?

I mean that the father grows accustomed to descend to the level of his sons and to fear them, and the son is on a level with his father, he having no respect or reverence for either of his parents; and this is his freedom, and metic is equal with the citizen and the citizen with the metic, and the stranger is quite as good as either.

Yes, he said, that is the way.

And these are not the only evils, I said—there are several lesser ones: In such a state of society the master fears and flatters his scholars, and the scholars despise their masters and tutors; young and old are all alike; and the young man is on a level with the old, and is ready to compete with him in word or deed; and old men condescend to the young and are full of pleasantry and gaiety; they are loth to be thought morose and authoritative, and therefore they adopt the manners of the young.

Quite true, he said.

The last extreme of popular liberty is when the slave bought with money, whether male or female, is just as free as his or her purchaser; nor must I forget to tell of the liberty and equality of the two sexes in relation to each other.

Why not, as Aeschylus says, utter the word which rises to our lips?

That is what I am doing, I replied; and I must add that no one who does not know would believe, how much greater is the liberty which the animals who are under the dominion of man have in a democracy than in any other State: for truly, the she-dogs, as the proverb says, are as good as their she-mistresses, and the horses and asses have a way of marching along with all the rights and dignities of freemen; and they will run at anybody who comes in their way if he does not leave the road clear for them: and all things are just ready to burst with liberty.

When I take a country walk, he said, I oft en experience what you describe. You and I have dreamed the same thing.

And above all, I said, and as the result of all, see how sensitive the citizens become; they chafe impatiently at the least touch of authority and at length, as you know, they cease to care even for the laws, written or unwritten; they will have no one over them.

Yes, he said, I know it too well.

Such, my friend, I said, is the fair and glorious beginning out of which springs tyranny.

Glorious indeed, he said. But what is the next step?

The ruin of oligarchy is the ruin of democracy; the same disease magnified and intensified by liberty overmasters democracy—the truth being that the excessive increase of anything oft en causes a reaction in the opposite direction; and this is the case not only in the seasons and in vegetable and animal life, but above all in forms of government.

True.

The excess of liberty, whether in States or individuals, seems only to pass into excess of slavery.

Yes, the natural order.

And so tyranny naturally arises out of democracy, and the most aggravated form of tyranny and slavery out of the most extreme form of liberty?

As we might expect.

That, however, was not, as I believe, your question—you rather desired to know what is that disorder which is generated alike in oligarchy and democracy, and is the ruin of both?

Just so, he replied.

Well, I said, I meant to refer to the class of idle spendthrift s, of whom the more courageous are the leaders and the more timid the followers, the same whom we were comparing to drones, some stingless, and others having stings.

A very just comparison.

These two classes are the plagues of every city in which they are generated, being what phlegm and bile are to the body. And the good physician and lawgiver of the State ought, like the wise bee-master, to keep them at a distance and prevent, if possible, their ever coming in; and if they have anyhow found a way in, then he should have them and their cells cut out as speedily as possible.

Yes, by all means, he said.

Then, in order that we may see clearly what we are doing, let us imagine democracy to be divided, as indeed it is, into three classes; for in the first place freedom creates rather more drones in the democratic than there were in the oligarchical State.

That is true.

And in the democracy they are certainly more intensified.

How so?

Because in the oligarchical State they are disqualified and driven from office, and therefore they cannot train or gather strength; whereas in a democracy they are almost the entire ruling power, and while the keener sort speak and act, the rest keep buzzing about the bema and do not suffer a word to be said on the other side; hence in democracies almost everything is managed by the drones.

Very true, he said.

Then there is another class which is always being severed from the mass.

What is that?

They are the orderly class, which in a nation of traders sure to be the richest.

Naturally so.

They are the most squeezable persons and yield the largest amount of honey to the drones.

Why, he said, there is little to be squeezed out of people who have little.

And this is called the wealthy class, and the drones feed upon them.

That is pretty much the case, he said.

The people are a third class, consisting of those who work with their own hands; they are not politicians, and have not much to live upon. This, when assembled, is the largest and most powerful class in a democracy.

True, he said; but then the multitude is seldom willing to congregate unless they get a little honey.

And do they not share? I said. Do not their leaders deprive the rich of their estates and distribute them among the people; at the same time taking care to reserve the larger part for themselves?

Why, yes, he said, to that extent the people do share.

And the persons whose property is taken from them are compelled to defend themselves before the people as they best can?

What else can they do?

And then, although they may have no desire of change, the others charge them with plotting against the people and being friends of oligarchy? True.

And the end is that when they see the people, not of their own accord, but through ignorance, and because they are deceived by informers, seeking to do them wrong, then at last they are forced to become oligarchs in reality; they do not wish to be, but the sting of the drones torments them and breeds revolution in them.

That is exactly the truth.

Then come impeachments and judgments and trials of one another.

True.

The people have always some champion whom they set over them and nurse into greatness.

Yes, that is their way.

This and no other is the root from which a tyrant springs; when he first appears above ground he is a protector.

Yes, that is quite clear.

How then does a protector begin to change into a tyrant? Clearly when he does what the man is said to do in the tale of the Arcadian temple of Lycaean Zeus.

What tale?

The tale is that he who has tasted the entrails of a single human victim minced up with the entrails of other victims is destined to become a wolf. Did you never hear it?

Oh, yes.

And the protector of the people is like him; having a mob entirely at his disposal, he is not restrained from shedding the blood of kinsmen; by the favourite method of false accusation he brings them into court and murders them, making the life of man to disappear, and with unholy tongue and lips tasting the blood of his fellow citizen; some he kills and others he banishes, at the same time hinting at the abolition of debts and partition of lands: and after this, what will be his destiny? Must he not either perish at the hands of his enemies, or from being a man become a wolf—that is, a tyrant?

Inevitably.

This, I said, is he who begins to make a party against the rich?

The same.

After a while he is driven out, but comes back, in spite of his enemies, a tyrant full grown.

That is clear.

And if they are unable to expel him, or to get him condemned to death by a public accusation, they conspire to assassinate him.

Yes, he said, that is their usual way.

Then comes the famous request for a bodyguard, which is the device of all those who have got thus far in their tyrannical career—'Let not the people's friend,' as they say, 'be lost to them.'

Exactly.

The people readily assent; all their fears are for him—they have none for themselves.

Very true.

And when a man who is wealthy and is also accused of being an enemy of the people sees this, then, my friend, as the oracle said to Croesus,

By pebbly Hermus' shore he flees and rests not and is not ashamed to be a coward.

And quite right too, said he, for if he were, he would never be ashamed again.

But if he is caught he dies.

Of course.

And he, the protector of whom we spoke, is to be seen, not 'larding the plain' with his bulk, but himself the overthrower of many, standing up in the chariot of State with the reins in his hand, no longer protector, but tyrant absolute.

No doubt, he said.

And now let us consider the happiness of the man, and also of the State in which a creature like him is generated.

Yes, he said, let us consider that.

At first, in the early days of his power, he is full of smiles, and he salutes every one whom he meets;—he to be called a tyrant, who is making promises in public and also in private! liberating debtors, and distributing land to the people and his followers, and wanting to be so kind and good to every one!

Of course, he said.

But when he has disposed of foreign enemies by conquest or treaty, and there is nothing to fear from them, then he is always stirring up some war or other, in order that the people may require a leader.

To be sure.

Has he not also another object, which is that they may be impoverished by payment of taxes, and thus compelled to devote themselves to their daily wants and therefore less likely to conspire against him? Clearly.

And if any of them are suspected by him of having notions of freedom, and of resistance to his authority, he will have a good pretext for destroying them by placing them at the mercy of the enemy; and for all these reasons the tyrant must be always getting up a war.

He must.

Now he begins to grow unpopular.

A necessary result.

Then some of those who joined in setting him up, and who are in power, speak their minds to him and to one another, and the more courageous of them cast in his teeth what is being done.

Yes, that may be expected.

And the tyrant, if he means to rule, must get rid of them; he cannot stop while he has a friend or an enemy who is good for anything.

He cannot.

And therefore he must look about him and see who is valiant, who is high-minded, who is wise, who is wealthy; happy man, he is the enemy of them all, and must seek occasion against them whether he will or no, until he has made a purgation of the State.

Yes, he said, and a rare purgation.

Yes, I said, not the sort of purgation which the physicians make of the body; for they take away the worse and leave the better part, but he does the reverse.

If he is to rule, I suppose that he cannot help himself.

What a blessed alternative, I said:—to be compelled to dwell only with the many bad, and to be by them hated, or not to live at all!

Yes, that is the alternative.

And the more detestable his actions are to the citizens the more satellites and the greater devotion in them will he require?

Certainly.

And who are the devoted band, and where will he procure them?

They will flock to him, he said, of their own accord, if lie pays them.

By the dog! I said, here are more drones, of every sort and from every land.

Yes, he said, there are.

But will he not desire to get them on the spot? How do you mean?

He will rob the citizens of their slaves; he will then set them free and enrol them in his bodyguard.

To be sure, he said; and he will be able to trust them best of all.

What a blessed creature, I said, must this tyrant be; he has put to death the others and has these for his trusted friends.

Yes, he said; they are quite of his sort.

Yes, I said, and these are the new citizens whom he has called into existence, who admire him and are his companions, while the good hate and avoid him.

# Politics

By Aristotle

## Nature and Origin of the State

Every state is a community of some kind, and every community is established with a view to some good; for mankind always act in order to obtain that which they think good. But, if all communities aim at some good, the state or political community, which is the highest of all, and which embraces all the rest, aims at good in a greater degree than any other, and at the highest good.

Some people think that the qualifications of a statesman, king, householder, and master are the same, and that they differ, not in kind, but only in the number of their subjects. For example, the ruler over a few is called a master; over more, the manager of a household; over a still larger number, a statesman or king, as if there were no difference between a great household and a small state. The distinction which is made between the king and the statesman is as follows: When the government is personal, the ruler is a king; when, according to the rules of the political science, the citizens rule and are ruled in turn, then he is called a statesman.

But all this is a mistake; for governments differ in kind, as will be evident to any one who considers the matter according to the method which has hitherto guided us. As in other departments of science, so in politics, the compound should always be resolved into the simple elements or least parts of the whole. We must therefore look at the elements of which the state is composed, in order that we may see in what the different kinds of rule differ from one another, and whether any scientific result can be attained about each one of them.

He who thus considers things in their first growth and origin, whether a state or anything else, will obtain the clearest view of them. In the first place there must be a union of those who cannot exist without each other; namely, of male and female, that the race may continue (and this is a union which is formed, not of deliberate purpose, but because, in common with other animals and with plants, mankind have a natural desire to leave behind them an image of themselves), and of natural ruler and subject, that both may be preserved. For that which can foresee by the exercise of mind is by nature intended to be lord and master, and that which can with its body give effect to such foresight is a subject, and by nature a slave;

53

hence master and slave have the same interest. Now nature has distinguished between the female and the slave. For she is not niggardly, like the smith who fashions the Delphian knife for many uses; she makes each thing for a single use, and every instrument is best made when intended for one and not for many uses. But among barbarians no distinction is made between women and slaves, because there is no natural ruler among them: they are a community of slaves, male and female.

Wherefore the poets say—

> It is meet that Hellenes should rule over barbarians; as if they thought that the barbarian and the slave were by nature one.

Out of these two relationships between man and woman, master and slave, the first thing to arise is the family, and Hesiod is right when he says—

> First house and wife and an ox for the plough,

for the ox is the poor man's slave. The family is the association established by nature for the supply of men's everyday wants, and the members of it are called by Charondas "companions of the cupboard," and by Epimenides the Cretan, "companions of the manger." But when several families are united, and the association aims at something more than the supply of daily needs, the first society to be formed is the village. And the most natural form of the village appears to be that of a colony from the family, composed of the children and grandchildren, who are said to be suckled "with the same milk." And this is the reason why Hellenic states were originally governed by kings; because the Hellenes were

under royal rule before they came together, as the barbarians still are. Every family is ruled by the eldest, and therefore in the colonies of the family the kingly form of government prevailed because they were of the same blood. As Homer says:

> Each one gives law to his children and to his wives.

For they lived dispersedly, as was the manner in ancient times. Wherefore men say that the Gods have a king, because they themselves either are or were in ancient times under the rule of a king. For they imagine, not only the forms of the Gods, but their ways of life to be like their own.

When several villages are united in a single complete community, large enough to be nearly or quite self-sufficing, the state comes into existence, originating in the bare needs of life, and continuing in existence for the sake of a good life. And therefore, if the earlier forms of society are natural, so is the state, for it is the end of them, and the nature of a thing is its end. For what each thing is when fully developed, we call its nature, whether we are speaking of a man, a horse, or a family. Besides, the final cause and end of a thing is the best, and to be self-sufficing is the end and the best.

Hence it is evident that the state is a creation of nature, and that man is by nature a political animal. And he who by nature and not by mere accident is without a state, is either a bad man or above humanity; he is like the

> Tribeless, lawless, heartless one,

whom Homer denounces—the natural outcast is forthwith a lover of war; he may be compared to an isolated piece at draughts.

Now, that man is more of a political animal than bees or any other gregarious animals is evident. Nature, as we often say, makes nothing in vain, and man is the only animal whom she has endowed with the gift of speech. And whereas mere voice is but an indication of pleasure or pain, and is therefore found in other animals (for their nature attains to the perception of pleasure and pain and the intimation of them to one another, and no further), the power of speech is intended to set forth the expedient and inexpedient, and therefore likewise the just and the unjust. And it is a characteristic of man that he alone has any sense of good and evil, of just and unjust, and the like, and the association of living beings who have this sense makes a family and a state.

Further, the state is by nature clearly prior to the family and to the individual, since the whole is of necessity prior to the part; for example, if the whole body be destroyed, there will be no foot or hand, except in an equivocal sense, as we might speak of a stone hand; for when destroyed the hand will be no better than that. But things are defined by their working and power; and we ought not to say that they are the same when they no longer have their proper quality, but only that they have the same name. The proof that the state is a creation of nature and prior to the individual is that the individual, when isolated, is not self-sufficing; and therefore he is like a part in relation to the whole. But he who is unable to live in society, or who has no need because he is sufficient for himself, must be either a beast or a god: he is no part of a state. A social instinct is implanted in all men by nature, and yet he who first founded the state was the greatest of benefactors.

For man, when perfected, is the best of animals, but, when separated from law and justice, he is the worst of all; since armed injustice is the more dangerous, and he is equipped at birth with arms, meant to be used by intelligence and virtue, which he may use for the worst ends. Wherefore, if he have not virtue, he is the most unholy and the most savage of animals, and the most full of lust and gluttony. But justice is the bond of men in states, for the administration of justice, which is the determination of what is just, is the principle of order in political society.

## Slavery

But is there any one thus intended by nature to be a slave, and for whom such a condition is expedient and right, or rather is not all slavery a violation of nature?

There is no difficulty in answering this question, on grounds both of reason and of fact. For that some should rule and others be ruled is a thing not only necessary, but expedient; from the hour of their birth, some are marked out for subjection, others for rule.

And there are many kinds both of rulers and subjects (and that rule is the better which is exercised over better subjects—for example, to rule over men is better than to rule over wild beasts; for the work is better which is executed by better workmen, and where one man rules and another is ruled, they may be said to have a work); for in all things which form a composite whole and which are made up of parts, whether continuous or discrete, a distinction between the ruling and the subject element comes to light. Such a duality exists in living creatures, but not in them only; it originates in the constitution of the universe; even in things which have no life there is a ruling principle, as in a musical mode. But we are wandering from the subject. We will therefore restrict ourselves to the living creature, which, in the first place, consists of soul and body: and of these two, the one is by nature the ruler, and the other the subject. But then we must look for the intentions of nature in things which retain their nature, and not in things which are corrupted. And therefore we must study the man who is in the most perfect state both of body and soul, for in him we shall see the true relation of the two; although in bad or corrupted natures the body will often appear to rule over the soul, because they are in an evil and unnatural condition. At all events we may firstly observe in living creatures both a despotical and a constitutional rule; for the soul rules the body with a despotical rule, whereas the intellect rules the appetites with a constitutional and royal rule. And it is clear that the rule of the soul over the body, and of the mind and the rational element over the passionate, is natural and expedient; whereas the equality of the two or the rule of the inferior is always hurtful. The same holds good of animals in relation to men; for tame animals have a better nature than wild, and all tame animals are better off when they are ruled by man; for then they are preserved. Again, the male is by nature superior, and the female inferior; and the one rules, and the other is ruled; this principle, of necessity, extends to all mankind. Where then there is such a difference as that between soul and body, or between men and animals (as in the case of those whose business is to use their body, and who can do nothing better), the lower sort are by nature slaves, and it is better for them as for all inferiors that they should be under the rule of a master. For he who can be, and therefore is, another's, and he who participates in rational principle enough to apprehend, but not to have, such a principle, is a slave by nature. Whereas the lower animals cannot even apprehend a principle, they obey their instincts. And indeed the use made of slaves and of tame animals is not very different; for both with their bodies minister to the needs of life. Nature would like to distinguish between the bodies of freemen and slaves, making the one strong for servile labour, the other upright, and although useless for such services, useful for political life in the arts both of war and peace. But the opposite often happens—that some have the souls and others have the bodies of freemen. And doubtless if men differed from one another in the mere forms of their bodies as much as the statues of the Gods do from men, all would acknowledge that the inferior class should be slaves of the superior. And if this is true of the body, how much more just that a similar distinction should exist in the soul? But the beauty of the body is seen, whereas the beauty of the soul is not seen. It is clear, then, that some men are by nature free, and others slaves, and that for these latter slavery is both expedient and right.

But that those who take the opposite view have in a certain way right on their side, may be easily seen. For the words slavery and slave are used in two senses. There is a slave or slavery by law as well as by nature. The law of which I speak is a sort of convention—the law by which whatever is taken in war is supposed to belong to the victors. But this right many jurists impeach, as they would an orator who brought forward an unconstitutional measure: they detest the notion that, because one man has the power of doing violence and is superior in brute strength, another shall be his slave and subject. Even among philosophers there is a difference of opinion. The origin of the dispute, and what makes the views invade each other's territory, is as follows: in some sense virtue, when furnished with means, has actually the greatest power of exercising force: and as superior power is only found where there is superior excellence of some kind, power seems to imply virtue, and the dispute to be simply one about justice (for it is due to one party identifying justice with goodwill, while the other identifies it with the mere rule of the stronger). If these views are thus set out separately, the other views have no force or plausibility against the view that the superior in virtue ought to rule, or be master. Others, clinging, as they think, simply to a principle of justice (for law and custom are a sort of justice), assume that slavery in accordance with the custom of war is justified by law, but at the same moment they deny this. For what if the cause of the war be unjust? And again, no one would ever say that he is a slave who is unworthy to be a slave. Were this the case, men of the highest rank would be slaves and the children of slaves if they or their parents chance to have been taken captive and sold. Wherefore Hellenes do not like to call Hellenes slaves, but confine the term to barbarians. Yet, in using this language, they really mean the natural slave of whom we spoke at first; for it must be admitted that some are slaves everywhere, others nowhere. The same principle applies to nobility. Hellenes regard themselves as noble everywhere, and not only in their own country, but they deem the barbarians noble only when at home, thereby implying that there are two sorts of nobility and freedom, the one absolute, the other relative. The Helen of Theodectes says:

Who would presume to call me servant who am on both sides sprung from the stem of the Gods?

What does this mean but that they distinguish freedom and slavery, noble and humble birth, by the two principles of good and evil? They think that as men and animals beget men and animals, so from good men a good man springs. But this is what nature, though she may intend it, cannot always accomplish.

We see then that there is some foundation for this difference of opinion, and that all are not either slaves by nature or freemen by nature, and also that there is in some cases a marked distinction between the two classes, rendering it expedient and right for the one to be slaves and the others to be masters: the one practising obedience, the others exercising the authority and lordship which nature intended them to have. The abuse of this authority is injurious to both; for the interests of part and whole, of body and soul, are the same, and the slave is a part of the master, a living but separated part of his bodily frame. Hence, where the relation of master and slave between them is natural they are friends and have a common interest, but where it rests merely on law and force the reverse is true.

## Critique of Plato's *Republic*

Our purpose is to consider what form of political community is best of all for those who are most able to realize their ideal of life. We must therefore examine not only this but other constitutions, both such as actually exist in well-governed states, and any theoretical forms which are held in esteem; that what is good and useful may be brought to light. And let no one suppose that in seeking for something beyond them we are anxious to make a sophistical display at any cost; we only undertake this inquiry because all the constitutions with which we are acquainted are faulty.

We will begin with the natural beginning of the subject. Three alternatives are conceivable: The members of a state must either have (1) all things or (2) nothing in common, or (3) some things in common and some not. That they should have nothing in common is clearly impossible, for the constitution is a community, and must at any rate have a common place—one city will be in one place, and the citizens are those who share in that one city. But should a well-ordered state have all things, as far as may be, in common, or some only and not others? For the citizens might conceivably have wives and children and property in common, as Socrates proposes in the *Republic* of Plato. Which is better, our present condition, or the proposed new order of society?

There are many difficulties in the community of women. And the principle on which Socrates rests the necessity of such an institution evidently is not established by his arguments. Further, as a means to the end which he ascribes to the state, the scheme, taken literally, is impracticable, and how we are to interpret it is nowhere precisely stated. I am speaking of the premiss from which the argument of Socrates proceeds, "that the greater the unity of the state the better." Is it not obvious that a state may at length attain such a degree of unity as to be no longer a state?—since the nature of a state is to be a plurality, and in tending to greater unity, from being a state, it becomes a family, and from being a family, an individual; for the family

may be said to be more than the state, and the individual than the family. So that we ought not to attain this greatest unity even if we could, for it would be the destruction of the state. Again, a state is not made up only of so many men, but of different kinds of men; for similars do not constitute a state. It is not like a military alliance. The usefulness of the latter depends upon its quantity even where there is no difference in quality (for mutual protection is the end aimed at), just as a greater weight of anything is more useful than a less (in like manner, a state differs from a nation, when the nation has not its population organized in villages, but lives an Arcadian sort of life); but the elements out of which a unity is to be formed differ in kind. Wherefore the principle of compensation, as I have already remarked in the *Ethics*, is the salvation of states. Even among freemen and equals this is a principle which must be maintained, for they cannot all rule together, but must change at the end of a year or some other period of time or in some order of succession. The result is that upon this plan they all govern; just as if shoemakers and carpenters were to exchange their occupations, and the same persons did not always continue shoemakers and carpenters. And since it is better that this should be so in politics as well, it is clear that while there should be continuance of the same persons in power where this is possible, yet where this is not possible by reason of the natural equality of the citizens, and at the same time it is just that all should share in the government (whether to govern be a good thing or a bad), an approximation to this is that equals should in turn retire from office and should, apart from official position, be treated alike. Thus the one party rule and the others are ruled in turn, as if they were no longer the same persons. In like manner when they hold office there is a variety in the offices held. Hence it is evident that a city is not by nature one in that sense which some persons affirm; and that what is said to be the greatest good of cities is in reality their destruction; but surely the good of things must be that which preserves them. Again, in another point of view, this extreme unification of the state is clearly not good; for a family is more self-sufficing than an individual, and a city than a family, and a city only comes into being when the community is large enough to be self-sufficing. If then self-sufficiency is to be desired, the lesser degree of unity is more desirable than the greater.

## Property: Equality or Inequality?

Next let us consider what should be our arrangements about property: should the citizens of the perfect state have their possessions in common or not? This question may be discussed separately from the enactments about women and children. Even supposing that the women and children belong to individuals, according to the custom which is at present universal, may there not be an advantage in having and using possessions in common? Three cases are possible: (1) the soil may be appropriated, but the produce may be thrown for consumption into the common stock; and this is the practice of some nations. Or (2), the soil may be common, and may be cultivated in common, but the produce divided among individuals for their private use; this is a form of common property which is said to exist among certain barbarians. Or (3), the soil and the produce may be alike common.

When the husbandmen are not the owners, the case will be different and easier to deal with; but when they till the ground for themselves the question of ownership will give a world of trouble. If they do not share equally in enjoyments and toils, those who labour much and get little will necessarily complain of those who labour little and receive or consume much. But indeed there is always a difficulty in men living together and having all human relations in common, but especially in their having common property. The partnerships of fellow-travelers are an example to the point; for they generally fall out over everyday matters and quarrel about any trifle which turns up. So with servants: we are most liable to take offense at those with whom we most frequently come into contact in daily life.

These are only some of the disadvantages which attend the community of property; the present arrangement, if improved as it might be by good customs and laws, would be far better, and would have the advantages of both systems. Property should be in a certain sense common, but, as a general rule, private; for, when every one has a distinct interest, men will not complain of one another, and they will make more progress, because every one will be attending to his own business. And yet by reason of goodness, and in respect of use, "Friends," as the proverb says, "will have all things common." Even now there are traces of such a principle, showing that it is not impracticable, but, in well-ordered states, exists already to a certain extent and may be carried further. For, although every man has his own property, some things he will place at the disposal of his friends, while of others he shares the use with them. The Lacedaemonians, for example, use one another's slaves, and horses, and dogs, as if they were their own; and when they lack provisions on a journey, they appropriate what they find in the fields throughout the country. It is clearly better that property should be private, but the use of it common; and the special business of the legislator is to create in men this benevolent disposition. Again, how immeasurably greater is the pleasure, when a man feels a thing to be his own; for surely the love of self is a feeling implanted by nature and not given in vain, although selfishness is rightly censured; this, however, is not the mere love of self, but the love of self in excess, like the miser's love of money; for all, or almost all, men love money and other such objects in a measure. And further, there is the greatest pleasure in doing a kindness or service to friends or guests or companions, which can only be rendered when a man has private property. These advantages are lost by excessive unification of the state. The exhibition of two virtues, besides, is visibly annihilated in such a state: first, temperance towards women (for it is an honourable action to abstain from another's wife for temperance sake); secondly, liberality in the matter of property. No one, when men have all things in common, will any longer set an example of liberality or do any liberal action; for liberality consists in the use which is made of property.

Such legislation may have a specious appearance of benevolence; men readily listen to it, and are easily induced to believe that in some wonderful manner everybody will become everybody's friend, especially when some one is heard denouncing the evils now existing in states, suits about contracts, convictions for perjury, flatteries of rich men and the like, which are said to arise out of the possession of private property. These evils, however, are due to a very different cause— the wickedness of human nature. Indeed, we see that there is much more quarrelling among those who have all things in common, though there are not many of them when compared with the vast numbers who have private property.

Again, we ought to reckon, not only the evils from which the citizens will be saved, but also the advantages which they will lose. The life which they are to lead appears to be quite impracticable. The error of Socrates must be attributed to the false notion of unity from which he starts. Unity there should be, both of the family and of the state, but in some respects only. For there is a point at which a state may attain such a degree of unity as to be no longer a state, or at which, without actually ceasing to exist, it will become an inferior state, like harmony passing into unison, or rhythm which has been reduced to a single foot. The state, as I was saying, is a plurality, which should be united and made into a community by education; and it is strange that the author of a system of education which he thinks will make the state virtuous should expect to improve his citizens by regulations of this sort, and not by philosophy or by customs and laws, like those which prevail at Sparta and Crete respecting common meals, whereby the legislator has made property common. Let us remember that we should not disregard the experience of ages; in the multitude of years these things, if they were good, would certainly not have been unknown; for almost everything has been found out, although sometimes they are not put together; in other cases men do not use the knowledge which they have. Great light would be thrown on this subject if we could see such a form of government in the actual process of construction; for the legislator could not form a state at all without distributing and dividing its constituents into associations for common meals, and into phratries and tribes. But all this legislation ends only in forbidding agriculture to the guardians, a prohibition which the Lacedaemonians try to enforce already.

But, indeed, Socrates has not said, nor is it easy to decide, what in such a community will be the general form of the state. The citizens who are not guardians are the majority, and about them nothing has been determined: are the husbandmen, too, to have their property in common? Or is each individual to have his own? and are the wives and children to be individual or common? If, like the guardians, they are to have all things in common, in what do they differ from them, or what will they gain by submitting to their government? Or, upon what principle would they submit, unless indeed the governing class adopt the ingenious policy of the Cretans, who give their slaves the same institutions as their own, but forbid them gymnastic exercises and the possession of arms. If, on the other hand, the inferior classes are to be like other cities in respect of marriage and property, what will be the form of the community? Must it not contain two states in one, each hostile to the other? He makes the guardians into a mere occupying garrison, while the husbandmen and artisans and the rest are the real citizens. But if so the suits and quarrels, and all the evils which Socrates affirms to exist in other states, will exist equally among them. He says indeed that, having so good an education, the citizens will not need many laws, for example laws about the city or about the markets; but then he confines his education to the guardians. Again, he makes the husbandmen owners of the property upon condition of their paying a tribute. But in that case they are likely to be much more unmanageable and conceited than the Helots, or Penestae, or slaves in general. And whether community of wives and property be necessary for the lower equally with the higher class or not, and the questions akin to this, what will be the education, form of government, laws of the lower class, Socrates has nowhere determined: neither is it easy to discover this, nor is their character of small importance if the common life of the guardians is to be maintained.

Again, if Socrates makes the women common, and retains private property, the men will see to the fields, but who will see to the house? And who will do so if the agricultural class have both their property and their wives in common? Once more: it is absurd to argue, from the analogy of the animals, that men and women should follow the same pursuits, for animals have not to manage a household. The government, too, as constituted by Socrates, contains elements of danger; for he makes the same persons always rule. And if this is often a cause of disturbance among the meaner sort, how much more among high-spirited warriors? But that the persons whom he makes rulers must be the same is evident; for the gold which the God mingles in the souls of men is not at one time given to one, at another time to another, but always to the same: as he says, "God mingles gold in some, and silver in others, from their very birth; but brass and iron in those who are meant to be artisans and husbandmen." Again, he deprives the guardians even of happiness, and says that the legislator ought to make the whole state happy. But the whole cannot be happy unless most, or all, or some of its parts enjoy happiness. In this respect happiness is not like the even principle in numbers, which may exist only in the whole, but in neither of the parts; not so happiness. And if the guardians are not happy, who are? Surely not the artisans, or the common people. The Republic of which Socrates discourses has all these difficulties, and others quite as great.

There is another point: Should not the amount of property be defined in some way which differs from this by being clearer? For Socrates says that a man should have so much property as will enable him to live temperately, which is only a way of saying "to live well"; this is too general a conception. Further, a man may live temperately and yet miserably. A better definition would be that a man must have so much property as will enable him to live not only temperately but liberally; if the two are parted, liberality will combine with luxury; temperance will be associated with toil. For liberality and temperance are the only eligible qualities which have to do with the use of property. A man cannot use property with mildness or courage, but temperately and liberally he may; and therefore the practice of these virtues is inseparable from property. There is an inconsistency, too, in equalizing the property and not regulating the number of the citizens; the population is to remain unlimited, and he thinks that it will be sufficiently equalized by a certain number of marriages being unfruitful, however many are born to others, because he finds this to be the case in existing states. But greater care will be required than now; for among ourselves, whatever may be the number of citizens, the property is always distributed among them, and therefore no one is in want; but, if the property were incapable of division as in the Laws, the supernumeraries, whether few or many, would get nothing. One would have thought that it was even more necessary to limit population than property; and that the limit should be fixed by calculating the chances of mortality in the children, and of sterility in married persons. The neglect of this subject, which in existing states is so common, is a never-failing cause of poverty among the citizens; and poverty is the parent of revolution and crime. Pheidon the Corinthian, who was one of the most ancient legislators, thought that the families and the number of citizens ought to remain the same, although originally all the lots may have been of different sizes: but in the Laws the opposite principle is maintained. What in our opinion is the right arrangement will have to be explained hereafter.

Other constitutions have been proposed; some by private persons, others by philosophers and statesmen, which all come nearer to established or existing ones than either of Plato's. No one else has introduced such novelties as the community of women and children, or public tables for women: other legislators begin with what is necessary. In the opinion of some, the regulation of property is the chief point of all, that being the question upon which all revolutions turn. This danger was recognized by Phaleas of Chalcedon, who was the first to affirm that the citizens of a state ought to have equal possessions. He thought that in a new colony the equalization might be accomplished without difficulty, not so easily when a state was already established; and that then the shortest way of compassing the desired end would be for the rich to give and not to receive marriage portions, and for the poor not to give but to receive them.

Plato in the Laws was of opinion that, to a certain extent, accumulation should be allowed, forbidding, as I have already observed, any citizen to possess more than five times the minimum qualification. But those who make such laws should remember what they are apt to forget—that the legislator who fixes the amount of property should also fix the number of children; for, if the children are too many for the property, the law must be broken. And, besides the violation of the law, it is a bad thing that many from being rich should become poor; for men of ruined fortunes are sure to stir up revolutions. That the equilization of property exercises an influence on political society was clearly understood even by some of the old legislators. Laws were made by Solon and others prohibiting an individual from possessing as much land as he pleased; and there are other laws in states which forbid the sale of property: among the Locrians, for example, there is a law that a man is not to sell his property unless he can prove unmistakably that some misfortune has befallen him. Again, there have been laws which enjoin the preservation of the original lots. Such a law existed in the island of Leucas, and the abrogation of it made the constitution too democratic, for the rulers no longer had the prescribed qualification. Again, where there is equality of property, the amount may be either too large or too small, and the possessor may be living either in luxury or penury. Clearly, then, the legislator ought not only to aim at the equalization of properties, but at moderation in their amount. Further, if he prescribe this moderate amount equally to all, he will be no nearer the mark; for it is not the possessions but the desires of mankind which require to be equalized, and this is impossible, unless a sufficient education is provided by the laws. But Phaleas will probably reply that this is precisely what he means; and that, in his opinion, there ought to be in states, not only equal property, but equal education. Still he should tell precisely what he means; and what, in his opinion, there ought to be in having one and the same for all, if it is of a sort that predisposes men to avarice, or ambition, or both. Moreover, civil troubles arise, not only out of the inequality of property, but out of the inequality of honour, though in opposite ways. For the common people quarrel about the inequality of property, the higher class about the equality of honour; as the poet says—

The bad and good alike in honour
share.

There are crimes of which the motive is want; and for these Phaleas expects to find a cure in the equalization of property, which will take away from a man the temptation to be a highwayman, because he is hungry or cold. But want is not the sole incentive to crime; men also wish to enjoy themselves and not to be in a state of desire—they wish to cure some desire, going beyond the necessities of life, which preys upon them; nay, this is not the only reason—they may desire superfluities in order to enjoy pleasures unaccompanied with pain, and therefore they commit crimes.

Now what is the cure of these three disorders? Of the first, moderate possessions and occupation; of the second, habits of temperance; as to the third, if any desire pleasures which depend on themselves, they will find the satisfaction of their desires nowhere but in philosophy; for all other pleasures we are dependent on others. The fact is that the greatest crimes are caused by excess and not by necessity. Men do not become tyrants in order that they may not suffer cold; and hence great is the honour bestowed, not on him who kills a thief, but on him who kills a tyrant. Thus we see that the institutions of Phaleas avail only against petty crimes.

There is another objection to them. They are chiefly designed to promote the internal welfare of the state. But the legislator should consider also its relation to neighbouring nations, and to all who are outside of it. The government must be organized with a view to military strength; and of this he has said not a word. And so with respect to property: there should not only be enough to supply the internal wants of the state, but also to meet dangers coming from without. The property of the state should not be so large that more powerful neighbours may be tempted by it, while the owners are unable to repel the invaders; nor yet so small that the state is unable to maintain a war even against states of equal power, and of the same character. Phaleas has not laid down any rule; but we should bear in mind that abundance of wealth is an advantage. The best limit will probably be, that a more powerful neighbour must have no inducement to go to war with you by reason of the excess of your wealth, but only such as he would have had if you had possessed less. There is a story that Eubulus, when Autophradates was going to besiege Atarneus, told him to consider how long the operation would take, and then reckon up the cost which would be incurred in the time. "For," said he, "I am willing for a smaller sum than that to leave Atarneus at once." These words of Eubulus made an impression on Autophradates, and he desisted from the siege.

The equalization of property is one of the things that tend to prevent the citizens from quarrelling. Not that the gain in this direction is very great. For the nobles will be dissatisfied because they think themselves worthy of more than an equal share of honours; and this is often found to be a cause of sedition and revolution. And the avarice of mankind is insatiable; at one time two obols was pay enough; but now, when this sum has become customary, men always want more and more without end; for it is of the nature of desire not to be satisfied, and most men live only for the gratification of it. The beginning of reform is not so much to equalize property as to train the nobler sort of natures not to desire more, and to prevent the lower from getting more; that is to say, they must be kept down, but not ill-treated. Besides, the equalization proposed by Phaleas is imperfect; for he only equalizes

land, whereas a man may be rich also in slaves, and cattle, and money, and in the abundance of what are called his movables. Now either all these things must be equalized, or some limit must be imposed on them, or they must all be let alone. It would appear that Phaleas is legislating for a small city only, if, as he supposes, all the artisans are to be public slaves and not to form a supplementary part of the body of citizens. But if there is a law that artisans are to be public slaves, it should only apply to those engaged on public works, as at Epidamnus, or at Athens on the plan which Diophantus once introduced.

From these observations any one may judge how far Phaleas was wrong or right in his ideas.

## Citizenship

He who would inquire into the essence and attributes of various kinds of governments must first of all determine "What is a state?" At present this is a disputed question. Some say that the state has done a certain act; others, no, not the state, but the oligarchy or the tyrant. And the legislator or statesman is concerned entirely with the state; a constitution or government being an arrangement of the inhabitants of a state. But a state is composite, like any other whole made up of many parts;—these are the citizens, who compose it. It is evident, therefore, that we must begin by asking, "Who is the citizen," and what is the meaning of the term? For here again there may be a difference of opinion. He who is a citizen in a democracy will often not be a citizen in an oligarchy. Leaving out of consideration those who have been made citizens, or who have obtained the name of citizen in any other accidental manner, we may say, first that a citizen is not a citizen because he lives in a certain place, for resident aliens and slaves share in the place; nor is he a citizen who has no legal right except that of suing and being sued; for this right may be enjoyed under the provisions of a treaty. Nay, resident aliens in many places do not possess even such rights completely, for they are obliged to have a patron, so that they do but imperfectly participate in citizenship, and we call them citizens only in a qualified sense, as we might apply the term to children who are too young to be on the register, or to old men who have been relieved from state duties. Of these we do not say quite simply that they are citizens, but add in the one case that they are not of age, and in the other, that they are past the age, or something of that sort; the precise expression is immaterial, for our meaning is clear. Similar difficulties to those which I have mentioned may be raised and answered about deprived citizens and about exiles. But the citizen whom we are seeking to define is a citizen in the strictest sense, against whom no such exception can be taken, and his special characteristic is that he shares in the administration of justice, and in offices. Now of offices some are discontinuous, and the same persons are not allowed to hold them twice, or can only hold them after a fixed interval; others have no limit of time—for example, the office of dicast or ecclesiast.1 It may, indeed, be argued that these are not magistrates at all, and that their functions give them no share in the government. But surely it is ridiculous to say that those who have the supreme power do not govern. Let us not dwell further upon

this, which is a purely verbal question; what we want is a common term including both dicast and ecclesiast. Let us, for the sake of distinction, call it "indefinite office," and we will assume that those who share in such office are citizens. This is the most comprehensive definition of a citizen, and best suits all those who are generally so called.

But we must not forget that things of which the underlying principles differ in kind, one of them being first, another second, another third, have, when regarded in this relation, nothing, or hardly anything, worth mentioning in common. Now we see that governments differ in kind, and that some of them are prior and that others are posterior; those which are faulty or perverted are necessarily posterior to those which are perfect. (What we mean by perversion will be hereafter explained.) The citizen then of necessity differs under each form of government; and our definition is best adapted to the citizen of a democracy; but not necessarily to other states. For in some states the people are not acknowledged, nor have they any regular assembly, but only extraordinary ones; and suits are distributed by sections among the magistrates. At Lacedaemon, for instance, the Ephors determine suits about contracts, which they distribute among themselves, while the elders are judges of homicide, and other causes are decided by other magistrates. A similar principle prevails at Carthage; there certain magistrates decide all causes. We may, indeed, modify our definition of the citizen so as to include these states. In them it is the holder of a definite, not of an indefinite office, who legislates and judges, and to some or all such holders of definite offices is reserved the right of deliberating or judging about some things or about all things. The conception of the citizen now begins to clear up.

1 "'Dicast" = juryman and judge in one: "ecclesiast" = member of the ecclesia or assembly of the citizens.

He who has the power to take part in the deliberative or judicial administration of any state is said by us to be a citizen of that state; and, speaking generally, a state is a body of citizens sufficing for the purposes of life.

There is a point nearly allied to the preceding: Whether the virtue of a good man and a good citizen is the same or not. But, before entering on this discussion, we must certainly first obtain some general notion of the virtue of the citizen. Like the sailor, the citizen is a member of a community. Now, sailors have different functions, for one of them is a rower, another a pilot, and a third a look-out man, a fourth is described by some similar term, and while the precise definition of each individual's virtue applies exclusively to him, there is, at the same time, a common definition applicable to them all. For they have all of them a common object, which is safety in navigation. Similarly, one citizen differs from another, but the salvation of the community is the common business of them all. This community is the constitution; the virtue of the citizen must therefore be relative to the constitution of which he is a member. If, then, there are many forms of government, it is evident that there is not one single virtue of the good citizen which is perfect virtue. But we say that the good man is he who has one single virtue which is perfect virtue. Hence it is evident that the good citizen need not of necessity possess the virtue which makes a good man.

The same question may also be approached by another road, from a consideration of the best constitution. If the state cannot be entirely composed of good men, and yet each citizen is expected to do his own business well, and must therefore have virtue, still, inasmuch as all the citizens cannot be alike, the virtue of the citizen and of the good man cannot coincide. All must have the virtue of the good citizen—thus, and thus only, can the state be perfect; but they will not have the virtue of a good man, unless we assume that in the good state all the citizens must be good.

Again, the state, as composed of unlikes, may be compared to the living being: as the first elements into which a living being is resolved are soul and body, as soul is made up of rational principle and appetite, the family of husband and wife, property of master and slave, so of all these, as well as other dissimilar elements, the state is composed; and, therefore, the virtue of all the citizens cannot possibly be the same, any more than the excellence of the leader of a chorus is the same as that of the performer who stands by his side. I have said enough to show why the two kinds of virtue cannot be absolutely and always the same.

But will there then be no case in which the virtue of the good citizen and the virtue of the good man coincide? To this we answer that the good *ruler* is a good and wise man, and that he who would be a statesman must be a wise man. And some persons say that even the education of the ruler should be of a special kind; for are not the children of kings instructed in riding and military exercises? As Euripides says:

> No subtle arts for me, but what the state requires.

As though there were a special education needed by a ruler. If then the virtue of a good ruler is the same as that of a good man, and we assume further that the subject is a citizen as well as the ruler, the virtue of the good citizen and the virtue of the good man cannot be absolutely the same, although in some cases they may; for the virtue of a ruler differs from that of a citizen. It was the sense of this difference which made Jason say that "he felt hungry when he was not a tyrant," meaning that he could not endure to live in a private station. But, on the other hand, it may be argued that men are praised for knowing both how to rule and how to obey, and he is said to be a citizen of approved virtue who is able to do both. Now if we suppose the virtue of a good man to be that which rules, and the virtue of the citizen to include ruling and obeying, it cannot be said that they are equally worthy of praise. Since, then, it is sometimes thought that the ruler and the ruled must learn different things and not the same, but that the citizen must know and share in them both, the inference is obvious. There is, indeed, the rule of a master, which is concerned with menial offices—the master need not know how to perform these, but may employ others, in the execution of them: the other would be degrading; and by the other I mean the power actually to do menial duties, which vary much in character and are executed by various classes of slaves, such, for example, as handicraftsmen, who, as their name signifies, live by the labour of their hands:—under these the mechanic is included. Hence in ancient times, and among some nations, the working classes had no share in the government—a privilege which they only acquired under the extreme democracy. Certainly the good man and the statesman and the good citizen ought not to learn the crafts of inferiors except for their own occasional use; if they habitually practice them, there will cease to be a distinction between master and slave.

This is not the rule of which we are speaking; but there is a rule of another kind, which is exercised over freemen and equals by birth—a constitutional rule, which the ruler must learn by obeying, as he would learn the duties of a general of cavalry by being under the orders of a general of cavalry, or the duties of a general of infantry by being under the orders of a general of infantry, and by having had the command of a regiment and of a company. It has been well said that "he who has never learned to obey cannot be a good commander." The two are not the same, but the good citizen ought to be capable of both; he should know how to govern like a freeman, and how to obey like a freeman—these are the virtues of a citizen. And, although the temperance and justice of a ruler are distinct from those of a subject, the virtue of a good man will include both; for the virtue of the good man who is free and also a subject, e.g. his justice, will not be one but will comprise distinct kinds, the one qualifying him to rule, the other to obey, and differing as the temperance and courage of men and women differ. For a man would be thought a coward if he had no more courage than a courageous woman, and a woman would be thought loquacious if she imposed no more restraint on her conversation than the good man; and indeed their part in the management of the household is different, for the duty of the one is to acquire, and of the other to preserve. Practical wisdom only is characteristic of the ruler: it would seem that all other virtues must equally belong to ruler and subject. The virtue of the subject is certainly not wisdom, but only true opinion; he may be compared to the maker of the flute, while his master is like the flute-player or user of the flute.

From these considerations may be gathered the answer to the question, whether the virtue of the good man is the same as that of the good citizen, or different, and how far the same, and how far different.

There still remains one more question about the citizen: Is he only a true citizen who has a share of office, or is the mechanic to be included? If they who hold no office are to be deemed citizens, not every citizen can have this virtue of ruling and obeying; for this man is a citizen. And if none of the lower class are citizens, in which part of the state are they to be placed? For they are not resident aliens, and they are not foreigners. May we not reply, that as far as this objection goes there is no more absurdity in excluding them than in excluding slaves and freedmen from any of the above-mentioned classes? It must be admitted that we cannot consider all those to be citizens who are necessary to the existence of the state; for example, children are not citizens equally with grown-up men, who are citizens absolutely, but children, not being grown up, are only citizens on a certain assumption. Nay, in ancient times, and among some nations, the artisan class were slaves or foreigners, and therefore the majority of them are so now. The best form of state will not admit them to citizenship; but if they are admitted, then our definition of the virtue of a citizen will not apply to every citizen, not to every free man as such, but only to those who are freed from necessary services. The necessary people are either slaves who minister to the wants of individuals, or mechanics and labourers who are the servants of the community. These reflections carried a little further will explain their position; and indeed what has been said already is of itself, when understood, explanation enough.

Since there are many forms of government there must be many varieties of citizens, and especially of citizens who are subjects; so that under some governments the mechanic and the labourer will be citizens, but not in others, as, for example, in aristocracy or the so-called government of the best (if there be such an one), in which honours are given according to virtue and merit; for no man can practise virtue who is living the life of a mechanic or labourer. In oligarchies the qualification for office is high, and therefore no labourer can ever be a citizen; but a mechanic may, for an actual majority of them are rich. At Thebes there was a law that no man could hold office who had not retired from business for ten years. But in many states the law goes to the length of admitting aliens; for in some democracies a man is a citizen though his mother only be a citizen; and a similar principle is applied to illegitimate children; the law is relaxed when there is a dearth of population. But when the number of citizens increases, first the children of a male or a female slave are excluded; then those whose mothers only are citizens; and at last the right of citizenship is confined to those whose fathers and mothers are both citizens.

Hence, as is evident, there are different kinds of citizens; and he is a citizen in the highest sense who shares in the honours of the state. Compare Homer's words "like some dishonoured stranger"; he who is excluded from the honours of the state is no better than an alien. But when this exclusion is concealed, then the object is that the privileged class may deceive their fellow inhabitants.

As to the question whether the virtue of the good man is the same as that of the good citizen, the considerations already adduced prove that in some states the good man and the good citizen are the same, and in others different. When they are the same it is not every citizen who is a good man, but only the statesman and those who have or may have, alone or in conjunction with others, the conduct of public affairs.

As in other natural compounds the conditions of a composite whole are not necessarily organic parts of it, so in a state or in any other combination forming a unity not everything is a part, which is a necessary condition. The members of an association have necessarily some one thing the same and common to all, in which they share equally or unequally; for example, food or land or any other thing. But where there are two things of which one is a means and the other an end, they have nothing in common except that the one receives what the other produces. Such, for example, is the relation in which workmen and tools stand to their work; the house and the builder have nothing in common, but the art of the builder is for the sake of the house. And so states require property, but property, even though living beings are included in it, is no part of a state; for a state is not a community of living beings only, but a community of equals, aiming at the best life possible. Now, whereas happiness is the highest good, being a realization and perfect practice of virtue, which some can attain, while others have little or none of it, the various qualities of men are clearly the reason why there are various kinds of states and many forms of government; for different men seek after happiness in different ways and by different means, and so make for themselves different modes of life and forms of government. We must see also how many things are indispensable to the existence of a state, for what we call the parts of a state will be found among the indispensables. Let us then enumerate the functions of a state, and we shall easily elicit what we want:

First, there must be food; secondly, arts, for life requires many instruments; thirdly, there must be arms, for the members of a community have need of them, and in their own hands, too, in order to maintain authority both against disobedient subjects and against external assailants; fourthly, there must be a certain amount of revenue, both for internal needs, and for the purposes of war; fifthly, or rather first, there must be a care of religion, which is commonly called worship; sixthly,

and most necessary of all, there must be a power of deciding what is for the public interest, and what is just in men's dealings with one another.

These are the services which every state may be said to need. For a state is not a mere aggregate of persons, but a union of them sufficing for the purposes of life; and if any of these things be wanting, it is as we maintain impossible that the community can be absolutely self-sufficing. A state then should be framed with a view to the fulfilment of these functions. There must be husbandmen to procure food, and artisans, and a warlike and a wealthy class, and priests, and judges to decide what is necessary and expedient.

Having determined these points, we have in the next place to consider whether all ought to share in every sort of occupation. Shall every man be at once husbandman, artisan, councillor, judge, or shall we suppose the several occupations just mentioned assigned to different persons? or, thirdly, shall some employments be assigned to individuals and others common to all? The same arrangement, however, does not occur in every constitution; as we were saying, all may be shared by all, or not all by all, but only by some; and hence arise the differences of constitutions, for in democracies all share in all, in oligarchies the opposite practice prevails. Now, since we are here speaking of the best form of government, i.e. that under which the state will be most happy (and happiness, as has been already said, cannot exist without virtue), it clearly follows that in the state which is best governed and possesses men who are just absolutely, and not merely relatively to the principle of the constitution, the citizens must not lead the life of mechanics or tradesmen, for such a life is ignoble, and inimical to virtue. Neither must they be husbandmen, since leisure is necessary both for the development of virtue and the performance of political duties.

Again, there is in a state a class of warriors, and another of councillors, who advise about the expedient and determine matters of law, and these seem in an especial manner parts of a state. Now, should these two classes be distinguished, or are both functions to be assigned to the same persons? Here again there is no difficulty in seeing that both functions will in one way belong to the same, in another, to different persons. To different persons in so far as these employments are suited to different primes of life, for the one requires wisdom and the other strength. But on the other hand, since it is an impossible thing that those who are able to use or to resist force should be willing to remain always in subjection, from this point of view the persons are the same; for those who carry arms can always determine the fate of the constitution. It remains therefore that both functions should be entrusted by the ideal constitution to the same persons, not, however, at the same time, but in the order prescribed by nature, who has given to young men strength and to older men wisdom. Such a distribution of duties will be expedient and also just, and is founded upon a principle of conformity to merit. Besides, the ruling class should be the owners of property, for they are citizens, and the citizens of a state should be in good circumstances; whereas mechanics or any other class which is not a producer of virtue have no share in the state. This follows from our first principle, for happiness cannot exist without virtue, and a city is not to be termed happy in regard to a portion of the citizens, but in regard to them all. And clearly property should be in their hands, since the husbandmen will of necessity be slaves or barbarian Perioeci.

Of the classes enumerated there remain only the priests, and the manner in which their office is to be regulated is obvious. No husbandman or mechanic should be appointed to it; for the Gods should receive honour from the citizens only. Now since the body of the citizens is divided into two classes, the warriors and the councillors, and it is beseeming that the worship of the Gods should be duly performed, and also a rest provided in their service for those who from age have given up active life, to the old men of these two classes should be assigned the duties of the priesthood.

We have shown what are the necessary conditions, and what the parts of a state: husbandmen, craftsmen, and labourers of all kinds are necessary to the existence of states, but the parts of the state are the warriors and councillors. And these are distinguished severally from one another, the distinction being in some cases permanent, in others not.

Since every political society is composed of rulers and subjects let us consider whether the relations of one to the other should interchange or be permanent. For the education of the citizens will necessarily vary with the answer given to this question. Now, if some men excelled others in the same degree in which gods and heroes are supposed to excel mankind in general (having in the first place a great advantage even in their bodies, and secondly in their minds), so that the superiority of the governors was undisputed and patent to their subjects, it would clearly be better that once for all the one class should rule and the others serve. But since this is unattainable, and kings have no marked superiority over their subjects, such as Scylax affirms to be found among the Indians, it is obviously necessary on many grounds that all the citizens alike should take their turn of governing and being governed. Equality consists in the same treatment of similar persons, and no government can stand which is not founded upon justice. For if the government be unjust every one in the country unites with the governed in the desire to have a revolution, and it is an impossibility that the members of the government can be so numerous as to be stronger than all their enemies put together. Yet that governors should excel their subjects is undeniable. How all this is to be effected, and in what way they will respectively share in the government, the legislator has to consider. The subject has been already mentioned. Nature herself has provided the distinction when she made a difference between old and young within the same species, of whom she fitted the one to govern and the other to be governed. No one takes offence at being governed when he is young, nor does he think himself better than his governors, especially if he will enjoy the same privilege when he reaches the required age.

We conclude that from one point of view governors and governed are identical, and from another different. And therefore their education must be the same and also different. For he who would learn to command well must, as men say, first of all learn to obey. As I observed in the first part of this treatise, there is one rule which is for the sake of the rulers and another rule which is for the sake of the ruled; the former is a despotic, the latter a free government. Some commands differ not in the thing commanded, but in the intention with which they are imposed. Wherefore, many apparently menial offices are an honour to the free youth by whom they are performed; for actions do not differ as honourable or dishonourable in themselves so much as in the end and intention of them. But since we say that the virtue of the citizen and ruler is the same as that of the good man, and that the same person must first be a subject and then a ruler, the legislator has to see that they become good men, and by what means this may be accomplished, and what is the end of the perfect life.

Now the soul of man is divided into two parts, one of which has a rational principle in itself, and the other, not having a rational principle in itself, is able to obey such a principle. And we call a man in any way good because he has the virtues of these two parts. In which of them the end is more likely to be found is no matter of doubt to those who adopt our division; for in the world both of nature and of art the inferior always exists for the sake of the better or superior, and the better or superior is that which has a rational principle. This principle, too, in our ordinary way of speaking, is divided into two kinds, for there is a practical and a speculative principle. This part, then, must evidently be similarly divided. And there must be a corresponding division of actions; the actions of the naturally better part are to be preferred by those who have it in their power to attain to two out of the three or to all, for that is always to every one the most eligible which is the highest attainable by him. The whole of life is further divided into two parts, business and leisure, war and peace, and of actions some aim at what is necessary and useful, and some at what is honourable. And the preference given to one or the other class of actions must necessarily be like the preference given to one or other part of the soul and its actions over the other; there must be war for the sake of peace, business for the sake of leisure, things useful and necessary for the sake of things honourable. All these points the statesman should keep in view when he frames his laws; he should consider the parts of the soul and their functions, and above all the better and the end; he should also remember the diversities of human lives and actions. For men must be able to engage in business and go to war, but leisure and peace are better; they must do what is necessary and indeed what is useful, but what is honourable is better. On such principles children and persons of every age which requires education should be trained. Whereas even the Hellenes of the present day who are reputed to be best governed, and the legislators who gave them their constitutions, do not appear to have framed their governments with a regard to the best end, or to have given them laws and education with a view to all the virtues, but in a vulgar spirit have fallen back on those which promised to be more useful and profitable. Many modern writers have taken a similar view: they commend the Lacedaemonian constitution, and praise the legislator for making conquest and war his sole aim, a doctrine which may be refuted by argument and has long ago been refuted by facts. For most men desire empire in the hope of accumulating the goods of fortune; and on this ground Thibron and all those who have written about the Lacedaemonian constitution have praised their legislator, because the Lacedaemonians, by being trained to meet dangers, gained great power. But surely they are not a happy people now that their empire has passed away, nor was their legislator right. How ridiculous is the result, if, while they are continuing in the observance of his laws and no one interferes with them, they have lost the better part of life! These writers further err about the sort of government which the legislator should approve, for the government of freemen is nobler and implies more virtue than despotic government. Neither is a city to be deemed happy or a legislator to be praised because he trains his citizens to conquer and obtain dominion over their neighbours, for there is great evil in this. On a similar principle any citizen who could, should obviously try to obtain the power in his own state—the crime which the Lacedaemonians accuse King Pausanias of attempting, although he had so great honour already. No such principle and no law having this object is either statesman-like or useful or right. For the same things are best both for individuals and for states, and these are the things which the legislator ought to implant in the minds of his citizens. Neither should men study war with a view to the enslavement of those who do not deserve to be enslaved; but first of all they should provide against their own enslavement, and in the second place obtain empire for the good of the governed, and not for the sake of exercising a general despotism, and in the third place they should seek to be masters only over those who deserve to be slaves. Facts, as well as arguments, prove that the legislator should direct all his military and other measures to the provision of leisure and the establishment of peace. For most of these military states are safe only while they are at war, but fall when they have acquired their empire; like unused iron they lose their temper in time of peace. And for this the legislator is to blame, he never having taught them how to lead the life of peace.

## Political Systems

Having determined these questions, we have next to consider whether there is only one form of government or many, and if many, what they are, and how many, and what are the differences between them.

A constitution is the arrangement of magistracies in a state, especially of the highest of all. The government is everywhere sovereign in the state, and the constitution is in fact the government. For example, in democracies the people are supreme, but in oligarchies, the few; and, therefore, we say that these two forms of government also are different: and so in other cases.

First, let us consider what is the purpose of a state, and how many forms of government there are by which human society is regulated. We have already said, in the first part of this treatise, when discussing household management and the rule of a master, that man is by nature a political animal. And therefore, men, even when they do not require one another's help, desire to live together; not but that they are also brought together by their common interests in proportion as they severally attain to any measure of well-being. This is certainly the chief end, both of individuals and of states. And also for the sake of mere life (in which there is possibly some noble element so long as the evils of existence do not greatly overbalance the good) mankind meet together and maintain the political community. And we all see that men cling to life even at the cost of enduring great misfortune, seeming to find in life a natural sweetness and happiness.

There is no difficulty in distinguishing the various kinds of authority; they have been often defined already in discussions outside the school. The rule of a master, although the slave by nature and the master by nature have in reality the same interests, is nevertheless exercised primarily with a view to the interest of the master, but accidentally considers the slave, since, if the slave perish, the rule of the master perishes with him. On the other hand,

the government of a wife and children and of a household, which we have called household management, is exercised in the first instance for the good of the governed or for the common good of both parties, but essentially for the good of the governed, as we see to be the case in medicine, gymnastic, and the arts in general, which are only accidentally concerned with the good of the artists themselves. For there is no reason why the trainer may not sometimes practise gymnastics, and the helmsman is always one of the crew. The trainer or the helmsman considers the good of those committed to his care. But, when he is one of the persons taken care of, he accidentally participates in the advantage, for the helmsman is also a sailor, and the trainer becomes one of those in training. And so in politics: when the state is framed upon the principle of equality and likeness, the citizens think that they ought to hold office by turns. Formerly, as is natural, every one would take his turn of service; and then again, somebody else would look after his interest, just as he, while in office, had looked after theirs. But nowadays, for the sake of the advantage which is to be gained from the public revenues and from office, men want to be always in office. One might imagine that the rulers, being sickly, were only kept in health while they continued in office; in that case we may be sure that they would be hunting after places. The conclusion is evident: that governments which have a regard to the common interest are constituted in accordance with strict principles of justice, and are therefore true forms; but those which regard only the interest of the rulers are all defective and perverted forms, for they are despotic, whereas a state is a community of freemen.

Having determined these points, we have next to consider how many forms of government there are, and what they are; and in the first place what are the true forms, for when they are determined the perversions of them will at once be apparent. The words constitution and government have the same meaning, and the government, which is the supreme authority in states, must be in the hands of one, or of a few, or of the many. The true forms of government, therefore, are those in which the one, or the few, or the many, govern with a view to the common interest; but governments which rule with a view to the private interest, whether of the one, or of the few, or of the many, are perversions. For the members of a state, if they are truly citizens, ought to participate in its advantages. Of forms of government in which one rules, we call that which regards the common interests, kingship or royalty; that in which more than one, but not many, rule, aristocracy; and it is so called, either because the rulers are the best men, or because they have at heart the best interests of the state and of the citizens. But when the citizens at large administer the state for the common interest, the government is called by the generic name—a constitution. And there is a reason for this use of language. One man or a few may excel in virtue; but as the number increases it becomes more difficult for them to attain perfection in every kind of virtue, though they may in military virtue, for this is found in the masses. Hence in a constitutional government the fighting-men have the supreme power, and those who possess arms are the citizens.

Of the above-mentioned forms, the perversions are as follows:—of royalty, tyranny; of aristocracy, oligarchy; of constitutional government, democracy. For tyranny is a kind of monarchy which has in view the interest of the monarch only; oligarchy has in view the interest of the wealthy; democracy,

of the needy: none of them the common good of all.

## Democracy and Oligarchy

Let us begin by considering the common definitions of oligarchy and democracy, and what is justice oligarchical and democratical. For all men cling to justice of some kind, but their conceptions are imperfect and they do not express the whole idea. For example, justice is thought by them to be, and is, equality, not, however, for all, but only for equals. And inequality is thought to be, and is, justice; neither is this for all, but only for unequals. When the persons are omitted, then men judge erroneously. The reason is that they are passing judgment on themselves, and most people are bad judges in their own case. And whereas justice implies a relation to persons as well as to things, and a just distribution, as I have already said in the *Ethics*, implies the same ratio between the persons and between the things, they agree about the equality of the things, but dispute about the equality of the persons, chiefly for the reason which I have just given—because they are bad judges in their own affairs; and secondly, because both the parties to the argument are speaking of a limited and partial justice, but imagine themselves to be speaking of absolute justice. For the one party, if they are unequal in one respect, for example wealth, consider themselves to be unequal in all; and the other party, if they are equal in one respect, for example free birth, consider themselves to be equal in all. But they leave out the capital point. For if men met and associated out of regard to wealth only, their share in the state would be proportioned to their property, and the oligarchical doctrine would then seem to carry the day. It would not be just that he who paid one mina should have the same share of a hundred minae, whether of the principal or of the profits, as he who paid the remaining ninety-nine. But a state exists for the sake of a good life, and not for the sake of life only: if life only were the object, slaves and brute animals might form a state, but they cannot, for they have no share in happiness or in a life of free choice. Nor does a state exist for the sake of alliance and security from injustice, nor yet for the sake of exchange and mutual intercourse; for then the Tyrrhenians and the Carthaginians, and all who have commercial treaties with one another, would be the citizens of one state. True, they have agreements about imports, and engagements that they will do no wrong to one another, and written articles of alliance. But there are no magistracies common to the contracting parties who will enforce their engagements; different states have each their own magistracies. Nor does one state take care that the citizens of the other are such as they ought to be, nor see that those who come under the terms of the treaty do no wrong or wickedness at all, but only that they do no injustice to one another. Whereas, those who care for good government take into consideration virtue and vice in states. Whence it may be further inferred that virtue must be the care of a state which is truly so called, and not merely enjoys the name: for without this end the community becomes a mere alliance which differs only in place from alliances of which the members live apart; and law is only a convention, "a surety to one another of justice," as the sophist Lycophron says, and has no real power to make the citizens good and just.

This is obvious; for suppose distinct places, such as Corinth and Megara, to be brought together so that their walls touched, still they would not be one city, not even if the citizens had the right to intermarry, which is one of the rights peculiarly characteristic of states. Again, if men dwelt at a distance from one another, but not so far off as to have no intercourse, and there were laws among them that they should not wrong each other in their exchanges, neither would this be a state. Let us suppose that one man is a carpenter, another a husbandman, another a shoemaker, and so on, and that their number is ten thousand: nevertheless, if they have nothing in common but exchange, alliance, and the like, that would not constitute a state. Why is this? Surely not because they are at a distance from one another: for even supposing that such a community were to meet in one place, but that each man had a house of his own, which was in a manner his state, and that they made alliance with one another, but only against evil-doers; still an accurate thinker would not deem this to be a state, if their intercourse with one another was of the same character after as before their union. It is clear then that a state is not a mere society, having a common place, established for the prevention of mutual crime and for the sake of exchange. These are conditions without which a state cannot exist; but all of them together do not constitute a state, which is a community of families and aggregations of families in well-being, for the sake of a perfect and self-sufficing life. Such a community can only be established among those who live in the same place and intermarry. Hence arise in cities family connexions, brotherhoods, common sacrifices, amusements which draw men together. But these are created by friendship, for the will to live together is friendship. The end of the state is the good life, and these are the means towards it. And the state is the union of families and villages in a perfect and self-sufficing life, by which we mean a happy and honourable life.

Our conclusion, then, is that political society exists for the sake of noble actions, and not of mere companionship. Hence they who contribute most to such a society have a greater share in it than those who have the same or a greater freedom or nobility of birth but are inferior to them in political virtue; or than those who exceed them in wealth but are surpassed by them in virtue.

From what has been said it will be clearly seen that all the partisans of different forms of government speak of a part of justice only.

There is also a doubt as to what is to be the supreme power in the state:—Is it the multitude? Or the wealthy? Or the good? Or the one best man? Or a tyrant? Any of these alternatives seems to involve disagreeable consequences. If the poor, for example, because they are more in number, divide among themselves the property of the rich—is not this unjust? No, by heaven (will be the reply), for the supreme authority justly willed it. But if this is not injustice, pray what is? Again, when in the first division all has been taken, and the majority divide anew the property of the minority, is it not evident, if this goes on, that they will ruin the state? Yet surely, virtue is not the ruin of those who possess her, nor is justice destructive of a state; and therefore this law of confiscation clearly cannot be just. If it were, all the acts of a tyrant must of necessity be just; for he only coerces other men by superior power, just as the multitude coerce the rich. But is it just then that the few and the wealthy should be the rulers? And what if they, in like manner, rob and plunder the people—is

this just? If so, the other case will likewise be just. But there can be no doubt that all these things are wrong and unjust.

Then ought the good to rule and have supreme power? But in that case everybody else, being excluded from power, will be dishonoured. For the offices of a state are posts of honour; and if one set of men always hold them, the rest must be deprived of them. Then will it be well that the one best man should rule? Nay, that is still more oligarchical, for the number of those who are dishonoured is thereby increased. Some one may say that it is bad in any case for a man, subject as he is to all the accidents of human passion, to have the supreme power, rather than the law. But what if the law itself be democratical or oligarchical, how will that help us out of our difficulties? Not at all; the same consequences will follow.

Most of these questions may be reserved for another occasion. The principle that the multitude ought to be supreme rather than the few best is one that is maintained, and, though not free from difficulty, yet seems to contain an element of truth. For the many, of whom each individual is but an ordinary person, when they meet together may very likely be better than the few good, if regarded not individually but collectively, just as a feast to which many contribute is better than a dinner provided out of a single purse. For each individual among the many has a share of virtue and prudence, and when they meet together, they become in a manner one man, who has many feet, and hands, and senses; that is a figure of their mind and disposition. Hence the many are better judges than a single man of music and poetry; for some understand one part, and some another, and among them they understand the whole. There is a similar combination of qualities in good men, who differ from any individual of the many, as the beautiful are said to differ from those who are not beautiful, and works of art from realities, because in them the scattered elements are combined, although, if taken separately, the eye of one person or some other feature in another person would be fairer than in the picture. Whether this principle can apply to every democracy, and to all bodies of men, is not clear. Or rather, by heaven, in some cases it is impossible of application; for the argument would equally hold about brutes; and wherein, it will be asked, do some men differ from brutes? But there may be bodies of men about whom our statement is nevertheless true. And if so, the difficulty which has been already raised, and also another which is akin to it—viz. what power should be assigned to the mass of freemen and citizens, who are not rich and have no personal merit—are both solved. There is still a danger in allowing them to share the great offices of state, for their folly will lead them into error, and their dishonesty into crime. But there is a danger also in not letting them share, for a state in which many poor men are excluded from office will necessarily be full of enemies. The only way of escape is to assign to them some deliberative and judicial functions. For this reason Solon and certain other legislators give them the power of electing to offices, and of calling the magistrates to account, but they do not allow them to hold office singly. When they meet together their perceptions are quite good enough, and combined with the better class they are useful to the state (just as impure food when mixed with what is pure sometimes makes the entire mass more wholesome than a small quantity of the pure would be), but each individual, left to himself, forms an imperfect judgment. On the other hand, the popular form of government involves certain difficulties. In the first place, it might be objected that he who can judge of the healing of a sick man would be one who could himself heal his disease, and make him whole—that is, in other words, the physician; and so in all professions and arts. As, then, the physician ought to be called to account by physicians, so ought men in general to be called to account by their peers. But physicians are of three kinds:—there is the ordinary practitioner, and there is the physician of the higher class, and thirdly the intelligent man who has studied the art: in all arts there is such a class; and we attribute the power of judging to them quite as much as to professors of the art. Secondly, does not the same principle apply to elections? For a right election can only be made by those who have knowledge; those who know geometry, for example, will choose a geometrician rightly, and those who know how to steer, a pilot; and, even if there be some occupations and arts in which private persons share in the ability to choose, they certainly cannot choose better than those who know. So that, according to this argument, neither the election of magistrates, nor the calling of them to account, should be entrusted to the many. Yet possibly these objections are to a great extent met by our old answer, that if the people are not utterly degraded, although individually they may be worse judges than those who have special knowledge—as a body they are as good or better. Moreover, there are some arts whose products are not judged of solely, or best, by the artists themselves, namely those arts whose products are recognized even by those who do not possess the art; for example, the knowledge of the house is not limited to the builder only; the user, or, in other words, the master, of the house will be even a better judge than the builder, just as the pilot will judge better of a rudder than the carpenter, and the guest will judge better of a feast than the cook.

This difficulty seems now to be sufficiently answered, but there is another akin to it. That inferior persons should have authority in greater matters than the good would appear to be a strange thing, yet the election and calling to account of the magistrates is the greatest of all. And these, as I was saying, are functions which in some states are assigned to the people, for the assembly is supreme in all such matters. Yet persons of any age, and having but a small property qualification, sit in the assembly and deliberate and judge, although for the great officers of state, such as treasurers and generals, a high qualification is required. This difficulty may be solved in the same manner as the preceding, and the present practice of democracies may be really defensible. For the power does not reside in the dicast, or senator, or ecclesiast, but in the court, and the senate, and the assembly, of which individual senators, or ecclesiasts, or dicasts, are only parts or members. And for this reason the many may claim to have a higher authority than the few; for the people, and the senate, and the courts consist of many persons, and their property collectively is greater than the property of one or of a few individuals holding great offices. But enough of this.

The discussion of the first question shows nothing so clearly as that laws, when good, should be supreme; and that the magistrate or magistrates should regulate those matters only on which the laws are unable to speak with precision owing to the difficulty of any general principle embracing all particulars. But what are good laws has not yet been clearly explained; the old difficulty remains. The goodness or badness, justice or injustice,

of laws varies of necessity with the constitutions of states. This, however, is clear, that the laws must be adapted to the constitutions. But if so, true forms of government will of necessity have just laws, and perverted forms of government will have unjust laws.

## Monarchy

If, however, there be some one person, or more than one, although not enough to make up the full complement of a state, whose virtue is so preeminent that the virtues or the political capacity of all the rest admit of no comparison with his or theirs, he or they can be no longer regarded as part of a state; for justice will not be done to the superior, if he is reckoned only as the equal of those who are so far inferior to him in virtue and in political capacity. Such an one may truly be deemed a God among men. Hence we see that legislation is necessarily concerned only with those who are equal in birth and in capacity; and that for men of preeminent virtue there is no law—they are themselves a law. Any one would be ridiculous who attempted to make laws for them: they would probably retort what, in the fable of Antisthenes, the lions said to the hares, when in the council of the beasts the latter began haranguing and claiming equality for all. And for this reason democratic states have instituted ostracism; equality is above all things their aim, and therefore they ostracized and banished from the city for a time those who seemed to predominate too much through their wealth, or the number of their friends, or through any other political influence. Mythology tells us that the Argonauts left Heracles behind for a similar reason; the ship Argo would not take him because she feared that he would have been too much for the rest of the crew. Wherefore those who denounce tyranny and blame the counsel which Periander gave to Thrasybulus cannot be held altogether just in their censure. The story is that Periander, when the herald was sent to ask counsel of him, said nothing, but only cut off the tallest ears of corn till he had brought the field to a level. The herald did not know the meaning of the action, but came and reported what he had seen to Thrasybulus, who understood that he was to cut off the principal men in the state; and this is a policy not only expedient for tyrants or in practice confined to them, but equally necessary in oligarchies and democracies. Ostracism is a measure of the same kind, which acts by disabling and banishing the most prominent citizens. Great powers do the same to whole cities and nations, as the Athenians did to the Samians, Chians, and Lesbians; no sooner had they obtained a firm grasp of the empire, than they humbled their allies contrary to treaty; and the Persian king has repeatedly crushed the Medes, Babylonians, and other nations, when their spirit has been stirred by the recollection of their former greatness.

The problem is a universal one, and equally concerns all forms of government, true as well as false; for, although perverted forms with a view to their own interests may adopt this policy, those which seek the common interest do so likewise. The same thing may be observed in the arts and sciences; for the painter will not allow the figure to have a foot which, however beautiful, is not in proportion, nor will the shipbuilder allow the stern or any other part of the vessel to be unduly large, any more than the chorus-master will allow any one who sings louder or better than all the rest to sing in the choir. Monarchs, too, may practise compulsion and still live in harmony with their cities, if their own government is for the interest of the state. Hence where there is an acknowledged superiority the argument in favor of ostracism is based upon a kind of political justice. It would certainly be better that the legislator should from the first so order his state as to have no need of such a remedy. But if the need arises, the next best thing is that he should endeavour to correct the evil by this or some similar measure. The principle, however, has not been fairly applied in states; for, instead of looking to the good of their own constitution, they have used ostracism for factious purposes. It is true that under perverted forms of government, and from their special point of view, such a measure is just and expedient, but it is also clear that it is not absolutely just. In the perfect state there would be great doubts about the use of it, not when applied to excess in strength, wealth, popularity, or the like, but when used against some one who is preeminent in virtue—what is to be done with him? Mankind will not say that such an one is to be expelled and exiled; on the other hand, he ought not to be a subject—that would be as if mankind should claim to rule over Zeus, dividing his offices among them. The only alternative is that all should joyfully obey such a ruler, according to what seems to be the order of nature, and that men like him should be kings in their state for life.

## Liberty and Equality

The basis of a democratic state is liberty; which, according to the common opinion of men, can only be enjoyed in such a state;—this they affirm to be the great end of every democracy. One principle of liberty is for all to rule and be ruled in turn, and indeed democratic justice is the application of numerical not proportionate equality; whence it follows that the majority must be supreme, and that whatever the majority approve must be the end and the just. Every citizen, it is said, must have equality, and therefore in a democracy the poor have more power than the rich, because there are more of them, and the will of the majority is supreme. This, then, is one note of liberty which all democrats affirm to be the principle of their state. Another is that a man should live as he likes. This, they say, is the privilege of a freeman, since, on the other hand, not to live as a man likes is the mark of a slave. This is the second characteristic of democracy, whence has arisen the claim of men to be ruled by none, if possible, or, if this is impossible, to rule and be ruled in turns; and so it contributes to the freedom based upon equality.

Such being our foundation and such the principle from which we start, the characteristics of democracy are as follows:—the election of officers by all out of all; and that all should rule over each, and each in his turn over all; that the appointment to all offices, or to all but those which require experience and skill, should be made by lot; that no property qualification should be required for offices, or only a very low one; that a man should not hold the same office twice, or not often, or in the case of few except military offices: that the tenure of all offices, or of as many as possible, should be brief; that all men should sit in judgment, or that judges selected out of all should judge, in all matters, or in most and in the greatest and most important—such as the scrutiny of accounts, the constitution,

and private contracts; that the assembly should be supreme over all causes, or at any rate over the most important, and the magistrates over none or only over a very few. Of all magistracies, a council is the most democratic when there is not the means of paying all the citizens, but when they are paid even this is robbed of its power; for the people then draw all cases to themselves, as I said in the previous discussion. The next characteristic of democracy is payment for services; assembly, law-courts, magistrates, everybody receives pay, when it is to be had; or when it is not to be had for all, then it is given to the law-courts and to the stated assemblies, to the council and to the magistrates, or at least to any of them who are compelled to have their meals together. And whereas oligarchy is characterized by birth, wealth, and education, the notes of democracy appear to be the opposite of these—low birth, poverty, mean employment. Another note is that no magistracy is perpetual, but if any such have survived some ancient change in the constitution it should be stripped of its power, and the holders should be elected by lot and no longer by vote. These are the points common to all democracies; but democracy and demos in their truest form are based upon the recognized principle of democratic justice, that all should count equally; for equality implies that the poor should have no more share in the government than the rich, and should not be the only rulers, but that all should rule equally according to their numbers. And in this way men think that they will secure equality and freedom in their state.

Next comes the question, how is this equality to be obtained? Are we to assign to a thousand poor men the property qualifications of five hundred rich men? and shall we give the thousand a power equal to that of the five hundred? or, if this is not to be the mode, ought we, still retaining the same ratio, to take equal numbers from each and give them the control of the elections and of the courts?—Which, according to the democratical notion, is the juster form of the constitution—this or one based on numbers only? Democrats say that justice is that to which the majority agree, oligarchs that to which the wealthier class; in their opinion the decision should be given according to the amount of property. In both principles there is some inequality and injustice. For if justice is the will of the few, any one person who has more wealth than all the rest of the rich put together, ought, upon the oligarchical principle, to have the sole power—but this would be tyranny; or if justice is the will of the majority, as I was before saying, they will unjustly confiscate the property of the wealthy minority. To find a principle of equality in which they both agree we must inquire into their respective ideas of justice.

Now they agree in saying that whatever is decided by the majority of the citizens is to be deemed law. Granted:—but not without some reserve; since there are two classes out of which a state is composed—the poor and the rich—that is to be deemed law, on which both or the greater part of both agree; and if they disagree, that which is approved by the greater number, and by those who have the higher qualification. For example, suppose that there are ten rich and twenty poor, and some measure is approved by six of the rich and is disapproved by fifteen of the poor, and the remaining four of the rich join with the party of the poor, and the remaining five of the poor with that of the rich; in such a case the will of those whose qualifications, when both sides are added up, are the greatest, should prevail. If they turn out to be equal, there is no

greater difficulty than at present, when, if the assembly or the courts are divided, recourse is had to the lot, or to some similar expedient. But, although it may be difficult in theory to know what is just and equal, the practical difficulty of inducing those to forbear who can, if they like, encroach, is far greater, for the weaker are always asking for equality and justice, but the stronger care for none of these things.

## The Rule of Law

At this place in the discussion there impends the inquiry respecting the king who acts solely according to his own will; he has now to be considered. The so-called limited monarchy, or kingship according to law, as I have already remarked, is not a distinct form of government, for under all governments, as, for example, in a democracy or aristocracy, there may be a general holding office for life, and one person is often made supreme over the administration of a state. A magistracy of this kind exists at Epidamnus, and also at Opus, but in the latter city has a more limited power. Now, absolute monarchy, or the arbitrary rule of a sovereign over all the citizens, in a city which consists of equals, is thought by some to be quite contrary to nature; it is argued that those who are by nature equals must have the same natural right and worth, and that for unequals to have an equal share, or for equals to have an uneven share, in the offices of state, is as bad as for different bodily constitutions to have the same food and clothing. Wherefore it is thought to be just that among equals every one be ruled as well as rule, and therefore that all should have their turn. We thus arrive at law; for an order of succession implies law. And the rule of the law, it is argued, is preferable to that of any individual. On the same principle, even if it be better for certain individuals to govern, they should be made only guardians and ministers of the law. For magistrates there must be—this is admitted; but then men say that to give authority to any one man when all are equal is unjust. Nay, there may indeed be cases which the law seems unable to determine, but in such cases can a man? Nay, it will be replied, the law trains officers for this express purpose, and appoints them to determine matters which are left undecided by it, to the best of their judgment. Further, it permits them to make any amendment of the existing laws which experience suggests. Therefore he who bids the law rule may be deemed to bid God and Reason alone rule, but he who bids man rule adds an element of the beast; for desire is a wild beast, and passion perverts the minds of rulers, even when they are the best of men. The law is reason unaffected by desire. We are told that a patient should call in a physician; he will not get better if he is doctored out of a book. But the parallel of the arts is clearly not in point; for the physician does nothing contrary to rule from motives of friendship; he only cures a patient and takes a fee; whereas magistrates do many things from spite and partiality. And, indeed, if a man suspected the physician of being in league with his enemies to destroy him for a bribe, he would rather have recourse to the book. But certainly physicians, when they are sick, call in other physicians, and training-masters, when they are in training, other trainingmasters, as if they could not judge truly about their own case and might be influenced by their feelings.

Hence it is evident that in seeking for justice men seek for the mean or neutral, for the law is the mean. Again, customary laws have more weight, and relate to more important matters, than written laws, and a man may be a safer ruler than the written law, but not safer than the customary law.

Again, it is by no means easy for one man to superintend many things; he will have to appoint a number of subordinates, and what difference does it make whether these subordinates always existed or were appointed by him because he needed them? If, as I said before, the good man has a right to rule because he is better, still two good men are better than one: this is the old saying—

two going together,

and the prayer of Agamemnon—

would that I had ten such counsellors!

And at this day there are magistrates, for example judges, who have authority to decide some matters which the law is unable to determine, since no one doubts that the law would command and decide in the best manner whatever it could. But some things can, and other things cannot, be comprehended under the law, and this is the origin of the vexed question whether the best law or the best man should rule. For matters of detail about which men deliberate cannot be included in legislation. Nor does any one deny that the decision of such matters must be left to man, but it is argued that there should be many judges, and not one only. For every ruler who has been trained by the law judges well; and it would surely seem strange that a person should see better with two eyes, or hear better with two ears, or act better with two hands or feet, than many with many; indeed, it is already the practice of kings to make to themselves many eyes and ears and hands and feet. For they make colleagues of those who are the friends of themselves and their governments. They must be friends of the monarch and of his government; if not his friends, they will not do what he wants; but friendship implies likeness and equality; and, therefore, if he thinks that his friends ought to rule, he must think that those who are equal to himself and like himself ought to rule equally with himself. These are the principal controversies relating to monarchy.

## Constitutional Government

Polity or constitutional government may be described generally as a fusion of oligarchy and democracy; but the term is usually applied to those forms of government which incline towards democracy, and the term aristocracy to those which incline towards oligarchy, because birth and education are commonly the accompaniments of wealth. Moreover, the rich already possess the external advantages the want of which is a temptation to crime, and hence they are called noblemen and gentlemen. And inasmuch as aristocracy seeks to give predominance to the best of the citizens, people say also of oligarchies that they are composed of noblemen and gentlemen. Now it appears to be an impossible thing that the state which is governed not by the best citizens but by the worst should be well-governed, and equally impossible that the state which is ill-governed should be governed by the best. But we must remember that good laws, if they are not obeyed, do not constitute good government. Hence there are two parts of good government; one is the actual obedience of citizens to the laws, the other part is the goodness of the laws which they obey; they may obey bad laws as well as good. And there may be a further subdivision; they may obey either the best laws which are attainable to them, or the best absolutely.

The distribution of offices according to merit is a special characteristic of aristocracy, for the principle of an aristocracy is virtue, as wealth is of an oligarchy, and freedom of a democracy. In all of them there of course exists the right of the majority, and whatever seems good to the majority of those who share in the government has authority. Now in most states the form called polity exists, for the fusion goes no further than the attempt to unite the freedom of the poor and the wealth of the rich, who commonly take the place of the noble. But as there are three grounds on which men claim an equal share in the government, freedom, wealth, and virtue (for the fourth or good birth is the result of the two last, being only ancient wealth and virtue), it is clear that the admixture of the two elements, that is to say, of the rich and poor, is to be called a polity or constitutional government; and the union of the three is to be called aristocracy or the government of the best, and more than any other form of government, except the true and ideal, has a right to this name.

Thus far I have shown the existence of forms of states other than monarchy, democracy, and oligarchy, and what they are, and in what aristocracies differ from one another, and polities from aristocracies—that the two latter are not very unlike is obvious.

Next we have to consider how by the side of oligarchy and democracy the so-called polity or constitutional government springs up, and how it should be organized. The nature of it will be at once understood from a comparison of oligarchy and democracy; we must ascertain their different characteristics, and taking a portion from each, put the two together, like the parts of an indenture. Now there are three modes in which fusions of government may be affected. In the first mode we must combine the laws made by both governments, say concerning the administration of justice. In oligarchies they impose a fine on the rich if they do not serve as judges, and to the poor they give no pay; but in democracies they give pay to the poor and do not fine the rich. Now (1) the union of these two modes is a common or middle term between them, and is therefore characteristic of a constitutional government, for it is a combination of both. This is one mode of uniting the two elements. Or (2) a mean may be taken between the enactments of the two: thus democracies require no property qualification, or only a small one, from members of the assembly, oligarchies a high one; here neither of these is the common term, but a mean between them. (3) There is a third mode, in which something is borrowed from the oligarchical and something from the democratical principle. For example, the appointment of magistrates by lot is thought to be democratical, and the election of them oligarchical; democratical again when there is no property qualification, oligarchical when there is. In the aristocratical or constitutional state, one element will be taken from each—from oligarchy the principle of electing to offices, from democracy the disregard of qualification. Such are the various modes of combination.

There is a true union of oligarchy and democracy when the same state may be termed either a democracy or an oligarchy; those who use both names evidently feel that the fusion is complete. Such a fusion there is also in the mean; for both extremes appear in it. The Lacedaemonian constitution, for example, is often described as a democracy, because it has many democratical features. In the first place the youth receive a democratical education. For the sons of the poor are brought up with the sons of the rich, who are educated in such a manner as to make it possible for the sons of the poor to be educated like them. A similar equality prevails in the following period of life, and when the citizens are grown up to manhood the same rule is observed; there is no distinction between the rich and poor. In like manner they all have the same food at their public tables, and the rich wear only such clothing as any poor man can afford. Again, the people elect to one of the two greatest offices of state, and in the other they share; for they elect the Senators and share in the Ephoralty. By others the Spartan constitution is said to be an oligarchy, because it has many oligarchical elements. That all offices are filled by election and none by lot, is one of these oligarchical characteristics; that the power of inflicting death or banishment rests with a few persons is another; and there are others. In a well attempered polity there should appear to be both elements and yet neither; also the government should rely on itself, and not on foreign aid, and on itself not through the good will of a majority—they might be equally well-disposed when there is a vicious form of government—but through the general willingness of all classes in the state to maintain the constitution.

Enough of the manner in which a constitutional government, and in which the so-called aristocracies ought to be framed.

## The Best State

In all arts and sciences which embrace the whole of any subject, and do not come into being in a fragmentary way, it is the province of a single art or science to consider all that appertains to a single subject. For example, the art of gymnastic considers not only the suitableness of different modes of training to different bodies (2) but what sort is absolutely the best (1); (for the absolutely best must suit that which is by nature best and best furnished with the means of life), and also what common form of training is adapted to the great majority of men (4). And if a man does not desire the best habit of body, or the greatest skill in gymnastics, which might be attained by him, still the trainer or the teacher of gymnastic should be able to impart any lower degree of either (3). The same principle equally holds in medicine and ship-building, and the making of clothes, and in the arts generally.

Hence it is obvious that government too is the subject of a single science, which has to consider what government is best and of what sort it must be, to be most in accordance with our aspirations, if there were no external impediment, and also what kind of government is adapted to particular states. For the best is often unattainable, and therefore the true legislator and statesman ought to be acquainted, not only with (1) that which is best in the abstract, but also with (2) that which is best relatively to circumstances. We should be able further to say how a state may be constituted under any given conditions (3); both how it is originally formed and, when formed, how it may be longest preserved; the supposed state being so far from having the best constitution that it is unprovided even with the conditions necessary for the best; neither is it the best under the circumstances, but of an inferior type.

He ought, moreover, to know (4) the form of government which is best suited to states in general; for political writers, although they have excellent ideas, are often unpractical. We should consider, not only what form of government is best, but also what is possible and what is easily attainable by all. There are some who would have none but the most perfect; for this many natural advantages are required. Others, again, speak of a more attainable form, and, although they reject the constitution under which they are living, they extol some one in particular, for example the Lacedaemonian. Any change of government which has to be introduced should be one which men, starting from their existing constitutions, will be both willing and able to adopt, since there is quite as much trouble in the reformation of an old constitution as in the establishment of a new one, just as to unlearn is as hard as to learn. And therefore, in addition to the qualifications of the statesman already mentioned, he should be able to find remedies for the defects of existing constitutions, as has been said before. This he cannot do unless he knows how many forms of government there are. It is often supposed that there is only one kind of democracy and one of oligarchy. But this is a mistake; and, in order to avoid such mistakes, we must ascertain what differences there are in the constitutions of states, and in how many ways they are combined. The same political insight will enable a man to know which laws are the best, and which are suited to different constitutions; for the laws are, and ought to be, relative to the constitution, and not the constitution to the laws. A constitution is the organization of offices in a state, and determines what is to be the governing body, and what is the end of each community. But laws are not to be confounded with the principles of the constitution; they are the rules according to which the magistrates should administer the state, and proceed against offenders. So that we must know the varieties, and the number of varieties, of each form of government, if only with a view to making laws. For the same laws cannot be equally suited to all oligarchies or to all democracies, since there is certainly more than one form both of democracy and of oligarchy.

## Political Moderation and Stability: The Middle Classes

We have now to inquire what is the best constitution for most states, and the best life for most men, neither assuming a standard of virtue which is above ordinary persons, nor an education which is exceptionally favoured by nature and circumstances, nor yet an ideal state which is an aspiration only, but having regard to the life in which the majority are able to share, and to the form of government which states in general can attain. As to those aristocracies, as they are called, of which we were just now speaking, they either lie beyond the possibilities of the greater number of states, or they approximate to the so-called constitutional

government, and therefore need no separate discussion. And in fact the conclusion at which we arrive respecting all these forms rests upon the same grounds. For if what was said in the *Ethics* is true, that the happy life is the life according to virtue lived without impediment, and that virtue is a mean, then the life which is in a mean, and in a mean attainable by every one, must be the best. And the same principles of virtue and vice are characteristic of cities and of constitutions; for the constitution is in a figure the life of the city.

Now in all states there are three elements: one class is very rich, another very poor, and a third in a mean. It is admitted that moderation and the mean are best, and therefore it will clearly be best to possess the gifts of fortune in moderation; for in that condition of life men are most ready to follow rational principle. But he who greatly excels in beauty, strength, birth, or wealth, or on the other hand who is very poor, or very weak, or very much disgraced, finds it difficult to follow rational principle. Of these two the one sort grow into violent and great criminals, the others into rogues and petty rascals. And two sorts of offences correspond to them, the one committed from violence, the other from roguery. Again, the middle class is least likely to shrink from rule, or to be overambitious for it; both of which are injuries to the state. Again, those who have too much of the goods of fortune, strength, wealth, friends, and the like, are neither willing nor able to submit to authority. The evil begins at home; for when they are boys, by reason of the luxury in which they are brought up, they never learn, even at school, the habit of obedience. On the other hand, the very poor, who are in the opposite extreme, are too degraded. So that the one class cannot obey, and can only rule despotically; the other knows not how to command and must be ruled like slaves. Thus arises a city, not of freemen, but of masters and slaves, the one despising, the other envying; and nothing can be more fatal to friendship and good fellowship in states than this: for good fellowship springs from friendship; when men are at enmity with one another, they would rather not even share the same path. But a city ought to be composed, as far as possible, of equals and similars; and these are generally the middle classes. Wherefore the city which is composed of middle-class citizens is necessarily best constituted in respect of the elements of which we say the fabric of the state naturally consists. And this is the class of citizens which is most secure in a state, for they do not, like the poor, covet their neighbours' goods; nor do others covet theirs, as the poor covet the goods of the rich; and as they neither plot against others, nor are themselves plotted against, they pass through life safely. Wisely then did Phocylides pray—"Many things are best in the mean; I desire to be of a middle condition in my city."

Thus it is manifest that the best political community is formed by citizens of the middle class, and that those states are likely to be well-administered, in which the middle class is large, and stronger if possible than both the other classes, or at any rate than either singly; for the addition of the middle class turns the scale, and prevents either of the extremes from being dominant. Great then is the good fortune of a state in which the citizens have a moderate and sufficient property; for where some possess much, and the others nothing, there may arise an extreme democracy, or a pure oligarchy; or a tyranny may grow out of either extreme—either out of the most rampant democracy, or out of an oligarchy; but it is not so likely to arise out of the middle constitutions and those akin to

them. I will explain the reason of this hereafter, when I speak of the revolutions of states. The mean condition of states is clearly best, for no other is free from faction; and where the middle class is large, there are least likely to be factions and dissensions. For a similar reason large states are less liable to faction than small ones, because in them the middle class is large; whereas in small states it is easy to divide all the citizens into two classes who are either rich or poor, and to leave nothing in the middle. And democracies are safer and more permanent than oligarchies, because they have a middle class which is more numerous and has a greater share in the government; for when there is no middle class, and the poor greatly exceed in number, troubles arise, and the state soon comes to an end. A proof of the superiority of the middle class is that the best legislators have been of a middle condition; for example, Solon, as his own verses testify; and Lycurgus, for he was not a king; and Charondas, and almost all legislators.

These considerations will help us to understand why most governments are either democratical or oligarchical. The reason is that the middle class is seldom numerous in them, and whichever party, whether the rich or the common people, transgresses the mean and predominates, draws the constitution its own way, and thus arises either oligarchy or democracy. There is another reason—the poor and the rich quarrel with one another, and whichever side gets the better, instead of establishing a just or popular government, regards political supremacy as the prize of victory, and the one party sets up a democracy and the other an oligarchy. Further, both the parties which had the supremacy in Hellas looked only to the interest of their own form of government and established in states, the one, democracies, and the other, oligarchies; they thought of their own advantage, of the public not at all. For these reasons the middle form of government has rarely, if ever, existed, and among a very few only. One man alone of all who ever ruled in Hellas was induced to give this middle constitution to states. But it has now become a habit among the citizens of states, not even to care about equality; all men are seeking for dominion, or, if conquered, are willing to submit.

What then is the best form of government and what makes it the best, is evident; and of other constitutions, since we say that there are many kinds of democracy and many of oligarchy, it is not difficult to see which has the first and which the second or any other place in the order of excellence, now that we have determined which is the best. For that which is nearest to the best must of necessity be better, and that which is furthest from it worse, if we are judging absolutely and not relatively to given conditions: I say "relatively to given conditions," since a particular government may be preferable, but another form may be better for some people.

## Causes of Revolution

In considering how dissensions and political revolutions arise, we must first of all ascertain the beginnings and causes of them which affect constitutions generally. They may be said to be three in number; and we have now

to given an outline of each. We want to know (1) what is the feeling? (2) what are the motives of those who make them? (3) whence arise political disturbances and quarrels? The universal and chief cause of this revolutionary feeling has been already mentioned; viz. the desire of equality, when men think that they are equal to others who have more than themselves; or, again, the desire of inequality and superiority, when conceiving themselves to be superior they think that they have not more but the same or less than their inferiors; pretensions which may and may not be just. Inferiors revolt in order that they may be equal, and equals that they may be superior. Such is the state of mind which creates revolutions. The motives for making them are the desire of gain and honour, or the fear of dishonour and loss; the authors of them want to divert punishment or dishonour from themselves or their friends. The causes and reasons of revolutions, whereby men are themselves affected in the way described, and about the things which I have mentioned, viewed in one way may be regarded as seven, and in another as more than seven. Two of them have been already noticed; but they act in a different manner, for men are excited against one another by the love of gain and honour—not, as in the case which I have just supposed, in order to obtain them for themselves, but at seeing others, justly or unjustly, engrossing them. Other causes are insolence, fear, excessive predominance, contempt, disproportionate increase in some part of the state; causes of another sort are election intrigues, carelessness, neglect about trifles, dissimilarity of elements.

# How To Prevent Revolution

We have next to consider what means there are of preserving constitutions in general, and in particular cases. In the first place it is evident that if we know the causes which destroy constitutions, we also know the causes which preserve them; for opposites produce opposites, and destruction is the opposite of preservation.

In all well-attempered governments there is nothing which should be more jealously maintained than the spirit of obedience to law, more especially in small matters; for transgression creeps in unperceived and at last ruins the state, just as the constant recurrence of small expenses in time eats up a fortune. The expense does not take place all at once, and therefore is not observed; the mind is deceived, as in the fallacy which says that "if each part is little, then the whole is little." And this is true in one way, but not in another, for the whole and the all are not little, although they are made up of littles.

In the first place, then, men should guard against the beginnings of change, and in the second place they should not rely upon the political devices of which I have already spoken invented only to deceive the people, for they are proved by experience to be useless. Further, we note that oligarchies as well as aristocracies may last not from any inherent stability in such forms of government, but because the rulers are on good terms both with the unenfranchised and with the governing classes, not maltreating any who are excluded from the government, but introducing into it the leading spirits among them. They should never wrong the ambitious in a matter of honour, or the common people in a matter of money; and they should treat one another and their fellow-citizens in a spirit of equality. The equality which the friends of democracy seek to establish for the multitude is not only just but likewise expedient among equals. Hence, if the governing class are numerous, many democratic institutions are useful; for example, the restriction of the tenure of offices to six months, that all those who are of equal rank may share in them. Indeed, equals or peers when they are numerous become a kind of democracy, and therefore demagogues are very likely to arise among them, as I have already remarked. The short tenure of office prevents oligarchies and aristocracies from falling into the hands of families, it is not easy for a person to do any great harm when his tenure of office is short, whereas long possession begets tyranny in oligarchies and democracies. For the aspirants to tyranny are either the principal men of the state, who in democracies are demagogues and in oligarchies members of ruling houses, or those who hold great offices, and have a long tenure of them.

Constitutions are preserved when their destroyers are at a distance, and sometimes also because they are near, for the fear of them makes the government keep in hand the constitution. Wherefore the ruler who has a care of the constitution should invent terrors, and bring distant dangers near, in order that the citizens may be on their guard, and, like sentinels in a night-watch, never relax their attention. He should endeavour too by help of the laws to control the contentions and quarrels of the notables, and to prevent those who have not hitherto taken part in them from catching the spirit of contention. No ordinary man can discern the beginning of evil, but only the true statesman.

As to the change produced in oligarchies and constitutional governments by the alteration of the qualification, when this arises, not out of any variation in the qualification but only out of the increase of money, it is well to compare the general valuation of property with that of past years, annually in those cities in which the census is taken annually, and in larger cities every third or fifth year. If the whole is many times greater or many times less than when the ratings recognized by the constitution were fixed, there should be power given by law to raise or lower the qualification as the amount is greater or less. Where this is not done a constitutional government passes into an oligarchy, and an oligarchy is narrowed to a rule of families; or in the opposite case constitutional government becomes democracy, and oligarchy either constitutional government or democracy.

It is a principle common to democracy, oligarchy, and every other form of government not to allow the disproportionate increase of any citizen, but to give moderate honour for a long time rather than great honour for a short time. For men are easily spoilt; not every one can bear prosperity. But if this rule is not observed, at any rate the honours which are given all at once should be taken away by degrees and not all at once. Especially should the laws provide against any one having too much power, whether derived from friends or money; if he has, he should be sent clean out of the country. And since innovations creep in through the private life of individuals also, there ought to be a magistracy which will have an eye to those whose life is not in harmony with the government, whether oligarchy or democracy or any other. And for a like reason an increase of prosperity in any part of the state should be carefully watched. The proper remedy for this evil is always to give the management of affairs and offices of state to opposite elements; such opposites are the virtuous and the many, or the rich and the poor. Another way is to combine the poor and the rich in one body, or to increase the middle class: thus an end will be put to the revolutions which arise from inequality.

But above all every state should be so administered and so regulated by law that its magistrates cannot possibly make money. In oligarchies special precautions should be used against this evil. For the people do not take any great offence at being kept out of the government—indeed they are rather pleased than otherwise at having leisure for their private business—but what irritates them is to think that their rulers are stealing the public money; then they are doubly annoyed; for they lose both honour and profit. If office brought no profit, then and then only could democracy and aristocracy be combined; for both notables and people might have their wishes gratified. All would be able to hold office, which is the aim of democracy, and the notables would be magistrates, which is the aim of aristocracy. And this result may be accomplished when there is no possibility of making money out of the offices; for the poor will not want to have them when there is nothing to be gained from them—they would rather be attending to their own concerns; and the rich, who do not want money from the public treasury, will be able to take them; and so the poor will keep to their work and grow rich, and the notables will not he governed by the lower class. In order to avoid peculation of the public money, the transfer of the revenue should be made at a general assembly of the citizens, and duplicates of the accounts deposited with the different brotherhoods, companies, and tribes. And honours should be given by law to magistrates who have the reputation of being incorruptible. In democracies the rich should be spared; not only should their property not be divided, but their incomes also, which in some states are taken from them imperceptibly, should be protected. It is a good thing to prevent the wealthy citizens, even if they are willing, from undertaking expensive and useless public services, such as the giving of choruses, torch-races, and the like. In an oligarchy, on the other hand, great care should be taken of the poor, and lucrative offices should go to them; if any of the wealthy classes insult them, the offender should be punished more severely than if he had wronged one of his own class. Provision should be made that estates pass by inheritance and not by gift, and no person should have more than one inheritance; for in this way properties will be equalized, and more of the poor rise to competency. It is also expedient both in a democracy and in an oligarchy to assign to those who have less share in the government (i.e. to the rich in a democracy and to the poor in an oligarchy) an equality or preference in all but the principal offices of state. The latter should be entrusted chiefly or only to members of the governing class.

# The Republic

By M. Tullius Cicero

## Book I

Then Laelius said: But you have not told us, Scipio, which of these three forms of government you yourself most approve.

Scipio: You are right to shape your question, which of the three I most approve, for there is not one of them which I approve at all by itself, since, as I told you, I prefer that government which is mixed and composed of all these forms, to any one of them taken separately. But if I must confine myself to one of the particular forms simply and exclusively, I must confess I prefer the royal one, and praise that as the first and best. In this, which I here choose to call the primitive form of government, I find the title of father attached to that of king, to express that he watches over the citizens as over his children, and endeavors rather to preserve them in freedom than reduce them to slavery. So that it is more advantageous for those who are insignificant in property and capacity to be supported by the care of one excellent and eminently powerful man. The nobles here present themselves, who profess that they can do all this in much better style; for they say that there is much more wisdom in many than

in one, and at least as much faith and equity. And, last of all, come the people, who cry with a loud voice, that they will render obedience neither to the one nor to the few; that even to brute beasts nothing is so dear as liberty; and that all men who serve either kings or nobles are deprived of it. Thus, the kings attract us by affection, the nobles by talent, the people by liberty; and in the comparison it is hard to choose the best.

Laelius: I think so, too, but yet it is impossible to dispatch the other branches of the question, if you leave this primary point undetermined.

36. Scipio: We must, then, I suppose, imitate Aratus, who, when he prepared himself to treat of great things, thought himself in duty bound to begin with Jupiter.

Laelius: Why Jupiter? And what is there in this discussion which resembles that poem?

Scipio: Why, it serves to teach us that we cannot better commence our investigations than by invoking him whom, with one voice, both learned and unlearned extol as the universal king of all gods and men.

Laelius: How so?

Scipio: Do you, then, believe in nothing which is not before your eyes? Whether these ideas have been established by the chiefs of states for the benefit of society, that there might be believed to exist one Universal Monarch in heaven, at whose nod (as Homer expresses it) all Olympus trembles, and that he might be accounted both king and father of all creatures; for there is great authority, and there are many witnesses, if you choose to call all many, who attest that all nations have unanimously recognized, by the decrees of their chiefs, that nothing is better than a king, since they think that all the gods are governed by the divine power of one sovereign; or if we suspect that this opinion rests on the error of the ignorant, and should be classed among the fables, let us listen to those universal testimonies of erudite men, who have, as it were, seen with their eyes those things to the knowledge of which we can hardly attain by report.

Laelius: What men do you mean?

Scipio: Those who, by the investigation of nature, have arrived at the opinion that the whole universe [is animated] by a single Mind. ... [Text missing].

37. Scipio: But if you please, my Laelius, I will bring forward evidences, which are neither too ancient, nor in any respect barbarous.

Laelius: Those are what I want.

Scipio: You are aware, that it is now not four centuries since this city of ours has been without kings.

Laelius: You are correct, it is less than four centuries.

Scipio: Well, then, what are four centuries in the age of a state or city; is it a long time?

Laelius: It hardly amounts to the age of maturity.

Scipio: You say truly, and yet not four centuries have elapsed since there was a king in Rome.

Laelius: And he was a proud king.

Scipio: But who was his predecessor?

Laelius: He was an admirably just one; and, indeed, we must bestow the same praise on all his predecessors, as far back as Romulus, who reigned about six centuries ago.

Scipio: Even he, then, is not very ancient.

Laelius: No, he reigned when Greece was already becoming old.

Scipio: Agreed. Was Romulus, then, think you, king of a barbarous people?

Laelius: Why, as to that, if we are to follow the example of the Greeks, who say that all people are either Greeks or barbarians, I am afraid that we must confess that he was a king of barbarians; but if this name belong rather to manners than to languages, then I believe the Greeks were just as barbarous as the Romans.

Scipio: But with respect to the present question, we do not so much need to inquire into the nation as into the disposition. For if intelligent men, at a period so little remote, desired the governing of kings, you will confess that I am producing authorities that are neither antiquated, rude, nor insignificant.

38. Laelius: I see, Scipio, that you are very sufficiently provided with authorities; but with me, as with every fair judge, authorities are worth less than arguments.

Scipio: Then, Laelius, you shall yourself make use of an argument derived from your own senses.

Laelius: What senses do you mean?

Scipio: The feelings which you experience when at any time you happen to feel angry at anyone.

Laelius: That happens rather oftener than I could wish.

Scipio: Well, then, when you are angry, do you permit your anger to triumph over your judgment?

Laelius: No, by Hercules! I imitate the famous Archytas of Tarentum, who, when he came to his villa, and found all its arrangements were contrary to his orders, said to his steward "Ah! you unlucky scoundrel, I would flog you to death, if it were not that I am in a rage with you."

Scipio: Capital. Archytas, then, regarded unreasonable anger as a kind of sedition and rebellion of nature, which he sought to appease by reflection. And so, if we examine avarice, the ambition of power or glory, or the lusts of concupiscence and licentiousness, we shall find a certain conscience in the mind of man, which, like a king, sways by the force of counsel all the inferior faculties and propensities; and this, in truth, is the noblest portion of our nature; for when conscience reigns, it allows no resting place to lust, violence, or temerity.

Laelius: You have spoken the truth.

Scipio: Well, then, does a mind thus governed and regulated meet your approbation?

Laelius: More than anything on earth.

Scipio: Then you would not approve that the evil passions, which are innumerable, should expel conscience, and that lusts and animal propensities should assume an ascendancy over us?

Laelius: For my part, I can conceive nothing more wretched than a mind thus degraded, or a man animated by a soul so licentious.

Scipio: You desire, then, that all the facilities of the mind should submit to a ruling power, and that conscience should reign over them all?

Laelius: Certainly, that is my wish.

Scipio: How, then, can you doubt what opinion to form on the subject of the commonwealth? in which, if the state is thrown into many hands, it is very plain that there will be no presiding authority; for if power be not united, it soon comes to nothing.

39. Laelius: But what difference is there, I should like to know, between the one and the many, if justice exists equally in many?

Scipio: Since I see, my Laelius, that the authorities I have adduced have no great influence on you, I must continue to employ yourself as my witness in proof of what I am saying.

Laelius: In what way are you going to make me again support your argument?

Scipio: Why thus. I recollect when we were lately at Formiae that you told your servants repeatedly to obey the orders of not more than one master only.

Laelius: To be sure, those of my steward.

Scipio: What do you at home? do you commit your affairs to the hands of many persons?

Laelius: No, I trust them to myself alone.

Scipio: Well, in your whole establishment, is there any other master but yourself?

Laelius: Not one.

Scipio: Then I think you must grant me that as respects the state, the government of single individuals, provided they are just, is superior to any other.

Laelius: You have conducted me to this conclusion, and I entertain very nearly that opinion.

40. Scipio: You would still further agree with me, my Laelius, if, omitting the common comparisons, that one pilot is better fitted to steer a ship, and a physician to treat an invalid, provided they be competent men in their respective professions, than many could be, I should come at once to more illustrious examples.

Laelius: What examples do you mean?

Scipio: Do you observe that it was the cruelty and pride of one single Tarquin only, that made the title of king unpopular among the Romans?

Laelius: Yes, I acknowledge that.

Scipio: You are also aware of this fact, on which I think I shall debate in the course of the coming discussion, that after the expulsion of King Tarquin, the people were transported by a wonderful excess of liberty. Then, innocent men were driven into banishment; then the estates of many individuals were pillaged, consulships were made annual, public authorities were overawed by mobs, popular appeals took place in all cases imaginable; then secessions of the lower orders ensued; and lastly, those proceedings which tended to place all powers in the hands of the populace.

Laelius: I must confess this all too true.

Scipio: All these things now happened during periods of peace and tranquility, for licence is wont to prevail when there is too little to fear, as in a calm voyage, or a trifling disease. But as we observe the voyager and invalid implore the aid of some competent director, as soon as the sea grows stormy and the disease alarming! so our nation in peace and security commands, threatens, resists, appeals from, and insults its magistrates, but in war obeys them as strictly as kings; for public safety is after all rather more valuable than popular licence. And in the most serious wars, our countrymen have even chosen the entire command to be deposited in the hands of some single chief, without a colleague; the very name of which magistrate indicates the absolute character of his power. For though he is evidently called dictator because he is appointed, yet do we still observe him, my Laelius, in our sacred books entitled Magister Populi, the master of the people.

Laelius: This is certainly the case.

Scipio: Our ancestors, therefore, acted wisely.

## Book VI (Scipio's Dream)

9. When I had arrived in Africa, where I was, as you are aware, military tribune of the fourth legion under the consul Manilius, there was nothing of which I was more earnestly desirous than to see King Massinissa, who, for very just reasons, had been always the especial friend of our family. When I was introduced to him, the old man embraced me, shed tears, and then, looking up to heaven, exclaimed I thank thee, O supreme Sun, and you also, you other celestial beings, that before I departed from this life I behold in my kingdom, and in my palace, Publius Cornelius Scipio, by whose mere name I seem to be reanimated; so complete and indelibly is the recollection of that best and most invincible of men, Africanus, imprinted in my mind.

After this, I inquired of him concerning the affairs of his kingdom. He, on the other hand, questioned me about the condition of our commonwealth, and in this mutual interchange of conversation we passed the whole of that day.

10. In the evening, we were entertained in a manner worthy the magnificence of a king, and carried on our discourse for a considerable part of the night. And during all this time the old man spoke of nothing but Africanus, all whose actions, and even remarkable sayings, he remembered distinctly. At last, when we retired to bed, I fell in a more profound sleep than usual, both because I was fatigued with my journey, and because I had sat up the greatest part of the night.

Here I had the following dream, occasioned, as I verily believe, by our preceding conversation—for it frequently happens that the thoughts and discourses which have employed us in the daytime, produce in our sleep an effect somewhat similar to that which Ennius writes happened to him about Homer, of whom, in his waking hours, he used frequently to think and speak.

Africanus, I thought, appeared to me in that shape, with which I was better acquainted from his picture, than from any personal knowledge of him. When I perceived it was he, I confess I trembled with consternation; but he addressed me, saying, Take courage, my Scipio, be not afraid, and carefully remember what I am saying to you.

11. Do you see that city Carthage, which, though brought under the Roman yoke by me, is now renewing former wars, and cannot live in peace? (and he pointed to Carthage from a loft y spot, full of stars, and brilliant and glittering;) to attack which city you are this day arrived in a station not much superior to that of a private soldier. Before two years, however, are elapsed, you shall be consul, and complete its overthrow; and you shall obtain, by your own merit, the surname of Africanus, which, as yet, belongs to you no otherwise than as derived from me. And when you have destroyed Carthage, and received the honor of a triumph, and been made censor, and, in quality of ambassador, visited Egypt, Syria, Asia, and Greece, you shall be elected a second time consul in your absence, and by utterly destroying Numantia, put an end to a most dangerous war.

But when you have entered the Capitol in your triumphal car, you shall find the Roman commonwealth all in a ferment, through the intrigues of my grandson Tiberius Gracchus.

12. It is on this occasion, my dear Africanus, that you show your country the greatness of your understanding, capacity and prudence. But I see that the destiny, however, of that time is, as it were, uncertain; for when your age shall have accomplished seven times eight revolutions of the sun, and your fatal hours shall be marked out by the natural product of these two numbers, each of which is esteemed a perfect one, but for different reasons,—then shall the whole city have recourse to you alone, and place its hopes in your auspicious name. On you the senate, all good citizens, the allies, the people of Latium, shall cast their eyes; on you the preservation of the state shall entirely depend. In a word, if you escape the impious machinations of your relatives, you will, in the quality of dictator, establish order and tranquility in the commonwealth.

When on this Laelius made an exclamation, and the rest of the company groaned loudly, Scipio, with a gentle smile, said—I entreat you, do not wake me out of my dream, but have patience, and hear the rest.

13. Now, in order to encourage you, my dear Africanus, continued the shade of my ancestor, to defend the state with the greater cheerfulness, be assured that for all those who have in any way conduced to the preservation, defense, and enlargement of their native country, there is a certain place in heaven, where they shall enjoy an eternity of happiness. For nothing on earth is more agreeable to God, the Supreme Governor of the universe, than the assemblies and societies of men united together by laws, which are called States. It is from heaven their rulers and preservers came, and there they return.

14. Though at these words I was extremely troubled, not so much at the fear of death, as at the perfidy of my own relations; yet I recollected myself enough to inquire, whether he himself, my father Paulus, and others whom we look upon as dead, were really living. Yes, truly, replied he, they all enjoy life who have escaped from the chains of the body as from a prison. But as to what you call life on earth, that is no more than one form of death. But see, here comes your father Paulus towards you! And as soon as I observed him, my eyes

burst out into a flood of tears; but he took me in his arms, and bade me not weep.

15. When my first transports subsided, and I regained the liberty of speech, I addressed my father thus: You best and most venerable of parents, since this, as I am informed by Africanus, is the only substantial life, why do I linger on earth, and not rather hasten to come hither where you are? That, replied he, is impossible; unless that God, whose temples is all that vast expanse you behold, shall free you from the fetters of the body, you can have no admission into this place. Mankind have received their being on this very condition, that they should labor for the preservation of that globe, which is situated, as you see, in the midst of this temple, and is called earth.

Men are likewise endowed with a soul, which is a portion of the eternal fires, which you call stars and constellations; and which, being round, spherical bodies, animated by divine intelligence, perform their cycles and revolutions with amazing rapidity. It is your duty, there fore, my Publius, and that of all who have any veneration for the gods, to preserve this wonderful union of soul and body; nor without the express command of him who gave you a soul, should the least thought be entertained of quitting human life, lest you seem to desert the post assigned to you by God himself.

But rather follow the example of your grandfather here, and of me, your father, in paying a strict regard to justice and piety; which is due in a great degree to parents and relations, but most of all to our country. Such a life as this is the true way to heaven, and to the company of those, who, after having lived on earth and escaped from the body, inhabit the place which you now behold.

16. This was the shining circle, or zone, whose remarkable brightness distinguishes it among the constellations, and which, after the Greeks, you call the Milky Way. From thence, as I took a view of the universe, everything appeared beautiful and admirable; for there, those stars are to be seen that are never visible from our globe, and everything appears of such magnitude as we could not have imagined. The least of all the stars, was that removed furthest from heaven, and situated next to earth; I mean our moon, which shines with a borrowed light. Now the globes of the stars far surpass the magnitude of our earth, which at that distance appeared so exceedingly small, that I could not but he sensibly affected on seeing our whole empire no larger than if we touched the earth with a point.

17. And as long as I continued to observe the earth with great attention, How long, I pray you, said Africanus, will your mind be fixed on that object; why don't you rather take a view of the magnificent temples among which you have arrived? The universe is composed of nine circles, or rather spheres, one of which is the heavenly one, and is exterior to all the rest, which it embraces; being itself the Supreme God, and bounding and containing the whole. In it are fixed those stars which revolve with never-varying courses. Below this are seven other spheres, which revolve in a contrary direction to that of the heavens. One of these is occupied by the globe which on earth they call Saturn. Next to that is the star of Jupiter, so benign and salutary to mankind. The third in order, is that fiery and terrible planet called Mars. Below this again, almost in the middle region, is the Sun—the leader, governor, the prince of the other luminaries; the soul of the world, which it regulates and illumines, being of such vast size that it pervades and gives light to all places. Then follow Venus and Mercury, which attend, as it were, on the Sun. Lastly,

the Moon, which shines only in the reflected beams of the Sun, moves in the lowest sphere of all. Below this, if we except that gift of the gods, the soul, which has been given by the liberality of the gods to the human race, every thing is mortal, and tends to dissolution, but above the moon all is eternal. For the Earth, which is in the ninth globe, and occupies the center, is immoveable, and being the lowest, all others gravitate towards it.

18. When I had recovered myself from the astonishment occasioned by such a wonderful prospect, I thus addressed Africanus Pray what is this sound that strikes my ears in so loud and agreeable a manner? To which he replied It is that which is called the music of the spheres, being produced by their motion and impulse; and being formed by unequal intervals, but such as are divided according to the most just proportion, it produces, by duly tempering acute with grave sounds, various concerts of harmony. For it is impossible that motions so great should be performed without any noise; and it is agreeable to nature that the extremes on one side should produce sharp, and on the other flat sounds. For which reason the sphere of the fixed stars, being the highest, and being carried with a more rapid velocity, moves with a shrill and acute sound; whereas that of the moon, being the lowest, moves with a very flat one. As to the Earth, which makes the ninth sphere, it remains immovably fixed in the middle or lowest part of the universe. But those eight revolving circles, in which both Mercury and Venus are moved with the same celerity, give out sounds that are divided by seven distinct intervals, which is generally the regulating number of all things.

This celestial harmony has been imitated by learned musicians, both on stringed instruments and with the voice, whereby they have opened to themselves a way to return to the celestial regions, as have likewise many others who have employed their sublime genius while on earth in cultivating the divine sciences.

By the amazing noise of this sound, the ears of mankind have been in some degree deafened, and indeed, hearing is the dullest of all the human senses. Thus, the people who dwell near the cataracts of the Nile, which are called Catadupa, are, by the excessive roar which that river makes in precipitating itself from those loft y mountains, entirely deprived of the sense of hearing. And so inconceivably great is this sound which is produced by the rapid motion of the whole universe, that the human ear is no more capable of receiving it, than the eye is able to look steadfastly and directly on the sun, whose beams easily dazzle the strongest sight.

While I was busied in admiring the scene of wonders, I could not help casting my eyes every now and then on the earth.

19. On which Africanus said, I perceive that you are still employed in contemplating the seat and residence of mankind. But if it appears to you so small, as in fact it really is, despise its vanities, and fix your attention for ever on these heavenly objects. Is it possible that you should attain any human applause or glory that is worth the contending for? The earth, you see, is peopled but in a very few places, and those too of small extent; and they appear like so many little spots of green scattered through vast uncultivated deserts. And those who inhabit the earth are not only so remote from each other as to be cut off from all mutual correspondence, but their situation being in oblique or contrary parts of the globe, or perhaps in those diametrically opposite to yours, all expectation of universal fame must fall to the ground.

20. You may likewise observe that the same globe of the earth is girt and surrounded with certain zones, whereof those two that are most remote from each other, and lie under the opposite poles of heaven, are congealed with frost; but that one in the middle, which is far the largest, is scorched with the intense heat of the sun. The other two are habitable, one towards the south—the inhabitants of which are your Antipodes, with whom you have no connection—the other, towards the north, is that which you inhabit, whereof a very small part, as you may see, falls to your share. For the whole extent of what you see, is as it were but a little island, narrow at both ends and wide in the middle, which is surrounded by the sea which on earth you call the great Atlantic ocean, and which, notwithstanding this magnificent name, you see is very insignificant. And even in these cultivated and well-known countries, has yours, or any of our names, ever passed the heights of the Caucasus, or the currents of the Ganges? In what other parts to the north or the south, or where the sun rises and sets, will your names ever be heard? And if we leave these out of the question, how small a space is there left for your glory to spread itself abroad? and how long will it remain in the memory of those whose minds are now full of it?

21. Besides all this, if the progeny of any future generation should wish to transmit to their posterity the praises of any one of us which they have heard from their forefathers, yet the deluges and combustions of the earth which must necessarily happen at their destined periods will prevent our obtaining, not only an eternal, but even a durable glory. And after all, what does it signify, whether those who shall hereafter be born talk of you, when those who have lived before you, whose number was perhaps not less, and whose merit certainly greater, were not so much as acquainted with your name?

22. Especially since not one of those who shall hear of us is able to retain in his memory the transactions of a single year. The bulk of mankind, indeed, measure their year by the return of the sun, which is only one star. But, when all the stars shall have returned to the place whence they set out, and after long periods shall again exhibit the same aspect of the whole heavens, that is what ought properly to be called the revolution of a year, though I scarcely dare attempt to enumerate the vast multitude of ages contained in it. For as the sun in old time was eclipsed, and seemed to be extinguished, at the time when the soul of Romulus penetrated into these eternal mansions, so, when all the constellations and stars shall revert to their primary position, and the sun shall at the same point and time be again eclipsed, then you may consider that the grand year is completed. Be assured, however, that the twentieth part of it is not yet elapsed.

23. Why, if you have no hopes of returning to this place, where great and good men enjoy all that their souls can wish for, of what value, pray, is all that human glory, which can hardly endure for a small portion of one year?

If, then, you wish to elevate your views to the contemplation of this eternal seat of splendor, you will not be satisfied with the praises of your fellow-mortals, nor with any human rewards that your exploits can obtain; but Virtue herself must point out to you the true and only object worthy of your pursuit. Leave to others to speak of you as they may, for speak they will. Their discourses will be confined to the narrow limits of the countries you see, nor will their duration be very extensive, for they will perish like those who utter them, and will be no more remembered by their posterity.

24. When he had ceased to speak in this manner, I said Oh, Africanus, if indeed the door of heaven is open to those who have deserved well of their country, although, indeed, from my childhood, I have always followed yours and my father's steps, and have not neglected to imitate your glory, still I will from henceforth strive to follow them more closely.

Follow them, then, said he, and consider your body only, not yourself, as mortal. For it is not your outward form which constitutes your being, but your mind; not that substance which is palpable to the senses, but your spiritual nature. Know, then, that you are a god—for a god it must be which flourishes, and feels, and recollects, and foresees, and governs, regulates and moves the body over which it is set, as the Supreme Ruler does the world which is subject to him. For as that Eternal Being moves whatever is mortal in this world, so the immortal mind of man moves the frail body with which it is connected.

25. For whatever is always moving must be eternal, but that which derives its motion from a power which is foreign to itself, when that motion ceases must itself lose its animation. That alone, then, which moves itself can never cease to be moved, because it can never desert itself. Moreover, it must be the source, and origin, and principle of motion in all the rest. There can be nothing prior to a principle, for all things must originate from it, and it cannot itself derive its existence from any other source, for if it did it would no longer be a principle. And if it had no beginning it can have no end, for a beginning that is put an end to will neither be renewed by any other cause, nor will it produce anything else of itself. All things, therefore, must originate from one source. Thus it follows, that motion must have its source in something which is moved by itself, and which can neither have a beginning nor an end. Otherwise all the heavens and all nature must perish, for it is impossible that they can of themselves acquire any power of producing motion in themselves.

26. As, therefore, it is plain that what is moved by itself must be eternal, who will deny that this is the general condition and nature of minds? For, as everything is inanimate which is moved by an impulse exterior to itself, so what is animated is moved by an interior impulse of its own; for this is the peculiar nature and power of mind. And if that alone has the power of self-motion it can neither have had a beginning, nor can it have an end.

Do you, therefore, exercise this mind of yours in the best pursuits. And the best pursuits are those which consist in promoting the good of your country. Such employments will speed the flight of your mind to this its proper abode; and its flight will be still more rapid, if, even while it is enclosed in the body, it will look abroad, and disengage itself as much as possible from its bodily dwelling, by the contemplation of things which are external to itself.

This it should do to the utmost of its power. For the minds of those who have given themselves up to the pleasures of the body, paying as it were a servile obedience to their lustful impulses, have violated the laws of God and man; and therefore, when they are separated from their bodies, flutter continually round the earth on which they lived, and are not allowed to return to this celestial region, till they have been purified by the revolution of many ages.

Thus saying he vanished, and I awoke from my dream.

# City of God

By St. Augustine

## Justice—The Foundation of the State

Justice being taken away, then, what are kingdoms but great robberies? For what are robberies themselves, but little kingdoms? The band itself is made up of men; it is ruled by the authority of a prince, it is knit together by the pact of the confederacy; the booty is divided by the law agreed on. If, by the admittance of abandoned men, this evil increases to such a degree that it holds places, fixes abodes, takes possession of cities, and subdues peoples, it assumes the more plainly the name of a kingdom, because the reality is now manifestly conferred on it, not by the removal of covetousness, but by the addition of impunity. Indeed, that was an apt and true reply which was given to Alexander the Great by a pirate who had been seized. For when that king had asked the man what he meant by keeping hostile possession of the sea, he answered with bold pride, "What thou meanest by seizing the whole earth; but because I do it with a petty ship, I am called a robber, whilst thou who dost it with a great fleet art styled emperor."[1]

## The True Happiness of the Ruler

For neither do we say that certain Christian emperors were therefore happy because they ruled a long time, or, dying a peaceful death, left their sons to succeed them in the empire, or subdued the enemies of the republic, or were able both to guard against and to suppress the attempt of hostile citizens rising against them. These and other gifts or comforts of this sorrowful life even certain worshippers of demons have merited to receive, who do not belong to the kingdom of God to which these belong; and this is to be traced to the mercy of God, who would not have those who believe in Him desire such things as the highest good. But we say that they are happy if they rule justly; if they are not lifted up amid the praises of those who pay them sublime honors, and

---

1   Cicero, *De Republica*, III.

103

the obsequiousness of those who salute them with an excessive humility, but remember that they are men; if they make their power the handmaid of His majesty by using it for the greatest possible extension of His worship; if they fear, love, worship God; if more than their own they love that kingdom in which they are not afraid to have partners; if they are slow to punish, ready to pardon; if they apply that punishment as necessary to government and defence of the republic, and not in order to gratify their own enmity; if they grant pardon, not that iniquity may go unpunished, but with the hope that the transgressor may amend his ways; if they compensate with the lenity of mercy and the liberality of benevolence for whatever severity they may be compelled to decree; if their luxury is as much restrained as it might have been unrestrained; if they prefer to govern depraved desires rather than any nation whatever; and if they do all these things, not through ardent desire of empty glory, but through love of eternal felicity, not neglecting to offer to the true God, who is their God, for their sins, the sacrifices of humility, contrition, and prayer. Such Christian emperors, we say, are happy in the present time by hope, and are destined to be so in the enjoyment of the reality itself, when that which we wait for shall have arrived.

## The Earthly and the Heavenly City

Accordingly, two cities have been formed by two loves: the earthly by the love of self, even to the contempt of God; the heavenly by the love of God, even to the contempt of self. The former, in a word, glories in itself, the latter in the Lord. For the one seeks glory from men; but the greatest glory of the other is God, the witness of conscience. The one lifts up its head in its own glory; the other says to its God, "Thou art my glory, and the lifter up of mine head."[2] In the one, the princes and the nations it subdues are ruled by the love of ruling; in the other, the princes and the subjects serve one another in love, the latter obeying, while the former take thought for all. The one delights in its own strength, represented in the persons of its rulers; the other says to its God, "I will love Thee, O Lord, my strength."[3] And therefore the wise men of the one city, living according to man, have sought for profit to their own bodies or souls, or both, and those who have known God "glorified Him not as God, neither were thankful, but became vain in their imaginations, and their foolish heart was darkened; professing themselves to be wise"—that is, glorying in their own wisdom, and being possessed by pride—"they became fools, and changed the glory of the incorruptible God into an image made like to corruptible man, and to birds, and four-footed beasts, and creeping things." For they were either leaders or followers of the people in adoring images, "and worshipped and served the creature more than the Creator, who is blessed for ever."[4] But in the other city there is no human wisdom, but only godliness, which offers due worship to the true God, and looks for its reward in the society of the saints, of holy angels as well as holy men, that God may be all in all.[5]

2 Ps. iii. 3.
3 Ps. xviii. 1.
4 Rom. i. 21–25.
5 I Cor. xv. 28.

## The Two Types of Man

Of the bliss of Paradise, of Paradise itself, and of the life of our first parents there, and of their sin and punishment, many have thought much, spoken much, written much. We ourselves, too, have spoken of these things in the foregoing books, and have written either what we read in the Holy Scriptures, or what we could reasonably deduce from them. And were we to enter into a more detailed investigation of these matters, an endless number of endless questions would arise, which would involve us in a larger work than the present occasion admits. We cannot be expected to find room for replying to every question that may be started by unoccupied and captious men, who are ever more ready to ask questions than capable of understanding the answer. Yet I trust we have already done justice to these great and difficult questions regarding the beginning of the world, or of the soul, or of the human race itself. This race we have distributed into two parts, the one consisting of those who live according to man, the other of those who live according to God. And these we also mystically call the two cities, or the two communities of men, of which the one is predestined to reign eternally with God, and the other to suffer eternal punishment with the devil. This, however, is their end, and of it we are to speak afterwards. At present, as we have said enough about their origin, whether among the angels, whose numbers we know not, or in the two first human beings, it seems suitable to attempt an account of their career, from the time when our two first parents began to propagate the race until all human generation shall cease. For this whole time or world-age, in which the dying give place and

those who are born succeed, is the career of these two cities concerning which we treat.

Of these two first parents of the human race, then, Cain was the first-born, and he belonged to the city of men; after him was born Abel, who belonged to the city of God. For as in the individual the truth of the apostle's statement is discerned, "that is not first which is spiritual, but that which is natural, and afterward that which is spiritual,"[6] whence it comes to pass that each man, being derived from a condemned stock, is first of all born of Adam evil and carnal, and becomes good and spiritual only afterwards, when he is grafted into Christ by regeneration: so was it in the human race as a whole. When these two cities began to run their course by a series of deaths and births, the citizen of this world was the first-born, and after him the stranger in this world, the citizen of the city of God, predestinated by grace, elected by grace, by grace a stranger below, and by grace a citizen above. By grace—for so far as regards himself he is sprung from the same mass, all of which is condemned in its origin: but God, like a potter (for this comparison is introduced by the apostle judiciously, and not without thought), of the same lump made one vessel to honor, another to dishonor.[7] But first the vessel to dishonor was made, and after it another to honor. For in each individual, as I have already said, there is first of all that which is reprobate, that from which we must begin, but in which we need not necessarily remain; afterwards is that which is well-approved, to which we may by advancing attain, and in which, when we have reached it, we may abide. Not, indeed, that every wicked man shall be good, but that no one will be good who was not first of all wicked; but the sooner any one becomes a

---

6 I Cor. xv. 46.
7 Rom. ix.21.

good man, the more speedily does he receive this title, and abolish the old name in the new. Accordingly, it is recorded of Cain that he built a city,[8] but Abel, being a sojourner, built none. For the city of the saints is above, although here below it begets citizens, in whom it sojourns till the time of its reign arrives, when it shall gather together all in the day of the resurrection; and then shall the promised kingdom be given to them, in which they shall reign with their Prince, the King of the ages, time without end.

## Conflict and Peace in the Earthly City

But the earthly city, which shall not be everlasting (for it will no longer be a city when it has been committed to the extreme penalty), has its good in this world, and rejoices in it with such joy as such things can afford. But as this is not a good which can discharge its devotees of all distresses, this city is often divided against itself by litigations, wars, quarrels, and such victories as are either life-destroying or short-lived. For each part of it that arms against another part of it seeks to triumph over the nations though itself in bondage to vice. If, when it has conquered, it is inflated with pride, its victory is life-destroying; but if it turns its thoughts upon the common casualties of our mortal condition, and is rather anxious concerning the disasters that may befall it than elated with the successes already achieved, this victory, though of a higher kind, is still only short-lived; for it

---

8  Gen. iv. 17.

cannot abidingly rule over those whom it has victoriously subjugated. But the things which this city desires cannot justly be said to be evil, for it is itself, in its own kind, better than all other human good. For it desires earthly peace for the sake of enjoying earthly goods, and it makes war in order to attain to this peace; since, if it has conquered, and there remains no one to resist it, it enjoys a peace which it had not while there were opposing parties who contested for the enjoyment of those things which were too small to satisfy both. This peace is purchased by toilsome wars; it is obtained by what they style a glorious victory. Now, when victory remains with the party which had the juster cause, who hesitates to congratulate the victor, and style it a desirable peace? These things, then, are good things, and without doubt the gifts of God. But if they neglect the better things of the heavenly city, which are secured by eternal victory and peace never-ending, and so inordinately covet these present good things that they believe them to be the only desirable things, or love them better than those things which are believed to be better—if this be so, then it is necessary that misery follow and ever increase.

## The Lust for Power in the Earthly City

Thus the founder of the earthly city was a fratricide. Overcome with envy, he slew his own brother, a citizen of the eternal city, and a sojourner on earth. So that we cannot be surprised that this first specimen, or, as the Greeks say, archetype of crime, should, long afterwards, find a corresponding crime at the foundation of that city which was destined to reign over so many nations, and be the head of this earthly city of which we speak. For of that city also, as one of their poets has mentioned, "the first walls were stained with a brother's blood."[9] or, as Roman history records, Remus was slain by his brother Romulus. And thus there is no difference between the foundation of this city and of the earthly city, unless it be that Romulus and Remus were both citizens of the earthly city. Both desired to have the glory of founding the Roman republic, but both could not have as much glory as if one only claimed it; for he who wished to have the glory of ruling would certainly rule less if his power were shared by a living consort. In order, therefore, that the whole glory might be enjoyed by one, his consort was removed; and by this crime the empire was made larger indeed, but inferior, while otherwise it would have been less, but better. Now these brothers, Cain and Abel, were not both animated by the same earthly desires, nor did the murderer envy the other because he feared that, by both ruling, his own dominion would be curtailed—for Abel was not solicitous to rule in that city which his brother built—he was moved by that diabolical, envious hatred with which the evil regard the good, for no other reason than because they are good while themselves are evil. For the possession of goodness is by no means diminished by being shared with a partner either permanent or temporarily assumed; on the contrary, the possession of goodness is increased in proportion to the concord and charity of each of those who share it. In short, he who is unwilling to share this possession cannot have it; and he who is most willing to admit others to a share of it will have the greatest abundance to himself. The quarrel, then, between Romulus and Remus shows how the earthly city is divided against itself; that which fell out between Cain and Abel illustrated the hatred that subsists between the two cities, that of God and that of men. The wicked war with the wicked; the good also war with the wicked. But with the good, good men, or at least perfectly good men, cannot war; though, while only going on towards perfection, they war to this extent, that every good man resists others in those points in which he resists himself. And in each individual "the flesh lusteth against the spirit, and the spirit against the flesh."[10] This spiritual lusting, therefore, can be at war with the carnal lust of another man; or carnal lust may be at war with the spiritual desires of another, in some such way as good and wicked men are at war; or, still more certainly, the carnal lusts of two men, good but not yet perfect, contend together, just as the wicked contend with the wicked, until the health of those who are under the treatment of grace attains final victory.

## Limitations of Social Life

We give a much more unlimited approval to their idea that the life of the wise man must be social. For how could the city of God either take a beginning or be developed, or attain its proper destiny, if the life of the saints were not a social life? But who can enumerate all the great grievances with which human society abounds in the misery of this mortal state? Who can weigh them? Hear how one of their comic writers makes one of his characters express

---

9   Lucan, Phar. i. 95.

10   Gal. v. 17.

the common feelings of all men in this matter: "I am married; this is one misery. Children are born to me; they are additional cares."[11] What shall I say of the miseries of love which Terence also recounts—"slights, suspicions, quarrels, war to-day, peace tomorrow?"[12] Is not human life full of such things? Do they not often occur even in honorable friendships? On all hands we experience these slights, suspicions, quarrels, war, all of which are undoubted evils; while, on the other hand, peace is a doubtful good, because we do not know the heart of our friend, and though we did know it to-day, we should be as ignorant of what it might be tomorrow. Who ought to be, or who are more friendly than those who live in the same family? And yet who can rely even upon this friendship, seeing that secret treachery has often broken it up, and produced enmity as bitter as the amity was sweet, or seemed sweet by the most perfect dissimulation? It is on this account that the words of Cicero so move the heart of every one, and provoke a sigh: "There are no snares more dangerous than those which lurk under the guise of duty or the name of relationship. For the man who is your declared foe you can easily baffle by precaution; but this hidden, intestine, and domestic danger not merely exists, but overwhelms you before you can foresee and examine it."[13] Is It is also to this that allusion is made by the divine saying, "A man's foes are those of his own household"[14]—words which one cannot hear without pain; for though a man have sufficient fortitude to endure it with equanimity, and sufficient sagacity to baffle the malice of a pretended friend, yet if he himself is a good man, he cannot but be

greatly pained at the discovery of the perfidy of wicked men, whether they have always been wicked and merely feigned goodness, or have fallen from a better to a malicious disposition. If, then, home, the natural refuge from the ills of life, is itself not safe, what shall we say of the city, which, as it is larger, is so much the more filled with lawsuits civil and criminal, and is never free from the fear, if sometimes from the actual outbreak, of disturbing and bloody insurrections and civil wars?

## Shortcomings of Human Justice

What shall I say of these judgments which men pronounce on men, and which are necessary in communities, whatever outward peace they enjoy? Melancholy and lamentable judgments they are, since the judges are men who cannot discern the consciences of those at their bar, and are therefore frequently compelled to put innocent witnesses to the torture to ascertain the truth regarding the crimes of other men. What shall I say of torture applied to the accused himself? He is tortured to discover whether he is guilty, so that, though innocent, he suffers most undoubted punishment for crime that is still doubtful, not because it is proved that he committed it, but because it is not ascertained that he did not commit it. Thus the ignorance of the judge frequently involves an innocent person in suffering. And what is still more unendurable—a thing, indeed, to be bewailed, and, if that were possible, watered with fountains of tears—is this, that when the judge puts the accused to the question, that he may not unwittingly put an innocent

---

11   Terent. *Adelph.* v. 4.

12   *Eunuch*, i. 1.

13   *In Verrem*, ii. I. 15.

14   Matt. x. 36.

man to death, the result of this lamentable ignorance is that this very person, whom he tortured that he might not condemn him if innocent, is condemned to death both tortured and innocent. For if he has chosen, in obedience to the philosophical instructions to the wise man, to quit this life rather than endure any longer such tortures, he declares that he has committed the crime which in fact he has not committed. And when he has been condemned and put to death, the judge is still in ignorance whether he has put to death an innocent or a guilty person, though he put the accused to the torture for the very purpose of saving himself from condemning the innocent; and consequently he has both tortured an innocent man to discover his innocence, and has put him to death without discovering it. If such darkness shrouds social life, will a wise judge take his seat on the bench or no? Beyond question he will. For human society, which he thinks it a wickedness to abandon, constrains him and compels him to this duty. And he thinks it no wickedness that innocent witnesses are tortured regarding the crimes of which other men are accused; or that the accused are put to the torture, so that they are often overcome with anguish, and, though innocent, make false confessions regarding themselves, and are punished; or that, though they be not condemned to die, they often die during, or in consequence of, the torture; or that sometimes the accusers, who perhaps have been prompted by a desire to benefit society by bringing criminals to stice, are themselves condemned through the ignorance of the judge, because they are unable to prove the truth of their accusations though they are true, and because the witnesses lie, and the accused endures the torture without being moved to confession. These numerous

and important evils he does not consider sins; for the wise judge does these things, not with any intention of doing harm, but because his ignorance compels him. and because human society claims him as a judge. But though we therefore acquit the judge of malice, we must none the less condemn human life as miserable. And if he is compelled to torture and punish the innocent because his office and his ignorance constrain him, is he a happy as well as a guiltless man? Surely it were proof of more profound considerateness and finer feeling were he to recognize the misery of these necessities, and shrink from his own implication in that misery; and had he any piety about him, he would cry to God "From my necessities deliver Thou me."[15]

## The Misery of War

After the state or city comes the world, the third circle of human society—the first being the house, and the second the city. And the world, as it is larger, so it is fuller of dangers, as the greater sea is the more dangerous. And here, in the first place, man is separated from man by the difference of languages. For if two men, each ignorant of the other's language, meet, and are not compelled to pass, but, on the contrary, to remain in company, dumb animals, though of different species, would more easily hold intercourse than they, humans though they be. For their common nature is no help to friendliness when they are prevented by diversity of language from conveying their

---

15  Ps. xxv. 17.

sentiments to one another; so that a man would more readily hold intercourse with his dog than with a foreigner. But the imperial city has endeavored to impose on subject nations not only her yoke, but her language, as a bond of peace, so that interpreters, far from being scarce, are numberless. This is true; but how many great wars, how much slaughter and bloodshed, have provided this unity! And though these are past, the end of these miseries has not yet come. For though there have never been wanting, nor are yet wanting, hostile nations beyond the empire, against whom wars have been and are waged, yet, supposing there were no such nations, the very extent of the empire itself has produced wars of a more obnoxious description—social and civil wars—and with these the whole race has been agitated, either by the actual conflict or the fear of a renewed outbreak. If I attempted to give an adequate description of these manifold disasters, these stern and lasting necessities, though I am quite unequal to the task, what limit could I set? But, say they, the wise man will wage just wars. As if he would not all the rather lament the necessity of just wars, if he remembers that he is a man; for if they were not just he would not wage them, and would therefore be delivered from all wars. For it is the wrong-doing of the opposing party which compels the wise man to wage just wars; and this wrongdoing, even though it gave rise to no war, would still be matter of grief to man because it is man's wrong-doing. Let every one, then, who thinks with pain on all these great evils, so horrible, so ruthless, acknowledge that this is misery. And if any one either endures or thinks of them without mental pain, this is a more miserable plight still, for he thinks himself happy because he has lost human feeling.

## The Objective of War: Peace

Whoever gives even moderate attention to human affairs and to our common nature, will recognize that if there is no man who does not wish to be joyful, neither is there any one who does not wish to have peace. For even they who make war desire nothing but victory—desire, that is to say, to attain to peace with glory. For what else is victory than the conquest of those who resist us? and when this is done there is peace. It is therefore with the desire for peace that wars are waged, even by those who take pleasure in exercising their warlike nature in command and battle. And hence it is obvious that peace is the end sought for by war. For every man seeks peace by waging war, but no man seeks war by making peace. For even they who intentionally interrupt the peace in which they are living have no hatred of peace, but only wish it changed into a peace that suits them better. They do not, therefore, wish to have no peace, but only one more to their mind. And in the case of sedition, when men have separated themselves from the community, they yet do not effect what they wish, unless they maintain some kind of peace with their fellow-conspirators. And therefore even robbers take care to maintain peace with their comrades, that they may with greater effect and greater safety invade the peace of other men. And if an individual happens to be of such unrivalled strength, and to be so jealous of partnership, that he trusts himself with no comrades, but makes his own plots, and commits depredations and murders on his own account, yet he maintains some shadow of peace with such persons as he is unable to kill, and from whom he wishes to conceal his deeds. In his own home, too, he makes it his aim to be at peace with his wife and children, and any other members of his household; for unquestionably their prompt obedience to his every look is a source of pleasure to him. And if this be not rendered, he is angry, he chides and punishes; and even by this storm he secures the calm peace of his own home, as occasion demands. For he sees that peace cannot be maintained unless all the members of the same domestic circle be subject to one head, such as he himself is in his own house. And therefore if a city or nation offered to submit itself to him, to serve him in the same style as he had made his household serve him, he would no longer lurk in brigand's hiding-places, but lift his head in open day as a king, though the same covetousness and wickedness should remain in him. And thus all men desire to have peace with their own circle whom they wish to govern as suits themselves. For even those whom they make war against they wish to make their own, and impose on them the laws of their own peace.

But let us suppose a man such as poetry and mythology speak of—a man so unsociable and savage as to be called rather a semi-man than a man.[16] Although, then, his kingdom was the solitude of a dreary cave, and he himself was so singularly bad-hearted that he was named Κακός, which is the Greek word for *bad;* though he had no wife to soothe him with endearing talk, no children to play with, no sons to do his bidding, no friend to enliven him with intercourse, not even his father Vulcan (though in one respect he was happier than his father, not having begotten a monster like himself); although he gave to no man, but took as he wished whatever he could, from whomsoever he could, when he could; yet in that solitary den, the floor

of which, as Virgil[17] says, was always reeking with recent slaughter, there was nothing else than peace sought, a peace in which no one should molest him, or disquiet him with any assault or alarm. With his own body he desired to be at peace, and he was satisfied only in proportion as he had this peace. For he ruled his members, and they obeyed him; and for the sake of pacifying his mortal nature, which rebelled when it needed anything, and of allaying the sedition of hunger which threatened to banish the soul from the body, he made forays, slew, and devoured, but used the ferocity and savageness he displayed in these actions only for the preservation of his own life's peace. So that, had he been willing to make with other men the same peace which he made with himself in his own cave, he would neither have been called bad, nor a monster, nor a semi-man. Or if the appearance of his body and his vomiting smoky fires frightened men from having any dealings with him, perhaps his fierce ways arose not from a desire to do mischief, but from the necessity of finding a living. But he may have had no existence, or, at least, he was not such as the poets fancifully describe him, for they had to exalt Hercules, and did so at the expense of Cacus. It is better, then, to believe that such a man or semi-man never existed, and that this, in common with many other fancies of the poets, is mere fiction. For the most savage animals (and he is said to have been almost a wild beast) encompass their own species with a ring of protecting peace. They cohabit, beget, produce, suckle, and bring up their young, though very many of them are not gregarious, but solitary—not like sheep, deer, pigeons, starlings, bees, but such as lions, foxes, eagles, bats. For what tigress

16  He refers to the giant Cacus.

17  *Aeneid*, viii. 195

does not gently purr over her cubs, and lay aside her ferocity to fondle them? What kite, solitary as he is when circling over his prey, does not seek a mate, build a nest, hatch the eggs, bring up the young birds, and maintain with the mother of his family as peaceful a domestic alliance as he can? How much more powerfully do the laws of man's nature move him to hold fellowship and maintain peace with all men so far as in him lies, since even wicked men wage war to maintain the peace of their own circle, and wish that, if possible, all men belonged to them, that all men and things might serve but one head, and might, either through love or fear, yield themselves to peace with him! It is thus that pride in its perversity apes God. It abhors equality with other men under Him; but, instead of His rule, it seeks to impose a rule of its own upon its equals. It abhors, that is to say, the just peace of God, and loves its own unjust peace; but it cannot help loving peace of one kind or other. For there is no vice so clean contrary to nature that it obliterates even the faintest traces of nature.

He, then, who prefers what is right to what is wrong, and what is well-ordered to what is perverted, sees that the peace of unjust men is not worthy to be called peace in comparison with the peace of the just. And yet even what is perverted must of necessity be in harmony with, and in dependence on, and in some part of the order of things, for otherwise it would have no existence at all. Suppose a man hangs with his head downwards, this is certainly a perverted attitude of body and arrangement of its members; for that which nature requires to be above is beneath, and *vice versa*. This perversity disturbs the peace of the body, and is therefore painful. Nevertheless the spirit is at peace with its body, and labors for its preservation, and hence the suffering; but

if it is banished from the body by its pains, then, so long as the bodily framework holds together, there is in the remains a kind of peace among the members, and hence the body remains suspended. And inasmuch as the earthly body tends towards the earth, and rests on the bond by which it is suspended, it tends thus to its natural peace, and the voice of its own weight demands a place for it to rest; and though now lifeless and without feeling, it does not fall from the peace that is natural to its place in creation, whether it already has it, or is tending towards it. For if you apply embalming preparations to prevent the bodily frame from mouldering and dissolving, a kind of peace still unites part to part, and keeps the whole body in a suitable place on the earth—in other words, in a place that is at peace with the body. If, on the other hand, the body receive no such care, but be left to the natural course, it is disturbed by exhalations that do not harmonize with one another, and that offend our senses; for it is this which is perceived in putrefaction until it is assimilated to the elements of the world, and particle by particle enters into peace with them. Yet throughout this process the laws of the most high Creator and Governor are strictly observed, for it is by Him the peace of the universe is administered. For although minute animals are produced from the carcass of a larger animal, all these little atoms, by the law of the same Creator, serve the animals they belong to in peace. And although the flesh of dead animals be eaten by others, no matter where it be carried, nor what it be brought into contact with, nor what it be converted and changed into, it still is ruled by the same laws which pervade all things for the conservation of every mortal race, and which bring things that fit one another into harmony.

## The Tranquillity of Order in the Universe

The peace of the body then consists in the duly proportioned arrangement of its parts. The peace of the irrational soul is the harmonious repose of the appetites, and that of the rational soul the harmony of knowledge and action. The peace of body and soul is the well-ordered and harmonious life and health of the living creature. Peace between man and God is the well-ordered obedience of faith to eternal law. Peace between man and man is well-ordered concord. Domestic peace is the well-ordered concord between those of the family who rule and those who obey. Civil peace is a similar concord among the citizens. The peace of the celestial city is the perfectly ordered and harmonious enjoyment of God, and of one another in God. The peace of all things is the tranquillity of order. Order is the distribution which allots things equal and unequal, each to its own place. And hence, though the miserable, in so far as they are such, do certainly not enjoy peace, but are severed from that tranquillity of order in which there is no disturbance, nevertheless, inasmuch as they are deservedly and justly miserable, they are by their very misery connected with order. They are not, indeed, conjoined with the blessed, but they are disjoined from them by the law of order. And though they are disquieted, their circumstances are notwithstanding adjusted to them, and consequently they have some tranquillity of order, and therefore some peace. But they are wretched because, although not wholly miserable, they are not in that place where any mixture of misery is impossible. They would, however, be more wretched if they had not that peace which arises from being in harmony with the natural order of things. When they suffer, their peace is in so far disturbed; but their peace continues in so far as they do not suffer, and in so far as their nature continues to exist. As, then, there may be life without pain, while there cannot be pain without some kind of life, so there may be peace without war, but there cannot be war without some kind of peace, because war supposes the existence of some natures to wage it, and these natures cannot exist without peace of one kind or other.

And therefore there is a nature in which evil does not or even cannot exist; but there cannot be a nature in which there is no good. Hence not even the nature of the devil himself is evil, in so far as it is nature, but it was made evil by being perverted. Thus he did not abide in the truth,[18] but could not escape the judgment of the truth; he did not abide in the tranquillity of order, but did not therefore escape the power of the Ordainer. The good imparted by God to his nature did not screen him from the justice of God by which order was preserved in his punishment; neither did God punish the good which He had created, but the evil which the devil had committed. God did not take back all He had imparted to his nature, but something He took and something He left, that there might remain enough to be sensible of the loss of what was taken. And this very sensibility to pain is evidence of the good which has been taken away and the good which has been left. For, were nothing good left, there could be no pain on account of the good which had been lost. For he who sins is still worse if he rejoices in his loss of righteousness. But he who is in pain, if he derives no benefit from it, mourns at least the loss of health. And as righteousness and

---

18  John viii. 44.

health are both good things, and as the loss of any good thing is matter of grief, not of joy—if, at least, there is no compensation, as spiritual righteousness may compensate for the loss of bodily health—certainly it is more suitable for a wicked man to grieve in punishment than to rejoice in his fault. As, then, the joy of a sinner who has abandoned what is good is evidence of a bad will, so his grief for the good he has lost when he is punished is evidence of a good nature. For he who laments the peace his nature has lost is stirred to do so by some relics of peace which make his nature friendly to itself. And it is very just that in the final punishment the wicked and godless should in anguish bewail the loss of the natural advantages they enjoyed, and should perceive that they were most justly taken from them by that God whose benign liberality they had despised. God, then, the most wise Creator and most just Ordainer of all natures, who placed the human race upon earth as its greatest ornament, imparted to men some good things adapted to this life, to wit, temporal peace, such as we can enjoy in this life from health and safety and human fellowship, and all things needful for the preservation and recovery of this peace, such as the objects which are accommodated to our outward senses, light, night, the air, and waters suitable for us, and everything the body requires to sustain, shelter, heal, or beautify it: and all under this most equitable condition, that every man who made a good use of these advantages suited to the peace of this mortal condition, should receive ampler and better blessings, namely, the peace of immortality, accompanied by glory and honor in an endless life made fit for the enjoyment of God and of one another in God; but that he who used the present blessings badly should both lose them and should not receive the others.

## Rulers as Servants of the Ruled

The whole use, then, of things temporal has a reference to this result of earthly peace in the earthly community, while in the city of God it is connected with eternal peace. And therefore, if we were irrational animals, we should desire nothing beyond the proper arrangement of the parts of the body and the satisfaction of the appetites—nothing, therefore, but bodily comfort and abundance of pleasures, that the peace of the body might contribute to the peace of the soul. For if bodily peace be wanting, a bar is put to the peace even of the irrational soul, since it cannot obtain the gratification of its appetites. And these two together help out the mutual peace of soul and body, the peace of harmonious life and health. For as animals, by shunning pain, show that they love bodily peace, and, by pursuing pleasure to gratify their appetites, show that they love peace of soul, so their shrinking from death is a sufficient indication of their intense love of that peace which binds soul and body in close alliance. But, as man has a rational soul, he subordinates all this which he has in common with the beasts to the peace of his rational soul, that his intellect may have free play and may regulate his actions, and that he may thus enjoy the well-ordered harmony of knowledge and action which constitutes, as we have said, the peace of the rational soul. And for this purpose he must desire to be neither molested by pain, nor disturbed by desire, nor extinguished by death, that he may arrive at some useful knowledge by which he may regulate his life and manners. But, owing to the liability of the human mind to fall into mistakes, this very pursuit of knowledge may be a snare to him unless he has a divine Master, whom he may obey without misgiving, and who may at the same time give him such help as to preserve his own freedom. And because, so long as he is in this mortal body, he is stranger to God, he walks by faith, not by sight; and he therefore refers all peace, bodily or spiritual or both, to that peace which mortal man has with the immortal God, so that he exhibits the well-ordered obedience of faith to eternal law. But as this divine Master inculcates two precepts—the love of God and the love of our neighbor—and as in these precepts a man finds three things he has to love—God, himself, and his neighbor—and that he who loves God loves himself thereby, it follows that he must endeavor to get his neighbor to love God, since he is ordered to love his neighbor as himself. He ought to make this endeavor in behalf of his wife, his children, his household, all within his reach, even as he would wish his neighbor to do the same for him if he needed it; and consequently he will be at peace, or in well-ordered concord, with all men, as far as in him lies. And this is the order of this concord, that a man, in the first place, injure no one, and, in the second, do good to every one he can reach. Primarily, therefore, his own household are his care, for the law of nature and of society gives him readier access to them and greater opportunity of serving them. And hence the apostle says, "Now, if any provide not for his own, and specially for those of his own house, he hath denied the faith, and is worse than an infidel."[19] This is the origin of domestic peace, or the well-ordered concord of those in the family who rule and those who obey. For they who care for the rest rule—the husband the wife, the parents the children, the masters the servants; and they who are cared for obey—the women their husbands, the children their parents, the servants their

masters. But in the family of the just man who lives by faith and is as yet a pilgrim journeying on to the celestial city, even those who rule serve those whom they seem to command; for they rule not from a love of power, but from a sense of the duty they owe to others—not because they are proud of authority, but because they love mercy.

## Liberty and Slavery

This is prescribed by the order of nature: it is thus that God has created man. For "let them," He says, "have dominion over the fish of the sea, and over the fowl of the air, and over every creeping thing which creepeth on the earth."[20] He did not intend that His rational creature, who was made in His image, should have dominion over anything but the irrational creation—not man over man, but man over the beasts. And hence the righteous men in primitive times were made shepherds of cattle rather than kings of men, God intending thus to teach us what the relative position of the creatures is, and what the desert of sin; for it is with justice, we believe, that the condition of slavery is the result of sin. And this is why we do not find the word "slave" in any part of Scripture until righteous Noah branded the sin of his son with this name. It is a name, therefore, introduced by sin and not by nature. The origin of the Latin word for slave is supposed to be found in the circumstance that those who by the law of war were liable to be killed were sometimes preserved by their victors, and were hence called servants. And

19 I Tim. v. 8.

20 "Gen. i. 26.

these circumstances could never have arisen save through sin. For even when we wage a just war, our adversaries must be sinning; and every victory, even though gained by wicked men, is a result of the first judgment of God, who humbles the vanquished either for the sake of removing or of punishing their sins. Witness that man of God, Daniel, who, when he was in captivity, confessed to God his own sins and the sins of his people, and declared with pious grief that these were the cause of the captivity.[21]

The prime cause, then, of slavery is sin, which brings man under the dominion of his fellow—that which does not happen save by the judgment of God, with whom is no unrighteousness, and who knows how to award fit punishments to every variety of offence. But our Master in heaven says, "Every one who doeth sin is the servant of sin."[22] And thus there are many wicked masters who have religious men as their slaves, and who are yet themselves in bondage; "for of whom a man is overcome, of the same is he brought in bondage."[23] And beyond question it is a happier thing to be the slave of a man than of a lust; for even this very lust of ruling, to mention no others, lays waste men's hearts with the most ruthless dominion. Moreover, when men are subjected to one another in a peaceful order, the lowly position does as much good to the servant as the proud position does harm to the master. But by nature, as God first created us, no one is the slave either of man or of sin. This servitude is, however, penal, and is appointed by that law which enjoins the preservation of the natural order and forbids its disturbance; for if nothing had been done in violation of that law, there would have been nothing to restrain by penal servitude. And therefore the apostle admonishes slaves to be subject to their masters, and to serve them heartily and with good-will, so that, if they cannot be freed by their masters, they may themselves make their slavery in some sort free, by serving not in crafty fear, but in faithful love, until all unrighteousness pass away, and all principality and every human power be brought to nothing, and God be all in all.

## Equitable Rule

And therefore, although our righteous fathers[24] had slaves, and administered their domestic affairs so as to distinguish between the condition of slaves and the heirship of sons in regard to the blessings of this life, yet in regard to the worship of God, in whom we hope for eternal blessings, they took an equally loving oversight of all the members of their household. And this is so much in accordance with the natural order, that the head of the household was called *paterfamilias;* and this name has been so generally accepted, that even those whose rule is unrighteous are glad to apply it to themselves. But those who are true fathers of their households desire and endeavor that all the members of their household, equally with their own children, should worship and win God, and should come to that heavenly home in which the duty of ruling men is no longer necessary, because the duty of caring for their everlasting happiness has also ceased; but, until they reach that home, masters ought to feel their position of

21  Dan. ix.
22  John viii. 34.
23  II Pet. ii. 19.

24  The patriarchs.

authority a greater burden than servants their service. And if any member of the family interrupts the domestic peace by disobedience, he is corrected either by word or blow, or some kind of just and legitimate punishment, such as society permits, that he may himself be the better for it, and be readjusted to the family harmony from which he had dislocated himself. For as it is not benevolent to give a man help at the expense of some greater benefit he might receive, so it is not innocent to spare a man at the risk of his failing into graver sin. To be innocent, we must not only do harm to no man, but also restrain him from sin or punish his sin, so that either the man himself who is punished may profit by his experience, or others be warned by his example. Since, then, the house ought to be the beginning or element of the city, and every beginning bears reference to some end of its own kind, and every element to the integrity of the whole of which it is an element, it follows plainly enough that domestic peace has a relation to civic peace—in other words, that the well-ordered concord of domestic obedience and domestic rule has a relation to the well-ordered concord of civic obedience and civic rule. And therefore it follows, further, that the father of the family ought to frame his domestic rule in accordance with the law of the city, so that the household may be in harmony with the civic order.

## The Supranational Character of the Heavenly City on Earth

But the families which do not live by faith seek their peace in the earthly advantages of this life; while the families which live by faith look for those eternal blessing which are promised, and use as pilgrims such advantages of time and of earth as do not fascinate and divert them from God, but rather aid them to endure with greater ease, and to keep down the number of those burdens of the corruptible body which weigh upon the soul. Thus the things necessary for this mortal life are used by both kinds of men and families alike, but each has its own peculiar and widely different aim in using them. The earthly city, which does not live by faith, seeks an earthly peace, and the end it proposes, in the well-ordered concord of civic obedience and rule, is the combination of men's wills to attain the things which are helpful to this life. The heavenly city, or rather the part of it which sojourns on earth and lives by faith, makes use of this peace only because it must, until this mortal condition which necessitates it shall pass away. Consequently, so long as it lives like a captive and a stranger in the earthly city, though it has already received the promise of redemption, and the gift of the Spirit as the earnest of it, it makes no scruple to obey the laws of the earthly city, whereby the things necessary for the maintenance of this mortal life are administered; and thus, as this life is common to both cities, so there is a harmony between them in regard to what belongs to it. But, as the earthly city has had some philosophers whose doctrine is condemned by the divine teaching, and who, being deceived either by their own conjectures or by demons, supposed that many gods must be invited to take an interest in human affairs, and assigned to each a separate function and a separate department—to one the body, to another the soul; and in the body itself, to one the head, to another the neck, and each of the other members to one of the gods; and in like manner, in the soul, to one god the natural capacity was assigned, to another education, to another anger, to another lust; and so the various affairs of life were assigned—cattle to one, corn to another, wine to another, oil to another, the woods to another, money to another, navigation to another, wars and victories to another, marriages to another, births and fecundity to another, and other things to other gods: and as the celestial city, on the other hand, knew that one God only was to be worshipped, and that to Him alone was due that service which the Greeks call *latreia*, and which can be given only to a god, it has come to pass that the two cities could not have common laws of religion, and that the heavenly city has been compelled in this matter to dissent, and to become obnoxious to those who think differently, and to stand the brunt of their anger and hatred and persecutions, except in so far as the minds of their enemies have been alarmed by the multitude of the Christians, and quelled by the manifest protection of God accorded to them. This heavenly city, then, while it sojourns on earth, calls citizens out of all nations, and gathers together a society of pilgrims of all languages, not scrupling about diversities in the manners, laws, and institutions whereby earthly peace is secured and maintained, but recognizing that, however various these are, they all tend to one and the same end of earthly peace. It therefore is so far from rescinding and abolishing these diversities, that it even preserves and adopts them, so long only as no hindrance to the worship of the one supreme and true God is thus introduced. Even the heavenly city, therefore, while in its state of pilgrimage, avails itself of the peace of earth, and, so far as it can without injuring faith and godliness, desires and maintains a common agreement among men regarding the acquisition of the necessaries of life, and makes this earthly peace bear upon the peace of heaven; for this alone can be truly called and esteemed the peace of the reasonable creatures, consisting as it does in the perfectly ordered and harmonious enjoyment of God and of one another in God. When we shall have reached that peace, this mortal life shall give place to one that is eternal, and our body shall be no more this animal body which by its corruption weighs down the soul, but a spiritual body feeling no want, and in all its members subjected to the will. In its pilgrim state the heavenly city possesses this peace by faith; and by this faith it lives righteously when it refers to the attainment of that peace every good action towards God and man; for the life of the city is a social life.

# The Prince

By Niccolo Machiavelli

## Chapter XIV

### Of the Duty of a Prince in Respect of Military Affairs

A prince, therefore, should have no care or thought but for war, and for the regulations and training it requires, and should apply himself exclusively to this as his peculiar province; for war is the sole art looked for in one who rules, and is of such efficacy that it not merely maintains those who are born Princes, but often enables men to rise to that eminence from a private station; while, on the other hand, we often see that when Princes devote themselves rather to pleasure than to arms, they lose their dominions. And as neglect of this art is the prime cause of such calamities, so to be a proficient in it is the surest way to acquire power. Francesco Sforza, from his renown in arms, rose from privacy to be Duke of Milan, while his descendants, seeking to avoid the hardships and fatigues of military life, from being Princes fell back into privacy. For among other causes of misfortune which your not being armed brings upon you, it makes you despised, and this is one of those reproaches against which, as shall presently be explained, a Prince ought most carefully to guard.

Between an armed and an unarmed man no proportion holds, and it is contrary to reason to expect that the armed man should voluntarily submit to him who is unarmed, or that the unarmed man should stand secure among armed retainers. For with contempt on one side, and distrust on the other, it is impossible that men should work well together. Wherefore, as has already been said, a Prince who is ignorant of military affairs, besides other disadvantages, can neither be respected by his soldiers, nor can he trust them. A Prince, therefore, ought never to allow his attention to be diverted from warlike pursuits, and should occupy himself with them even more in peace than in war. This he can do in two ways, by practice or by study.

As to the practice, he ought, besides keeping his soldiers well trained and disciplined, to be constantly engaged in the chase, that he may inure his body to hardships and fatigue, and gain at the same time a knowledge of places, by observing how the mountains slope, the valleys open, and the plains spread; acquainting himself with the characters of rivers and marshes, and giving the greatest attention to this subject. Such knowledge is useful to him in two ways; for first, he learns thereby to know his own country, and to understand better how it may be defended; and next, from his familiar acquaintance with its localities, he readily comprehends the character of other districts when obliged to observe them for the first time. For the hills, valleys, plains, rivers, and marshes of Tuscany, for example, have a certain resemblance to those elsewhere; so that from a knowledge of the natural features of that province, similar knowledge in respect of other provinces may readily be gained. The Prince who is wanting in this kind of knowledge, is wanting in the first qualification of a good captain for by it he is taught how to surprise an enemy, how to choose an encampment, how to lead his army on a march, how to array it for battle, and how to post it to the best advantage for a siege.

Among the commendations which Philopoemon, Prince of the Achaians, has received from historians is this—that in times of peace he was always thinking of methods of warfare, so that when walking in the country with his friends he would often stop and talk with them on the subject. 'If the enemy,' he would say, 'were posted on that hill, and we found ourselves here with our army, which of us would have the better position? How could we most safely and in the best order advance to meet them? If we had to retreat, what direction should we take? If they retired, how should we pursue?' In this way he put to his friends, as he went along, all the contingencies that can befall an army. He listened to their opinions, stated his own, and supported them with reasons; and from his being constantly occupied with such meditations, it resulted, that when in actual command no complication could ever present itself with which he was not prepared to deal.

As to the mental training of which we have spoken, a Prince should read histories, and in these should note the actions of great men, observe how they conducted themselves in their wars, and examine the causes of their victories and defeats, so as to avoid the latter and imitate them in the former. And above all, he should, as many great men of past ages have done, assume for his models those persons who before his time have been renowned and celebrated, whose deeds and achievements he should constantly keep in mind, as it is related that Alexander the Great sought to resemble Achilles, Caesar Alexander, and Scipio Cyrus. And any one who reads the life of this last-named hero, written by Xenophon, recognizes afterwards in the life of Scipio, how much this imitation was the source of his glory, and how nearly in his chastity, affability, kindliness, and generosity, he conformed to the character of Cyrus as Xenophon describes it.

A wise Prince, therefore, should pursue such methods as these, never resting idle in times of peace, but strenuously seeking to turn them to account, so that he may derive strength from them in the hour of danger, and find himself ready should Fortune turn against him, to resist her blows.

## Chapter XV

### Of the Qualities in Respect of Which Men, and Most of All Princes, Are Praised or Blamed

It now remains for us to consider what ought to be the conduct and bearing of a Prince in relation to his subjects and friends. And since I know that many have written on this subject, I fear it may be thought presumptuous in me to write of it also; the more so, because in my treatment of it, I depart from the views that others have taken.

But since it is my object to write what shall be useful to whosoever understands it, it seems to me better to follow the real truth of things than an imaginary view of them. For many Republics and Princedoms have been imagined that were never seen or known to exist in reality. And the manner in which we live, and that in which we ought to live, are things so wide asunder, that he who quits the one to betake himself to the other is more likely to destroy than to save himself; since any one who would act up to a perfect standard of goodness in everything, must be ruined among so many who are not good. It is essential, therefore, for a Prince who desires to maintain his position, to have learned how to be other than good, and to use or not to use his goodness as necessity requires.

Laying aside, therefore, all fanciful notions concerning a Prince, and considering those only that are true, I say that all men when they are spoken of, and Princes more than others from their being set so high, are characterized by some one of those qualities which attach either praise or blame. Thus one is accounted liberal, another miserly (which word I use, rather than *avaricious*, to denote the man who is too sparing of what is his own, *avarice* being the disposition to take wrongfully what is another's); one is generous, another greedy; one cruel, another tender-hearted; one is faithless, another true to his word; one effeminate and cowardly, another high-spirited and courageous; one is courteous, another haughty; one impure, another chaste; one simple, another crafty; one firm, another facile; one grave, another frivolous; one devout, another unbelieving; and the like. Every one, I know, will admit that it would be most laudable for a Prince to be endowed with all of the above qualities that are reckoned good; but since it is impossible for him to possess or constantly practise them all, the conditions of human nature not allowing it, he must be discreet enough to know how to avoid the infamy of those vices that would deprive him of his government, and, if possible, be on his guard also against those which might not deprive him of it; though if he cannot wholly restrain himself, he may with less scruple indulge in the latter. He need never hesitate, however, to incur the reproach of those vices without which his authority can hardly be preserved; for if he well consider the whole matter, he will find that there may be a line of conduct having the appearance of virtue, to follow which would be his ruin, and that there may be another course having the appearance of vice, by following which his safety and well-being are secured.

# Chapter XVI

## Of Liberality and Miserliness

Beginning, then, with the first of the qualities above noticed, I say that it may be a good thing to be reputed liberal, but, nevertheless, that liberality without the reputation of it is hurtful; because, though it be worthily and rightly used, still if it be not known, you escape not the reproach of its opposite vice. Hence, to have credit for liberality with the world at large, you must neglect no circumstance of sumptuous display; the result being, that a Prince of a liberal disposition will consume his whole substance in things of this sort, and, after all, be obliged, if he would maintain his reputation for liberality, to burden his subjects with extraordinary taxes, and to resort to confiscations and all the other shifts whereby money is raised. But in this way he becomes hateful to his subjects, and growing impoverished is held in little esteem by any. So that in the end, having by his liberality offended many and obliged few, he is worse off than when he began, and is exposed to all his original dangers. Recognizing this, and endeavouring to retrace his steps, he at once incurs the infamy of miserliness.

A Prince, therefore, since he cannot without injury to himself practise the virtue of liberality so that it may be known, will not, if he be wise, greatly concern himself though he be called miserly. Because in time he will come to be regarded as more and more liberal, when it is seen that through his parsimony his revenues are sufficient; that he is able to defend himself against any who make war on him; that he can engage in enterprises against others without burdening his subjects; and thus exercise liberality towards all from whom he does not take, whose number is infinite, while he is miserly in respect of those only to whom he does not give, whose number is few.

In our own days we have seen no Princes accomplish great results save those who have been accounted miserly. All others have been ruined. Pope Julius II, after availing himself of his reputation for liberality to arrive at the Papacy, made no effort to preserve that reputation when making war on the King of France, but carried on all his numerous campaigns without levying from his subjects a single extraordinary tax, providing for the increased expenditure out of his long-continued savings. Had the present King of Spain been accounted liberal, he never could have engaged or succeeded in so many enterprises.

A Prince, therefore, if he is enabled thereby to forbear from plundering his subjects, to defend himself, to escape poverty and contempt, and the necessity of becoming rapacious, ought to care little though he incur the reproach of miserliness, for this is one of those vices which enable him to reign.

And should any object that Caesar by his liberality rose to power, and that many others have been advanced to the highest dignities from their having been liberal and so reputed, I reply, 'Either you are already a Prince or you seek to become one; in the former case liberality is hurtful, in the latter it is very necessary that you be thought liberal; Caesar was one of those who sought the sovereignty of Rome; but if after obtaining it he had lived on without retrenching his expenditure, he must have ruined the Empire.' And if it be further urged that many Princes reputed to have been most liberal have achieved great things with their armies, I answer that a Prince spends either what belongs to himself and his subjects, or what belongs to others; and that in the former case he ought to be sparing, but in the latter ought not to refrain from any kind of liberality. Because for a Prince who leads his armies in person and maintains them by plunder, pillage, and forced contributions, dealing as he does with the property of others this liberality is necessary, since otherwise he would not be followed by his soldiers. Of what does not belong to you or to your subjects you should, therefore, be a lavish giver, as were Cyrus, Caesar, and Alexander; for to be liberal with the property of others does not take from your reputation, but adds to it. What injures you is to give away what is your own. And there is no quality so self-destructive as liberality; for while you practise it you lose the means whereby it can be practised, and become poor and despised, or else, to avoid poverty, you become rapacious and hated. For liberality leads to one or other of these two results, against which, beyond all others, a Prince should guard.

Wherefore it is wiser to put up with the name of being miserly, which breeds ignominy, but without hate, than to be obliged, from the desire to be reckoned liberal, to incur the reproach of rapacity, which breeds hate as well as ignominy.

# Chapter XVII

## Of Cruelty and Clemency, and Whether It Is Better to Be Loved or Feared

Passing to the other qualities above referred to, I say that every Prince should desire to be accounted merciful and not cruel. Nevertheless, he should be on his guard against the abuse of this quality of mercy. Cesare Borgia was reputed cruel, yet his cruelty restored Romagna, united it, and brought it to order and obedience; so that if we look at things in their true light, it will be seen that he was in reality far more merciful than the people of Florence, who, to avoid the imputation of cruelty, suffered Pistoja to be torn to pieces by factions.

A Prince should therefore disregard the reproach of being thought cruel where it enables him to keep his subjects united and obedient. For he who quells disorder by a very few signal examples will in the end be more merciful than he who from too great leniency permits things to take their course and so to result in rapine and bloodshed; for these hurt the whole State, whereas the severities of the Prince injure individuals only.

And for a new Prince, of all others, it is impossible to escape a name for cruelty, since new States are full of dangers. Wherefore Virgil, by the mouth of Dido, excuses the harshness of her reign on the plea that it was new, saying:—

A fate unkind, and newness in my reign Compel me thus to guard a wide domain.

Nevertheless, the new Prince should not be too ready of belief, nor too easily set in motion; nor should he himself be the first to raise alarms; but should so temper prudence with kindliness that too great confidence in others shall not throw him off his guard, nor groundless distrust render him insupportable.

And here comes in the question whether it is better to be loved rather than feared, or feared rather than loved. It might perhaps be answered that we should wish to be both; but since love and fear can hardly exist together, if we must choose between them, it is far safer to be feared than loved. For of men it may generally be affirmed, that they are thankless, fickle, false studious to avoid danger, greedy of gain, devoted to you while you are able to confer benefits upon them, and ready, as I said before, while danger is distant, to shed their blood, and sacrifice their property, their lives, and their children for you; but in the hour of need they turn against you. The Prince, therefore, who without otherwise securing himself builds wholly on their professions is undone. For the friendships which we buy with a price, and do not gain by greatness and nobility of character, though they be fairly earned are not made good, but fail us when we have occasion to use them.

Moreover, men are less careful how they offend him who makes himself loved than him who makes himself feared. For love is held by the tie of obligation, which, because men are a sorry breed, is broken on every whisper of private interest; but fear is bound by the apprehension of punishment which never relaxes its grasp.

Nevertheless a Prince should inspire fear in such a fashion that if he do not win love he may escape hate. For a man may very well be feared and yet not hated, and this will be the case so long as he does not meddle with the property or with the women of his citizens and subjects. And if constrained to put any to death, he should do so only when there is manifest cause or reasonable justification. But, above all, he must abstain from the property of others. For men will sooner forget the death of their father than the loss of their patrimony. Moreover, pretexts for confiscation are never to seek, and he who has once begun to live by rapine always finds reasons for taking what is not his; whereas reasons for shedding blood are fewer, and sooner exhausted.

But when a Prince is with his army, and has many soldiers under his command, he must needs disregard the reproach of cruelty, for without such a reputation in its Captain, no army can be held together or kept under any kind of control. Among other things remarkable in Hannibal this has been noted, that having a very great army, made up of men of many different nations and brought to fight in a foreign country, no dissension ever arose among the soldiers themselves, nor any mutiny against their leader, either in his good or in his evil fortunes. This we can only ascribe to the transcendent cruelty, which, joined with numberless great qualities, rendered him at once venerable and terrible in the eyes of his soldiers; for without this reputation for cruelty these other virtues would not have produced the like results.

Unreflecting writers, indeed, while they praise his achievements, have condemned the chief cause of them; but that his other merits would not by themselves have been so efficacious we may see from the case of Scipio, one of the greatest Captains, not of his own time only but of all times of which we have record, whose armies rose against him in Spain from no other cause than his too great leniency in allowing them a freedom inconsistent with military strictness. With which weakness Fabius Maximus taxed him in the Senate House, calling him the corrupter of the Roman soldiery. Again, when the Locrians were shamefully outraged by one of his lieutenants, he neither avenged them, nor punished the insolence of his officer; and this from the natural easiness of his disposition. So that it was said in the Senate by one who sought to excuse him, that there were many who knew better how to refrain from doing wrong themselves than how to correct the wrong-doing of others. This temper, however, must in time have marred the name and fame even of Scipio, had he continued in it, and retained his command. But living as he did under the control of the Senate, this hurtful quality was not merely disguised, but came to be regarded as a glory.

Returning to the question of being loved or feared, I sum up by saying, that since his being loved depends upon his subjects, while his being feared depends upon himself, a wise Prince should build on what is his own, and not on what rests with others. Only, as I have said, he must do his utmost to escape hatred.

## Chapter XVIII

### How Princes Should Keep Faith

Every one understands how praiseworthy it is in a Prince to keep faith, and to live uprightly and not craftily. Nevertheless, we see from what has taken place in our own days that Princes who have set little store by their word, but have known how to overreach men by their cunning, have accomplished great things, and in the end got the better of those who trusted to honest dealing.

Be it known, then, that there are two ways of contending, one in accordance with the laws, the other by force; the first of which is proper to men, the second to beasts. But since the first method is often ineffectual, it becomes necessary to resort to the second. A Prince should, therefore, understand how to use well both the man and the beast. And this lesson has been covertly taught by the ancient writers, who relate how Achilles and many others of these old Princes were given over to be brought up and trained by Chiron the Centaur; since the only meaning of their having for instructor one who was half man and half beast is, that it is necessary for a Prince to know how to use both natures, and that the one without the other has no stability.

But since a Prince should know how to use the beast's nature wisely, he ought of beasts to choose both the lion and the fox; for the lion cannot guard himself from the toils, nor the fox from wolves. He must therefore be a fox to discern toils, and a lion to drive off wolves.

To rely wholly on the lion is unwise; and for this reason a prudent Prince neither can nor ought to keep his word when to keep it is hurtful to him and the causes which led him to pledge it are removed. If all men were good, this would not be good advice, but since they are dishonest and do not keep faith with you, you in return, need not keep faith with them; and no prince was ever at a loss for plausible reasons to cloak a breach of faith. Of this numberless recent instances could be given, and it might be shown how many solemn treaties and engagements have been rendered inoperative and idle through want of faith in Princes, and that he who was best known to play the fox has had the best success.

It is necessary, indeed, to put a good colour on this nature, and to be skilful in simulating and dissembling. But men are so simple, and governed so absolutely by their present needs, that he who wishes to deceive will never fail in finding willing dupes. One recent example I will not omit. Pope Alexander VI had no care or thought but how to deceive, and always found material to work on. No man ever had a more effective manner of asseverating, or made promises with more solemn protestations, or observed them less. And yet, because he understood this side of human nature, his frauds always succeeded.

It is not essential, then, that a Prince should have all the good qualities which I have enumerated above, but it is most essential that he should seem to have them; I will even venture to affirm that if he has and invariably practises them all, they are hurtful, whereas the appearance of having them is useful. Thus, it is well to seem merciful, faithful, humane, religious, and upright, and also to be so; but the mind should remain so balanced that were it needful not to be so, you should be able and know how to change to the contrary.

And you are to understand that a Prince, and most of all a new Prince, cannot observe all those rules of conduct in respect whereof men are accounted good, being often forced, in order to preserve his Princedom, to act in opposition to good faith, charity, humanity, and religion. He must therefore keep his mind ready to shift as the winds and tides of Fortune turn, and, as I have already said, he ought not to quit good courses if he can help it, but should know how to follow evil courses if he must.

A Prince should therefore be very careful that nothing ever escapes his lips which is not replete with the five qualities above named, so that to see and hear him, one would think him the embodiment of mercy, good faith, integrity, humanity, and religion. And there is no virtue which it is more necessary for him to seem to possess than this last; because men in general judge rather by the eye than by the hand, for every one can see but few can touch. Every one sees what you seem, but few know what you are, and these few dare not oppose themselves to the opinion of the many who have the majesty of the State to back them up.

Moreover, in the actions of all men, and most of all of Princes, where there is no tribunal to which we can appeal, we look to results. Wherefore if a Prince succeeds in establishing and maintaining his authority, the means will always be judged honourable and be approved by every one. For the vulgar are always taken by appearances and by results, and the world is made up of the vulgar, the few only finding room when the many have no longer ground to stand on.

A certain Prince of our own days, whose name it is as well not to mention, is always preaching peace and good faith, although the mortal enemy of both; and both, had he practised them as he preaches them, would, oftener than once, have lost him his kingdom and authority.

# Chapter XIX

## That a Prince Should Seek to Escape Contempt and Hatred

Having now spoken of the chief of the qualities above referred to, the rest I shall dispose of briefly with these general remarks, that a Prince, as has already in part been said, should consider how he may avoid such courses as would make him hated or despised; and that whenever he succeeds in keeping clear of these, he has performed his part, and runs no risk though he incur other infamies.

A Prince, as I have said before, sooner becomes hated by being rapacious and by interfering with the property and with the women of his subjects, than in any other way. From these, therefore, he should abstain. For so long as neither their property nor their honour is touched, the mass of mankind live contentedly, and the Prince has only to cope with the ambition of a few, which can in many ways and easily be kept within bounds.

A Prince is despised when he is seen to be fickle, frivolous, effeminate, pusillanimous, or irresolute, against which defects he ought therefore most carefully to guard, striving so to bear himself that greatness, courage, wisdom, and strength may appear in all his actions. In his private dealings with his subjects his decisions should be irrevocable, and his reputation such that no one would dream of overreaching or cajoling him.

The Prince who inspires such an opinion of himself is greatly esteemed, and against one who is greatly esteemed conspiracy is difficult; nor, when he is known to be an excellent Prince and held in reverence by his subjects, will it be easy to attack him. For a Prince is exposed to two dangers, from within in respect of his subjects, from without in respect of foreign powers. Against the latter he will defend himself with good arms and good allies, and if he have good arms he will always have good allies; and when things are settled abroad, they will always be settled at home, unless disturbed by conspiracies; and even should there be hostility from without, if he has taken those measures, and has lived in the way I have recommended, and if he never abandons hope, he will withstand every attack; as I have said was done by Nabis the Spartan.

As regards his own subjects, when affairs are quiet abroad, he has to fear they may engage in secret plots; against which a Prince best secures himself when he escapes being hated or despised, and keeps on good terms with his people; and this, as I have already shown at length, it is essential he should do. Not to be hated or despised by the body of his subjects, is one of the surest safeguards that a Prince can have against conspiracy. For he who conspires always reckons on pleasing the people by putting the Prince to death; but when he sees that instead of pleasing he will offend them, he cannot summon courage to carry out his design. For the difficulties that attend conspirators are infinite, and we know from experience that while there have been many conspiracies, few of them have succeeded.

He who conspires cannot do so alone, nor can he assume as his companions any save those whom he believes to be discontented; but so soon as you impart your design to a discontented man, you supply him with the means of removing his discontent, since by betraying you he can procure for himself every advantage; so that seeing on the one hand certain gain, and on the other a doubtful and dangerous risk, he must either be a rare friend to you, or the mortal enemy of his Prince, if he keep your secret.

To put the matter shortly, I say that on the side of the conspirator there are distrust, jealousy, and dread of punishment to deter him, while on the side of the Prince there are the laws, the majesty of the throne, the protection of friends and of the government to defend him; to which if the general good-will of the people be added, it is hardly possible that any should be rash enough to conspire. For while in ordinary cases, the conspirator has ground for fear only before the execution of his villainy, in this case he has also cause to fear after the crime has been perpetrated, since he has the people for his enemy, and is thus cut off from every hope of shelter.

Of this, endless instances might be given, but I shall content myself with one that happened within the recollection of our fathers. Messer Annibale Bentivoglio, Lord of Bologna and grandfather of the present Messer Annibale, was conspired against and murdered by the Canneschi, leaving behind none belonging to him save Messer Giovanni, then an infant in arms. Immediately upon the murder, the people rose and put all the Canneschi to death. This resulted from the general goodwill with which the House of the Bentivogli was then regarded in Bologna; which feeling was so strong, that when upon the death of Messer Annibale no one was left who could govern the State, there being reason to believe that a descendant of the family (who up to that time had been thought to be the son of a smith), was living in Florence, the citizens of Bologna came there for him, and entrusted him with the government of their city; which he retained until Messer Giovanni was old enough to govern.

To be brief, a Prince has little to fear from conspiracies when his subjects are well disposed towards him; but when they are hostile and hold him in detestation, he has then reason to fear everything and every one. And well ordered States and wise Princes have provided with extreme care that the nobility shall not be driven to desperation, and that the commons shall be kept satisfied and contented; for this is one of the most important matters that a Prince has to look to.

Among the well ordered and governed Kingdoms of our day is that of France, wherein we find an infinite number of wise institutions, upon which depend the freedom and the security of the King, and of which the most important are the Parliament and its authority. For he who gave its constitution to this Realm, knowing the ambition and arrogance of the nobles, and judging it necessary to bridle and restrain them, and on the other hand knowing the hatred, originating in fear, entertained against them by the commons, and desiring that they should be safe, was unwilling that the responsibility for this should rest on the King; and to relieve him of the ill-will which he might incur with the nobles by favouring the commons, or with the commons by favouring the nobles, appointed a third party to be arbitrator, who without committing the King, might depress the nobles and uphold the commons. Nor could there be any better, wiser, or surer safeguard for the King and the Kingdom. And hence we may draw another notable lesson, namely, that Princes should devolve on others those matters that entail responsibility, and reserve to themselves those that relate to grace and favour. And again I say that a Prince should esteem the great, but must not make himself odious to the people.

To some it may perhaps appear, that if the lives and deaths of many of the Roman Emperors be considered, they offer examples opposed to the views expressed by me; since we find that some among them who had always lived good lives, and shown themselves possessed of great qualities, were nevertheless deposed and even put to death by their subjects who had conspired against them.

In answer to such objections, I shall examine the characters of several Emperors, and show that the causes of their downfall were in no way different from those which I have indicated. In doing this I shall submit for consideration such matters only as must strike every one who reads the history of these times; and it will be enough for my purpose to take those Emperors who reigned from the time of Marcus the Philosopher to the time of Maximinus, who were, inclusively, Marcus, Commodus his son, Pertinax, Julianus, Severus, Caracalla his son, Macrinus, Heliogabalus, Alexander, and Maximinus.

In the first place, then, we have to note that while in other Princedoms the Prince has only to contend with the ambition of the nobles and the insubordination of the people, the Roman Emperors had a further difficulty to encounter in the cruelty and rapacity of their soldiers, which were so distracting as to cause the ruin of many of these Princes. For it was hardly possible for them to satisfy both the soldiers and the people; the latter loving peace and therefore preferring sober Princes, while the former preferred a Prince of a warlike spirit, however harsh, haughty, or rapacious; being willing that he should exercise these qualities against the people, as the means of procuring for themselves double pay, and indulging their greed and cruelty.

Whence it followed that those Emperors who had not inherited or won for themselves such authority as enabled them to keep both people and soldiers in check, were always ruined. The most of them, and those especially who came to the Empire new and without

experience, seeing the difficulty of dealing with these conflicting humours, set themselves to satisfy the soldiers, and made little account of offending the people. And for them this was a necessary course to take; for as Princes cannot escape being hated by some, they should, in the first place, endeavour not to be hated by a class; failing in which, they must do all they can to escape the hatred of that class which is the stronger. Wherefore those Emperors who, by reason of their newness, stood in need of extraordinary support, sided with the soldiery rather than with the people; a course which turned out advantageous or otherwise, according as the Prince knew, or did not know, how to maintain his authority over them.

From the causes indicated it resulted that Marcus, Pertinax, and Alexander, being Princes of a temperate disposition, lovers of justice, enemies of cruelty, gentle, and kindly, had all, save Marcus, an unhappy end. Marcus alone lived and died honoured in the highest degree; and this because he had succeeded to the Empire by right of inheritance, and not through the favour either of the soldiery or of the people; and also because, being endowed with many virtues which made him revered, he kept, while he lived, both factions within bounds, and was never either hated or despised.

But Pertinax was chosen Emperor against the will of the soldiery, who being accustomed to a licentious life under Commodus, could not tolerate the stricter discipline to which his successor sought to bring them back. And having thus made himself hated, and being at the same time despised by reason of his advanced age, he was ruined at the very outset of his reign.

And here it is to be noted that hatred is incurred as well on account of good actions as of bad; or which reason, as I have already said, a Prince who would maintain his authority is often compelled to be other than good. For when the class, be it the people, the soldiers, or the nobles, on whom you judge it necessary to rely for your support, is corrupt, you must needs adapt yourself to its humours, and satisfy these, in which case virtuous conduct will only prejudice you.

Let us now come to Alexander, who was so just a ruler that among the praises ascribed to him it is recorded, that, during the fourteen years he held the Empire, no man was ever put to death by him without trial. Nevertheless, being accounted effeminate, and thought to be governed by his mother, he fell into contempt, and the army conspiring against him, slew him.

When we turn to consider the characters of Commodus, Severus, and Caracalla, we find them all to have been most cruel and rapacious Princes, who to satisfy the soldiery, scrupled not to inflict every kind of wrong upon the people. And all of them, except Severus, came to a bad end. But in Severus there was such strength of character, that, keeping the soldiers his friends, he was able, although he oppressed the people, to reign on prosperously to the last; because his great qualities made him so admirable in the eyes both of the people and the soldiers, that the former remained in a manner amazed and awestruck, while the latter were respectful and contented.

And because his actions, for one who was a new Prince, were thus remarkable, I will point out shortly how well he understood to play the part both of the lion and of the fox, each of which natures, as I have observed before, a Prince should know how to assume.

Knowing the indolent disposition of the Emperor Julianus, Severus persuaded the army which he commanded in Illyria that it was their duty to go to Rome to avenge the death of Pertinax, who had been slain by the Pretorian guards. Under this pretext, and without disclosing his design on the Empire, he put his army in march, and reached Italy before it was known that he had set out. On his arrival in Rome, the Senate, through fear, elected him Emperor and put Julianus to death. After taking this first step, two obstacles still remained to his becoming sole master of the Empire; one in Asia, where Niger who commanded the armies of the East had caused himself to be proclaimed Emperor; the other in the West, where Albinus, who also aspired to the Empire, was in command. And as Severus judged it dangerous to declare open war against both, he resolved to proceed against Niger by arms, and against Albinus by artifice. To the latter, accordingly, he wrote, that having been chosen Emperor by the Senate, he desired to share the dignity with him; that he therefore sent him the title of Caesar, and in accordance with a resolution of the Senate assumed him as his colleague. All which statements Albinus accepted as true. But so soon as Severus had defeated and slain Niger, and restored tranquillity in the East, returning to Rome he complained in the Senate that Albinus, all unmindful of the favours he had received from him, had treacherously sought to destroy him; for which cause he was compelled to go and punish his ingratitude. Whereupon he set forth to seek Albinus in Gaul, where he at once deprived him of his dignities and his life.

Whoever, therefore, examines carefully the actions of this Emperor, will find in him all the fierceness of the lion and all the craft of the fox, and will note how he was feared and respected by the people, yet not hated by the army, and will not be surprised that though a new man, he was able to maintain his hold of so great an Empire. For the splendour of his reputation always shielded him from the odium which the people might otherwise have conceived against him by reason of his cruelty and rapacity.

Caracalla, his son, was likewise a man of great parts, endowed with qualities that made him admirable in the sight of the people, and endeared him to the army, being of a warlike spirit, most patient of fatigue, and contemning all luxury in food and every other effeminacy. Nevertheless, his ferocity and cruelty were so extravagant and unheard of (he having put to death a vast number of the inhabitants of Rome at different times, and the whole of those of Alexandria at a stroke), that he came to be detested by all the world, and so feared even by those whom he had about him, that at the last he was slain by a centurion in the midst of his army.

And here let it be noted that deaths like this which are the result of a deliberate and fixed resolve, cannot be escaped by Princes, since any one who disregards his own life can effect them. A Prince, however, needs the less to fear them as they are seldom attempted. The only precaution he can take is to avoid doing grave wrong to any of those who serve him, or whom he has near him as officers of his Court, a precaution which Caracalla neglected in putting to a shameful death the brother of this centurion, and in using daily threats against the man himself, whom he nevertheless retained as one of his bodyguard. This, as the event showed, was a rash and fatal course.

We come next to Commodus, who, as he took the Empire by hereditary right, ought to have held it with much ease. For being the son of Marcus, he had only to follow in his father's footsteps to content both the people and the soldiery. But being of a cruel and brutal nature, to sate his rapacity at the expense of the people, he sought support from the army, and indulged it in every kind of excess. On the other hand, by an utter disregard of his dignity, in frequently descending into the arena to fight with gladiators, and by other base acts wholly unworthy of the Imperial station, he became contemptible in the eyes of the soldiery; and being on the one hand hated, on the other despised, was at last conspired against and murdered.

The character of Maximinus remains to be touched upon. He was of a very warlike disposition, and on the death of Alexander, of whom we have already spoken, was chosen Emperor by the army who had been displeased with the effeminacy of that Prince. But this dignity he did not long enjoy, since two causes concurred to render him at once odious and contemptible; the one the baseness of his origin, he having at one time herded sheep in Thrace, a fact well known to all, and which led all to look on him with disdain; the other that on being proclaimed Emperor, delaying to repair to Rome and enter on possession of the Imperial throne, he incurred the reputation of excessive cruelty by reason of the many atrocities perpetrated by his prefects in Rome and other parts of the Empire. The result was that the whole world, stirred at once with scorn of his mean birth and with the hatred which the dread of his ferocity inspired, combined against him, Africa leading the way, the Senate and people of Rome and the whole of Italy following. In which conspiracy his own army joined. For they, being engaged in the siege of Aquileja and finding difficulty in reducing it, disgusted with his cruelty, and less afraid of him when they saw so many against him, put him to death.

I need say nothing of Heliogabalus, Macrinus, or Julianus, all of whom being utterly despicable, came to a speedy downfall, but shall conclude these remarks by observing, that the Princes of our own days are less troubled with the difficulty of having to make constant efforts to keep their soldier in good humour. For though they must treat them with some indulgence, the need for doing so is soon over, since none of these Princes possesses a standing army which, like the armies of the Roman Empire, has strengthened with the growth of his government and the administration of his State. And if it was then necessary to satisfy the soldiers rather than the people, because the soldiers were more powerful than the people, now it is more necessary for all Princes, except the Turk and the Soldan, to satisfy the people rather than the soldiery, since the former are more powerful than the latter.

I except the Turk because he has always about him some twelve thousand foot soldiers and fifteen thousand horse, on whom depend the security and strength of his kingdom, and with whom he must needs keep on good terms, all regard for the people being subordinate. The government of the Soldan is similar, so that he too being wholly in the hands of his soldiers, must keep well with them without regard to the people.

And here you are to note that the State of the Soldan, while it is unlike all other Princedoms, resembles the Christian Pontificate in this, that it can neither be classed as new, nor as hereditary. For the sons of a Soldan who dies do not succeed to the kingdom as his heirs, but he who is elected to the post by those who have authority to make such elections. And this being the ancient and established order of things, the Princedoms cannot be accounted new, since none of the difficulties that attend new Princedoms are found in it. For although the Prince be new, the institutions of the State

are old, and are so contrived that the elected Prince is accepted as though he were an hereditary Sovereign.

But returning to the matter in hand, I say that whoever reflects on the above reasoning will see that either hatred or contempt was the ruin of the Emperors whom I have named; and will also understand how it happened that some taking one way and some the opposite, one only by each of these roads came to a happy, and all the rest to an unhappy end. Because for Pertinax and Alexander, they being new Princes, it was useless and hurtful to try to imitate Marcus, who was an hereditary Prince; and similarly for Caracalla, Commodus, and Maximinus it was a fatal error to imitate Severus, since they lacked the qualities that would have enabled them to tread in his footsteps.

In short, a Prince new to the Princedom cannot imitate the actions of Marcus, nor is it necessary that he should imitate all those of Severus; but he should borrow from Severus those parts of his conduct which are needed to serve as a foundation for his government, and from Marcus those suited to maintain it, and render it glorious when once established.

## Chapter XXI

### How a Prince Should Bear Himself So as to Acquire Reputation

Nothing makes a Prince so well thought of as to undertake great enterprises and give striking proofs of his capacity.

Among the Princes of our time Ferdinand of Aragon, the present King of Spain, may almost be accounted a new Prince, since from one of the weakest he has become, for fame and glory, the foremost King in Christendom. And if you consider his achievements you will find them all great and some extraordinary.

In the beginning of his reign he made war on Granada, which enterprise was the foundation of his power. At first he carried on the war leisurely, without fear of interruption, and kept the attention and thoughts of the Barons of Castile so completely occupied with it, that they had no time to think of changes at home. Meanwhile he insensibly acquired reputation among them and authority over them. With the money of the Church and of his subjects he was able to maintain his armies, and during the prolonged contest to lay the foundations of that military discipline which afterwards made him so famous. Moreover, to enable him to engage in still greater undertakings, always covering himself with the cloak of religion, he had recourse to what may be called *pious cruelty*, in driving out and clearing his Kingdom of the Moors; than which exploit none could be more wonderful or uncommon. Using the same pretext he made war on Africa, invaded Italy, and finally attacked France; and being thus constantly busied in planning and executing vast designs, he kept the minds of his subjects in suspense and admiration, and occupied with the results of his actions, which arose one out of another in such close succession as left neither time nor opportunity to oppose them.

Again, it greatly profits a Prince in conducting the internal government of his State, to follow striking methods, such as are recorded of Messer Bernabo of Milan, whenever the remarkable actions of any one in civil life, whether for good or for evil, afford him occasion; and to choose such ways of rewarding and punishing as cannot fail to be much spoken of. But above all, he should strive by all his actions to inspire a sense of his greatness and goodness.

A Prince is likewise esteemed who is a stanch friend and a thorough foe, that is to say, who without reserve openly declares for one against another, this being always a more advantageous course than to stand neutral. For supposing two of your powerful neighbours come to blows, it must either be that you have, or have not, reason to fear the one who comes off victorious. In either case it will always be well for you to declare yourself, and join in frankly with one side or other. For should you fail to do so you are certain, in the former of the cases put, to become the prey of the victor to the satisfaction and delight of the vanquished, and no reason or circumstance that you may plead will avail to shield or shelter you; for the victor dislikes doubtful friends, and such as will not help him at a pinch; and the vanquished will have nothing to say to you, since you would not share his fortunes sword in hand.

When Antiochus, at the instance of the Aetolians, passed into Greece in order to drive out the Romans, he sent envoys to the Achaians, who were friendly to the Romans, exhorting them to stand neutral. The Romans, on the other hand, urged them to take up arms on their behalf. The matter coming to be discussed in the Council of the Achaians, the legate of Antiochus again urged neutrality, whereupon the Roman envoy answered— 'Nothing can be less to your advantage than the course which has been recommended as the best and most useful for your State, namely, to refrain from taking any part in our war, for by standing aloof you will gain neither favour nor fame, but remain the prize of the victor.'

And it will always happen that he who is not your friend will invite you to neutrality, while he who is your friend will call on you to declare yourself openly in arms. Irresolute Princes, to escape immediate danger, commonly follow the neutral path, in most instances to their destruction. But when you pronounce valiantly in favour of one side or other, if he to whom you give your adherence conquers, although he be powerful and you are at his mercy, still he is under obligations to you, and has become your friend; and none are so lost to shame as to destroy with manifest ingratitude, one who has helped them. Besides which, victories are never so complete that the victor can afford to disregard all considerations whatsoever, more especially considerations of justice. On the other hand, if he with whom you take part should lose, you will always be favourably regarded by him; while he can he will aid you, and you become his companion in a cause which may recover.

In the second case, namely, when both combatants are of such limited strength that whichever wins you have no cause to fear, it is all the more prudent for you to take a side, for you will then be ruining the one with the help of the other, who were he wise would endeavour to save him. If he whom you help conquers, he remains in your power, and with your aid he cannot but conquer.

And here let it be noted that a Prince should be careful never to join with one stronger than himself in attacking others, unless, as already said, he be driven to it by necessity. For if he whom you join prevails, you are at his mercy; and Princes, so far as in them lies, should avoid placing themselves at the mercy of others. The Venetians, although they might have declined the alliance, joined with France against the Duke of Milan, which brought about their ruin. But when an alliance cannot be avoided, as was the case with the Florentines when the Pope and Spain together led their armies to attack Lombardy, a Prince, for the reasons given, must take a side. Nor let it be supposed that any State can choose for itself a perfectly safe line of policy. On the contrary, it must reckon on every course which it may take being doubtful; for it happens in all human affairs that we never seek to escape one mischief without falling into another. Prudence therefore consists in knowing how to distinguish degrees of disadvantage, and in accepting a less evil as a good.

Again, a Prince should show himself a patron of merit, and should honour those who excel in every art. He ought accordingly to encourage his subjects by enabling them to pursue their callings, whether mercantile, agricultural, or any other, in security, so that this man shall not be deterred from beautifying his possessions from the apprehension that they may be taken from him, or that other refrain from opening a trade through fear of taxes; and he should provide rewards for those who desire so to employ themselves, and for all who are disposed in any way to add to the greatness of his City or State.

He ought, moreover, at suitable seasons of the year to entertain the people with festivals and shows. And because all cities are divided into guilds and companies, he should show attention to these societies, and sometimes take part in their meetings; offering an example of courtesy and munificence, but always maintaining the dignity of his station, which must under no circumstances be compromised.

## Chapter XXII

### Of the Secretaries of Princes

The choice of Ministers is a matter of no small moment to a Prince. Whether they shall be good or no depends on his prudence, so that the readiest conjecture we can form of the character and sagacity of a Prince, is from seeing what sort of men he has about him. When they are at once capable and faithful, we may always account him wise, since he has known to recognize their merit and to retain their fidelity. But if they be otherwise, we must pronounce unfavourably of him, since he has committed a first fault in making this selection.

There was none who knew Messer Antonio of Venafro, as Minister of Pandolfo Petrucci, Lord of Siena, but thought Pandolfo a most prudent ruler in having him for his servant. And since there are three scales of intelligence, one which understands by itself, a second which understands what is shown it by others, and a third which understands neither by itself nor on the showing of others, the first of which is most excellent, the second good, but the third worthless, we must needs admit that if Pandolfo was not in the first of these degrees, he was in the second; for when one has the judgment to discern the good from the bad in what another says or does, though he be devoid of invention, he can recognize the merits and demerits of his servant, and will commend the former while he corrects the latter. The servant cannot hope to deceive such a master, and will continue good.

As to how a Prince is to know his Minister, this unerring rule may be laid down. When you see a Minister thinking more of himself than of you, and in all his actions seeking his own ends, that man can never be a good Minister or one that you can trust. For he who has the charge of the State committed to him, ought not to think of himself, but only of his Prince, and should never bring to the notice of the latter what does not directly concern him. On the other hand, to keep his Minister good, the Prince should be considerate of him, dignifying him, enriching him, binding him to himself by benefits, and sharing with him the honours as well as the burthens of the State, so that the abundant honours and wealth bestowed upon him may divert him from seeking them at other hands; while the great responsibilities wherewith he is charged may lead him to dread change, knowing that he cannot stand alone without his master's support. When Prince and Minister are upon this footing they can mutually trust one another; but when the contrary is the case, it will always fare ill with one or other of them.

## Chapter XXIII

### That Flatterers Should Be Shunned

One error into which Princes, unless very prudent or very fortunate in their choice of friends, are apt to fall, is of so great importance that I must not pass it over. I mean in respect of flatterers. These abound in Courts, because men take such pleasure in their own concerns, and so deceive themselves with regard to them, that they can hardly escape this plague; while even in the effort to escape it there is risk of their incurring contempt.

For there is no way to guard against flattery but by letting it be seen that you take no offense in hearing the truth: but when every one is free to tell you the truth respect falls short. Wherefore a prudent Prince should follow a middle course, by choosing certain discreet men from among his subjects, and allowing them alone free leave to speak their minds on any matter on which he asks their opinion, and on none other. But he ought to ask their opinion on everything, and after hearing what they have to say, should reflect and judge for himself. And with these counsellors collectively, and with each of them separately, his bearing should be such, that each and all of them may know that the more freely they declare their thoughts the better they will be liked. Besides these, the Prince should hearken to no others, but should follow the course determined on, and afterwards adhere firmly to his resolves. Whoever acts otherwise is either undone by flatterers, or from continually vacillating as opinions vary, comes to be held in light esteem.

With reference to this matter, I shall cite a recent instance. Father Luke, who is attached to the Court of the present Emperor Maximilian, in speaking of his Majesty told me, that he seeks advice from none, yet never has his own way; and this from his following a course contrary to that above recommended. For being of a secret disposition, he never discloses his intentions to any, nor asks their opinion; and it is only when his plans are to be carried out that they begin to be discovered and known, and at the same time they begin to be thwarted by those he has about him, when he being facile gives way. Hence it happens that what he does one day, he undoes the next; that his wishes and designs are never fully ascertained; and that it is impossible to build on his resolves.

A Prince, therefore, ought always to take counsel, but at such times and reasons only as he himself pleases, and not when it pleases others; nay, he should discourage every one from obtruding advice on matters on which it is not sought. But he should be free in asking advice, and afterwards as regards the matters on which he has asked it, a patient hearer of the truth, and even displeased should he perceive that any one, from whatever motive, keeps it back.

But those who think that every Prince who has a name for prudence owes it to the wise counsellors he has around him, and not to any merit of his own, are certainly mistaken; since it is an unerring rule and of universal application that a Prince who is not wise himself cannot be well advised by others, unless by chance he surrender himself to be wholly governed by some one adviser who happens to be supremely prudent; in which case he may, indeed, be well advised; but not for long, since such an adviser will soon deprive him of his Government. If he listen to a multitude of advisers, the Prince who is not wise will never have consistent counsels, nor will he know of himself how to reconcile them. Each of his counsellors will study his own advantage, and the Prince will be unable to detect or correct them. Nor could it well be otherwise, for men will always grow rogues on your hands unless they find themselves under a necessity to be honest.

Hence it follows that good counsels, whencesoever they come, have their origin in the prudence of the Prince, and not the prudence of the Prince in wise counsels.

## Chapter XXIV

### Why the Princes of Italy Have Lost Their States

The lessons above taught if prudently followed will make a new Prince seem like an old one, and will soon seat him in his place more firmly and securely than if his authority had the sanction of time. For the actions of a new Prince are watched much more closely than those of an hereditary Prince; and when seen to be good are far more effectual than antiquity of blood in gaining men over and attaching them to his cause. For men are more nearly touched by things present than by things past, and when they find themselves well off as they are, enjoy their felicity and seek no further; nay, are ready to do their utmost in defence of the new Prince, provided he be not wanting to himself in other respects. In this way there accrues to him a twofold glory, in having laid the foundations of the new Princedom, and in having strengthened and adorned it with good laws and good arms, with faithful friends and great deeds; as, on the other hand, there is a double disgrace in one who has been born to a Princedom losing it by his own want of wisdom.

And if we contemplate those Lords who in our own times have lost their dominions in Italy, such as the King of Naples, the Duke of Milan, and others, in the first place we shall see, that in respect of arms they have, for reasons already dwelt on, been all alike defective; and next, that some of them have either had the people against them, or if they have had the people with them, have not known how to secure themselves against their nobles. For without such defects as these, States powerful enough to keep an army in the field are never overthrown.

Philip of Macedon, not the father of Alexander the Great, but he who was vanquished by Titus Quintius, had no great State as compared with the strength of the Romans and Greeks who attacked him. Nevertheless, being a Prince of a warlike spirit, and skilful in gaining the good will of the people and in securing the fidelity of the nobles, he maintained himself for many years against his assailants, and in the end, though he lost some towns, succeeded in saving his Kingdom.

Let those Princes of ours, therefore, who, after holding them for a length of years, have lost their dominions, blame not Fortune but their own inertness. For never having reflected in tranquil times that there might come a change (and it is human nature when the sea is calm not to think of storms), when adversity overtook them, they thought not of defence but only of escape, hoping that their people, disgusted with the arrogance of the conqueror, would some day recall them.

This course may be a good one to follow when all others fail, but it were the height of folly, trusting to it, to abandon every other; since none would wish to fall on the chance of some one else being found to lift him up. It may not happen that you are recalled by your people, or if it happen, it gives you no security. It is an ignoble resource, since it does not depend on you for its success; and those modes of defence are alone good, certain and lasting, which depend upon yourself and your own worth.

# Chapter XXV

## What Fortune Can Effect in Human Affairs, and How She May Be Withstood

I am not ignorant that many have been and are of the opinion that human affairs are so governed by Fortune and by God, that men cannot alter them by any prudence of theirs, and indeed have no remedy against them, and for this reason have come to think that it is not worth while to labour much about anything, but that they must leave everything to be determined by chance.

Often when I turn the matter over, I am in part inclined to agree with this opinion, which has had the readier acceptance in our own times from the great changes in things which we have seen, and every day see happen contrary to all human expectation. Nevertheless, that our free will be not wholly set aside, I think it may be the case that Fortune is the mistress of one half our actions, and yet leaves the control of the other half, or a little less, to ourselves. And I would liken her to one of those wild torrents which, when angry, overflow the plains, sweep away trees and houses, and carry off soil from one bank to throw it down upon the other. Every one flees before them, and yields to their fury without the least power to resist. And yet, though this be their nature, it does not follow that in seasons of fair weather, men cannot, by constructing weirs and moles, take such precautions as will cause them when again in flood to pass off by some artificial channel, or at least prevent their course from being so uncontrolled and destructive. And so it is with Fortune, who displays her might where there is no organized strength to resist her, and directs her onset where she knows that there is neither barrier nor embankment to confine her.

And if you look at Italy, which has been at once the seat of these changes and their cause, you will perceive that it is a field without embankment or barrier. For if, like Germany, France, and Spain, it had been guarded with sufficient skill, this inundation, if it ever came upon us, would never have wrought the violent changes which we have witnessed.

This I think enough to say generally touching resistance to Fortune. But confining myself more closely to the matter in hand, I note that one day we see a Prince prospering and the next day overthrown, without detecting any change in his nature or character. This, I believe, comes chiefly from a cause already dwelt upon, namely, that a Prince who rests wholly on Fortune is ruined when she changes. Moreover, I believe that he will prosper most whose mode of acting best adapts itself to the character of the times; and conversely that he will be unprosperous, with whose mode of acting the times do not accord. For we see that men in these matters which lead to the end that each has before him, namely, glory and wealth, proceed by different ways, one with caution, another with impetuosity, one with violence, another with subtlety, one with patience, another with its contrary; and that by one or other of these different courses each may succeed.

Again, of two who act cautiously, you shall find that one attains his end, the other not, and that two of different temperament, the one cautious, the other impetuous, are equally successful. All which happens from no other cause than that the character of the times accords or does not accord with their methods of acting. And hence it comes, as I have already said, that two operating differently arrive at the same result, and two operating similarly, the one succeeds and the other not. On this likewise depend the vicissitudes of Fortune. For if to one who conducts himself with caution and patience, time and circumstances are propitious, so that his method of acting is good, he goes on prospering; but if these change he is ruined, because he does not change his method of acting.

For no man is found so prudent as to know how to adapt himself to these changes, both because he cannot deviate from the course to which nature inclines him, and because, having always prospered while adhering to one path, he cannot be persuaded that it would be well for him to forsake it. And so when occasion requires the cautious man to act impetuously, he cannot do so and is undone: whereas, had he changed his nature with time and circumstances, his fortune would have been unchanged.

Pope Julius II proceeded with impetuosity in all his undertakings, and found time and circumstances in such harmony with his mode of acting that he always obtained a happy result. Witness his first expedition against Bologna, when Messer Giovanni Bentivoglio was yet living. The Venetians were not favourable to the enterprise; nor was the King of Spain. Negotiations respecting it with the King of France were still open. Nevertheless, the Pope with his wonted hardihood and impetuosity marched in person on the expedition, and by this movement brought the King of Spain and the Venetians to a check, the latter through fear, the former from his eagerness to recover the entire Kingdom of Naples; at the same time, he dragged after him the King of France, who, desiring to have the Pope for an ally in humbling the Venetians, on finding him already in motion saw that he could not refuse him his soldiers without openly offending him.

By the impetuosity of his movements, therefore, Julius effected what no other Pontiff endowed with the highest human prudence could. For had he, as any other Pope would have done, put off his departure from Rome until terms had been settled and everything duly arranged, he never would have succeeded. For the King of France would have found a thousand pretexts to delay him, and the others would have menaced him with a thousand alarms. I shall not touch upon his other actions, which were all of a like character, and all of which had a happy issue, since the shortness of his life did not allow him to experience reverses. But if times had overtaken him, rendering a cautious line of conduct necessary, his ruin must have ensued, since he never could have departed from those methods to which nature inclined him.

To be brief, I say that since Fortune changes and men stand fixed in their old ways, they are prosperous so long as there is congruity between them, and the reverse when there is not. Of this, however, I am well persuaded, that it is better to be impetuous than cautious. For Fortune is a woman who to be kept under must be beaten and roughly handled; and we see that she suffers herself to be more readily mastered by those who so treat her than by those who are more timid in their approaches. And always, like a woman, she favours the young, because they are less scrupulous and fiercer, and command her with greater audacity.

# Chapter XXVI

## An Exhortation to Liberate Italy from the Barbarians

Turning over in my mind all the matters which have above been considered, and debating with myself whether in Italy at the present hour the times are such as might serve to confer honour on a new Prince, and whether a fit opportunity now offers for a prudent and valiant leader to bring about changes glorious for himself and beneficial to the whole Italian people, it seems to me that so many conditions combine to further such an enterprise, that I know of no time so favourable to it as the present. And if, as I have said, it was necessary in order to display the valour of Moses that the children of Israel should be slaves in Egypt, and to know the greatness and courage of Cyrus that the Persians should be oppressed by the Medes, and to illustrate the excellence of Theseus that the Athenians should be scattered and divided, so at this hour, to prove the worth of some Italian hero, it was required that Italy should be brought to her present abject condition, to be more a slave than the Hebrew, more oppressed than the Persian, more disunited than the Athenian, without a head, without order, beaten, spoiled, torn in pieces, over-run and abandoned to destruction in every shape.

But though, heretofore, glimmerings may have been discerned in this man or that, whence it might be conjectured that he was ordained by God for her redemption, nevertheless it has afterwards been seen in the further course of his actions that Fortune has disowned him; so that our country, left almost without life, still waits to know who it is that

is to heal her bruises, to put an end to the devastation and plunder of Lombardy, to the exactions and imposts of Naples and Tuscany, and to stanch those wounds of hers which long neglect has changed into running sores.

We see how she prays God to send some one to rescue her from these barbarous cruelties and oppressions. We see too how ready and eager she is to follow any standard were there only some one to raise it. But at present we see no one except in your illustrious House (pre-eminent by its virtues and good fortune, and favoured by God and by the Church whose headship it now holds), who could undertake the part of a deliverer.

But for you this will not be too hard a task, if you keep before your eyes the lives and actions of those whom I have named above. For although these men were singular and extraordinary, after all they were but men, not one of whom had so great an opportunity as now presents itself to you. For their undertakings were not more just than this, nor more easy, nor was God more their friend than yours. The justice of the cause is conspicuous; for that war is just which is necessary, and those arms are sacred from which we derive our only hope. Everywhere there is the strongest disposition to engage in this cause; and where the disposition is strong the difficulty cannot be great, provided you follow the methods observed by those whom I have set before you as models.

But further, we see here extraordinary and unexampled proofs of Divine favour. The sea has been divided; the cloud has attended you on your way; the rock has flowed with water; the manna has rained from heaven; everything has concurred to promote your greatness. What remains to be done must be done by you; since in order not to deprive us of our free will and such share of glory as belongs to us, God will not do everything himself.

Nor is to be marvelled at if none of those Italians I have named has been able to effect what we hope to see effected by your illustrious House; or that amid so many revolutions and so many warlike movements it should always appear as though the military virtues of Italy were spent; for this comes her old system being defective, and from no one being found among us capable to strike out a new. Nothing confers such honour on the reformer of a State, as do the new laws and institutions which he devises; for these when they stand on a solid basis and have a greatness in their scope, make him admired and venerated. And in Italy material is not wanting for improvement in every form. If the head be weak the limbs are strong, and we see daily in single combats, or where few are engaged, how superior are the strength, dexterity, and intelligence of Italians. But when it comes to armies, they are nowhere, and this from no other reason than the defects of their leaders. For those who are skilful in arms will not obey, and every one thinks himself skillful, since hitherto we have had none among us so raised by merit or by fortune above his fellows that they should yield him the palm. And hence it happens that for the long period of twenty years, during which so many wars have taken place, whenever there has been an army purely Italian it has always been beaten. To this testify, first Taro, then Alessandria, Capua, Genoa, Vaila, Bologna, Mestri.

If then your illustrious House should seek to follow the example of those great men who have delivered their country in past ages, it is before all things necessary, as the true foundation of every such attempt, to be provided with national troops, since you can have no braver, truer, or more faithful soldiers; and although every single man of them be good, collectively they will be better, seeing themselves commanded by their own Prince, and honoured and esteemed by him. That you may be able, therefore, to defend yourself against the foreigner with Italian valour, the first step is to provide yourself with an army such as this.

And although the Swiss and the Spanish infantry are each esteemed formidable, there are yet defects in both, by reason of which troops trained on a different system might not merely withstand them, but be certain of defeating them. For the Spaniards cannot resist cavalry and the Swiss will give way before infantry if they find them as resolute as themselves at close quarters. Whence it has been seen, and may be seen again, that the Spaniards cannot sustain the onset of the French men-at-arms and that the Swiss are broken by the Spanish foot. And although of this last we have no complete instance, we have yet an indication of it in the battle of Ravenna, where the Spanish infantry confronted the German companies who have the same discipline as the Swiss; on which occasion the Spaniards by their agility and with the aid of their bucklers forced their way under the pikes, and stood ready to close with the Germans, who were no longer in a position to defend themselves; and had they not been charged by cavalry, they must have put the Germans to utter rout. Knowing, then, the defects of each of these kinds of troops, you can train your men on some different system, to withstand cavalry and not to fear infantry. To effect this, will not require the creation of any new forces, but simply a change in the discipline of the old. And these are matters in reforming which the new Prince acquires reputation and importance.

This opportunity then, for Italy at last to look on her deliverer, ought not to be allowed to pass away. With what love he would be received in all those Provinces which have suffered from the foreign inundation, with what thirst for vengeance, with what fixed fidelity, with what devotion, and what tears, no words of mine can declare. What gates would be closed against him? What people would refuse him obedience? What jealousy would stand in his way? What Italian but would yield him homage? This barbarian tyranny stinks in all nostrils.

Let your illustrious House therefore take upon itself this enterprise with all the courage and all the hopes with which a just cause is undertaken; so that under your standard this our country may be ennobled, and under your auspices be fulfilled the words of Petrarch:—

> Brief will be the strife
> When valour arms against barbaric rage;
> For the bold spirit of the bygone age
> Still warms Italian hearts with life.

# On Secular Authority

By Martin Luther

## Temporal Authority: To What Extent It Should Be Obeyed

To the illustrious high born prince and lord, Lord John, Duke of Saxony, Landgrave of Thuringia Margrave of Meissen, my gracious lord.

Grace and peace in Christ. Again, illustrious, highborn prince, gracious lord, necessity is laid upon me, and the entreaties of many, and above all your Princely Grace's wishes, impel me to write about temporal authority and the sword it bears, how to use it in a Christian manner, and to what extent men are obligated to obey it. You are perturbed over Christ's injunction in Matthew 5 [:39, 25, 40], "Do not resist evil, but make friends with your accuser; and if any one should take your coat, let him have your cloak as well"; and Romans 12[:19], "Vengeance is mine, I will repay, says the Lord." These very texts were used long ago against St. Augustine by the prince Volusian, who charged that Christian teaching permits the wicked to do evil, and is incompatible with the temporal sword.

The sophists in the universities have also been perplexed by these texts, because they could not reconcile the two things. In order not to make heathen of the princes, they taught that Christ did not demand these things but merely offered them as advice or counsel to those who would be perfect. So Christ had to become a liar and be in error in order that the princes might come off with honor, for they could not exalt the princes without degrading Christ-wretched blind sophists that they are. And their poisonous error has spread thus to the whole world until everyone regards these teachings of Christ not as precepts binding on all Christians alike but as mere counsels for the perfect. It has gone so far that they have granted the imperfect estate of the sword and of the temporal authority not only to the estate of the bishops, but even to the pope, that most perfect estate of all; in fact, they have ascribed it to no one on earth so completely as to him! So thoroughly has the devil taken control of the sophists and the universities that they themselves do not know how they speak or teach.

I hope, however, that I may instruct the princes and the temporal authorities in such a way that they will remain Christians—and Christ will remain Lord—and yet Christ's

143

commands will not for their sake have to become mere counsels.

I do this as a humble service to your Princely Grace, for the benefit of everyone who may need it, and to the praise and glory of Christ our Lord. I commend your Princely Grace with all your kin to the grace of God. May he mercifully have you in his keeping.

At Wittenberg, New Year's Day, 1523.
Your Princely Grace's obedient servant,
    Martin Luther

Some time ago I addressed a little book to the German nobility, setting forth their Christian office and functions. How far they acted on my suggestions is only too evident. Hence, I must change my tactics and write them, this time, what they should omit and not do. I fear this new effort will have as little effect on them as the other, and that they will continue to be princes and never become Christians. For God the Almighty has made our rulers mad; they actually think they can do—and order their subjects to do—whatever they please. And the subjects make the mistake of believing that they, in turn, are bound to obey their rulers in everything. It has gone so far that the rulers have begun ordering the people to get rid of certain books, and to believe and conform to what the rulers prescribe. They are thereby presumptuously setting themselves in God's place, lording it over men's consciences and faith, and schooling the Holy Spirit according to their own crackbrained ideas. Nevertheless, they let it be known that they are not to be contradicted, and are to be called gracious lords all the same.

They issue public proclamations, and say that this is the emperor's command and that they want to be obedient Christian princes, just as if they really meant it and no one noticed the scoundrel behind the mask. If the emperor were to take a castle or a city from them or command some other injustice, we should then see how quickly they would find themselves obliged to resist the emperor and disobey him. But when it comes to fleecing the poor or venting their spite on the word of God, it becomes a matter of "obedience to the imperial command." Such people were formerly called scoundrels; now they have to be called obedient Christian princes. Still they will not permit anyone to appear before them for a hearing or to defend himself, no matter how humbly he may petition. If the emperor or anyone else were to treat them this way, they would regard it as quite intolerable. Such are the princes who today rule the empire in the German lands. This is also why things are going so well in all the lands, as we see!.

Because the raging of such fools tends toward the suppression of the Christian faith, the denying of the divine word, and the blaspheming of the Divine Majesty, I can and will no longer just look at my ungracious lords and angry nobles; I shall have to resist them, at least with words. And since I have not been in terror of their idol, the pope, who threatens to deprive me of soul and heaven, I must show that I am not in terror of his lackeys and bullies who threaten to deprive me of body and of earth. God grant that they may have the rage until the gray coats perish, and help us that we may not die of their threatenings. Amen.

First, we must provide a sound basis for the civil law and sword so no one will doubt that it is in the world by God's will and ordinance. The passages which do this are the following: Romans 12, "Let every soul [seele] be subject to the governing authority, for their in no authority except from God; the authority which everywhere [allenthalben] exists has been ordained by God. He then who resists the governing authority resists the ordinance of God, and he who resists God's ordinance will incur judgment." Again, in I Peter 2 [:13–14], "Be subject to every kind of human ordinance, whether it be to the king as supreme, or to governors, as those who have been sent by him to punish the wicked and to praise the righteous."

The law of this temporal sword has existed from the beginning of the world. For when Cain slew his brother Abel, he was in such great terror of being killed in turn that God even placed a special prohibition on it and suspended the sword for his sake, so that no one was to slay him [Gen. 4:14–15]. He would not have had this fear if he had not seen and heard from Adam that murderers are to be slain. Moreover, after the Flood, God reestablished and confirmed this in unmistakable terms when he said in Genesis 9[:6], "Whoever sheds the blood of man, by man shall his blood be shed." This cannot be understood as a plague or punishment of God upon murderers, for many murderers who are punished in other ways or pardoned altogether continue to live, and eventually die by means other than the sword. Rather, it is said of the law of the sword, that a murderer is guilty of death and in justice is to be slain by the sword. Now if justice should be hindered or the sword have become negligent so that the murderer dies a natural death, Scripture in not on that account false when it says, "Whoever sheds the blood of man, by man shall his blood be shed." The credit or blame belongs to men if this law instituted by God is not carried out; just as other commandments of God, too, are broken.

Afterward it was also confirmed by the law of Moses, Exodus 21 [:14], "If a man willfully kills another, you shall take him from my altar, that he may die." And again, in the same chapter, "A life for a life, an eye for an eye, a tooth for a tooth, a foot for a foot, a hand for a hand, a wound for a wound, a stripe for a stripe." In addition, Christ also confirms it when he says to Peter in the garden, "He that takes the sword will perish by the sword" [Matt. 26:52], which is to be interpreted exactly like the Genesis 9 [:6] passage, "Whoever sheds the blood of man," etc. Christ is undoubtedly referring in these words to that very passage which he thereby wishes to cite and confirm. John the Baptist also teaches the same thing. When the soldiers asked him what they should do, he answered, "Do neither violence nor injustice to any one, and be content with your wages" [Luke 3:14]. If the sword were not a godly estate, he should have directed them to get out of it, since he was suppose to make the people perfect and instruct them in a proper Christian way. Hence, it is certain and clear enough that it is God's will that the temporal sword and law be used for the punishment of the wicked and the protection of the upright.

Second. There appear to be powerful arguments to the contrary. Christ says in Matthew 5[:38–41], "You have heard that it was said to them of old: An eye for an eye, a tooth for a tooth. But I say to you, Do not resist evil; but if anyone strikes you on the right cheek, turn to him the other also. And if anyone would sue you and take your coat, let them have your cloak as well. And if anyone forces you to go one mile, go with him two miles," etc. Likewise Paul in Romans 12 [:19], "Beloved, defend not yourselves, but leave it to the wrath of God; for it is written, 'Vengeance is mine; I will repay says the Lord.'" And in Matthew 5 [:44], "Love your enemies, do good to them that hate you." And again in I Peter 2 [3:9], "Do not return evil for evil, or reviling for reviling," etc. These and similar passages would certainly make it appear as though in the New Testament Christians were to have no temporal sword.

Hence, the sophists also say that Christ has thereby abolished the law of Moses. Of such commandments they make "counsels" for the perfect. They divide Christian teaching and Christians into two classes. One part they call the perfect, and assign to it such counsels. The other they call the imperfect, and assign to it the commandments. This they do out of sheer wantonness and caprice, without any scriptural basis. They fail to see that in the same passage Christ lays such stress on his teachings that he is unwilling to have the least word of it set aside, and condemns to hell those who do not love their enemies. Therefore, we must interpret these passages differently, so that Christ's words may apply to everyone alike, be he perfect, or imperfect. For perfection and imperfection are do not consist in works, and do not establish any distinct external order among Christians. They exist in the heart, in faith and love, so that those who believe and love the most are the perfect ones, whether they be outwardly male or female, prince or peasant, monk or layman. For the love and faith produce no sects or outward differences.

Third. Here we must divide the children of Adam and all mankind into two classes, the first belonging to the kingdom of God, the second to the kingdom of the world. Those who belong to the kingdom of God are all true believers who are in Christ and under Christ, for Christ is King and Lords in the kingdom of God, as Psalm 2 [:6] and all of Scripture says. For this reason he came into the world, that he might begin God's kingdom and establish it in the world. Therefore, he says before Pilate, "My kingdom is not of the world, but every one who is of the truth hears my voice." [John 18:36–37]. In the gospel he continually refers to the kingdom of God, and says, "Amend your ways, the kingdom of God and his righteousness" [Matt. 6:33]. He also calls the gospel a gospel of the kingdom of God; because it teaches, governs, and upholds God's kingdom.

Now observe, these people need no temporal law or sword. If all the world were composed of real Christians, that is, true believers, there would be no need for benefits from prince, king, lord, sword, or law. They would serve no purpose, since Christians have in their heart the Holy Spirit, who both teaches and makes them to do injustice to no one, to love everyone, and to suffer injustice and even death willingly and cheerfully at the hands of anyone. Where there is nothing but the unadulterated doing of right and bearing of wrong, there is no need for any suit, litigation, court, judge, penalty, law, or sword. For this reason it is impossible that the temporal sword and law should find any work to do among Christians, since they do of their own accord much more than all the laws and teachings can demand, just as Paul says in I Timothy 1 [:9], "The law is not laid down for the just but for the lawless."

Why is this? It is because the righteous man of his own accord does all and more than the law demands. But the unrighteous do nothing that the law demands; therefore, they need the law to instruct, constrain, and compel them to do good. A good tree needs no instruction or law to bear good fruit; its nature causes it to bear according to its kind without any law or instruction. I would take to be quite a fool any man who would make a book full of laws and statutes for an apple tree telling it how to bear apples and not thorns, when the tree is able by its own nature to do this better than the man with all his books can describe and demand. Just so, by the Spirit and by faith all Christians are so thoroughly disposed and conditioned in their very nature that they do right and keep the law better than one can teach them with all manner of statutes; so far as they themselves are concerned, no statutes or laws are needed.

You ask: Why, then, did God give so many commandments to all mankind, and why does Christ prescribe in the gospel so many things for us to do? Of this I have written at length in the Postils and elsewhere. To put it here as briefly as possible, Paul says that the law has been laid down for the sake of the lawless [I Tim. 1:9], that is, so that those who are not Christians may through the law be restrained outwardly from evil deeds, as we shall later. Now since no one is by nature Christians or righteous, but altogether sinful and wicked, God through the law puts them all under restraint so they dare not willfully implement their wickedness in actual deeds. In addition, Paul ascribes to the law another function in Romans 7 and Galatians 2, that of teaching men to recognize sin in order that it may make them humble unto grace and unto faith in Christ. Christ does the same thing here in Matthew 5 [:39], where he teaches that we should not resist evil; by this he is interpreting the law and teaching what ought to be and must be the state and temper of a true Christian, as we shall hear further later on.

Fourth. All who are not Christians belong to the kingdom of the world and are under the law. There are few true believers, and still fewer who live a Christian life, who do not resist evil and indeed themselves do no evil. For this reason God has provided for them a different government beyond the Christian estate and kingdom of God. He has subjected them to the sword so that, even though they would like to, they are unable to practice their wickedness, and if they do practice it they cannot do so without their wickedness, and if they do practice it they cannot do so without fear or with success and impunity. In the same way a savage wild beast is bound with chains and ropes so that is cannot bite and tear as it would normally do, even though it would like to; whereas a tame and gentle animal needs no restraint, but is harmless despite the lack of chains and ropes.

If this were not so, men would devour one another, seeing that the whole world is evil and that among thousands there is scarcely a single true Christian. No one could support wife and child, feed himself, and serve God. The world would be reduced to chaos. For this reason God has ordained two governments: the spiritual, by which the Holy Spirit produces Christians and righteous people under Christ; and the temporal, which restrains the un-Christian and wicked so that—no thanks to them—they are obliged to keep still and to maintain an outward peace. Thus does St. Paul interpret the temporal sword in Romans 13 [:3], when he says it is not a terror to good conduct but to bad. And Peter says it is for the punishment of the wicked [I Peter 2:14].

If anyone attempted to rule the world by the gospel and to abolish all temporal law and sword on the plea that all are baptized and Christian, and that, according to the gospel, there shall be among them no law or sword—or need for either—pray tell me, friend, what would he be doing? He would be loosing the ropes and chains of the savage wild beasts and letting them bite and mangle everyone, meanwhile insisting that they were harmless, tame, and gentle creatures; but I would have the proof in my wounds. Just so would the wicked under the name of Christian abuse evangelical freedom, carrying on their rascality, and insist that they were Christians subject neither to the law not sword, as some are already raving and ranting.

To such a one we must say: Certainly it is true that Christians, so far as they themselves are concerned, are subject neither to law nor sword, have need of either. But take heed and first fill the world with real Christian before you attempt to rule it in a Christian or evangelical manner. This you will never accomplish; for the world and the masses are and always will be un-Christian, even if they are all baptized and Christian in names. Christians are few and far between (as they say is). Therefore, it is out of the question that there should be a common Christian government over the whole world, or indeed over a single country or any considerable body of the people, for the wicked always outnumber the good. Hence, a man who would venture to govern an entire country or the world with the gospel would be like a shepherd who should put together in one fold wolves, lions, eagles, and sheep, and let them mingle freely with one another, saying, "Help yourselves, and be good and peaceful toward one another. The fold is open, there is plenty of food. You need have no fear of dogs and clubs." The sheep would doubtless keep the peace and allow themselves to be fed and governed peacefully, but they would not live long, nor would one beast survive another.

For this reason one must carefully distinguish between these two governments. Both must be permitted to remain; the one to produce righteousness, the other to bring about external peace and prevent evil deeds. Neither one is sufficient in the world without the other. No one can become righteous in the sight of God by means of the temporal government, without Christ's spiritual government. Christ's government does not extend over all men; rather, Christians are always a minority in the midst of non-Christians. Now

where temporal government or law alone prevails, there sheer hypocrisy is inevitable, even though the commandments be God's own. For without the Holy Spirit in the heart no one becomes truly righteous, no matter how fine the works he does. On the other hand, where the spiritual government alone prevails over land and people, there wickedness is given free rein and the door is open for all manner of rascality, for the world as a whole cannot receive or comprehend it.

Now you see the intent of Christ's words which we quoted above from Matthew 5, that Christians should not go to law or use the temporal sword among themselves. Actually, he says this only to his beloved Christians, those who alone accept it and act accordingly, who do not make "counsels" out of it as the sophists do, but in their heart are so disposed and conditioned [genaturt] by the Spirit that they do evil to no one and willingly endure evil at the hands of others. If now the whole world were Christian in this sense, then these words would apply to all, and all would act accordingly. Since the world in un-Christian, however, these words do not apply to all; and all do not act accordingly, but are under another government in which those who are not Christian are kept under external constraint and compelled to keep the peace and do what is good.

This is also why Christ did not wield the sword, or give it a place in his kingdom. For he is a king over Christians and rulers by his Holy Spirit alone, without law. Although he sanctions the sword, he did not make use of it, for it serves no purpose in his kingdom, in which there are none but the upright. Hence, David of old was not permitted to build the temple [II Sam. 7:4–13], because he had wielded the sword and had shed much blood. Not that he had done wrong thereby, but because he could not be a type of Christ, who without the sword was to have a kingdom of peace. It had to be built instead by Solomon, whose name in German means "Frederich" or "peaceful"; he had a peaceful kingdom, by which the truly peaceful kingdom of Christ, the real Frederich and Solomon, could be represented. Again, "during the entire building of the temple no tool of iron was heard," as the text says [I Kings 6:7]; all for this reason, that Christ, without constraint and force, without law and sword, was to have a people who would serve him willingly.

That it is what the prophets mean in Psalm 110 [:3], "Your people will act of their own free volition"; and in Isaiah 11 [:9], "They shall not hurt or destroy in all my holy mountain"; and again in Isaiah 2 {:4}, "They shall beat their swords into plowshares and their spears into pruning hooks, and no one shall lift up the sword against another, neither shall they put their efforts into war anymore," etc. Whoever would extend the application of these and similar passages to wherever Christ's name is mentioned, would entirely pervert the Scripture; rather, they are spoken only of true Christians, who really do this among themselves.

Fifth, But you say: if Christians then do not need the temporal sword or law, why does Paul say to all Christians in Romans 13 [:1], "Let all souls be subject to the governing authority," and St. Peter, "Be subject to every human ordinance" [I Pet. 2:13], etc., as quoted? Answer: I have just said that Christians, among themselves, need no law or sword, since it is neither necessary nor useful for them. Since a true Christian lives and labors on earth not for himself alone but for his neighbor, he does by the very nature of his spirit even what he himself has no need of, but it is needful and useful to his neighbor. Because the sword is most beneficial and necessary for the whole world in order to preserve peace, punish sin, and restrain the wicked, the Christian submits most willingly to the rule of the sword, pays his taxes, honors those in, serves, helps, and does all he can to assist the governing authority, that it may continue to function and be held in honor and fear. Although he has no need of these things for himself—to him they are not essential—nevertheless, he concerns himself about what is serviceable and of benefit to others, as Paul teaches in Ephesians 5 [:21–6:9].

Just as he performs all other works of love which he himself does not need—he does not visit the sick in order that he himself might be made well, or feed others because he himself needs food—so he serves the governing authority not because he needs it but for the sake of others, that they may be protected and that the wicked may not become worse. He loses nothing by this; such service in no way harms him, yet it is of great benefit to the world. If he did not serve he would be acting not as a Christian but even contrary to love; he would also be setting a bad example to others who in like manner would not submit to authority, even though they were not Christians. In this way the gospel would be brought into disrepute, as though it taught insurrection and produced self-willed people unwilling to benefit or serve others, when in fact it make a Christian the servant of all. Thus in Matthew 17 [:27} Christ paid the half-shelked tax that he might not offend them, although he had no need to do so.

Thus you observe in the words of Christ quoted above from Matthew 5 that he clearly teaches that Christians among themselves should have no temporal sword or law. He does not, however, forbid one to serve and be subject to those who do have the secular sword or law. Rather, since you do not need it and should not have it, you are to serve all the more those who have not to such heights as you and who therefore do still need it. Although you do not need to have your enemy punished, your afflicted neighbor does. You should help him that he may have peace and that his enemy might be curbed, but this is not possible unless the governing authority is honored and feared. Christ does not say, "You shall not serve the governing authority or be subject to it," but rather, "Do not resist evil" [Matt. 5:39], as much to say, "Behave in such a way that you bear everything, so that you may not need the governing authority to help you and serve you or be beneficial or essential for you, but that you in turn may help and serve it, being beneficial and essential to it. I would have you be too exalted and far too noble to have any need of it; it should rather have need of you."

Sixth. You ask whether a Christian too may bear the temporal sword and punish the wicked, since Christ's words, "Do not resist evil," are so clear and definite that the sophists have had to make of them a "counsel." Answer: You have now heard two propositions. One is that the sword can have no place among Christians; therefore, you cannot bear it among Christians or hold it over them, for they do not need it. The question, therefore, must be referred to the other group, the non-Christians, whether you may bear it there in a Christian manner. Here the other proposition applies, that you are under obligation to serve and assist the sword by whatever means you can, with body, goods, honor, and soul. For it is something which you do not need, but which is very beneficial and essential for the whole world and for your neighbor. Therefore, if you see that there is a lack of hangmen, constables, judges, lords, or princes, and you find that you

are qualified, you should offer your services and seek the position, that the essential government authority may not be despised and become enfeebled or perish. The world cannot and dare not dispense with it.

Here is the reason why you should do this: In such a case you should be entering entirely into the service and work of others, which would be of advantage neither to yourself nor your property or honor, but only to your neighbor and to others. You would be doing it not with the purpose of avenging yourself or returning evil for evil, but for the good of your neighbor and for the maintenance of the safety and peace of others. For yourself, you would abide by the gospel and govern yourself according to Christ's word [Matt. 5:39–40], gladly turning the other cheek and letting the cloak go with the coat when the matter concerned you and your cause.

In this way two propositions are brought into harmony with one another: at one and the same time you satisfy God's kingdom inwardly and the kingdom of the world outwardly. You suffer evil and injustice, and yet at the same time you punish evil and injustice; you do not resist evil, and yet at the same time, you do resist it. In the one case, you consider yourself and what is yours; in the other, you consider your neighbor and what is his. In what concerns you and yours, you govern yourself by the gospel and suffer injustice toward yourself as a true Christian; in what concerns the person or property of others, you govern yourself according to love and tolerate no injustice toward your neighbor. The gospel does not forbid this; in fact, in other places it actually commands it.

From the beginning of the world all the saints have wielded the sword in this way: Adam and his descendants; Abraham when he rescued Lot, his brother's son, and routed the four kings as related in Genesis 14 [:8–16], although he was a thoroughly evangelical man. Thus did Samuel, the holy prophet, slay King Agag, as we read in I Samuel 15 [:33]; and Elijah slew the prophets of Baal, I Kings 18 [:40]. So too did Moses, Joshua, the children of Israel, Samson, David, and all the kings and princes in the Old Testament wield the sword; also Daniel and his associates, Hananiah, Azariah, and Mishael, in Babylon; and Joseph in Egypt, and so on.

Should anyone contend that the Old Testament is abrogated and no longer in effect, and that therefore such examples cannot be set before Christians, I answer: That is not so. St. Paul says in I Corinthians 10 [:3–4], " they ate the same spiritual food as we, and drank the same spiritual drink from the Rock, which is Christ." That is, they had the same Spirit and faith in Christ as we have, and were just as much Christians as we are. Therefore, wherein they did right, all Christians do right, from the beginning of the world unto the end. For time and external circumstances make no difference among Christians. Neither is it true that the Old Testament was abrogated in such a way that it must not be kept, or that whoever kept it fully would be doing wrong, as St. Jerome and many others mistakenly held. Rather, it is abrogated in the sense that we are free to keep it or not to keep it, and it is no longer necessary to keep it on penalty of losing one's soul, as was the case at that time.

Paul says in I Corinthians 7 [:19] and Galatians 6 [:15] that neither uncircumcision nor circumcision counts for anything, but only a new creature in Christ. That is, it is not sin to be uncircumcised, as the Jews thought, nor is it sin to be circumcised, as the Gentiles thought. Either is right and permissible for him who does not think he will thereby become righteous or be saved. The same is true of all other parts of the Old Testament; it is not wrong to ignore

them and it is not wrong to abide by them, but it is permissible to and proper either to follow them or to omit them. Indeed, if it were necessary or profitable for the salvation of one's neighbor, it would be necessary to keep all of them. For everyone is under obligation to do what is for his neighbor's good, be it Old Testament or New, Jewish or Gentile, as Paul teaches in I Corinthians 12. For love pervades all and transcends all; it considers only what is necessary and beneficial to others, and does not ask whether it is old or new. Hence, the precedents for the use of the sword also are matters of freedom, and you may follow them or not. But where you see that your neighbor needs it, there love constrains you to do as a matter of necessity that which would otherwise be optional and not necessary for you either to do or to leave undone.

Only so not suppose that you will thereby become righteous or be saved—as the Jews presumed to be saved by their works—but leave this to faith, which without works makes you a new creature.

To prove our position also by the New Testament, the testimony of John the Baptist in Luke 3 [:14] stands unshaken on this point. There can be no doubt that it was his task to point to Christ, witness for him, and teach about him; that is to say, the teaching of the man who was to lead a truly perfected people to Christ had of necessity to be purely New Testament and evangelical. John confirms the soldiers' calling, saying they should be content with their wages. Now if it had been un-Christian to bear the sword, he ought to have censured them for it and told them to abandon both wages and sword, else he would not have been teaching Christianity aright. So likewise, when St. Peter in Acts 10 [:33–34] preached Christ to Cornelius, he did not tell him to abandon his profession, which he would have had to do if it had prevented Cornelius from being a Christian. Moreover, before he was baptized the Holy Spirit came upon him [Acts 10:44–48].

St. Luke also praises him as an upright man prior to St. Peter's sermon, and does not criticize him for being a soldier, the centurion of a pagan emperor [Acts 10:1–2]. It is only right that what the Holy Spirit permitted to remain and did not censure in the case of Cornelius, we too should permit and not censure.

A similar case is that of the Ethiopian captain, the eunuch in Acts 8 [:27–39], whom Philip the evangelist converted and baptized and permitted to return home and remain in office, although without the sword he could not possibly have been so high an official under the queen of Ethiopia. It was the same too with the proconsul of Cyprus, Sergius Paulus, in Acts 13 [:7–12]; St. Paul converted him, and yet permitted him to remain proconsul over and among the heathen. The same policy was followed by many holy martyrs who continued obedient to pagan Roman emperors, went into battle under them, and undoubtedly slew people for the sake of preserving peace, as it is written of St. Maurice, St. Acacius, St. Gereon, and many others under the emperor Julian.

Moreover, we have the clear and compelling text of St. Paul in Romans 13 [:1], where he says, "The governing authority has been ordained by God"; and further, "The governing authority does not bear the sword in vain. It is God's servant for your good, an avenger upon him who does evil" [Rom. 13:4]. Be not so wicked, my friend, as to say, "A christian may not do that which is God's own peculiar work, ordinance, and creation." Else you must also say, "A Christian must not eat, drink, or be married," for these are also God's work and ordinance. If it is God's work and creation, then it is good, so good that everyone can use it in a Christian and salutary way, as Paul and says in II Timothy 4 [I Tim. 4:4,3], "Everything created by God is good, and nothing is to be rejected by those who believe and know the truth." Under "everything created by God' you must include not simply food and drink, clothing and shoes, but also authority and subjection, protection and punishment.

In short, since Paul says here that the governing authority is God's servant, we must allow it to be exercised not only by the heathen but by all men. What can be the meaning of the phrase, "It is God's servant," except that the governing authority is by its very nature such that through it one may serve God? Now it would be quite un-Christian to say that there is any service of God in which a Christian should not or must not take part, when service of God is actually more characteristic of Christians than of anyone else. It would even be fine and fitting if all princes were good, true Christians. For the sword and authority, as a particular service of God, belong more appropriately to Christians than to any other men on earth. Therefore, you should esteem the sword or governmental authority as highly as the state of marriage, or husbandry, or any other calling which God has instituted. Just as one can serve God in the estate of marriage, or in farming or a trade, for the benefit of others—and must so serve if his neighbor needs it—so one can serve God in government, and should there serve if the needs of his neighbor demand it. For those who punish evil and protect the good are God's servants and workmen. Only, one should also be set free not to do it if there is no need for it, just as we are free not to marry or farm where there is no need for them.

You ask: Why did not Christ and the apostles bear the sword? Answer: You tell me, why did Christ not take a wife, or become a cobbler or a tailor. If an office or vocation were to be regarded as disreputable on the ground that Christ did not pursue it himself, what would become of all the offices and vocations other than the ministry, the one occupation he did follow? Christ pursued his own office and vocation, but he did not thereby reject any other. It was not incumbent upon him to bear the sword, for he was to exercise only that function by which his kingdom is governed and which properly serves his kingdom. Now, it is not essential to his kingdom that he be a married man, a cobbler, tailor, farmer, prince, hangman, or constable; neither is the temporal sword or law essential to it, but only God's Word and Spirit. It is by these that his people are ruled inwardly. This is the office which he also exercised then and still exercises now, always bestowing God's Word and Spirit. And in this office the apostles and all spiritual rulers had to follow him. For in order to do their job right they are so busily occupied with the spiritual sword, the Word of God, that they must perforce neglect the temporal sword and leave it to others who do not have to preach, although it is not contrary to their calling to use it, as I have said. For each one must attend to the duties of his own calling.

Therefore, although Christ did not bear or prescribe the sword, it is sufficient that he did not forbid or abolish it, but actually confirmed it; just as it is sufficient that he did not abolish the state of marriage but confirmed it, though without himself taking a wife or setting forth a teaching concerning it. He had to manifest himself wholly in connection with that estate and calling which alone expressly served his kingdom, lest from his example there should be deduced the justification or necessity of teaching or believing that the kingdom of God could not exist without matrimony and the sword and similar externals (since Christ's example is necessarily binding), when in fact it exists solely by God's Word and Spirit. This was and had to be Christ's peculiar function as the Supreme King in this kingdom. Since not all Christians have this same function (although they are entitled to it), it is fitting that they should have some other external office by which God may also be served.

From all this we gain the true meaning of Christ's words in Matthew 5 [:39], "Do not resist evil," etc. It is this: A Christian should be so disposed that he will suffer every evil and injustice without avenging himself; neither will he seek every evil and injustice without avenging himself; neither will he seek legal redress in the courts but have utterly no need of temporal authority and law for his own sake. On behalf of others, however, he may and should seek vengeance, justice, protection, and help, and do as much as he can to achieve it. Likewise, the governing authority should, on its own initiative or through the instigation of others, help and protect him too, without any complaint, application, or instigation on his own part. If it fails to do this, he should permit himself to be despoiled and slandered; he should not resist evil, as Christ's words say.

Be certain too that this teaching of Christ is not a counsel for those who would be perfect, as our sophists blasphemously and falsely say, but a universally obligatory command for all Christians. Then you will realize that all those who avenge themselves or go to law and wrangle in the courts over their property and honor are nothing but heathen masquerading under the name of Christians. It cannot be otherwise, I tell you. Do not be dissuaded by the multitude and common practice; for there are few Christians on earth—have no doubt about it—and God's word is something very different from the common practice.

Here you see that Christ is not abrogating the law when he says, "You have heard that it was said to them of old, 'An eye for an eye'; but I say to you: Do not resist evil," etc. [Matt. 5:38–39]. On the contrary, he is expounding the meaning of the law as it is to be understood, as if he were to say, "You Jews think that it is right and proper in the sight of God to recover by law what is yours. You rely on what Moses said, 'an eye for an eye,' etc. But I say to you that Moses set this law over the wicked, who do not belong to God's kingdom, in order that they might not avenge themselves or worse but be compelled by such outward law to desist from evil, in order that by outward law and rule they might be kept subordinate to the governing authority. You, however, should so conduct yourselves that you neither need nor resort to such law. Although the temporal authority must have such a law by which to judge unbelievers, and although you yourselves may also use it for judging others, still you should not invoke or use it for yourselves and in you own affairs. You have the kingdom of heaven; therefore, you should leave the kingdom of earth to anyone who wants to take it."

There you see that Christ does not interpret his words to mean that he is abrogating the law of Moses or prohibiting temporal authority. He is rather making an exception of his own people. They are not to use the secular authority for themselves but to leave it to the unbelievers. Yet they may also serve these unbelievers, even with their own law, since they are not Christians and no one can be forced into Christianity. That Christ's words apply only to his own is evident from the fact that later on he says they should love their enemies and be perfect like their heavenly Father [Matt. 5:44, 48]. But he who loves his enemies and is perfect leaves the law alone and does not use

it to demand and eye for an eye. Neither does he restrain the non-Christians, however, who do not love their enemies and who do wish to make use of the law; indeed, he lends his help that these laws may hinder the wicked from doing worse.

Thus the word of Christ is now reconciled, I believe, with the passages which establish the sword, and the meaning is this: No Christian shall wield or invoke the sword for himself and his cause. In behalf of another, however, he may and should wield it and invoke it to restrain wickedness and to defend godliness. Even as the Lord says in the same chapter [Matt. 5:34–37], "A Christian should not swear, but his word should be Yes, yes; No, no." That is, for himself and of his own volition and desire, he should not swear. When it is needful or necessary, however, and salvation or the honor of God demands it, he should swear. Thus, he uses the forbidden oath to serve another. Christ and Paul oft en swore in order to make their teaching and testimony valuable and credible to others, as men do and have the right to do in covenants and compacts, etc., of which Psalms 63 [:11] says, "They shall be praised who swear by his name."

Here you inquire further, whether constables, hangmen, jurists, lawyers, and others of similar function can also be Christians and in a state of salvation. Answer: If the governing authority and its sword are a divine service, as was proved above, then everything that is essential for the authority's bearing of the sword must also be divine service. There must be those who arrest, prosecute, execute, and destroy the wicked, and who protect, acquit, defend, and save the good. Therefore, when they perform their duties, not with the intention of seeking their own ends but only of helping the law and the governing authority function to coerce the wicked, there is no peril in that; they may use their office like anybody else would use his trade, as a means of livelihood. For, as has been said, love of neighbor is not concerned about its own; it considers not how great or humble, but how profitable and needful the works are for neighbor or community.

You may ask, "Why may I not use the sword for myself and for my own cause, so long as it is my intention not to seek my own advantage but to punish evil?" Answer: Such a miracle is not impossible, but very rare and hazardous. Where the Spirit is so richly present it may well happen. For we read thus of Samson in Judges 15 [:11], that he said, "As they did to me, so have I done to them," even though Proverbs 24 [:29] says to the contrary, "Do not say, I will do to him as he has done to me," and Proverbs 20 [:22] adds, "Do not say, I will repay him his evil." Samson was called of God to harass the Philistines and deliver the children of Israel. Although he used them as an occasion to further his own cause, still he did not do so in order to avenge himself or to seek his own interests, but to serve others and to punish the Philistines [Judg. 14:4]. No one but a true Christian, filled with the Spirit, will follow this example. Where reason too tries to do likewise, it will probably contend that it is not trying to seek its own, but this will be basically untrue, for it cannot be done without grace. Therefore first become like Samson, and then you can also do as Samson did.

## Part Two

## How Far Temporal Authority Extends

We come now to the main part of this treatise. Having learned that there must be temporal authority on earth, and how it is to be exercised in a Christian and salutary manner, we must now learn how far its arm extends and how widely its hand stretches, lest it extent too far and encroach upon God's kingdom and government. It is essential for us to know this, for where it is given too wide a scope, intolerable and terrible injury follows; on the other hand, injury is also inevitable where it is restricted too narrowly. In the former case, the temporal authority punishes too much; in the latter case, it punishes too little. To err in this direction, however, and punish too little is more tolerable, for it is always better to let a scoundrel live than to put a godly man to death. The world has plenty of scoundrels anyway and must continue to have them, but godly men are scarce.

It is to be noted that the two classes of Adam's children—the one in God's kingdom under Christ and the other in the kingdom of the world under governing authority, as was said above—have two kinds of law. For every kingdom must have its own laws and statutes: without law no kingdom or government can survive, as everyday experience amply shows. The temporal government has laws which extend no further than to life and property and external affairs on earth, for God cannot and will not permit anyone but himself to rule over the soul. Therefore, where the temporal authority presumes to prescribe laws for the soul, it encroaches upon God's government and only misleads souls and destroys them.

We want to make this so clear that everyone will grasp it, and that our fine gentlemen, the princes and bishops, will see what fools they are when they seek to coerce the people with their laws and commandments into believing this or that.

When a man-made law is imposed upon the soul to make it believe this or that as its human author may prescribe, there is certainly no word of God for it. If there is no word of God for it, then we cannot be sure whether God wishes to have it so, for we cannot be certain that something which he does not command is pleasing to him. Indeed, we are sure that it does not please him, for he desires that our faith be based simply and entirely on his divine word alone. He says in Matthew 18 [16:18], "On this rock I will build my church."; and in John 10 [:27,14,5], "My sheep hear my voice and know me; however, they will not hear the voice of a stranger, but flee from him." From this is follows that with such a wicked command the temporal power is driving souls to eternal death. For it compels them to believe as right and certainly pleasing to God that which is in fact uncertain, indeed, certain to be displeasing to him since there is no clear word of God for it. Whoever believes something to be right which is wrong or uncertain is denying that truth, which is God himself. He is believing in lies and errors, and counting as right that which is wrong.

Hence, it is the height of folly when they command that one shall believe the Church, the fathers, and the councils, though there be no word of God for it. It is not the church but the devil's apostles who command such things, for the church commands nothing unless it knows for certain that it is God's word. As St. Peter puts it, "Whoever speaks, let him speak as the word of God" [I Pet. 4:11]. It will be a long time, however, before they can ever prove that the decrees of the councils are God's word. Still more foolish is it when the assert that kings, princes, and the mass of mankind believe thus and so. My dear man, we are not baptized into kings, or princes, or even into the mass of mankind, but into Christ and God himself. Neither are we called kings, princes, or common folk, but Christians. No one shall or can command the soul unless he is able to show it the way to heaven; but this no man can do, only God alone. Therefore, in matters which concern the salvation of souls nothing but God's word shall be taught and accepted.

Again, consummate fools though they are, they must confess that they have no power over souls. For no human being can kill a soul or give it life, or conduct it to heaven or hell. If they will not take our word for it, Christ himself will attend to it strongly enough where he says in the tenth chapter of Matthew, "Do not fear those who kill the body, and after that have nothing that they can do; rather fear him who after he has killed the body, has power to condemn to hell." I think it is clear enough here that the soul is taken out of all human hands and is placed under the authority of God alone.

Now tell me: How much wit must there be in the head of a person who imposes commands in an area where he has no authority whatsoever? Would you not judge the person insane who commanded the moon to shine whenever he wanted to? How well would it go if Leipzigers were to impose laws on us Wittenbergers, or if, conversely, we in Wittenberg were to legislate for the people of Leipzig! They would certainly send the lawmakers a thank—offering of hellebore to purge their brains and cure their sniffles. Yet our emperor and clever princes are doing just that today. They are allowing pope, bishop, and sophists to lead them on—one blind man leading the other—to command their subjects to believe, without God's word, whatever they please. And still they would be known as Christian princes, God forbid!

Besides, we cannot conceive how an authority could or should act in a situation except where it can see, know, judge, condemn, change, and modify. What would I think of a judge who should blindly decide cases which he neither hears nor sees? Tell me then: How can a mere man see, know, judge, condemn, and change hearts? That is reserved for God alone, as Psalm 7 [:9] says, "God tries the hearts and reins"; and [v.8], "The Lord judges the peoples." And acts 10 says, "God knows the hearts"; and Jeremiah 1 [17:9–10], "Wicked and unsearchable is the human heart; who can understand it? I the Lord, who search the heart and reins." A court should and must be quite certain and clear about everything if it is to render judgment. But the thoughts and inclinations of the soul can be known to no one but God. Therefore, it is futile and impossible to command or compel anyone by force to believe this or that. The matter must be approached in a different way. Force will not accomplish it. And I am surprised at the big fools, for they themselves all say: *De occultis non Ecclesia*, the church does not judge secret matters. If the spiritual rule of the church governs only public matters, how dare the mad temporal authority judge and control such a secret, spiritual, hidden matter as faith?

Furthermore, every man runs his own risk in believing as he does, and he must see to it himself that he believes rightly. As nobody else can go to heaven or hell for me, so nobody else can believe or disbelieve for me; as nobody else can open or close heaven or hell for me, so nobody else can drive me to belief or unbelief. How he believes or disbelieves is a matter for the conscience of each individual,

and since this takes nothing away from the temporal authority the latter should be content to attend to its own affairs and let men believe this or that as they are able and willing, and constrain no one by force. For faith is a free act, to which no one can be forced. Indeed, it is a work of God in the spirit, not something which outward authority should compel or create. Hence arises the common saying, found also in Augustine, "No one can or ought to be forced to believe."

Moreover, the blind, wretched fellows fail to see how utterly hopeless and impossible a thing they are attempting. For no matter how harshly they lay down the law, or how violently they rage, they can do no more than force an outward compliance of the mouth and the hand; the heart they cannot compel, though they work themselves to a frazzle. For the proverb is true: :Thoughts are tax free." Why do they persist in trying to force people to believe from the heart when they see that it is impossible? In so doing they only compel weak consciences to lie, to disavow, and to utter what is not in their hearts. They thereby load themselves down with dreadful alien sins, for all the lies and false confessions which such weak consciences utter fall back upon him who compels them. Even if their subjects were in error, it would be much easier simply to let them err than to compel them to lie and to utter what is not in their hearts. In addition, it is not right to prevent evil by something even worse.

Would you like to know why God ordains that the temporal princes must offend so frightfully? I will tell you. God has given them to a base mind [Rom. 1:28] and will make an end of them just as he does of the spiritual nobility. For my ungracious lords, the pope and the bishops, are supposed to be bishops and preach God's word. This they leave undone, and have become temporal princes who govern with laws which concern only life and property. How completely they have turned things topsy-turvy! They are supposed to be ruling souls inwardly by God's word; so they rule castles, cities, lands, and people outwardly, torturing, souls with unspeakable outrages.

Similarly, the temporal lords are suppose to govern lands and people outwardly. This they leave undone. They can do no more than strip and fleece, heap tax upon tax and tribute upon tribute, letting loose here a bear and there a wolf. Besides this, there is no justice, integrity, or truth to be found among them. They behave worse than any thief or scoundrel, and their temporal rule has sunk quite as low as that of the spiritual tyrants. For this reason God so perverts their minds also, that they rush on into the absurdity of trying to exercise a spiritual rule over souls, just as their counterparts try to establish temporal rule. They blithely heap alien sins upon themselves and incur the hatred of God and man, one scoundrel with the other. Then they lay all the blame on the gospel, and instead of confessing their sin they blaspheme God and say that our preaching has brought about that which their perverse wickedness has deserved—and still unceasingly serves— just as the Romans did when they were destroyed. Here then you have God's decree concerning the high and mighty. They are not to believe it, however, lest this stern decree of God be hindered by their repentance.

But, you say: Paul said in Romans 13 [:1] that every soul [seele] should be subject to the governing authority; and Peter says that we should be subject to every human ordinance [I Pet. 2:13]. Answer: Now you are on the right track, for these passages are in my favor. St. Paul is speaking of the governing authority.

Now you have just heard that no one but God can have authority over souls. Hence, St. Paul cannot possibly be speaking of any obedience except where there can be corresponding authority. From this it follows that he is not speaking of faith, to the effect that temporal authority should have the right to command faith. He is speaking rather of external things, that they should be ordered and governed on earth. His words too make this perfectly clear, where he prescribes limits for both authority and obedience, saying, "Pay all of them their dues, taxes to whom taxes are due, revenue to whom revenue is due, honor to whom honor is due, respect to whom respect is due" [Rom. 13:7], Temporal obedience and authority, you see, apply only to taxes revenue, honor, and respect. Again, where he says, "The governing authority is not a terror to good conduct, but to bad" [Rom. 13:3], he again so limits the governing authority that it is not to have the mastery over faith or the word of God, but over evil works.

This is also what St. Peter means by the phrase, "Human ordinance" [I Pet. 2:13]. A human ordinance cannot possibly extend its authority into heaven and over souls; it is limited to the earth, to external dealings men have with one another, where they can see, know, judge, evaluate, punish, and acquit.

Christ himself made this distinction, and summed it all up very nicely when he said in Matthew 22 [:21], "Render to Caesar the things that are Caesar's and to God the things that are God's." Now, if the imperial power extended into God's kingdom and authority, and were not something separate, Christ would not have made this distinction. For, as has been the said, the soul is not under the authority of Caesar; he can neither teach it nor guide it, neither kill it nor give it life, neither bind it or loose it, neither judge nor condemn it, neither hold it fast nor release it. All this he would have to do, had he the authority to command it and to impose laws upon it. But with respect to body, property, and honor he has indeed to do these things, for such matters are under his authority.

David too summarized all this long ago in an excellent brief passage, when he said in Psalm 113 [115:16], "He has given heaven to the Lord of heaven, but the earth he has given to the sons of men." That is, over what is on earth and belongs to the temporal, earthly kingdom, man has authority from God; but whatever belongs to heaven and to the eternal kingdom is exclusively under the Lord of heaven. Neither did Moses forget this when he said in Genesis 1 [:26], "God said, 'Let us make man to have dominion over the beasts of the earth, the fish of the sea, and the birds of the air.'" There only external dominion is ascribed to man. In short, this is the meaning as St. Peter says in Acts 4 [5:29], "We must obey God rather than men." Thereby, he clearly sets a limit to the temporal authority, for if we had to do everything that the temporal authority wanted there would have been no point in saying, "We must obey God rather than men."

If your prince or temporal ruler commands you to side with the pope, to believe thus and so, or to get rid of certain books, you should say, "It is not fitting that Lucifer should sit at the side of God. Gracious sir, I owe you obedience in body and property; command me within the limits of your authority on earth, and I will obey. But if you command me to believe or to get rid of certain books, I will not obey; for then you are a tyrant and overreach yourself, commanding where you have neither the right or the authority," etc. Should he seize your property on account of this and punish such disobedience, then blessed are you; thank God that you are worthy to suffer

for the sake of the divine word. Let him rage, fool that he is; he will meet his judge. For I tell you, if you fail to withstand him, if you give in to him and let him take away your faith and your books, you have truly denied God.

Let me illustrate. In Meissen, Bavaria, the Mark, and other places, the tyrants have issued an order that all copies of the New Testament are everywhere to be turned in to the officials. This should not turn in a single page, not even a letter, on pain of losing their salvation. Whoever does so is delivering Christ up into the hands of Herod, for these tyrants act as murderers of Christ just like Herod. If their homes are ordered searched and books or property taken by force, they suffer it to be done. Outrage is not to be resisted but endured; yet we should not sanction it, or lift a little finger to conform, or obey. For such tyrants are acting as worldly princes are supposed to act, and worldly princes they surely are. But the world is God's enemy; hence, they too have to do what is antagonistic to God and agreeable to the world, that they may not be bereft of honor, but remain worldly princes. Do not wonder, therefore, that they rage and mock at the gospel; they have to live up to their name and title.

You must know that since the beginning of the world a wise prince is a mighty rare bird, and an upright prince ever rarer. They are generally the biggest fools or the worst scoundrels on earth; therefore, one must constantly expect the worst from them and look for little good, especially in divine matters which concern the salvation of souls. They are God's executioners and hangmen; his divine wrath uses them to punish the wicked and to maintain outward peace. Our God is a great lord and ruler; this is why he must also have such noble, highborn, and rich hangmen and constables. He desires that everyone shall copiously accord them to riches, honor, and fear in abundance. It pleases his divine will that we call his hangmen gracious lords, fall at their feet, and be subject to them in all humility, so long as they do not ply their trade too far and try to become shepherds instead of hangmen. If a prince should happen to be wise, upright, or a Christian, that is one of the great miracles, the most precious token of divine grace upon that land. Ordinarily the course of events is in accordance with the passage from Isaiah 3 [:4], "I will make boys their princes and gaping fools shall rule over them"; and in Hosea 13 [:11], "I will give you a king in my anger, and take him away in my wrath." The world is too wicked, and does not deserve to have many wise and upright princes. Frogs must have their storks.

Again, you say, "The temporal power is not forcing men to believe; it is simply seeing to it externally that no one deceives the people by false doctrine; how could heretics otherwise be restrained?" Answer: This the bishops should do; it is a function entrusted to them and not to the princes. Heresy can never be restrained by force. One will have to tackle the problem in some other way, for heresy must be opposed and dealt with otherwise than with the sword. Here God's word must do the fighting. If it does not succeed, certainly the temporal power will not succeed either, even if it were to drench the world in blood. Heresy is a spiritual matter which you cannot hack to pieces with iron, consume with fire, or drown in water. God's word alone avails here, as Paul says in II Corinthians 10 {:4–5], "our weapons are not carnal, but mighty in God to destroy every argument and proud obstacle that exalts itself against the knowledge of God, and to take every thought captive in the service of Christ."

Moreover, faith and heresy are never so strong as when men oppose them by sheer force, without God's word. For men count it certain that such force is for a wrong cause and is directed against the right, since it proceeds without God's word and knows not how to further its cause except by naked force, as brute beasts do. Even in temporal affairs force can be used only after the wrong has been legally condemned. How much less possible it is to act with force, without justice and God's word, in these lofty spiritual matters! See, therefore, what fine, clever nobles they are! They would drive out heresy, but set about it in such a way that they only strengthen the opposition, rousing suspicion against themselves and justifying the heretics. My friend, if you wish to drive out heresy, you must find some way to tear it first of all from the heart and completely turn men's wills away from it. With force you will not stop it, but only strengthen it. What do you gain by strengthening heresy in the heart, while weakening only its outward expression and forcing the tongue to lie? God's word, however, enlightens the heart, and so all heresies and errors vanish from the heart of their own accord.

This way of destroying heresy was proclaimed by Isaiah in his eleventh chapter where he says, "He shall smite the earth with the rod of his mouth, and with the breath of his lips he shall slay the wicked." There you see that if the wicked are to be slain and converted, it will be accomplished with the mouth. In short, these princes and tyrants do not realize that to fight against heresy is to fight against the devil, who fills men's hearts with error, as Paul says in Ephesians 6 [:12], "We are no contending against flesh and blood, but against spiritual wickedness, against the principalities which rule this present darkness," etc. Therefore, so long as the devil is not repelled and driven from the heart, it is agreeable to him that I destroy his vessels with fire of sword; it's as if

I were to fight lightning with a straw. Job bore abundant witness to this when in his forty-first chapter he said that the devil counts iron as straw, and fears no power on earth. We learn it is also from experience, for even if all Jews and heretics were forcibly burned no one ever has been or will be convinced or converted thereby.

Nevertheless, such a world as this deserves such princes, none of whom attends to his duties. The bishops are to leave God's word alone and not use it to rule souls; instead they are to turn over to the worldly princes the job of ruling souls with the sword. The worldly princes, in turn, are to permit usury, robbery, adultery, murder, and other evil deeds, and even commit these offenses themselves, and then allow the bishops to punish with letters of excommunication. Thus, they neatly put the shoe on the wrong foot: they rule the souls with iron and the bodies with letters, so that worldly princes rule in a spiritual way, and spiritual princes rule in a worldly way. What else does the devil have to do on earth than to masquerade and play the fool with his people? These are our Christian princes, who defend the faith and devour the Turk! Fine fellows, indeed, whom we may well trust to accomplish something by such refined wisdom, namely, to break their necks and plunge land and people into misery and want.

I would in all good faith advise these blind fellows to take heed to a little phrase that occurs in Psalm 107: *"Effundit contemptum super principes."* ("He pours contempt upon princes.") I swear to you by God that if you fail to see that this little text is applicable to you, then you are lost, even though each one of you be as mighty as the Turk; and your fuming and raging will avail you nothing. A goodly part of it has already come true. For there are very few princes who are not regarded as

fools or scoundrels; that is because they show themselves to be so. The common man is learning to think, and the scourge of princes (that which God calls *contemptum*) is gathering force among the mob and with the common man. I fear there will be no way to avert it, unless the princes conduct themselves in a princely manner and begin again to rule decently and reasonably. Men will not, men cannot, men refuse to endure your tyranny and wantonness much longer. Dear princes and lords be wise and guide yourselves accordingly. God will no longer tolerate it. The world is no longer what it once was, when you hunted and drove people like game. Abandon therefore your wicked use of force, give thought to dealing justly, and let God's word have its way, as it will anyway and must and shall; you cannot prevent it. If there is heresy somewhere, let it be overcome, as is proper, with God's word. But if you can continue to brandish the sword, take heed lest someone come and compel you to sheathe it—and not in God's name!

But you might say, "Since There is to be no temporal sword among Christians, how then are they to be ruled outwardly? There certainly must be authority even among Christians." Answer: Among Christians there shall and can be no authority; rather all are alike subject to one another, as Paul says in Romans 12: "Each shall consider the other his superior"; and Peter says in I Peter 5 [:5], "All of you be subject to one another." This is also what Christ means in Luke 14 [:10], "When you are invited to a wedding, go and sit in the lowest place." Among Christians there is no superior but Christ himself, and him alone. What kind of authority can there be where all are equal and have the same right, power, possessions, and honor, and where no one desires to be the other's superior, but each the other's subordinate? Where there are such people, one could not establish authority even if he wanted to, since in the nature of things it is impossible to have superiors where no one is willing to be a superior. Where there are no such people, however, there are no real Christians either.

What, then, are the priests and bishop? Answer: The government is not a matter of authority or power, but a service and an office, for they are neither higher nor better than other Christians. Therefore, they should impose no law or decree on others without their will and consent. Their ruling is rather nothing more than the inculcating of God's word, by which they guide Christians and overcome heresy. As we have said, Christians can be ruled in faith, not with outward works. Faith, however, can come through no word of man, but only through the word of God, as Paul says in Romans 10 [:17], "Faith comes through hearing, and hearing through the word of God." Those who do not believe are not Christians; they do not belong to Christ's kingdom, but to the worldly kingdom where they are constrained and governed by the sword and by outward rule. Christians do every good thing of their own accord and without constraint, and find God's word alone sufficient for them. Of this I have written frequently and at length elsewhere.

## Part Three

Now that we know the limits of temporal authority, it is time to inquire also how a prince should use it. We do this for the sake of those very few who would also like very much to

be Christian princes and lords, who desire to enter into the life in heaven. Christ himself describes the nature of worldly princes in Luke 22 [:25], where he says, "The princes of this world exercise lordship, and those that are in authority proceed with force." For if they are lords by birth or by election they think it only right that they should be served and should rule by force. For cursed and condemned is every sort of life lived and sought for the benefit and good of self; cursed are all works not done in love. They are done in love, however, when they are directed wholeheartedly toward the benefit, honor, and salvation of others, and not toward the pleasure, benefit, honor, comfort, and salvation of self.

I will say nothing here of the temporal dealings and laws of the governing authority. That is a large subject, and there are too many lawbooks already, although if a prince is himself no wiser than his jurist and knows no more than what is in the lawbooks, he will surely rule according to the saying in Proverbs 28: "A prince who lacks understanding will oppress many with injustice." For no matter how good and equitable the laws are, they all make an exception in the case of necessity, in the face of which they cannot insist upon being strictly enforced. Therefore, a prince must have the law as firmly in hand as the sword, and determine in his own mind when and where the law is to be applied strictly or with moderation, so that law may prevail at all times and in all cases, and reason may be the highest law and the master of all administration of law. To take an analogy, the head of a family fixes both the time and the amount when it comes to matters of work and of food for his servants and children; still, he must reserve the right to modify or suspend these regulations if his servants happen to be ill, imprisoned, detained, deceived, or otherwise hindered; he must not deal as severely with the sick as with the well. I say this in order that men may not think it sufficiently praiseworthy merely to follow the written law or the opinions of the jurists. There is more to it than that.

What, then, is a prince to do if he lacks the requisite wisdom and has to be guided by the jurists and the lawbooks? Answer: This is why I said that the princely estate is a perilous one. If he be not wise enough himself to master both his laws and his advisers, then the maxim of Solomon applies, "Woe to the land whose prince is a child" [Eccles. 10:16]. Solomon recognized this too. This is why he despaired of all law—even of that which Moses through God had prescribed for him—and of all his princes and counselors. He turned to God himself and besought him for an understanding heart to govern the people [I Kings 3:9]. A prince must follow this example and proceed in fear; he must depend neither upon the dead books nor living heads, but cling solely to God, and be at him constantly, praying for a right understanding, beyond that of all books and teachers, to rule his subjects wisely. For this reason I know of no law to prescribe for a prince; instead, I will simply instruct his heart and mind on what his attitude should be toward all laws, counsels, judgments, and actions. If he governs himself accordingly, God will surely grant him the ability to carry out all laws, counsels, and actions in a proper and godly way.

**First.** He must give consideration and attention to his subjects, and really devote himself to it. This he does when he directs his every thought to making himself useful and beneficial to them; when instead of thinking, "The land and people belong to me, I will do what best pleases me," he thinks rather, "I belong to the land and the people, I shall do what is useful and good for them. My concern will not be how to lord it over them and dominate them, but how to protect and maintain them in peace and plenty." He should picture Christ to himself, and say, "Behold, Christ, the supreme ruler. Came to serve me; he did not seek to gain power, estate, and honor from me, but considered only my need, and directed all things to the end that I should gain power, estate, and honor form him and through him. I will do likewise, seeking from my subjects not my own advantage but theirs. I will use my office to serve and protect them, listen to their problems and defend them, and govern to the sole end that they, not I, may benefit and profit from my rule." In such manner should a prince in his heart empty himself of his power and authority, and take unto himself the needs of his subjects, dealing with them as though they were his own needs. For this is what Christ is to us [Phil. 2:7]; and these are the proper works of Christian love.

Now you will say, "Who would then want to be a prince? That would make the princely estate the worst on earth, full of trouble, labor, and sorrow. What would become of the princely amusements—dancing, hunting, racing, gaming, and similar worldly pleasures?" I answer: We are not here teaching how a temporal prince is to live, but how a temporal prince is to be a Christian, such that he may also reach heaven. Who is not aware that a prince is a rare prize in heaven? I do not speak with any hope that temporal princes will give heed, but on the chance that there might be one who would also like to be Christian, and to know how he should act. Of this I am certain, that God's word will neither turn nor bend for princes, but princes must bend themselves to God's word.

I am satisfied simply to point out that it is not impossible for a prince to be a Christian, although it is a rare thing and beset with difficulties. If they would so manage that their dancing, hunting, and racing were done without injury to their subjects, and if they would otherwise conduct their office in love toward them, God would not be so harsh as to begrudge them their dancing and hunting and racing. But they would soon find out for themselves that if they gave their subjects the care and attention required by their office, many a fine dance, hunt, race, and game would have to be missed.

**Second.** He must beware of the high and mighty and of his counselors, and so conduct himself toward them that he despises none, but also trusts none enough to leave everything to him. God cannot tolerate either course. He once spoke through the mouth of an ass [Num. 22:28]; therefore, no man is to be despised, however humble he may be. On the other hand, he permitted the highest angel to fall from heaven; therefore, no man is to be trusted, no matter how wise, holy, or great he may be. One should rather give a hearing to all, and wait to see through which one of them God will speak and act. The greatest harm is done at court when the prince gives his mind into the captivity of the high and mighty and of the flatterers, and does not look into things himself. When a prince fails and plays the fool, not just one person is affected, but land and people must bear the result of such foolishness.

Therefore, a prince should trust his officials and allow them to act, but only in such a way that he will still keep the reins of government in his own hands. He must not be overconfident but keep his eyes open and attend to things, and (like Jehoshaphat did [II Chron. 19:4–7]) ride through the land and observe everywhere how the government and the law are being administered. In this way he will learn for himself that one cannot place complete trust in any man. You have no

right to assume that somebody else will take as deep and interest in you and your land as you do yourself, unless he be a good Christian filled with the Spirit. The natural man will not. And since you cannot know whether he is a Christian or how long he will remain one, you cannot safely depend upon him.

Beware especially of those who say, "Oh, gracious lord, does your grace not have greater confidence in me? Who is so willing to serve your grace?" etc. Such a person is certainly not guileless; he wants to be lord in the land and make a monkey of you. If he were a true and devout Christian he would be glad that you entrust nothing to him, and would praise and approve you for keeping such a close watch on him. Since he acts in accord with God's will, he is willing and content to have his actions brought to light by you or anyone else. As Christ says in John 8 [3:21], "He who does what is good comes to the light, that it may be clearly seen that his deeds have been wrought in God." The former, however, would blind your eyes, and act under cover of darkness; as Christ also says in the same place, "He who does evil shuns the light, lest his deeds should be exposed" [John 3:20]. Therefore, beware of him. And if he complains about it, say to him, "Friend, I do you no wrong; God is unwilling that I trust myself or any other man. Find fault with Him because He will have it so, or because He has not made you something more than a man. But even if you were an angel, I still would not fully trust you—Lucifer was not to be trusted—for we should trust God alone."

Let no prince think that he will fare better than David, who is an example to all princes. He had so wise a counselor, Ahithophel by name, that the text says: The counsel which Ahithophel gave was as if one had consulted God himself [II Sam. 16:23]. Yet Ahithophel fell, and sank so low that he tried to betray, slay, and destroy David, his own lord {II Sam. 17:1–23]. Thus did David at that time have to learn that no man is to be trusted. Why do you suppose God permitted such a horrible incident to occur and be recorded? It could only be in order to warn princes and lords against putting their trust in any man, which is the most perilous misfortune that could befall them. For it is most deplorable when flatterers reign at court, or when the prince relies upon others and puts himself in their hands, and lets everyone do as he will.

Now you will say, "If no one is to be trusted, how can land and people be governed?" Answer: You are to take the risk of entrusting matters to others, but you are yourself to trust and rely upon God alone. You will certainly have to entrust duties to somebody else and take a chance on him, but you must continue to watch with unceasing vigilance. A coachman has confidence in the horses and wagon he drives; yet he does not let them proceed on their own, but holds rein and lash in his hands and keeps his eyes open. Remember the old proverbs—which are the sure fruit of experience—"The master's eye makes the horse fat"; and, "The master's footprints fertilize the soil best." That is, if the master does not look after things himself but depends on advisers and servants, things never go right. God also wills it that way and causes it to be so in order that the lords may be driven of necessity to care for their office themselves, just as everyone has to fulfill his own calling and every creature do its own work. Otherwise, the lords will become fatted pigs and worthless fellows, or benefit to no one but themselves.

**Third.** He must take care to deal justly with evildoers. Here he must be very wise and prudent, so he can inflict punishment without injury to others. Again, I know of no better example of this than David. He had a commander, Joab by name, who committed two underhanded crimes when he treacherously murdered two upright commanders [II Sam. 3:27; 20:10], whereby he justly merited death twice over. Yet David, during his own lifetime, did not have him put to death but commanded his son Solomon to do so without fail [I Kings 2:5–6], doubtless because he himself could not do it without causing even greater damage and tumult. A prince must punish the wicked in such a way that he does not step on the dish while picking up the spoon, and for the sake of one man's head plunge country and people into want and fill the land with widows and orphans. Therefore, he must not follow the advice of those counselors and fire-eaters who would stir and incite him to start a war, saying, What, must we suffer such insult for the sake of a single castle would put the whole land in jeopardy.

In short, here one must go by the proverb, "He cannot govern who cannot wink at faults." Let this be his rule: Where wrong cannot be punished without greater wrong, there let him waive his rights, however just they may be. He should not have regard to his own injury, but to the wrong others must suffer in consequence of the penalty he imposes. What have the many women and children done to deserve being made widows and orphans in order that you may avenge yourself on a worthless tongue or an evil hand which has injured you.

Here you will ask: "Is a prince then not to go to war, and are his subjects not to follow him into battle?" Answer: This is a far-reaching question, but let me answer it very briefly. To act here as a Christian, I say, a prince should not go to war against his overlord—king, emperor, or other liege lord—but let him who takes, take. For the governing authority must not be resisted by force, but only by confession of the truth. If it is influenced by this, well and good; if not, you are excused, you suffer wrong for God's sake. If, however, the antagonist is your equal, your inferior, or of a foreign government, you should first offer him justice and peace, as Moses taught his children of Israel. If he refuses, then—mindful of what is best for you—defend yourself against force by force, as Moses so well describes it in Deuteronomy 20 [:10–12]. But in doing this you must not consider your personal interests and how you may remain lord, but those of your subjects to whom you owe help and protection, that such action may proceed in love. Since your entire land is in peril you must take the venture, so that with God's help all may not be lost. If you cannot prevent some from becoming widows and orphans as a consequence, you must at least see that not everything goes to ruin until there is nothing left except widows and orphans.

In this matter subjects are not in duty bound to follow, and to devote their life and property, for in such a case one must risk his goods and himself for the sake of others. In a war of this sort it is both Christian and an act of love to kill the enemy without hesitation, to plunder and burn and inquire him by every method of warfare until he is conquered (except that one must beware of sin, and violate wives and virgins). And when victory has been achieved, one should offer mercy and peace to those who surrender and humble themselves. In such a case let the proverb apply, "God helps the strongest." This is what Abraham did when he smote the four kings, Genesis 14; he certainly slaughtered many, and showed little mercy until he conquered them. Such a case must be regarded as sent by God as a means to cleanse the land for once and drive out the rascals.

What if a prince is in the wrong? Are his people bound to follow him then too? Answer:

No, for it is no one's duty to do wrong; we must obey God (who desires the right) rather than men [acts 5:29]. What if the subjects do not know whether their prince is in the right or not? Answer: So long as they do not know, and cannot with all possible diligence find out, they may obey him without peril to their souls. For in such a case one must apply the law of Moses in Exodus 21, where he writes that a murderer who has unknowingly and unintentionally killed a man shall through flight to a city of refuge and by judgment of a court be declared acquitted. Whichever side then suffers defeat, whether it be in the right or in the wrong, must accept it as a punishment from God. Whichever side fights and wins in such ignorance, however, must regard its battle as though someone fell from a roof and killed another, and leave the matter to God. It is all the same to God whether he deprives you of life and property by a just or by an unjust lord. You are His creature and He can do with you as He wills, just so your conscience is clear. Thus in Genesis 20 [:2–7] God himself excuses Abimelech for taking Abraham's wife; not because he had done right, but because he had not known that she was Abraham's wife.

**Fourth.** Here we come to what should really have been placed first, and of which we spoke above. A prince must act in a Christian way toward his God also; that is, he must subject himself to him in an entire confidence and pray for wisdom to rule well, as Solomon did [Kings 3:9]. But of faith and trust in God I have written so much that it is not necessary to say more here. Therefore, we will close with this brief summation, that a prince's duty is fourfold: First, toward God there must be true confidence and earnest prayer; second, toward his subjects there must be love and Christian service; third, with respect to his counselors and officials he must maintain an untrammeled reason and unfettered judgment; fourth, with respect to evildoers he must manifest a restrained severity and firmness. Then the prince's job will be done right, both outwardly and inwardly; it will be pleasing to God and to the people. But he will have to expect much envy and sorrow on account of it; the cross will soon rest on the shoulders of such a prince.

Finally, I must add an appendix in answer to those who raise questions about restitution, that is, about the return of goods wrongfully acquired. This is a matter about which the temporal sword is commonly concerned; much has been written about it, and many fantastically severe judgments have been sought in cases of this sort. I will put it all in a few words, however, and at one fell swoop dispose of all such laws and of the harsh judgments based upon them, thus: No surer law can be found in this matter than the law of love. In the first place, when a case of this sort is brought before you in which one is to make restitution to another, if they are both Christians the matter is soon settled; neither will withhold what belongs to the other, and neither will demand that it be returned. If only one of them is a Christian, namely, the one to whom restitution is due, it is again easy to settle, for he does not care whether restitution is ever made to him. The same is true if the one who is suppose to make restitution is a Christian, for he will do so.

But whether one be a Christian on not a Christian, you should decide the question of restitution as follows. If the debtor is poor and unable to make restitution as follows. If the debtor is poor and unable to make restitution, and the other party is not poor, then you should let the law of love prevail and acquit the debtor; for according to the law of love the other party is in any event obliged to relinquish the debt and, if necessary, to give him something besides. But if the debtor is not poor, then have him restore as much as he can, whether it be all, a half, a third, or a fourth of it, provided that you leave him enough to assure a house, food, and clothing for himself, his wife, and his children. This much you would owe him in any case, if you could afford it; so much the less ought you to take it away now, since you do not need it and he cannot get along without it.

If neither party is Christian, or if one of them is unwilling to be judged by the law of love, then you may have them call in some other judge, and tell the obstinate or that they are acting contrary to God and natural law, even if they obtain a strict judgment in terms of human law. For nature teaches—as does love—that I should do as I would be done by [Luke 6:31]. Therefore, I cannot strip another of his possessions, no matter how clear a right I have, so long as I am unwilling myself to be stripped of my goods. Rather, just as I would that another, in such circumstances, should relinquish his right in my favor, even so should I relinquish my rights.

Thus should one deal with all property unlawfully held, whether in public or in private, that love and natural law may always prevail. For when you judge according to love you will easily decide and adjust matters without any lawbooks. But when you ignore love and natural law you will never hit upon the solution that pleases God, though you may have devoured all the lawbooks and jurists. Instead, the more you depend on them, the further they will lead you astray. A good and just decision must not and cannot be pronounced out of books, but must come from a free mind, as though there were no books. Such a free decision is given, however, by love and by natural law, with which all reason is filled; out of the books come extravagant and untenable judgments. Let me give you an example of this.

This story is told of Duke Charles of Burgundy. A certain nobleman took an enemy prisoner. The prisoner's wife came to ransom her husband. The nobleman promised to give back the husband on condition that she would lie with him. The woman was virtuous, yet wished to set her husband free; so she goes and asks her husband whether she should do this thing in order to set him free. The husband wished to be set free and to save his life, so he gives his wife permission. After the nobleman had lain with the wife, he had the husband beheaded the next day and gave him to her as a corpse. She laid the whole case before Duke Charles. He summoned the nobleman and commanded him to marry the woman. When the wedding day was over he had the nobleman beheaded, gave the woman possession of his property, and restored her to honor. Thus he punished the crime in a princely way.

Observe: No pope, no jurist, no lawbook could have given him such a decision. It sprang from untrammeled reason, above the law in all books, and is so excellent that everyone must approve of it and find the justice of it written in his own heart. St. Augustine relates a similar story in *The Lord's Sermon on the Mount*. Therefore, we should keep written laws subject to reason, from which they originally welled forth as from the spring of justice. We should not make the spring dependent on its rivulets, or make reason a captive of letters.

# Of Civil Government

By John Calvin

## Book IV, Chapter XX

**1.** Having shown above that there is a twofold government in man, and having fully considered the one which, placed in the soul or inward man, relates to eternal life, we are here called to say something of the other, which pertains only to civil institutions and the external regulation of manners. For although this subject seems from its nature to be unconnected with the spiritual doctrine of faith, which I have undertaken to treat, it will appear as we proceed, that I have properly connected them, nay, that I am under the necessity of doing so, especially while, on the one hand, frantic and barbarous men are furiously endeavouring to overturn the order established by God, and, on the other, the flatterers of princes, extolling their power without measure, hesitate not to oppose it to the government of God. Unless we meet both extremes, the purity of the faith will perish. We may add, that it in no small degree concerns us to know how kindly God has here consulted for the human race, that pious zeal may the more strongly urge us to testify our gratitude. And first, before entering on the subject itself, it is necessary to attend to the distinction which we formerly laid down, lest, as oft en happens to many, we imprudently confound these two things, the nature of which is altogether different. For some, on hearing that liberty is promised in the gospel, a liberty which acknowledges no king and no magistrate among men, but looks to Christ alone, think that they can receive no benefit from their liberty so long as they see any power placed over them. Accordingly, they think that nothing will be safe until the whole world is changed into a new form, when there will be neither courts, nor laws, nor magistrates, nor anything of the kind to interfere, as they suppose, with their liberty. But he who knows to distinguish between the body and the soul, between the present fleeting life and that which is future and eternal, will have no difficulty in understanding that the spiritual kingdom of Christ and civil government are things very widely separated. Seeing, therefore, it is a Jewish vanity to seek and include the kingdom of Christ under the elements of this world, let us, considering, as Scripture clearly teaches, that the blessings which we derive from Christ are spiritual, remember to confine the liberty which is promised and offered to us in him within its proper limits. For why is it that the very same apostle who bids us "stand fast in the liberty wherewith Christ hath made us free, and be not again entangled with the yoke of bond-age" (Gal. 5:1), in another passage forbids slaves to be solicitous about their state (1 Cor. 7:21) unless it be that spiritual liberty is perfectly compatible with civil servitude? In this sense the following passages are to be understood: "There is neither Jew nor Greek, there is neither bond nor free, there is neither male nor female" (Gal. 3:28). Again, "There is neither Greek nor Jew, circumcision nor un-circumcision, barbarian, Scythian, bond nor free: but Christ is all and in all" (Col 3:11). It is thus intimated, that it matters not what your condition is among men, nor under what laws you live, since in them the kingdom of Christ does not at all consist.

2. Still the distinction does not go so far as to justify us in supposing that the whole scheme of civil government is matter of pol-lution, with which Christian men have nothing to do. Fanatics, indeed, delighting in unbridled license, insist and vociferate that, after we are dead by Christ to the elements of this world, and being translated into the kingdom of God sit among the celestials, it is unworthy of us, and far beneath our dignity, to be occupied with those profane and impure cares which relate to matters alien from a Christian man. To what end, they say, are laws without courts and tribunals? But what has a Christian man to do with courts? Nay, if it is unlawful to kill, what have we to do with laws and courts? But as we lately taught that that kind of government is distinct from the spiritual and internal king-dom of Christ, so we ought to know that they are not adverse to each other. The former, in some measure, begins the heavenly kingdom in us, even now upon earth, and in this mortal and evanescent life commences immortal and incorruptible blessedness, while to the latter it is assigned, so long as we live among men, to foster and maintain the external worship of God, to defend sound doctrine and the condi-tion of the Church, to adapt our conduct to human society, to form our manners to civil justice, to conciliate us to each other, to cher-ish common peace and tranquillity. All these I confess to be superfluous, if the kingdom of God, as it now exists within us, extinguishes the present life. But if it is the will of God that while we aspire to true piety we are pilgrims upon the earth, and if such pilgrimage stands in need of such aids, those who take them away from man rob him of his humanity. As to their allegation that there ought to be such perfection in the Church of God that her guidance should suffice for law, they stupidly imagine her to be such as she never can be found in the community of men. For while the insolence of the wicked is so great, and their iniquity so stillborn, that it can scarcely be curbed by any severity of laws, what do we expect would be done by those whom force can scarcely repress from doing ill, were they to see perfect impunity for their wickedness?

3. But we shall have a fitter opportunity of speaking of the use of civil government. All we wish to be understood at present is, that it is perfect barbarism to think of exterminating it, its use among men being not less than that of bread and water, light and air, while its dignity is much more excellent. Its object is not mere-ly, like those things, to enable men to breathe, eat, drink, and be warmed (though it certainly included all these, while it enables them to live together); this, I say, is not its only object, but it is, that no idolatry, no blasphemy against the name of God, no calumnies against his truth, nor other offences to religion, break out and be disseminated among the people; that the

public quiet be not disturbed, that every man's property be kept secure, that men may carry on innocent commerce with each other, that honesty and modesty be cultivated; in short, that a public form of religion may exist among Christians, and humanity among men. Let no one be surprised that I now attribute the task of constituting religion aright to human polity, though I seem above to have placed it beyond the will of man, since I no more than formerly allow men at pleasure to enact laws concerning religion and the worship of God, when I approve of civil order which is directed to this end—viz. to prevent the true religion, which is contained in the law of God, from being with impunity openly violated and polluted by public blasphemy. But the reader, by the help of perspicuous arrangement, will better understand what view is to be taken of the whole order of civil government, if we treat of each of its parts separately. Now these are three: The Magistrate, who is president and guardian of the laws; the Laws, according to which he governs; and the People, who are governed by the laws, and obey the magistrate. Let us consider, then, first, What is the function of the magistrate? Is it a lawful calling approved by God? What is the nature of his duty? What the extent of his power? Secondly, What are the laws by which Christian polity is to be regulated? And, lastly, What is the use of laws as regards the people? And, What obedience is due to the magistrate?

4. With regard to the function of magistrates, the Lord has not only declared that he approves and is pleased with it, but, moreover, has strongly recommended it to us by the very honourable titles which he has conferred upon it. To mention a few. When those who bear the office of magistrate are called gods, let no one suppose that there is little weight in that appellation. It is thereby intimated that they have a commission from God, that they are invested with divine authority, and, in fact, represent the person of God, as whose substitutes they in a manner act. This is not a quibble of mine, but is the interpretation of Christ. "If Scripture," says he, "called them Gods, to whom the word of God came." What is this but that the business was committed to them by God, to serve him in their office, and (as Moses and Jehoshaphat said to the judges whom they were appointing over each of the cities of Judah) to exercise judgment, not for man, but for God? To the same effect Wisdom affirms, by the mouth of Solomon, "By me kings reign, and princes decree justice. By me princes rule, and nobles, even all the judges of the earth" (Prov. 8:15,16). For it is just as if it had been said, that it is not owing to human perverseness that supreme power on earth is lodged in kings and other governors, but by Divine Providence, and the holy decree of Him to whom it has seemed good so to govern the affairs of men, since he is present, and also presides in enacting laws and exercising judicial equity. This Paul also plainly teaches when he enumerates offices of rule among the gift s of God, which, distributed variously, according to the measure of grace, ought to be employed by the servants of Christ for the edification of the Church (Rom. 12:8). In that place, however, he is properly speaking of the senate of grave men who were appointed in the primitive Church to take charge of public discipline. This office, in the Epistle to the Corinthians, he calls governments, (1 Cor. 12:28). Still, as we see that civil power has the same end in view, there can be no doubt that he is recommending every kind of just government. He speaks much more clearly when he comes to a proper discussion of the subject. For he says that "there is no power but of God: the powers that be are ordained of God;" that

rulers are the ministers of God, "not a terror to good works, but to the evil" (Rom. 13:1,3). To this we may add the examples of saints, some of whom held the offices of kings, as David, Josiah, and Hezekiah; others of governors, as Joseph and Daniel; others of civil magistrates among a free people, as Moses, Joshua, and the Judges. Their functions were expressly approved by the Lord. Therefore no man can doubt that civil authority is, in the sight of God, not only sacred and lawful, but the most sacred, and by far the most honourable, of all stations in mortal life.

5. Those who are desirous to introduce anarchy object that, though anciently kings and judges presided over a rude people, yet that, in the present day, that servile mode of governing does not at all accord with the perfection which Christ brought with his gospel. Herein they betray not only their ignorance, but their devilish pride, arrogating to themselves a perfection of which not even a hundredth part is seen in them. But be they what they may, the refutation is easy. For when David says, "Be wise now therefore, O ye kings: be instructed, ye judges of the earth;" "Kiss the Son, lest he be angry" (Ps. 2:10,12), he does not order them to lay aside their authority and return to private life, but to make the power with which they are invested subject to Christ, that he may rule over all. In like manner, when Isaiah predicts of the Church, "Kings shall be thy nursing-fathers, and their queens thy nursing-mothers" (Isaiah 49:23), he does not bid them abdicate their authority; he rather gives them the honourable appellation of patrons of the pious worshippers of God; for the prophecy refers to the advent of Christ. I intentionally omit very many passages which occur throughout Scripture, and especially in the Psalms, in which the due authority of all rulers is asserted. The most celebrated passage of all is that in which Paul, admonishing Timothy, that prayers are to be offered up in the public assembly for kings, subjoins the reason, "that we may lead a quiet and peaceable life in all godliness and honesty" (1 Tim. 2:2). In these words, he recommends the condition of the Church to their protection and guardianship.

6. This consideration ought to be constantly present to the minds of magistrates, since it is fitted to furnish a strong stimulus to the discharge of duty, and also afford singular consolation, smoothing the difficulties of their office, which are certainly numerous and weighty. What zeal for integrity, prudence, meekness, continence, and innocence, ought to sway those who know that they have been appointed ministers of the divine justice! How will they dare to admit iniquity to their tribunal, when they are told that it is the throne of the living God? How will they venture to pronounce an unjust sentence with that mouth which they understand to be an ordained organ of divine truth? With what conscience will they subscribe impious decrees with that hand which they know has been appointed to write the acts of God? In a word, if they remember that they are the vicegerents of God, it behooves them to watch with all care, vigilance, and industry, that they may in themselves exhibit a kind of image of the Divine Providence, guardianship, goodness, benevolence, and justice. And let them constantly keep the additional thought in view, that if a curse is pronounced on him that "doeth the work of the Lord deceitfully," a much heavier curse must lie on him who deals deceitfully in a righteous calling. Therefore, when Moses and Jehoshaphat would urge their judges to the discharge of duty, they had nothing by which they could more powerfully stimulate their minds than the consideration to which we have already referred,–"Take heed what ye

do: for ye judge not for man, but for the Lord, who is with you in the judgment. Wherefore now let the fear of the Lord be upon you; take heed and do it: for there is no iniquity with the Lord our God, nor respect of persons, nor taking of gifts" (2 Chr. 19:6,7, compared with Deut. 1:16, etc.). And in another passage it is said, "God standeth in the congregation of the mighty; he judgeth among the gods" (Psalm 82:1; Isaiah 3:14), that they may be animated to duty when they hear that they are the ambassadors of God, to whom they must one day render an account of the province committed to them. This admonition ought justly to have the greatest effect upon them; for if they sin in any respect, not only is injury done to the men whom they wickedly torment, but they also insult God himself, whose sacred tribunals they pollute. On the other hand, they have an admirable source of comfort when they reflect that they are not engaged in profane occupations, unbefitting a servant of God, but in a most sacred office, inasmuch as they are the ambassadors of God.

7. In regard to those who are not debarred by all these passages of Scripture from presuming to inveigh against this sacred ministry as if it were a thing abhorrent from religion and Christian piety, what else do they than assail God himself, who cannot but be insulted when his servants are disgraced? These men not only speak evil of dignities, but would not even have God to reign over them (1 Sam. 7:7). For if this was truly said of the people of Israel, when they declined the authority of Samuel, how can it be less truly said in the present day of those who allow themselves to break loose against all the authority established by God? But it seems that when our Lord said to his disciples, "The kings of the gentiles exercise lordship over them; and they that exercise authority upon them are called benefactors.

But ye shall not be so: but he that is greatest among you, let him be as the younger; and he that is chief; as he that doth serve" (Luke 22:25,26); he by these words prohibited all Christians from becoming kings or governors. Dexterous expounders! A dispute had arisen among the disciples as to which of them should be greatest. To suppress this vain ambition, our Lord taught them that their ministry was not like the power of earthly sovereigns, among whom one greatly surpasses another. What, I ask, is there in this comparison disparaging to royal dignity? nay, what does it prove at all unless that the royal office is not the apostolic ministry? Besides, though among magisterial offices themselves there are different forms, there is no difference in this respect, that they are all to be received by us as ordinances of God. For Paul includes all together when he says that "there is no power but of God," and that which was by no means the most pleasing of all, was honored with the highest testimonial—I mean the power of one. This, as carrying with it the public servitude of all (except the one to whose despotic will all is subject), was anciently disrelished by heroic and more excellent natures. But Scripture, to obviate these unjust judgments, affirms expressly that it is by divine wisdom that "kings reign," and gives special command "to honour the king" (1 Peter 2:17).

8. And certainly it were a very idle occupation for private men to discuss what would be the best form of polity in the place where they live, seeing these deliberations cannot have any influence in determining any public matter. Then the thing itself could not be defined absolutely without rashness, since the nature of the discussion depends on circumstances. And if you compare the different states with each other, without regard to circumstances, it is not easy to determine which of these has

the advantage in point of utility, so equal are the terms on which they meet. Monarchy is prone to tyranny. In an aristocracy, again, the tendency is not less to the faction of a few, while in popular ascendancy there is the strongest tendency to sedition. When these three forms of government, of which philosophers treat, are considered in themselves, I, for my part, am far from denying that the form which greatly surpasses the others is aristocracy, either pure or modified by popular government not indeed in itself, but because it very rarely happens that kings so rule themselves as never to dissent from what is just and right, or are possessed of so much acuteness and prudence as always to see correctly. Owing, therefore, to the vices or defects of men, it is safer and more tolerable when several bear rule, that they may thus mutually assist, instruct, and admonish each other, and should any one be disposed to go too far, the others are censors and masters to curb his excess. This has already been proved by experience, and confirmed also by the authority of the Lord himself, when he established an aristocracy bordering on popular government among the Israelites, keeping them under that as the best form, until he exhibited an image of the Messiah in David. And as I willingly admit that there is no kind of government happier than where liberty is framed with becoming moderation, and duly constituted so as to be durable, so I deem those very happy who are permitted to enjoy that form, and I admit that they do nothing at variance with their duty when they strenuously and constantly labour to preserve and maintain it. Nay, even magistrates ought to do their utmost to prevent the liberty, of which they have been appointed guardians, from being impaired, far less violated. If in this they are sluggish or little careful, they are perfidious traitors to

their office and their country. But should those to whom the Lord has assigned one form of government, take it upon them anxiously to long for a change, the wish would not only be foolish and superfluous, but very pernicious. If you fix your eyes not on one state merely, but look around the world, or at least direct your view to regions widely separated from each other you will perceive that Divine Providence has not, without good cause, arranged that different countries should be governed by different forms of polity. For as only elements of unequal temperature adhere together, so in different regions a similar inequality in the form of government is best. All this, however, is said unnecessarily to those to whom the will of God is a sufficient reason. For if it has pleased him to appoint kings over kingdoms, and senates or burgomasters over free states, whatever be the form which he has appointed in the places in which we live, our duty is to obey and submit.

9. The duty of magistrates, its nature, as described by the word of God, and the things in which it consists, I will here indicate in passing. That it extends to both tables of the law, did Scripture not teach, we might learn from profane writers; for no man has discoursed of the duty of magistrates, the enacting of laws, and the common weal, without beginning with religion and divine worship. Thus all have confessed that no polity can be successfully established unless piety be its first care, and that those laws are absurd which disregard the rights of God, and consult only for men. Seeing then that among philosophers religion holds the first place, and that the same thing has always been observed with the universal consent of nations, Christian princes and magistrates may be ashamed of their heartlessness if they make it not their care. We have already shown that this office is specially assigned

them by God, and indeed it is right that they exert themselves in asserting and defending the honour of him whose vicegerents they are, and by whose favour they rule. Hence in Scripture holy kings are especially praised for restoring the worship of God when corrupted or overthrown, or for taking care that religion flourished under them in purity and safety. On the other hand, the sacred history sets down anarchy among the vices, when it states that there was no king in Israel, and, therefore, every one did as he pleased (Judges 21:25). This rebukes the folly of those who would neglect the care of divine things, and devote themselves merely to the administration of justice among men; as if God had appointed rulers in his own name to decide earthly controversies, and omitted what was of far greater moment, his own pure worship as prescribed by his law. Such views are adopted by turbulent men, who, in their eagerness to make all kinds of innovations with impunity, would fain get rid of all the vindicators of violated piety. In regard to the second table of the law, Jeremiah addresses rulers, "Thus saith the Lord, Execute ye judgment and righteousness, and deliver the spoiled out of the hand of the oppressor: and do no wrong, do no violence to the stranger, the fatherless, nor the widow, neither shed innocent blood" (Jer. 22:3). To the same effect is the exhortation in the Psalm, "Defend the poor and fatherless; do justice to the afflicted and needy. Deliver the poor and needy; rid them out of the hand of the wicked" (Psalm 82:3,4). Moses also declared to the princes whom he had substituted for himself, "Hear the causes between your brethren, and judge righteously between every man and his brother, and the stranger that is with him. Ye shall not respect persons in judgment; but ye shall hear the small as well as the great: ye shall not be afraid of the face of man, for the judgment is God's" (Deut. 1:16). I say nothing as to such passages as these, "He shall not multiply horses to himself, nor cause the people to return to Egypt;" "neither shall he multiply wives to himself; neither shall he greatly multiply to himself silver and gold;" "he shall write him a copy of this law in a book;" "and it shall be with him, and he shall read therein all the days of his life, that he may learn to fear the Lord his God;" "that his heart be not lifted up above his brethren" (Deut. 17:16-20). In here explaining the duties of magistrates, my exposition is intended not so much for the instruction of magistrates themselves, as to teach others why there are magistrates, and to what end they have been appointed by God. We say, therefore, that they are the ordained guardians and vindicators of public innocence, modesty, honour, and tranquillity, so that it should be their only study to provide for the common peace and safety. Of these things David declares that he will set an example when he shall have ascended the throne. "A froward heart shall depart from me: I will not know a wicked person. Whoso privily slandereth his neighbour, him will I cut off: him that hath an high look and a proud heart will not I suffer. Mine eyes shall be upon the faithful of the land, that they may dwell with me: he that walketh in a perfect way, he shall serve me" (Psalm 101:4-6). But as rulers cannot do this unless they protect the good against the injuries of the bad, and give aid and protection to the oppressed, they are armed with power to curb manifest evil-doers and criminals, by whose misconduct the public tranquillity is disturbed or harassed. For we have full experience of the truth of Solon's saying, that all public matters depend on reward and punishment; that where these are wanting, the whole discipline of states totters and falls to pieces. For in the minds of many the love of equity and justice grows cold, if due honour be not paid to virtue, and the licentiousness of the wicked cannot be restrained, without strict discipline and the infliction of punishment. The two things are comprehended by the prophet when he enjoins kings and other rulers to execute "judgment and righteousness" (Jer. 21:12; 22:3). It is righteousness (justice) to take charge of the innocent, to defend and avenge them, and set them free: it is judgment to withstand the audacity of the wicked, to repress their violence, and punish their faults.

10. But here a difficult, and, as it seems, a perplexing question arises. If all Christians are forbidden to kill, and the prophet predicts concerning the holy mountain of the Lord, that is, the Church, "They shall not hurt or destroy," how can magistrates be at once pious and yet shedders of blood? But if we understand that the magistrate, in inflicting punishment, acts not of himself, but executes the very judgments of God, we shall be disencumbered of every doubt. The law of the Lord forbids to kill; but, that murder may not go unpunished, the Lawgiver himself puts the sword into the hands of his ministers, that they may employ it against all murderers. It belongs not to the pious to afflict and hurt; but to avenge the afflictions of the pious, at the command of God, is neither to afflict nor hurt. I wish it could always be present to our mind, that nothing is done here by the rashness of men but all in obedience to the authority of God. When it is the guide, we never stray from the right path, unless, indeed, divine justice is to be placed under restraint, and not allowed to take punishment on crimes. But if we dare not give the law to it, why should we bring a charge against its ministers? "He beareth not the sword in vain," says Paul, "for he is the minister of God, a revenger to execute wrath on him that doeth evil" (Rom. 13:4). Wherefore, if princes and other rulers know that nothing will be more acceptable to God than their obedience, let them give themselves to this service if they are desirous to improve their piety, justice, and integrity to God. This was the feeling of Moses when, recognizing himself as destined to deliver his people by the power of the Lord, he laid violent hands on the Egyptian, and afterwards took vengeance on the people for sacrilege, by slaying three thousand of them in one day. This was the feeling of David also, when, towards the end of his life, he ordered his son Solomon to put Joab and Shimei to death. Hence, also, in an enumeration of the virtues of a king one is to cut off the wicked from the earth, and banish all workers of iniquity from the city of God. To the same effect is the praise which is bestowed on Solomon, "Thou lovest righteousness, and hatest wickedness." How is it that the meek and gentle temper of Moses becomes so exasperated, that, besmeared and reeking with the blood of his brethren, he runs through the camp making new slaughter? How is it that David, who, during his whole life, showed so much mildness, almost at his last breath, leaves with his son the bloody testament, not to allow the grey hairs of Joab and Shimei to go to the grave in peace? Both, by their sternness, sanctified the hands which they would have polluted by showing mercy, inasmuch as they executed the vengeance committed to them by God. Solomon says, "It is an abomination to kings to commit wickedness; for the throne is established by righteousness." Again, "A king that sitteth in the throne of judgment, scattereth away all evil with his eyes." Again, "A wise king scattereth the wicked, and bringeth the wheel over them." Again, "Take away the dross from the silver, and there shall come forth a vessel for the finer. Take away the wicked men

from before the king, and his throne shall be established in righteousness." Again, "He that justifieth the wicked, and he that condemneth the just, even they both are an abomination to the Lord." Again, "An evil man seeketh only rebellion, therefore an evil messenger shall be sent against him." Again, "He that saith unto the wicked, Thou art righteous; him shall the people curse, nations shall abhor him." Now, if it is true justice in them to pursue the guilty and impious with drawn sword, to sheath the sword, and keep their hands pure from blood, while nefarious men wade through murder and slaughter, so far from redounding to the praise of their goodness and justice, would be to incur the guilt of the greatest impiety; provided always they eschew reckless and cruel asperity, and that tribunal which may be justly termed a rock on which the accused must founder. For I am not one of those who would either favour an unseasonable severity, or think that my tribunal could be accounted just that is not presided over by mercy, that best and surest counsellor of kings, and, as Solomon declares, "upholder of the throne" (Prov. 20:28). This, as was truly said by one of old, should be the primary endowment of princes. The magistrate must guard against both extremes; he must neither, be excessive severity, rather wound than cure, nor by a superstitious affectation of clemency, fall into the most cruel inhumanity, by giving way to soft and dissolute indulgence to the destruction of many. It was well said by one under the empire of Nerva, It is indeed a bad thing to live under a prince with whom nothing is lawful, but a much worse to live under one with whom all things are lawful.

11. As it is sometimes necessary for kings and states to take up arms in order to execute public vengeance, the reason assigned furnishes us with the means of estimating how far the wars which are thus undertaken are lawful. For if power has been given them to maintain the tranquillity of their subjects, repress the seditious movements of the turbulent, assist those who are violently oppressed, and animadvert on crimes, can they use it more opportunely than in repressing the fury of him who disturbs both the ease of individuals and the common tranquillity of all; who excites seditious tumult, and perpetrates acts of violent oppression and gross wrongs? If it becomes them to be the guardians and maintainers of the laws, they must repress the attempts of all alike by whose criminal conduct the discipline of the laws is impaired. Nay, if they justly punish those robbers whose injuries have been afflicted only on a few, will they allow the whole country to be robbed and devastated with impunity? Since it makes no difference whether it is by a king or by the lowest of the people that a hostile and devastating inroad is made into a district over which they have no authority, all alike are to be regarded and punished as robbers. Natural equity and duty, therefore, demand that princes be armed not only to repress private crimes by judicial inflictions, but to defend the subjects committed to their guardianship whenever they are hostilely assailed. Such even the Holy Spirit, in many passages of Scripture, declares to be lawful.

12. But if it is objected, that in the New Testament there is no passage or example teaching that war is lawful for Christians, I answer, first, that the reason for carrying on war, which anciently existed, still exists in the present day, and that, on the other hand, there is no ground for debarring magistrates from the defence of those under them; and, secondly, that in the Apostolical writings we are not to look for a distinct exposition of those matters, their object being not to form a civil polity, but

to establish the spiritual kingdom of Christ; lastly, that there also it is indicated, in passing, that our Saviour, by his advent, made no change in this respect. For (to use the words of Augustine) "if Christian discipline condemned all wars, when the soldiers ask counsel as to the way of salvation, they would have been told to cast away their arms, and withdraw altogether from military service. Whereas it was said (Luke 3:14), concuss no one, do injury to no one, be contented with your pay. Those whom he orders to be contented with their pay he certainly does not forbid to serve" (August. Ep. v. ad Marcell.) But all magistrates must here be particularly cautious not to give way, in the slightest degree, to their passions. Or rather, whether punishments are to be inflicted, they must not be borne headlong by anger, nor hurried away by hatred, nor burn with implacable severity they must, as Augustine says (De Civit. Dei. Lib. v. cap. 24), "even pity a common nature in him in whom they punish an individual fault;" or whether they have to take up arms against an enemy that is, an armed robber, they must not readily catch at the opportunity, nay, they must not take it when offered, unless compelled by the strongest necessity. For if we are to do far more than that heathen demanded, who wished war to appear as desired peace, assuredly all other means must be tried before having recourse to arms. In fine, in both cases, they must not allow themselves to be carried away by any private feeling, but be guided solely by regard for the public. Acting otherwise, they wickedly abuse their power which was given them, not for their own advantage, but for the good and service of others. On this right of war depends the right of garrisons, leagues, and other civil munitions. By garrisons, I mean those which are stationed in states for defence of the frontiers; by leagues, the alliances which are made by neighbouring princes, on the ground that if any disturbance arise within their territories, they will mutually assist each other, and combine their forces to repel the common enemies of the human race; under civil munitions, I include everything pertaining to the military art.

13. Lastly, we think it proper to add, that taxes and imposts are the legitimate revenues of princes, which they are chiefly to employ in sustaining the public burdens of their office. These, however, they may use for the maintenance of their domestic state, which is in a manner combined with the dignity of the authority which they exercise. Thus we see that David, Hezekiah, Josiah, Jehoshaphat, and other holy kings, Joseph also, and Daniel, in proportion to the office which they sustained, without offending piety, expended liberally of the public funds; and we read in Ezekiel, that a very large extent of territory was assigned to kings (Ezek. 48:21). In that passage, indeed, he is depicting the spiritual kingdom of Christ, but still he borrows his representation from lawful dominion among men Princes, however, must remember, in their turn, that their revenues are not so much private chests as treasuries of the whole people (this Paul testifies, Rom. 13:6), which they cannot, without manifest injustice, squander or dilapidate; or rather, that they are almost the blood of the people, which it were the harshest inhumanity not to spare. They should also consider that their levies and contributions, and other kinds of taxes, are merely subsidies of the public necessity, and that it is tyrannical rapacity to harass the poor people with them without cause. These things do not stimulate princes to profusion and luxurious expenditure (there is certainly no need to inflame the passions, when they are already, of their own accord, inflamed more than enough), but seeing it is

of the greatest consequence that, whatever they venture to do, they should do with a pure conscience, it is necessary to teach them how far they can lawfully go, lest, by impious confidence, they incur the divine displeasure. Nor is this doctrine superfluous to private individuals, that they may not rashly and petulantly stigmatize the expenditure of princes, though it should exceed the ordinary limits.

14. In states, the thing next in importance to the magistrates is laws, the strongest sinews of government, or, as Cicero calls them after Plato, the soul, without which, the office of the magistrate cannot exist; just as, on the other hand, laws have no vigour without the magistrate. Hence nothing could be said more truly than that the law is a dumb magistrate, the magistrate a living law. As I have undertaken to describe the laws by which Christian polity is to be governed, there is no reason to expect from me a long discussion on the best kind of laws. The subject is of vast extent, and belongs not to this place. I will only briefly observe, in passing, what the laws are which may be piously used with reference to God, and duly administered among men. This I would rather have passed in silence, were I not aware that many dangerous errors are here committed. For there are some who deny that any commonwealth is rightly framed which neglects the law of Moses, and is ruled by the common law of nations. How perilous and seditious these views are, let others see: for me it is enough to demonstrate that they are stupid and false. We must attend to the well known division which distributes the whole law of God, as promulgated by Moses, into the moral, the ceremonial, and the judicial law, and we must attend to each of these parts, in order to understand how far they do, or do not, pertain to us. Meanwhile, let no one be moved by the thought that the judicial and ceremonial laws relate to morals. For the ancients who adopted this division, though they were not unaware that the two latter classes had to do with morals, did not give them the name of moral, because they might be changed and abrogated without affecting morals. They give this name specially to the first class, without which, true holiness of life and an immutable rule of conduct cannot exist.

15. The moral law, then (to begin with it), being contained under two heads, the one of which simply enjoins us to worship God with pure faith and piety, the other to embrace men with sincere affection, is the true and eternal rule of righteousness prescribed to the men of all nations and of all times, who would frame their life agreeably to the will of God. For his eternal and immutable will is, that we are all to worship him and mutually love one another. The ceremonial law of the Jews was a tutelage by which the Lord was pleased to exercise, as it were the childhood of that people, until the fullness of the time should come when he was fully to manifest his wisdom to the world, and exhibit the reality of those things which were then adumbrated by figures (Gal. 3:24; 4:4). The judicial law, gives them as a kind of polity, delivered certain forms of equity and justice, by which they might live together innocently and quietly. And as that exercise in ceremonies properly pertained to the doctrine of piety, inasmuch as it kept the Jewish Church in the worship and religion of God, yet was still distinguishable from piety itself, so the judicial form, though it looked only to the best method of preserving that charity which is enjoined by the eternal law of God, was still something distinct from the precept of love itself. Therefore, as ceremonies might be abrogated without at all interfering with piety, so, also, when these judicial arrangements are

removed, the duties and precepts of charity can still remain perpetual. But if it is true that each nation has been left at liberty to enact the laws which it judges to be beneficial still these are always to be tested by the rule of charity, so that while they vary in form, they must proceed on the same principle. Those barbarous and savage laws, for instance, which conferred honour on thieves, allowed the promiscuous intercourse of the sexes, and other things even fouler and more absurd, I do not think entitled to be considered as laws, since they are not only altogether abhorrent to justice, but to humanity and civilized life.

16. What I have said will become plain if we attend, as we ought, to two things connected with all laws–viz. the enactment of the law, and the equity on which the enactment is founded and rests. Equity, as it is natural, cannot be the same in all, and therefore ought to be proposed by all laws, according to the nature of the thing enacted. As constitutions have some circumstances on which they partly depend, there is nothing to prevent their diversity, provided they all alike aim at equity as their end. Now, as it is evident that the law of God which we call moral, is nothing else than the testimony of natural law, and of that conscience which God has engraven on the minds of men, the whole of this equity of which we now speak is prescribed in it. Hence it alone ought to be the aim, the rule, and the end of all laws. Wherever laws are formed after this rule, directed to this aim, and restricted to this end, there is no reason why they should be disapproved by us, however much they may differ from the Jewish law, or from each other (August. de Civit. Dei, Lib. xix. c. 17). The law of God forbids to steal. The punishment appointed for theft in the civil polity of the Jews may be seen in Exodus 22. Very ancient laws of other nations punished theft by exacting

the double of what was stolen, while subsequent laws made a distinction between theft, manifest and not manifest. Other laws went the length of punishing with exile, or with branding, while others made the punishment capital. Among the Jews, the punishment of the false witness was to "do unto him as he had thought to have done with his brother" (Deut. 19:19). In some countries, the punishment is infamy, in others hanging, in others crucifixion. All laws alike avenge murder with blood, but the kinds of death are different. In some countries, adultery was punished more severely, in others more leniently. Yet we see that amidst this diversity they all tend to the same end. For they all with one mouth declare against those crimes which are condemned by the eternal law of God—viz. murder, theft, adultery, and false witness; though they agree not as to the mode of punishment. This is not necessary, nor even expedient. There may be a country which, if murder were not visited with fearful punishments, would instantly become a prey to robbery and slaughter. There may be an age requiring that the severity of punishments should be increased. If the state is in troubled condition, those things from which disturbances usually arise must be corrected by new edicts. In time of war, civilization would disappear amid the noise of arms, were not men overawed by an unwonted severity of punishment. In sterility, in pestilence, were not stricter discipline employed, all things would grow worse. One nation might be more prone to a particular vice, were it not most severely repressed. How malignant were it, and invidious of the public good, to be offended at this diversity, which is admirably adapted to retain the observance of the divine law. The allegation, that insult is offered to the law of God enacted by Moses, where it is abrogated, and other new laws are preferred to it, is most absurd. Others are not preferred when they are more approved, not absolutely, but from regard to time and place, and the condition of the people, or when those things are abrogated which were never enacted for us. The Lord did not deliver it by the hand of Moses to be promulgated in all countries, and to be everywhere enforced; but having taken the Jewish nation under his special care, patronage, and guardianship, he was pleased to be specially its legislator, and as became a wise legislator, he had special regard to it in enacting laws.

17. It now remains to see, as was proposed in the last place, what use the common society of Christians derive from laws, judicial proceedings, and magistrates. With this is connected another question—viz. What difference ought private individuals to pay to magistrates, and how far ought obedience to proceed? To very many it seems that among Christians the office of magistrate is superfluous, because they cannot piously implore his aid, inasmuch as they are forbidden to take revenge, cite before a judge, or go to law. But when Paul, on the contrary, clearly declares that he is the minister of God to us for good (Rom. 13:4), we thereby understand that he was so ordained of God, that, being defended by his hand and aid against the dishonesty and injustice of wicked men, we may live quiet and secure. But if he would have been appointed over us in vain, unless we were to use his aid, it is plain that it cannot be wrong to appeal to it and implore it. Here, indeed, I have to do with two classes of men. For there are very many who boil with such a rage for litigation, that they never can be quiet with themselves unless they are fighting with others. Law-suits they prosecute with the bitterness of deadly hatred, and with an insane eagerness to hurt and revenge, and they persist in them with

implacable obstinacy, even to the ruin of their adversary. Meanwhile, that they may be thought to do nothing but what is legal, they use this pretext of judicial proceedings as a defence of their perverse conduct. But if it is lawful for brother to litigate with brother, it does not follow that it is lawful to hate him, and obstinately pursue him with a furious desire to do him harm.

18. Let such persons then understand that judicial proceedings are lawful to him who makes a right use of them; and the right use, both for the pursuer and for the defender, is for the latter to sist himself on the day appointed, and, without bitterness, urge what he can in his defence, but only with the desire of justly maintaining his right; and for the pursuer, when undeservedly attacked in his life or fortunes, to throw himself upon the protection of the magistrate, state his complaint, and demand what is just and good; while, far from any wish to hurt or take vengeance—far from bitterness or hatred—far from the ardour of strife, he is rather disposed to yield and suffer somewhat than to cherish hostile feelings towards his opponent. On the contrary, when minds are filled with malevolence, corrupted by envy, burning with anger, breathing revenge, or, in fine, so inflamed by the heat of the contest, that they, in some measure, lay aside charity, the whole pleading, even of the justest cause, cannot but be impious. For it ought to be an axiom among all Christians, that no plea, however equitable, can be rightly conducted by any one who does not feel as kindly towards his opponent as if the matter in dispute were amicably transacted and arranged. Some one, perhaps, may here break in and say, that such moderation in judicial proceedings is so far from being seen, that an instance of it would be a kind of prodigy. I confess that in these times it is rare to meet with an example of an

honest litigant; but the thing itself, untainted by the accession of evil, ceases not to be good and pure. When we hear that the assistance of the magistrate is a sacred gift from God, we ought the more carefully to beware of polluting it by our fault.

19. Let those who distinctly condemn all judicial distinction know, that they repudiate the holy ordinance of God, and one of those gifts which to the pure are pure, unless, indeed, they would charge Paul with a crime, because he repelled the calumnies of his accusers, exposing their craft and wickedness, and, at the tribunal, claimed for himself the privilege of a Roman citizen, appealing, when necessary, from the governor to Caesar's judgment-seat. There is nothing contrary to this in the prohibition, which binds all Christians to refrain from revenge, a feeling which we drive far away from all Christian tribunals. For whether the action be of a civil nature, he only takes the right course who, with innocuous simplicity, commits his cause to the judge as the public protector, without any thought of returning evil for evil (which is the feeling of revenge); or whether the action is of a graver nature, directed against a capital offence, the accuser required is not one who comes into court, carried away by some feeling of revenge or resentment from some private injury, but one whose only object is to prevent the attempts of some bad men to injure the commonweal. But if you take away the vindictive mind, you offend in no respect against that command which forbids Christians to indulge revenge. But they are not only forbidden to thirst for revenge, they are also enjoined to wait for the hand of the Lord, who promises that he will be the avenger of the oppressed and afflicted. But those who call upon the magistrate to give assistance to themselves or others, anticipate the vengeance of the heavenly Judge.

By no means, for we are to consider that the vengeance of the magistrate is the vengeance not of man, but of God, which, as Paul says, he exercises by the ministry of man for our good (Rom. 13:8).

20. No more are we at variance with the words of Christ, who forbids us to resist evil, and adds, "Whosoever shall smite thee on thy right cheek, turn to him the other also. And if any man will sue thee at the law, and take away thy coat, let him have thy cloak also" (Matt. 5:39,40). He would have the minds of his followers to be so abhorrent to everything like retaliation, that they would sooner allow the injury to be doubled than desire to repay it. From this patience we do not dissuade them. For verily Christians were to be a class of men born to endure affronts and injuries, and be exposed to the iniquity, imposture, and derision of abandoned men, and not only so, but were to be tolerant of all these evils; that is, so composed in the whole frame of their minds, that, on receiving one offence, they were to prepare themselves for another, promising themselves nothing during the whole of life but the endurance of a perpetual cross. Meanwhile, they must do good to those who injure them, and pray for those who curse them, and (this is their only victory) strive to overcome evil with good (Rom. 12:20,21). Thus affected, they will not seek eye for eye, and tooth for tooth (as the Pharisees taught their disciples to long for vengeance), but (as we are instructed by Christ), they will allow their body to be mutilated, and their goods to be maliciously taken from them, prepared to remit and spontaneously pardon those injuries the moment they have been inflicted. This equity and moderation, however, will not prevent them, with entire friendship for their enemies, from using the aid of the magistrate for the preservation of their goods, or, from

zeal for the public interest, to call for the punishment of the wicked and pestilential man, whom they know nothing will reform but death. All these precepts are truly expounded by Augustine, as tending to prepare the just and pious man patiently to sustain the malice of those whom he desires to become good, that he may thus increase the number of the good, not add himself to the number of the bad by imitating their wickedness. Moreover, it pertains more to the preparation of the heart which is within, than to the work which is done openly, that patience and good-will may be retained within the secret of the heart, and that may be done openly which we see may do good to those to whom we ought to wish well (August. Ep. v. ad. Marcell.).

21. The usual objection, that law-suits are universally condemned by Paul (1 Cor. 6:6), is false. It may easily be understood from his words, that a rage for litigation prevailed in the Church of Corinth to such a degree, that they exposed the gospel of Christ, and the whole religion which they professed, to the calumnies and cavils of the ungodly. Paul rebukes them, first for traducing the gospel to unbelievers by the intemperance of their dissensions; and, secondly, for so striving with each other while they were brethren. For so far were they from bearing injury from another, that they greedily coveted each other's effects, and voluntarily provoked and injured them. He inveighs, therefore, against that madness for litigation, and not absolutely against all kinds of disputes. He declares it to be altogether a vice or infirmity, that they do not submit to the loss of their effects, rather than strive, even to contention, in preserving them; in other words, seeing they were so easily moved by every kind of loss, and on every occasion, however slight, ran off to the forum and to law-suits, he says, that in this

way they showed that they were of too irritable a temper, and not prepared for patience. Christians should always feel disposed rather to give up part of their right than to go into court, out of which they can scarcely come without a troubled mind, a mind inflamed with hatred of their brother. But when one sees that his property, the want of which he would grievously feel, he is able, without any loss of charity, to defend, if he should do so, he offends in no respect against that passage of Paul. In short, as we said at first, every man's best adviser is charity. Everything in which we engage without charity, and all the disputes which carry us beyond it, are unquestionably unjust and impious.

22. The first duty of subjects towards their rulers, is to entertain the most honourable views of their office, recognizing it as a delegated jurisdiction from God, and on that account receiving and reverencing them as the ministers and ambassadors of God. For you will find some who show themselves very obedient to magistrates, and would be unwilling that there should be no magistrates to obey, because they know this is expedient for the public good, and yet the opinion which those persons have of magistrates is, that they are a kind of necessary evils. But Peter requires something more of us when he says, "Honour the king" (1 Pet. 2:17); and Solomon, when he says, "My son, fear thou the Lord and the king" (Prov. 24:21). For, under the term honour, the former includes a sincere and candid esteem, and the latter, by joining the king with God, shows that he is invested with a kind of sacred veneration and dignity. We have also the remarkable injunction of Paul, "Be subject not only for wrath, but also for conscience sake" (Rom. 13:5). By this he means, that subjects, in submitting to princes and governors, are not to be influenced merely by fear (just as

those submit to an armed enemy who see vengeance ready to be executed if they resist), but because the obedience which they yield is rendered to God himself inasmuch as their power is from God. I speak not of the men as if the mask of dignity could cloak folly, or cowardice, or cruelty, or wicked or flagitious manners, and thus acquire for vice the praise of virtue; but I say that the station itself is deserving of honour and reverence, and that those who rule should, in respect of their office, be held by us in esteem and veneration.

23. From this, a second consequence is, that we must with ready minds prove our obedience to them, whether in complying with edicts, or in paying tribute, or in undertaking public offices and burdens, which relate to the common defence, or in executing any other orders. "Let every soul," says Paul, "be subject unto the higher powers." "Whosoever, therefore, resisteth the power, resisteth the ordinance of God" (Rom. 13:1,2). Writing to Titus, he says, "Put them in mind to be subject to principalities and powers, to obey magistrates, to be ready to every good work" (Tit. 3:1). Peter also says, "Submit yourselves to every human creature" (or rather, as I understand it, "ordinance of man"), "for the Lord's sake: whether it be to the king, as supreme; or unto governors, as unto them that are sent by him for the punishment of evil-doers, and for the praise of them that do well" (1 Pet. 2:13). Moreover, to testify that they do not feign subjection, but are sincerely and cordially subject, Paul adds, that they are to commend the safety and prosperity of those under whom they live to God. "I exhort, therefore," says he, "that, first of all, supplications, prayers, intercessions, and giving of thanks, be made for all men; for kings, and for all that are in authority: that we may lead a quiet and peaceable life in all godliness and honesty" (1 Tim. 2:1,2). Let no man, here deceive himself,

since we cannot resist the magistrate without resisting God. For, although an unarmed magistrate may seem to be despised with impunity, yet God is armed, and will signally avenge this contempt. Under this obedience, I comprehend the restraint which private men ought to impose on themselves in public, not interfering with public business, or rashly encroaching on the province of the magistrate, or attempting anything at all of a public nature. If it is proper that anything in a public ordinance should be corrected, let them not act tumultuously, or put their hands to a work where they ought to feel that their hands are tied, but let them leave it to the cognisance of the magistrate, whose hand alone here is free. My meaning is, let them not dare to do it without being ordered. For when the command of the magistrate is given, they too are invested with public authority. For as, according to the common saying, the eyes and ears of the prince are his counsellors, so one may no' improperly say that those who, by his command, have the charge of managing affairs, are his hands.

24. But as we have hitherto described the magistrate who truly is what he is called—viz. the father of his country, and (as the Poet speaks) the pastor of the people, the guardian of peace, the president of justice, the vindicator of innocence, he is justly to be deemed a madman who disapproves of such authority. And since in almost all ages we see that some princes, careless about all their duties on which they ought to have been intent, live, without solicitude, in luxurious sloth; others, bent on their own interest, venally prostitute all rights, privileges, judgments, and enactments; others pillage poor people of their money, and afterwards squander it in insane largesses; others act as mere robbers, pillaging houses, violating matrons, and slaying the innocent; many cannot be persuaded to recognize such

persons for princes, whose command, as far as lawful, they are bound to obey. For while in this unworthy conduct, and among atrocities so alien, not only from the duty of the magistrate, but also of the man, they behold no appearance of the image of God which ought to be conspicuous in the magistrate, while they see not a vestige of that minister of God, who was appointed to be a praise to the good and a terror to the bad, they cannot recognize the ruler whose dignity and authority Scripture recommends to us. And, undoubtedly, the natural feeling of the human mind has always been not less to assail tyrants with hatred and execration, than to look up to just kings with love and veneration.

25. But if we have respect to the word of God, it will lead us farther, and make us subject not only to the authority of those princes who honestly and faithfully perform their duty toward us, but all princes, by whatever means they have so become, although there is nothing they less perform than the duty of princes. For though the Lord declares that a ruler to maintain our safety is the highest gift of his beneficence, and prescribes to rulers themselves their proper sphere, he at the same time declares, that of whatever description they may be, they derive their power from none but him. Those, indeed, who rule for the public good, are true examples and specimens of his beneficence, while those who domineer unjustly and tyrannically are raised up by him to punish the people for their iniquity. Still all alike possess that sacred majesty with which he has invested lawful power. I will not proceed further without subjoining some distinct passages to this effect. We need not labour to prove that an impious king is a mark of the Lord's anger, since I presume no one will deny it, and that this is not less true of a king than of a robber who plunders your goods, an adulterer who defiles your bed, and an assassin who aims at your life, since all such calamities are classed by Scripture among the curses of God. But let us insist at greater length in proving what does not so easily fall in with the views of men, that even an individual of the worst character, one most unworthy of all honour, if invested with public authority, receives that illustrious divine power which the Lord has by his word devolved on the ministers of his justice and judgment, and that, accordingly, in so far as public obedience is concerned, he is to be held in the same honour and reverence as the best of kings.

26. And, first, I would have the reader carefully to attend to that Divine Providence which, not without cause, is so often set before us in Scripture, and that special act of distributing kingdoms, and setting up as kings whomsoever he pleases. In Daniel it is said, "He changeth the times and the seasons: he removeth kings, and setteth up kings" (Dan. 2:21,37). Again, "That the living may know that the Most High ruleth in the kingdom of men, and giveth it to whomsoever he will" (Dan. 4:17,25). Similar sentiments occur throughout Scripture, but they abound particularly in the prophetical books. What kind of king Nebuchadnezzar, he who stormed Jerusalem, was, is well known. He was an active invader and devastator of other countries. Yet the Lord declares in Ezekiel that he had given him the land of Egypt as his hire for the devastation which he had committed. Daniel also said to him, "Thou, O king, art a king of kings: for the God of heaven hath given thee a kingdom, power, and strength, and glory. And wheresoever the children of men dwell, the beasts of the field and the fowls of the heaven hath he given into thine hand, and hath made thee ruler over them all" (Dan. 2:37,38). Again,

he says to his son Belshazzar, "The most high God gave Nebuchadnezzar thy father a kingdom, and majesty and glory, and honour: and for the majesty that he gave him, all people, nations, and languages, trembled and feared before him" (Dan. 5:18,19). When we hear that the king was appointed by God, let us, at the same time, call to mind those heavenly edicts as to honouring and fearing the king, and we shall have no doubt that we are to view the most iniquitous tyrant as occupying the place with which the Lord has honoured him. When Samuel declared to the people of Israel what they would suffer from their kings, he said, "This will be the manner of the king that shall reign over you: He will take your sons, and appoint them for himself, for his chariots, and to be his horsemen; and some shall run before his chariots. And he will appoint him captains over thousands, and captains over fifties; and will set them to ear his ground, and to reap his harvest and to make his instruments of war, and instruments of his chariots And he will take your daughters to be confectionaries, and to be cooks, and to be bakers. And he will take your fields, and your vineyards, and your olive-yards, even the best of them, and give them to his servants. And he will take the tenth of your seed, and of your vineyards, and give to his officers, and to his servants. And he will take your men-servants, and your maidservants, and your goodliest young men, and your asses, and put them to his work. He will take the tenth of your sheep: and ye shall be his servants" (1 Sam. 8:11-17). Certainly these things could not be done legally by kings, whom the law trained most admirably to all kinds of restraint; but it was called justice in regard to the people, because they were bound to obey, and could not lawfully resist: as if Samuel had said, To such a degree will

kings indulge in tyranny, which it will not be for you to restrain. The only thing remaining for you will be to receive their commands, and be obedient to their words.

27. But the most remarkable and memorable passage is in Jeremiah. Though it is rather long, I am not indisposed to quote it, because it most clearly settles this whole question. "I have made the earth, the man and the beast that are upon the ground, by my great power, and by my outstretched arm, and have given it unto whom it seemed meet unto me. And now have I given all these lands into the hand of Nebuchadnezzar the king of Babylon, my servant: and the beasts of the field have I given him also to serve him. And all nations shall serve him, and his son, and his son's son, until the very time of his land come: and then many nations and great kings shall serve themselves of him. And it shall come to pass, that the nation and kingdom which will not serve the same Nebuchadnezzar the king of Babylon, and that will not put their neck under the yoke of the king of Babylon, that nation will I punish, saith the Lord, with the sword, and with famine, and with pestilence, until I have consumed them by his hand" (Jer. 27:5-8). Therefore "bring your necks under the yoke of the king of Babylon, and serve him and his people, and live" (v. 12). We see how great obedience the Lord was pleased to demand for this dire and ferocious tyrant, for no other reason than just that he held the kingdom. In other words, the divine decree had placed him on the throne of the kingdom, and admitted him to regal majesty, which could not be lawfully violated. If we constantly keep before our eyes and minds the fact, that even the most iniquitous kings are appointed by the same decree which establishes all regal authority, we will never entertain the seditious thought, that a king is to be treated according to his

deserts, and that we are not bound to act the part of good subjects to him who does not in his turn act the part of a king to us.

28. It is vain to object, that that command was specially given to the Israelites. For we must attend to the ground on which the Lord places it—" I have given the kingdom to Nebuchadnezzar; therefore serve him and live." Let us doubt not that on whomsoever the kingdom has been conferred, him we are bound to serve. Whenever God raises any one to royal honour, he declares it to be his pleasure that he should reign. To this effect we have general declarations in Scripture. Solomon says—"For the transgression of a land, many are the princes thereof" (Prov. 28:2). Job says—"He looseth the bond of kings, and girdeth their loins with a girdle" (Job. 12:18). This being confessed, nothing remains for us but to serve and live. There is in Jeremiah another command in which the Lord thus orders his people—"Seek the peace of the city whither I have caused you to be carried away captives, and pray unto the Lord for it: for in the peace thereof shall ye have peace" (Jer. 29:7). Here the Israelites, plundered of all their property, torn from their homes, driven into exile, thrown into miserable bondage, are ordered to pray for the prosperity of the victor, not as we are elsewhere ordered to pray for our persecutors, but that his kingdom may be preserved in safety and tranquillity, that they too may live prosperously under him. Thus David, when already king elect by the ordination of God, and anointed with his holy oil, though causelessly and unjustly assailed by Saul, holds the life of one who was seeking his life to be sacred, because the Lord had invested him with royal honour. "The Lord forbid that I should do this thing unto my master, the Lord's anointed, to stretch forth mine hand against him, seeing he is the anointed of the Lord." "Mine eyes spare thee; and I said, I will not put forth mine hand against my lord; for he is the Lord's anointed" (1 Sam. 24:6,11). Again,—" Who can stretch forth his hand against the Lord's anointed, and be guiltless"? "As the Lord liveth the Lord shall smite him, or his day shall come to die, or he shall descend into battle, and perish. The Lord forbid that I should stretch forth mine hand against the Lord's anointed" (1 Sam. 24:9-11).

29. This feeling of reverence, and even of piety, we owe to the utmost to all our rulers, be their characters what they may. This I repeat the oftener, that we may learn not to consider the individuals themselves, but hold it to be enough that by the will of the Lord they sustain a character on which he has impressed and engraven inviolable majesty. But rulers, you will say, owe mutual duties to those under them. This I have already confessed. But if from this you conclude that obedience is to be returned to none but just governors, you reason absurdly. Husbands are bound by mutual duties to their wives, and parents to their children. Should husbands and parents neglect their duty; should the latter be harsh and severe to the children whom they are enjoined not to provoke to anger, and by their severity harass them beyond measure; should the former treat with the greatest contumely the wives whom they are enjoined to love and to spare as the weaker vessels; would children be less bound in duty to their parents, and wives to their husbands? They are made subject to the froward and undutiful. Nay, since the duty of all is not to look behind them, that is, not to inquire into the duties of one another, but to submit each to his own duty, this ought especially to be exemplified in the case of those who are placed under the power of others. Wherefore, if we are cruelly tormented by a savage, if we are rapaciously

pillaged by an avaricious or luxurious, if we are neglected by a sluggish, if, in short, we are persecuted for righteousness' sake by an impious and sacrilegious prince, let us first call up the remembrance of our faults, which doubtless the Lord is chastising by such scourges. In this way humility will curb our impatience. And let us reflect that it belongs not to us to cure these evils, that all that remains for us is to implore the help of the Lord, in whose hands are the hearts of kings, and inclinations of kingdoms. "God stand-eth in the congregation of the mighty; he judgeth among the gods." Before his face shall fall and be crushed all kings and judges of the earth, who have not kissed his anointed, who have enacted unjust laws to oppress the poor in judgment, and do violence to the cause of the humble, to make widows a prey, and plunder the fatherless.

30. Herein is the goodness, power, and providence of God wondrously displayed. At one time he raises up manifest avengers from among his own servants, and gives them his command to punish accursed tyranny, and deliver his people from calamity when they are unjustly oppressed; at another time he employs, for this purpose, the fury of men who have other thoughts and other aims. Thus he rescued his people Israel from the tyranny of Pharaoh by Moses; from the violence of Chusa, king of Syria, by Othniel; and from other bondage by other kings or judges. Thus he tamed the pride of Tyre by the Egyptians; the insolence of the Egyptians by the Assyrians; the ferocity of the Assyrians by the Chaldeans; the confidence of Babylon by the Medes and Persians,—Cyrus having previously subdued the Medes, while the ingratitude of the kings of Judah and Israel, and their impious contumacy after all his kindness, he subdued and punished,—at one time by the Assyrians, at another by the Babylonians.

All these things, however, were not done in the same way. The former class of deliverers being brought forward by the lawful call of God to perform such deeds, when they took up arms against kings, did not at all violate that majesty with which kings are invested by divine appointment, but armed from heaven, they, by a greater power, curbed a less, just as kings may lawfully punish their own satraps. The latter class, though they were directed by the hand of God, as seemed to him good, and did his work without knowing it, had nought but evil in their thoughts.

31. But whatever may be thought of the acts of the men themselves, the Lord by their means equally executed his own work, when he broke the bloody scepters of insolent kings, and overthrew their intolerable dominations. Let princes hear and be afraid; but let us at the same time guard most carefully against spurning or violating the venerable and majestic authority of rulers, an authority which God has sanctioned by the surest edicts, although those invested with it should be most unworthy of it, and, as far as in them lies, pollute it by their iniquity. Although the Lord takes vengeance on unbridled domination, let us not therefore suppose that that vengeance is committed to us, to whom no command has been given but to obey and suffer. I speak only of private men. For when popular magistrates have been appointed to curb the tyranny of kings (as the Ephori, who were opposed to kings among the Spartans, or Tribunes of the people to consuls among the Romans, or Demarchs to the senate among the Athenians; and perhaps there is something similar to this in the power exercised in each kingdom by the three orders, when they hold their primary diets). So far am I from forbidding these officially to check the undue license of kings, that if they connive at kings when they tyrannize

and insult over the humbler of the people, I affirm that their dissimulation is not free from nefarious perfidy, because they fraudulently betray the liberty of the people, while knowing that, by the ordinance of God, they are its appointed guardians.

32. But in that obedience which we hold to be due to the commands of rulers, we must always make the exception, nay, must be particularly careful that it is not incompatible with obedience to Him to whose will the wishes of all kings should be subject, to whose decrees their commands must yield, to whose majesty their scepters must bow. And, indeed, how preposterous were it, in pleasing men to incur the offence of Him for whose sake you obey men! The Lord, therefore, is King of kings. When he opens his sacred mouth, he alone is to be heard, instead of all and above all. We are subject to the men who rule over us, but subject only in the Lord. If they command anything against him let us not pay the least regard to it, nor be moved by all the dignity which they possess as magistrates—a dignity to which no injury is done when it is subordinated to the special and truly supreme power of God. On this ground Daniel denies that he had sinned in any respect against the king when he refused to obey his impious decree (Dan. 6:22), because the king had exceeded his limits, and not only been injurious to men, but, by raising his horn against God, had virtually abrogated his own power. On the other hand, the Israelites are condemned for having too readily obeyed the impious edict of the king. For, when Jeroboam made the golden calf, they forsook the temple of God, and, in submissiveness to him, revolted to new superstitions (1 Kings 12:28). With the same facility posterity had bowed before the decrees of their kings. For this they are severely upbraided by the Prophet (Hosea. 5:11). So far is the praise of modesty from being due to that pretence by which flattering courtiers cloak themselves, and deceive the simple, when they deny the lawfulness of declining anything imposed by their kings, as if the Lord had resigned his own rights to mortals by appointing them to rule over their fellows, or as if earthly power were diminished when it is subjected to its author, before whom even the principalities of heaven tremble as suppliants. I know the imminent peril to which subjects expose themselves by this firmness, kings being most indignant when they are contemned. As Solomon says, "The wrath of a king is as messengers of death" (Prov. 16:14). But since Peter, one of heaven's heralds, has published the edict, "We ought to obey God rather than men" (Acts 5:29), let us console ourselves with the thought, that we are rendering the obedience which the Lord requires, when we endure anything rather than turn aside from piety. And that our courage may not fail, Paul stimulates us by the additional consideration (1 Cor. 7:23), that we were redeemed by Christ at the great price which our redemption cost him, in order that we might not yield a slavish obedience to the depraved wishes of men, far less do homage to their impiety.

# Leviathan

By Thomas Hobbes

## Chapter XIII

### Of the Natural Condition of Mankind as Concerning their Felicity and Misery

**N**ature hath made men so equal, in the faculties of the body and mind; as that though there be found one man sometimes manifestly stronger in body, or of quicker mind than another, yet when all is reckoned together, the difference between man and man, is not so considerable, as that one man can thereupon claim to himself any benefit, to which another may not pretend, as well as he. For as to the strength of body, the weakest has strength enough to kill the strongest, either by secret machination, or by confederacy with others, that are in the same danger with himself.

And as to the faculties of the mind, setting aside the arts grounded upon words, and especially that skill of proceeding upon general and infallible rules, called science; which very few have, and but in few things; as being not a native faculty, born with us; nor attained, as prudence, while we look after somewhat else, I find yet a greater equality amongst men than that of strength. For prudence is but experience; which equal time, equally bestows on all men, in those things they equally apply themselves unto. That which may perhaps make such equality incredible, is but a vain conceit of one's own wisdom, which almost all men think they have in a greater degree than the vulgar; that is, than all men but themselves, and a few others, whom by fame or for concurring with themselves, they approve. For such is the nature of men, that howsoever they may acknowledge many others to be more witty, or more eloquent, or more learned; yet they will hardly believe there be many so wise as themselves; for they see their own wit at hand, and other men's at a distance. But this proveth rather that men are in that point equal, than unequal. For there is not ordinarily a greater sign of the equal distribution of anything, than that every man is contented with his share.

From this equality of ability, ariseth equality of hope in the attaining of our ends. And therefore if any two men desire the same thing, which nevertheless they cannot both enjoy, they become enemies; and in the way to their end, which is principally their own conservation, and sometimes their delectation only, endeavour to destroy or subdue one another. And from hence it comes to pass, that where an invader hath no more to fear than another man's single power; if one plant, sow, build, or possess a convenient seat, others may probably be expected to come prepared with forces united, to dispossess and deprive him, not only of the fruit of his labour, but also of his life or liberty. And the invader again is in the like danger of another.

And from this diffidence of one another, there is no way for any man to secure himself, so reasonable, as anticipation; that is, by force, or wiles, to master the persons of all men he can, so long, till he see no other power great enough to endanger him: and this is no more than his own conservation requireth, and is generally allowed. Also because there be some, that taking pleasure in contemplating their own power in the acts of conquest, which they pursue farther than their security requires; if others, that otherwise would be glad to be at ease within modest bounds, should not by invasion increase their power, they would not be able, long time, by standing only on their defence, to subsist. And by consequence, such augmentation of dominion over men being necessary to a man's conservation, it ought to be allowed him.

Again, men have no pleasure, but on the contrary a great deal of grief, in keeping company, where there is no power able to overawe them all. For every man looketh that his companion should value him, at the same rate he sets upon himself: and upon all signs of contempt, or undervaluing, naturally endeavours, as far as he dares, (which amongst them that have no common power to keep them in quiet, is far enough to make them destroy each other,) to extort a greater value from his contemners, by damage; and from others, by the example.

So that in the nature of man, we find three principal causes of quarrel. First, competition; secondly, diffidence; thirdly, glory.

The first, maketh men invade for gain; the second, for safety; and the third, for reputation. The first use violence, to make themselves masters of other men's persons, wives, children, and cattle; the second, to defend them; the third, for trifles, as a word, a smile, a different opinion, and any other sign of undervalue, either direct in their persons, or by reflection in their kindred, their friends, their nation, their profession, or their name.

Hereby it is manifest, that during the time men live without a common power to keep them all in awe, they are in that condition which is called war; and such a war, as is of every man, against every man. For "war" consisteth not in battle only, or the act of fighting; but in a tract of time, wherein the will to contend by battle is sufficiently known: and therefore the notion of "time" is to be considered in the nature of war, as it is in the nature of weather. For as the nature of foul weather lieth not in a shower or two of rain, but in an inclination thereto of many days together; so the nature of war consisteth not in actual fighting, but in the known disposition thereto during all the time there is no assurance to the contrary. All other time is "peace."

Whatsoever therefore is consequent to a time of war, where every man is enemy to every man, the same is consequent to the time wherein men live without other security than what their own strength and their own invention shall furnish them withal. In such condition there is no place for industry, because the fruit thereof is uncertain, and consequently no culture of the earth; no navigation, nor use of the commodities that may be imported by sea; no commodious building; no instruments of moving and removing such things as require much force; no knowledge of the face of the earth; no account of time; no arts; no letters; no society; and, which is worst of all, continual fear and danger of violent death; and the life of man, solitary, poor, nasty, brutish, and short.

It may seem strange to some man, that has not well weighed these things, that Nature should thus dissociate, and render men apt to invade and destroy one another; and he may therefore, not trusting to this inference, made from the passions, desire perhaps to have the same confirmed by experience. Let him therefore consider with himself, when taking a journey, he arms himself, and seeks to go well accompanied; when going to sleep, he locks his doors; when even in his house, he locks his chests; and this when he knows there be laws, and public officers, armed, to revenge all injuries shall be done him; what opinion he has of his fellow-subjects, when he rides armed; of his fellow-citizens, when he locks his doors; and of his children and servants, when he locks his chests. Does he not there as much accuse mankind by his actions as I do by my words ? But neither of us accuse man's nature in it. The desires and other passions of man are in themselves no sin. No more are the actions that proceed from those passions, till they know a law that forbids them; which till laws be made they cannot know, nor can any law be made till they have agreed upon the person that shall make it.

It may peradventure be thought there was never such a time nor condition of war as this; and I believe it was never generally so, over all the world, but there are many places where they live so now. For the savage people in many places of America, except the government of small families, the concord whereof dependeth on natural lust, have no government at all, and live at this day in that brutish manner, as I said before. Howsoever, it may be perceived what manner of life there would be, where there were no common power to fear, by the manner of life which men that have formerly lived under a peaceful government, use to degenerate into in a civil war.

But though there had never been any time, wherein particular men were in a condition of war one against another; yet in all times, kings, and persons of sovereign authority, because of their independency, are in continual jealousies, and in the state and posture of gladiators; having their weapons pointing, and their eyes fixed on one another; that is, their forts, garrisons, and guns upon the frontiers of their kingdoms; and continual spies upon their neighbours; which is a posture of war. But because they uphold thereby the industry of their subjects; there does not follow from it that misery which accompanies the liberty of particular men.

To this war of every man, against every man, this also is consequent; that nothing can be unjust. The notions of right and wrong, justice and injustice, have there no place. Where there is no common power, there is no law; where no law, no injustice. Force and fraud, are in war the two cardinal virtues. Justice and injustice are none of the faculties neither of the body nor mind. If they were, they might be in a man that were alone in the world, as well as his senses, and passions. They are qualities that relate to men in society, not in solitude. It is consequent also to the same condition, that there be no propriety, no dominion, no "mine" and "thine" distinct; but only that to be every man's, that he can get; and for so long, as he can keep it. And thus much for the ill condition, which man by mere nature is actually placed in; though with a possibility to come out of it, consisting partly in the passions, partly in his reason.

The passions that incline men to peace, are fear of death; desire of such things as are necessary to commodious living; and a hope by their industry to obtain them. And reason suggesteth convenient articles of peace, upon which men may be drawn to agreement. These articles are they which otherwise are called the Laws of Nature: whereof I shall speak more particularly, in the two following chapters.

# Chapter XIV

## Of the First and Second Natural Laws, and of Contracts

"The right of Nature," which writers commonly call *jus naturale,* is the liberty each man hath, to use his own power, as he will himself, for the preservation of his own nature; that is to say, of his own life; and consequently, of doing anything, which in his own judgment and reason he shall conceive to be the aptest means thereunto.

By "liberty," is understood, according to the proper signification of the word, the absence of external impediments: which impediments may oft take away part of a man's power to do what he would; but cannot hinder him from using the power left him, according as his judgment and reason shall dictate to him.

A "law of Nature," *lex naturalis,* is a precept or general rule, found out by reason, by which a man is forbidden to do that which is destructive of his life, or taketh away the means of preserving the same; and to omit that, by which he thinketh it may be best preserved. For though they that speak of this subject, use to confound *jus* and *lex,* "right" and "law:" yet they ought to be distinguished; because "right," consisteth in liberty to do, or to forbear; whereas "law," determineth and bindeth to one of them; so that law and right differ as much as obligation and liberty; which in one and the same matter are inconsistent.

And because the condition of man, as hath been declared in the precedent chapter, is a condition of war of every one against every one; in which case every one is governed by his own reason; and there is nothing he can make use of, that may not be a help unto him, in preserving his life against his enemies; it followeth, that in such a condition, every man has a right to everything; even to one another's body. And therefore, as long as this natural right of every man to everything endureth, there can be no security to any man, how strong or wise soever he be, of living out the time, which Nature ordinarily alloweth men to live. And consequently it is a precept, or general rule of reason, "that every man ought to endeavour peace, as far as he has hope of obtaining it; and when he cannot obtain it, that he may seek, and use, all helps, and advantages of war." The first branch of which rule, containeth the first, and fundamental law of Nature; which is, "to seek peace, and follow it." The second, the sum of the right of Nature: which is, "by all means we can, to defend ourselves."

From this fundamental law of Nature, by which men are commanded to endeavour peace, is derived this second law; "that a man be willing, when others are so too, as far-forth, as for peace, and defence of himself he shall think it necessary, to lay down this right to all things; and be contented with so much liberty against other men, as he would allow other men against himself." For as long as every man holdeth this right, of doing anything he liketh; so long are all men in the condition of war. But if other men will not lay down their right, as well as he; then there is no reason for any one to divest himself of his: for that were to expose himself to prey, which no man is bound to, rather than to dispose himself to peace. This is that law of the Gospel; "whatsoever you require that others should do to you, that do ye to them." And that law of all men, *quod tibi fieri non vis, alteri ne feceris.*

To "lay down" a man's "right" to anything, is to "divest" himself of the "liberty," of hindering another of the benefit of his own right to the same. For he that renounceth, or passeth away his right, giveth not to any other man a right which he had not before; because there is nothing to which every man had not right by Nature: but only standeth out of his way, that he may enjoy his own original right, without hindrance from him; not without hindrance from another. So that the effect which redoundeth to one man, by another man's defect of right, is but so much diminution of impediments to the use of his own right original.

Right is laid aside, either by simply renouncing it; or by transferring it to another. By "simply renouncing;" when he cares not to whom the benefit thereof redoundeth. By "transferring;" when he intendeth the benefit thereof to some certain person or persons. And when a man hath in either manner abandoned, or granted away his right; then is he said to be "obliged," or "bound," not to hinder those, to whom such right is granted, or abandoned, from the benefit of it: and that he "ought," and it is his "duty," not to make void that voluntary act of his own: and that such hindrance is "injustice," and "injury," as being

*sine jure;* the right being before renounced, or transferred. So that "injury," or "injustice," in the controversies of the world, is somewhat like to that, which in the disputations of scholars is called "absurdity." For as it is there called an absurdity, to contradict what one maintained in the beginning: so in the world it is called injustice and injury voluntarily to undo that from the beginning he had voluntarily done. The way by which a man either simply renounceth, or transferreth his right, is a declaration, or signification, by some voluntary and sufficient sign, or signs, that he doth so renounce, or transfer; or hath so renounced, or transferred the same, to him that accepteth it. And these signs are either words only, or actions only; or, as it happeneth most often, both words and actions. And the same are the "bonds," by which men are bound, and obliged: bonds, that have their strength, not from their own nature, for nothing is more easily broken than a man's word, but from fear of some evil consequence upon the rupture.

Whensoever a man transferreth his right, or renounceth it, it is either in consideration of some right reciprocally transferred to himself; or for some other good he hopeth for thereby. For it is a voluntary act: and of the voluntary acts of every man, the object is some "good to himself." And therefore there be some rights, which no man can be understood by any words, or other signs, to have abandoned or transferred. As first a man cannot lay down the right of resisting them that assault him by force, to take away his life; because he cannot be understood to aim thereby at any good to himself. The same may be said of wounds, and chains, and imprisonment; both because there is no benefit consequent to such patience; as there is to the patience of suffering another to be wounded, or imprisoned; as also because a man cannot tell, when he seeth men proceed against him by violence, whether they intend his death or not. And lastly the motive and end for which this renouncing, and transferring of right is introduced, is nothing else but the security of a man's person, in his life, and in the means of so preserving life, as not to be weary of it. And therefore if a man by words, or other sigus, seem to despoil himself of the end, for which those signs were intended; he is not to be understood as if he meant it, or that it was his will; but that he was ignorant of how such words and actions were to be interpreted.

The mutual transferring of right, is that which men call "contract."

There is difference between transferring of right to the thing; and transferring, or tradition, that is delivery of the thing itself. For the thing may be delivered together with the translation of the right; as in buying and selling with ready money; or exchange of goods, or lands; and it may be delivered some time after.

Again, one of the contractors may deliver the thing contracted for on his part, and leave the other to perform his part at some determinate time after, and in the meantime be trusted; and then the contract on his part is called "pact," or "covenant:" or both parts may contract now, to perform hereafter; in which cases, he that is to perform in time to come, being trusted, his performance is called "keeping of promise," or faith; and the failing of performance, if it be voluntary, "violation of faith."

When the transferring of right, is not mutual: but one of the parties transferreth, in hope to gain thereby friendship, or service from another, or from his friends; or in hope to gain the reputation of charity, or magnanimity, or to deliver his mind from the pain of compassion; or in hope of reward in heaven; this is not contract, but "gift," "free gift," "grace," which words signify one and the same thing.

Signs of contract, are either "express," or "by inference." Express, are words spoken with understanding of what they signify; and such words are either of the time "present," or "past;" as, "I give," "I grant," "I have given," "I have granted," "I will that this be yours;" or of the future, as, "I will give," "I will grant;" which words of the future are called "promise."

Signs by inference are sometimes the consequence of words; sometimes the consequence of silence; sometimes the consequence of actions; sometimes the consequence of forbearing an action: and generally a sign by inference, of any contract, is whatsoever sufficiently argues the will of the contractor.

Words alone, if they be of the time to come, and contain a bare promise, are an insufficient sign of a free gift, and therefore not obligatory. For if they be of the time to come, as "to-morrow I will give," they are a sign I have not given yet, and consequently that my right is not transferred, but remaineth till I transfer it by some other act. But if the words be of the time present, or past, as, "I have given," or, "do give to be delivered tomorrow," then is my to-morrow's right given away to-day; and that by the virtue of the words, though there were no other argument of my will. And there is a great difference in the signification of these words, *volo hoc tuum esse cras,* and *cras dabo;* that is, between "I will that this be thine to-morrow," and, "I will give it thee to-morrow for the word "I will," in the former manner of speech, signifies an act of the will present; but in the latter, it signifies a promise of an act of the will to come: and therefore the former words, being of the present, transfer a future right; the latter, that be of the future, transfer nothing. But if there be other signs of the will to transfer a right, besides words, then, though the gift be free, yet may the right be understood to pass by words of the future: as if a man propound a prize to him that comes first to the end of a race, the gift is free; and though the words be of the future, yet the right passeth: for if he would not have his words so be understood, he should not have let them run.

In contracts, the right passeth, not only where the words are of the time present, or past, but also where they are of the future: because all contract is mutual translation, or change of right; and therefore he that promiseth only, because he hath already received the benefit for which he promiseth, is to be understood as if he intended the right should pass: for unless he had been content to have his words so understood, the other would not have performed his part first. And for that cause, in buying and selling, and other acts of contracts, a promise is equivalent to a covenant; and therefore obligatory.

He that performeth first in the case of a contract, is said to "merit" that which he is to receive by the performance of the other; and he hath it as "due." Also when a prize is propounded to many, which is to be given to him only that winneth; or money is thrown amongst many, to be enjoyed by them that catch it; though this be a free gift; yet so to win, or so to catch, is to "merit," and to have it as "due." For the right is transferred in the propounding of the prize, and in throwing down the money; though it be not determined to whom, but by the event of the contention. But there is between these two sorts of merit, this difference, that in contract, I merit by virtue of my own power, and the contractor's need; but in this case of free gift, I am enabled to merit only by the benignity of the giver: in contract, I merit at the contractor's hand that he should depart with his right; in this case of gift, I merit not that the giver should part with

his right; but that when he has parted with it, it should be mine, rather than another's. And this I think to be the meaning of that distinction of the schools, between *meritum congrui*, and *meritum condigni*. For God Almighty, having promised Paradise to those men, hoodwinked with carnal desires, that can walk through this world according to the precepts and limits prescribed by Him; they say, he that shall so walk, shall merit Paradise *ex congruo*. But because no man can demand a right to it, by his own righteousness, or any other power in himself, but by the free grace of God only; they say, no man can merit Paradise *ex condigno*. This I say, I think is the meaning of that distinction; but because disputers do not agree upon the signification of their own terms of art, longer than it serves their turn; I will not affirm anything of their meaning: only this I say; when a gift is given indefinitely, as a prize to be contended for, he that winneth meriteth, and may claim the prize as due.

If a convenant be made, wherein neither of the parties perform presently, but trust one another; in the condition of mere nature, which is a condition of war of every man against every man, upon any reasonable suspicion, it is void; but if there be a common power set over them both, with right and force sufficient to compel performance, it is not void. For he that per formeth first, has no assurance the other will perform after; because the bonds of words are too weak to bridle men's ambition, avarice, anger, and other passions, without the fear of some coercive power; which in the condition of mere nature, where all men are equal, and judges of the justness of their own fears, cannot possibly be supposed. And therefore he which performeth first, does but betray himself to his enemy; contrary to the right, he can never abandon, of defending his life and means of living.

But in a civil estate, where there is a power set up to constrain those that would otherwise violate their faith, that fear is no more reasonable, and for that cause, he which by the covenant is to perform first, is obliged so to do.

The cause of fear, which maketh such a covenant invalid, must be always something arising after the covenant made; as some new fact, or other sign of the will not to perform: else it cannot make the covenant void. For that which could not hinder a man from promising, ought not to be admitted as a hindrance of performing.

He that transferreth any right, transferreth the means of enjoying it, as far as lieth in his power. As he that selleth land, is understood to transfer the herbage, and whatsoever grows upon it: nor can he that sells a mill turn away the stream that drives it. And they that give to a man the right of government in sovereignty, are understood to give him the right of levying money to maintain soldiers; and of appointing magistrates for the administration of justice.

To make covenants with brute beasts, is impossible; because not understanding our speech, they understand not, nor accept of any translation of right; nor can translate any right to another: and without mutual acceptation, there is no covenant.

To make covenant with God, is impossible, but by mediation of such as God speaketh to, either by revelation supernatural, or by His lieutenants that govern under Him, and in His name: for otherwise we know not whether our covenants be accepted, or not. And therefore they that vow anything contrary to any law of Nature, vow in vain; as being a thing unjust to pay such vow. And if it be a thing commanded by the law of Nature, it is not the vow, but the law that binds them.

The matter, or subject of a covenant, is always something that falleth under deliberation; for to covenant is an act of the will; that is to say, an act, and the last act of deliberation; and is therefore always understood to be something to come; and which is judged possible for him that covenanteth to perform.

And therefore, to promise that which is known to be impossible, is no covenant. But if that prove impossible afterwards, which before was thought possible, the covenant is valid, and bindeth, though not to the thing itself, yet to the value; or, if that also be impossible, to the unfeigned endeavour of performing as much as is possible: for to more no man can be obliged.

Men are freed of their covenants two ways; by performing, or by being forgiven. For performance is the natural end of obligation; and forgiveness the restitution of liberty; as being a retransferring of that right, in which the obligation consisted.

Covenants entered into by fear, in the condition of mere nature, are obligatory. For example, if I covenant to pay a ransom, or service for my life, to an enemy, I am bound by it, for it is a contract, wherein one receiveth the benefit of life; the other is to receive money, or service for it; and consequently, where no other law, as in the condition of mere nature, forbiddeth the performance, the covenant is valid. Therefore prisoners of war, if trusted with the payment of their ransom, are obliged to pay it: and if a weaker prince make a disadvantageous peace with a stronger, for fear, he is bound to keep it; unless, as hath been said before, there ariseth some new and just cause of fear, to renew the war. And even in commonwealths, if I be forced to redeem myself from a thief by promising him money, I am bound to pay it, till the civil law discharge me. For whatsoever I may lawfully do without obligation, the same I may lawfully covenant to do through fear, and what I lawfully covenant, I cannot lawfully break.

A former covenant makes void a later. For a man that hath passed away his right to one man to-day, hath it not to pass to-morrow to another, and therefore the later promise passeth no right, but is null.

A covenant not to defend myself from force, by force, is always void. For, as I have shown before, no man can transfer, or lay down his right to save himself from death, wounds, and imprisonment, the avoiding whereof is the only end of laying down any right; and therefore the promise of not resisting force, in no covenant transferreth any right, nor is obliging. For though a man may covenant thus, "unless I do so, or so, kill me," he cannot covenant thus, "unless I do so, or so, I will not resist you when you come to kill me." For man by nature chooseth the lesser evil, which is danger of death in resisting, rather than the greater, which is certain and present death in not resisting. And this is granted to be true by all men, in that they lead criminals to execution and prison, with armed men, notwithstanding that such criminals have consented to the law by which they are condemned.

A covenant to accuse oneself, without assurance of pardon, is likewise invalid. For in the condition of nature, where every man is judge, there is no place for accusation: and in the civil state, the accusation is followed with punishment; which being force, a man is not obliged not to resist. The same is also true of the accusation of those by whose condemnation a man falls into misery; as of a father, wife, or benefactor. For the testimony of such an accuser, if it be not willingly given, is presumed to be corrupted by nature, and therefore not to be received: and where a man's testimony is not to be credited, he is not bound to give it. Also accusations upon torture, are not to be reputed as testimonies. For torture is to be used but as means of conjecture and light, in the further examination and search of truth; and what is in that case confessed, tendeth to the ease of him that is tortured, not to the informing of the torturers, and therefore ought not to have the credit of a sufficient testimony; for whether he deliver himself by true or false accusation, he does it by the right of preserving his own life.

The force of words being, as I have formerly noted, too weak to hold men to the performance of their covenants; there are in man's nature but two imaginable helps to strengthen it. And those are either a fear of the consequence of breaking their word, or a glory or pride in appearing not to need to break it. This latter is a generosity too rarely found to be presumed on, especially in the pursuers of wealth, command, or sensual pleasure, which are the greatest part of mankind. The passion to be reckoned upon is fear; whereof there be two very general objects: one, the power of spirits invisible; the other, the power of those men they shall therein offend. Of these two, though the former be the greater power, yet the fear of the latter is commonly the greater fear. The fear of the former is in every man his own religion, which hath place in the nature of man before civil society. The latter hath not so, at least not place enough to keep men to their promises; because in the condition of mere nature, the inequality of power is not discerned, but by the event of battle. So that before the time of civil society, or in the interruption thereof by war, there is nothing can strengthen a covenant of peace agreed on, against the temptations of avarice, ambition, lust, or other strong desire, but the fear of that invisible power, which they every one worship as God, and fear as a revenger of their perfidy.

All therefore that can be done between two men not subject to civil power, is to put one another to swear by the God he feareth, which "swearing," or "oath," is "a form of speech, added to a promise; by which he that promiseth, signifieth, that unless he perform, he renouneeth the mercy of his God, or calleth to Him for vengeance on himself." Such was the heathen form, "Let Jupiter kill me else, as I kill this beast." So is our form, "I shall do thus, and thus, so help me God." And this, with the rites and ceremonies, which every one useth in his own religion, that the fear of breaking faith might be the greater.

By this it appears, that an oath taken according to any other form, or rite, than his that sweareth, is in vain; and no oath: and that there is no swearing by anything which the swearer thinks not God. For though men have sometimes used to swear by their kings, for fear, or flattery; yet they would have it thereby understood, they attributed to them divine honour. And that swearing unnecessarily by God, is but profaning of His name: and swearing by other things, as men do in common discourse, is not swearing, but an impious custom, gotten by too much vehemence of talking.

It appears also, that the oath adds nothing to the obligation. For a covenant, if lawful, binds in the sight of God, without the oath, as much as with it: if unlawful, bindeth not at all; though it be confirmed with an oath.

# Chapter XV

## Of Other Laws of Nature

From that law of Nature, by which we are obliged to transfer to another, such rights, as being retained, hinder the peace of mankind, there followeth a third; which is this, "that men perform their covenants made;" without which, covenants are in vain, and but empty words; and the right of all men to all things remaining, we are still in the condition of war.

And in this law of Nature consisteth the fountain and original of "justice." For where no covenant hath preceded, there hath no right been transferred, and every man has right to everything; and consequently, no action can be unjust. But when a covenant is made, then to break it is "unjust:" and the definition of "injustice," is no other than "the not performance of covenant." And whatsoever is not unjust, is "just."

But because covenants of mutual trust, where there is a fear of not performance on either part, as hath been said in the former chapter, are invalid; though the original of justice be the making of covenants; yet injustice actually there can be none, till the cause of such fear be taken away; which while men are in the natural condition of war, cannot be done. Therefore before the names of just and unjust can have place, there must be some coercive power, to compel men equally to the performance of their covenants, by the terror of some punishment, greater than the benefit they expect by the breach of their covenant; and to make good that propriety, which by mutual contract men acquire, in recompense of the universal right they abandon: and such power there is none before the erection of a commonwealth. And this is also to be gathered out of the ordinary definition of justice in the schools: for they say, that "justice is the constant will of giving to every man his own." And therefore where there is no "own," that is no propriety, there is no injustice; and where there is no coercive power erected, that is, where there is no commonwealth, there is no propriety; all men having right to all things: therefore where there is no commonwealth, there nothing is unjust. So that the nature of justice, consisteth in keeping of valid covenants: but the validity of covenants begins not but with the constitution of a civil power, sufficient to compel men to keep them; and then it is also that propriety begins.

The fool hath said in his heart, there is no such thing as justice; and sometimes also with his tongue; seriously alleging, that every man's conservation, and contentment, being committed to his own care, there could be no reason why every man might not do what he thought conduced thereunto: and therefore also to make, or not make; keep, or not keep covenants, was not against reason, when it conduced to one's benefit. He does not therein deny, that there be covenants; and that they are sometimes broken, sometimes kept; and that such breach of them may be called injustice, and the observance of them justice; but he questioneth, whether injustice, taking away the fear of God, for the same fool hath said in his heart there is no God, may not sometimes stand with that reason, which dictateth to every man his own good; and particularly then, when it conduceth to such a benefit, as shall put a man in a condition to neglect not only the dispraise, and revilings, but also the power of other men. The kingdom of God is gotten by violence; but what if it could be gotten by unjust violence? were it against reason so to get it, when it is impossible to receive hurt by it?

and if it be not against reason, it is not against justice; or else justice is not to be approved for good. From such reasoning as this, successful wickedness hath obtained the name of virtue; and some that in all other things have disallowed the violation of faith; yet have allowed it, when it is for the getting of a kingdom. And the heathen that believed that Saturn was deposed by his son Jupiter, believed nevertheless the same Jupiter to be the avenger of injustice; somewhat like to a piece of law in Coke's "Commentaries on Littleton;" where he says, if the right heir of the crown be attainted of treason; yet the crown shall descend to him, and *eo instante* the attainder be void: from which instances a man will be very prone to infer, that when the heir apparent of a kingdom shall kill him that is in possession, though his father; you may call it injustice, or by what other name you will; yet it can never be against reason, seeing all the voluntary actions of men tend to the benefit of themselves; and those actions are most reasonable, that conduce most to their ends. This specious reasoning is nevertheless false.

For the question is not of promises mutual, where there is no security of performance on either side; as when there is no civil power erected over the parties promising; for such promises are no covenants: but either where one of the parties has performed already; or where there is a power to make him perform; there is the question whether it be against reason, that is, against the benefit of the other to perform, or not. And I say it is not against reason. For the manifestation whereof, we are to consider; first, that when a man doth a thing, which notwithstanding anything can be foreseen and reckoned on, tendeth to his own destruction, howsoever some accident which he could not expect, arriving may turn it to his benefit; yet such events do not make it reasonably or wisely done. Secondly, that in a condition of war, wherein every man to every man, for want of a common power to keep them all in awe, is an enemy, there is no man who can hope by his own strength, or wit, to defend himself from destruction, without the help of confederates; where every one expects the same defence by the confederation, that any one else does: and therefore he which declares he thinks it reason to deceive those that help him, can in reason expect no other means of safety than what can be had from his own single power. He therefore that breaketh his covenant, and consequently declareth that he thinks he may with reason do so, cannot be received into any society, that unite themselves for peace and defence, but by the error of them that receive him; nor when he is received, be retained in it, without seeing the danger of their error; which errors a man cannot reasonably reckon upon as the means of his security; and therefore if he be left, or cast out of society, he perisheth; and if he live in society, it is by the errors of other men, which he could not foresee, nor reckon upon; and consequently against the reason of his preservation; and so, as all men that contribute not to his destruction, forbear him only out of ignorance of what is good for themselves.

As for the instance of gaining the secure and perpetual felicity of heaven, by any way, it is frivolous: there being but one way imaginable; and that is not breaking, but keeping of covenant.

And for the other instance of attaining sovereignty by rebellion; it is manifest, that though the event follow, yet because it cannot reasonably be expected, but rather the contrary; and because by gaining it so, others are taught to gain the same in like manner, the attempt thereof is against reason. Justice

therefore, that is to say, keeping of covenant, is a rule of reason, by which we are forbidden to do anything destructive to our life; and consequently a law of Nature.

There be some that proceed further; and will not have the law of Nature to be those rules which conduce to the preservation of man's life on earth; but to the attaining of an eternal felicity after death; to which they think the breach of government may conduce; and consequently be just and reasonable; such are they that think it a work of merit to kill, or depose, or rebel against the sovereign power constituted over them by their own consent. But because there is no natural knowledge of man's estate after death; much less of the reward that is then to be given to breach of faith; but only a belief grounded upon other men's saying, that they know it supernaturally, or that they know those that knew them, that knew others, that knew it supernaturally; breach of faith cannot be called a precept of reason, or nature.

Others, that allow for a law of Nature the keeping of faith, do nevertheless make exception of certain persons; as heretics, and such as use not to perform their covenant to others; and this also is against reason. For if any fault of a man be sufficient to discharge our covenant made; the same ought in reason to have been sufficient to have hindered the making of it.

The names of just, and unjust, when they are attributed to men, signify one thing; and when they are attributed to actions, another. When they are attributed to men, they signify conformity, or inconformity of manners, to reason. But when they are attributed to actions they signify the conformity or inconformity to reason, not of manners or manner of life, but of particular actions. A just man, therefore, is he that taketh all the care he can that his actions may be all just, and an unjust man is he that neglecteth it. And such men are more often in our language styled by the names of righteous and unrighteous than just and unjust, though the meaning be the same. Therefore, a righteous man does not lose that title by one or a few unjust actions that proceed from sudden passion or mistake of things or persons; nor does an unrighteous man lose his character for such actions as he does, or forbears to do, for fear, because his will is not framed by the justice, but by the apparent benefit of what he is to do. That which gives to human actions the relish of justice is a certain nobleness or gallantness of courage, rarely found, by which a man scorns to be beholden, for the contentment of his life, to fraud or breach of promise. This justice of the manners is that which is meant, where justice is called a virtue, and injustice a vice.

But the justice of actions denominates men, not just, but "guiltless;" and the injustice of the same, which is also called injury, gives them but the name of "guilty."

Again, the injustice of manners is the disposition or aptitude to do injury; and is injustice before it proceeds to act, and without supposing any individual person injured. But the injustice of an action, that is to say injury, supposeth an individual person injured, namely, him to whom the covenant was made; and therefore many times the injury is received by one man when the damage redoundeth to another. As when the master commandeth his servant to give money to a stranger: if it be not done, the injury is done to the master, whom he had before covenanted to obey; but the damage redoundeth to the stranger, to whom he had no obligation, and therefore could not injure him. And so also in commonwealths. Private men may remit to one another their debts, but not robberies or other violences, whereby they are endamaged, because the detaining of debt is an injury to themselves, but robbery and violence are injuries to the person of the commonwealth.

Whatsoever is done to a man, conformable to his own will signified to the doer, is no injury to him. For if he that doeth it, hath not passed away his original right to do what he please, by some antecedent covenant, there is no breach of covenant; and therefore no injury done him. And if he have, then his will to have it done being signified, is a release of that covenant; and so again there is no injury done him.

Justice of actions, is by writers divided into "commutative," and "distributive:" and the former they say consisteth in proportion arithmetical; the latter in proportion geometrical. Commutative, therefore, they place in the equality of value of the things contracted for; and distributive, in the distribution of equal benefit, to men of equal merit. As if it were injustice to sell dearer than we buy; or to give more to a man than he merits. The value of all things contracted for, is measured by the appetite of the contractors: and therefore the just value is that which they be contented to give. And merit, besides that which is by covenant, where the performance on one part, meriteth the performance of the other part, and falls under justice commutative, not distributive, is not due by justice; but is rewarded of grace only. And therefore this distinction, in the sense wherein it useth to be expounded, is not right. To speak properly, commutative justice is the justice of a contractor; that is, a performance of covenant, in buying and selling; hiring, and letting to hire; lending, and borrowing; exchanging, bartering, and other acts of contract.

And distributive justice, the justice of an arbitrator; that is to say, the act of defining what is just. Wherein, being trusted by them that make him arbitrator, if he perform his trust, he is said to distribute to every man his own: and this is indeed just distribution, and may be called, though improperly, distributive justice; but more properly equity; which also is a law of Nature, as shall be shown in due place.

As justice dependeth on antecedent covenant; so does "gratitude" depend on antecedent grace; that is to say, antecedent free gift: and is the fourth law of Nature; which may be conceived in this form, "that a man which receiveth benefit from another of mere grace, endeavour that he which giveth it, have no reasonable cause to repent him of his good will." For no man giveth, but with intention of good to himself; because gift is voluntary; and of all voluntary acts, the object is to every man his own good; of which if men see they shall be frustrated, there will be no beginning of benevolence, or trust, nor consequently of mutual help; nor of reconciliation of one man to another; and therefore they are to remain still in the condition of "war," which is contrary to the first and fundamental law of Nature, which commandeth men to "seek peace." The breach of this law, is called "ingratitude," and hath the same relation to grace that injustice hath to obligation by covenant.

A fifth law of Nature, is "complaisance:" that is to say, "that every man strive to accommodate himself to the rest." For the understanding whereof, we may consider, that there is in men's aptness to society, a diversity of nature, rising from their diversity of affections; not unlike to that we see in stones brought together for building of an edifice. For as that stone which by the asperity, and irregularity of figure, takes more room from others than itself fills; and for the hardness, cannot be easily made plain, and thereby hindereth the building, is by the builders cast away as unprofitable and troublesome: so also, a man that by asperity of nature, will strive to retain those things which to himself are superfluous, and to others necessary; and for the stubbornness of his passions, cannot be corrected, is to be left, or cast out of society, as cumbersome thereunto. For seeing every man, not only by right, but also by necessity of nature, is supposed to endeavour all he can, to obtain that which is necessary for his conservation; he that shall oppose himself against it, for things superfluous, is guilty of the war that thereupon is to follow; and therefore doth that which is contrary to the fundamental law of Nature, which commandeth "to seek peace." The observers of this law, maybe called "sociable," the Latins call them *commodi;* the contrary, "stubborn," "insociable," "froward," "intractable."

A sixth law of Nature is this, "that upon caution of the future time, a man ought to pardon the offences past of them that repenting, desire it." For "pardon" is nothing but granting of peace; which though granted to them that persevere in their hostility, be not peace, but fear; yet not granted to them that give caution of the future time, is sign of an aversion to peace; and therefore contrary to the law of Nature.

A seventh is, "that in revenges," that is, retribution of evil for evil, "men look not at the greatness of the evil past, but the greatness of the good to follow." Whereby we are forbidden to inflict punishment with any other design, than for correction of the offender, or direction of others. For this law is consequent to the next before it, that commandeth pardon, upon security of the future time. Besides, revenge, without respect to the example and profit to come, is a triumph or glorying in the hurt of another, tending to no end; for the end is always somewhat to come; and glorying to no end, is vain-glory, and contrary to reason, and to hurt without reason, tendeth to the introduction of war; which is against the law of Nature; and is commonly styled by the name of "cruelty."

And because all signs of hatred, or contempt, provoke to fight; insomuch as most men choose rather to hazard, their life than not to be revenged; we may in the eighth place, for a law of Nature, set down this precept, "that no man by deed, word, countenance, or gesture, declare hatred or contempt of another." The breach of which law is commonly called "contumely."

The question who is the better man, has no place in the condition of mere nature; where, as has been shown before, all men are equal. The inequality that now is, has been introduced by the laws civil. I know that Aristotle in the first book of his "Politics," for a foundation of his doctrine, maketh men by nature, some more worthy to command, meaning the wiser sort, such as he thought himself to be for his philosophy; others to serve, meaning those that had strong bodies, but were not philosophers as he; as if master and servant were not introduced by consent of men, but by difference of wit; which is not only against reason, but also against experience. For there are very few so foolish, that had not rather govern themselves than be governed by others: nor when the wise in their own conceit, contend by force with them who distrust their own wisdom, do they always, or often, or almost at any time, get the victory. If Nature therefore have made men equal, that equality is to be acknowledged: or if Nature have made men unequal; yet because men that think themselves equal, will not enter into conditions of peace, but upon equal terms, such equality must be admitted. And therefore for the ninth law of Nature. I put this, "that every man

acknowledge another for his equal by nature." The breach of this precept is "pride."

On this law dependeth another, "that at the entrance into conditions of peace, no man require to reserve to himself any right which he is not content should be reserved to every one of the rest." As it is necessary for all men that seek peace to lay down certain rights of nature; that is to say, not to have liberty to do all they list: so is it necessary for man's life to retain some, as right to govern their own bodies; enjoy air, water, motion, ways to go from place to place; and all things else, without which a man cannot live, or not live well. If in this case, at the making of peace, men require for themselves that which they would not have to be granted to others, they do contrary to the precedent law, that commandeth the acknowledgment of natural equality, and therefore also against the law of Nature. The observers of this law are those we call "modest," and the breakers "arrogant" men. The Greeks call the violation of this law πλεονεξια; that is, a desire of more than their share.

Also if "a man be trusted to judge between man and man," it is a precept of the law of Nature, "that he deal equally between them." For without that, the controversies of men cannot be determined but by war. He therefore that is partial in judgment, doth what in him lies, to deter men from the use of judges and arbitrators; and consequently, against the fundamental law of Nature, is the cause of war.

The observance of this law, from the equal distribution to each man, of that which in reason belongeth to him, is called "equity," and as I have said before, distributive justice: the violation, "acception of persons," προσωποληψια.

And from this followeth another law, "that such things as cannot be divided, be enjoyed in common, if it can be; and if the quantity of the thing permit, without stint; otherwise proportionably to the number of them that have right." For otherwise the distribution is unequal, and contrary to equity.

But some things there be that can neither be divided nor enjoyed in common. Then, the law of Nature, which prescribeth equity, requireth "that the entire right, or else, making the use alternate, the first possession, be determined by lot." For equal distribution is of the law of Nature, and other means of equal distribution cannot be imagined.

Of "lots" there be two sorts, "arbitrary," and "natural." Arbitrary is that which is agreed on by the competitors: natural, is either "primogeniture," which the Greeks call κληρονομία, which signifies "given by lot," or "first seizure."

And therefore those things which cannot be enjoyed in common, nor divided, ought to be adjudged to the first possessor; and in some cases to the first born, as acquired by lot.

It is also a law of Nature, "that all men that mediate peace, be allowed safe conduct." For the law that commandeth peace, as the end, commandeth intercession, as the "means;" and to intercession the means is safe conduct.

And because, though men be never so willing to observe these laws, there may nevertheless arise questions concerning a man's action; first, whether it were done, or not done; secondly, if done, whether against the law, or not against the law; the former whereof, is called a question "of fact;" the latter a question "of right," therefore unless the parties to the question covenant mutually to stand to the sentence of another, they are as far from peace as ever. This other to whose sentence they submit is called an "arbitrator." And therefore it is of the law of Nature, "that they that are at controversy, submit their right to the judgment of an arbitrator. '

And seeing every man is presumed to do all things in order to his own benefit, no man is a fit arbitrator in his own cause; and if he were never so fit; yet equity allowing to each party equal benefit, if one be admitted to be judge, the other is to be admitted also; and so the controversy, that is, the cause of war, remains against the law of Nature.

For the same reason no man in any cause ought to be received for arbitrator, to whom greater profit, or honour, or pleasure apparently ariseth out of the victory of one party than of the other: for he hath taken, though an unavoidable bribe, yet a bribe; and no man can be obliged to trust him. And thus also the controversy, and the condition of war remaineth, contrary to the law of Nature.

And in a controversy of "fact," the judge being to give no more credit to one than to the other, if there be no other arguments, must give credit to a third; or to a third and fourth; or more: for else the question is undecided, and left to force, contrary to the law of Nature.

These are the laws of Nature, dictating peace, for a means of the conservation of men in multitudes; and which only concern the doctrine of civil society. There be other things tending to the destruction of particular men; as drunkenness, and all other parts of intemperance; which may therefore also be reckoned amongst those things which the law of Nature hath forbidden; but are not necessary to be mentioned, nor are pertinent enough to this place.

And though this may seem too subtle a deduction of the laws of Nature, to be taken notice of by all men; whereof the most part are too busy in getting food, and the rest too negligent to understand; yet to leave all men inexcusable, they have been contracted into one easy sum, intelligible even to the meanest capacity; and that is, "Do not that to another, which thou wouldst not have done to thyself;" which showeth him that he has no more to do in learning the laws of Nature, but when weighing the actions of other men with his own, they seem too heavy, he put them into the other part of the balance, and his own into their place, that his own passions and self-love may add nothing to the weight; and then there is none of these laws of Nature that will not appear unto him very reasonable.

The laws of Nature oblige *in foro interno;* that is to say, they bind to a desire they should take place: but *in foro externo;* that is, to the putting them in act, not always. For he that should be modest, and tractable, and perform all he promises, in such time and place where no man else should do so, should but make himself a prey to others, and procure his own certain ruin, contrary to the ground of all laws of Nature, which tend to Nature's preservation. And again, he that having sufficient security, that others shall observe the same laws towards him, observes them not himself, seeketh not peace, but war; and consequently the destruction of his nature by violence.

And whatsoever laws bind *in foro interno,* may be broken, not only by a fact contrary to the law, but also by a fact according to it, in case a man think it contrary. For though his action in this case be according to the law, yet his purpose was against the law; which, where the obligation is *in foro interno,* is a breach.

The laws of Nature are immutable and eternal; for injustice, ingratitude, arrogance, pride, iniquity, acception of persons, and the rest, can never be made lawful. For it can never be that war shall preserve life, and peace destroy it.

The same laws, because they oblige only to a desire and endeavour, I mean an unfeigned and constant endeavour, are easy to be observed. For in that they require nothing but endeavour, he that endeavoureth their performance, fulfilleth them; and he that fulfilleth the law, is just.

And the science of them is the true and only moral philosophy. For moral philosophy is nothing else but the science of what is "good" and "evil," in the conversation and society of mankind. "Good" and "evil" are names that signify our appetites, and aversions; which in different tempers, customs, and doctrines of men, are different: and divers men, differ not only in their judgment, on the senses of what is pleasant and unpleasant to the taste, smell, hearing, touch, and sight; but also of what is conformable or disagreeable to reason, in the actions of common life. Nay, the same man, in divers times, differs from himself; and one time praiseth, that is, calleth good, what another time he dispraiseth, and calleth evil: from whence arise disputes, controversies, and at last war. And therefore so long as a man is in the condition of mere nature, which is a condition of war, as private appetite is the measure of good and evil: and consequently all men agree on this, that peace is good, and therefore also the way or means of peace, which, as I have showed before, are "justice," "gratitude," "modesty," "equity," "mercy," and the rest of the laws of Nature, are good; that is to say, "moral virtues;" and their contrary "vices," evil. Now the science of virtue and vice is moral philosophy; and therefore the true doctrine of the laws of Nature, is the true moral philosophy. But the writers of moral philosophy, though they acknowledge the same virtues and vices; yet not seeing wherein consisted their goodness; nor that they come to be praised, as the means of peaceable, sociable, and comfortable living, place them in a mediocrity of passions: as if not the cause, but the degree of daring, made fortitude; or not the cause, but the quantity of a gift, made liberality.

These dictates of reason, men used to call by the name of laws, but improperly: for they are but conclusions, or theorems concerning what conduceth to the conservation and defence of themselves; whereas law, properly, is the word of him that by right hath command over others. But yet if we consider the same theorems, as delivered in the word of God, that by right commandeth all things; then are they properly called laws.

<h1 style="text-align:center">Chapter XVI</h1>

## Of Persons, Authors, and Things Personated

A person is he, "whose words or actions are considered, either as his own, or as representing the words or actions of another man, or of any other thing, to whom they are attributed, whether truly or by fiction."

When they are considered as his own, then is he called a "natural person:" and when they are considered as representing the words and actions of another, then is he a "feigned" or "artificial person."

The word person is Latin: instead whereof the Greeks have πρόσωπον, which signifies the "face," as persona in Latin signifies the "disguise," or "outward appearance" of a man, counterfeited on the stage; and sometimes more particularly that part of it, which disguiseth the face, as a mask or vizard: and from the stage, hath been translated to any representer of speech and action, as well in tribunals as theatres. So that a "person," is the same that an "actor" is, both on the stage and in common conversation; and to "personate," is to "act," or "represent" himself or another; and he that acteth another, is said to bear his person, or act in his name; in which sense Cicero useth it where he says, Unus sustineo tres personas; mei, adversarii, et judicis: I bear three persons: my own, my adversary's, and the judge's; and is called in divers occasions, diversely; as a "representer," or "representative," a "lieutenant,"a "vicar," an "attorney," a "deputy," a "procurator," an "actor," and the like.

Of persons artificial, some have their words and actions "owned" by those whom they represent. And then the person is the "actor;" and he that owneth his words and actions, is the "author:" in which case the actor acteth by authority. For that which in speaking of goods and possessions is called an "owner," and in Latin dominus, in Greek kýplos speaking of actions, is called author. And as the right of possession, is called dominion; so the right of doing any action, is called "authority." So that by authority, is always understood a right of doing any act; and "done by authority," done by commission, or licence from him whose right it is.

From hence it followeth, that when the actor maketh a covenant by authority, he bindeth thereby the author, no less than if he had made it himself; and no less subjecteth him to all the consequences of the same. And therefore all that hath been said formerly (chap. xiv.) of the nature of covenants between man and man in their natural capacity, is true also when they are made by their actors, representers, or procurators, that have authority from them, so far forth as is in their commission, but no further.

And therefore he that maketh a covenant with the actor or representer, not knowing the authority he hath, doth it at his own peril. For no man is obliged by a covenant whereof he is not author; nor consequently by a covenant made against or beside the authority he gave.

When the actor doth anything against the law of Nature by command of the author, if he be obliged by former covenant to obey him, not he but the author breaketh the law of Nature; for though the action be against the law of Nature, yet it is not his: but contrarily, to refuse to do it, is against the law of Nature, that forbiddeth breach of covenant.

And he that maketh a covenant with the author by mediation of the actor, not knowing what authority he hath, but only takes his word, in case such authority be not made manifest unto him upon demand, is no longer obliged, for the covenant made with the author is not valid without his counter-assurance. But if he that so covenanteth knew beforehand he was to expect no other assurance than the actor's word, then is the covenant valid, because the actor in this case maketh himself the author. And therefore, as when the authority is evident, the covenant obligeth the author, not the actor; so when the authority is feigned, it obligeth the actor only, there being no author but himself.

There are few things that are incapable of being represented by fiction. Inanimate things, as a church, an hospital, a bridge, may be personated by a rector, master, or overseer. But things inanimate cannot be authors, nor therefore give authority to their actors; yet the actors may have authority to procure their maintenance, given them by those that are owners or governors of those things. And therefore such things cannot be personated before there be some state of civil government.

Likewise children, fools, and madmen, that have no use of reason, may be personated by guardians or curators; but can be no authors, during that time, of any action done by them longer than, when they shall recover the use of reason, they shall judge the same reasonable. Yet during the folly, he that hath right of governing them may give authority to the guardian. But this again has no place but in a state civil, because before such estate there is no dominion of persons.

An idol, or mere figment of the brain, may be personated, as were the gods of the heathen, which, by such officers as the state appointed, were personated, and held possessions, and other goods and rights, which men from time to time dedicated and consecrated unto them. But idols cannot be authors, for an idol is nothing. The authority proceeded from the state; and therefore, before introduction of civil government, the gods of the heathen could not be personated.

The true God may be personated. As He was, first, by Moses; who governed the Israelites, that were not his, but God's people, not in his own name, with *hoc dicit Moses;* but in God's name, with *hoc dicit Dominus.* Secondly, by the Son of man, His own Son, our blessed Saviour Jesus Christ, that came to reduce the Jews, and induce all nations into the kingdom of His Father, not as of Himself, but as sent from His Father. And thirdly, by the Holy Ghost or Comforter, speaking and working in the Apostles; which Holy Ghost was a Comforter that came not of Himself; but was sent, and proceeded from them both.

A multitude of men are made "one" person, when they are by one man or one person represented; so that it be done with the consent of every one of that multitude in particular. For it is the "unity" of the representer, not the "unity" of the represented, that maketh the person "one." And it is the representer that beareth the person, and but one person: and "unity" cannot otherwise be understood in multitude.

And because the multitude naturally is not "one," but "many," they cannot be understood for one; but many authors, of everything their representative saith, or doth in their name; every man giving their common representer authority from himself in particular, and owning all the actions the representer doth, in case they give him authority without stint: otherwise, when they limit him in what and how far he shall represent them, none of them owneth more than they gave him commission to act.

And if the representative consist of many men, the voice of the greater number must be considered as the voice of them all. For if the lesser number pronounce, for example, in the affirmative, and the greater in the negative, there will be negatives more than enough to destroy the affirmatives; and thereby the excess of negatives, standing uncontradicted, are the only voice the representative hath.

And a representative of even number, especially when the number is not great, whereby the contradictory voices are oftentimes equal, is therefore oftentimes mute and incapable of action. Yet in some cases contradictory voices equal in number may determine a question; as in condemning, or absolving, equality of votes, even in that they condemn not, do absolve; but not on the contrary condemn, in that they absolve not. For when a cause is heard, not to condemn is to absolve: but on the contrary, to say that not absolving, is condemning, is not true. The like it is in a deliberation of executing presently, or deferring till another time: for when the voices are equal, the not decreeing execution is a decree of dilation.

Or if the number be odd, as three or more, men or assemblies; whereof every one has by a negative voice authority to take away the effect of all the affirmative voices of the rest, this number is no representative; because by the diversity of opinions, and interests of men, it becomes oftentimes, and in cases of the greatest consequence, a mute person, and unapt, as for many things else, so for the government of a multitude, especially in time of war.

Of authors there be two sorts. The first simply so called; which I have before defined to be him, that owneth the action of another simply. The second is he that owneth an action or covenant of another conditionally; that is to say, he undertaketh to do it if the other doth it not at or before a certain time. And these authors conditional, are generally called "sureties," in Latin, *fidejussores*, and *sponsores*; and particularly for debt, *prades*; and for appearance before a judge, or magistrate, *vades*.

## Part II—Of Commonwealth, Chapter XVII

### Of the Causes, Generation, and Definition of a Commonwealth

The final cause, end, or design of men, who naturally love liberty, and dominion over others, in the introduction of that restraint upon themselves, in which we see them live in commonwealths, is the foresight of their own preservation, and of a more contented life thereby; that is to say, of getting themselves out from that miserable condition of war, which is necessarily consequent, as hath been shown in chapter xiii., to the natural passions of men, when there is no visible power to keep them in awe, and tie them by fear of punishment to the performance of their covenants, and observation of those laws of Nature set down in the fourteenth and fifteenth chapters.

For the laws of Nature, as "justice," "equity," "modesty," "mercy," and, in sum, "doing toothers, as we would be done to," of themselves, without the terror of some power, to cause them to be observed, are contrary to our natural passions, that carry us to partiality, pride, revenge, and the like. And covenants, without the sword, are but words, and of no strength to secure a man at all. Therefore notwithstanding the laws of Nature, which everyone hath then kept, when he has the will to keep them, when he can do it safely, if there be no power erected, or not great enough for our security; every man will, and may lawfully rely on his own strength and art, for caution against all other men. And in all places, where men have lived by small families, to rob and spoil one another, has been a trade, and so far from being reputed against the law of Nature, that the greater spoils they gained, the greater was their honour; and men observed no other laws therein, but the laws of honour; that is, to abstain from cruelty, leaving to men their lives, and instruments of husbandry. And as small families did then; so now do cities and kingdoms, which are but greater families, for their own security, enlarge their dominions, upon all pretences of danger, and fear of invasion, or assistance that may be given to invaders, and endeavour as much as they can, to subdue, or weaken their neighbours, by open force and secret arts, for want of other caution, justly;

and are remembered for it in after ages with honour.

Nor is it the joining together of a small number of men, that gives them this security; because in small numbers, small additions on the one side or the other, make the advantage of strength so great, as is sufficient to carry the victory; and therefore gives encouragement to an invasion. The multitude sufficient to confide in for our security, is not determined by any certain number, but by comparison with the enemy we fear; and is then sufficient, when the odds of the enemy is not of so visible and conspicuous moment, to determine the event of war, as to move him to attempt.

And be there never so great a multitude; yet if their actions be directed according to their particular judgments and particular appetites, they can expect thereby no defence, nor protection, neither against a common enemy, nor against the injuries of one another. For being distracted in opinions concerning the best use and application of their strength, they do not help but hinder one another; and reduce their strength by mutual opposition to nothing: whereby they are easily, not only subdued by a very few that agree together; but also when there is no common enemy, they make war upon each other, for their particular interests. For if we could suppose a great multitude of men to consent in the observation of justice, and other laws of Nature, without a common power to keep them all in awe; we might as well suppose all mankind to do the same; and then there neither would be, nor need to be any civil government or commonwealth at all; because there would be peace without subjection.

Nor is it enough for the security, which men desire should last all the time of their life, that they be governed and directed by one judgment, for a limited time: as in one battle, or one war. For though they obtain a victory by their unanimous endeavour against a foreign enemy; yet afterwards, when either they have no common enemy, or he that by one part is held for an enemy, is by another part held for a friend, they must needs by the difference of their interests dissolve, and fall again into a war amongst themselves.

It is true that certain living creatures, as bees and ants, live sociably one with another, which are therefore by Aristotle numbered amongst political creatures; and yet have no other direction, than their particular judgments and appetites; nor speech, whereby one of them can signify to another, what he thinks expedient for the common benefit: and therefore some man may perhaps desire to know, why mankind cannot do the same. To which I answer,

First, that men are continually in competition for honour and dignity, which these creatures are not; and consequently amongst men there ariseth on that ground, envy and hatred, and finally war; but amongst these not so.

Secondly, that amongst these creatures, the common good differeth not from the private; and being by nature inclined to their private, they procure thereby the common benefit. But man, whose joy consisteth in comparing himself with other men, can relish nothing but what is eminent.

Thirdly, that these creatures, having not, as man, the use of reason, do not see, nor think they see any fault, in the administration of their common business; whereas amongst men, there are very many that think themselves wiser, and abler to govern the public, better than the rest; and these strive to reform and innovate, one this way, another that way; and thereby bring it into distraction and civil war.

Fourthly, that these creatures, though they have some use of voice, in making known to one another their desires and other affections; yet they want that art of words, by which some men can represent to others that which is good in the likeness of evil; and evil in the likeness of good; and augment or diminish the apparent greatness of good and evil; discontenting men, and troubling their peace at their pleasure.

Fifthly, irrational creatures cannot distinguish between "injury" and "damage;" and therefore as long as they be at ease, they are not offended with their fellows: whereas man is then most troublesome, when he is most at ease; for then it is that he loves to show his wisdom, and control the actions of them that govern the commonwealth.

Lastly, the agreement of these creatures is natural; that of men is by covenant only, which is artificial: and therefore it is no wonder if there be somewhat else required, besides covenant, to make their agreement constant and lasting; which is a common power, to keep them in awe, and to direct their actions to the common benefit.

The only way to erect such a common power, as may be able to defend them from the invasion of foreigners, and the injuries of one another, and thereby to secure them in such sort, as that by their own industry, and by the fruits of the earth, they may nourish themselves and live contentedly, is to confer all their power and strength upon one man, or upon one assembly of men, that may reduce all their wills, by plurality of voices, unto one will: which is as much as to say, to appoint one man, or assembly of men, to bear their person; and every one to own, and acknowledge himself to be author of whatsoever he that so beareth their person, shall act, or cause to be acted, in those things which concern the common peace and safety; and therein to submit their wills, every one to his will, and their judgments, to his judgment. This is more than consent, or concord; it is a real unity of them all, in one and the same person, made by covenant of every man with every man, in such manner, as if every man should say to every man, "I authorize and give up my right of governing myself, to this man, or to this assembly of men, on this condition, that thou give up thy right to him, and authorize all his actions in like manner." This done, the multitude so united in one person is called a "commonwealth," in Latin *civitas*. This is the generation of that great "leviathan," or rather, to speak more reverently, of that "mortal god," to which we owe under the "immortal God," our peace and defence. For by this authority, given him by every particular man in the commonwealth, he hath the use of so much power and strength conferred on him, that by terror thereof, he is enabled to perform the wills of them all, to peace at home, and mutual aid against their enemies abroad. And in him consisteth the essence of the commonwealth; which, to define it, is "one person, of whose acts a great multitude, by mutual covenants one with another, have made themselves every one the author, to the end he may use the strength and means of them all, as he shall think expedient, for their peace and common defence."

And he that carrieth this person is called "sovereign," and said to have "sovereign power;" and every one besides, his "subject."

The attaining to this sovereign power is by two ways. One, by natural force; as when a man maketh his children to submit themselves, and their children, to his government, as being able to destroy them if they refuse; or by war subdueth his enemies to his will,

giving them their lives on that condition. The other is, when men agree amongst themselves to submit to some man, or assembly of men, voluntarily, on confidence to be protected by him against all others. This latter may be called a political commonwealth, or commonwealth by "institution;" and the former, a commonwealth by "acquisition." And first, I shall speak of a commonwealth by institution.

## Chapter XVIII

### Of the Rights of Sovereigns by Institution

A "COMMONWEALTH" is said to be "instituted," when a "multitude" of men do agree, and "covenant, every one, with every one," that to whatsoever "man," or "assembly of men," shall be given by the major part, the "right " to "present" the person of them all, that is to say, to be their "representative;" every one, as well he that "voted for it," as he that "voted against it," shall "authorize" all the actions and judgments, of that man, or assembly of men, in the same manner, as if they were his own, to the end, to live peaceably amongst themselves, and be protected against other men.

From this institution of a commonwealth are derived all the "rights" and "faculties" of him, or them, on whom sovereign power is conferred by the consent of the people assembled.

First, because they covenant, it is to be understood, they are not obliged by former covenant to anything repugnant hereunto. And consequently they that have already instituted a commonwealth, being thereby bound by covenant, to own the actions and judgments of one, cannot lawfully make a new covenant, amongst themselves, to be obedient to any other, in any thing whatsoever, without his permission. And therefore, they that are subjects to a monarch, cannot without his leave cast off monarchy, and return to the confusion of a disunited multitude; nor transfer their person from him that beareth it, to another man, or other assembly of men: for they are bound, every man to every man, to own, and be reputed author of all, that he that already is their sovereign, shall do, and judge fit to be done: so that any one man dissenting, all the rest should break their covenant made to that man, which is injustice: and they have also every man given the sovereignty to him that beareth their person; and therefore if they depose him, they take from him that which is his own, and so again it is injustice. Besides, if he that attempteth to depose his sovereign, be killed, or punished by him for such attempt, he is author of his own punishment, as being by the institution, author of all his sovereign shall do: and because it is injustice for a man to do anything for which he may be punished by his own authority, he is also upon that title unjust. And whereas some men have pretended for their disobedience to their sovereign, a new covenant, made not with men, but with God; this also is unjust: for there is no covenant with God but by mediation of somebody that representeth God's person; which none doth but God's lieutenant, who hath the sovereignty under God. But this pretence of covenant with God, is so evident a lie, even in the pretenders' own consciences, that it is not only an act of an unjust, but also of a vile and unmanly disposition.

Secondly, because the right of bearing the person of them all, is given to him they make sovereign, by covenant only of one to another, and not of him to any of them; there can happen no breach of covenant on the part of the sovereign: and consequently none of his subjects, by any pretence of forfeiture, can be freed from his subjection. That he which is made sovereign maketh no covenant with his subjects beforehand, is manifest; because either he must make it with the whole multitude, as one party to the covenant; or he must make a several covenant with every man. With the whole, as one party, it is impossible; because as yet they are not one person; and if he make so many several covenants as there be men, those covenants after he hath the sovereignty are void; because what act soever can be pretended by any one of them for breach thereof, is the act both of himself and of all the rest, because done in the person and by the right of every one of them in particular. Besides, if any one or more of them, pretend a breach of the covenant made by the sovereign at his institution; and others, or one other of his subjects, or himself alone, pretend there was no such breach, there is in this case no judge to decide the controversy; it returns therefore to the sword again; and every man recovereth the right of protecting himself by his own strength, contrary to the design they had in the institution. It is therefore in vain to grant sovereignty by way of precedent covenant. The opinion that any monarch receiveth his power by covenant, that is to say, on condition, proceedeth from want of understanding this easy truth, that covenants being but words and breath, have no force to oblige, contain, constrain, or protect any man, but what it has from the public sword; that is, from the united hands of that man, or assembly of men that hath the sovereignty, and whose actions are avouched by them all, and performed by the strength of them all, in him united. But when an assembly of men is made sovereign; then no man imagineth any such covenant to have passed in the institution; for no man is so dull as to say, for example, the people of Rome made a covenant with the Romans, to hold the sovereignty on such or such conditions; which not performed, the Romans might lawfully depose the Roman people. That men see not the reason to be alike in a monarchy, and in a popular government, proceedeth from the ambition of some, that are kinder to the government of an assembly, whereof they may hope to participate, than of monarchy, which they despair to enjoy.

Thirdly, because the major part hath by consenting voices declared a sovereign; he that dissented must now consent with the rest; that is, be contented to avow all the actions he shall do, or else justly be destroyed by the rest. For if he voluntarily entered into the congregation of them that were assembled, he sufficiently declared thereby his will, and therefore tacitly covenanted to stand to what the major part should ordain: and therefore if he refuse to stand thereto, or make protestation against any of their decrees, he does contrary to his covenant, and therefore unjustly. And whether he be of the congregation or not; and whether his consent be asked or not, he must either submit to their decrees, or be left in the condition of war he was in before; wherein he might without injustice be destroyed by any man whatsoever.

Fourthly, because every subject is by this institution author of all the actions and judgments of the sovereign instituted, it follows, that whatsoever he doth it can be no injury to any of his subjects, nor ought he to be by any of them accused of injustice. For he that doth anything by authority from another doth therein no injury to him by whose authority he acteth: but by this institution of a commonwealth every particular man is author of all the sovereign doth; and consequently, he that complaineth of injury from his sovereign complaineth of that whereof he himself is author, and therefore ought not to accuse any man but himself; no, nor himself of injury; because to do injury to one's self is impossible. It is true that they that have sovereign power may commit iniquity, but not injustice or injury in the proper signification.

Fifthly, and consequently to that which was said last, no man that hath sovereign power can justly be put to death, or otherwise in any manner by his subjects punished. For seeing every subject is author of the actions of his sovereign, he punisheth another for the actions committed by himself.

And because the end of this institution is the peace and defence of them all; and whosoever has right to the end has right to the means; it belongeth of right to whatsoever man or assembly that hath the sovereignty to be judge both of the means of peace and defence, and also of the hindrances and disturbances of the same, and to do whatsoever he shall think necessary to be done, both beforehand, for the preserving of peace and security, by prevention of discord at home and hostility from abroad; and, when peace and security are lost, for the recovery of the same. And therefore,

Sixthly, it is annexed to the sovereignty to be judge of what opinions and doctrines are averse and what conducing to peace; and consequently, on what occasions, how far, and what men are to be trusted withal, in speaking to multitudes of people, and who shall examine the doctrines of all books before they be published. For the actions of men proceed from their opinions, and in the well governing of opinions consisteth the well-governing of men's actions, in order to their peace and concord. And though in matter of doctrine nothing ought to be regarded but the truth; yet this is not repugnant to regulating the same by peace. For doctrine repugnant to peace can be no more true than peace and concord can be against the law of Nature. It is true that in a commonwealth, where, by the negligence or unskilfulness of governors and teachers, false doctrines are by time generally received; the contrary truths may be generally offensive. Yet the most sudden and rough bursting in of a new truth that can be, does never break the peace, but only sometimes awake the war. For those men that are so remissly governed, that they dare take up arms to defend or introduce an opinion, are still in war; and their condition not peace, but only a cessation of arms for fear of one another; and they live, as it were, in the precincts of battle continually. It belongeth therefore to him that hath the sovereign power to be judge, or constitute all judges of opinions and doctrines, as a thing necessary to peace, thereby to prevent discord and civil war.

Seventhly, is annexed to the sovereignty, the whole power of prescribing the rules, whereby every man may know what goods he may enjoy, and what actions he may do, without being molested by any of his fellow-subjects; and this is it men call "propriety." For before constitution of sovereign power, as hath already been shown, all men had right to all things, which necessarily causeth war: and therefore this propriety, being necessary to peace, and depending on sovereign power, is the act of that power, in order to the public peace. These rules of propriety, or *meum* and *tuum,* and of "good," "evil," "lawful," and "unlawful" in the actions of subjects, are the civil laws; that is to say, the laws of each commonwealth in particular; though the name of civil law be now restrained to the ancient civil laws of the city of Rome, which being the head of a great part of the world, her laws at that time were in these parts the civil law.

Eighthly, is annexed to the sovereignty, the right of judicature; that is to say, of hearing and deciding all controversies, which may arise concerning law, either civil or natural, or concerning fact. For without the decision of controversies, there is no protection of one subject against the injuries of another; the laws concerning *meum* and *tuum* are in vain, and to every man remaineth, from the natural and necessary appetite of his own conservation, the right of protecting himself by his private strength, which is the condition of war, and contrary to the end for which every commonwealth is instituted.

Ninthly, is annexed to the sovereignty, the right of making war and peace with other nations and commonwealths; that is to say, of judging when it is for the public good, and how great forces are to be assembled, armed, and paid for that end; and to levy money upon the subjects to defray the expenses thereof. For the power by which the people are to be defended consisteth in their armies, and the strength of an army, in the union of their strength under one command, which command the sovereign instituted, therefore hath; because the command of the "militia, without other institution, maketh him that hath it sovereign. And therefore whosoever is made general of an army, he that hath the sovereign power is always generalissimo.

Tenthly, is annexed to the sovereignty, the choosing of all counsellors, ministers, magistrates, and officers, both in peace and war. For seeing the sovereign is charged with the end, which is the common peace and defence, he is understood to have power to use such means as he shall think most fit for his discharge.

Eleventhly, to the sovereign is committed the power of rewarding with riches or honour, and of punishing with corporal or pecuniary punishment, or with ignominy, every subject according to the law he hath formerly made; or if there be no law made, according as he shall judge most to conduce to the encouraging of men to serve the commonwealth, or deterring of them from doing disservice to the same.

Lastly, considering what value men are naturally apt to set upon themselves; what respect they look for from others; and how little they value other men; from whence continually arise amongst them, emulation, quarrels, factions, and at last war, to the destroying of one another, and diminution of their strength against a common enemy; it is necessary that there be laws of honour, and a public rate of the worth of such men as have deserved, or are able to deserve well of the commonwealth; and that there be force in the hands of some or other, to put those laws in execution. But it hath already been shown, that not only the whole "militia," or forces of the commonwealth; but also the judicature of all controversies, is annexed to the sovereignty. To the sovereign therefore it belongeth also to give titles of honour; and to appoint what order of place and dignity each man shall hold; and what signs of respect, in public or private meetings, they shall give to one another.

These are the rights, which make the essence of sovereignty; and which are the marks whereby a man may discern in what man, or assembly of men, the sovereign power is placed and resideth. For these are incommunicable, and inseparable. The power to coin money; to dispose of the estate and persons of infant heirs; to have pre-emption in markets; and all other statute prerogatives, may be transferred by the sovereign; and yet the power to protect his subjects be retained. But if he transfer the "militia," he retains the judicature in vain, for want of execution of the laws: or if he grant away the power of raising money, the "militia" is in vain; or if he give away the government of doctrines, men will be frighted into rebellion with the fear of spirits. And so if we consider any one of the said rights, we shall presently see, that the holding of all the rest will produce no effect, in the conservation of peace and justice, the end for which all commonwealths are instituted. And this divisiou is it, whereof it is said, "a kingdom divided in itself cannot stand:" for unless this division precede, division into opposite armies can never happen. If there had not first been an opinion received of the greatest part of England, that these powers were divided between the King, and the Lords, and the House of Commons, the people had never been divided and fallen into this civil war; first between those that disagreed in politics; and after between the dissenters about the liberty of religion; which have so instructed men in this point of sovereign right, that there be few now in England that do not see that these rights are inseparable, and will be so generally acknowledged at the next return of peace; and so continue, till their miseries are forgotten; and no longer, except the vulgar be better taught than they have hitherto been.

And because they are essential and inseparable rights, it follows necessarily, that in whatsoever words any of them seem to be granted away, yet if the sovereign power itself be not in direct terms renounced, and the name of sovereign no more given by the grantees to him that grants them, the grant is void: for when he has granted all he can, if we grant back the sovereignty, all is restored, as inseparably annexed thereunto.

This great authority being indivisible, and inseparably annexed to the sovereignty, there is little ground for the opinion of them that say of sovereign kings, though they be *singulis majores,* of greater power than every one of their subjects, yet they be *universis minores,* of less power than them all together. For if by "all together," they mean not the collective body as one person, then "all together," and "every one," signify the same; and the speech is absurd. But if by "all together," they understand them as one person, which person the sovereign bears, then the power of all together, is the same with the sovereign's power; and so again the speech is absurd: which absurdity they see well enough, when the sovereignty is in an assembly of the people; but in a monarch they see it not; and yet the power of sovereignty is the same in whomsoever it be placed.

And as the power, so also the honour of the sovereign, ought to be greater, than that of any, or all the subjects. For in the sovereignty is the fountain of honour. The dignities of lord, earl, duke, and prince are his creatures. As in the presence of the master, the servants are equal, and without any honour at all; so are the subjects in the presence of the sovereign. And though they shine some more, some less, when they are out of his sight; yet in his presence, they shine no more than the stars in the presence of the sun.

But a man may here object, that the condition of subjects is very miserable; as being obnoxious to the lusts, and other irregular passions of him or them that have so unlimited a power in their hands. And commonly they that live under a monarch, think it the fault of monarchy; and they that live under the government of democracy, or other sovereign assembly, attribute all the inconvenience to that form of commonwealth; whereas the power in all forms, if they be perfect enough to protect them, is the same: not considering that the state of man can never be without some incommodity or other; and that the greatest, that in any form of government can possibly happen to the people in general, is scarce sensible, in respect of the miseries, and horrible calamities, that accompany a civil war, or that dissolute condition of masterless men, without subjection to laws, and a coercive power to tie their hands from rapine and revenge: nor considering that the greatest pressure of sovereign governors proceedeth not from any delight, or profit they can expect in the damage or weakening of their subjects, in whose vigour consisteth their own strength and glory; but in the restiveness of themselves, that unwillingly contributing to their own defence, make it necessary for their governors to draw from them what they can in time of peace, that they may have means on any emergent occasion, or sudden need, to resist, or take advantage on their enemies. For all men are by nature provided of notable multiplying glasses, that is their passions and self-love, through which every little payment appeareth a great grievance; but are destitute of those prospective glasses, namely, moral and civil science, to see afar off the miseries that hang over them, and cannot without such payments be avoided.

## Chapter XX

## Of Dominion Paternal, and Despotical

A commonwealth "by acquisition," is that, where the sovereign power is acquired by force; and it is acquired by force when men singly, or many together by plurality of voices, for fear of death, or bonds, do authorize all the actions of that man, or assembly, that hath their lives and liberty in his power.

And this kind of dominion, or sovereignty, differeth from sovereignty by institution only in this, that men who choose their sovereign do it for fear of one another, and not of him whom they institute: but in this case, they subject themselves to him they are afraid of. In both cases they do it for fear: which is to be noted by them that hold all such covenants as proceed from fear of death or violenee, void: which if it were true, no man, in any kind of commonwealth, could be obliged to obedience. It is true, that in a commonwealth once instituted, or acquired, promises proceeding from fear of death or violence, are no covenants, nor obliging, when the thing promised is contrary to the laws; but the reason is not because it was made upon fear, but because he that promiseth hath no right in the thing promised. Also, when he may lawfully perform, and doth not, it is not the invalidity of the covenant that absolveth him, but the sentence of the sovereign. Otherwise, whensoever a man lawfully promiseth, he unlawfully breaketh: but when the sovereign, who is the actor, acquitteth him, then he is acquitted by him that extorted the promise, as by the author of such absolution.

But the rights and consequences of sovereignty, are the same in both. His power cannot, without his consent, be transferred to another; he cannot forfeit it: he cannot be accused by any of his subjects of injury: he cannot be punished by them; he is judge of what is necessary for peace; and judge of doctrines: he is sole legislator; and supreme judge of controversies; and of the times, and occasions of war, and peace: to him it belongeth to choose magistrates, counsellors, commanders, and all other officers and ministers; and to determine of rewards and punishments, honour, and order. The reasons whereof, are the same which are alleged in the precedent chapter, for the same rights and consequences of sovereignty by institution.

Dominion is acquired two ways; by generation and by conquest. The right of dominion by generation is that, which the parent hath over his children, and is called "paternal." And is not so derived from the generation, as if therefore the parent had dominion over his child because he begat him; but from the child's consent, either express, or by other sufficient arguments declared. For as to the generation, God hath ordained to man a helper; and there be always two that are equally parents: the dominion therefore over the child should belong equally to both; and he be equally subject to both, which is impossible, for no man can obey two masters. And whereas some have attributed the dominion to the man only, as being of the more excellent sex; they misreckon in it. For there is not always that difference of strength or prudence between the man and the woman, as that the right can be determined without war. In commonwealths, this controversy is decided by the civil law; and for the most part, but not always, the sentence is in favour of the father; because for the most part commonwealths have been erected by the fathers, not by the mothers of families. But the question lieth now in the state of mere nature; where there are supposed no laws of matrimony; no laws for the education of children; but the law of Nature, and the natural inclination of the sexes, one to another, and to their children. In this condition of mere nature, either the parents between themselves dispose of the dominion over the child by contract; or do not dispose thereof at all. If they dispose thereof, the right passeth according to the contract. We find in history that the Amazons contracted with the men of the neighbouring countries, to whom they had recourse for issue, that the issue male should be sent back, but the female remain with themselves: so that the dominion of the females was in the mother.

If there be no contract, the dominion is in the mother. For in the condition of mere nature, where there are no matrimonial laws, it cannot be known who is the father, unless it be declared by the mother: and therefore the right of dominion over the child dependeth on her will, and is consequently hers. Again, seeing the infant is first in the power of the mother, so as she may either nourish or expose it; if she nourish it, it oweth its life to the mother; and is therefore obliged to obey her, rather than any other; and by consequence the dominion over it is hers. But if she expose it, and another find and nourish it, the dominion is in him that nourisheth it. For it ought to obey him by whom it is preserved; because preservation of life being the end, for which one man becomes subject to another, every man is supposed to promise obedience to him, in whose power it is to save, or destroy him.

If the mother be the father's subject, the child is in the father's power: and if the father be the mother's subject, as when a sovereign queen marrieth one of her subjects, the child is subject to the mother; because the father also is her subject.

If a man and woman, monarchs of two several kingdoms, have a child, and contract concerning who shall have the dominion of him, the right of the dominion passeth by the contract. If they contract not, the dominion followeth the dominion of the place of his residence. For the sovereign of each country hath dominion over all that reside therein.

He that hath the dominion over the child, hath dominion also over the children of the child; and over their children's children. For he that hath dominion over the person of a man, hath dominion over all that is his; without which, dominion were but a title, without the effect.

The right of succession to paternal dominion, proceedeth in the same manner as doth the right of succession of monarchy; of which I have already sufficiently spoken in the precedent chapter.

Dominion acquired by conquest, or victory in war, is that which some writers call "despotical," from Δεσπότης, which signifieth a "lord," or "master;" and is the dominion of the master over his servant. And this dominion is then acquired to the victor, when the vanquished, to avoid the present stroke of death, covenanteth either in express words, or by other sufficient signs of the will, that so long as his life and the liberty of his body is allowed him, the victor shall have the use thereof, at his pleasure. And after such covenant made, the vanquished is a "servant," and not before: for by the word "servant," whether it be derived from servire, to serve, or from servare, to save, which I leave to grammarians to dispute, is not meant a captive, which is kept in prison or bonds, till the owner of him that took him, or bought him of one that did, shall consider what to do with him: for such men, commonly called slaves, have no obligation at all; but may break their bonds or the prison; and kill, or carry away captive their master, justly: but one, that being taken, hath corporal liberty allowed him; and upon promise not to run away, nor to do violence to his master, is trusted by him.

It is not therefore the victory that giveth the right of dominion over the vanquished, but his own covenant. Nor is he obliged because he is conquered; that is to say, beaten and taken, or put to flight; but because he cometh in and submitteth to the victor; nor is the victor obliged by an enemy's rendering himself without promise of life, to spare him for this his yielding to discretion, which obliges not the victor longer than in his own discretion he shall think fit.

And that which men do when they demand, as it is now called, "quarter," which the Greeks called Ζωγρία, "taking alive," is to evade the present fury of the victor by submission, and to compound for their life with ransom, or service; and therefore he that hath quarter, hath not his life given, but deferred till farther deliberation; for it is not a yielding on condition of life, but to discretion. And then only is his life in security, and his service due, when the victor hath trusted him with his corporal liberty. For slaves that work in prisons, or fetters, do it not of duty, but to avoid the cruelty of their taskmasters.

The master of the servant is master also of all he hath, and may exact the use thereof, that is to say, of his goods, of his labour, of his servants, and of his children, so often as he shall think fit. For he holdeth his life of his master by the covenant of obedience; that is, of owning and authorizing whatsoever the master shall do. And in case the master, if he refuse, kill him, or cast him into bonds, or otherwise punish him for his disobedience, he is himself the author of the same, and cannot accuse him of injury.

In sum, the rights and consequences of both "paternal" and "despotical" dominion, are the very same with those of a sovereign by institution; and for the same reasons: which reasons are set down in the precedent chapter. So that for a man that is monarch of divers nations, whereof he hath in one the sovereignty by institution of the people assembled, and in another by conquest, that is by the submission of each particular, to avoid death or bonds; to demand of one nation more than of the other from the title of conquest, as being a conquered nation, is an act of ignorance of the rights of sovereignty; for the sovereign is absolute over both alike, or else there is no sovereignty at all; and so every man may lawfully protect himself, if he can, with his own sword, which is the condition of war.

By this it appears that a great family, if it be not part of some commonwealth, is of itself, as to the rights of sovereignty, a little monarchy; whether that family consist of a man and his children, or of a man and his servants; or of a man, and his children and servants together, wherein the father or master is the sovereign. But yet a family is not properly a commonwealth, unless it be of that power by its own number, or by other opportunities, as not to be subdued without the hazard of war. For where a number of men are manifestly too weak to defend themselves united, every one may use his own reason in time of danger to save his own life, either by flight or by submission to the enemy, as he shall think best; in the same manner as a very small company of soldiers, surprised by an army, may cast down their arms and demand quarter, or run away, rather than be put to the sword. And thus much shall suffice concerning what I find by speculation, and deduction of sovereign rights, from the nature, need, and designs of men, in erecting of commonwealths, and putting themselves under monarchs, or assemblies entrusted with power euough for their protection.

Let us now consider what the Scripture teacheth in the same point. To Moses, the children of Israel say thus: "Speak thou to us, and we will hear thee; but let not God speak to us, lest we die" (Exod. xx. 19). This is absolute obedience to Moses. Concerning the right of kings, God Himself by the mouth of Samuel, saith (1 Sam. viii. 11, 12, &c.): "This shall be the right of the king you will have to reign over you. He shall take your sons, and set them to drive his chariots, and to be his horsemen, and to run before his chariots; and gather in his harvest; and to make his engines of war, and instruments of his chariots; and shall take your daughters to make perfumes, to be his cooks, and bakers. He shall take your fields, your vineyards, and your olive yards, and give them to his servants. He shall take the tithe of your corn and wine, and give it to the men of his chamber, and to his other servants. He shall take your manservants and your maidservants, and the choice of your youth, and employ them in his business. He shall take the tithe of your flocks, and you shall be his servants." This is absolute power, and summed up in the last words, "you shall be his servants." Again, when the people heard what power their king was to have, yet they consented thereto, and say thus (verse 10): "We will be as all other nations, and our king shall judge our causes, and go before us, to conduct our wars." Here is confirmed the right that sovereigns have both to the "militia" and to all "judicature;" in which is contained as absolute power as one man can possibly transfer to another. Again, the prayer of king Solomon to God was this (1 Kings III. 9): "Give to thy servant understanding, to judge thy people, and to discern between good and evil." It belongeth therefore to the sovereign to be "judge," and to prescribe the rules of "discerning good" and "evil;" which rules are laws; and therefore in him is the legislative power. Saul sought the life of David; yet when it was in his power to slay Saul, and his servants would have done it, David forbad them, saying (1 Sam. xxiv. 6): "God forbid I should do such an act against my lord, the anointed of God." For obedience of servants St. Paul saith (Col. iii. 22): "Servants obey your masters in all things;" and (Col. iii. 20): "Children obey your parents in all things." There is simple obedience in those that are subject to paternal or despotical dominion. Again (Matt. xxiii. 2, 3): "The Scribes and Pharisees sit in Moses' chair, and therefore all that they shall bid you observe, that observe and do." There again is simple obedience, And St. Paul (Titus iii. 2): "Warn them that they subject themselves to princes, and to those that are in authority, and obey them." This obedience is also simple. Lastly, our Saviour Himself acknowledges, that men ought to pay such taxes as are by kings imposed, where he says, "Give to Caesar that which is Caesar's;" and paid such taxes Himself. And that the king's word is sufficient to take anything from any subject, when there is need; and that the king is judge of that need, for He Himself, as king of the Jews, commanded His disciples to take the ass, and ass's colt, to carry Him into Jerusalem, saying (Matt. xxi. 2, 3): "Go into the village over against you, and you shall find a she-ass tied, and her colt with her; untie them, and bring them to me. And if any man ask you what you mean by it, say the Lord hath need of them: and they will let them go." They will not ask whether His necessity be a sufficient title; nor whether He be judge of that necessity; but acquiesce in the will of the Lord.

To these places may be added also that of Genesis (iii. 5): "Ye shall be as gods, knowing good and evil." And (verse 11): "Who told thee that thou wast naked? hast thou eaten of the tree, of which I commanded thee thou shouldest not eat?" For the cognizance or judicature of "good" and "evil," being forbidden by the name of the fruit of the tree of knowledge, as a trial of Adam's obedience; the devil to inflame the ambition of the woman, to whom that fruit already seemed beautiful, told her that by tasting it they should be as gods, knowing "good" and "evil." Whereupon having both eaten, they did indeed take upon them God's office, which is judicature of good and evil; but acquired no new ability to distinguish between them aright. And whereas it is said, that having eaten, they saw they were naked; no man hath so interpreted that place, as if they had been formerly blind, and saw not their own skins: the meaning is plain, that it was then they first judged their nakedness, wherein it was God's will to create them, to be uncomely; and by being ashamed, did tacitly censure God Himself. And thereupon God saith: "Hast thou eaten, &c.," as if He should say, doest thou that owest me obedience, take upon thee to judge of my commandments? Whereby it is clearly, though allegorically, signified that the commands of them that have the right to command, are not by their subjects to be censured nor disputed.

So that it appeareth plainly, to my understanding, both from reason and Scripture, that the sovereign power, whether placed in one man, as in monarchy, or in one assembly of men, as in popular and aristocratical commonwealths, is as great as possibly men can be imagined to make it. And though of so unlimited a power, men may fancy many evil consequences, yet the consequences of the want of it, which is perpetual war of every man against his neighbour, are much worse. The condition of man in this life shall never be without inconveniences; but there happeneth in no commonwealth any great inconvenience but what proceeds from the subject's disobedience, and breach of those covenants, from which the commonwealth has its being. And whosoever thinking sovereign power too great, will seek to make it less, must subject himself to the power that can limit it; that is to say, to a greater.

The greatest objection is, that of the practice; when men ask where and when such power has by subjects been acknowledged. But one may ask them again, when or where has there been a kingdom long free from sedition and civil war. In those nations whose commonwealths have been long-lived, and not being destroyed but by foreign war, the subjects never did dispute of the sovereign power. But howsoever, an argument from the practice of men, that have not sifted to the bottom, and with exact reason weighed the causes and nature of commonwealths, and suffer daily those miseries that proceed from the ignorance thereof, is invalid. For though in all places of the world men should lay the foundation of their houses on the sand, it could not thence be inferred that so it ought to be. The skill of making and maintaining commonwealths, consisteth in certain rules, as doth arithmetic and geometry; not, as tennis-play, on practice only: which rules neither poor men have the leisure, nor men that have had the leisure, have hitherto had the curiosity, or the method to find out.

# Chapter XXI

## Of the Liberty of Subjects

Liberty, or "freedom," signifieth, properly, the absence of opposition; by opposition, I mean external impediments of motion; and may be applied no less to irrational and inanimate creatures than to rational. For whatsoever is so tied, or environed, as it cannot move but within a certain space, which space is determined by the opposition of some external body, we say it hath not liberty to go further. And so of all living creatures whilst they are imprisoned, or restrained, with walls or chains; and of the water whilst it is kept in by banks or vessels, that otherwise would spread itself into a larger space, we use to say, they are not at liberty to move in such manner, as without those external impediments they would. But when the impediment of motion is in the constitution of the thing itself, we use not to say, it wants the liberty, but the power to move; as when a stone lieth still, or a man is fastened to his bed by sickness.

And according to this proper and generally received meaning of the word, a "freeman, is he, that in those things, which by his strength and wit he is able to do, is not hindered to do what he has a will to." But when the words "free," and "liberty," are applied to anything but "bodies," they are abused; for that which is not subject to motion, is not subject to impediment; and therefore, when it is said for example, the way is free, no liberty of the way is signified, but of those that walk in it without stop. And when we say a gift is free, there is not meant any liberty of the gift, but of the giver, that was not bound by any law or covenant to give it. So when we "speak freely,"

it is not the liberty of voice, or pronunciation, but of the man, whom no law hath obliged to speak otherwise than he did. Lastly, from the use of the word "free-will," no liberty can be inferred of the will, desire, or inclination, but the liberty of the man; which consisteth in this, that he finds no stop, in doing what he has the will, desire, or inclination to do.

Fear and liberty are consistent; as when a man throweth his goods into the sea for "fear" the ship should sink, he doth it nevertheless very willingly, and may refuse to do it if he will: it is therefore the action of one that was "free;" so a man sometimes pays his debt, only for "fear" of imprisonment, which because nobody hindered him from detaining, was the action of a man at "liberty." And generally all actions which men do in commonwealths, for "fear" of the law, are actions which the doers had "liberty" to omit.

"Liberty" and "necessity" are consistent, as in the water that hath not only "liberty," but a "necessity" of descending by the channel; so likewise in the actions which men voluntarily do: which, because they proceed from their will, proceed from "liberty;" and yet, because every act of man's will, and every desire and inclination proceedeth from some cause, and that from another cause, in a continual chain, whose first link is in the hand of God the first of all causes, proceed from "necessity." So that to him that could see the connection of those causes, the "necessity" of all men's voluntary actions would appear manifest. And therefore God, that seeth and disposeth all things, seeth also that the "liberty" of man in doing what he will, is accompanied with the "necessity" of doing that which God will, and no more nor less. For though men may do many things which God does not command, nor is therefore author of them; yet they can have no passion, nor appetite to anything, of which appetite

God's will is not the cause. And did not His will assure the "necessity" of man's will, and consequently of all that on man's will dependeth, the "liberty" of men would be a contradiction, and impediment to the omnipotence and "liberty" of God. And this shall suffice, as to the matter in hand, of that natural "liberty," which only is properly called "liberty."

But as men, for the attaining of peace, and conservation of themselves thereby, have made an artificial man, which we call a commonwealth; so also have they made artificial chains, called "civil laws," which they themselves, by mutual covenants, have fastened at one end, to the lips of that man, or assembly, to whom they have given the sovereign power; and at the other end to their own ears. These bonds, in their own nature but weak, may nevertheless be made to hold, by the danger, though not by the difficulty of breaking them.

In relation to these bonds only it is, that I am to speak now, of the "liberty" of "subjects." For seeing there is no commonwealth in the world, wherein there be rules enough set down for the regulating of all the actions and words of men, as being a thing impossible; it followeth necessarily, that in all kinds of actions by the laws pretermitted, men have the liberty of doing what their own reasons shall suggest, for the most profitable to themselves. For if we take liberty in the proper sense, for corporal liberty; that is to say, freedom from chains and prison; it were very absurd for men to clamour as they do for the liberty they so manifestly enjoy. Again, if we take liberty for an exemption from laws, it is no less absurd for men to demand as they do that liberty by which all other men may be masters of their lives. And yet, as absurd as it is, this is it they demand; not knowing that the laws are of no power to protect them, without a sword in the hands of a man, or men, to cause those laws to be put in execution. The liberty of a subject lieth therefore only in those things which in regulating their actions, the sovereign hath pretermitted: such as is the liberty to buy and sell, and otherwise contract with one another; to choose their own abode, their own diet, their own trade of life, and institute their children as they themselves think fit; and the like.

Nevertheless we are not to understand, that by such liberty, the sovereign power of life and death is either abolished or limited. For it has been already shown, that nothing the sovereign representative can do to a subject, on what pretence soever, can properly be called injustice or injury; because every subject is author of every act the sovereign doth; so that he never wanteth right to anything, otherwise than as he himself is the subject of God, and bound thereby to observe the laws of Nature. And therefore it may, and doth often happen in commonwealths, that a subject may be put to death by the command of the sovereign power; and yet neither do the other wrong: as when Jephtha caused his daughter to be sacrificed; in which, and the like cases, he that so dieth, had liberty to do the action, for which he is nevertheless without injury put to death. And the same holdeth also in a sovereign prince that putteth to death an innocent subject. For though the action be against the law of Nature, as being contrary to equity, as was the killing of Uriah, by David; yet it was not an injury to Uriah, but to God. Not to Uriah, because the right to do what he pleased was given him by Uriah himself: and yet to God, because David was God's subject, and prohibited all iniquity by the law of Nature: which distinction, David himself, when he repented the fact, evidently confirmed, saying, "To thee only have I sinned." In the same manner the people of Athens, when they banished the most potent of their commonwealth for ten years, thought they committed no injustice; and yet they never questioned what crime he had done; but what hurt he would do: nay they commanded the banishment of they knew not whom; and every citizen bringing his oyster-shell into the market-place, written with the name of him he desired should be banished, without actually accusing him, sometimes banished an Aristides, for his reputation of justice; and sometimes a scurrilous jester, as Hyperbolus, to make a jest of it. And yet a man cannot say, the sovereign people of Athens wanted right to banish them; or an Athenian the liberty to jest, or to be just.

The liberty, whereof there is so frequent and honourable mention in the histories and philosophy of the ancient Greeks and Romans, and in the writings and discourse of those that from them have received all their learning in the politics, is not the liberty of particular men; but the liberty of the commonwealth: which is the same with that which every man then should have, if there were no civil laws, nor commonwealth at all. And the effects of it also be the same. For as amongst masterless men there is perpetual war, of every man against his neighbour; no inheritance, to transmit to the son, nor to expect from the father; no propriety of goods, or lands; no security; but a full and absolute liberty in every particular man: so in states and commonwealths not dependent on one another, every commonwealth, not every man, has an absolute liberty to do what it shall judge, that is to say, what that man, or assembly that representeth it, shall judge most conducing to their benefit. But withal, they live in the condition of a perpetual war, and upon the confines of battle, with their frontiers armed, and cannons planted against their neighbours round about. The Athenians and Romans were free; that is, free commonwealths: not that any particular men had the liberty to resist their own representative; but that their representative had the liberty to resist, or invade other people. There is written on the turrets of the city of Lucca, in great characters, at this day, the word "Libertas;" yet no man can thence infer, that a particular man has more liberty, or immunity from the service of the commonwealth there, than in Constantinople. Whether a commonwealth be monarchical, or popular, the freedom is still the same.

But it is an easy thing for men to be deceived by the specious name of liberty; and for want of judgment to distinguish, mistake that for their private inheritance and birthright, which is the right of the public only. And when the same error is confirmed by theauthority of men in reputation for their writings on this subject, it is no wonder if it produce sedition, and change of government. In these western parts of the world, we are made to receive our opinions concerning the institution and rights of commonwealths, from Aristotle, Cicero, and other men, Greeks and Romans, that living under popular states, derived those rights, not from the principles of Nature, but transcribed them into their books, out of the practice of their own commonwealths, which were popular; as the grammarians describe the rules of language out of the practice of the time; or the rules of poetry out of the poems of Homer and Virgil. And because the Athenians were taught to keep them from desire of changing their government, that they were free men, and all that lived under monarchy were slaves; therefore Aristotle put it down in his "Politics" (lib. 6, cap. ii.): "In democracy, 'liberty" is to be supposed: for it is commonly held, that no man is ' free ' in any other government." And as Aristotle, so Cicero and other writers have grounded their civil doctrine on the opinions of the Romans, who were taught to hate monarchy, at first, by them that having deposed their sovereign, shared amongst them the sovereignty of Rome; and afterwards by their successors. And by reading of these Greek and Latin authors, men from their childhood have gotten a habit, under a false show of liberty, of favouring tumults, and of licentious controlling the actions of their sovereigns, and again of controlling those controllers; with the effusion of so much blood, as I think I may truly say, there was never anything so dearly bought as these western parts have bought the learning of the Greek and Latin tongues.

To come now to the particulars of the true liberty of a subject; that is to say, what are the things, which though commanded by the sovereign, he may nevertheless, without injustice, refuse to do; we are to consider what rights we pass away, when we make a commonwealth; or, which is all one, what liberty we deny ourselves, by owning all the actions, without exception, of the man, or assembly, we make our sovereign. For in the act of our "submission," consisteth both our "obligation," and our "liberty;" which must therefore be inferred by arguments taken from thence; there being no obligation on any man, which ariseth not from some act of his own; for all men equally, are by Nature free. And because such arguments must either be drawn from the express words, I "authorize all his actions," or from the intention of him that submitteth himself to his power, which intention is to be understood by the end for which he so submitteth; the obligation and liberty of the subject, is to be derived, either from those words, or others equivalent; or else from the end of the institution of sovereignty, namely, the peace of the subjects within themselves, and their defence against a common enemy.

First therefore, seeing sovereignty by institution, is by covenant of every one to every one; and sovereignty by acquisition, by covenants of the vanquished to the victor, or child to the parent; it is manifest, that every subject has liberty in all those things, the right whereof cannot by covenant be transferred. I have shown before in the 14th chapter, that covenants, not to defend a man's own body, are void. Therefore,

If the sovereign command a man, though justly condemned, to kill, wound, or maim himself; or not to resist those that assault him; or to abstain from the use of food, air, medicine, or any other thing, without which he cannot live; yet hath that man the liberty to disobey.

If a man be interrogated by the sovereign, or his authority, concerning a crime done by himself, he is not bound, without assurance of pardon, to confess it; because no man, as I have shown in the same chapter, can be obliged by covenant to accuse himself.

Again, the consent of a subject to sovereign power, is contained in these words, "I authorize, or take upon me, all his actions;" in which there is no restriction at all, of his own former natural liberty: for by allowing him to "kill me," I am not bound to kill myself when he commands me. It is one thing to say, "kill me, or my fellow, if you please;" another thing to say, "I will kill myself, or my fellow." It followeth therefore, that

No man is bound by the words themselves, either to kill himself, or any other man; and consequently, that the obligation a man may sometimes have, upon the command of the sovereign to execute any dangerous or dishonourable office, dependeth not on the words of our submission; but on the intention, which is to be understood by the end thereof. When therefore our refusal to obey, frustrates the end for which the sovereignty was ordained; then there is no liberty to refuse: otherwise there is.

Upon this ground, a man that is commanded as a soldier to fight against the enemy, though his sovereign have right enough to punish his refusal with death, may nevertheless in many cases refuse, without injustice; as when he substituteth a sufficient soldier in his place: for in this case he deserteth not the service of the commonwealth. And there is allowance to be made for natural timorousness; not only to women, of whom no such dangerous duty is expected, but also to men of feminine courage. When armies fight, there is on one side, or both, a running away; yet when they do it not out of treachery, but fear, they are not esteemed to do it unjustly, but dishonourably. For the same reason, to avoid battle, is not injustice, but cowardice. But he that enrolleth himself a soldier, or taketh impressed money, taketh away the excuse of a timorous nature; and is obliged, not only to go to the battle, but also not to run from it, without his captain's leave. And when the defence of the commonwealth requireth at once the help of all that are able to bear arms, every one is obliged; because otherwise the institution of the commonwealth, which they have not the purpose or courage to preserve, was in vain.

To resist the sword of the commonwealth in defence of another man, guilty or innocent, no man hath liberty; because such liberty takes away from the sovereign the means of protecting us; and is therefore destructive of the very essence of government. But in case a great many men together have already resisted the sovereign power unjustly, or committed some capital crime for which every one of them expecteth death, whether have they not the liberty then to join together, and assist and defend one another? Certainly they have;

for they but defend their lives, which the guilty man may as well do as the innocent. There was indeed injustice in the first breach of their duty; their bearing of arms subsequent to it, though it be to maintain what they have done, is no new unjust act. And if it be only to defend their persons, it is not unjust at all. But the offer of pardon taketh from them to whom it is offered the plea of self-defence, and maketh their perseverance in assisting or defending the rest unlawful.

As for other liberties, they depend on the silence of the law. In cases where the sovereign has prescribed no rule, there the subject hath the liberty to do, or forbear, according to his own discretion. And therefore such liberty is in some places more, and in some less; and in some times more, in other times less, according as they that have the sovereignty shall think most convenient. As for example, there was a time when, in England, a man might enter into his own land, and dispossess such as wrongfully possessed it, by force. But in aftertimes, that liberty of forcible entry was taken away by a statute made by the king in parliament. And in some places of the world, men have the liberty of many wives; in other places such liberty is not allowed.

If a subject have a controversy with his sovereign, of debt, or of right of possession of lands or goods, or concerning any service required at his hands, or concerning any penalty, corporal or pecuniary, grounded on a precedent law; he hath the same liberty to sue for his right as if it were against a subject, and before such judges as are appointed by the sovereign. For seeing the sovereign demandeth by force of a former law, and not by virtue of his power; he declareth thereby that he requireth no more than shall appear to be due by that law. The suit therefore is not contrary to the will of the sovereign;

and consequently the subject hath the liberty to demand the hearing of his cause; and sentence, according to that law. But if he demand, or take anything by pretence of his power there lieth, in that case, no action of law; for all that is done by him in virtue of his power, is done by the authority of every subject, and consequently he that brings an action against the sovereign, brings it against himself.

If a monarch, or sovereign assembly, grant a liberty to all or any of his subjects, which grant standing, he is disabled to provide for their safety, the grant is void, unless he directly renounce or transfer the sovereignty to another. For in that he might openly, if it had been his will, and in plain terms, have renounced or transferred it, and did not; it is to be understood it was not his will, but that the grant proceeded from ignorance of the repugnancy between such a liberty and the sovereign power, and therefore the sovereignty is still retained; and consequently all those powers, which are necessary to the exercising thereof; such as are the power of war and peace, of judicature, of appointing officers and councillors, of levying money, and the rest named in the 18th chapter.

The obligation of subjects to the sovereign is understood to last as long, and no longer, than the power lasteth by which he is able to protect them. For the right men have by nature to protect themselves, when none else can protect them, can by no covenant be relinquished. The sovereignty is the soul of the commonwealth, which once departed from the body, the members do no more receive their motion from it. The end of obedience is protection, which, wheresoever a man seeth it, either in his own or in another's sword, nature applieth his obedience to it, and his endeavour to maintain it. And though sovereignty, in the intention of them that make it, be immortal, yet is it in its own nature not only subject to violent death by foreign war, but also, through the ignorance and passions of men, it hath in it, from the very institution, many seeds of a natural mortality, by intestine discord.

If a subject be taken prisoner in war, or his person, or his means of life be within the guards of the enemy, and hath his life and corporal liberty given him on condition to be subject to the victor, he hath liberty to accept the condition; and having accepted it, is the subject of him that took him, because he had no other way to preserve himself. The case is the same, if he be detained on the same terms, in a foreign country. But if a man be held in prison, or bonds, or is not trusted with the liberty of his body, he cannot be understood to be bound by covenant to subjection; and therefore may, if he can, make his escape by any means whatsoever.

If a monarch shall relinquish the sovereignty, both for himself and his heirs, his subjects return to the absolute libert of rature; because, though nature may declare who are his sons, and who are the nearest of his kin, yet it dependeth on his own will, as hath been said in the precedent chapter, who shall be his heir. If therefore he will have no heir, there is no sovereignty, nor subjection. The case is the same if he die without known kindred, and without declaration of his heir. For then there can no heir be known, and consequently no subjection be due.

If the sovereign banish his subject, during the banishment he is not subject. But he that is sent on a message, or hath leave to travel, is still subject; but it is, by contract between sovereigns, not by virtue of the covenant of subjection. For whosoever entereth into another's dominion, is subject to all the laws thereof, unless he have a privilege by the amity of the sovereigns, or by special license.

If a monarch subdued by war render himself subject to the victor, his subjects are delivered from their former obligation, and become obliged to the victor. But if he be held prisoner, or have not the liberty of his own body, he is not understood to have given away the right of sovereignty; and therefore his subjects are obliged to yield obedience to the magistrates formerly placed, governing not in their own name, but in his. For, his right remaining, the question is only of the administration; that is to say, of the magistrates and officers, which, if we have not means to name, he is supposed to approve those which he himself had formerly appointed.

# Chapter XXV

## Of Counsel

How fallacious it is to judge of the nature of things by the ordinary and inconstant use of words, appeareth in nothing more than in the confusion of counsels and commands, arising from the imperative manner of speaking in them both, and in many other occasions besides. For the words "do this," are the words not only of him that commandeth, but also of him that giveth counsel, and of him that exhorteth; and yet there are but few that see not that these are very different things, or that cannot distinguish between them when they perceive who it is that speaketh, and to whom the speech is directed, and upon what occasion. But finding those phrases in men's writings, and being not able or not willing to enter into a consideration of the circumstances, they mistake sometimes the precepts of counsellors for the precepts of them that command; and sometimes the contrary, according as it best agreeth with the conclusions they would infer, or the actions they approve. To avoid which mistakes, and render to those terms of commanding, counselling, and exhorting their proper and distinct significations, I define them thus.

"Command" is, where a man saith "do this," or "do not this," without expecting other reason than the will of him that says it. From this it followeth manifestly, that he that commandeth, pretendeth thereby his own benefit: for the reason of his command is his own will only, and the proper object of every man's will, is some good to himself.

"Counsel," is where a man saith, "do," or "do not this," and deduceth his reasons from the benefit that arriveth by it to him to whom he saith it. And from this it is evident, that he that giveth counsel, pretendeth only, whatsoever he intendeth, the good of him to whom he giveth it.

Therefore between counsel and command, one great difference is, that command is directed to a man's own benefit; and counsel to the benefit of another man. And from this ariseth another difference, that a man may be obliged to do what he is commanded; as when he hath covenanted to obey: but he cannot be obliged to do as he is counselled, because the hurt of not following it, is his own; or if he should covenant to follow it, then is the counsel turned into the nature of a command. A third difference between them is, that no man can pretend a right to be of another man's counsel; because he is not to pretend benefit by it to himself: but to demand right to counsel another, argues a will to know his designs, or to gain some other good to himself: which, as I said before, is of every man's will the proper object.

This also is incident to the nature of counsel; that whatsoever it be, he that asketh it, cannot in equity accuse or punish it: for to ask counsel of another, is to permit him to give such counsel as he shall think best; and consequently, he that giveth counsel to his sovereign, whether a monarch, or an assembly, when he asketh it, cannot in equity be punished for it, whether the same be conformable to the opinion of the most, or not, so it be to the proposition in debate. For if the sense of the assembly can be taken notice of, before the debate be ended, they should neither ask nor take any further counsel; for the sense of the assembly is the resolution of the debate, and end of all deliberation. And generally he that demandeth counsel, is author of it; and therefore cannot punish it; and what the sovereign cannot, no man else can. But if one subject giveth counsel to another, to do anything contrary to the laws, whether that counsel proceed from evil intention, or from ignorance only, it is punishable by the commonwealth; because ignorance of the law is no good excuse, where every man is bound to take notice of the laws to which he is subject.

"Exhortation" and "dehortation" is counsel, accompanied with signs in him that giveth it, of vehement desire to have it followed: or to say it more briefly, "counsel vehemently pressed." For he that exhorteth, doth not deduce the consequences of what he adviseth to be done, and tie himself therein to the rigour of true reasoning; but encourages him he counselleth to action: as he that dehorteth, deterreth him from it. And therefore they have in their speeches, a regard to the common passions and opinions of men, in deducing their reasons; and make use of similitudes, metaphors, examples, and other tools of oratory, to persuade their hearers of the utility, honour, or justice of following their advice.

From whence may be inferred, first, that exhortation and dehortation is directed to the good of him that giveth the counsel, not of him that asketh it, which is contrary to the duty of a counsellor; who, by the definition of counsel, ought to regard not his own benefit, but his whom he adviseth. And that he directeth his counsel to his own benefit, is manifest enough, by the long and vehement urging, or by the artificial giving thereof; which being not required of him, and consequently proceeding from his own occasions, is directed principally to his own benefit, and but accidentally to the good of him that is counselled, or not at all.

Secondly, that the use of exhortation and dehortation lieth only where a man is to speak to a multitude; because when the speech is addressed to one, he may interrupt him, and examine his reasons more rigorously than can be done in a multitude; which are too many to enter into dispute and dialogue with him that speaketh indifferently to them all at once.

Thirdly, that they that exhort and dehort, where they are required to give counsel, are corrupt counsellors, and as it were bribed by their own interest. For though the counsel they give be never so good; yet he that gives it, is no more a good counsellor than he that giveth a just sentence for a reward is a just judge. But where a man may lawfully command, as a father in his family, or a leader in an army, his exhortations and dehortations are not only lawful, but also necessary and laudable. But then they are no more counsels but commands; which when they are for execution of sour labour, sometimes necessity and always humanity requireth to be sweetened in the delivery by encouragement, and in the tune and phrase of counsel, rather than in harsher language of command.

Examples of the difference between command and counsel we may take from the forms of speech that express them in Holy Scripture. "Have no other gods but me;" "make to thyself no graven image;" "take not God's name in vain;" "sanctify the Sabbath;" "honour thy parents;" "kill not;" "steal not," &c., are commands; because the reason for which we are to obey them is drawn from the will of God our king, whom we are obliged to obey. But these words, "Sell all thou hast; give it to the poor; and follow me," are counsel; because the reason for which we are to do so, is drawn from our own benefit; which is this, that we shall have "treasure in heaven." These words, "Go into the village over against you, and you shall find an ass tied, and her colt; loose her, and bring her to me," are a command; for the reason of their fact is drawn from the will of their Master: but these words, "Repent and be baptized in the name of Jesus," are counsel; because the reason why we should so do, tendeth not to any benefit of God Almighty, who shall still be king in what manner soever we rebel; but of ourselves, who have no other means of avoiding the punishment hanging over us for our sins.

As the difference of counsel from command hath been now deduced from the nature of counsel, consisting in a deducing of the benefit, or hurt that may arise to him that is to be counselled, by the necessary or probable consequences of the action he propoundeth: so may also the differences between "apt" and "inept" counsellors be derived from the same. For experience, being but memory of the consequences of like actions formerly observed, and counsel but the speech whereby that experience is made known to another; the virtues and defects of counsel are the same with the virtues and defects intellectual: and to the person of a commonwealth, his counsellors serve him in the place of memory and mental discourse. But with this resemblance of the commonwealth to a natural man, there is one dissimilitude joined of great importance; which is, that a natural man receiveth his experience from the natural objects of sense, which work upon him without passion or interest of their own; whereas they that give counsel to the representative person of a commonwealth may have, and have often their particular ends and passions, that render their counsels always suspected, and many times unfaithful. And therefore we may set down for the first condition of a good counsellor, "that his ends and interests be not inconsistent with the ends and interests of him he counselleth."

Secondly, because the office of a counsellor, when an action comes into deliberation, is to make manifest the consequences of it, in such manner as he that is counselled may be truly and evidently informed; he ought to propound his advice in such form of speech as may make the truth most evidently appear; that is to say, with as firm ratiocination, as significant and proper language, and as briefly as the evidence will permit. And therefore "rash and unevident inferences," such as are fetched only from examples or authority of books, and are not arguments of what is good or evil, but witnesses of fact or of opinion; "obscure, confused, and ambiguous expressions, also all metaphorical speeches, tending to the stirring up of passions," (because such reasoning and such expressions are useful only to deceive, or to lead him we counsel towards other ends than his own,) "are repugnant to the office of a counsellor."

Thirdly, because the ability of counselling proceedeth from experience and long study;

and no man is presumed to have experience in all those things that to the administration of a great commonwealth are necessary to be known, "no man is presumed to be a good counsellor, but in such business as he hath not only been much versed in, but hath also much meditated on, and considered." For seeing the business of a commonwealth is this, to preserve the people in peace at home, and defend them against foreign invasion, we shall find it requires great knowledge of the disposition of mankind, of the rights of government, and of the nature of equity, law, justice, and honour, not to be attained without study; and of the strength, commodities, places, both of their own country, and their neighbours; as also of the inclinations and designs of all nations that may any way annoy them. And this is not attained to without much experience. Of which things, not only the whole sum, but every one of the particulars requires the age and observation of a man in years, and of more than ordinary study. The wit required for counsel, as I have said before (chap. viii.), is judgment. And the differences of men in that point come from different education, of some to one kind of study or business, and of others to another. When for the doing of anything there be infallible rules, as in engines and edifices, the rules of geometry, all the experience of the world cannot equal his counsel that has learnt or found out the rule. And when there is no such rule, he that hath most experience in that particular kind of business has therein the best judgment, and is the best counsellor.

Fourthly, to be able to give counsel to a commonwealth, in a business that hath reference to another commonwealth, "it is necessary to be acquainted with the intelligences, and letters" that come from thence, "and with all the records of treaties, and other transactions of state" between them; which none can do, but such as the representative shall think fit. By which we may see, that they who are not called to counsel, can have no good counsel in such cases to obtrude.

Fifthly, supposing the number of counsellors equal, a man is better counselled by hearing them apart than in an assembly; and that for many causes. First, in hearing them apart you have the advice of every man; but in an assembly many of them deliver their advice with "aye," or "no," or with their hands or feet, not moved by their own sense, but by the eloquence of another, or for fear of displeasing some that have spoken, or the whole assembly, by contradiction; or for fear of appearing duller in apprehension than those that have applauded the contrary opinion. Secondly, in an assembly of many, there cannot choose but be some whose interests are contrary to that of the public; and these their interests make passionate, and passion eloquent, and eloquence draws others into the same advice. For the passions of men, which asunder are moderate, as the heat of one brand; in an assembly are like many brands, that inflame one another, especially when they blow one another with orations, to the setting of the commonwealth on fire, under pretence of counselling it, Thirdly, in hearing every man apart, one may examine, when there is need, the truth or probability of his reasons, and of the grounds of the advice he gives, by frequent interruptions and objections; which cannot be done in an assembly, where in every difficult question a man is rather astonied and dazzled with the variety of discourse upon it, than informed of the course he ought to take. Besides, there cannot be an assembly of many called together for advice, wherein there be not some that have the ambition to be thought eloquent, and also learned in the politics; and give not their advice with care of the business propounded, but of the applause of their motley orations, made of the divers coloured threads or shreds of authors; which is an impertinence at least, that takes away the time of serious consultation, and in the secret way of counselling apart, is easily avoided. Fourthly, in deliberations that ought to be kept secret, whereof there be many occasions in public business, the counsels of many, and especially in assemblies, are dangerous; and therefore great assemblies are necessitated to commit such affairs to lesser numbers, and of such persons as are most versed, and in whose fidelity they have most confidence.

To conclude, who is there that so far approves the taking of counsel from a great assembly of counsellors, that wisheth for, or would accept of their pains, when there is a question of marrying his children, disposing of his lands, governing his household, or managing his private estate, especially if there be amongst them such as wish not his prosperity? A man that doth his business by the help of many and prudent counsellors, with every one consulting apart in his proper element, does it best, as he that useth able seconds at tennis-play, placed in their proper stations. He does next best that useth his own judgment only, as he that has no second at all. But he that is carried up and down to his business in a framed counsel, which cannot move but by the plurality of consenting opinions, the execution whereof is commonly, out of envy or interest, retarded by the part dissenting, does it worst of all, and like one that is carried to the ball, though by good players, yet in a wheelbarrow or other frame, heavy of itself, and retarded also by the inconcurrent judgments and endeavours

of them that drive it; and so much the more, as they be more that set their hands to it; and most of all, when there is one, or more amongst them, that desire to have him lose. And though it be true that many eyes see more than one; yet it is not to be understood of many counsellors, but then only when the final resolution is in one man. Otherwise, because many eyes see the same thing in divers lines, and are apt to look asquint towards their private benefit; they that desire not to miss their mark, though they look about with two eyes, yet they never aim but with one; and therefore no great popular commonwealth was ever kept up but either by a foreign enemy that united them, or by the reputation of some eminent man amongst them, or by the secret counsel of a few, or by the mutual fear of equal factions, and not by the open consultations of the assembly. And as for very little commonwealths, be they popular or monarchical, there is no human wisdom can uphold them longer than the jealousy lasteth of their potent neighbours.

## Chapter XXVI

### Of Civil Laws

By "civil laws," I understand the laws that men are therefore bound to observe, because they are members, not of this or that commonwealth in particular, but of a commonwealth. For the knowledge of particular laws belongeth to them that profess the study of the laws of their several countries; but the knowledge of civil law in general to any man. The ancient law of Rome was called their "civil law," from the word *civitas*, which signifies a commonwealth: and those countries which having been under the Roman empire, and governed by that law, retain still such part thereof as they think fit, call that part the civil law, to distinguish it from the rest of their own civil laws. But that is not it I intend to speak of here; my design being not to show what is law here and there; but what is law; as Plato, Aristotle, Cicero, and divers others have done, without taking upon them the profession of the study of the law.

And first it is manifest, that the law in general is not counsel, but command; nor a command of any man to any man; but only of him, whose command is addressed to one formerly obliged to obey him. And as for civil law, it addeth only the name of the person commanding, which is *persona civitatis*, the person of the commonwealth.

Which considered, I define civil law in this manner. "'Civil law,' is to every subject, those rules, which the commonwealth hath commanded him, by word, writing, or other sufficient sign of the will, to make use of, for the distinction of right and wrong; that is to say, of what is contrary and what is not contrary to the rule."

In which definition, there is nothing that is not at first sight evident. For every man seeth, that some laws are addressed to all the subjects in general; some to particular provinces; some to particular vocations; and some to particular men; and are therefore laws to every of those to whom the command is directed, and to none else. As also, that laws are the rules of just and unjust; nothing being reputed unjust that is not contrary to some law. Likewise, that none can make laws but the commonwealth; because our subjection is to the commonwealth only: and that commands are to be signified by sufficient signs; because a man

knows not otherwise how to obey them. And therefore, whatsoever can from this definition by necessary consequence be deduced, ought to be acknowledged for truth. Now I deduce from it this that followeth.

1. The legislator in all commonwealths, is only the sovereign, be he one man, as in a monarchy, or one assembly of men, as in a democracy, or aristocracy. For the legislator is he that maketh the law. And the commonwealth only prescribes and commandeth the observation of those rules, which we call law: therefore the commonwealth is the legislator. But the commonwealth is no person, nor has capacity to do anything, but by the representative, that is, the sovereign; and therefore the sovereign is the sole legislator. For the same reason, none can abrogate a law made, but the sovereign; because a law is not abrogated, but by another law, that forbiddeth it to be put in execution.

2. The sovereign of a commonwealth, be it an assembly or one man, is not subject to the civil laws. For having power to make and repeal laws, he may when he pleaseth free himself from that subjection, by repealing those laws that trouble him and making of new; and consequently he was free before. For he is free, that can be free when he will: nor is it possible for any person to be bound to himself; because he that can bind, can release; and therefore he that is bound to himself only, is not bound.

3. When long use obtaineth the authority of a law, it is not the length of time that maketh the authority, but the will of the sovereign signified by his silence, for silence is sometimes an argument of consent; and it is no longer law, than the sovereign shall be silent therein. And therefore if the sovereign

shall have a question of right grounded, not upon his present will, but upon the laws formerly made; the length of time shall bring no prejudice to his right; but the question shall be judged by equity. For many unjust actions and unjust sentences go uncontrolled a longer time than any man can remember. And our lawyers account no customs law but such as are reasonable, and that evil customs are to be abolished. But the judgment of what is reasonable and of what is to be abolished belongeth to him that maketh the law, which is the sovereign assembly or monarch.

4. The law of Nature and the civil law, contain each other, and are of equal extent. For the laws of Nature, which consist in equity, justice, gratitude, and other moral virtues on these depending, in the condition of mere nature, as I have said before in the end of the fifteenth chapter, are not properly laws, but qualities that dispose men to peace and obedience. When a commonwealth is once settled, then are they actually laws, and not before; as being then the commands of the commonwealth; and therefore also civil laws: for it is the sovereign power that obliges men to obey them. For in the differences of private men, to declare what is equity, what is justice, and what is moral virtue, and to make them binding, there is need of the ordinances of sovereign power, and punishments to be ordained for such as shall break them; which ordinances are therefore part of the civil law. The law of Nature therefore is a part of the civil law in all commonwealths of the world. Reciprocally also, the civil law is a part of the dictates of Nature. For justice, that is to say, performance of covenant, and giving to every man his own, is a dictate of the law of Nature. But every subject in a commonwealth hath covenanted to obey the civil law; either one with another, as when they assemble to make a common representative, or with the representative itself one by one, when subdued by the sword they promise obedience, that they may receive life; and therefore obedience to the civil law is part also of the law of Nature. Civil and natural law are not different kinds, but different parts of law; whereof one part being written, is called civil, the other unwritten, natural. But the right of nature, that is, the natural liberty of man, may by the civil law be abridged and restrained: nay, the end of making laws is no other but such restraint; without the which there cannot possibly be any peace. And law was brought into the world for nothing else but to limit the natural liberty of particular men, in such manner as they might not hurt, but assist one another, and join together against a common enemy.

5. If the sovereign of one commonwealth subdue a people that have lived under other written laws, and afterwards govern them by the same laws by which they were governed before; yet those laws are the civil laws of the victor, and not of the vanquished commonwealth. For the legislator is he, not by whose authority the laws were first made, but by whose authority they now continue to be laws. And therefore where there be divers provinces within the dominion of a commonwealth, and in those provinces diversity of laws, which commonly are called the customs of each several province, we are not to understand that such customs have their force only from length of time; but that they were anciently laws written, or

otherwise made known, for the constitutions and statutes of their sovereigns; and are now laws, not by virtue of the prescription of time, but by the constitutions of their present sovereigns. But if an unwritten law, in all the provinces of a dominion, shall be generally observed, and no iniquity appear in the use thereof; that law can be no other but a law of Nature, equally obliging all mankind.

6. Seeing then all laws, written and unwritten, have their authority and force from the will of the commonwealth, that is to say, from the will of the representative, which in a monarchy is the monarch, and in other commonwealths the sovereign assembly; a man may wonder from whence proceed such opinions as are found in the books of lawyers of eminence in several commonwealths, directly or by consequence making the legislative power depend on private men, or subordinate judges. As for example, "that the common law hath no controller but the parliament;" which is true only where a parliament has the sovereign power, and cannot be assembled nor dissolved but by their own discretion. For if there be a right in any else to dissolve them, there is a right also to control them, and consequently to control their controllings. And if there be no such right, then the controller of laws is not *parliamentum*, but *rex in parliamento.* And where a parliament is sovereign, if it should assemble never so many or so wise men from the countries subject to them, for whatsoever cause; yet there is no man will believe that such an assembly hath thereby acquired to themselves a legislative power. "Item" that the two arms of a commonwealth, are "force and justice; the first whereof is in the king, the other

deposited in the hands of the parliament." As if a commonwealth could consist, where the force were in any hand, which justice had not the authority to command and govern.

7. That law can never be against reason our lawyers are agreed; and that not the letter that is every construction of it, but that which is according to the intention of the legislator, is the law. And it is true, but the doubt is of whose reason it is that shall be received for law. It is not meant of any private reason, for then there would be as much contradiction in the laws as there is in the schools; nor yet, as Sir Edward Coke makes it, an "artificial perfection of reason, gotten by long study, observation, and experience," as his was. For it is possible long study may increase and confirm erroneous sentences, and where men build on false grounds, the more they build the greater is the ruin: and of those that study and observe with equal time and diligence, the reason and resolutions are, and must remain, discordant, and therefore it is not that *juris prudentia* or wisdom of subordinate judges; but the reason of this our artificial man the commonwealth, and his command that maketh law: and the commonwealth being in their representative but one person, there cannot easily arise any contradiction in the laws; and when there doth, the same reason is able, by interpretation or alteration, to take it away. In all courts of justice, the sovereign, which is the person of the commonwealth, is he that judgeth; the subordinate judge ought to have regard to the reason which moved his sovereign to make such law that his sentence may be according thereunto, which then is his

sovereign's sentence, otherwise it is his own, and an unjust one.

8. From this that the law is a command, and a command consisteth in declaration or manifestation of the will of him that commandeth, by voice, writing, or some other sufficient argument of the same, we may understand that the command of the commonwealth is law only to those that have means to take notice of it. Over natural fools, children, or madmen, there is no law, no more than over brute beasts, nor are they capable of the title of just or unjust; because they had never power to make any covenant, or to understand the consequences thereof, and consequently never took upon them to authorize the actions of any sovereign, as they must do that make to themselves a commonwealth. And as those from whom nature or accident hath taken away the notice of all laws in general; so also every man from whom any accident, not proceeding from his own default, hath taken away the means to take notice of any particular law, is excused if he observe it not, and, to speak properly, that law is no law to him. It is therefore necessary to consider in this place what arguments and signs be sufficient for the knowledge of what is the law, that is to say, what is the will of the sovereign as well in monarchies as in other forms of government.

And first, if it be a law that obliges all the subjects without exception, and is not written, nor otherwise published in such places as they may take notice thereof, it is a law of Nature. For whatsoever men are to take knowledge of for law, not upon other men's words, but every one from his own reason, must be such as is agreeable to the reason of all men; which

no law can be, but the law of Nature. The laws of Nature therefore need not any publishing, nor proclamation; as being contained in this one sentence, approved by all the world, "Do not that to another, which thou thinkest unreasonable to be done by another to thyself."

Secondly, if it be a law that obliges only some condition of men, or one particular man, and be not written, nor published by word, then also it is a law of Nature; and known by the same arguments and signs that distinguish those in such a condition from other subjects. For whatsoever law is not written, or some way published by him that makes it law, can be known no way, but by the reason of him that is to obey it; and is therefore also a law not only civil, but natural. For example, if the sovereign employ a public minister, without written instructions what to do; he is obliged to take for instructions the dictates of reason; as if he make a judge, the judge is to take notice that his sentence ought to be according to the reason of his sovereign, which being always understood to be equity, he is bound to it by the law of Nature: or if an ambassador, he is, in all things not contained in his written instructions, to take for instruction that which reason dictates to be most conducing to his sovereign's interest; and so of all other ministers of the sovereignty, public and private. All which instructions of natural reason may be comprehended under one name of "fidelity;" which is a branch of natural justice.

The law of Nature excepted, it belongeth to the essence of all other laws, to be made known, to every man that shall be obliged to obey them, either by word, or writing, or some other act, known to proceed from the sovereign authority. For the will of another cannot be understood, but by his own word, or act, or by conjecture taken from his scope and purpose; which in the person of the commonwealth is to be supposed always consonant to equity and reason. And in ancient time, before letters were in common use, the laws were many times put into verse; that the rude people taking pleasure in singing or reciting them, might the more easily retain them in memory. And for the same reason Solomon (Prov. vii. 3) adviseth a man to bind the ten commandments upon his ten fingers. And for the law which Moses gave to the people of Israel at the renewing of the covenant (Deut. xi. 19), he biddeth them to teach it their children, by discoursing of it both at home and upon the way; at going to bed, and at rising from bed; and to write it upon the posts and doors of their houses; and (Deut. xxxi. 12) to assemble the people, man, woman, and child, to hear it read.

Nor is it enough the law be written and published; but also that there be manifest signs that it proceedeth from the will of the sovereign. For private men, when they have, or think they have, force enough to secure their unjust designs, and convoy them safely to their ambitious ends, may publish for laws what they please, without or against the legislative authority. There is therefore requisite, not only a declaration of the law, but also sufficient signs of the author and authority. The author or legislator is supposed in every commonwealth to be evident, because he is the sovereign, who having been constituted by the consent of every one, is supposed by every one to be sufficiently known. And though the ignorance and security of men be such, for the most part, as that when the memory of the first constitution of their commonwealth is worn out, they do not consider by whose power they used to be defended against their enemies, and to have their industry protected, and to be righted when injury is done them; yet because no man that considers, can make

question of it, no excuse can be derived from the ignorance of where the sovereignty is placed. And it is a dictate of natural reason, and consequently an evident law of Nature, that no man ought to weaken that power, the protection whereof he hath himself demanded, or wittingly received against others. Therefore of who is sovereign, no man, but by his own fault (whatsoever evil men suggest), can make any doubt. The difficulty consisteth in the evidence of the authority derived from him; the removing whereof dependeth on the knowledge of the public registers, public counsels, public ministers, and public seals; by which all laws are sufficiently verified; verified, I say, not authorized: for the verification is but the testimony and record, not the authority of the law; which consisteth in the command of the sovereign only.

If therefore a man have a question of injury, depending on the law of Nature; that is to say, on common equity; the sentence of the judge, that by commission hath authority to take cognizance of such causes, is a sufficient verification of the law of Nature in that individual case. For though the advice of one that professeth the study of the law be useful for the avoiding of contention; yet it is but advice: it is the judge must tell men what is law, upon the hearing of the controversy.

But when the question is of injury, or crime, upon a written law; every man by recourse to the registers, by himself or others, may, if he will, be sufficiently informed, before he do such injury, or commit the crime, whether it be an injury or not: nay, he ought to do so: for when a man doubts whether the act he goeth about be just or unjust; and may inform himself, if he will; the doing is unlawful. In like manner, he that supposeth himself injured, in a case determined by the written law, which he may, by himself or others, see and consider;

if he complain before he consults with the law, he does unjustly, and bewrayeth a disposition rather to vex other men than to demand his own right.

If the question be of obedience to a public officer; to have seen his commission, with the public seal, and heard it read; or to have had the means to be informed of it, if a man would, is a sufficient verification of his authority. For every man is obliged to do his best endeavour to inform himself of all written laws, that may concern his own future actions.

The legislator known; and the laws, either by writing or by the light of Nature, sufficiently published; there wanteth yet another very material circumstance to make them obligatory. For it is not the letter, but the intendment or meaning, that is to say, the authentic interpretation of the law (which is the sense of the legislator), in which the nature of the law consisteth; and therefore the interpretation of all laws dependeth on the authority sovereign; and the interpreters can be none but those which the sovereign, to whom only the subject oweth obedience, shall appoint. For else, by the craft of an interpreter, the law may be made to bear a sense contrary to that of the sovereign, by which means the interpreter becomes the legislator.

All laws, written and unwritten, have need of interpretation. The unwritten law of Nature, though it be easy to such as, without partiality and passion, make use of their natural reason, and therefore leaves the violators thereof without excuse; yet considering there be very few, perhaps none, that in some cases are not blinded by self-love or some other passion, it is now become of all laws the most obscure, and has consequently the greatest need of able interpreters.) The written laws, if they be short, are easily misinterpreted, from the divers significations of a word or two: if long, they be more obscure by the divers significations of many words: insomuch as no written law, delivered in few or many words, can be well understood, without a perfect understanding of the final causes for which the law was made, the knowledge of which final causes is in the legislator. To him therefore there cannot be any knot in the law insoluble; either by finding out the ends, to undo it by; or else by making what ends he will, as Alexander did with his sword in the Gordian knot, by the legislative power, which no other interpreter can do.

The interpretation of the laws of Nature in a commonwealth dependeth not on the books of moral philosophy. The authority of writers, without the authority of the commonwealth, maketh not their opinions law, be they never so true. That which I have written in this treatise concerning the moral virtues, and of their necessity for the procuring and maintaining peace, though it be evident truth, is not therefore presently law; but because in all commonwealths in the world it is part of the civil law. For though it be naturally reasonable, yet it is by the sovereign power that it is law: otherwise, it were a great error to call the laws of Nature unwritten law; whereof we see so many volumes published, and in them so many contradictions of one another and of themselves.

The interpretation of the law of Nature, is the sentence of the judge constituted by the sovereign authority, to hear and determine such controversies as depend thereon; and consisteth in the application of the law to the present case. For in the act of judicature, the judge doth no more but consider whether the demand of the party be consonant to natural reason and equity; and the sentence he giveth is therefore the interpretation of the law of Nature; which interpretation is authentic; not because it is his private sentence; but because he giveth it by authority of the sovereign, whereby it becomes the sovereign's sentence, which is law for that time, to the parties pleading.

But because there is no judge subordinate, nor sovereign, but may err in a judgment of equity; if afterward in another like case he find it more consonant to equity to give a contrary sentence, he is obliged to do it. No man's error becomes his own law; nor obliges him to persist in it. Neither, for the same reason, becomes it a law to other judges, though sworn to follow it. For though a wrong sentence given by authority of the sovereign, if he know and allow it, in such laws as are mutable, be a constitution of a new law, in cases in which every little circumstance is the same; yet in laws immutable, such as are the laws of Nature, they are no laws to the same or other judges, in the like cases for ever after. Princes succeed one another; and one judge passeth, another cometh; nay, heaven and earth shall pass; but not one tittle of the law of Nature shall pass; for it is the eternal law of God. Therefore all the sentences of precedent judges that have ever been, cannot altogether make a law contrary to natural equity: nor any examples of former judges, can warrant an unreasonable sentence, or discharge the present judge of the trouble of studying what is equity, in the case he is to judge, from the principles of his own natural reason. For example sake, it is against the law of Nature "to punish the innocent;" and innocent is he that acquitteth himself judicially, and is acknowledged for innocent by the judge. Put the case now, that a man is accused of a capital crime, and seeing the power and malice of some enemy, and the frequent corruption and partiality of judges, runneth away for fear of the event, and afterwards is taken, and brought to a legal trial, and maketh it sufficiently appear he was not guilty of the crime, and being thereof acquitted, is nevertheless condemned to lose his goods; this is a manifest condemnation of the innocent. I say therefore that there is no place in the world, where this can be an interpretation of a law of Nature, or be made a law by the sentences of precedent judges, that had done the same. For he that judged it first, judged unjustly; and no injustice can be a pattern of judgment to succeeding judges. A written law may forbid innocent men to fly, and they may be punished for flying: but that flying for fear of injury should be taken for presumption of guilt, after a man is already absolved of the crime judicially, is contrary to the nature of a presumption, which hath no place after judgment given. Yet this is set down by a great lawyer for the common law of England. "If a man," saith he, "that is innocent, be accused of felony, and for fear flyeth for the same; albeit he judicially acquitteth himself of the felony; yet if it be found that he fled for the felony, he shall notwithstanding, his innocency, forfeit all his goods, chattels, debts, and duties. For as to the forfeiture of them, the law will admit no proof against the presumption in law, grounded upon his flight." Here you see "an innocent man judicially acquitted, notwithstanding his innocency," when no written law forbad him to fly, after his acquittal, "upon a presumption in law," condemned to lose all the goods he hath. If the law ground upon his flight a presumption of the fact, which was capital, the sentence ought to have been capital: if the presumption were not of the fact, for what then ought he to lose his goods ? This therefore is no law of England; nor is the condemnation grounded upon a presumption of law, but upon the presumption of the judges. It is also against law, to say that proof shall be admitted against a presumption of law. For all judges, sovereign and subordinate, if they refuse to hear proof, refuse to do justice: for though the sentence be just, yet the judges that condemn without hearing the proofs offered, are unjust judges; and their presumption is but prejudice; which no man ought to bring with him to the seat of justice, whatsoever precedent judgments or examples he shall pretend to follow. There be other things of this nature, wherein men's judgments have been perverted, by trusting to precedents: but this is enough to show, that though the sentence of the judge be a law to the party pleading, yet it is no law to any judge that shall succeed him in that office.

In like manner, when question is of the meaning of written laws, he is not the interpreter of them, that writeth a commentary upon them. For commentaries are commonly more subject to cavil than the text; and therefore need other commentaries; and so there will be no end of such interpretation. And therefore unless there be an interpreter authorized by the sovereign, from which the subordinate judges are not to recede, the interpreter can be no other than the ordinary judges, in the same manner as they are in cases of the unwritten law; and their sentences are to be taken by them that plead for laws in that particular case; but not to bind other judges in like cases to give like judgments. For a judge may err in the interpretation even of written laws; but no error of a subordinate judge can change the law, which is the general sentence of the sovereign.

In written laws, men use to make a difference between the letter and the sentence of the law: and when by the letter is meant whatsoever can be gathered by the bare words, it is well distinguished. For the significations of almost all words are either in themselves, or in the metaphorical use of them, ambiguous; and may be drawn in argument, to make many senses; but there is only one sense of the law. But if by the letter be meant the literal sense, then the letter and the sentence or intention of the law, is all one. For the literal sense is that which the legislator intended should by the letter of the law be signified. Now the intention of the legislator is always supposed to be equity: for it were a great contumely for a judge to think otherwise of the sovereign. He ought therefore, if the word of the law do not fully authorize a reasonable sentence, to supply it with the law of Nature; or if the case be difficult, to respite judgment till he have received more ample authority. For example, a written law ordaineth that he which is thrust out of his house by force shall be restored by force: it happens that a man by negligence leaves his house empty, and returning is kept out by force, in which case there is no special law ordained. It is evident that this case is contained in the same law: for else there is no remedy for him at all; which is to be supposed against the intention of the legislator. Again, the word of the law commandeth to judge according to the evidence: a man is accused falsely of a fact, which the judge himself saw done by another, and not by him that is accused. In this case neither shall the letter of the law be followed to the condemnation of the innocent, nor shall the judge give sentence against the evidence of the witnesses; because the letter of the law is to the contrary; but procure of the sovereign that another be made judge, and himself witness. So that the incommodity that follows the bare words of a written law may lead him to the intention of the law, whereby to interpret the same the better; though no incommodity can warrant a sentence against the law. For every judge of right and wrong is not judge of what is commodious or incommodious to the commonwealth.

The abilities required in a good interpreter of the law, that is to say, in a good judge, are not the same with those of an advocate; namely, the study of the laws. For a judge, as he ought to take notice of the fact from none but the witnesses; so also he ought to take notice of the law from nothing but the statutes and constitutions of the sovereign, alleged in the pleading, or declared to him by some that have authority from the sovereign power to declare them; and need not take care beforehand what he shall judge; for it shall be given him what he shall say concerning the fact, by witnesses; and what he shall say in point of law, from those that shall in their pleadings show it, and by authority interpret it upon the place. The Lords of parliament in England were judges, and most difficult causes have been heard and determined by them; yet few of them were much versed in the study of the laws, and fewer had made profession of them; and though they consulted with lawyers, that were appointed to be present there for that purpose, yet they alone had the authority of giving sentence. In like manner, in the ordinary trials of right, twelve men of the common people are the judges, and give sentence, not only of the fact, but of the right; and pronounce simply for the complainant, or for the defendant; that is to say, are judges, not only of the fact, but also of the right: and in a question of crime, not only determine whether done, or not done; but also whether it be "murder," "homicide," "felony, "assault," and the like, which are determinations of law: but because they are not supposed to know the law of themselves, there is one that hath authority to inform them of it, in the particular case they are to judge of. But yet if they judge not according to that he tells them, they are not subject thereby to any penalty; unless it be made appear that they did it against their consciences, or had been corrupted by reward.

The things that make a good judge or good interpreter of the laws are, first, "a right understanding" of that principal law of Nature called "equity," which depending not on the reading of other men's writings, but on the goodness of a man's own natural reason and meditation, is presumed to be in those most that have had most leisure, and had the most inclination to meditate thereon. Secondly, "contempt of unnecessary riches and preferments." Thirdly, "to be able in judgment to divest himself of all fear, anger, hatred, love, and compassion." Fourthly, and lastly, "patience to hear, diligent attention in hearing, and memory to retain, digest and apply what he hath heard."

The difference and division of the laws has been made in divers manners, according to the different methods of those men that have written of them. For it is a thing that dependeth not on nature, but on the scope of the writer, and is subservient to every man's proper method. In the Institutions of Justinian, we find seven sorts of civil laws.

1. The "edicts," "constitutions," and "epistles of the prince," that is, of the emperor, because the whole power of the people was in him. Like these are the proclamations of the kings of England.
2. "The decrees of the whole people of Rome," comprehending the senate, when they were put to the question by the "senate." These were laws at first by the virtue of the sovereign power residing in the people; and such of them as by the emperors were not abrogated, remained laws by the authority imperial. For all laws that bind are understood to be laws by his authority that has power to repeal them.

Somewhat like to these laws are the acts of parliament in England.

3. "The decrees of the common people," excluding the senate, when they were put to the question by the "tribune" of the people. For such of them as were not abrogated by the emperors remained laws by the authority imperial. Like to these were the orders of the House of Commons in England.

4. *Senatus consulta,* the "orders of the senate;" because when the people of Rome grew so numerous as it was inconvenient to assemble them; it was thought fit by the emperor that men should consult the senate, instead of the people; and these have some resemblance with the acts of council.

5. "The edicts of praetors," and in some cases of "aediles;" such as are the chief justices in the courts of England.

6. *Responsa prudentum,* which were the sentences and opinion of those lawyers to whom the emperor gave authority to interpret the law, and to give answer to such as in matter of law demanded their advice; which answers, the judges in giving judgment were obliged by the constitutions of the emperor to observe, and should be like the reports of cases judged, if other judges be by the law of England bound to observe them. For the judges of the common law of England are not properly judges, but *juris consulti,* of whom the judges, who are either the Lords, or twelve men of the country, are in point of law to ask advice.

7. Also "unwritten customs," which in their own nature are an imitation of law, by the tacit consent of the emperor, in case they be not contrary to the law of Nature, are very laws.

Another division of laws is into "natural" and "positive." "Natural" are those which have been laws from all eternity; and are called not only "natural" but also "moral" laws; consisting in the moral virtues, as justice, equity, and all habits of the mind that conduce to peace and charity, of which I have already spoken in the fourteenth and fifteenth chapters.

"Positive" are those which have not been from eternity; but have been made laws by the will of those that have had the sovereign power over others; and are either written or made known to men by some other argument of the will of their legislator.

Again, of positive laws some are "human," some "divine;" and of human positive laws some are "distributive," some "penal." "Distributive" are those that determine the rights of the subjects, declaring to every man what it is by which he acquireth and holdeth a propriety in lands or goods, and a right or liberty of action: and these speak to all the subjects. "Penal" are those which declare what penalty shall be inflicted on those that violate the law; and speak to the ministers and officers ordained for execution. For though every one ought to be informed of the punishments ordained beforehand for their transgression, nevertheless the command is not addressed to the delinquent, who cannot be supposed will faithfully punish himself, but to public ministers appointed to see the penalty executed. And these penal laws are for the most part written together with the laws distributive; and are sometimes called judgments. For all laws are general judgments, or sentences of the legislator; as also every particular judgment is a law to him whose case is judged.

"Divine positive laws" (for natural laws being eternal and universal are all divine) are those which being the commandments of God, not from all eternity, nor universally addressed to all men, but only to a certain people, or to certain persons, are declared for such by those whom God hath authorized to declare them. But this authority of man to declare what be these positive laws of God, how can it be known? God may command a man by a supernatural way to deliver laws to other men. But because it is of the essence of law, that he who is to be obliged be assured of the authority of him that declareth it, which we cannot naturally take notice to be from God, "how can a man without supernatural revelation be assured of the revelation received by the declarer?" and "how can he be bound to obey them?" For the first question, how a man can be assured of the revelation of another, without a revelation particularly to himself, it is evidently impossible. For though a man may be induced to believe such revelation from the miracles they see him do, or from seeing the extraordinary sanctity of his life, or from seeing the extraordinary wisdom or extraordinary felicity of his actions, all which are marks of God's extraordinary favour; yet they are not assured evidences of special revelation. Miracles are marvellous works; but that which is marvellous to one, may not be so to another. Sanctity may be feigned; and the visible felicities of this world are most often the work of God by natural and ordinary causes. And therefore no man can infallibly know by natural reason that another has had a supernatural revelation of God's will, but only a belief; every one, as the signs thereof shall appear greater or lesser, a firmer or a weaker belief.

But for the second, how can he be bound to obey them; it is not so hard. For if the law declared be not against the law of Nature, which is undoubtedly God's law, and he undertake to obey it, he is bound by his own act; bound I say to obey it, but not bound to believe it:

for men's belief and interior cogitations are not subject to the commands, but only to the operation of God, ordinary or extraordinary. Faith of supernatural law is not a fulfilling, but only an assenting to the same; and not a duty that we exhibit to God, but a gift which God freely giveth to whom He pleaseth; as also unbelief is not a breach of any of His laws; but a rejection of them all, except the laws natural. But this that I say, will be made yet clearer by the examples and testimonies concerning this point in Holy Scripture. The covenant God made with Abraham, in a supernatural manner, was thus (Gen. xvii. 10): "This is the covenant which thou shalt observe between me and thee, and thy seed after thee." Abraham's seed had not this revelation, nor were yet in being; yet they are a party to the covenant, and bound to obey what Abraham should declare to them for God's law; which they could not be, but in virtue of the obedience they owed to their parents; who, if they be subject to no other earthly power, as here in the case of Abraham, have sovereign power over their children and servants. Again, where God saith to Abraham, "In thee shall all nations of the earth be blessed; for I know thou wilt command thy children, and thy house after thee, to keep the way of the Lord, and to observe righteousness and judgment," it is manifest, the obedience of his family, who had no revelation, depended on their former obligation to obey their sovereign. At Mount Sinai Moses only went up to God; the people were forbidden to approach on pain of death; yet they were bound to obey all that Moses declared to them for God's law. Upon what ground, but on this submission of their own, "Speak thou to us and we will hear thee; but let not God speak to us, lest we die?" By which two places it sufficiently appeareth, that in a commonwealth, a subject that has no certain and assured revelation particularly to himself concerning the will of God, is to obey for such the command of the commonwealth: for if men were at liberty to take for God's commandments their own dreams and fancies, or the dreams and fancies of private men; scarce two men would agree upon what is God's commandment; and yet in respect of them, every man would despise the commands ments of the commonwealth. I conclude therefore, that in all things not contrary to the moral law, that is to say, to the law of Nature, all subjects are bound to obey that for divine law, which is declared to be so by the laws of the commonwealth. Which also is evident to any man's reason; for whatsoever is not against the law of Nature, may be made law in the name of them that have the sovereign power; and there is no reason men should be the less obliged by it, when it is propounded in the name of God, Besides, there is no place in the world where men are permitted to pretend other commandments of God than are declared for such by the commonwealth. Christian states punish those that revolt from the Christian religion, and all other states those that set up any religion by them forbidden. For in whatsoever is not regulated by the commonwealth, it is equity, which is the law of Nature, and therefore an eternal law of God, that every man equally enjoy his liberty.

There is also another distinction of laws into "fundamental" and "not fundamental;" but I could never see in any author what a fundamental law signifieth. Nevertheless one may very reasonably distinguish laws in that manner.

For a fundamental law in every commonwealth is that, which being taken away, the commonwealth faileth and is utterly dissolved; as a building whose foundation is destroyed. And therefore a fundamental law is that, by which subjects are bound to uphold whatsoever power is given to the sovereign, whether a monarch or a sovereign assembly, without which the commonwealth cannot stand; such as is the power of war and peace, of judicature, of election of officers, and of doing whatsoever he shall think necessary for the public good. Not fundamental is that, the abrogating whereof draweth not with it the dissolution of the commonwealth; such as are the laws concerning controversies between subject and subject. Thus much of the division of laws.

I find the words *lex civilis* and *jus civile*, that is to say "law" and "right civil," promiscuously used for the same thing, even in the most learned authors; which nevertheless ought not to be so. For "right" is "liberty," namely that liberty which the civil law leaves us: but "civil law" is an "obligation," and takes from us the liberty which the law of Nature gave us. Nature gave a right to every man to secure himself by his own strength, and to invade a suspected neighbour, by way of prevention: but the civil law takes away that liberty, in all cases where the protection of the law may be safely stayed for. Insomuch as *lex* and *jus* are as different as "obligation" and "liberty."

Likewise "laws" and "charters" are taken promiscuously for the same thing. Yet charters are donations of the sovereign; and not laws, but exemptions from law. The phrase of a law is, *jubeo, injungo,* "I command" and "enjoin:" the phrase of a charter is, *dedi, concessi,* "I have given," "I have granted:" but what is given or granted to a man is not forced upon him by a law. A law may be made to bind all the subjects of a commonwealth: a liberty or charter is only to one man, or some one part of the people. For to say all the people of a commonwealth have liberty in any case whatsoever, is to say, that in such case there hath been no law made; or else having been made, is now abrogated.

# Chapter XXIX

## Of Those Things that Weaken, or Tend to the Dissolution of a Commonwealth

Though nothing can be immortal which mortals make, yet if men had the use of reason they pretend to, their commonwealths might be secured, at least from perishing by internal diseases. For by the nature of their institution, they are designed to live as long as mankind, or as the laws of Nature or as justice itself, which gives them life. Therefore when they come to be dissolved, not by external violence, but intestine disorder, the fault is not in men, as they are the "matter;" but as they are the "makers," and orderers of them. For men, as they become at last weary of irregular jostling and hewing one another, and desire with all their hearts to conform themselves into one firm and lasting edifice: so for want, both of the art of making fit laws, to square their actions by, and also of humility and patience, to suffer the rude and cumbersome points of their present greatness to be taken off, they cannot without the help of a very able architect, be compiled into any other than a crazy building, such as hardly lasting out their own time, must assuredly fall upon the heads of their posterity.

Amongst the "infirmities" therefore of a commonwealth, I will reckon in the first place, those that arise from an imperfect institution, and resemble the diseases of a natural body, which proceed from a defectuous procreation.

Of which this is one, "that a man to obtain a kingdom, is sometimes content with less power, than to the peace and defence of the commonwealth is necessarily required." From whence it cometh to pass, that when the exercise of the power laid by is for the public safety to be resumed, it hath the resemblance of an unjust act; which disposeth great numbers of men, when occasion is presented, to rebel; in the same manner as the bodies of children, gotten by diseased parents, are subject either to untimely death, or to purge the ill quality, derived from their vicious conception, by breaking out into boils and scabs. And when kings deny themselves some such necessary power, it is not always, though sometimes, out of ignorance of what is necessary to the office they undertake; but many times out of a hope to recover the same again at their pleasure. Wherein they reason not well; because such as will hold them to their promises, shall be maintained against them by foreign commonwealths; who in order to the good of their own subjects let slip few occasions to "weaken" the estate of their neighbours. So was Thomas Becket, Archbishop of Canterbury, supported against Henry the Second, by the Pope; the subjection of ecclesiastics to the commonwealth, having been dispensed with by William the Conqueror at his reception, when he took an oath not to infringe the liberty of the Church. And so were the barons, whose power was by William Rufus, to have their help in transferring the succession from his elder brother to himself, increased to a degree inconsistent with the sovereign power, maintained in their rebellion against king John, by the French.

Nor does this happen in monarchy only. For whereas the style of the ancient Roman commonwealth was "the senate and people of Rome," neither senate nor people pretended to the whole power; which first caused the seditions of Tiberius Gracchus, Caius Gracchus, Lucius Saturninus, and others; and afterwards the wars between the senate and the people, under Marius and Sylla; and again under Pompey and Caesar, to the extinction of their democracy, and the setting up of monarchy.

The people of Athens bound themselves but from one only action; which was, that no man on pain of death should propound the renewing of the war for the island of Salamis; and yet thereby, if Solon had not caused to be given out he was mad, and afterwards in gesture and habit of a madman, and in verse, propounded it to the people that flocked about him, they had had an enemy perpetually in readiness, even at the gates of their city; such damage or shifts are all commonwealths forced to, that have their power so little limited.

In the second place, I observe the "diseases" of a commonwealth, that proceed from the poison of seditious doctrines, whereof one is, "That every private man is judge of good and evil actions." This is true in the condition of mere nature, where there are no civil laws; and also under civil government, in such cases as are not determined by the law. But otherwise, it is manifest, that the measure of good and evil actions, is the civil law; and the judge the legislator, who is always representative of the commonwealth. From this false doctrine, men are disposed to debate with themselves and dispute the commands of the commonwealth; and afterwards to obey or disobey them, as in their private judgments they shall think fit; whereby the commonwealth is distracted and "weakened."

Another doctrine repugnant to civil society, is, that "whatsoever a man does against his conscience is sin;" and it dependeth on the presumption of making himself judge of good and evil. For a man's conscience and his judgment is the same thing, and as the judgment,so also the conscience may be erroneous. Therefore, though he that is subject to no civil law, sinneth in all he does against his conscience, because he has no other rule to follow but his own reason; yet it is not so with him that lives in a commonwealth; because the law is the public conscience, by which he hath already undertaken to be guided. Otherwise in such diversity, as there is of private consciences, which are but private opinions, the commonwealth must needs be distracted, and no man dare to obey the sovereign power, further than it shall seem good in his own eyes.

It hath been also commonly taught, "that faith and sanctity, are not to be attained by study and reason, but by supernatural inspiration or infusion." Which granted, I see not why any man should render a reason of his faith; or why every Christian should not be also a prophet; or why any man should take the law of his country rather than his own inspiration for the rule of his action. And thus we fall again in the fault of taking upon us to judge of good and evil; or to make judges of it, such private men as pretend to be supernaturally inspired, to the dissolution of all civil government. Faith comes by hearing, and hearing by those accidents which guide us into the presence of them that speak to us; which accidents are all contrived by God Almighty; and yet are not supernatural, but only, for the great number of them that concur to every effect, unobservable. Faith and sanctity are indeed not very frequent; but yet they are not miracles, but brought to pass by education, discipline, correction, and other natural ways, by which God worketh them in His elect, at such times as He thinketh fit. And these three opinions, pernicious to peace and government, have in this part of the world, proceeded chiefly from the tongues and pens of unlearned divines, who joining the words of Holy Scripture together, otherwise than is agreeable to reason, do what they can to make men think that sanctity and natural reason cannot stand together.

A fourth opinion, repugnant to the nature of a commonwealth, is this "that he that hath the sovereign power is subject to the civil laws." It is true, that sovereigns are all subject to the laws of Nature; because such laws be divine, and cannot by any man or commonwealth be abrogated. But to those laws which the sovereign himself, that is, which the commonwealth, maketh, he is not subject. For to be subject to laws is to be subject to the commonwealth, that is to the sovereign representative, that is to himself; which is not subjection, but freedom from the laws. Which error, because it setteth the laws above the sovereign, setteth also a judge above him and a power to punish him; which is to make a new sovereign; and again for the same reason a third, to punish the second; and so continually without end, to the confusion and dissolution of the commonwealth.

A fifth doctrine that tendeth to the dissolution of a commonwealth is, "that every private man has an absolute propriety in his goods; such as excludeth the right of the sovereign." Every man has indeed a propriety that excludes the right of every other subject: and he has it only from the sovereign power; without the protection whereof every other man should have equal right to the same. But if the right of the sovereign also be excluded, he cannot perform the office they have put him into; which is, to defend them both from foreign enemies, and from the injuries of one another; and consequently there is no longer a commonwealth.

And if the propriety of subjects exclude not the right of the sovereign representative to their goods; much less to their offices of judicature or execution, in which they represent the sovereign himself.

There is a sixth doctrine plainly and directly against the essence of a commonwealth; and it is this, "that the sovereign power may be divided." For what is it to divide the power of a commonwealth, but to dissolve it; for powers divided mutually destroy each other. And for these doctrines men are chiefly beholding to some of those that making profession of the laws, endeavour to make them depend upon their own learning, and not upon the legislative power.

And as false doctrine, so also oftentimes the example of different government in a neighbouring nation, disposeth men to alteration of the form already settled. So the people of the Jews were stirred up to reject God, and to call upon the prophet Samuel for a king after the manner of the nations: so also the lesser cities of Greece were continually disturbed with seditions of the aristocratical and democratical factions; one part of almost every commonwealth desiring to imitate the Lacedemonians; the other the Athenians. And I doubt not but many men have been contented to see the late troubles in England out of an imitation of the Low Countries; supposing there needed no more to grow rich than to change, as they had done, the form of their government. For the constitution of man's nature is of itself subject to desire novelty. When therefore they are provoked to the same by the neighbourhood also of those that have been enriched by it, it is almost impossible for them not to be content with those that solicit them to change; and love the first beginnings, though they be grieved with the continuance of disorder; like hot bloods, that having gotten the itch, tear themselves with their own nails, till they can endure the smart no longer.

And as to rebellion in particular against monarchy; one of the most frequent causes of it is the reading of the books of policy and histories of the ancient Greeks and Romans; from which young men, and all others that are unprovided of the antidote of solid reason, receiving a strong and delightful impression of the great exploits of war, achieved by the conductors of their armies, receive withal a pleasing idea of all they have done besides; and imagine their great prosperity, not to have proceeded from the emulation of particular men, but from the virtue of their popular form of government: not considering the frequent seditions, and civil wars, produced by the imperfection of their policy. From the reading, I say, of such books, men have undertaken to kill their kings, because the Greek and Latin writers, in their books and discourses of policy, make it lawful and laudable for any man so to do; provided, before he do it, he call him tyrant. For they say not "regicide," that is, killing a king, but "tyrannicide," that is, killing of a tyrant is lawful. From the same books, they that live under a monarch conceive an opinion, that the subjects in a popular commonwealth enjoy liberty; but that in a monarchy they are all slaves. I say, they that live under a monarchy conceive such an opinion; not they that live under a popular government: for they find no such matter. In sum, I cannot imagine how anything can be more prejudicial to a monarchy than the allowing of such books to be publicly read, without present applying such correctives of discreet masters, as are fit to take away their venom: which venom I will not doubt to compare to the biting of a mad dog, which is a disease the physicians call "hydrophobia," or "fear of water." For as he that is so bitten has a continual torment of thirst, and yet abhorreth water; and is in such an estate, as if the poison endeavoured to convert him into a dog: so when a monarchy is once bitten to the quick by those democratical writers, that continually snarl at that estate; it wanteth nothing more than a strong monarch, which nevertheless out of a certain "tyrannophobia," or fear of being strongly governed, when they have him, they abhor.

As there have been doctors that hold there be three souls in a man; so there be also that think there may be more souls, that is, more sovereigns, than one in a commonwealth; and set up a "supremacy" against the "sovereignty;" "canons" against "laws;" and a "ghostly authority" against the "civil;" working on men's minds with words and distinctions, that of themselves signify nothing, but bewray by their obscurity; that there walketh, as some think, invisibly another kingdom, as it were a kingdom of fairies, in the dark. Now seeing it is manifest that the civil power and the power of the commonwealth is the same thing; and that supremacy, and the power of making canons, and granting faculties, implieth a commonwealth; it followeth that where one is sovereign, another supreme; where one can make laws, and another make canons; there must needs be two commonwealths, of one and the same subjects; which is a kingdom divided in itself, and cannot stand. For notwithstanding the insignificant distinction of "temporal" and "ghostly," they are still two kingdoms, and every subject is subject to two masters. For seeing the "ghostly" power challengeth the right to declare what is sin, it challengeth by consequence to declare what is law, sin being nothing but the transgression of the law; and again, the civil power challenging to declare what is law, every subject must obey two masters, who both will have their commands be observed as law; which is impossible. Or, if it be but one kingdom, either the "civil," which is the power of the commonwealth, must be subordinate to the "ghostly," and then there is no sovereignty but the "ghostly;" or the "ghostly" must be subordinate to the "temporal," and then there is no "supremacy" but the "temporal." When therefore these two powers oppose one another, the commonwealth cannot but be in great danger of civil war and dissolution. For the "civil" authority being more visible, and standing in the clearer light of natural reason, cannot choose but draw to it in all times a very considerable part of the people: and the "spiritual," though it stand in the darkness of school distinctions, and hard words, yet because the fear of darkness and ghosts is greater than other fears, cannot want a party sufficient to trouble, and sometimes to destroy a commonwealth. And this is a disease which may not unfitly be compared to the epilepsy, or falling sickness, which the Jews took to be one kind of possession by spirits, in the body natural. For as in this disease, there is an unnatural spirit, or wind in the head that obstructeth the roots of the nerves, and moving them violently, taketh away the motion which naturally they should have from the power of the soul in the brain, and thereby causeth violent and irregular motions which men call convulsions in the parts; insomuch that he that is seized therewith, falleth down sometimes into the water, and sometimes into the fire, as a man deprived of his senses; so also in the body politic, when the spiritual power moveth the members of a commonwealth, by the terror of punishments and hope of rewards, which are the nerves of it, otherwise than by the civil power, which is the soul of the commonwealth, they ought to be moved; and by strange and hard words suffocate their understanding, it must needs thereby distract the people, and either overwhelm the commonwealth with oppression, or cast it into the fire of a civil war.

Sometimes also in the merely civil government, there be more than one soul; as when the power of levying money, which is the nutritive faculty, has depended on a general assembly; the power of conduct and command, which is the motive faculty, on one man; and the power of making laws, which is the rational faculty, on the accidental consent, not only of those two, but also of a third; this endangereth the commonwealth, sometimes for want of consent to good laws, but most often for want of such nourishment as is necessary to life and motion. For although few perceive that such government is not government, but division of the commonwealth into three factions, and call it mixed monarchy; yet the truth is that it is not one independent commonwealth, but three independent factions; nor one representative person, but three. In the kingdom of God, there may be three persons independent, without breach of unity in God that reigneth; but where men reign that be subject to diversity of opinions, it cannot be so. And therefore if the king bear the person of the people, and the general assembly bear also the person of the people, and another assembly bear the person of a part of the people, they are not one person, nor one sovereign, but three persons, and three sovereigns.

To what disease in the natural body of man I may exactly compare this irregularity of a commonwealth, I know not. But I have seen a man, that had another man growing out of his side, with a head, arms, breast and stomach of his own; if he had had another man growing out of his other side, the comparison might then have been exact.

Hitherto I have named such diseases of a commonwealth as are of the greatest and most present danger. There be other not so great, which nevertheless are not unfit to be observed. As first, the difficulty of raising money for the necessary uses of the commonwealth, especially in the approach of war. This difficulty ariseth from the opinion that every subject hath a propriety in his lands and goods, exclusive of the sovereign's right to the use of the same. From whence it cometh to pass that the sovereign power, which foreseeth the necessities and dangers of the commonwealth, finding the passage of money to the publie treasury obstructed by the tenacity of the people, whereas it ought to extend itself to encounter and prevent such dangers in their beginnings, contracteth itself as long as it can, and when it cannot longer, struggles with the people by stratagems of law, to obtain little sums, which not sufficing, he is fain at last violently to open the way for present supply, or perish; and being put often to these extremities; at last reduceth the people to their due temper, or else the commonwealth must perish. Insomuch as we may compare this distemper very aptly to an ague, wherein, the fleshy parts being congealed, or by venomous matter obstructed, the veins which by their natural course empty themselves into the heart, are not, as they ought to be, supplied from the arteries, whereby there succeedeth at first a cold contraction and trembling of the limbs; and afterward a hot and strong endeavour of the heart, to force a passage for the blood; and before it can do that, contenteth itself with the small refreshments of such things as cool for a time, till, if nature be strong enough, it break at last the contumacy of the parts obstructed, and

dissipateth the vemon into sweat; or, if nature be too weak, the patient dieth.

Again, there is sometimes in a commonwealth, a disease which resembleth the pleurisy; and that is, when the treasure of the commonwealth, flowing out of its due course, is gathered together in too much abundance, in one or a few private men, by monopolies or by farms of the public revenues; in the same manner as the blood in a pleurisy, getting into the membrane of the breast, breedeth there inflammation, accompanied with a fever and painful stitches.

Also the popularity of a potent subject, unless the commonwealth have very good caution of his fidelity, is a dangerous disease; because the people which should receive their motion from the authority of the sovereign, by the flattery and by the reputation of an ambitious man are drawn away from their obedience to the laws, to follow a man, of whose virtues and designs they have no knowledge. And this is commonly of more danger in a popular government than in a monarchy; because an army is of so great force and multitude, as it may easily be made believe they are the people. By this means it was that Julius Caesar, who was set up by the people against the senate, having won to himself the affections of his army, made himself master both of senate and people. And this proceeding of popular and ambitious men, is plain rebellion; and may be resembled to the effects of witchcraft.

Another infirmity of a commonwealth is the immoderate greatness of a town, when it is able to furnish out of its own circuit the number and expense of a great army: as also the great number of corporations; which are as it were many lesser commonwealths in the bowels of a greater, like worms in the entrails of a natural man. To which may be added the liberty of disputing against absolute power, by pretenders to political prudence; which though bred for the most part in the lees of the people, yet animated by false doctrines are perpetually meddling with the fundamental laws, to the molestation of the commonwealth; like the little worms, which physicians call *ascarides*.

We may further add, the insatiable appetite, or βουλιμια, of enlarging dominion; with the incurable "wounds" thereby many times received from the enemy; and the "wens" of ununited conquests, which are many times a burthen, and with less danger lost than kept: as also the "lethargy" of ease and "consumption" of riot and vain expense.

Lastly, when in a war, foreign or intestine, the enemies get a final victory; so as, the forces of the commonwealth keeping the field no longer, there is no further protection of subjects in their loyalty; then is the commonwealth "dissolved," and every man at liberty to protect himself by such courses as his own discretion shall suggest unto him. For the sovereign is the public soul, giving life and motion to the commonwealth; which expiring, the members are governed by it no more, than the carcase of a man, by his departed, though immortal soul. For though the right of a sovereign monarch cannot be extinguished by the act of another; yet the obligation of the members may. For he that wants protection may seek it anywhere; and when he hath it, is obliged, without fraudulent pretence of having submitted himself out of fear, to protect his protection as long as he is able. But when the power of an assembly is once suppressed, the right of the same perisheth utterly; because the assembly itself is extinct; and consequently there is no possibility for the sovereignty to re-enter.

# Chapter XXX

## Of the Office of the Sovereign Representative

The office of the sovereign, be it a monarch or an assembly, consisteth in the end for which he was trusted with the sovereign power, namely, the procuration of "the safety of the people;" to which he is obliged by the law of Nature, and to render an account thereof to God, the author of that law, and to none but Him. But by safety here, is not meant a bare preservation, but also all other contentments of life, which every man by lawful industry, without danger or hurt to the commonwealth, shall acquire to himself.

And this is intended should be done, not by care applied to individuals, further than their protection from injuries when they shall complain; but by a general providence contained in public instruction, both of doctrine and example; and in the making and executing of good laws, to which individual persons may apply their own cases.

And because, if the essential rights of sovereignty, specified before in the eighteenth chapter, be taken away, the commonwealth is thereby dissolved, and every man returneth into the condition and calamity of a war with every other man, which is the greatest evil that can happen in this life; it is the office of the sovereign to maintain those rights entire; and consequently against his duty, first, to transfer to another, or to lay from himself any of them. For he that deserteth the means, deserteth the ends; and he deserteth the means, that being the sovereign, acknowledgeth himself subject to the civil laws; and renounceth the power of supreme judicature, or of making war or peace by his own authority; or of judging of the necessities of the commonwealth; or of levying money and soldiers, when, and as much as in his own conscience he shall judge necessary; or of making officers, and ministers both of war and peace; or of appointing teachers, and examining what doctrines are conformable or contrary to the defence, peace, and good of the people. Secondly, it is against his duty to let the people be ignorant, or misinformed of the grounds and reasons of those his essential rights; because thereby men are easy to be seduced, and drawn to resist him, when the commonwealth shall require their use and exercise.

And the grounds of these rights have the rather need to be diligently and truly taught; because they cannot be maintained by any civil law, or terror of legal punishment. For a civil law that shall forbid rebellion, (and such is all resistance to the essential rights of the sovereignty,) is not, as a civil law, any obligation, but by virtue only of the law of Nature, that forbiddeth the violation of faith: which natural obligation, if men know not, they cannot know the right of any law the sovereign maketh. And for the punishment, they take it but for an act of hostility; which when they think they have strength enough, they will endeavour by acts of hostility to avoid.

As I have heard some say, that justice is but a word, without substance; and that whatsoever a man can by force or art acquire to himself, not only in the condition of war, but also in a commonwealth, is his own, which I have already showed to be false: so there be also that maintain, that there are no grounds, nor principles of reason, to sustain those essential rights which make sovereignty absolute. For if there were, they would have been found out in some place or other; whereas we see there has not hitherto been any commonwealth, where those rights have been acknowledged or challenged. Wherein they argue as ill, as if the savage people of America should deny there were any grounds, or principles of reason, so to build a house as to last as long as the materials, because they never yet saw any so well built. Time and industry produce every day new knowledge. And as the art of well building is derived from principles of reason, observed by industrious men, that had long studied the nature of materials, and the divers effects of figure and proportion, long after mankind began, though poorly, to build; so, long time after men have begun to constitute commonwealths, imperfect, and apt to relapse into disorder, there may principles of reason be found out, by industrious meditation, to make their constitution, excepting by external violence, everlasting. And such are those which I have in this discourse set forth: which whether they come not into the sight of those that have power to make use of them, or be neglected by them, or not, concerneth my particular interests, at this day, very little. But supposing that these of mine are not such principles of reason; yet I am sure they are principles from authority of Scripture; as I shall make it appear, when I shall come to speak of the kingdom of God, administered by Moses, over the Jews, His peculiar people by covenant.

But they say again, that though the principles be right, yet common people are not of capacity enough to be made to understand them. I should be glad that the rich and potent subjects of a kingdom, or those that are accounted the most learned, were no less incapable than they. But all men know that the obstructions to this kind of doctrine proceed, not so much from the difficulty of the matter as from the interest of them that are to learn. Potent men digest hardly anything that setteth up a power to bridle their affections; and learned men anything that discovereth their errors, and thereby lesseneth their authority: whereas the common people's minds, unless they be tainted with dependence on the potent, or scribbled over with the opinions of their doctors, are like clean paper, fit to receive whatsoever by public authority shall be imprinted in them. Shall whole nations be brought to "acquiesce" in the great mysteries of the Christian religion, and millions of men be made believe that the same body may be in innumerable places at one and the same time, which is against reason, and shall not men be able, by their teaching and preaching, protected by the law, to make that received which is so consonant to reason, that any unprejudicated man needs no more to learn it than to hear it? I conclude therefore that in the instruction of the people in the essential rights which are the natural and fundamental laws of sovereignty there is no difficulty, whilst a sovereign has his power entire, but what proceeds from his own fault, or the fault of those whom he trusteth in the administration of the commonwealth; and consequently it is his duty to cause them so to be instructed; and not only his duty, but his benefit also, and security against the danger that may arrive to himself in his natural person from rebellion.

And to descend to particulars, the people are to be taught, first, that they ought not to be in love with any form of government they see in their neighbour nations more than with their own, nor whatsoever present prosperity they behold in nations that are otherwise governed than they, to desire change. For the prosperity of a people ruled by an aristocratical or democratical assembly, cometh not from aristocracy nor from democracy, but from the obedience and concord of the subjects: nor do the people flourish in a monarchy because one man has the right to rule them, but because they obey him. Take away in any kind of state the obedience, and consequently the concord of the people, and they shall not only not flourish, but in short time be dissolved. And they that go about by disobedience to do no more than reform the commonwealth, shall find they do thereby destroy it; like the foolish daughters of Peleus, in the fable; which desiring to renew the youth of their decrepid father, did by the counsel of Medea cut him in pieces, and boil him, together with strange herbs, but made not of him a new man. This desire of change is like the breach of the first of God's commandments: for there God says, *Non habebis Deos alienos;* Thou shalt not have the gods of other nations; and in another place concerning "kings," that they are "gods."

Secondly, they are to be taught that they ought not to be led with admiration of the virtue of any of their fellow-subjects, how high soever he stand, or how conspicuously soever he shine in the commonwealth; nor of any assembly, except the sovereign assembly, so as to defer to them any obedience or honour, appropriate to the sovereign only, whom, in their particular stations, they represent; nor to receive any influence from them, but such as is conveyed by them from the sovereign authority. For that sovereign cannot be imagined to love his people as he ought, that is not jealous of them, but suffers them by the flattery of popular men to be seduced from their loyalty, as they have often been, not only secretly, but openly, so as to proclaim marriage with them *in facie ecclesiæ* by preachers, and by publishing the same in the open streets, which may fitly be compared to the violation of the second of the ten commandments.

Thirdly, in consequence to this, they ought to be informed how great a fault it is to speak evil of the sovereign representative, whether one man, or an assembly of men; or to argue and dispute his power, or any way to use his name irreverently, whereby he may be brought into contempt with his people, and their obedience, in which the safety of the commonwealth consisteth, slackened. Which doctrine the third commandent by resemblance pointeth to.

Fourthly, seeing people cannot be taught this, nor when it is taught, remember it, nor after one generation past, so much as know in whom the sovereign power is placed, without setting apart from their ordinary labour, some certain times, in which they may attend those that are appointed to instruct them; it is necessary that some such times be determined, wherein they may assemble together, and, after prayers and praises given to God, the Sovereign of sovereigns, hear those their duties told them, and the positive laws, such as generally concern them all, read and expounded, and be put in mind of the authority that maketh them laws. To this end had the Jews every seventh day a sabbath, in which the law was read and expounded; and in the solemnity whereof they were put in mind that their king was God; that having created the world in six days, He rested the seventh day; and by their resting on it from their labour, that that God was their king, which redeemed them from their servile and painful labour in Egypt, and gave them a time, after they had rejoiced in God, to take joy also in themselves by lawful recreation. So that the first table of the commandments is spent all in setting down the sum of God's absolute power, not only as God, but as king by pact in peculiar of the Jews; and may therefore give light to those that have sovereign power conferred on them by the consent of men, to see what doctrine they ought to teach their subjects.

And because the first instruction of children dependeth on the care of their parents, it is necessary that they should be obedient to them whilst they are under their tuition; and not only so, but that also afterwards, as gratitude requireth, they acknowledge the benefit of their education by external signs of honour. To which end they are to be taught that originally the father of every man was also his sovereign lord, with power over him of life and death; and that the fathers of families, when by instituting a commonwealth, they resigned that absolute power, yet it was never intended they should lose the honour due unto them for their education. For to relinquish such right was not necessary to the institution of sovereign power; nor would there be any reason why any man should desire to have children, or take the care to nourish and instruct them, if they were afterwards to have no other benefit from them than from other men. And this accordeth with the fifth commandment.

Again, every sovereign ought to cause justice to be taught, which, consisting in taking from no man what is his, is as much as to say, to cause men to be taught not to deprive their neighbours, by violence or fraud, of anything which by the sovereign authority is theirs. Of things held in propriety, those that are dearest to a man are his own life and limbs; and in the next degree, in most men, those that concern conjugal affection; and after them, riches and means of living. Therefore the people are to be taught to abstain from violence to one another's person, by private revenges; from violation of conjugal honour; and from forcible rapine and fraudulent surreption of one another's goods. For which purpose also it is necessary they be showed the evil consequences of false judgment, by corruption either of judges or witnesses, whereby the distinction of propriety is taken away, and justice becomes of no effect: all which things are intimated in the sixth, seventh, eighth, and ninth commandments.

Lastly, they are to be taught that not only the unjust facts, but the designs and intentions to do them, though by accident hindered, are injustice; which consisteth in the pravity of the will, as well as in the irregularity of the act. And this is the intention of the tenth commandment, and the sum of the second table; which is reduced all to this one commandment of mutual charity, "thou shalt love thy neighbour as thyself:" as the sum of the first table is reduced to "the love of God;" whom they had then newly received as their king.

As for the means and conduits, by which the people may receive this instruction, we are to search by what means so many opinions, contrary to the peace of mankind, upon weak and false principles, have nevertheless been so deeply rooted in them. I mean those which I have in the precedent chapter specified: as that men shall judge of what is lawful and unlawful, not by the law itself, but by their own consciences; that is to say, by their own private judgments: that subjects sin in obeying the commands of the commonwealth, unless they themselves have first judged them to be lawful: that their propriety in their riches is such, as to exclude the dominion which the commonwealth hath over the same: that it is lawful for subjects to kill such as they call tyrants: that the sovereign power may be divided, and the like; which come to be instilled into the people by this means. They whom necessity or covetousness keepeth attent on their trades and labour; and they, on the other side, whom superfluity or sloth carrieth after their sensual pleasures; which two sorts of men take up the greatest part of mankind; being diverted from the deep meditation, which the learning of truth, not

only in the matter of natural justice, but also of all other sciences necessarily requireth, receive the notions of their duty, chiefly from divines in the pulpit, and partly from such of their neighbours or familiar acquaintance, as having the faculty of discoursing readily and plausibly, seem wiser and better learned in cases of law and conscience, than themselves. And the divines and such others as make show of learning, derive their knowledge from the universities, and from the schools of law, or from the books, which by men, eminent in those schools and universities, have been published. It is therefore manifest that the instruction of the people dependeth wholly on the right teaching of youth in the universities. But are not, may some man say, the universities of England learned enough already to do that? or is it you will undertake to teach the universities? Hard questions. Yet to the first I doubt not to answer; that till towards the latter end of Henry the Eighth, the power of the Pope was always upheld against the power of the commonwealth, principally by the universities; and that the doctrines maintained by so many preachers against the sovereign power of the king, and by so many lawyers and others that had their educatiou there, is a sufficient argument, that though the universities were not authors of those false doctrines, yet they knew not how to plant the true. For in such a contradiction of opinions, it is most certain that they have not been sufficiently instructed; and it is no wonder if they yet retain a relish of that subtle liquor, wherewith they were first seasoned, against the civil authority. But to the latter question it is not fit nor needful for me to say either aye or no: for any man that sees what I am doing, may easily perceive what I think.

The safety of the people requireth further, from him or them that have the sovereign power, that justice be equally administered to all degrees of people; that is, that as well the rich and mighty, as poor and obscure persons, may be righted of the injuries done them; so as the great may have no greater hope of impunity, when they do violence, dishonour, or any injury to the meaner sort, than when one of these does the like to one of them: for in this consisteth equity; to which, as being a precept of the law of Nature, a sovereign is as much subject as any of the meanest of his people. All breaches of the law are offences against the commonwealth: but there be some that are also against private persons. Those that concern the commonwealth only may without breach of equity be pardoned, for every man may pardon what is done against himself, according to his own discretion. But an offence against a private man cannot in equity be pardoned, without the consent of him that is injured, or reasonable satisfaction.

The inequality of subjects proceedeth from the acts of sovereign power; and therefore has no more place in the presence of the sovereign, that is to say, in a court of justice, than the inequality between kings and their subjects, in the presence of the King of kings. The honour of great persons is to be valued for their beneficence and the aids they give to men of inferior rank, or not at all. And the violences, oppressions, and injuries they do, are not extenuated, but aggravated by the greatness of their persons; because they have least need to commit them. The consequences of this partiality towards the great, proceed in this manner. Impunity maketh insolence; insolence, hatred; and hatred, an endeavour to pull down all oppressing and contumelious greatness, though with the ruin of the commonwealth.

To equal justice appertaineth also the equal imposition of taxes; the equality whereof dependeth not on the equality of riches, but on the equality of the debt that every man oweth to the commonwealth for his defence. It is not enough for a man to labour for the maintenance of his life; but also to fight, if need be, for the securing of his labour. They must either do as the Jews did after their return from captivity, in re-edifying the temple, build with one hand, and hold the sword in the other; or else they must hire others to fight for them. For the impositions that are laid on the people by the sovereign power, are nothing else but the wages due to them that hold the public sword to defend private men in the exercise of their several trades and callings. Seeing then the benefit that every one receiveth thereby, is the enjoyment of life, which is equally dear to poor and rich; the debt which a poor man oweth them that defend his life, is the same which a rich man oweth for the defence of his; saving that the rich, who have the service of the poor, may be debtors not only for their own persons but for many more. Which considered, the equality of imposition, consisteth rather in the equality of that which is consumed than of the riches of the persons that consume the same. For what reason is there that he which laboureth much, and sparing the fruits of his labour, consumeth little, should be more charged than he that living idly, getteth little, and spendeth all he gets; seeing the one hath no more protection from the commonwealth than the other? But when the impositions are laid upon those things which men consume, every man payeth equally for what he useth: nor is the commonwealth defrauded by the luxurious waste of private men.

And whereas many men, by accident inevitable, become unable to maintain themselves by their labour; they ought not to be left to the charity of private persons; but to be provided for, as far forth as the necessities of nature require by the laws of the commonwealth. For as it is uncharitableness in any man to neglect the impotent; so it is in the sovereign of a commonwealth to expose them to the hazard of such uncertain charity.

But for such as have strong bodies, the case is otherwise: they are to be forced to work: and to avoid the excuse of not finding employment, there ought to be such laws as may encourage all manner of arts, as navigation, agriculture, fishing, and all manner of manufacture that requires labour. The multitude of poor and yet strong people still increasing, they are to be transplanted into countries not sufficiently inhabited: where nevertheless, they are not to exterminate those they find there; but constrain them to inhabit closer together, and not to range a great deal of ground to snatch what they find; but to court each little plot with art and labour, to give them their sustenance in due season. And when all the world is overcharged with inhabitants, then the last remedy of all is war; which provideth for every man, by victory or death.

To the care of the sovereign belongeth the making of good laws. But what is a good law ? By a good law I mean not a just law, for no law can be unjust. The law is made by the sovereign power, and all that is done by such power is warranted and owned by every one of the people; and that which every man will have so, no man can say is unjust. It is in the laws of a commonwealth as in the laws of gaming: whatsoever the gamesters all agree on, is injustice to none of them. A good law is that which is "needful" for the "good of the people," and withal "perspicuous."

For the use of laws, which are but rules authorized, is not to bind the people from all voluntary actions; but to direct and keep them in such a motion as not to hurt themselves by their own impetuous desires, rashness, or indiscretion; as hedges are set, not to stop travellers, but to keep them in their way. And therefore a law that is not needful, having not the true end of a law, is not good. A law may be conceived to be good, when it is for the benefit of the sovereign; though it be not necessary for the people; but it is not so. For the good of the sovereign and people cannot be separated. It is a weak sovereign that has weak subjects; and a weak people, whose sovereign wanteth power to rule them at his will. Unnecessary laws are not good laws; but traps for money; which where the right of sovereign power is acknowledged, are superfluous; and where it is not acknowledged, insufficient to defend the people.

The perspicuity consisteth not so much in the words of the law itself, as in a declaration of the causes and motives for which it was made. That is it that shows the meaning of the legislator; and the meaning of the legislator known, the law is more easily understood by few than many words. For all words are subject to ambiguity; and therefore multiplication of words in the body of the law is multiplication of ambiguity: besides it seems to imply, by too much diligence, that whosoever can evade the words, is without the compass of the law. And this is a cause of many unnecessary processes. For when I consider how short were the laws of ancient times, and how they grew by degrees still longer, methinks I see a contention between the penners and pleaders of the law; the former seeking to circumscribe the latter, and the latter to evade their circumscriptions, and that the pleaders have got the victory. It belongeth therefore to the office of a legislator (such as is in all commonwealths the supreme representative, be it one man or an assembly) to make the reason perspicuous why the law was made; and the body of the law itself as short, but in as proper and significant terms, as may be.

It belongeth also to the office of the sovereign to make a right application of punishments and rewards. And seeing the end of punishing is not revenge and discharge of choler; but correction either of the offender or of others by his example; the severest punishments are to be inflicted for those crimes that are of most danger to the public; such as are those which proceed from malice to the government established; those that spring from contempt of justice; those that provoke indignation in the multitude; and those, which unpunished, seem authorized, as when they are committed by sons, servants, or favourites of men in authority. For indignation carrieth men not only against the actors and authors of injustice; but against all power that is likely to protect them; as in the case of Tarquin; when for the insolent act of one of his sons, he was driven out of Rome, and the monarchy itself dissolved. But crimes of infirmity, such as are those which proceed from great provocation, from great fear, great need, or from ignorance whether the fact be a great crime or not, there is place many times for lenity, without prejudice to the commonwealth; and lenity, when there is such place for it, is required by the law of Nature. The punishment of the leaders and teachers in a commotion, not the poor seduced people, when they are punished, can profit the commonwealth by their example. To be severe to the people, is to punish that ignorance which may in great part be imputed to the sovereign, whose fault it was that they were no better instructed.

In like manner it belongeth to the office and duty of the sovereign, to apply his rewards always so, as there may arise from them benefit to the commonwealth; wherein consisteth their use and end; and is then done, when they that have well served the commonwealth, are with as little expense of the common treasure as is possible, so well recompensed as others thereby may be encouraged, both to serve the same as faithfully as they can, and to study the arts by which they may be enabled to do it better. To buy with money, or preferment, from a popular ambitious subject, to be quiet and desist from making ill impressions in the minds of the people, has nothing of the nature of reward; (which is ordained not for disservice, but for service past;) nor a sign of gratitude, but of fear; nor does it tend to the benefit, but to the damage of the public. It is a contention with ambition, like that of Hercules with the monster Hydra, which having many heads, for every one that was vanquished, there grew up three. For in like manner, when the stubbornness of one popular man is overcome with reward, there arise many more by the example, that do the same mischief in hope of like benefit: and as all sorts of manufacture, so also malice increaseth by being vendible. And though sometimes a civil war may be deferred by such ways as that, yet the danger grows still the greater, and the public ruin more assured. It is therefore against the duty of the sovereign, to whom the public safety is committed, to reward those that aspire to greatness by disturbing the peace of their country, and not rather to oppose the beginnings of such men with a little danger, than after a longer time with greater.

Another business of the sovereign, is to choose good counsellors; I mean such, whose advice he is to take in the government of the commonwealth. For this word counsel, *consilium*, corrupted from *considium*, is of a large signification, and comprehendeth all assemblies of men that sit together, not only to deliberate what is to be done hereafter, but also to judge of facts past, and of law for the present. I take it here in the first sense only: and in this sense, there is no choice of counsel, neither in a democracy nor aristocracy; because the persons counselling are members of the person counselled. The choice of counsellors therefore is proper to monarchy; in which, the sovereign that endeavoureth not to make choice of those that in every kind are the most able, dischargeth not his office as he ought to do. The most able counsellors are they that have least hope of benefit by giving evil counsel, and most knowledge of those things that conduce to the peace and defence of the commonwealth. It is a hard matter to know who expecteth benefit from public troubles; but the signs that guide to a just suspicion is the soothing of the people in their unreasonable or irremediable grievances, by men whose estates are not sufficient to discharge their accustomed expenses, and may easily be observed by any one whom it concerns to know it. But to know who has most knowledge of the public affairs, is yet harder; and they that know them, need them a greal deal the less. For to know who knows the rules almost of any art, is a great degree of the knowledge of the same a r t ; because no man can be assured of the truth of another's rules, but he that is first taught to understand them. But the best signs of knowledge of any art, are, much conversing in it, and constant good effects of it. Good counsel comes not by lot, nor by inheritance; and therefore there is no more reason to expect good advice from the rich or noble, in matter of state, than in delineating the dimensions of a fortress; unless we shall think there needs no method in the study of the politics, as there does in the study of geometry, but only to be lookers-on; which is not so. For the politics is the harder study of the two. Whereas in these parts of Europe, it hath been taken for a right of certain persons, to have place in the highest council of state by inheritance; it is derived from the conquests of the ancient Germans; wherein many absolute lords joining together to conquer other nations, would not enter into the confederacy, without such privileges as might be marks of difference in time following, between their posterity and the posterity of their subjects; which privileges being inconsistent with the sovereign power, by the favonr of the sovereign, they may seem to keep; but contending for them as their right, they must needs by degrees let them go, and have at last no further honour than adhereth naturally to their abilities.

And how able soever be the counsellors in any affair, the benefit of their counsel is greater when they give every one his advice and the reasons of it apart, than when they do it in an assembly, by way of orations; and when they have premeditated, than when they speak on the sudden; both because they have more time to survey the consequences of action, and are less subject to be carried away to contradiction, through envy, emulation, or other passions arising from the difference of opinion.

The best counsel in those things that concern not other nations, but only the ease and benefit the subjects may enjoy, by laws that look only inward, is to be taken from the general informations and complaints of the people of each province, who are best acquainted with their own wants, and ought therefore, when they demand nothing in derogation of the essential rights of sovereignty, to be diligently taken notice of. For without those essential rights, as I have often before said, the commonwealth cannot at all subsist.

A commander of an army in chief, if he be not popular, shall not be beloved nor feared as he ought to be by his army, and consequently cannot perform that office with good success. He must therefore be industrious, valiant, affable, liberal, and fortunate, that he may gain an opinion both of sufficiency, and of loving his soldiers. This is popularity, and breeds in the soldiers both desire and courage to recommend themselves to his favour, and protects the severity of the general in punishing, when need is, the mutinous or negligent soldiers. But this love of soldiers, if caution be not given of the commander's fidelity, is a dangerous thing to sovereign power; especially when it is in the hands of an assembly not popular. It belongeth therefore to the safety of the people, both that they be good conductors and faithful subjects to whom the sovereign commits his armies.

But when the sovereign himself is popular; that is, reverenced and beloved of his people, there is no danger at all from the popularity of a subject. For soldiers are never so generally unjust as to side with their captain, though they love him, against their sovereign, when they love not only his person, but also his cause. And therefore those who by violence have at any time suppressed the power of their lawful sovereign, before they could settle themselves in his place, have been always put to the trouble of contriving their titles, to save the people from the shame of receiving them. To have a known right to sovereign power is so popular a quality, as he that has it needs no more, for his own part, to turn the hearts of his subjects to him, but that they see him able absolutely to govern his own family; nor, on the part of his enemies, but a disbanding of their armies. For the greatest and most active part of mankind has never hitherto been well contented with the present.

Concerning the offices of one sovereign to another, which are comprehended in that law, which is commonly called the "law of nations," I need not say anything in this place, because the law of nations, and the law of Nature, is the same thing. And every sovereign hath the same right, in procuring the safety of his people, that any particular man can have in procuring the safety of his own body. And the same law that dictateth to men that have no civil government, what they ought to do, and what to avoid in regard of one another, dictateth the same to commonwealths, that is, to the consciences of sovereign princes and sovereign assemblies; there being no court of natural justice but in the conscience only: where not man, but God reigneth; whose laws, such of them as oblige all mankind in respect of God, as He is the author of Nature, are "natural;" and in respect of the same God, as He is King of kings, are "laws." But of the kingdom of God, as King of kings, and as King also of a peculiar people, I shall speak in the rest of this discourse.

# Two Treatises of Government

By John Locke

## The State of Nature

To understand political power aright, and derive it from its original, we must consider, what state all men are naturally in, and that is, a state of perfect freedom to order their actions, and dispose of their possessions and persons, as they think fit, within the bounds of the law of nature, without asking leave, or depending upon the will of any other man.

A state also of equality, wherein all the power and jurisdiction is reciprocal, no one having more than another; there being nothing more evident, than that creatures of the same species and rank, promiscuously born to all the same advantages of nature, and the use of the same faculties, should also be equal one amongst another without subordination or subjection, unless the lord and master of them all should, by any manifest declaration of his will, set one above another, and confer on him, by an evident and clear appointment, an undoubted right to dominion and sovereignty.

This equality of men by nature, the judicious Hooker looks upon as so evident in itself, and beyond all question, that he makes it the foundation of that obligation to mutual love amongst men, on which he builds the duties they owe one another, and from whence he derives the great maxims of justice and charity. His words are:

> The like natural inducement hath brought men to know that it is no less their duty, to love others than themselves; for seeing those things which are equal, must needs all have one measure; if I cannot but wish to receive good, even as much at every man's hands, as any man can wish unto his own soul, how should I look to have any part of my desire herein satisfied, unless myself be careful to satisfy the like desire, which is undoubtedly in other men. We all being of one and the same nature; to have any thing offered them repugnant to this desire, must needs in all respects grieve them as much as me; so that if I do harm, I must look to suffer, there being no reason that others should shew greater measure of love to me, than they have by me shewed unto them; my desire therefore to be loved of my equals in nature, as

263

much as possible may be, imposeth upon me a natural duty of bearing to themward fully the like affection; from which relation of equality between ourselves and them that are as ourselves, what several rules and canons natural reason hath drawn, for direction of life, no man is ignorant.

—*Eccl. Pol.*, lib.i.

But though this be a state of liberty, yet it is not a state of licence: though man in that state have an uncontrollable liberty to dispose of his person or possessions, yet he has not liberty to destroy himself, or so much as any creature in his possession, but where some nobler use than its bare preservation calls for it. The state of nature has a law of nature to govern it, which obliges every one, and reason, which is that law, teaches all mankind, who will but consult it, that being all equal and independent, no one ought to harm another in his life, health, liberty, or possessions: for men being all the workmanship of one omnipotent, and infinitely wise maker; all the servants of one sovereign master, sent into the world by his order, and about his business; they are his property, whose workmanship they are, made to last during his, not one another's pleasure: and being furnished with like faculties, sharing all in one community of nature, there cannot be supposed any such subordination among us, that may authorize us to destroy one another, as if we were made for one another's uses, as the inferior ranks of creatures are for ours. Every one, as he is bound to preserve himself, and not to quit his station wilfully, so by the like reason, when his own preservation comes not in competition, ought he as much as he can to preserve the rest of mankind, and

not unless it be to do justice on an offender, take away, or impair the life, or what tends to the preservation of the life, the liberty, health, limb or goods of another.

And that all men may be restrained from invading others rights, and from doing hurt to one another, and the law of nature be observed, which willeth the peace and preservation of all mankind, the execution of the law of nature is, in that state, put into every man's hands, whereby every one has a right to punish the transgressors of that law to such a degree, as may hinder its violation. For the law of nature would, as all other laws that concern men in this world, be in vain, if there were nobody that in the state of nature had a power to execute that law, and thereby preserve the innocent and restrain offenders. And if any one in the state of nature may punish another for any evil he has done, every one may do so: for in that state of perfect equality where naturally there is no superiority or jurisdiction of one over another, what any may do in prosecution of that law, every one must needs have a right to do.

And thus, in the state of nature, one man comes by a power over another; but yet no absolute or arbitrary power, to use a criminal, when he has got him in his hands, according to the passionate heats, or boundless extravagancy of his own will; but only to retribute to him, so far as calm reason and conscience dictates, what is proportionate to his transgression, which is so much as may serve for reparation and restraint: for these two are the only reasons why one man may lawfully do harm to another, which is that we call punishment. In transgressing the law of nature, the offender declares himself to live by another rule than that of reason and common equity, which is that measure God has set to the actions of men for their mutual security, and so he becomes dangerous to mankind, the tie, which is to secure them from injury and violence, being slighted and broken by him, which being a trespass against the whole species, and the peace and safety of it, provided for by the law of nature, every man upon this score, by the right he hath to preserve mankind in general, may restrain, or where it is necessary, destroy things noxious to them, and so may bring such evil on any one, who hath transgressed that law, as may make him repent the doing of it, and thereby deter him, and, by his example others, from doing the like mischief. And in this case, and upon this ground, every man hath a right to punish the offender, and be executioner of the law of nature.

I doubt not but this will seem a very strange doctrine to some men; but before they condemn it, I desire them to resolve me, by what right any prince or state can put to death, or punish an alien, for any crime he commits in their country. 'Tis certain their laws, by virtue of any sanction they receive from the promulgated will of the legislative, reach not a stranger: they speak not to him, nor, if they did, is he bound to hearken to them. The legislative authority, by which they are in force over the subjects of that commonwealth, hath no power over him. Those who have the supreme power of making laws in England, France or Holland, are to an Indian, but like the rest of the world, men without authority: and therefore, if by the law of nature every man hath not a power to punish offences against it, as he soberly judges the case to require, I see not how the magistrates of any community can punish an alien of another country; since, in reference to him, they can have no more power than what every man naturally may have over another.

Besides the crime which consists in violating the law, and varying from the right rule of reason, whereby a man so far becomes degenerate, and declares himself to quit the principles of human nature and to be a noxious creature, there is commonly injury done, and some person or other, some other man receives damage by his transgression; in which case he who hath received any damage, has, besides the right of punishment common to him with other men, a particular right to seek reparation from him that has done it: and any other person, who finds it just, may also join with him that is injured, and assist him in recovering from the offender so much as may make satisfaction for the harm he has suffered.

From these two distinct rights, the one of punishing the crime for restraint, and preventing the like offence, which right of punishing is in everybody; the other of taking reparation, which belongs only to the injured party, comes it to pass that the magistrate, who by being magistrate hath the common right of punishing put into his hands, can often, where the public good demands not the execution of the law, remit the punishment of criminal offences by his own authority, but yet cannot remit the satisfaction due to any private man for the damage he has received. That, he who has suffered the damage has a right to demand in his own name, and he alone can remit: the damnified person has this power of appropriating to himself the goods or service of the offender, by right of self-preservation, as every man has a power to punish the crime, to prevent its being committed again, by the right he has of preserving all mankind, and doing all reasonable things he can in order to that end: and thus it is, that every man, in the state of nature, has a power to kill a murderer, both to deter others from doing the like injury, which no reparation can compensate, by the example of the punishment that attends it from every body, and also to secure men from the attempts of a criminal, who having renounced reason, the common rule and measure God hath given to mankind, hath, by the unjust violence and slaughter he hath committed upon one, declared war against all mankind, and therefore may be destroyed as a lion or a tiger, one of those wild savage beasts, with whom men can have no society nor security: and upon this is grounded that great law of nature, *Whoso sheddeth man's blood, by man shall his blood be shed*. And Cain was so fully convinced, that every one had a right to destroy such a criminal, that after the murder of his brother, he cries out. *Every one that findeth me shall slay me;* so plain was it writ in the hearts of all mankind.

By the same reason may a man in the state of nature punish the lesser breaches of that law. It will perhaps be demanded, with death? I answer, each transgression may be punished to that degree, and with so much severity, as will suffice to make it an ill bargain to the offender, give him cause to repent, and terrify others from doing the like. Every offence, that can be committed in the state of nature, may in the state of nature be also punished equally, and as far forth as it may, in a commonwealth: for though it would be besides my present purpose, to enter here into the particulars of the law of nature, or its measures of punishment; yet, it is certain there is such a law, and that too as intelligible and plain to a rational creature, and a studier of that law, as the positive laws of commonwealths: nay, possibly plainer; as much as reason is easier to be understood, than the fancies and intricate contrivances of men, following contrary and hidden interests put into words; for so truly are a great part of the municipal laws of countries, which are only so far right, as they are founded on the law of nature, by which they are to be regulated and interpreted.

To this strange doctrine, *viz.,* that in the state of nature every one has the executive power of the law of nature, I doubt not but it will be objected, that it is unreasonable for men to be judges in their own cases, that self-love will make men partial to themselves and their friends: and on the other side, ill-nature, passion and revenge will carry them too far in punishing others; and hence nothing but confusion and disorder will follow; and that therefore God hath certainly appointed government to restrain the partiality and violence of men. I easily grant that civil government is the proper remedy for the inconveniences of the state of nature, which must certainly be great where men may be judges in their own case, since 'tis easy to be imagined, that he who was so unjust as to do his brother an injury, will scarce be so just as to condemn himself for it; but I shall desire those who make this objection, to remember, that absolute monarchs are but men; and if government is to be the remedy of those evils, which necessarily follow from men's being judges in their own cases, and the state of nature is therefore not to be endured, I desire to know what kind of government that is, and bow much better it is than the state of nature, where one man commanding a multitude, has the liberty to be judge in his own case, and may do to all his subjects whatever he pleases, without the least question or control of those who execute his pleasure? and in whatsoever he doth, whether led by reason, mistake or passion, must be submitted to? which men in the state of nature are not bound to do one to another. And if he that judges, judges amiss in his own, or any other case, he is answerable for it to the rest of mankind.

'Tis often asked as a mighty objection, where are, or ever were there any men in such a state of nature? To which it may suffice as an answer at present, that since all princes and rulers of *independent* governments all through the world, are in a state of nature, 'tis plain the world never was, nor never will be, without numbers of men in that state. I have named all governors of *independent* communities, whether they are, or are not, in league with others: for 'tis not every compact that puts an end to the state of nature between men, but only this one of agreeing together mutually to enter into one community, and make one body politic; other promises, and compacts, men may make one with another, and yet still be in the state of nature. The promises and bargains for truck, etc., between the two men in the desert island, mentioned by Garcilasso de la Vega, in his history of Peru; or between a Swiss and an Indian, in the woods of America, are binding to them, though they are perfectly in a state of nature, in reference to one another: for truth and keeping of faith belongs to men as men, and not as members of society.

To those that say, there were never any men in the state of nature, I will not only oppose the authority of the judicious Hooker, *Eccl. Pol.* lib. i. *sect.* 10, where he *says,*

> the laws which have been hitherto mentioned, *i.e.,* the laws of nature, do bind men absolutely, even as they are men, although they have never any settled fellowship, never any solemn agreement amongst themselves what to do, or not to do: but forasmuch as we are not by ourselves sufficient to furnish ourselves with competent store of things, needful for such a life as our nature doth desire, a life fit for the dignity of man; therefore to supply those defects and imperfections which are in us, as living singly and solely by ourselves, we are naturally induced to seek communion and fellowship with others: this was the cause of men uniting themselves at first in politic societies.

But I moreover affirm, that all men are naturally in that state, and remain so, till by their own consents they make themselves members of some politic society; and I doubt not in the sequel of this discourse, to make it very clear.

## The State of War

The state of war is a state of enmity and destruction; and therefore declaring by word or action, not a passionate and hasty, but sedate, settled design upon another man's life, puts him in a state of war with him against whom he has declared such an intention, and so has exposed his life to the other's power to be taken away by him, or any one that joins with him in his defence, and espouses his quarrel, it being reasonable and just I should have a right to destroy that which threatens me with destruction; for by the fundamental law of nature, man being to be preserved, as much as possible, when all cannot be preserved, the safety of the innocent is to be preferred; and one may destroy a man who makes war upon him, or has discovered an enmity to his being, for the same reason that he may kill a wolf or a lion, because such men are not under the ties of the common law of reason, have no other rule but that of force and violence, and so may be treated as beasts of prey, those dangerous and noxious creatures that will be sure to destroy him whenever he falls into their power.

And hence it is that he who attempts to get another man into his absolute power does thereby put himself into a state of war with him; it being to be understood as a declaration of a design upon his life. For I have reason to conclude that he who would get me into his power without my consent would use me as he pleased when he had got me there, and destroy me too when he had a fancy to it, for nobody can desire to have me in his absolute power unless it be to compel me by force to that which is against the right of my freedom—*i.e.*, make me a slave. To be free from such force is the only security of my preservation, and reason bids me look on him as an enemy to my preservation who would take away that freedom which is the fence to it; so that he who makes an attempt to enslave me thereby puts himself into a state of war with me. He that in the state of nature would take away the freedom that belongs to any one in that state must necessarily be supposed to have a design to take away everything else, that freedom being the foundation of all the rest; as he that in the state of society would take away the freedom belonging to those of that society or commonwealth must be supposed to design to take away from them everything else, and so be looked on as in a state of war.

This makes it lawful for a man to kill a thief who has not in the least hurt him, nor declared any design upon his life, any farther than by the use of force, so to get him in his power as to take away his money, or what he pleases, from him; because using force, where he has no right to get me into his power, let his pretence be what it will, I have no reason to suppose that he who would take away my liberty would not, when he had me in his power, take away everything else. And therefore it is lawful for me to treat him as one who has put himself into a state of war with me—*i.e.*, kill him if I can; for to that hazard does he justly expose himself whoever introduces a state of war, and is aggressor in it.

And here we have the plain difference between the state of nature and the state of war, which however some men have confounded, are as far distant as a state of peace, goodwill, mutual assistance, and preservation; and a state of enmity, malice, violence and mutual destruction are one from another. Men living together according to reason without a common superior on earth, with authority to judge between them, are properly in the state of nature. But force, or a declared design of force upon the person of another, where there is no common superior on earth to appeal to for relief, is the state of war; and 'tis the want of such an appeal gives a man the right of war even against an aggressor, though he be in society and a fellow-subject. Thus, a thief whom I cannot harm, but by appeal to the law, for having stolen all that I am worth, I may kill when he sets on me to rob me but of my horse or coat, because the law, which was made for my preservation, where it cannot interpose to secure my life from present force, which if lost is capable of no reparation, permits me my own defence and the right of war, a liberty to kill the aggressor, because the aggressor allows not time to appeal to our common judge, nor the decision of the law, for remedy in a case where the mischief may be irreparable. Want of a common judge with authority puts all men in a state of nature; force without right upon a man's person makes a state of war both where there is, and is not, a common judge.

But when the actual force is over, the state of war ceases between those that are in society and are equally on both sides subjected to the fair determination of the law; because then there lies open the remedy of appeal for the past injury, and to prevent future harm; but where no such appeal is, as in the state of nature, for want of positive laws, and judges with authority to appeal to, the state of war, once begun, continues with a right to the innocent party to destroy the other whenever he can, until the aggressor offers peace, and desires reconciliation on such terms as may repair any wrongs he has already done, and secure the innocent for the future; nay, where an appeal to the law and constituted judges lies open, but the remedy is denied by a manifest perverting of justice, and a barefaced wresting of the laws to protect or indemnify the violence or injuries of some men or party of men, there it is hard to imagine any thing but a state of war: for wherever violence is used, and injury done, though by hands appointed to administer justice, it is still violence and injury, however coloured with the name, pretences, or forms of law, the end whereof being to protect and redress the innocent, by an unbiased application of it, to all who are under it; wherever that is not *bona fide* done, war is made upon the sufferers, who having no appeal on earth to right them, they are left to the only remedy in such cases, an appeal to heaven.

To avoid this state of war (wherein there is no appeal but to heaven, and wherein every the least difference is apt to end, where there is no authority to decide between the contenders) is one great reason of men's putting themselves into society, and quitting the state of nature. For where there is an authority, a power on earth from which relief can be had by appeal, there the continuance of the state of war is excluded, and the controversy is decided by that power.

# Slavery

The natural liberty of man is to be free from any superior power on earth, and not to be under the will or legislative authority of man, but to have only the law of nature for his rule. The liberty of man in society is to be under no other legislative power but that established by consent in the commonwealth, nor under the dominion of any will, or restraint of any law, but what the legislative shall enact according to the trust put in it. Freedom, then, is not what Sir Robert Filmer tells us, *O.A. 55. A liberty for every one to do what he lists, to live as he pleases, and not to be tied by any laws,* but freedom of men under government is to have a standing rule to live by, common to every one of that society, and made by the legislative power erected in it. A liberty to follow my own will in all things where the rule prescribes not, not to be subject to the inconstant, uncertain, unknown, arbitrary will of another man, as freedom of nature is to be under no other restraint but the law of nature.

This freedom from absolute, arbitrary power is so necessary to, and closely joined with, a man's preservation, that he cannot part with it but by what forfeits his preservation and life together. For a man, not having the power of his own life, cannot, by compact or his own consent, enslave himself to any one, nor put himself under the absolute, arbitrary power of another to take away his life when he pleases. Nobody can give more power than he has himself, and he that cannot take away his own life cannot give another power over it. Indeed, having by his fault forfeited his own life by some act that deserves death, he to whom he has forfeited it may, when he has him in his power, delay to take it, and make use of him to his own service; and he does him no injury by it. For, whenever he finds the hardship of his slavery outweigh the value of his life, 'tis in his power, by resisting the will of his master, to draw on himself the death he desires.

## Property

God, who hath given the world to men in common, hath also given them reason to make use of it to the best advantage of life and convenience. The earth and all that is therein is given to men for the support and comfort of their being. And though all the fruits it naturally produces, and beasts it feeds, belong to mankind in common, as they are produced by the spontaneous hand of nature, and no body has originally a private dominion exclusive of the rest of mankind in any of them, as they are thus in their natural state, yet being given for the use of men, there must of necessity be a means to appropriate them some way or other before they can be of any use, or at all beneficial, to any particular man. The fruit or venison which nourishes the wild Indian, who knows no enclosure, and is still a tenant in common, must be his, and so his—*i.e.*, a part of him, that another can no longer have any right to it before it can do him any good for the support of his life.

Though the earth and all inferior creatures be common to all men, yet every man has a *property* in his own *person*. This nobody has any right to but himself. The *labour* of his body and the work of his hands, we may say, are properly his. Whatsoever, then, he removes out of the state that nature hath provided and left it in, he hath mixed his labour with it, and joined to it something that is his own, and thereby makes it his property. It being by him removed from the common state nature placed it in, it hath by this labour something annexed to it that excludes the common right of other men. For this labour being the unquestionable property of the labourer, no man but he can have a right to what that is once joined to, at least where there is enough, and as good left in common for others.

He that is nourished by the acorns he picked up under an oak, or the apples he gathered from the trees in the wood, has certainly appropriated them to himself.

Nobody can deny but the nourishment is his. I ask, then, when did they begin to be his? when he digested? or when he ate? or when he boiled? or when he brought them home? or when he picked them up? And 'tis plain, if the first gathering made them not his, nothing else could. That labour put a distinction between them and common. That added something to them more than Nature, the common mother of all, had done, and so they became his private right. And will any one say he had no right to those acorns or apples he thus appropriated because he had not the consent of all mankind to make them his? Was it a robbery thus to assume to himself what belonged to all in common? If such a consent as that was necessary, man had starved, notwithstanding the plenty God had given him. We see in commons, which remain so by compact, that 'tis the taking any part of what is common, and removing it out of the state Nature leaves it in, which begins the property, without which the common is of no use. And the taking of this or that part does not depend on the express consent of all the commoners. Thus, the grass my horse has bit, the turfs my servant has cut, and the ore I have digged in any place, where I have a right to them in common with others, become my property without the assignation or consent of any body. The labour that was mine, removing them out of that common state they were in, hath fixed my property in them.

It will perhaps be objected to this, that if gathering the acorns or other fruits of the earth, etc., makes a right to them, then any one may engross as much as he will. To which I answer, Not so. The same law of nature that does by this means give us property, does also bound that property too. *God has given us all things richly,* I *Tim.* vi. 12. Is the voice of reason confirmed by inspiration? But how far has he given it us, *to enjoy?* As much as any one can make use of to any advantage of life before it spoils, so much he may by his labour fix a property in. Whatever is beyond this is more than his share, and belongs to others. Nothing was made by God for man to spoil or destroy. And thus considering the plenty of natural provisions there was a long time in the world, and the few spenders, and to how small a part of that provision the industry of one man could extend itself and engross it to the prejudice of others, especially keeping within the bonds set by reason of what might serve for his use, there could be then little room for quarrels or contentions about property so established.

But the chief matter of property being now not the fruits of the earth and the beasts that subsist on it, but the earth itself, as that which takes in and carries with it all the rest, I think it is plain that property in that too is acquired as the former. As much land as a man tills, plants, improves, cultivates, and can use the product of, so much is his property. He by his labour does, as it were, enclose it from the common. Nor will it invalidate his right to say, Every body else has an equal title to it, and therefore he cannot appropriate, he cannot enclose, without the consent of all his fellow commoners, all mankind. God, when he gave the world

in common to all mankind, commanded man also to labour, and the penury of his condition required it of him. God and his reason commanded him to subdue the earth—*i.e.,* improve it for the benefit of life and therein lay out something upon it that was his own, his labour. He that, in obedience to this command of God, subdued, tilled, and sowed any part of it, thereby annexed to it something that was his property, which another had no title to, nor could without injury take from him.

Nor was this appropriation of any parcel of land, by improving it, any prejudice to any other man, since there was still enough and as good left, and more than the yet unprovided could use. So that, in effect, there was never the less left for others because of his enclosure for himself. For he that leaves as much as another can make use of does as good as take nothing at all. No body could think himself injured by the drinking of another man, though he took a good draught, who had a whole river of the same water left him to quench his thirst. And the case of land and water, where there is enough of both, is perfectly the same.

God gave the world to men in common, but since he gave it them for their benefit and the greatest conveniences of life they were capable to draw from it, it cannot be supposed he meant it should always remain common and uncultivated. He gave it to the use of the industrious and rational (and labour was to be his title to it); not to the fancy or covetousness of the quarrelsome and contentious. He that had as good left for his improvement as was already taken up needed not complain, ought not to meddle with what was already improved by another's labour; if he did 'tis plain he desired the benefit of another's pains, which he had no right to, and not the ground which God had given him, in common with others, to labour on, and whereof there was as good left as that already possessed, and more than he knew what to do with, or his industry could reach to.

Nor is it so strange as perhaps before consideration, it may appear, that the property of labour should be able to overbalance the community of land, for 'tis labour indeed that puts the difference of value on every thing; and let any one consider what the difference is between an acre of land planted with tobacco or sugar, sown with wheat or barley, and an acre of the same land lying in common without any husbandry upon it, and he will find that the improvement of labour makes the far greater part of the value. I think it will be but a very modest computation to say, that of the products of the earth useful to the life of man, nine-tenths are the effects of labour: nay, if we will rightly estimate things as they come to our use, and cast up the several expenses about them, what in them is purely owing to nature and what to labour, we shall find that in most of them ninety-nine hundredths are wholly to be put on the account of labour.

There cannot be a clearer demonstration of any thing than several nations of the Americans are of this, who are rich in land and poor in all the comforts of life; whom nature, having furnished as liberally as any other people with the materials of plenty, *i.e.*, a fruitful soil, apt to produce in abundance what might serve for food, raiment, and delight; yet, for want of improving it by labour, have not one hundredth part of the conveniences we enjoy. And a king of a large and fruitful territory there feeds, lodges, and is clad worse than a day labourer in England.

From all which it is evident, that though the things of nature are given in common, man (by being master of himself, and proprietor of his own person, and the actions or labour of it) had still in himself the great foundation of property; and that which made up the great part of what he applied to the support or comfort of his being, when invention and arts had improved the conveniences of life, was perfectly his own, and did not belong in common to others.

Thus labour, in the beginning, gave a right of property, wherever any one was pleased to employ it, upon what was common, which remained a long while, the far greater part, and is yet more than mankind makes use of. Men at first, for the most part, contented themselves with what unassisted nature offered to their necessities, and though afterwards, in some parts of the world, where the increase of people and stock, with the use of money, had made land scarce, and so of some value, the several communities settled the bounds of their distinct territories, and, by laws, within themselves, regulated the properties of the private men of their society, and so, by compact and agreement, settled the property which labour and industry began; and the leagues that have been made between several states and kingdoms, either expressly or tacitly disowning all claim and right to the land in the other's possession, have, by common consent, given up their pretences to their natural common right, which originally they had to those countries; and so have, by positive agreement, settled a property amongst themselves, in distinct parts of the world; yet there are still great tracts of ground to be found, which the inhabitants thereof, not having joined with the rest of mankind in the consent of the use of their common money, lie waste, and are more than the people who dwell on it, do, or can make use of, and so still lie in common; though this can scarce happen amongst that part of mankind that have consented to the use of money.

The greatest part of things really useful to the life of man, and such as the necessity of subsisting made the first commoners of the world look after, as it doth the Americans now, are generally things of short duration, such as, if they are not consumed by use, will decay and perish of themselves. Gold, silver, and diamonds are things that fancy or agreement hath put the value on, more than real use and the necessary support of life. Now of those good things which nature hath provided in common, every one had a right (as hath been said) to as much as he could use, and had a property in all that he could effect with his labour; all that his industry could extend to, to alter from the state nature had put it in, was his. He that gathered a hundred bushels of acorns or apples had thereby a property in them, they were his goods as soon as gathered. He was only to look that he used them before they spoiled, else he took more than his share, and robbed others. And, indeed, it was a foolish thing, as well as dishonest, to hoard up more than he could make use of. If he gave away a part to any body else, so that it perished not uselessly in his possession, these he also made use of. And if he also bartered away plums that would have rotted in a week, for nuts that would last good for his eating a whole year, he did no injury; he wasted not the common stock; destroyed no part of the portion of goods that belonged to others, so long as nothing perished uselessly in his hands. Again, if he would give his nuts for a piece of metal, pleased with its colour, or exchange his sheep for shells, or wool for a sparkling pebble or a diamond, and keep those by him all his life, he invaded not the right of others; he might heap up as much of these durable things as he pleased; the exceeding of the bounds of his just property not lying in the largeness of his possession, but the perishing of anything uselessly in it.

And thus came in the use of money, some lasting thing that men might keep without spoiling, and that, by mutual consent, men would take in exchange for the truly useful but perishable supports of life.

And as different degrees of industry were apt to give men possessions in different proportions, so this invention of money gave them the opportunity to continue and enlarge them. For supposing an island, separate from all possible commerce with the rest of the world, wherein there were but a hundred families, but there were sheep, horses, and cows, with other useful animals, wholesome fruits, and land enough for corn for a hundred thousand times as many, but nothing in the island, either because of its commonness or perishableness, fit to supply the place of money. What reason could any one have there to enlarge his possessions beyond the use of his family, and a plentiful supply to its consumption, either in what their own industry produced, or they could barter for like perishable, useful commodities with others? Where there is not something both lasting and scarce, and so valuable to be hoarded up, there men will not be apt to enlarge their possessions of land, were it never so rich, never so free for them to take. For I ask, what would a man value ten thousand or an hundred thousand acres of excellent land, ready cultivated and well stocked, too, with cattle, in the middle of the inland parts of America, where he had no hopes of commerce with other parts of the world, to draw money to him by the sale of the product? It would not be worth the enclosing, and we should see him give up again to the wild common of nature whatever was more than would supply the conveniences of life, to be had there for him and his family.

Thus, in the beginning, all the world was America, and more so than that is now; for no such thing as money was any where known. Find out something that hath the use and value of money amongst his neighbours, you shall see the same man will begin presently to enlarge his possessions.

But since gold and silver, being little useful to the life of man, in proportion to food, raiment, and carriage, has its value only from the consent of men, whereof labour yet makes in great part the measure, it is plain that the consent of men have agreed to a disproportionate and unequal possession of the earth, I mean out of the bounds of society and compact; for in governments the laws regulate it, they having, by consent, found out and agreed in a way how a man may rightfully, and without injury, possess more than he himself can make use of by receiving gold and silver, which may continue long in a man's possession without decaying for the overplus, and agreeing those metals should have a value.

## Political Society

Man being born, as has been proved, with a title to perfect freedom and an uncontrolled enjoyment of all the rights and privileges of the law of nature, equally with any other man, or number of men in the world, hath by nature a power not only to preserve his property, that is, his life, liberty, and estate, against the injuries and attempts of other men, but to judge of and punish the breaches of that law in others, as he is persuaded the offence deserves, even with death itself, in crimes where the heinousness of the fact, in his opinion, requires it. But because no political society can be, nor subsist, without having in itself the power to preserve the property, and in order thereunto punish the offences of all those of that society: there, and there only, is political society, where every one of the members hath quitted this natural power, resigned it up into the hands of the community in all cases that exclude him not from appealing for protection to the law established by it. And thus all private judgement of every particular member being excluded, the community comes to be umpire, by settled standing rules; indifferent, and the same to all parties: And by men having authority from the community for the execution of those rules, decides all the differences that may happen between any members of that society concerning any matter of right, and punishes those offences which any member hath committed against the society with such penalties as the law has established; whereby it is easy to discern who are, and who are not, in political society together. Those who are united into one body, and have a common established law and judicature to appeal to, with authority to decide controversies between them and punish offenders, are in civil society one with, another; but those who have no such common appeal, I mean on earth, are still in the state of nature, each being, where there is no other, judge for himself and executioner; which is, as I have before showed it, the perfect state of nature.

And thus the commonwealth comes by a power to set down what punishment shall belong to the several transgressions they think worthy of it, committed amongst the members of that society (which is the power of making laws) as well as it has the power to punish any injury done unto any of its members by anyone that is not of it (which is the power of war and peace); and all this for the preservation of the property of all the members of that society, as far as is possible. But though every man entered into society has quitted his power to punish offences against the law of nature in prosecution of his own private judgement, yet with the judgement of offences which he has given up to the legislative in all cases where he can appeal to the magistrate, he has given up a right to the commonwealth to employ his force for the execution of the judgements of the commonwealth whenever he shall be called to it, which, indeed, are his own judgements, they being made by himself or his representative. And herein we have the original of the legislative and executive power of civil society, which is to judge by standing laws how far offences are to be punished when committed within the commonwealth; and also by occasional judgements founded on the present circumstances of the fact, how far injuries from without are to be vindicated, and in both these to employ all the force of all the members when there shall be need.

Wherever therefore any number of men are so united into one society as to quit every one his executive power of the law of nature, and to resign it to the public, there and there only is a political or civil society. And this is done wherever any number of men, in the state of nature, enter into society to make one people, one body politic under one supreme government: or else when anyone joins himself to and incorporates with any government already made. For hereby he authorizes the society, or which is all one, the legislative thereof, to make laws for him as the public good of the society shall require, to the execution whereof his own assistance (as to his own decrees) is due. And this puts men out of a state of nature into that of a commonwealth, by setting up a judge on earth with authority to determine all the controversies and redress the injuries that

may happen to any member of the commonwealth; which judge is the legislative or magistrates appointed by it. And wherever there are any number of men, however associated, that have no such decisive power to appeal to, there they are still in the state of nature.

And hence it is evident that absolute monarchy, which by some men is counted for the only government in the world, is indeed inconsistent with civil society, and so can be no form of civil government at all. For the end of civil society being to avoid and remedy those inconveniences of the state of nature which necessarily follow from every man's being judge in his own case, by setting up a known authority, to which everyone of that society may appeal upon any injury received, or controversy that may arise, and which everyone of the society ought to obey, wherever any persons are who have not such an authority to appeal to, for the decision of any difference between them there, those persons are still in the state of nature. And so is every absolute prince in respect of those who are under his *dominion*.

For he being supposed to have all, both legislative and executive, power in himself alone, there is no judge to be found, no appeal lies open to anyone, who may fairly and indifferently, and with authority decide, and from whence relief and redress may by expected of any injury or inconveniency that may be suffered from him, or by his order. So that such a man, however entitled, Czar, or Grand Signior, or how you please, is as much in the state of nature, with all under his dominion, as he is with the rest of mankind. For wherever any two men are, who have no standing rule and common judge to appeal to on earth, for the determination of controversies of right betwixt them, there they are still in the state of nature, and under all the inconveniences of it, with only this woeful difference to the subject, or rather slave of an absolute prince. That whereas, in the ordinary state of nature, he has a liberty to judge of his right, and according to the best of his power, to maintain it; but whenever his property is invaded by the will and order of his monarch, he has not only no appeal, as those in society ought to have, but, as if he were degraded from the common state of rational creatures, is denied a liberty to judge of, or defend his right, and so is exposed to all the misery and inconveniences that a man can fear from one, who being in the unrestrained state of nature, is yet corrupted with flattery and armed with power.

## The End of Government

If man in the state of nature be so free as has been said; if he be absolute lord of his own person and possessions; equal to the greatest and subject to no body, why will he part with his freedom? Why will he give up this empire, and subject himself to the dominion and control of any other power? To which 'tis obvious to answer, that though in the state of nature he hath such a right, yet the enjoyment of it is very uncertain and constantly exposed to the invasion of others; for all being kings as much as he, every man his equal, and the greater part no strict observers of equity and justice, the enjoyment of the property he has in this state is very unsafe, very unsecure. This makes him willing to quit this condition which, however free, is full of fears and continual dangers; and 'tis not without reason that he seeks out and is willing to join in society with others who are already united, or have a mind

to unite for the mutual preservation of their lives, liberties, and estates, which I call by the general name, property.

The great and chief end therefore, of men's uniting into commonwealths, and putting themselves under government, is the preservation of their property; to which in the state of nature there are many things wanting.

*First,* There wants an established, settled, known law, received and allowed by common consent to be the standard of right and wrong, and the common measure to decide all controversies between them. For though the law of nature be plain and intelligible to all rational creatures, yet men, being biased by their interest, as well as ignorant for want of study of it, are not apt to allow of it as a law binding to them in the application of it to their particular cases.

*Secondly,* In the state of nature there wants a known and indifferent judge, with authority to determine all differences according to the established law. For everyone in that state being both judge and executioner of the law of nature, men being partial to themselves, passion and revenge is very apt to carry them too far, and with too much heat in their own cases, as well as negligence and unconcernedness, make them too remiss in other men's.

*Thirdly,* In the state of nature there often wants power to back and support the sentence when right, and to give it due execution. They who by any injustice offended, will seldom fail where they are able by force to make good their injustice. Such resistance many times makes the punishment dangerous, and frequently destructive to those who attempt it.

Thus mankind, notwithstanding all the privileges of the state of nature, being but in an ill condition while they remain in it, are quickly driven into society. Hence it comes to pass, that we seldom find any number of men live any time together in this state. The inconveniences that they are therein exposed to by the irregular and uncertain exercise of the power every man has of punishing the transgressions of others, make them take sanctuary under the established laws of government, and therein seek the preservation of their property. 'Tis this makes them so willingly give up every one his single power of punishing to be exercised by such alone as shall be appointed to it amongst them, and by such rules as the community, or those authorized by them to that purpose, shall agree on. And in this we have the original right and rise of both the legislative and executive power as well as of the governments and societies themselves.

## The Limits of Government

The great end of men's entering into society being the enjoyment of their properties in peace and safety, and the great instrument and means of that being the laws established in that society, the first and fundamental positive law of all commonwealths is the establishing of the legislative power; as the first and fundamental natural law, which is to govern even the legislative itself, is the preservation of the society, and (as far as will consist with the public good) of every person in it. This legislative is not only the supreme power of the commonwealth, but sacred and unalterable in the hands where the community have once placed it; nor can any edict of anybody else, in what form soever conceived, or by what power soever backed, have the force and obligation of a law which has not its

sanction from that legislative which the public has chosen and appointed; for without this the law could not have that which is absolutely necessary to its being a law, the consent of the society, over whom nobody can have a power to make laws but by their own consent and by authority received from them; and therefore all the obedience, which by the most solemn ties anyone can be obliged to pay, ultimately terminates in this supreme power, and is directed by those laws which it enacts. Nor can any oaths to any foreign power whatsoever, or any domestic subordinate power, discharge any member of the society from his obedience to the legislative, acting pursuant to their trust, nor oblige him to any obedience contrary to the laws so enacted or farther than they do allow, it being ridiculous to imagine one can be tied ultimately to obey any power in the society which is not the supreme.

Though the legislative, whether placed in one or more, whether it be always in being or only by intervals, though it be the supreme power in every commonwealth, yet.

*First,* It is not, nor can possibly be, absolutely arbitrary over the lives and fortunes of the people. For it being but the joint power of every member of the society given up to that person or assembly which is legislator, it can be no more than those persons had in a state of nature before they entered into society, and gave it up to the community. For nobody can transfer to another more power than he has in himself, and nobody has an absolute arbitrary power over himself, or over any other, to destroy his own life, or take away the life or property of another. A man, as has been proved, cannot subject himself to the arbitrary power of another; and having, in the state of nature, no arbitrary power over the life, liberty, or possession of another, but only so much as the law of nature gave him for the preservation of himself and the rest of mankind, this is all he doth, or can give up to the commonwealth, and by it to the legislative power, so that the legislative can have no more than this. Their power in the utmost bounds of it is limited to the public good of the society. It is a power that hath no other end but preservation, and therefore can never have a right to destroy, enslave, or designedly to impoverish the subjects; the obligations of the law of nature cease not in society, but only in many cases are drawn closer, and have, by human laws, known penalties annexed to them to enforce their observation. Thus the law of nature stands as an eternal rule to all men, legislators as well as others. The rules that they make for other men's actions must, as well as their own and other men's actions, be conformable to the law of nature, *i.e.*, to the will of God, of which that is a declaration, and the fundamental law of nature being the preservation of mankind, no human sanction can be good or valid against it.

*Secondly,* The legislative or supreme authority cannot assume to itself a power to rule by extemporary arbitrary decrees, but is bound to dispense justice and decide the rights of the subject by promulgated standing laws, and known authorized judges. For the law of nature being unwritten, and so nowhere to be found but in the minds of men, they who, through passion or interest, shall miscite or misapply it, cannot so easily be convinced of their mistake where there is no established judge; and so it serves not as it ought, to determine the rights and fence the properties of those that live under it, especially where everyone is judge, interpreter, and executioner of it too, and that in his own case; and he that has right on his side, having ordinarily but his own single strength, hath not force enough to defend himself from injuries or to punish delinquents. To avoid these inconveniencies which disorder men's properties in the state of nature, men unite into societies that they may have the united strength of the whole society to secure and defend their properties, and may have standing rules to bound it by which everyone may know what is his. To this end it is that men give up all their natural power to the society they enter into, and the community put the legislative power into such hands as they think fit, with this trust, that they shall be governed by declared laws, or else their peace, quiet, and property will still be at the same uncertainty as it was in the state of nature.

Absolute arbitrary power, or governing without settled standing laws, can neither of them consist with the ends of society and government, which men would not quit the freedom of the state of nature for, and tie themselves up under, were it not to preserve their lives, liberties, and fortunes, and by stated rules of right and property to secure their peace and quiet. It cannot be supposed that they should intend, had they a power so to do, to give to any one or more an absolute arbitrary power over their persons and estates, and put a force into the magistrate's hand to execute his unlimited will arbitrarily upon them; this were to put themselves into a worse condition than the state of nature, wherein they had a liberty to defend their right against the injuries of others, and were upon equal terms of force to maintain it, whether invaded by a single man or many in combination. Whereas by supposing they have given up themselves to the absolute arbitrary power and will of a legislator, they have disarmed themselves, and armed him to make a prey of them when he pleases; he being in a much worse condition that is exposed to the arbitrary power of one man who has the command of a hundred thousand than he that is exposed to the arbitrary power of a hundred thousand single men, nobody being secure, that his will who has such a command is better than that of other men, though his force be a hundred thousand times stronger. And, therefore, whatever form the commonwealth is under, the ruling power ought to govern by declared and received laws, and not by extemporary dictates and undetermined resolutions, for then mankind will be in a far worse condition than in the state of nature if they shall have armed one or a few men with the joint power of a multitude, to force them to obey at pleasure the exorbitant and unlimited decrees of their sudden thoughts, or unrestrained, and till that moment, unknown wills, without having any measures set down which may guide and justify their actions. For all the power the government has, being only for the good of the society, as it ought not to be arbitrary and at pleasure, so it ought to be exercised by established and promulgated laws, that both the people may know their duty, and be safe and secure within the limits of the law, and the rulers, too, kept within their due bounds, and not to be tempted by the power they have in their hands to employ it to purposes, and by such measures as they would not have known, and own not willingly.

*Thirdly,* The supreme power cannot take from any man any part of his property without his own consent. For the preservation of property being the end of government, and that for which men enter into society, it necessarily supposes and requires that the people should have property, without which they must be supposed to lose that by entering into society which was the end for which they entered into it; too gross an absurdity for any man to own. Men therefore in society having property, they have such a right to the goods, which by the

law of the community are theirs, that nobody hath a right to their substance, or any part of it, from them without their own consent; without this they have no property at all. For I have truly no property in that which another can by right take from me when he pleases against my consent. Hence it is a mistake to think that the supreme or legislative power of any commonwealth can do what it will, and dispose of the estates of the subject arbitrarily, or take any part of them at pleasure. This is not much to be feared in governments where the legislative consists wholly or in part in assemblies which are variable, whose members upon the dissolution of the assembly are subjects under the common laws of their country, equally with the rest. But in governments where the legislative is in one lasting assembly, always in being, or in one man as in absolute monarchies, there is danger still, that they will think themselves to have a distinct interest from the rest of the community, and so will be apt to increase their own riches and power by taking what they think fit from the people. For a man's property is not at all secure, though there be good and equitable laws to set the bounds of it between him and his fellow-subjects, if he who commands those subjects have power to take from any private man what part he pleases of his property, and use and dispose of it as he thinks good.

But government, into whatsoever hands it is put, being as I have before showed, entrusted with this condition, and for this end, that men might have and secure their properties, the prince or senate, however it may have power to make laws for the regulating of property between the subjects one amongst another, yet can never have a power to take to themselves the whole, or any part of the subjects' property, without their own consent; for this would be in effect to leave them no property at all. And to let us see that even absolute power, where it is necessary, is not arbitrary by being absolute, but is still limited by that reason, and confined to those ends which required it in some cases to be absolute, we need look no farther than the common practice of martial discipline. For the preservation of the army, and in it of the whole commonwealth, requires an absolute obedience to the command of every superior officer, and it is justly death to disobey or dispute the most dangerous or unreasonable of them; but yet we see that neither the sergeant that could command a soldier to march up to the mouth of a cannon, or stand in a breach where he is almost sure to perish, can command that soldier to give him one penny of his money; nor the general that can condemn him to death for deserting his post, or not obeying the most desperate orders, cannot yet with all his absolute power of life and death dispose of one farthing of that soldier's estate, or seize one jot of his goods; whom yet be can command anything, and hang for the least disobedience. Because such a blind obedience is necessary to that end for which the commander has his power, *viz.* the preservation of the rest, but the disposing of his goods has nothing to do with it.

'Tis true, governments cannot be supported without great charge, and 'tis fit everyone who enjoys his share of the protection should pay out of his estate his proportion for the maintenance of it. But still it must be with his own consent, *i.e.,* the consent of the majority, giving it either by themselves or their representatives chosen by them; for if anyone shall claim a power to lay and levy taxes on the people by his own authority, and without such consent of the people, he thereby invades the fundamental law of property, and subverts the end of government. For what property have I

in that which another may by right take when he pleases himself?

*Fourthly,* The legislative cannot transfer the power of making laws to any other hands, for it being but a delegated power from the people, they who have it cannot pass it over to others. The people alone can appoint the form of the commonwealth, which is by constituting the legislative, and appointing in whose hands that shall be. And when the people have said, We will submit, and be governed by laws made by such men, and in such forms, nobody else can say other men shall make laws for them; nor can they be bound by any laws but such as are enacted by those whom they have chosen and authorized to make laws for them. The power of the legislative being derived from the people by a positive voluntary grant and institution, can be no other than what that positive grant conveyed, which being only to make laws, and not to make legislators, the legislative can have no power to transfer their authority of making laws, and place it in other hands.

These are the bounds which the trust that is put in them by the society and the law of God and nature have set to the legislative power of every commonwealth, in all forms of government.

*First,* They are to govern by promulgated established laws, not to be varied in particular cases, but to have one rule for rich and poor, for the favourite at Court, and the countryman at plough.

*Secondly,* These laws also ought to be designed for no other end ultimately but the good of the people.

*Thirdly,* They must not raise taxes on the property of the people without the consent of the people given by themselves or their deputies. And this properly concerns only such governments where the legislative is always in being, or at least where the people have not reserved any part of the legislative to deputies, to be from time to time chosen by themselves.

*Fourthly,* The legislative neither must nor can transfer the power of making laws to anybody else, or place it anywhere but where the people have.

## The Right to Rebel

The reason why men enter into society is the preservation of their property; and the end why they choose and authorize a legislative is that there may be laws made, and rules set, as guards and fences to the properties of all the members of the society, to limit the power and moderate the dominion of every part and member of the society. For since it can never be supposed to be the will of the society that the legislative should have a power to destroy that which every one designs to, secure by entering into society, and for which the people submitted themselves to legislators of their own making: whenever the legislators endeavour to take away and destroy the property of the people, or to reduce them to slavery under arbitrary power, they put themselves into a state of war with the people, who are thereupon absolved from any farther obedience, and are left to the common refuge which God hath provided for all men against force and violence. Whensoever therefore the legislative shall transgress this fundamental rule of society, and either by ambition, fear, folly, or corruption, endeavour to grasp themselves, or put into the hands of any other, an absolute power over the lives, liberties, and estates of the people, by this breach of trust they forfeit the power the people had put into their hands for quite contrary ends, and it devolves to the people; who have a right to resume their original liberty, and by the establishment of a new legislative (such as they shall think fit), provide for their own safety and security, which is the end for which they are in society. What I have said here concerning the legislative in general holds true also concerning the supreme executor, who having a double trust put in him, both to have a part in the legislative and the supreme execution of the law, acts against both, when he goes about to set up his own arbitrary will as the law of the society. He acts also contrary to his trust when he employs the force, treasure, and offices of the society to corrupt the representatives and gain them to his purposes, when he openly pre-engages the electors, and prescribes, to their choice, such whom he has, by solicitations, threats, promises, or otherwise, won to his designs, and employs them to bring in such who have promised beforehand what to vote and what to enact. Thus to regulate candidates and electors, and new model the ways of election, what is it but to cut up the government by the roots, and poison the very fountain of public security? For the people having reserved to themselves the choice of their representatives as the fence to their properties, could do it for no other end but that they might always be freely chosen, and so chosen, freely act and advise as the necessity of the commonwealth and the public good should, upon examination and mature debate, be judged to require. This, those who give their votes before they hear the debate, and have weighed the reasons on all sides, are not capable of doing. To prepare such an assembly as this, and endeavour to set up the declared abettors of his own will, for the true representatives of the people, and the law-makers of the society, is certainly as great a breach of trust, and as perfect a declaration of a design to subvert the government, as is possible to be met with. To which, if one shall add rewards and punishments visibly employed to the same end, and all the arts of perverted law made use of to take off and destroy all that stand in the way of such a design, and will not comply and consent to betray the liberties of their country, 'twill be past doubt what is doing. What power they ought to have in the society who thus employ it contrary to the trust went along with it in its first institution, is easy to determine; and one cannot but see that he who has once attempted any such thing as this cannot any longer be trusted.

To this, perhaps, it will be said, that the people being ignorant and always discontented, to lay the foundation of government in the unsteady opinion and uncertain humour of the people, is to expose it to certain ruin; and no government will be able long to subsist if the people may set up a new legislative whenever they take offence at the old one. To this I answer, quite the contrary. People are not so easily got out of their old forms as some are apt to suggest. They are hardly to be prevailed with to amend the acknowledged faults in the frame they have been accustomed to. And if there be any original defects, or adventitious ones introduced by time or corruption, 'tis not an easy thing to get them changed, even when all the world sees there is an opportunity for it. This slowness and aversion in the people to quit their old constitutions has in the many revolutions [that] have been seen in this kingdom, in this and former ages, still kept us to, or after some interval of fruitless attempts, still brought us back again to our old legislative king, lords and commons; and whatever provocations have made the crown be taken from some of our princes' heads,

they never carried the people so far as to place it in another line.

But 'twill be said, this hypothesis lays a ferment for frequent rebellion. To which I answer:

*First,* No more than any other hypothesis. For when the people are made miserable, and find themselves exposed to the ill usage of arbitrary power; cry up their governors as much as you will for sons of *Jupiter,* let them be sacred and divine, descended or authorized from Heaven; give them out for whom or what you please, the same will happen. The people generally ill treated, and contrary to right, will be ready upon any occasion to ease themselves of a burden that sits heavy upon them. They will wish and seek for the opportunity, which in the change, weakness, and accidents of human affairs, seldom delays long to offer itself. He must have lived but a little while in the world, who has not seen examples of this in his time; and he must have read very little who cannot produce examples of it in all sorts of governments in the world.

*Secondly,* I answer, such revolutions happen not upon every little mismanagement in public affairs. Great mistakes in the ruling part, many wrong and inconvenient laws, and all the slips of human frailty will be borne by the people without mutiny or murmur. But if a long train of abuses, prevarications, and artifices, all tending the same way, make the design visible to the people, and they cannot but feel what they lie under, and see whither they are going, 'tis not to be wondered that they should then rouse themselves, and endeavour to put the rule into such hands which may secure to them the ends for which government was at first erected, and without which, ancient names and specious forms are so far from being better, that they are much worse than the state of nature or pure anarchy; the inconveniencies being all as great and as near, but the remedy farther off and more difficult.

*Thirdly,* I answer, That this power in the people of providing for their safety anew by a new legislative when their legislators have acted contrary to their trust by invading their property, is the best fence against rebellion, and the probablest means to hinder it. For rebellion being an opposition, not to persons, but authority, which is founded only in the constitutions and laws of the government; those, whoever they be, who by force break through, and by force justify their violation of them, are truly and properly rebels. For when men, by entering into society and civil government, have excluded force, and introduced laws for the preservation of property, peace, and unity amongst themselves; those who set up force again in opposition to the laws, do *rebellare*—that is, bring back again the state of war, and are properly rebels, which they who are in power, by the pretence they have to authority, the temptation of force they have in their hands, and the flattery of those about them being likeliest to do, the properest way to prevent the evil is to show them the danger and injustice of it who are under the greatest temptation to run into it.

In both the forementioned cases, when either the legislative is changed, or the legislators act contrary to the end for which they were constituted, those who are guilty are guilty of rebellion. For if any one by force takes away the established legislative of any society, and the laws by them made, pursuant to their trust, he thereby takes away the umpirage which every one had consented to for a peaceable decision of all their controversies, and a bar to the state of war amongst them. They who remove or change the legislative take away this decisive power, which no body can have but by the appointment and consent of the people; and so destroying the authority which the people did, and no body else can set up, and introducing a power which the people hath not authorized, actually introduce a state of war, which is that of force without authority; and thus by removing the legislative established by the society, in whose decisions the people acquiesced and united as to that of their own will, they untie the knot, and expose the people anew to the state of war. And if those, who by force take away the legislative, are rebels, the legislators themselves, as has been shown, can be no less esteemed so, when they who were set up for the protection and preservation of the people, their liberties and properties shall by force invade and endeavour to take them away; and so they putting themselves into a state of war with those who made them the protectors and guardians of their peace, are properly, and with the greatest aggravation, *rebellantes*, rebels.

But if they who say it lays a foundation for rebellion mean that it may occasion civil wars or intestine broils to tell the people they are absolved from obedience when illegal attempts are made upon their liberties or properties, and may oppose the unlawful violence of those who were their magistrates when they invade their properties, contrary to the trust put in them; and that, therefore, this doctrine is not to be allowed, being so destructive to the peace of the world; they may as well say, upon the same ground, that honest men may not oppose robbers or pirates, because this may occasion disorder or bloodshed. If any mischief come in such cases, it is not to be charged upon him who defends his own right, but on him that invades his neighbour's. If the innocent honest man must quietly quit all he has for peace sake to him who will lay violent hands upon it, I desire it may be considered what a kind of peace there will be in the world which consists only in violence and rapine, and which is to be maintained only for the benefit of robbers and oppressors. Who would not think it an admirable peace betwixt the mighty and the mean, when the lamb, without resistance, yielded his throat to be torn by the imperious wolf? *Polyphemus's* den gives us a perfect pattern of such a peace. Such a government wherein *Ulysses* and his companions had nothing to do but quietly to suffer themselves to be devoured. And no doubt, *Ulysses*, who was a prudent man, preached up passive obedience, and exhorted them to a quiet submission by representing to them of what concernment peace was to mankind, and by showing the inconveniences might happen if they should offer to resist *Polyphemus*, who had now the power over them.

The end of government is the good of mankind; and which is best for mankind, that the people should be always exposed to the boundless will of tyranny, or that the rulers should be sometimes liable to be opposed when they grow exorbitant in the use of their power, and employ it for the destruction, and not the preservation, of the properties of their people?

Nor let any one say that mischief can arise from hence as often as it shall please a busy head or turbulent spirit to desire the alteration of the government. 'Tis true such men may stir whenever they please, but it will be only to their own just ruin and perdition. For till the mischief be grown general, and the ill designs of the rulers become visible, or their attempts sensible to the greater part, the people, who are more disposed to suffer than right themselves by resistance, are not apt to stir. The examples of particular injustice or oppression of here and there an unfortunate man moves them not. But if they universally have a persuasion grounded upon manifest evidence that designs are carrying on against their liberties, and the general course and tendency of things cannot but give them strong suspicions of the evil intention of their governors, who is to be blamed for it? Who can help it if they, who might avoid it, bring themselves into this suspicion? Are the people to be blamed if they have the sense of rational creatures, and can think of things no otherwise than as they find and feel them? And is it not rather their fault who put things in such a posture that they would not have them thought as they are? I grant that the pride, ambition, and turbulency of private men have sometimes caused great disorders in commonwealths, and factions have been fatal to states and kingdoms. But whether the mischief has oftener begun in the people's wantonness, and a desire to cast off the lawful authority of their rulers, or in the rulers' insolence and endeavours to get and exercise an arbitrary power over their people, whether oppression or disobedience gave the first rise to the disorder, I leave it to impartial history to determine. This I am sure, whoever, either ruler or subject, by force goes about to invade the rights of either prince 'or people, and lays the foundation for overturning the constitution and frame of any just government, he is guilty of the greatest crime I think a man is capable of, being to answer for all those mischiefs of blood, rapine, and desolation, which the breaking to pieces of governments bring on a country; and he who does it is justly to be esteemed the common enemy and pest of mankind, and is to be treated accordingly.

That subjects or foreigners attempting by force on the properties of any people may be resisted with force is agreed on all hands; but that magistrates doing the same thing may be resisted, has of late been denied; as if those who had the greatest privileges and advantages by the law had thereby a power to break those laws by which alone they were set in a better place than their brethren; whereas their offence is thereby the greater, both as being ungrateful for the greater share they have by the law, and breaking also that trust which is put into their hands by their brethren.

Whosoever uses force without right, as every one does in society who does it without law, puts himself into a state of war with those against whom he so uses it, and in that state all former ties are cancelled, all other rights cease, and every one has a right to defend himself, and to resist the aggressor.

Here 'tis like the common question will be made, Who shall be judge whether the prince or legislative act contrary to their trust? This, perhaps, ill-affected and factious men may spread amongst the people, when the prince only makes use of his due prerogative. To this I reply, The people shall be judge; for who shall be judge whether his trustee or deputy acts well and according to the trust reposed in him, but he who deputes him and must, by having deputed him, have still a power to discard him when he fails in his trust? If this be reasonable in particular cases of private men, why should it be otherwise in that of the greatest moment, where the welfare of millions is concerned and also where the evil, if not prevented, is greater, and the redress very difficult, dear, and dangerous?

But, farther, this question, (Who shall be judge?) cannot mean that there is no judge at all. For where there is no judicature on earth to decide controversies amongst men, God in Heaven is judge. He alone, 'tis true, is judge of the right. But every man is judge for himself, as in all other cases so in this, whether another hath put himself into a state of war with him,

and whether he should appeal to the supreme Judge, as *Jephtha* did.

If a controversy arise betwixt a prince and some of the people in a matter where the law is silent or doubtful, and the thing be of great consequence, I should think the proper umpire, in such a case, should be the body of the people. For in such cases where the prince hath a trust reposed in him, and is dispensed from the common, ordinary rules of the law; there, if any men find themselves aggrieved, and think the prince acts contrary to, or beyond that trust, who so proper to judge as the body of the people (who at first lodged that trust in him) how far they meant it should extend? But if the prince, or whoever they be in the administration, decline that way of determination, the appeal then lies nowhere but to Heaven. Force between either persons, who have no known superior on earth, or which permits no appeal to a judge on earth, being properly a state of war, wherein the appeal lies only to Heaven; and in that state the injured party must judge for himself when he will think fit to make use of that appeal and put himself upon it.

To conclude, The power that every individual gave the society when he entered into it, can never revert to the individuals again, as long as the society lasts, but will always remain in the community; because without this there can be no community, no commonwealth, which is contrary to the original agreement; so also when the society hath placed the legislative in any assembly of men, to continue in them and their successors, with direction and authority for providing such successors, the legislative can never revert to the people whilst that government lasts; because, having provided a legislative with power to continue for ever, they have given up their political power to the legislative, and cannot resume it. But if they have set limits to the duration of their legislative, and made this supreme power in any person or assembly only temporary; or else when, by the miscarriages of those in authority, it is forfeited; upon the forfeiture of their rulers or at the determination of the time set, it reverts to the society, and the people have a right to act as supreme, and continue the legislative in themselves or place it in a new form, or new hands, as they think good.

# Federalist Papers, #9

### By Alexander Hamilton

## The Union as a Safeguard Against Domestic Faction and Insurrection

*For the Independent Journal.*

To the People of the State of New York:

A firm Union will be of the utmost moment to the peace and liberty of the States, as a barrier against domestic faction and insurrection. It is impossible to read the history of the petty republics of Greece and Italy without feeling sensations of horror and disgust at the distractions with which they were continually agitated, and at the rapid succession of revolutions by which they were kept in a state of perpetual vibration between the extremes of tyranny and anarchy. If they exhibit occasional calms, these only serve as short-lived contrast to the furious storms that are to succeed. If now and then intervals of felicity open to view, we behold them with a mixture of regret, arising from the reflection that the pleasing scenes before us are soon to be overwhelmed by the tempestuous waves of sedition and party rage. If momentary rays of glory break forth from the gloom, while they dazzle us with a transient and fleeting brilliancy, they at the same time admonish us to lament that the vices of government should pervert the direction and tarnish the lustre of those bright talents and exalted endowments for which the favored soils that produced them have been so justly celebrated.

From the disorders that disfigure the annals of those republics the advocates of despotism have drawn arguments, not only against the forms of republican government, but against the very principles of civil liberty. They have decried all free government as inconsistent with the order of society, and have indulged themselves in malicious exultation over its friends and partisans. Happily for mankind, stupendous fabrics reared on the basis of liberty, which have flourished for ages, have, in a few glorious instances, refuted their gloomy sophisms. And, I trust, America will be the broad and solid foundation of other edifices, not less magnificent, which will be equally permanent monuments of their errors.

But it is not to be denied that the portraits they have sketched of republican government were too just copies of the originals from which they were taken. If it had been found impracticable to have devised models of a more perfect structure, the enlightened friends to liberty would have been obliged to abandon the cause of that species of government as indefensible. The science of politics, however, like most other sciences, has received great improvement. The efficacy of various principles is now well understood, which were either not known at all, or imperfectly known to the ancients. The regular distribution of power into distinct departments; the introduction of legislative balances and checks; the institution of courts composed of judges holding their offices during good behavior; the representation of the people in the legislature by deputies of their own election: these are wholly new discoveries, or have made their principal progress towards perfection in modern times. They are means, and powerful means, by which the excellences of republican government may be retained and its imperfections lessened or avoided. To this catalogue of circumstances that tend to the amelioration of popular systems of civil government, I shall venture, however novel it may appear to some, to add one more, on a principle which has been made the foundation of an objection to the new Constitution; I mean the ENLARGEMENT of the ORBIT within which such systems are to revolve, either in respect to the dimensions of a single State or to the consolidation of several smaller States into one great Confederacy. The latter is that which immediately concerns the object under consideration. It will, however, be of use to examine the principle in its application to a single State, which shall be attended to in another place.

The utility of a Confederacy, as well to suppress faction and to guard the internal tranquillity of States, as to increase their external force and security, is in reality not a new idea. It has been practiced upon in different countries and ages, and has received the sanction of the most approved writers on the subject of politics. The opponents of the plan proposed have, with great assiduity, cited and circulated the observations of Montesquieu on the necessity of a contracted territory for a republican government. But they seem not to have been apprised of the sentiments of that great man expressed in another part of his work, nor to have adverted to the consequences of the principle to which they subscribe with such ready acquiescence.

When Montesquieu recommends a small extent for republics, the standards he had in view were of dimensions far short of the limits of almost every one of these States. Neither Virginia, Massachusetts, Pennsylvania, New York, North Carolina, nor Georgia can by any means be compared with the models from which he reasoned and to which the terms of his description apply. If we therefore take his ideas on this point as the criterion of truth, we shall be driven to the alternative either of taking refuge at once in the arms of monarchy, or of splitting ourselves into an infinity of little, jealous, clashing, tumultuous commonwealths, the wretched nurseries of unceasing discord, and the miserable objects of universal pity or contempt. Some of the writers who have come forward on the other side of the question seem to have been aware of the dilemma; and have even been bold enough to hint at the division of the larger States as a desirable thing. Such an infatuated policy, such a desperate expedient, might, by the multiplication of petty offices, answer the views of men who possess not qualifications to extend their influence beyond the narrow circles of personal intrigue, but it could never promote the greatness or happiness of the people of America.

Referring the examination of the principle itself to another place, as has been already mentioned, it will be sufficient to remark here that, in the sense of the author who has been most emphatically quoted upon the occasion, it would only dictate a reduction of the SIZE of the more considerable MEMBERS of the Union, but would not militate against their being all comprehended in one confederate government. And this is the true question, in the discussion of which we are at present interested.

So far are the suggestions of Montesquieu from standing in opposition to a general Union of the States, that he explicitly treats of a CONFEDERATE REPUBLIC as the expedient for extending the sphere of popular government, and reconciling the advantages of monarchy with those of republicanism. "It is very probable," (says he1) "that mankind would have been obliged at length to live constantly under the government of a single person, had they not contrived a kind of constitution that has all the internal advantages of a republican, together with the external force of a monarchical government. I mean a CONFEDERATE REPUBLIC.

"This form of government is a convention by which several smaller STATES agree to become members of a larger ONE, which they intend to form. It is a kind of assemblage of societies that constitute a new one, capable of increasing, by means of new associations, till they arrive to such a degree of power as to be able to provide for the security of the united body.

"A republic of this kind, able to withstand an external force, may support itself without any internal corruptions. The form of this society prevents all manner of inconveniences.

"If a single member should attempt to usurp the supreme authority, he could not be supposed to have an equal authority and credit in all the confederate states. Were he to have too great influence over one, this would alarm the rest. Were he to subdue a part, that which would still remain free might oppose him with forces independent of those which he had usurped and overpower him before he could be settled in his usurpation.

"Should a popular insurrection happen in one of the confederate states the others are able to quell it. Should abuses creep into one part, they are reformed by those that remain sound. The state may be destroyed on one side, and not on the other; the confederacy may be dissolved, and the confederates preserve their sovereignty.

"As this government is composed of small republics, it enjoys the internal happiness of each; and with respect to its external situation, it is possessed, by means of the association, of all the advantages of large monarchies."

I have thought it proper to quote at length these interesting passages, because they contain a luminous abridgment of the principal arguments in favor of the Union, and must effectually remove the false impressions which a misapplication of other parts of the work was calculated to make. They have, at the same time, an intimate connection with the more immediate design of this paper; which is, to illustrate the tendency of the Union to repress domestic faction and insurrection.

A distinction, more subtle than accurate, has been raised between a CONFEDERACY and a CONSOLIDATION of the States. The essential characteristic of the first is said to be, the restriction of its authority to the members in their collective capacities, without reaching to the individuals of whom they are composed. It is contended that the national council ought to have no concern with any object of internal administration. An exact equality of suffrage between the members has also been insisted upon as a leading feature of a confederate government. These positions are, in the main, arbitrary; they are supported neither by principle nor precedent. It has indeed happened, that governments of this kind have generally operated in the manner which the distinction taken notice of, supposes to be inherent in their nature; but there have been in most of them extensive exceptions to the practice, which serve to prove, as far as example will go, that there is no absolute rule on the subject. And it will be clearly shown in the course of this investigation that as far as the principle contended for has prevailed, it has been the cause of incurable disorder and imbecility in the government.

The definition of a CONFEDERATE REPUBLIC seems simply to be "an assemblage of societies," or an association of two or more states into one state. The extent, modifications, and objects of the federal authority are mere matters of discretion. So long as the separate organization of the members be not abolished; so long as it exists, by a constitutional necessity, for local purposes; though it should be in perfect subordination to the general authority of the union, it would still be, in fact and in theory, an association of states, or a confederacy. The proposed Constitution, so far from implying an abolition of the State governments, makes them constituent parts of the national sovereignty, by allowing them a direct representation in the Senate, and leaves in their possession certain exclusive and very important portions of sovereign power. This fully corresponds, in every rational import of the terms, with the idea of a federal government.

In the Lycian confederacy, which consisted of twenty-three CITIES or republics, the largest were entitled to THREE votes in the COMMON COUNCIL, those of the middle class to TWO, and the smallest to ONE. The COMMON COUNCIL had the appointment of all the judges and magistrates of the respective CITIES. This was certainly the most, delicate species of interference in their internal administration; for if there be any thing that seems exclusively appropriated to the local jurisdictions, it is the appointment of their own officers. Yet Montesquieu, speaking of this association, says: "Were I to give a model of an excellent Confederate Republic, it would be that of Lycia." Thus we perceive that the distinctions insisted upon were not within the contemplation of this enlightened civilian; and we shall be led to conclude, that they are the novel refinements of an erroneous theory.

**PUBLIUS.**

1.  "Spirit of Lawa," vol. I., book IX., chap. I.

# Federalist Papers, #10

By James Madison

## The Same Subject Continued (The Union as a Safeguard Against Domestic Faction and Insurrection)

*From the New York Packet.*
*Friday, November 23, 1787.*

To the People of the State of New York:
Among the numerous advantages promised by a well-constructed Union, none deserves to be more accurately developed than its tendency to break and control the violence of faction. The friend of popular governments never finds himself so much alarmed for their character and fate, as when he contemplates their propensity to this dangerous vice. He will not fail, therefore, to set a due value on any plan which, without violating the principles to which he is attached, provides a proper cure for it. The instability, injustice, and confusion introduced into the public councils, have, in truth, been the mortal diseases under which popular governments have everywhere perished; as they continue to be the favorite and fruitful topics from which the adversaries to liberty derive their most specious declamations. The valuable improvements made by the American constitutions on the popular models, both ancient and modern, cannot certainly be too much admired; but it would be an unwarrantable partiality, to contend that they have as effectually obviated the danger on this side, as was wished and expected. Complaints are everywhere heard from our most considerate and virtuous citizens, equally the friends of public and private faith, and of public and personal liberty, that our governments are too unstable, that the public good is disregarded in the conflicts of rival parties, and that measures are too often decided, not according to the rules of justice and the rights of the minor party, but by the superior force of an interested and overbearing majority. However anxiously we may wish that these complaints had no foundation, the evidence, of known facts will not permit us to deny that they are in some degree true. It will be found, indeed, on a candid review of our situation, that some of the distresses under which we labor have been erroneously charged on the operation of our governments; but it will be found, at the same time, that other causes will not alone account for many of our heaviest misfortunes; and, particularly,

for that prevailing and increasing distrust of public engagements, and alarm for private rights, which are echoed from one end of the continent to the other. These must be chiefly, if not wholly, effects of the unsteadiness and injustice with which a factious spirit has tainted our public administrations.

By a faction, I understand a number of citizens, whether amounting to a majority or a minority of the whole, who are united and actuated by some common impulse of passion, or of interest, adversed to the rights of other citizens, or to the permanent and aggregate interests of the community.

There are two methods of curing the mischiefs of faction: the one, by removing its causes; the other, by controlling its effects.

There are again two methods of removing the causes of faction: the one, by destroying the liberty which is essential to its existence; the other, by giving to every citizen the same opinions, the same passions, and the same interests.

It could never be more truly said than of the first remedy, that it was worse than the disease. Liberty is to faction what air is to fire, an aliment without which it instantly expires. But it could not be less folly to abolish liberty, which is essential to political life, because it nourishes faction, than it would be to wish the annihilation of air, which is essential to animal life, because it imparts to fire its destructive agency.

The second expedient is as impracticable as the first would be unwise. As long as the reason of man continues fallible, and he is at liberty to exercise it, different opinions will be formed. As long as the connection subsists between his reason and his self-love, his opinions and his passions will have a reciprocal influence on each other; and the former will be objects to which the latter will attach themselves. The diversity in the faculties of men, from which the rights of property originate, is not less an insuperable obstacle to a uniformity of interests. The protection of these faculties is the first object of government. From the protection of different and unequal faculties of acquiring property, the possession of different degrees and kinds of property immediately results; and from the influence of these on the sentiments and views of the respective proprietors, ensues a division of the society into different interests and parties.

The latent causes of faction are thus sown in the nature of man; and we see them everywhere brought into different degrees of activity, according to the different circumstances of civil society. A zeal for different opinions concerning religion, concerning government, and many other points, as well of speculation as of practice; an attachment to different leaders ambitiously contending for pre-eminence and power; or to persons of other descriptions whose fortunes have been interesting to the human passions, have, in turn, divided mankind into parties, inflamed them with mutual animosity, and rendered them much more disposed to vex and oppress each other than to co-operate for their common good. So strong is this propensity of mankind to fall into mutual animosities, that where no substantial occasion presents itself, the most frivolous and fanciful distinctions have been sufficient to kindle their unfriendly passions and excite their most violent conflicts. But the most common and durable source of factions has been the various and unequal distribution of property. Those who hold and those who are without property have ever formed distinct interests in society. Those who are creditors, and those who are debtors, fall under a like discrimination. A landed interest, a manufacturing interest, a mercantile interest, a moneyed interest, with many lesser interests, grow up of necessity in civilized nations, and divide them into different classes, actuated by different sentiments and views. The regulation of these various and interfering interests forms the principal task of modern legislation, and involves the spirit of party and faction in the necessary and ordinary operations of the government.

No man is allowed to be a judge in his own cause, because his interest would certainly bias his judgment, and, not improbably, corrupt his integrity. With equal, nay with greater reason, a body of men are unfit to be both judges and parties at the same time; yet what are many of the most important acts of legislation, but so many judicial determinations, not indeed concerning the rights of single persons, but concerning the rights of large bodies of citizens? And what are the different classes of legislators but advocates and parties to the causes which they determine? Is a law proposed concerning private debts? It is a question to which the creditors are parties on one side and the debtors on the other. Justice ought to hold the balance between them. Yet the parties are, and must be, themselves the judges; and the most numerous party, or, in other words, the most powerful faction must be expected to prevail. Shall domestic manufactures be encouraged, and in what degree, by restrictions on foreign manufactures? are questions which would be differently decided by the landed and the manufacturing classes, and probably by neither with a sole regard to justice and the public good. The apportionment of taxes on the various descriptions of property is an act which seems to require the most exact impartiality; yet there is, perhaps, no legislative act in which greater opportunity and temptation are given to a predominant party to trample on the rules of justice. Every

shilling with which they overburden the inferior number, is a shilling saved to their own pockets.

It is in vain to say that enlightened statesmen will be able to adjust these clashing interests, and render them all subservient to the public good. Enlightened statesmen will not always be at the helm. Nor, in many cases, can such an adjustment be made at all without taking into view indirect and remote considerations, which will rarely prevail over the immediate interest which one party may find in disregarding the rights of another or the good of the whole.

The inference to which we are brought is, that the CAUSES of faction cannot be removed, and that relief is only to be sought in the means of controlling its EFFECTS.

If a faction consists of less than a majority, relief is supplied by the republican principle, which enables the majority to defeat its sinister views by regular vote. It may clog the administration, it may convulse the society; but it will be unable to execute and mask its violence under the forms of the Constitution. When a majority is included in a faction, the form of popular government, on the other hand, enables it to sacrifice to its ruling passion or interest both the public good and the rights of other citizens. To secure the public good and private rights against the danger of such a faction, and at the same time to preserve the spirit and the form of popular government, is then the great object to which our inquiries are directed. Let me add that it is the great desideratum by which this form of government can be rescued from the opprobrium under which it has so long labored, and be recommended to the esteem and adoption of mankind.

By what means is this object attainable? Evidently by one of two only. Either the existence of the same passion or interest in a majority at the same time must be prevented, or the majority, having such coexistent passion or interest, must be rendered, by their number and local situation, unable to concert and carry into effect schemes of oppression. If the impulse and the opportunity be suffered to coincide, we well know that neither moral nor religious motives can be relied on as an adequate control. They are not found to be such on the injustice and violence of individuals, and lose their efficacy in proportion to the number combined together, that is, in proportion as their efficacy becomes needful.

From this view of the subject it may be concluded that a pure democracy, by which I mean a society consisting of a small number of citizens, who assemble and administer the government in person, can admit of no cure for the mischiefs of faction. A common passion or interest will, in almost every case, be felt by a majority of the whole; a communication and concert result from the form of government itself; and there is nothing to check the inducements to sacrifice the weaker party or an obnoxious individual. Hence it is that such democracies have ever been spectacles of turbulence and contention; have ever been found incompatible with personal security or the rights of property; and have in general been as short in their lives as they have been violent in their deaths. Theoretic politicians, who have patronized this species of government, have erroneously supposed that by reducing mankind to a perfect equality in their political rights, they would, at the same time, be perfectly equalized and assimilated in their possessions, their opinions, and their passions.

A republic, by which I mean a government in which the scheme of representation takes place, opens a different prospect, and promises the cure for which we are seeking. Let us examine the points in which it varies from pure democracy, and we shall comprehend both the nature of the cure and the efficacy which it must derive from the Union.

The two great points of difference between a democracy and a republic are: first, the delegation of the government, in the latter, to a small number of citizens elected by the rest; secondly, the greater number of citizens, and greater sphere of country, over which the latter may be extended.

The effect of the first difference is, on the one hand, to refine and enlarge the public views, by passing them through the medium of a chosen body of citizens, whose wisdom may best discern the true interest of their country, and whose patriotism and love of justice will be least likely to sacrifice it to temporary or partial considerations. Under such a regulation, it may well happen that the public voice, pronounced by the representatives of the people, will be more consonant to the public good than if pronounced by the people themselves, convened for the purpose. On the other hand, the effect may be inverted. Men of factious tempers, of local prejudices, or of sinister designs, may, by intrigue, by corruption, or by other means, first obtain the suffrages, and then betray the interests, of the people. The question resulting is, whether small or extensive republics are more favorable to the election of proper guardians of the public weal; and it is clearly decided in favor of the latter by two obvious considerations:

In the first place, it is to be remarked that, however small the republic may be, the representatives must be raised to a certain number, in order to guard against the cabals of a few; and that, however large it may be, they must be limited to a certain number, in order to guard against the confusion of a multitude.

Hence, the number of representatives in the two cases not being in proportion to that of the two constituents, and being proportionally greater in the small republic, it follows that, if the proportion of fit characters be not less in the large than in the small republic, the former will present a greater option, and consequently a greater probability of a fit choice.

In the next place, as each representative will be chosen by a greater number of citizens in the large than in the small republic, it will be more difficult for unworthy candidates to practice with success the vicious arts by which elections are too often carried; and the suffrages of the people being more free, will be more likely to centre in men who possess the most attractive merit and the most diffusive and established characters.

It must be confessed that in this, as in most other cases, there is a mean, on both sides of which inconveniences will be found to lie. By enlarging too much the number of electors, you render the representatives too little acquainted with all their local circumstances and lesser interests; as by reducing it too much, you render him unduly attached to these, and too little fit to comprehend and pursue great and national objects. The federal Constitution forms a happy combination in this respect; the great and aggregate interests being referred to the national, the local and particular to the State legislatures.

The other point of difference is, the greater number of citizens and extent of territory which may be brought within the compass of republican than of democratic government; and it is this circumstance principally which renders factious combinations less to be dreaded in the former than in the latter. The smaller the society, the fewer probably will be the distinct parties and interests composing it; the fewer the distinct parties and interests, the more frequently will a majority be found of the same party; and the smaller the number of individuals composing a majority, and the smaller the compass within which they are placed, the more easily will they concert and execute their plans of oppression. Extend the sphere, and you take in a greater variety of parties and interests; you make it less probable that a majority of the whole will have a common motive to invade the rights of other citizens; or if such a common motive exists, it will be more difficult for all who feel it to discover their own strength, and to act in unison with each other. Besides other impediments, it may be remarked that, where there is a consciousness of unjust or dishonorable purposes, communication is always checked by distrust in proportion to the number whose concurrence is necessary.

Hence, it clearly appears, that the same advantage which a republic has over a democracy, in controlling the effects of faction, is enjoyed by a large over a small republic, is enjoyed by the Union over the States composing it. Does the advantage consist in the substitution of representatives whose enlightened views and virtuous sentiments render them superior to local prejudices and schemes of injustice? It will not be denied that the representation of the Union will be most likely to possess these requisite endowments. Does it consist in the greater security afforded by a greater variety of parties, against the event of any one party being able to outnumber and oppress the rest? In an equal degree does the increased variety of parties comprised within the Union, increase this security. Does it, in fine, consist in the greater obstacles opposed to the concert and accomplishment of the secret wishes of an unjust and interested majority? Here, again, the extent of the Union gives it the most palpable advantage.

The influence of factious leaders may kindle a flame within their particular States, but will be unable to spread a general conflagration through the other States. A religious sect may degenerate into a political faction in a part of the Confederacy; but the variety of sects dispersed over the entire face of it must secure the national councils against any danger from that source. A rage for paper money, for an abolition of debts, for an equal division of property, or for any other improper or wicked project, will be less apt to pervade the whole body of the Union than a particular member of it; in the same proportion as such a malady is more likely to taint a particular county or district, than an entire State.

In the extent and proper structure of the Union, therefore, we behold a republican remedy for the diseases most incident to republican government. And according to the degree of pleasure and pride we feel in being republicans, ought to be our zeal in cherishing the spirit and supporting the character of Federalists.

**PUBLIUS**.

# Federalist Papers, #51

By Alexander Hamilton or James Madison

## The Structure of the Government Must Furnish the Proper Checks and Balances Between the Different Departments

*From the New York Packet.*
*Friday, February 8, 1788.*

To the People of the State of New York:
To what expedient, then, shall we finally resort, for maintaining in practice the necessary partition of power among the several departments, as laid down in the Constitution? The only answer that can be given is, that as all these exterior provisions are found to be inadequate, the defect must be supplied, by so contriving the interior structure of the government as that its several constituent parts may, by their mutual relations, be the means of keeping each other in their proper places. Without presuming to undertake a full development of this important idea, I will hazard a few general observations, which may perhaps place it in a clearer light, and enable us to form a more correct judgment of the principles and structure of the government planned by the convention.

In order to lay a due foundation for that separate and distinct exercise of the different powers of government, which to a certain extent is admitted on all hands to be essential to the preservation of liberty, it is evident that each department should have a will of its own; and consequently should be so constituted that the members of each should have as little agency as possible in the appointment of the members of the others. Were this principle rigorously adhered to, it would require that all the appointments for the supreme executive, legislative, and judiciary magistracies should be drawn from the same fountain of authority, the people, through channels having no communication whatever with one another. Perhaps such a plan of constructing the several departments would be less difficult in practice than it may in contemplation appear. Some difficulties, however, and some additional expense would attend the execution of it. Some deviations, therefore, from the principle must be admitted. In the constitution of the judiciary department in particular, it might be inexpedient to insist rigorously on the principle: first, because peculiar qualifications being essential in the members, the primary consideration ought to be to select that mode of choice which best secures these qualifications; secondly, because the permanent tenure by which the appointments are held in that department, must soon destroy all sense of dependence on the authority conferring them.

It is equally evident, that the members of each department should be as little dependent as possible on those of the others, for the emoluments annexed to their offices. Were the executive magistrate, or the judges, not independent of the legislature in this particular, their independence in every other would be merely nominal.

But the great security against a gradual concentration of the several powers in the same department, consists in giving to those who administer each department the necessary constitutional means and personal motives to resist encroachments of the others. The provision for defense must in this, as in all other cases, be made commensurate to the danger of attack. Ambition must be made to counteract ambition. The interest of the man must be connected with the constitutional rights of the place. It may be a reflection on human nature, that such devices should be necessary to control the abuses of government. But what is government itself, but the greatest of all reflections on human nature? If men were angels, no government would be necessary. If angels were to govern men, neither external nor internal controls on government would be necessary. In framing a government which is to be administered by men over men, the great difficulty lies in this: you must first enable the government to control the governed; and in the next place oblige it to control itself. A dependence on the people is, no doubt, the primary control on the government; but experience has taught mankind the necessity of auxiliary precautions.

This policy of supplying, by opposite and rival interests, the defect of better motives, might be traced through the whole system of human affairs, private as well as public. We see it particularly displayed in all the subordinate distributions of power, where the constant aim is to divide and arrange the several offices in such a manner as that each may be a check on the other that the private interest of every individual may be a sentinel over the public rights. These inventions of prudence cannot be less requisite in the distribution of the supreme powers of the State.

But it is not possible to give to each department an equal power of self-defense. In republican government, the legislative authority necessarily predominates. The remedy for this inconveniency is to divide the legislature into different branches; and to render them, by different modes of election and different principles of action, as little connected with each other as the nature of their common functions and their common dependence on the society will admit. It may even be necessary to guard against dangerous encroachments by still further precautions. As the weight of the legislative authority requires that it should be thus divided, the weakness of the executive may require, on the other hand, that it should be fortified. An absolute negative on the legislature appears, at first view, to be the natural defense with which the executive magistrate should be armed. But perhaps it would be neither altogether safe nor alone sufficient. On ordinary occasions it might not be exerted with the requisite firmness, and on extraordinary occasions it might be perfidiously abused. May not this defect of an absolute negative be supplied by some qualified connection between this weaker department and the weaker branch of the stronger department, by which the latter may be led to support the constitutional rights of the former, without being too much detached from the rights of its own department?

If the principles on which these observations are founded be just, as I persuade myself they are, and they be applied as a criterion to the several State constitutions, and to the federal Constitution it will be found that if the latter does not perfectly correspond with them, the former are infinitely less able to bear such a test.

There are, moreover, two considerations particularly applicable to the federal system of America, which place that system in a very interesting point of view.

**First.** In a single republic, all the power surrendered by the people is submitted to the administration of a single government; and the usurpations are guarded against by a division of the government into distinct and separate departments. In the compound republic of America, the power surrendered by the people is first divided between two distinct governments, and then the portion allotted to each subdivided among distinct and separate departments. Hence a double security arises to the rights of the people. The different governments will control each other, at the same time that each will be controlled by itself.

**Second.** It is of great importance in a republic not only to guard the society against the oppression of its rulers, but to guard one part of the society against the injustice of the other part. Different interests necessarily exist in different classes of citizens. If a majority be united by a common interest, the rights of the minority will be insecure. There are but two methods of providing against this evil: the one by creating a will in the community independent of the majority that is, of the society itself; the other, by comprehending in the society so many separate descriptions of citizens as will render an unjust combination of a majority of the whole very improbable, if not impracticable. The first method prevails in all governments possessing an hereditary or self-appointed authority. This, at best, is but a precarious security; because a power independent of the society may as well espouse the unjust views of the major, as the rightful interests of the minor party, and may possibly be turned against both parties. The second method will be exemplified in the federal republic of the United States. Whilst all authority in it will be derived from and dependent on the society, the society itself will be broken into so many parts, interests, and classes of citizens, that the rights of individuals, or of the minority, will be in little danger from interested combinations of the majority. In a free government the security for civil rights must be the same as that for religious rights. It consists in the one case in the multiplicity of interests, and in the other in the multiplicity of sects. The degree of security in both cases will depend on the number of interests and sects; and this may be presumed to depend on the extent of country and number of people comprehended under the same government. This view of the subject must particularly recommend a proper federal system to all the sincere and considerate friends of republican government, since it shows that in exact proportion as the territory of the Union may be formed into more circumscribed Confederacies, or States oppressive combinations of a majority will be facilitated: the best security, under the republican forms, for the rights of every class of citizens, will be diminished: and consequently the stability and independence of some member of the government, the only other security, must be proportionately increased. Justice is the end of government. It is the end of civil society.

It ever has been and ever will be pursued until it be obtained, or until liberty be lost in the pursuit. In a society under the forms of which the stronger faction can readily unite and oppress the weaker, anarchy may as truly be said to reign as in a state of nature, where the weaker individual is not secured against the violence of the stronger; and as, in the latter state, even the stronger individuals are prompted, by the uncertainty of their condition, to submit to a government which may protect the weak as well as themselves; so, in the former state, will the more powerful factions or parties be gradually induced, by a like motive, to wish for a government which will protect all parties, the weaker as well as the more powerful. It can be little doubted that if the State of Rhode Island was separated from the Confederacy and left to itself, the insecurity of rights under the popular form of government within such narrow limits would be displayed by such reiterated oppressions of factious majorities that some power altogether independent of the people would soon be called for by the voice of the very factions whose misrule had proved the necessity of it. In the extended republic of the United States, and among the great variety of interests, parties, and sects which it embraces, a coalition of a majority of the whole society could seldom take place on any other principles than those of justice and the general good; whilst there being thus less danger to a minor from the will of a major party, there must be less pretext, also, to provide for the security of the former, by introducing into the government a will not dependent on the latter, or, in other words, a will independent of the society itself. It is no less certain than it is important, notwithstanding the contrary opinions which have been entertained, that the larger the society, provided it lie within a practical sphere, the more duly capable it will be of self-government. And happily for the REPUBLICAN CAUSE, the practicable sphere may be carried to a very great extent, by a judicious modification and mixture of the FEDERAL PRINCIPLE.

**PUBLIUS.**

# "John DeWitt"

By John DeWitt

*Massachusetts, October 27, 1787*

To the Free Citizens of the Commonwealth of Massachusetts:

In my last address upon the proceedings of the Federal Convention I endeavored to convince you of the importance of the subject, that it required a cool, dispassionate examination, and a thorough investigation, previous to its adoption—that it was not a mere revision and amendment of our first Confederation, but a compleat System for the future government of the United States, and I may now add in preference to, and in exclusion of, all others heretofore adopted.—It is not TEMPORARY, but in its nature, PERPETUAL.—It is not designed that you shall be annually called, either to revise, correct, or renew it; but, that your posterity shall grow up under, and be governed by it, as well as ourselves.—It is not so capable of alterations as you would at the first reading suppose; and I venture to assert, it never can be, unless by force of arms. The fifth article in the proceedings, it is true, expressly provides for an alteration under certain conditions, whenever "it shall be ratified by the Legislatures of three fourths of the several States, or by Conventions in three fourths thereof, as the one or the other mode of ratification may be proposed by Congress."—Notwithstanding which, such are the "*heterogeneous materials from which this System was formed,*" such is the difference of interest, different manners, and different local prejudices, in the different parts of the United States, that to obtain that majority of three fourths to any one single alteration, essentially affecting this or any other State, amounts to an absolute impossibility. The conduct of the Delegates in dissolving the Convention, plainly speaks this language, and no other.—Their sentiments in their Letter to his Excellency the President of Congress are—That this Constitution was the result of a spirit of amity—that the parties came together disposed to concede as much as possible each to the other—that mutual concessions and compromises did, in fact, take place, and all those which could, consistent with the peculiarity of their political situation. Their dissolution enforces the same sentiment, by confining you to the alternative of taking or refusing their doings in the gross. In this view, who is there to be found among us, who can seriously assert, that this Constitution, after ratification and being practiced upon, will be so easy of alteration? Where is the probability that a future Convention, in any future day, will be found possessed of a greater spirit of amity and mutual concession than the present? Where is the probability that three fourths of the States in that Convention, or three fourths of the Legislatures of the different States, whose interests differ scarcely in nothing short of every thing, will be so very ready or willing materially to change any part of this System, which shall be to the emolument of an individual State only? No, my fellow-citizens, as you are now obliged to take it in the whole, so you must hereafter administer it in whole, without the prospect of change, unless by again reverting to, a state of Nature, which will be ever opposed with success by those who approve of the Government in being.

That the want of a Bill of Rights to accompany this proposed System, is a solid objection to it, provided there is nothing exceptionable in the System itself, I do not assert.—If, however, there is at any time, a propriety in having one, it would not have been amiss here. A people, entering into society, surrender such a part of their natural rights, as shall be necessary for the existence of that society. They are so precious in themselves, that they would never be parted with, did not the preservation of the remainder require it. They are entrusted in the hands of those, who are very willing to receive them, who are naturally fond of exercising of them, and whose passions are always striving to make a bad use of them.—They are conveyed by a written compact, expressing those which are given up, and the mode in which those reserved shall be secured. Language is so easy of explanation, and so difficult is it by words to convey exact ideas, that the party to be governed cannot be too explicit. The line cannot be drawn with too much precision and

accuracy. The necessity of this accuracy and this precision increases in proportion to the greatness of the sacrifice and the numbers who make it.—That a Constitution for the United States does not require a Bill of Rights, when it is considered, that a Constitution for an individual State would, I cannot conceive. —The difference between them is only in the numbers of the parties concerned they are both a compact between the Governors and Governed the letter of which must be adhered to in discussing their powers. That which is not expressly granted, is of course retained.

The Compact itself is a recital upon paper of that proportion of the subject's natural rights, intended to be parted with, for the benefit of adverting to it in case of dispute. Miserable indeed would be the situation of those individual States who have not prefixed to their Constitutions a Bill of Rights, if, as a very respectable, learned Gentleman at the Southward observes, "the People, when they established the powers of legislation under their separate Governments, invested their Representatives with every right and authority which they did not, in explicit terms, reserve; and therefore upon every question, respecting the jurisdiction of the House of Assembly, if the Frame of Government is silent, the jurisdiction of the House of Assembly, if the Frame of Government is silent, the jurisdiction is efficient and complete."[1] In other words, those powers which the people by their Constitutions expressly give them; they enjoy by positive grant, and those remaining ones, which they never meant to give them, and which the Constitutions say nothing about, they enjoy by tacit implication, so that by one means and by the other, they became possessed of the whole.—This doctrine is but poorly calculated for the meridian of America, where the nature of compact, the mode of construing them, and the principles upon which society is founded, are so accurately known and universally diffused. That insatiable thirst for unconditional controul over our fellow-creatures, and the facility of sounds to convey essentially different ideas, produced the first Bill of Rights ever prefixed to a Frame of Government. The people, although fully sensible that they reserved every tittle of power they did not expressly grant away, yet afraid that the words made use of, to express those rights so granted might convey more than they originally intended, they chose at the same moment to express in different language those rights which the agreement did not include, and which they never designed to part with, endeavoring thereby to prevent any cause for future altercation and the intrusion into society of that doctrine of tacit implication which has been the favorite theme of every tyrant from the origin of all governments to the present day.

The proceedings of the Convention are now handed to you by your Legislature, and the second Wednesday in January is appointed for your final answer. To enable you to give that with propriety; that your future reflections may produce peace, however opposed the present issue of your present conduct may be to your present expectations, you must determine, that, in order to support with dignity the Federal Union, it is proper and fit, that the present Confederation shall be annihilated: —That the future Congress of the United States shall be armed with the powers of Legislation, Judgment and Execution.—That annual elections in this Congress shall not be known, and the most powerful body, the Senate, in which a due proportion of representation is not preserved, and in which the smallest State has equal weight with the largest, be the longest in duration:—That it is not necessary for the public good, that persons habituated to the exercise of power should ever be reminded from whence they derive it, by a return to the station of private citizens, but that they shall at all times at the expiration of the term for which they were elected to an office, be capable of immediate re-election to that same office:—That you will hereafter risk the probability of having the Chief Executive Branch chosen from among you; and that it is wholly indifferent, both to you and your children after you, whether this future Government shall be administered within the territories of your own State, or at the distance of four thousand miles from them.—You must also determine, that they shall have the exclusive power of imposts and the duties on imports and exports, the power of laying excises and other duties, and the additional power of laying internal taxes upon your lands, your goods, your chattels, as well as your persons at their sovereign pleasure: —That the produce of these several funds shall be appropriated to the use of the United States, and collected by their own officers, armed with a military force, if a civil aid should not prove sufficient:—that the power of organizing, arming and disciplining the militia shall be lodged in them, and this through fear that they shall not be sufficiently attentive to keeping so respectable a body of men as the yeomanry of this Commonwealth, compleatly armed, organized and disciplined; they shall have also the power of raising, supporting and establishing a standing army in time of peace in your several towns, and I see not why in your several houses:—That should an insurrection or an invasion, however small, take place, in Georgia, the extremity of the Continent, it is highly expedient they should have the power of suspending the writ of Habeas Corpus in Massachusetts, and as long as they shall judge the public safety requires it:—You must also say, that your present Supreme Judicial Court shall be an Inferior Court to a Continental Court, which is to be inferior to the Supreme Court of the United States:—that from an undue bias which they are supposed to have for the citizens of their own States, they shall not be competent to determine title to your real estate, disputes which may arise upon a protested Bill of Exchange, a simple note of hand, or book debt, wherein your citizens shall be unfortunately involved with disputes of such or any other kind, with citizens either of other States or foreign States: In all such cases they shall have a right to carry their causes to the Supreme Court of the United States, whether for delay only or vexation; however distant from the place of your abode, or inconsistent with your circumstances:—That such appeals shall be extended to matters of fact as well as law, and a trial of the cause by jury you shall not have a right to insist upon.—In short, my fellow-citizens, previous to a capacity of giving a compleat answer to these proceedings, you must determine that the Constitution of your Commonwealth, which is instructive, beautiful and consistent in practice, which has been justly admired in Europe, as a model of perfection, and which the present Convention have affected to imitate, a Constitution which is especially calculated for your territory, and is made conformable to your genius, your habits, the mode of holding your estates, and your particular interests, shall be reduced in its powers to those of a City Corporation: —The skeleton of it may remain, but its vital principle shall be transferred to the new Government: Nay, you must go still further, and agree to invest the new Congress with powers, which you have yet thought proper to withhold from your own present Government.—All these, and more, which are contained in the proceedings of the Federal Convention, may be highly proper and necessary.—In this overturn of all individual governments, in this new-fashioned set of ideas, and in this total dereliction of those sentiments which animated us in 1775, the Political Salvation of the United States may be very deeply interested, but BE CAUTIOUS.

1.  Speech of James Wilson, October 6, 1787.

# The Social Contract

By Jean Jacques Rousseau

## Man Is Born Free

Man is born free; and everywhere he is in chains. One thinks himself the master of others, and still remains a greater slave than they. How did this change come about? I do not know. What can make it legitimate? That question I think I can answer.

If I took into account only force, and the effects derived from it, I should say: "As long as a people is compelled to obey, and obeys, it does well; as soon as it can shake off the yoke, and shakes it off, it does still better; for, regaining its liberty by the same right as took it away, either it is justified in resuming it, or there was no justification for those who took it away." But the social order is a sacred right which is the basis of all other rights. Nevertheless, this right does not come from nature, and must therefore be founded on conventions. Before coming to that, I have to prove what I have just asserted.

## The Right of the Strongest

The strongest is never strong enough to be always the master, unless he transforms strength into right, and obedience into duty. Hence the right of the strongest, which, though to all seeming meant ironically, is really laid down as a fundamental principle. But are we never to have an explanation of this phrase? Force is a physical power, and I fail to see what moral effect it can have. To yield to force is an act of necessity, not of will—at the most, an act of prudence. In what sense can it be a duty?

Suppose for a moment that this so-called "right" exists. I maintain that the sole result is a mass of inexplicable nonsense. For, if force creates right, the effect changes with the cause: every force that is greater than the first succeeds to its right. As soon as it is possible to disobey with impunity, disobedience is legitimate; and, the strongest being always in the right, the only thing that matters is to act so as to become the strongest. But what kind of right is that which perishes when force fails? If we must obey perforce, there is no need to obey because we ought; and if we are not forced to obey, we are under no obligation to do so. Clearly, the word "right" adds nothing to force: in this connection, it means absolutely nothing.

Obey the powers that be. If this means yield to force, it is a good precept, but superfluous: I can answer for its never being violated. All power comes from God, I admit; but so does all sickness: does that mean that we are forbidden to call in the doctor? A brigand surprises me at the edge of a wood: must I not merely surrender my purse on compulsion; but, even if I cou withhold it, am I in conscience bound give it up? For certainly the pistol he hoi is also a power.

Let us then admit that force does not c ate right, and that we are obliged to o' only legitimate powers. In that case, original question recurs.

## Slavery

Since no man has a natural authority his fellow, and force creates no right must conclude that conventions form the basis of all legitimate authority among men.

If an individual, says Grotius, can alienate his liberty and make himself the slave of a master, why could not a whole people do the same and make itself subject to a king? There are in this passage plenty of ambiguous words which would need explaining; but let us confine ourselves to the word *alienate*. To alienate is to give or to sell. Now, a man who becomes the slave of another does not give himself; he sells himself, at the least for his subsistence: but for what does a people sell itself? A king is so far from furnishing his subjects with their subsistence that he gets his own only from them; and, according to Rabelais, kings do not live on nothing. Do subjects then give their persons on condition that the king takes their goods also? I fail to see what they have left to preserve.

It will be said that the despot assures his subjects civil tranquillity. Granted; but what do they gain, if the wars his ambition brings down upon them, his insatiable avidity, and the vexatious conduct of his ministers press harder on them than their own dissensions would have done? What do they gain, if the very tranquillity they enjoy is one of their miseries? Tranquillity is found also in dungeons; but is that enough to make them desirable places to live in? The Greeks imprisoned in the cave of the Cyclops lived there very tranquilly, while they were awaiting their turn to be devoured.

To say that a man gives himself gratuitously, is to say what is absurd and inconceivable; such an act is null and illegitimate, from the mere fact that he who does it is out of his mind. To say the same of a whole people is to suppose a people of madmen; and madness creates no right.

Even if each man could alienate himself, he could not alienate his children: they are born men and free; their liberty belongs to them, and no one but they has the right to dispose of it. Before they come to years of discretion, the father can, in their name, lay down conditions for their preservation and well-being, but he cannot give them irrevocably and without conditions: such a gift is contrary to the ends of nature, and exceeds the rights of paternity. It would therefore be necessary, in order to legitimize an arbitrary government, that in every generation the people should be in a position to accept or reject it; but, were this so, the government would be no longer arbitrary.

To renounce liberty is to renounce being a man, to surrender the rights of humanity and even its duties. For him who renounces everything no indemnity is possible. Such a renunciation is incompatible with man's nature; to remove all liberty from his will is to remove all morality from his acts. Finally, it is an empty and contradictory convention that sets up, on the one side, absolute authority, and, on the other, unlimited obedience. Is it not clear that we can be under no obligation to a person from whom we have the right to exact everything? Does not this condition alone, in the absence of equivalence or exchange, in itself involve the nullity of the act? For what right can my slave have against me, when all that he has belongs to me, and, his right being mine, this right of mine against myself is a phrase devoid of meaning?

Grotius and the rest find in war another origin for the so-called right of slavery. The victor having, as they hold, the right of killing the vanquished, the latter can buy back his life at the price of his liberty; and this convention is the more legitimate because it is to the advantage of both parties.

But it is clear that this supposed right to kill the conquered is by no means deducible from the state of war. Men, from the mere fact that, while they are living in their primitive independence, they have no mutual relations stable enough to constitute either the state of peace or the state of war, cannot be naturally enemies. War is constituted by a relation between things, and not between persons; and, as the state of war cannot arise out of simple personal relations, but only out of real relations, private war, or war of man with man, can exist neither in the state of nature, where there is no constant property, nor in the social state, where everything is under the authority of the laws.

Individual combats, duels, and encounters, are acts which cannot constitute a state; while the private wars, authorized by the Establishments of Louis IX, King of France, and suspended by the Peace of God, are abuses of feudalism, in itself an absurd system if ever there was one, and contrary to the principles of natural right and to all good polity.

War then is a relation, not between man and man, but between State and State, and individuals are enemies only accidentally, not as men, nor even as citizens,[1] but as soldiers; not as members of their country, but as its defenders. Finally, each State can have for enemies only other States, and not men; for between things disparate in nature there can be no real relation.

Furthermore, this principle is in conformity with the established rules of all times and the constant practice of all civilized peoples. Declarations of war are intimations less to powers than to their subjects. The foreigner, whether king, individual, or people, who robs, kills, or detains the subjects, without declaring war on the prince, is not an enemy, but a brigand. Even in real war, a just prince, while laying hands, in the enemy's country, on all that belongs to the public, respects the lives

---

1 The Romans, who understood and respected the right of war more than any other nation on earth, carried their scruples on this head so far that a citizen was not allowed to serve as a volunteer without engaging himself expressly against the enemy, and against such and such an enemy by name. A legion in which the younger Cato was seeing his first service under Popilius having been reconstructed, the elder Cato wrote to Popilius that, if he wished his son to continue serving under him, he must administer to him a new military oath, because, the first having been annulled, he was no longer able to bear arms against the enemy. The same Cato wrote to his son telling him to take great care not to go into battle before taking this new oath. I know that the siege of Clusium and other isolated events can be quoted against me; but I am citing laws and customs. The Romans are the people that least often transgressed its laws; and no other people has had such good ones.

and goods of individuals: he respects rights on which his own are founded. The object of the war being the destruction of the hostile State, the other side has a right to kill its defenders, while they are bearing arms; but as soon as they lay them down and surrender, they cease to be enemies or instruments of the enemy, and become once more merely men, whose life no one has any right to take. Sometimes it is possible to kill the State without killing a single one of its members; and war gives no right which is not necessary to the gaining of its object. These principles are not those of Grotius: they are not based on the authority of poets, but derived from the nature of reality and based on reason.

The right of conquest has no foundation other than the right of the strongest. If war does not give the conqueror the right to massacre the conquered peoples, the right to enslave them cannot be based upon a right which does not exist. No one has a right to kill an enemy except when he cannot make him a slave, and the right to enslave him cannot therefore be derived from the right to kill him. It is accordingly an unfair exchange to make him buy at the price of his liberty his life, over which the victor holds no right. Is it not clear that there is a vicious circle in founding the right of life and death on the right of slavery, and the right of slavery on the right of life and death?

Even if we assume this terrible right to kill everybody, I maintain that a slave made in war, or a conquered people, is under no obligation to a master, except to obey him as far as he is compelled to do so. By taking an equivalent for his life, the victor has not done him a favour; instead of killing him without profit, he has killed him usefully. So far then is he from acquiring over him any authority in addition to that of force, that the state of war continues to subsist between them: their mutual relation is the effect of it, and the usage of the right of war does not imply a treaty of peace. A convention has indeed been made; but this convention, so far from destroying the state of war, presupposes its continuance.

So, from whatever aspect we regard the question, the right of slavery is null and void, not only as being illegitimate, but also because it is absurd and meaningless. The words *slave* and *right* contradict each other, and are mutually exclusive. It will always be equally foolish for a man to say to a man or to a people: "I make with you a convention wholly at your expense and wholly to my advantage; I shall keep it as long as I like, and you will keep it as long as I like."

## The First Convention of Society

Even if I granted all that I have been refuting, the friends of despotism would be no better off. There will always be a great difference between subduing a multitude and ruling a society. Even if scattered individuals were successively enslaved by one man, however numerous they might be, I still see no more than a master and his slaves, and certainly not a people and its ruler; I see what may be termed an aggregation, but not an association; there is as yet neither public good nor body politic. The man in question, even if he has enslaved half the world, is still only an individual; his interest, apart from that of others, is still a purely private interest. If this same man comes to die, his empire, after him, remains scattered and without unity, as an oak falls and dissolves into a heap of ashes when the fire has consumed it.

A people, says Grotius, can give itself to a king. Then, according to Grotius, a people is a people before it gives itself. The gift is itself a civil act, and implies public deliberation. It would be better, before examining the act by which a people gives itself to a king, to examine that by which it has become a people; for this act, being necessarily prior to the other, is the true foundation of society.

Indeed, if there were no prior convention, where, unless the election were unanimous, would be the obligation on the minority to submit to the choice of the majority? How have a hundred men who wish for a master the right to vote on behalf of ten who do not? The law of majority voting is itself something established by convention, and presupposes unanimity, on one occasion at least.

## The Social Compact

I suppose men to have reached the point at which the obstacles in the way of their preservation in the state of nature show their power of resistance to be greater than the resources at the disposal of each individual for his maintenance in that state, The primitive condition can then subsist no longer; and the human race would perish unless it changed its manner of existence.

But, as men cannot engender new forces, but only unite and direct existing ones, they have no other means of preserving themselves than the formation, by aggregation, of a sum of forces great enough to overcome the resistance. These they have to bring into play by means of a single motive power, and cause to act in concert.

This sum of forces can arise only where several persons come together: but, as the force and liberty of each man are the chief instruments of his self-preservation, how can he pledge them without harming his own interests, and neglecting the care he owes to himself? This difficulty, in its bearing on my present subject, may be stated in the following terms:

"The problem is to find a form of association which will defend and protect with the whole common force the person and goods of each associate, and in which each, while uniting himself with all, may still obey himself alone, and remain as free as before." This is the fundamental problem of which the *Social Contract* provides the solution.

The clauses of this contract are so determined by the nature of the act that the slightest modification would make them vain and ineffective; so that, although they have perhaps never been formally set forth, they are everywhere the same and everywhere tacitly admitted and recognized, until, on the violation of the social compact, each regains his original rights and resumes his natural liberty, while losing the conventional liberty in favour of which he renounced it.

These clauses, properly understood, may be reduced to one—the total alienation of each associate, together with all his rights, to the whole community; for, in the first place, as each gives himself absolutely, the conditions are the same for all; and, this being so, no one has any interest in making them burdensome to others.

Moreover, the alienation being without reserve, the union is as perfect as it can be, and no associate has anything more to demand: for, if the individuals retained certain rights, as there would be no common superior to decide between them and the public, each, being on one point his own judge, would ask to be so on all; the state of nature would thus continue, and the association would necessarily become inoperative or tyrannical.

Finally, each man, in giving himself to all, gives himself to nobody; and as there is no associate over which he does not acquire the same right as he yields others over himself, he gains an equivalent for everything he loses, and an increase of force for the preservation of what he has.

If then we discard from the social compact what is not of its essence, we shall find that it reduces itself to the following terms:

*"Each of us puts his person and all his power in common under the supreme direction of the general will, and, in our corporate capacity, we receive each member as an indivisible part of the whole."*

At once, in place of the individual personality of each contracting party, this act of association creates a moral and collective body, composed of as many members as the assembly contains voters, and receiving from this act its unity, its common identity, its life, and its will. This public person, so formed by the union of all other persons, formerly took the name of city,[2] and now takes that of *Republic* or *body politic;* it is called by its members *State* when passive, *Sovereign* when active, and *Power* when compared with others like itself. Those who are associated in it take collectively the name of *people*, and severally are called *citizens,* as sharing in the sovereign power, and *subjects,* as being under the laws of the State. But these terms are often confused and taken one for another: it is enough to know how to distinguish them when they are being used with precision.

## The Sovereign

This formula shows us that the act of association comprises a mutual undertaking between the public and the individuals, and that each individual, in making a contract, as we may say, with himself, is bound in a double capacity; as a member of the Sovereign he is bound to the individuals, and as a member of the State to the Sovereign. But the maxim of civil right, that no one is bound by undertakings made to himself, does not apply in this case; for there is a great difference between incurring an obligation to yourself and incurring one to a whole of which you form a part.

Attention must further be called to the fact that public deliberation, while competent to bind all the subjects to the Sovereign, because of the two different capacities in which each of them may be regarded, cannot, for the opposite reason, bind the Sovereign to itself; and that it is consequently against the

---

2   The real meaning of this word has been almost wholly lost in modern times; most people mistake a town for a city, and a townsman for a citizen. They do not know that houses make a town, but citizens a city. The same mistake long ago cost the Carthaginians dear. I have never read of the title of citizens being given to the subjects of any prince, not even the ancient Macedonians or the English of to-day, though they are nearer liberty than any one else. The French alone everywhere familiarly adopt the name of citizens, because, as can be seen from their dictionaries, they have no idea of its meaning, otherwise they would be guilty in usurping it, of the crime of *lèse-majestè:* among them, the name expresses a virtue, and not a right. When Bodin spoke of our citizens and townsmen, he fell into a bad blunder in taking the one class for the other. M. d'Alembert has avoided the error, and, in his article on Geneva, has clearly distinguished the four orders of men

(or even five, counting mere foreigners) who dwell in our town, of which two only compose the Republic. No other French writer, to my knowledge, has understood the real meaning of the word citizen.

nature of the body politic for the Sovereign to impose on itself a law which it cannot infringe. Being able to regard itself in only one capacity, it is in the position of an individual who makes a contract with himself; and this makes it clear that there neither is nor can be any kind of fundamental law binding on the body of the people—not even the social contract itself. This does not mean that the body politic cannot enter into undertakings with others, provided the contract is not infringed by them; for in relation to what is external to it, it becomes a simple being, an individual.

But the body politic or the Sovereign, drawing its being wholly from the sanctity of the contract, can never bind itself, even to an outsider, to do anything derogatory to the original act, for instance, to alienate any part of itself, or to submit to another Sovereign. Violation of the act by which it exists would be self-annihilation; and that which is itself nothing can create nothing.

As soon as this multitude is so united in one body, it is impossible to offend against one of the members without attacking the body, and still more to offend against the body without the members resenting it. Duty and interest therefore equally oblige the two contracting parties to give each other help; and the same men should seek to combine, in their double capacity, all the advantages dependent upon that capacity.

Again, the Sovereign, being formed wholly of the individuals who compose it, neither has nor can have any interest contrary to theirs; and consequently the sovereign power need give no guarantee to its subjects, because it is impossible for the body to wish to hurt all its members. We shall also see later on that it cannot hurt any in particular. The Sovereign, merely by virtue of what it is, is always what it should be.

This, however, is not the case with the relation of the subjects to the Sovereign, which, despite the common interest, would have no security that they would fulfil their undertakings, unless it found means to assure itself of their fidelity.

In fact, each individual, as a man, may have a particular will contrary or dissimilar to the general will which he has as a citizen. His particular interest may speak to him quite differently from the common interest: his absolute and naturally independent existence may make him look upon what he owes to the common cause as a gratuitous contribution, the loss of which will do less harm to others than the payment of it is burdensome to himself; and, regarding the moral person which constitutes the State as a *persona ficta*, because not a man, he may wish to enjoy the rights of citizenship without being ready to fulfil the duties of a subject. The continuance of such an injustice could not but prove the undoing of the body politic.

In order then that the social compact may not be an empty formula, it tacitly includes the undertaking, which alone can give force to the rest, that whoever refuses to obey the general will shall be compelled to do so by the whole body. This means nothing less than that he will be forced to be free; for this is the condition which, by giving each citizen to his country, secures him against all personal dependence. In this lies the key to the working of the political machine; this alone legitimizes civil undertakings, which, without it, would be absurd, tyrannical, and liable to the most frightful abuses.

## The Civil State

The passage from the state of nature to the civil state produces a very remarkable change in man, by substituting justice for instinct in his conduct, and giving his actions the morality they had formerly lacked. Then only, when the voice of duty takes the place of physical impulses and right of appetite, does man, who so far had considered only himself, find that he is forced to act on different principles, and to consult his reason before listening to his inclinations. Although, in this state, he deprives himself of some advantages which he got from nature, he gains in return others so great, his faculties are so stimulated and developed, his ideas so extended, his feelings so ennobled, and his whole soul so uplifted, that, did not the abuses of this new condition often degrade him below that which he left, he would be bound to bless continually the happy moment which took him from it for ever, and, instead of a stupid and unimaginative animal, made him an intelligent being and a man.

Let us draw up the whole account in terms easily commensurable. What man loses by the social contract is his natural liberty and an unlimited right to everything he tries to get and succeeds in getting; what he gains is civil liberty and the proprietorship of all he possesses. If we are to avoid mistakes in weighing one against the other, we must clearly distinguish natural liberty, which is bounded only by the strength of the individual, from civil liberty, which is limited by the general will; and possession, which is merely the effect of force or the right of the first occupier, from property, which can be founded only on a positive title.

We might, over and above all this, add, to what man acquires in the civil state, moral liberty, which alone makes him truly master of himself; for the mere impulse of appetite is slavery, while obedience to a law which we prescribe to ourselves is liberty. But I have already said too much on this head, and the philosophical meaning of the word liberty does not now concern us.

## The Inalienability of Sovereignty

The first and most important deduction from the principles we have so far laid down is that the general will alone can direct the State according to the object for which it was instituted, i.e. the common good: for if the clashing of particular interests made the establishment of societies necessary, the agreement of these very interests made it possible. The common element in these different interests is what forms the social tie; and, were there no point of agreement between them all, no society could exist. It is solely on the basis of this common interest that every society should be governed.

I hold then that Sovereignty, being nothing less than the exercise of the general will, can never be alienated, and that the Sovereign, who is no less than a collective being, cannot be represented except by himself: the power indeed may be transmitted, but not the will.

In reality, if it is not impossible for a particular will to agree on some point with the general will, it is at least impossible for the agreement to be lasting and constant; for the particular will tends, by its very nature, to partiality, while the general will tends to equality. It is even more impossible to have any guarantee of this agreement; for even if it should always exist, it would be the effect not of art, but of chance. The Sovereign may indeed say: "I now will actually what this man wills, or at least what he says he wills"; but it cannot say: "What he wills to-morrow, I too shall will" because it is absurd for the will to bind itself for the future, nor is it incumbent on any will to consent to anything that is not for the good of the being who wills. If then the people promises simply to obey, by that very act it dissolves itself and loses what makes it a people; the moment a master exists, there is no longer a Sovereign, and from that moment the body politic has ceased to exist.

This does not mean that the commands of the rulers cannot pass for general wills, so long as the Sovereign, being free to oppose them, offers no opposition. In such a case, universal silence is taken to imply the consent of the people. This will be explained later on.

## The Indivisibility of Sovereignty

Sovereignty, for the same reason as makes it inalienable, is indivisible; for will either is, or is not, general;[3] it is the will either of the body of the people, or only of a part of it. In the first case, the will, when declared, is an act of Sovereignty and constitutes law: in the second, it is merely a particular will, or act of magistracy—at the most a decree.

But our political theorists, unable to divide Sovereignty in principle, divide it according to its object: into force and will; into legislative power and executive power; into rights of taxation, justice, and war; into internal administration and power of foreign treaty. Sometimes they confuse all these sections, and sometimes they distinguish them; they turn the Sovereign into a fantastic being composed of several connected pieces: it is as if they were making man of several bodies, one with eyes, one with arms, another with feet, and each with nothing besides. We are told that the jugglers of Japan dismember a child before the eyes of the spectators; then they throw all the members into the air one after another, and the child falls down alive and whole. The conjuring tricks of our political theorists are very like that; they first dismember the body politic by an illusion worthy of a fair, and then join it together again we know not how.

This error is due to a lack of exact notions concerning the Sovereign authority, and to taking for parts of it what are only emanations from it. Thus, for example, the acts of declaring war and making peace have been regarded as acts of Sovereignty; but this is not the case, as these acts do not constitute law, but merely the application of a law, a particular act which decides how the law applies, as we shall see clearly when the idea attached to the word "law" has been defined.

If we examined the other divisions in the same manner, we should find, that, whenever Sovereignty seems to be divided, there is an illusion: the rights which are taken as being part of Sovereignty are really all subordinate, and always imply supreme wills of which they only sanction the execution.

It would be impossible to estimate the obscurity this lack of exactness has thrown over the decisions of writers who have dealt with political right, when they have used the principles laid down by them to pass judgment on the respective rights of kings and peoples. Every one can see, in Chapters III and IV of the

---

3  To be general, a will need not always be unanimous; but every vote must be counted: any exclusion is a breach of generality.

first book of Grotius, how the learned man and his translator, Barbeyrac, entangle and tie themselves up in their own sophistries, for fear of saying too little or too much of what they think, and so offending the interests they have to conciliate. Grotius, a refugee in France, ill content with his own country, and desirous of paying his court to Louis XIII, to whom his book is dedicated, spares no pains to rob the peoples of all their rights and invest kings with them by every conceivable artifice. This would also have been much to the taste of Barbeyrac, who dedicated his translation to George I of England. But unfortunately the expulsion of James II, which he called his "abdication," compelled him to use all reserve, to shuffle and to tergiversate, in order to avoid making William out a usurper. If these two writers had adopted the true principles, all difficulties would have been removed, and they would have been always consistent; but it would have been a sad truth for them to tell, and would have paid court for them to no one save the people. Moreover, truth is no road to fortune, and the people dispenses neither ambassador-ships, nor professorships, nor pensions.

## Infallibility of the General Will

It follows from what has gone before that the general will is always right and tends to the public advantage; but it does not follow that the deliberations of the people are always equally correct. Our will is always for our own good, but we do not always see what that is; the people is never corrupted, but it is often deceived, and on such occasions only does it seem to will what is bad.

There is often a great deal of difference between the will of all and the general will; the latter considers only the common interest, while the former takes private interest into account, and is no more than a sum of particular wills: but take away from these same wills the pluses and minuses that cancel one another,[4] and the general will remains as the sum of the differences.

If, when the people, being furnished with adequate information, held its deliberations, the citizens had no communication one with another, the grand total of the small differences would always give the general will, and the decision would always be good. But when factions arise, and partial associations are formed at the expense of the great association, the will of each of these associations becomes general in relation to its members, while it remains particular in relation to the State: it may then be said that there are no longer as many votes as there are men, but only as many as there are associations. The differences become less numerous and give a less general result. Lastly, when one of these associations is so great as to prevail over all the rest, the result is no longer a sum of small differences, but a single difference; in this case there is no longer a general will, and the opinion which prevails is purely particular.

It is therefore essential, if the general will is to be able to express itself, that there should be no partial society within the State, and that each citizen should think only his

---

4 "Every interest," says the Marquis d'Argenson, "has different principles. The agreement of two particular interests is formed by opposition to a third." He might have added that the agreement of all interests is formed by opposition to that of each. If there were no different interests, the common interest would be barely felt, as it would encounter no obstacle; all would go on of its own accord, and politics would cease to be an art.

own thoughts[5] which was indeed the sublime and unique system established by the great Lycurgus. But if there are partial societies, it is best to have as many as possible and to prevent them from being unequal, as was done by Solon, Numa, and Servius. These precautions are the only ones than can guarantee that the general will shall be always enlightened, and that the people shall in no way deceive itself.

## Limits of the Sovereign Power

If the State is a moral person whose life is in the union of its members, and if the most important of its cares is the care for its own preservation, it must have a universal and compelling force, in order to move and dispose each part as may be most advantageous to the whole. As nature gives each man absolute power over all his members, the social compact gives the body politic absolute power over all its members also; and it is this power which, under the direction of the general will, bears, as I have said, the name of Sovereignty.

But, besides the public person, we have to consider the private persons composing it, whose life and liberty are naturally independent of it. We are bound then to distinguish clearly between the respective rights of the citizens and the Sovereign,[6] and between the duties the former have to fulfil as subjects, and the natural rights they should enjoy as men.

Each man alienates, I admit, by the social compact, only such part of his powers, goods, and liberty as it is important for the community to control; but it must also be granted that the Sovereign is sole judge of what is important.

Every service a citizen can render the State he ought to render as soon as the Sovereign demands it; but the Sovereign, for its part, cannot impose upon its subjects any fetters that are useless to the community, nor can it even wish to do so; for no more by the law of reason than by the law of nature can anything occur without a cause.

The undertakings which bind us to the social body are obligatory only because they are mutual; and their nature is such that in fulfilling them we cannot work for others without working for ourselves. Why is it that the general will is always in the right, and that all continually will the happiness of each one, unless it is because there is not a man who does not think of "each" as meaning him, and consider himself in voting for all? This proves that equality of rights and the idea of justice which such equality creates originate in the preference each man gives to himself, and accordingly in the very nature of man. It proves that the general will, to be really such, must be general in its object as well as its essence; that it must both come from all and apply to all; and that it loses its natural rectitude when it is directed to some particular and determinate object, because in such a case we are judging of something foreign to us, and have no true principle of equity to guide us.

Indeed, as soon as a question of particular fact or right arises on a point not previously regulated by a general convention, the matter

---

5 "In fact," says Machiavelli, "there are some divisions that are harmful to a Republic and some that are advantageous. Those which stir up sects and parties are harmful; those attended by neither are advantageous. Since, then, the founder of a Republic cannot help enmities arising, he ought at least to prevent them from growing into sects" (*History of Florence,* Book VII).

6 Attentive readers, do not, I pray, be in a hurry to charge me with contradicting myself. The terminology made it unavoidable, considering the poverty of the language; but wait and see.

becomes contentious. It is a case in which the individuals concerned are one party, and the public the other, but in which I can see neither the law that ought to be followed nor the judge who ought to give the decision. In such a case, it would be absurd to propose to refer the question to an express decision of the general will, which can be only the conclusion reached by one of the parties and in consequence will be, for the other party, merely an external and particular will, inclined on this occasion to injustice and subject to error. Thus, just as a particular will cannot stand for the general will, the general will, in turn, changes its nature, when its object is particular, and, as general, cannot pronounce on a man or a fact. When, for instance, the people of Athens nominated or displaced its rulers, decreed honours to one, and imposed penalties on another, and, by a multitude of particular decrees, exercised all the functions of government indiscriminately, it had in such cases no longer a general will in the strict sense; it was acting no longer as Sovereign, but as magistrate. This will seem contrary to current views; but I must be given time to expound my own.

It should be seen from the foregoing that what makes the will general is less the number of votes than the common interest uniting them; for, under this system, each necessarily submits to the conditions he imposes on others: and this admirable agreement between interest and justice gives to the common deliberations an equitable character which at once vanishes when any particular question is discussed, in the absence of a common interest to unite and identify the ruling of the judge with that of the party.

From whatever side we approach our principle, we reach the same conclusion, that the social compact sets up among the citizens an equality of such a kind, that they all bind themselves to observe the same conditions and should therefore all enjoy the same rights. Thus, from the very nature of the compact, every act of Sovereignty, i.e. every authentic act of the general will, binds or favours all the citizens equally; so that the Sovereign recognizes only the body of the nation, and draws no distinctions between those of whom it is made up. What, then, strictly speaking, is an act of Sovereignty? It is not a convention between a superior and an inferior, but a conviction between the body and each of its members. It is legitimate, because based on the social contract, and equitable, because common to all; useful, because it can have no other object than the general good, and stable, because guaranteed by the public force and the supreme power. So long as the subjects have to submit only to conventions of this sort, they obey no one but their own will; and to ask how far the respective rights of the Sovereign and the citizens extend, is to ask up to what point the latter can enter into undertakings with themselves, each with all, and all with each.

We can see from this that the sovereign power, absolute, sacred, and inviolable as it is, does not and cannot exceed the limits of general conventions, and that every man may dispose at will of such goods and liberty as these conventions leave him; so that the Sovereign never has a right to lay more charges on one subject than on another, because, in that case, the question becomes particular, and ceases to be within its competency.

When these distinctions have once been admitted, it is seen to be so untrue that there is, in the social contract, any real renunciation on the part of the individuals, that the position in which they find themselves as a result of the contract is really preferable to that in which they were before. Instead of a renunciation, they have made an advantageous exchange: instead of an uncertain and precarious way of living they have got one that is better and more secure; instead of natural independence they have got liberty, instead of the power to harm others security for themselves, and instead of their strength, which others might overcome, a right which social union makes invincible. Their very life, which they have devoted to the State, is by it constantly protected; and when they risk it in the State's defence, what more are they doing than giving back what they have received from it? What are they doing that they would not do more often and with greater danger in the state of nature, in which they would inevitably have to fight battles at the peril of their lives in defence of that which is the means of their preservation? All have indeed to fight when their country needs them; but then no one has ever to fight for himself. Do we not gain something by running, on behalf of what gives us our security, only some of the risks we should have to run for ourselves, as soon as we lost it?

## Law

By the social compact we have given the body politic existence and life; we have now by legislation to give it movement and will. For the original act by which the body is formed and united still in no respect determines what it ought to do for its preservation.

What is well and in conformity with order is so by the nature of things and independently of human conventions. All justice comes from God, who is its sole source; but if we knew how to receive so high an inspiration, we should need neither government nor laws. Doubtless, there is a universal justice emanating from reason alone; but this justice, to be admitted among us, must be mutual. Humanly speaking, in default of natural sanctions, the laws of justice are ineffective among men: they merely make for the good of the wicked and the undoing of the just, when the just man observes them towards everybody and nobody observes them towards him. Conventions and laws are therefore needed to join rights to duties and refer justice to its object. In the state of nature, where everything is common, I owe nothing to him whom I have promised nothing; I recognize as belonging to others only what is of no use to me. In the state of society all rights are fixed by law, and the case becomes different.

But what, after all, is a law? As long as we remain satisfied with attaching purely metaphysical ideas to the word, we shall go on arguing without arriving at an understanding; and when we have defined a law of nature, we shall be no nearer the definition of a law of the State,

I have already said that there can be no general will directed to a particular object. Such an object must be either within or outside the State. If outside, a will which is alien to it cannot be, in relation to it, general; if within, it is part of the State, and in that case there arises a relation between whole and part which makes them two separate beings, of which the part is one, and the whole minus the part the other. But the whole minus a part cannot be the whole; and while this relation persists, there can be no whole, but only two unequal parts; and it follows that the will of one is no longer in any respect general in relation to the other.

But when the whole people decrees for the whole people, it is considering only itself; and if a relation is then formed, it is between two aspects of the entire object, without there being any division of the whole. In that case the matter about which the decree is made is, like the decreeing will, general. This act is what I call a law.

When I say that the object of laws is always general, I mean that law considers subjects *en masse* and actions in the abstract, and never a particular person or action. Thus the law may indeed decree that there shall be privileges, but cannot confer them on anybody by name. It may set up several classes of citizens, and even lay down the qualifications for membership of these classes, but it cannot nominate such and such persons as belonging to them; it may establish a monarchical government and hereditary succession, but it cannot choose a king, or nominate a royal family. In a word, no function which has a particular object belongs to the legislative power.

On this view, we at once see that it can no longer be asked whose business it is to make laws, since they are acts of the general will; nor whether the prince is above the law, since he is a member of the State; nor whether the law can be unjust, since no one is unjust to himself; nor how we can be both free and subject to the laws, since they are but registers of our wills.

We see further that, as the law unites universality of will with universality of object, what a man, whoever he be, commands of his own motion cannot be a law; and even what the Sovereign commands with regard to a particular matter is no nearer being a law, but is a decree, an act, not of sovereignty, but of magistracy.

I therefore give the name "Republic" to every State that is governed by laws, no matter what the form of its administration may be: for only in such a case does the public interest govern, and the *res publica* rank as a *reality*. Every legitimate government is republican;[7] what government is I will explain later on.

Laws are, properly speaking, only the conditions of civil association. The people, being subject to the laws, ought to be their author: the conditions of the society ought to be regulated solely by those who come together to form it. But how are they to regulate them? Is it to be by common agreement, by a sudden inspiration? Has the body politic an organ to declare its will? Who can give it the foresight to formulate and announce its acts in advance? Or how is it to announce them in the hour of need? How can a blind multitude, which often does not know what it wills, because it rarely knows what is good for it, carry out for itself so great and difficult an enterprise as a system of legislation? Of itself the people wills always the good, but of itself it by no means always sees it. The general will is always in the right, but the judgment which guides it is not always enlightened. It must be got to see objects as they are, and sometimes as they ought to appear to it; it must be shown the good road it is in search of, secured from the seductive influences of individual wills, taught to see times and spaces as a series, and made to weigh the attractions of present and sensible advantages against the danger of distant and hidden evils. The individuals see the good they reject; the public wills the good it does not see. All stand equally in need of guidance. The former must be compelled to bring their wills into conformity with their reason; the latter must be taught to know what it wills. If that is done,

---

7  I understand by this word, not merely an aristocracy or a democracy, but generally any government directed by the general will, which is the law. To be legitimate, the government must be, not one with the Sovereign, but its minister. In such a case even a monarchy is a Republic.

public enlightenment leads to the union of understanding and will in the social body: the parts are made to work exactly together, and the whole is raised to its highest power. This makes a legislator necessary.

## The Legislator

In order to discover the rules of society best suited to nations, a superior intelligence beholding all the passions of men without experiencing any of them would be needed. This intelligence would have to be wholly unrelated to our nature, while knowing it through and through; its happiness would have to be independent of us, and yet ready to occupy itself with ours; and lastly, it would have, in the march of time, to look forward to a distant glory, and, working in one century, to be able to enjoy in the next.[8] It would take gods to give men laws.

What Caligula argued from the facts, Plato, in the dialogue called the *Politicus,* argued in defining the civil or kingly man, on the basis of right. But if great princes are rare, how much more so are great legislators! The former have only to follow the pattern which the latter have to lay down. The legislator is the engineer who invents the machine, the prince merely the mechanic who sets it up and makes it go. "At the birth of societies," says Montesquieu, "the rulers of Republics establish institutions, and afterwards the institutions mould the rulers."[9]

He who dares to undertake the making of a people's institutions ought to feel himself capable, so to speak, of changing human nature, of transforming each individual, who is by himself a complete and solitary whole, into part of a greater whole from which he in a manner receives his life and being; of altering man's constitution for the purpose of strengthening it; and of substituting a partial and moral existence for the physical and independent existence nature has conferred on us all. He must, in a word, take away from man his own resources and give him instead new ones alien to him, and incapable of being made use of without the help of other men. The more completely these natural resources are annihilated, the greater and more lasting are those which he acquires, and the more stable and perfect the new institutions; so that if each citizen is nothing and can do nothing without the rest, and the resources acquired by the whole are equal or superior to the aggregate of the resources of all the individuals, it may be said that legislation is at the highest possible point of perfection.

The legislator occupies in every respect an extraordinary position in the State. If he should do so by reason of his genius, he does so no less by reason of his office, which is neither magistracy, nor Sovereignty. This office, which sets up the Republic, nowhere enters into its constitution; it is an individual and superior function, which has nothing in common with human empire; for if he who holds command over men ought not to have command over the laws, he who has command over the laws ought not any more to have it over men; or else his laws would be

---

8 A people becomes famous only when its legislation begins to decline. We do not know for how many centuries the system of Lycurgus made the Spartans happy before the rest of Greece took any notice of it.

9 Montesquieu, *The Greatness and Decadence of the Romans,* chap. i.

the ministers of his passions and would often merely serve to perpetuate his injustices: his private aims would inevitably mar the sanctity of his work.

When Lycurgus gave laws to his country, he began by resigning the throne. It was the custom of most Greek towns to entrust the establishment of their laws to foreigners. The Republics of modern Italy in many cases followed this examples; Geneva did the same and profited by it.[10] Rome, when it was most prosperous, suffered a revival of all the crimes of tyranny, and was brought to the verge of destruction, because it put the legislative authority and the sovereign power into the same hands.

Nevertheless, the decemvirs themselves never claimed the right to pass any law merely on their own authority. "Nothing we propose to you," they said to the people, "can pass into law without your consent. Romans, be yourselves the authors of the laws which are to make you happy."

He, therefore, who draws up the laws has, or should have, no right of legislation, and the people cannot, even if it wishes, deprive itself of this incommunicable right, because, according to the fundamental compact, only the general will can bind the individuals, and there can be no assurance that a particular will is in conformity with the general will, until it has been put to the free vote of the people. This I have said already; but it is worth while to repeat it.

Thus in the task of legislation we find together two things which appear to be incompatible; an enterprise too difficult for human powers, and, for its execution, an authority that is no authority.

There is a further difficulty that deserves attention. Wise men, if they try to speak their language to the common herd instead of its own, cannot possibly make themselves understood. There are a thousand kinds of ideas which it is impossible to translate into popular language. Conceptions that are too general and objects that are too remote are equally out of its range: each individual, having no taste for any other plan of government than that which suits his particular interest, finds it difficult to realize the advantages he might hope to draw from the continual privations good laws impose. For a young people to be able to relish sound principles of political theory and follow the fundamental rules of statecraft, the effect would have to become the cause; the social spirit, which should be created by these institutions, would have to preside over their very foundation; and men would have to be before law what they should become by means of law. The legislator therefore, being unable to appeal to either force or reason, must have recourse to an authority of a different order, capable of constraining without violence and persuading without convincing.

This is what has, in all ages, compelled the fathers of nations to have recourse to divine intervention and credit the gods with their own wisdom, in order that the peoples, submitting to the laws of the State as to those of nature, and recognizing the same power in the formation of the city as in that of man, might obey freely, and bear with docility the yoke of the public happiness.

This sublime reason, far above the range of the common herd, is that whose decisions the legislator puts into the mouth of the

---

10 Those who know Calvin only as a theologian much underestimate the extent of his genius. The codification of our wise edicts, in which he played a large part, does him no less honour than his *Institutes*. Whatever revolution time may bring in our religion, so long as the spirit of patriotism and liberty still lives among us, the memory of this great man will be for ever blessed.

immortals, in order to constrain by divine authority those whom human prudence could not move.[11] But it is not anybody who can make the gods speak, or get himself believed when he proclaims himself their interpreter. The great soul of the legislator is the only miracle that can prove his mission. Any man may grave tablets of stone, or buy an oracle, or feign secret intercourse with some divinity, or train a bird to whisper in his ear, or find other vulgar ways of imposing on the people. He whose knowledge goes no further may perhaps gather round him a band of fools; but he will never found an empire, and his extravagances will quickly perish with him. Idle tricks form a passing tie; only wisdom can make it lasting. The Judaic law, which still subsists, and that of the child of Ishmael, which, for ten centuries, has ruled half the world, still proclaim the great men who laid them down; and, while the pride of philosophy or the blind spirit of faction sees in them no more than lucky impostures, the true political theorist admires, in the institutions they set up, the great and powerful genius which presides over things made to endure.

We should not, with Warburton, conclude from this that politics and religion have among us a common object, but that, in the first periods of nations, the one is used as an instrument for the other.

---

11  "In truth," says Machiavelli, "there has never been, in any country, an extraordinary legislator who has not had recourse to God; for otherwise his laws would not have been accepted: there are, in fact, many useful truths of which a wise man may have knowledge without their having in themselves such clear reasons for their being so as to be able to convince others" (*Discourses on Livy*, Bk. V, chap. xi).

# The People

As nature has set bounds to the stature of a well-made man, and, outside those limits, makes nothing but giants or dwarfs, similarly, for the constitution of a State to be at its best, it is possible to fix limits that will make it neither too large for good government, nor too small for self-maintenance. In every body politic there is a maximum strength which it cannot exceed and which it only loses by increasing in size. Every extension of the social tie means its relaxation; and, generally speaking, a small State is stronger in proportion than a great one.

A thousand arguments could be advanced in favour of this principle. First, long distances make administration more difficult, just as a weight becomes heavier at the end of a longer lever. Administration therefore becomes more and more burdensome as the distance grows greater; for, in the first place, each city has its own, which is paid for by the people: each district its own, still paid for by the people: then comes each province, and then the great governments, satrapies, and viceroyalties, always costing more the higher you go, and always at the expense of the unfortunate people. Last of all comes the supreme administration, which eclipses all the rest. All these overcharges are a continual drain upon the subjects; so far from being better governed by all these different orders, they are worse governed than if there were only a single authority over them. In the meantime, there scarce remain resources enough to meet emergencies; and, when recourse must be had to these, the State is always on the eve of destruction.

This is not all; not only has the government less vigour and promptitude for securing the observance of the laws, preventing nuisances, correcting abuses, and guarding against seditious undertakings begun in distant places; the people has less affection for its rulers, whom it never sees, for its country, which, to its eyes, seems like the world, and for its fellow citizens, most of whom are unknown to it. The same laws cannot suit so many diverse provinces with different customs, situated in the most various climates, and incapable of enduring a uniform government. Different laws lead only to trouble and confusion among peoples which, living under the same rulers and in constant communication one with another, intermingle and intermarry, and, coming under the sway of new customs, never know if they can call their very patrimony their own. Talent is buried, virtue unknown, and vice unpunished, among such a multitude of men who do not know one another, gathered together in one place at the seat of the central administration. The leaders, overwhelmed with business, see nothing for themselves; the State is governed by clerks. Finally, the measures which have to be taken to maintain the general authority, which all these distant officials wish to escape or to impose upon, absorb all the energy of the public, so that there is none left for the happiness of the people. There is hardly enough to defend it when need arises, and thus a body which is too big for its constitution gives way and falls crushed under its own weight.

Again, the State must assure itself a safe foundation, if it is to have stability, and to be able to resist the shocks it cannot help experiencing, as well as the efforts it will be forced to make for its maintenance; for all peoples have a kind of centrifugal force that makes them continually act one against another, and tend to aggrandize themselves at their neighbours' expense, like the vortices of Descartes. Thus the weak run the risk of being soon swallowed up; and it is almost impossible for any one

to preserve itself except by putting itself in a state of equilibrium with all, so that the pressure is on all sides practically equal.

It may therefore be seen that there are reasons for expansion and reasons for contraction; and it is no small part of the statesman's skill to hit between them the mean that is most favourable to the preservation of the State. It may be said that the reason for expansion, being merely external and relative, ought to be subordinate to the reasons for contraction, which are internal and absolute. A strong and healthy constitution is the first thing to look for; and it is better to count on the vigour which comes of good government than on the resources a great territory furnishes.

It may be added that there have been known States so constituted that the necessity of making conquests entered into their very constitution, and that, in order to maintain themselves, they were forced to expand ceaselessly. It may be that they congratulated themselves greatly on this fortunate necessity, which none the less indicated to them, along with the limits of their greatness, the inevitable moment of their fall.

## Government in General

I warn the reader that this chapter requires careful reading, and that I am unable to make myself clear to those who refuse to be attentive.

Every free action is produced by the concurrence of two causes; one moral, i.e. the will which determines the act; the other physical, i.e. the power which executes it. When I walk towards an object, it is necessary first that

I should will to go there, and, in the second place, that my feet should carry me. If a paralytic wills to run and an active man wills not to, they will both stay where they are. The body politic has the same motive powers; here too force and will are distinguished, will under the name of legislative power and force under that of executive power. Without their concurrence, nothing is, or should be, done.

We have seen that the legislative power belongs to the people, and can belong to it alone. It may, on the other hand, readily be seen, from the principles laid down above, that the executive power cannot belong to the generality as legislature or Sovereign, because it consists wholly of particular acts which fall outside the competency of the law, and consequently of the Sovereign, whose acts must always be laws.

The public force therefore needs an agent of its own to bind it together and set it to work under the direction of the general will, to serve as a means of communication between the State and the Sovereign, and to do for the collective person more or less what the union of soul and body does for man.

Here we have what is, in the State, the basis of government, often wrongly confused with the Sovereign, whose minister it is.

What then is government? An intermediate body set up between the subjects and the Sovereign, to secure their mutual correspondence, charged with the execution of the laws and the maintenance of liberty, both civil and political.

The members of this body are called magistrates or *kings,* that is to say *governors,* and the whole body bears the name *prince.*[12] Thus those who hold that the act, by which a people puts itself under a prince, is not a contract, are certainly right. It is simply and solely a commission, an employment, in which the rulers, mere officials of the Sovereign, exercise in their own name the power of which it makes them depositaries. This power it can limit, modify, or recover at pleasure; for the alienation of such a right is incompatible with the nature of the social body, and contrary to the end of association.

I call then *government,* or supreme administration, the legitimate exercise of the executive power, and prince or magistrate the man or the body entrusted with that administration.

In government reside the intermediate forces whose relations make up that of the whole to the whole, or of the Sovereign to the State. This last relation may be represented as that between the extreme terms of the continuous proportion, which has government as its mean proportional. The government gets from the Sovereign the orders it gives the people, and, for the State to be properly balanced, there must, when everything is reckoned in, be equality between the product or power of the government taken in itself, and the product or power of the citizens, who are on the one hand sovereign and on the other subject.

Furthermore, none of these three terms can be altered without the equality being instantly destroyed. If the Sovereign desires to govern, or the magistrate to give laws, or if the subjects refuse to obey, disorder takes the place of regularity, force and will no longer act together, and the State is dissolved and falls into despotism or anarchy. Lastly, as there is only one mean proportional between each relation, there is also only one good government possible for a State. But, as countless events may change the relations of a people, not only may different governments be good

---

12  Thus at Venice the College, even in the absence of the Doge, is called "Most Serene Prince."

for different peoples, but also for the same people at different times.

In attempting to give some idea of the various relations that may hold between these two extreme terms, I shall take as an example the number of a people, which is the most easily expressible.

Suppose the State is composed of ten thousand citizens. The Sovereign can only be considered collectively and as a body; but each member, as being a subject, is regarded as an individual: thus the Sovereign is to the subject as ten thousand to one, i.e. each member of the State has as his share only a ten-thousandth part of the sovereign authority, although he is wholly under its control. If the people numbers a hundred thousand, the condition of the subject undergoes no change, and each equally is under the whole authority of the laws, while his vote, being reduced to one hundred thousandth part, has ten times less influence in drawing them up. The subject therefore remaining always a unit, the relation between him and the Sovereign increases with the number of citizens. From this it follows that, the larger the State, the less the liberty.

When I say the relation increases, I mean that it grows more unequal. Thus the greater it is in the geometrical sense, the less relation there is in the ordinary sense of the word. In the former sense, the relation, considered according to quantity, is expressed by the quotient; in the latter, considered according to identity, it is reckoned by similarity.

Now, the less relation the particular wills have to the general will, that is, morals and manners to laws, the more should the repressive force be increased The government, then, to be good, should be proportionately stronger as the people is more numerous.

On the other hand, as the growth of the State gives the depositaries of the public authority more temptations and chances of abusing their power, the greater the force with which the government ought to be endowed for keeping the people in hand, the greater too should be the force at the disposal of the Sovereign for keeping the government in hand. I am speaking, not of absolute force, but of the relative force of the different parts of the state.

It follows from this double relation that the continuous proportion between the Sovereign, the prince, and the people, is by no means an arbitrary idea, but a necessary consequence of the nature of the body politic. It follows further that, one of the extreme terms, viz. the people, as subject, being fixed and represented by unity, whenever the duplicate ratio increases or diminishes, the simple ratio does the same, and is changed accordingly. From this we see that there is not a single unique and absolute form of government, but as many governments differing in nature as there are States differing in size.

If, ridiculing this system, any one were to say that, in order to find the mean proportional and give form to the body of the government, it is only necessary, according to me, to find the square root of the number of the people, I should answer that I am here taking this number only as an instance; that the relations of which I am speaking are not measured by the number of men alone, but generally by the amount of action, which is a combination of a multitude of causes; and that, further, if, to save words, I borrow for a moment the terms of geometry, I am none the less well aware that moral quantities do not allow of geometrical accuracy.

The government is on a small scale what the body politic which includes it is on a great one. It is a moral person endowed with certain faculties, active like the Sovereign and passive like the State, and capable of being resolved into other similar relations. This accordingly gives rise to a new proportion, within which there is yet another, according to the arrangement of the magistracies, till an indivisible middle term is reached, i.e. a single ruler or supreme magistrate, who may be represented, in the midst of this progression, as the unity between the fractional and the ordinal series.

Without encumbering ourselves with this multiplication of terms, let us rest content with regarding government as a new body within the State, distinct from the people and the Sovereign, and intermediate between them.

There is between these two bodies this essential difference, that the State exists by itself, and the government only through the Sovereign. Thus the dominant will of the prince is, or should be, nothing but the general will or the law; his force is only the public force concentrated in his hands, and, as soon as he tries to base any absolute and independent act on his own authority, the tie that binds the whole together begins to be loosened. If finally the prince should come to have a particular will more active than the will of the Sovereign, and should employ the public force in his hands in obedience to this particular will, there would be, so to speak, two Sovereigns, one rightful and the other actual, the social union would evaporate instantly, and the body politic would be dissolved.

However, in order that the government may have a true existence and a real life distinguishing it from the body of the State, and in order that all its members may be able to act in concert and fulfil the end for which it was set up, it must have a particular personality, a sensibility common to its members, and a force and will of its own making for its preservation. This particular existence implies assemblies, councils, power of deliberation and decision, rights, titles, and privileges belonging exclusively to the prince and making the office of magistrate more honourable in proportion as it is more troublesome. The difficulties lie in the manner of so ordering this subordinate whole within the whole, that it in no way alters the general constitution by affirmation of its own, and always distinguishes the particular force it possesses, which is destined to aid in its preservation, from the public force, which is destined to the preservation of the State; and, in a word, is always ready to sacrifice the government to the people, and never to sacrifice the people to the government.

Furthermore, although the artificial body of the government is the work of another artificial body, and has, we may say, only a borrowed and subordinate life, this does not prevent it from being able to act with more or less vigour or promptitude, or from being, so to speak, in more or less robust health. Finally, without departing directly from the end for which it was instituted, it may deviate more or less from it, according to the manner of its constitution.

From all these differences arise the various relations which the government ought to bear to the body of the State, according to the accidental and particular relations by which the State itself is modified, for often the government that is best in itself will become the most pernicious, if the relations in which it stands have altered according to the defects of the body politic to which it belongs.

# Democracy

He who makes the law knows better than any one else how it should be executed and interpreted. It seems then impossible to have a better constitution than that in which the executive and legislative powers are united; but this very fact renders the government in certain respects inadequate, because things which should be distinguished are confounded, and the prince and the Sovereign, being the same person, form, so to speak, no more than a government without government.

It is not good for him who makes the laws to execute them, or for the body of the people to turn its attention away from a general standpoint and devote it to particular objects. Nothing is more dangerous than the influence of private interests in public affairs, and the abuse of the laws by the government is a less evil than the corruption of the legislator, which is the inevitable sequel to a particular standpoint. In such a case, the State being altered in substance, all reformation becomes impossible. A people that would never misuse governmental powers would never misuse independence; a people that would always govern well would not need to be governed.

If we take the term in the strict sense, there never has been a real democracy, and there never will be. It is against the natural order for the many to govern and the few to be governed. It is unimaginable that the people should remain continually assembled to devote their time to public affairs, and it is clear that they cannot set up commissions for that purpose without the form of administration being changed.

In fact, I can confidently lay down as a principle that, when the functions of government are shared by several tribunals, the less numerous sooner or later acquire the greatest authority, if only because they are in position to expedite affairs, and power thus naturally comes into their hands.

Besides, how many conditions that are difficult to unite does such a government presuppose! First, a very small State, where the people can readily be got together and where each citizen can with ease know all the rest; secondly, great simplicity of manners, to prevent business from multiplying and raising thorny problems; next, a large measure of equality in rank and fortune, without which equality of rights and authority cannot long subsist; lastly, little or no luxury—for luxury either comes of riches or makes them necessary; it corrupts at once rich and poor, the rich by possession and the poor by covetousness; it sells the country to softness and vanity, and takes away from the State all its citizens, to make them slaves one to another, and one and all to public opinion.

This is why a famous writer has made virtue the fundamental principle of Republics; for all these conditions could not exist without virtue. But, for want of the necessary distinctions, that great thinker was often inexact, and sometimes obscure, and did not see that, the sovereign authority being everywhere the same, the same principle should be found in every well-constituted State, in a greater or less degree, it is true, according to the form of the government.

It may be added that there is no government so subject to civil wars and intestine agitations as democratic or popular government, because there is none which has so strong and continual a tendency to change to another form, or which demands more vigilance and courage for its maintenance as it is. Under such a constitution above all, the citizen should arm himself with strength and constancy, and say, every day of his life, what a virtuous Count Palatine said in the Diet of Poland: "Malo periculosam libertatem quam quieturn servitium."

Were there a people of gods, their government would be democratic. So perfect a government is not for men.

## Deputies or Representatives

As soon as public service ceases to be the chief business of the citizens, and they would rather serve with their money than with their persons, the State is not far from its fall. When it is necessary to march out to war, they pay troops and stay at home: when it is necessary to meet in council, they name deputies and stay at home. By reason of idleness and money, they end by having soldiers to enslave their country and representatives to sell it.

It is through the hustle of commerce and the arts, through the greedy self-interest of profit, and through softness and love of amenities that personal services are replaced by money payments. Men surrender a part of their profits in order to have time to increase them at leisure. Make gifts of money, and you will not be long without chains. The word "finance" is a slavish word, unknown in the city-state. In a country that is truly free, the citizens do everything with their own arms and nothing by means of money; so far from paying to be exempted from their duties, they would even pay for the privilege of fulfilling them themselves. I am far from taking the common view: I hold enforced labour to be less opposed to liberty than taxes.

The better the constitution of a State is, the more do public affairs encroach on private in the minds of the citizens. Private affairs are even of much less importance, because the aggregate of the common happiness furnishes a greater proportion of that of each individual, so that there is less for him to seek in particular cares. In a well-ordered city every man flies to the assemblies: under a bad government no one cares to stir a step to get to them, because no one is interested in what happens there, because it is foreseen that the general will not prevail, and lastly because domestic cares are all-absorbing. Good laws lead to the making of better ones; bad ones bring about worse. As soon as any man says of the affairs of the State *What does it matter to me?* the State may be given up for lost.

The lukewarmness of patriotism, the activity of private interest, the vastness of States, conquest, and the abuse of government suggested the method of having deputies or representatives of the people in the national assemblies. These are what, in some countries, men have presumed to call the Third Estate. Thus the individual interest of two orders is put first and second; the public interest occupies only the third place.

Sovereignty, for the same reason as makes it inalienable, cannot be represented; it lies essentially in the general will, and will does not admit of representation: it is either the same, or other; there is no intermediate possibility. The deputies of the people, therefore, are not and cannot be its representatives: they are merely its stewards, and can carry through no definitive acts. Every law the people has not ratified in person is null and void—is, in fact, not a law. The people of England regards itself as free; but it is grossly mistaken; it is free only during the election of members of parliament.

As soon as they are elected, slavery overtakes it, and it is nothing. The use it makes of the short moments of liberty it enjoys shows indeed that it deserves to lose them.

The idea of representation is modern; it comes to us from feudal government, from that iniquitous and absurd system which degrades humanity and dishonours the name of man. In ancient republics and even in monarchies, the people never had representatives; the word itself was unknown. It is very singular that in Rome, where the tribunes were so sacrosanct, it was never even imagined that they could usurp the functions of the people, and that in the midst of so great a multitude they never attempted to pass on their own authority a single *plebiscitum*. We can, however, form an idea of the difficulties caused sometimes by the people being so numerous, from what happened in the time of the Gracchi, when some of the citizens had to cast their votes from the roofs of buildings.

Where right and liberty are everything, disadvantages count for nothing. Among this wise people everything was given its just value, its lictors were allowed to do what its tribunes would never have dared to attempt; for it had no fear that its lictors would try to represent it.

To explain, however, in what way the tribunes did sometimes represent it, it is enough to conceive how the government represents the Sovereign. Law being purely the declaration of the general will, it is clear that, in the exercise of the legislative power, the people cannot be represented; but in that of the executive power, which is only the force that is applied to give the law effect, it both can and should be represented. We thus see that if we looked closely into the matter we should find that very few nations have any laws. However that may be, it is certain that the tribunes, possessing no executive power, could never represent the Roman people by right of the powers entrusted to them, but only by usurping those of the senate.

In Greece, all that the people had to do, it did for itself; it was constantly assembled in the public square. The Greeks lived in a mild climate; they had no natural greed; slaves did their work for them; their great concern was with liberty. Lacking the same advantages, how can you preserve the same rights? Your severer climates add to your needs;[13] for half the year your public squares are uninhabitable; the flatness of your languages unfits them for being heard in the open air; you sacrifice more for profit than for liberty, and fear slavery less than poverty.

What then? Is liberty maintained only by the help of slavery? It may be so. Extremes meet. Everything that is not in the course of nature has its disadvantages, civil society most of all. There are some unhappy circumstances in which we can only keep our liberty at others' expense, and where the citizen can be perfectly free only when the slave is most a slave. Such was the case with Sparta. As for you, modern peoples, you have no slaves, but you are slaves yourselves; you pay for their liberty with your own. It is in vain that you boast of this preference; I find in it more cowardice than humanity.

I do not mean by all this that it is necessary to have slaves, or that the right of slavery is legitimate: I am merely giving the reason why modern peoples, believing themselves to be free, have representatives, while ancient peoples had none. In any case, the moment a people allows itself to be represented, it is no longer free: it no longer exists.

---

13  To adopt in cold countries the luxury and effeminacy of the East is to desire to submit to its chains; it is indeed to bow to them far more inevitably in our case than in theirs.

All things considered, I do not see that it is possible henceforth for the Sovereign to preserve among us the exercise of its rights, unless the city is very small. But if it is very small, it will be conquered? No. I will show later on how the external strength of a great people may be combined with the convenient polity and good order of a small State.

## Voting

It may be seen that the way in which general business is managed may give a clear enough indication of the actual state of morals and the health of the body politic. The more concert reigns in the assemblies, that is, the nearer opinion approaches unanimity, the greater is the dominance of the general will. On the other hand, long debates, dissensions, and tumult proclaim the ascendancy of particular interests and the decline of the State.

This seems less clear when two or more orders enter into the constitution, as patricians and plebeians did at Rome; for quarrels between these two orders often disturbed the comitia, even in the best days of the Republic. But the exception is rather apparent than real; for then, through the defect that is inherent in the body politic, there were, so to speak, two States in one, and what is not true of the two together is true of either separately. Indeed, even in the most stormy times, the *plebiscita* of the people, when the senate did not interfere with them, always went through quietly and by large majorities. The citizens having but one interest, the people had but a single will.

At the other extremity of the circle, unanimity recurs; this is the case when the citizens, having fallen into servitude, have lost both liberty and will. Fear and flattery then change votes into acclamation; deliberation ceases, and only worship or malediction is left. Such was the vile manner in which the senate expressed its views under the emperors. It did so sometimes with absurd precautions. Tacitus observes that, under Otho, the senators, while they heaped curses on Vitellius, contrived at the same time to make a deafening noise, in order that, should he ever become their master, he might not know what each of them had said.

On these various considerations depend the rules by which the methods of counting votes and comparing opinions should be regulated, according as the general will is more or less easy to discover, and the State more or less in its decline.

There is but one law which, from its nature, needs unanimous consent. This is the social compact; for civil association is the most voluntary of all acts. Every man being born free and his own master, no one, under any pretext whatsoever, can make any man subject without his consent. To decide that the son of a slave is born a slave is to decide that he is not born a man.

If then there are opponents when the social compact is made, their opposition does not invalidate the contract, but merely prevents them from being included in it. They are foreigners among citizens. When the State is instituted, residence constitutes consent; to dwell within its territory is to submit to the Sovereign.[14]

---

14  This should of course be understood as applying to a free State; for elsewhere family, goods, lack of a refuge, necessity, or violence may detain a man in a country against his will; and then his dwelling there no longer by itself implies his consent to the contract or to its violation.

Apart from this primitive contract, the vote of the majority always binds all the rest. This follows from the contract itself. But it is asked how a man can be both free and forced to conform to wills that are not his own. How are the opponents at once free and subject to laws they have not agreed to?

I retort that the question is wrongly put. The citizen gives his consent to all the laws, including those which are passed in spite of his opposition, and even those which punish him when he dares to break any of them. The constant will of all the members of the State is the general will; by virtue of it they are citizens and free.[15] When in the popular assembly a law is proposed, what the people is asked is not exactly whether it approves or rejects the proposal, but whether it is in conformity with the general will, which is their will. Each man, in giving his vote, states his opinion on that point; and the general will is found by counting votes. When therefore the opinion that is contrary to my own prevails, this proves neither more nor less than that I was mistaken, and that what I thought to be the general will was not so. If my particular opinion had carried the day I should have achieved the opposite of what was my will; and it is in that case that I should not have been free.

This presupposes, indeed, that all the qualities of the general will still reside in the majority; when they cease to do so, whatever side a man may take, liberty is no longer possible.

In my earlier demonstration of how particular wills are substituted for the general will in public deliberation, I have adequately pointed out the practicable methods of avoiding this abuse; and I shall have more to say of them later on. I have also given the principles for determining the proportional number of votes for declaring that will. A difference of one vote destroys equality; a single opponent destroys unanimity; but between equality and unanimity, there are several grades of unequal division, at each of which this proportion may be fixed in accordance with the condition and the needs of the body politic.

There are two general rules that may serve to regulate this relation. First, the more grave and important the questions discussed, the nearer should the opinion that is to prevail approach unanimity. Secondly, the more the matter in hand calls for speed, the smaller the prescribed difference in the numbers of votes may be allowed to become: where an instant decision has to be reached, a majority of one vote should be enough. The first of these two rules seems more in harmony with the laws, and the second with practical affairs. In any case, it is the combination of them that gives the best proportions for determining the majority necessary.

---

15  At Genoa, the word "Liberty" may be read over the front of the prisons and on the chains of the galley-slaves. This application of the device is good and just. It is indeed only malefactors of all estates who prevent the citizen from being free. In the country in which all such men were in the galleys, the most perfect liberty would be enjoyed.

# The Communist Manifesto

By Karl Marx and Friedrich Engels

**A** spectre is haunting Europe—the spectre of Communism. All the powers of old Europe have entered into a holy alliance to exorcise this spectre: Pope and Czar, Metternich and Guizot, French Radicals and German police-spies.

Where is the party in opposition that has not been decried as communistic by its opponents in power? Where the Opposition that has not hurled back the branding reproach of Communism, against the more advanced opposition parties, as well as against its reactionary adversaries?

Two things result from this fact:

I. Communism is already acknowledged by all European powers to be itself a power.

II. It is high time that Communists should openly, in the face of the whole world, publish their views, their aims, their tendencies, and meet this nursery tale of the spectre of Communism with a manifesto of the party itself.

To this end, Communists of various nationalities have assembled in London, and sketched the following manifesto, to be published in the English, French, German, Italian, Flemish and Danish languages.

## Bourgeois and Proletarians

The history of all hitherto existing society is the history of class struggles.

Freeman and slave, patrician and plebeian, lord and serf, guild-master and journeyman, in a word, oppressor and oppressed, stood in constant opposition to one another, carried on an uninterrupted, now hidden, now open fight, a fight that each time ended, either in a revolutionary reconstitution of society at large, or in the common ruin of the contending classes.

In the earlier epochs of history, we find almost everywhere a complicated arrangement of society into various orders, a manifold gradation of social rank. In ancient Rome we have patricians, knights, plebeians, slaves; in the Middle Ages, feudal lords, vassals, guild-masters, journeymen, apprentices, serfs; in almost all of these classes, again, subordinate gradations.

The modern bourgeois society that has sprouted from the ruins of feudal society, has not done away with class antagonisms. It has but established new classes, new conditions of oppression, new forms of struggle in place of the old ones.

Our epoch, the epoch of the bourgeoisie, possesses, however, this distinctive feature: It has simplified the class antagonisms. Society as a whole is more and more splitting up into two great hostile camps, into two great classes directly facing each other—bourgeoisie and proletariat.

From the serfs of the Middle Ages sprang the chartered burghers of the earliest towns. From these burgesses the first elements of the bourgeoisie were developed.

The discovery of America, the rounding of the Cape, opened up fresh ground for the rising bourgeoisie. The East-Indian and Chinese markets, the colonisation of America, trade with the colonies, the increase in the means of exchange and in commodities generally, gave to commerce, to navigation, to industry, an impulse never before known, and thereby, to the revolutionary element in the tottering feudal society at rapid development.

The feudal system of industry, in which industrial production was monopolised by closed guilds, now no longer sufficed for the growing wants of the new markets. The manufacturing system took its place. The guild-masters were pushed aside by the manufacturing middle class; division of labour between the different corporate guilds vanished in the face of division of labour in each single workshop.

Meantime the markets kept ever growing, the demand ever rising. Even manufacture no longer sufficed. Thereupon, steam and machinery revolutionised industrial production. The place of manufacture was taken by the giant, modern industry, the place of the industrial middle class, by industrial millionaires—the leaders of whole industrial armies, the modern bourgeoisie.

Modern industry has established the world market, for which the discovery of America paved the way. This market has given an immense development to commerce, to navigation, to communication by land. This development has, in its turn, reacted on the extension of industry; and in proportion as industry, commerce, navigation, railways extended, in the same proportion the bourgeoisie developed, increased its capital, and pushed into the background every class handed down from the Middle Ages.

We see, therefore, how the modern bourgeoisie is itself the product of a long course of development, of a series of revolutions in the modes of production and of exchange.

Each step in the development of the bourgeoisie was accompanied by a corresponding political advance of that class. An oppressed class under the sway of the feudal nobility, it became an armed and self-governing association in the mediaeval commune; here independent urban republic (as in Italy and Germany), there taxable "third estate" of the monarchy (as in France); afterwards, in the period of manufacture proper, serving either the semi-feudal or the absolute monarchy as a counterpoise against the nobility, and, in fact, cornerstone of the great monarchies in general—the bourgeoisie has at last, since the establishment of modern industry and of the world market, conquered for itself, in the modern representative state, exclusive political sway. The executive of the modern state is but a committee for managing the common affairs of the whole bourgeosie.

The bourgeoisie has played a most revolutionary rôle in history.

The bourgeoisie, wherever it has got the upper hand, has put an end to all feudal, patriarchal, idyllic relations. It has pitilessly torn asunder the motley feudal ties that bound man to his "natural superiors," and has left no other bond between man and man than naked self-interest, than callous "cash payment." It has drowned the most heavenly ecstasies of religious fervour, of chivalrous enthusiasm, of philistine sentimentalism, in the icy water of egotistical calculation. It has resolved personal worth into exchange value, and in place of the numberless indefeasible chartered freedoms, has set up that single, unconscionable freedom—Free Trade. In one word, for exploitation, veiled by religious and political illusions, it has substituted naked, shameless, direct, brutal exploitation.

The bourgeoisie has stripped of its halo every occupation hitherto honoured and looked up to with reverent awe. It has converted the physician, the lawyer, the priest, the poet, the man of science, into its paid wage-labourers.

The bourgeoisie has torn away from the family its sentimental veil, and has reduced the family relation to a mere money relation.

The bourgeoisie has disclosed how it came to pass that the brutal display of vigour in the Middle Ages, which reactionaries so much admire, found its fitting complement in the most slothful indolence. It has been the first to show what man's activity can bring about. It has accomplished wonders far surpassing Egyptian pyramids, Roman aqueducts, and Gothic cathedrals; it has conducted expeditions that put in the shade all former migrations of nations and crusades.

The bourgeoisie cannot exist without constantly revolutionising the instruments of production, and thereby the relations of production, and with them the whole relations of society. Conservation of the old modes of production in unaltered form, was, on the contrary, the first condition of existence for all earlier industrial classes. Constant revolutionising of production, uninterrupted disturbance of all social conditions, everlasting uncertainty and agitation distinguish the bourgeois epoch from all earlier ones. All fixed, fast-frozen relations, with their train of ancient and venerable prejudices and opinions, are swept away, all new-formed ones become antiquated before they can ossify. All that is solid melts into air, all that is holy is profaned, and man is at last compelled to face with sober senses his real conditions of life and his relations with his kind.

The need of a constantly expanding market for its products chases the bourgeoisie over the whole surface of the globe. It must nestle everywhere, settle everywhere, establish connections everywhere.

The bourgeoisie has through its exploitation of the world market given a cosmopolitan character to production and consumption in every country. To the great chagrin of reactionaries, it has drawn from under the feet of industry the national ground on which it stood. All old-established national industries have been destroyed or are daily being destroyed. They are dislodged by new industries, whose introduction becomes a life and death question for all civilised nations, by industries that no longer work up indigenous raw material, but raw material drawn from the remotest zones; industries whose products are consumed, not only at home, but in every quarter of the globe. In place of the old wants, satisfied by the production of the country, we find new wants, requiring for their satisfaction the products of distant lands and climes. In place of the old local and national seclusion and self-sufficiency, we have intercourse in every direction, universal interdependence of nations. And as in material, so also in intellectual production. The intellectual creations of individual nations become common property. National onesidedness and narrow-mindedness become more and more impossible, and from the numerous national and local literatures there arises a world literature.

The bourgeoisie, by the rapid improvement of all instruments of production, by the immensely facilitated means of communication, draws all nations, even the most barbarian, into civilisation. The cheap prices of its commodities are the heavy artillery with which it batters down all Chinese walls, with which it forces the barbarians' intensely obstinate hatred of foreigners to capitulate. It compels all nations, on pain of extinction, to adopt the bourgeois mode of production; it compels them to introduce what it calls civilisation into their midst, *i.e.,* to become bourgeois themselves. In a word, it creates a world after its own image.

The bourgeoisie has subjected the country to the rule of the towns. It has created enormous cities, has greatly increased the urban population as compared with the rural, and has thus rescued a considerable part of the population from the idiocy of rural life. Just as it has made the country dependent on the towns, so it has made barbarian and semi-barbarian countries dependent on the civilised ones, nations of peasants on nations of bourgeois, the East on the West.

The bourgeoisie keeps more and more doing away with the scattered state of the population, of the means of production, and of property. It has agglomerated population, centralised means of production, and has concentrated property in a few hands. The necessary consequence of this was political centralisation. Independent, or but loosely connected provinces, with separate interests, laws, governments and systems of taxation, became lumped together into one nation, with one government, one code of laws, one national class interest, one frontier and one customs tariff.

The bourgeoisie, during its rule of scarce one hundred years, has created more massive and more colossal productive forces than have all preceding generations together. Subjection of nature's forces to man, machinery, application of chemistry to industry and agriculture, steam-navigation, railways, electric telegraphs, clearing of whole continents for cultivation, canalisation of rivers, whole populations conjured out of the ground—what earlier century had even a presentiment that such productive forces slumbered in the lap of social labour?

We see then that the means of production and of exchange, which served as the foundation for the growth of the bourgeoisie, were generated in feudal society. At a certain stage in the development of these means of production and of exchange, the conditions under which feudal society produced and exchanged, the feudal organisation of agriculture and manufacturing industry, in a word, the feudal relations of property became no longer compatible with the already developed productive forces; they became so many fetters. They had to be burst asunder; they were burst asunder.

Into their place stepped free competition, accompanied by a social and political constitution adapted to it, and by the economic and political sway of the bourgeois class.

A similar movement is going on before our own eyes. Modern bourgeois society with its relations of production, of exchange and of property, a society that has conjured up such gigantic means of production and of exchange, is like the sorcerer who is no longer able to control the powers of the nether world whom he has called up by his spells. For many a decade past the history of industry and commerce is but the history of the revolt of modern productive forces against modern conditions of production, against the property relations that are the conditions for the existence of the bourgeoisie and of its rule. It is enough to mention the commercial crises that by their periodical return put the existence of the entire bourgeois society on trial, each time more threateningly. In these crises a great part not only of the existing products, but also of the previously created productive forces, are periodically destroyed. In these crises there breaks out an epidemic that, in all earlier epochs, would have seemed an absurdity—the epidemic of over-production. Society suddenly finds itself put back into a state of momentary barbarism; it appears as if a famine, a universal war of devastation had cut off the supply of every means of subsistence; industry and commerce seem to be destroyed. And why? Because there is too much civilization, too much means of subsistence, too much industry, too much commerce. The productive forces at the disposal of society no longer tend to further the development of the conditions of bourgeois property; on the contrary, they have become too powerful for these conditions, by which they are fettered, and no sooner do they overcome these fetters than they bring disorder into the whole of bourgeois society, endanger the existence of bourgeois property. The conditions of bourgeois society are too narrow to comprise the wealth created by them. And how does the bourgeoisie get over these crises? On the one hand by enforced destruction of a mass of productive forces; on the other, by the conquest of new markets, and by the more thorough exploitation of the old ones. That is to say, by paving the way for more extensive and more destructive crises, and by diminishing the means whereby crises are prevented.

The weapons with which the bourgeoisie felled feudalism to the ground are now turned against the bourgeoisie itself.

But not only has the bourgeoisie forged the weapons that bring death to itself; it has also called into existence the men who are to wield those weapons—the modern working class—the proletarians.

In proportion as the bourgeoisie, *i.e.*, capital, is developed, in the same proportion is the proletariat, the modern working class, developed—a class of labourers, who live only so long as they find work, and who find work only so long as their labour increases capital. These labourers, who must sell themselves piecemeal, are a commodity, like every other article of commerce, and are consequently exposed to all the vicissitudes of competition, to all the fluctuations of the market.

Owing to the extensive use of machinery and to division of labour, the work of the proletarians has lost all individual character, and, consequently, all charm for the workman. He becomes an appendage of the machine, and it is only the most simple, most monotonous, and most easily acquired knack, that is required of him. Hence, the cost of production of a workman is restricted, almost entirely, to the means of subsistence that he requires for his maintenance, and for the propagation of his race. But the price of a commodity, and therefore also of labour, is equal to its cost of production. In proportion, therefore, as the repulsiveness of the work increases, the wage decreases. Nay more, in proportion as the use of machinery and division of labour increases, in the same proportion the burden of toil also increases, whether by prolongation of the working hours, by increase of the work exacted in a given time, or by increased speed of the machinery, etc.

Modern industry has converted the little workshop of the patriarchal master into the great factory of the industrial capitalist. Masses of labourers, crowded into the factory, are organised like soldiers. As privates of the industrial army they are placed under the command of a perfect hierarchy of officers and sergeants. Not only are they slaves of the bourgeois class, and of the bourgeois state; they are daily and hourly enslaved by the machine, by the overseer, and, above all, by the individual bourgeois manufacturer himself. The more openly this despotism proclaims gain to be its end and aim, the more petty, the more hateful and the more embittering it is.

The less the skill and exertion of strength implied in manual labour, in other words, the more modern industry develops, the more is the labour of men superseded by that of women. Differences of age and sex have no longer any distinctive social validity for the working class. All are instruments of labour, more or less expensive to use, according to their age and sex.

No sooner has the labourer received his wages in cash, for the moment escaping exploitation by the manufacturer, than he is set upon by the other portions of the bourgeoisie, the landlord, the shopkeeper, the pawnbroker, etc.

The lower strata of the middle class—the small tradespeople, shopkeepers, and retired tradesman generally, the handicraftsmen and peasants—all these sink gradually into the proletariat, partly because their diminutive capital does not suffice for the scale on which modern industry is carried on, and is swamped in the competition with the large capitalists, partly because their specialised skill is rendered worthless by new methods of production. Thus the proletariat is recruited from all classes of the population.

The proletariat goes through various stages of development. With its birth begins its struggle with the bourgeoisie. At first the contest is carried on by individual labourers, then by the work people of a factory, then by the operatives of one trade, in one locality, against the individual bourgeois who directly exploits them. They direct their attacks not against the bourgeois conditions of production, but against the instruments of production themselves; they destroy imported wares that compete with their labour, they smash machinery to pieces, they set factories ablaze, they seek to restore by force the vanished status of the workman of the Middle Ages.

At this stage the labourers still form an incoherent mass scattered over the whole country, and broken up by their mutual competition. If anywhere they unite to form more compact bodies, this is not yet the consequence of their own active union, but of the union of the bourgeoisie, which class, in order to attain its own political ends, is compelled to set the whole proletariat in motion, and is moreover still able to do so for a time. At this stage, therefore, the proletarians do not fight their enemies, but the enemies of their enemies, the remnants of absolute monarchy, the landowners, the nonindustrial bourgeois, the petty bourgeoisie. Thus the whole historical movement is concentrated in the hands of the bourgeoisie; every victory so obtained is a victory for the bourgeoisie.

But with the development of industry the proletariat not only increases in number; it becomes concentrated in greater masses, its strength grows, and it feels that strength more. The various interests and conditions of life within the ranks of the proletariat are more and more equalised, in proportion as machinery obliterates all distinctions of labour and nearly everywhere reduces wages to the same low level. The growing competition among the bourgeois, and the resulting commercial crises, makes the wages of the workers ever more fluctuating. The unceasing improvement of machinery, ever more rapidly developing, makes their livelihood more and more precarious; the collisions between individual workmen and individual bourgeois take more and more the character of collisions between two classes. Thereupon the workers begin to form combinations (trade unions) against the bourgeoisie; they club together in order to keep up the rate of wages; they found permanent associations in order to make provision beforehand for these occasional revolts. Here and there the contest breaks out into riots.

Now and then the workers are victorious, but only for a time. The real fruit of their battles lies, not in the immediate result, but in the ever expanding union of the workers. This union is furthered by the improved means of communication which are created by modern industry, and which place the workers of different localities in contact with one another. It was just this contact that was needed to centralise the numerous local struggles, all of the same character, into one national struggle between classes. But every class struggle is a political struggle. And that union, to attain which the burghers of the Middle Ages, with their miserable highways, required centuries, the modern proletarians, thanks to railways, achieve in a few years.

This organisation of the proletarians into a class, and consequently into a political party, is continually being upset again by the competition between the workers themselves. But it ever rises up again, stronger, firmer, mightier.

It compels legislative recognition of particular interests of the workers, by taking advantage of the divisions among the bourgeoisie itself. Thus the ten-hour bill in England was carried.

Altogether, collisions between the classes of the old society further the course of development of the proletariat in many ways. The bourgeoisie finds itself involved in a constant battle. At first with the aristocracy; later on, with those portions of the bourgeoisie itself whose interests have become antagonistic to the progress of industry; at all times with the bourgeoisie of foreign countries. In all these battles it sees itself compelled to appeal to the proletariat, to ask for its help, and thus, to drag it into the political arena. The bourgeoisie itself, therefore, supplies the proletariat with its own elements of political and general education, in other words, it furnishes the proletariat with weapons for fighting the bourgeoisie.

Further, as we have already seen, entire sections of the ruling classes are, by the advance of industry, precipitated into the proletariat, or are at least threatened in their conditions of existence. These also supply the proletariat with fresh elements of enlightenment and progress.

Finally, in times when the class struggle nears the decisive hour, the process of dissolution going on within the ruling class, in fact within the whole range of old society, assumes such a violent, glaring character, that a small section of the ruling class cuts itself adrift, and joins the revolutionary class, the class that holds the future in its hands. Just as, therefore, at an earlier period, a section of the nobility went over to the bourgeoisie, so now a portion of the bourgeoisie goes over to the proletariat, and in particular, a portion of the bourgeois ideologists, who have raised themselves to the level of comprehending theoretically the historical movement as a whole.

Of all the classes that stand face to face with the bourgeoisie today, the proletariat alone is a really revolutionary class. The other classes decay and finally disappear in the face of modern industry: the proletariat is its special and essential product.

The lower middle class, the small manufacturer, the shopkeeper, the artisan, the peasant, all these fight against the bourgeoisie, to save from extinction their existence as fractions of the middle class. They are therefore not revolutionary but conservative. Nay more, they are reactionary, for they try to roll back the wheel of history. If by chance they are revolutionary, they are so only in view of their impending transfer into the proletariat; they thus defend not their present, but their future interests; they desert their own standpoint to adopt that of the proletariat.

The "dangerous class," the social scum (Lumpenproletariat), that passively rotting mass thrown off by the lowest layers of old society, may, here and there, be swept into the movement by a proletarian revolution; its conditions of life, however, prepare it far more for the part of a bribed tool of reactionary intrigue.

The social conditions of the old society no longer exist for the proletariat. The proletarian is without property; his relation to his wife and children has no longer anything in common with bourgeois family relations; modern industrial labour, modern subjection to capital, the same in England as in France, in America as in Germany, has stripped him of every trace of national character. Law, morality, religion, are to him so many bourgeois prejudices, behind which lurk in ambush just as many bourgeois interests.

All the preceding classes that got the upper hand, sought to fortify their already acquired status by subjecting society at large to their conditions of appropriation. The proletarians cannot become masters of the productive forces of society, except by abolishing their own previous mode of appropriation, and thereby also every other previous mode of appropriation. They have nothing of their own to secure and to fortify; their mission is to destroy all previous securities for, and insurances of, individual property.

All previous historical movements were movements of minorities, or in the interest of minorities. The proletarian movement is the self-conscious, independent movement of the immense majority, in the interest of the immense majority. The proletariat, the lowest stratum of our present society, cannot stir, cannot raise itself up, without the whole super-incumbent strata of official society being sprung into the air.

Though not in substance, yet in form, the struggle of the proletariat with the bourgeoisie is at first a national struggle. The proletariat of each country must, of course, first of all settle matters with its own bourgeoisie.

In depicting the most general phases of the development of the proletariat, we traced the more or less veiled civil war, raging within existing society, up to the point where that war breaks out into open revolution, and where the violent overthrow of the bourgeoisie lays the foundation for the sway of the proletariat.

Hitherto, every form of society has been based, as we have already seen, on the antagonism of oppressing and oppressed classes. But in order to oppress a class, certain conditions must be assured to it under which it can, at least, continue its slavish existence. The serf, in the period of serfdom, raised himself to membership in the commune, just as the petty bourgeois, under the yoke of feudal absolutism, managed to develop into a bourgeois. The modern labourer, on the contrary, instead of rising with the progress of industry, sinks deeper and deeper below the conditions of existence of his own class. He becomes a pauper, and pauperism develops more rapidly than population and wealth. And here it becomes evident, that the bourgeoisie is unfit any longer to be the ruling class in society, and to impose its conditions of existence upon society as an over-riding law. It is unfit to rule because it is incompetent to assure an existence to its slave within his slavery, because it cannot help letting him sink into such a state, that it has to feed him, instead of being fed by him. Society can no longer live under this bourgeoisie, in other words, its existence is no longer compatible with society.

The essential condition for the existence and sway of the bourgeois class, is the formation and augmentation of capital; the condition for capital is wage-labour. Wage-labour rests exclusively on competition between the labourers. The advance of industry, whose involuntary promoter is the bourgeoisie, replaces the isolation of the labourers, due to competition, by their revolutionary combination, due to association. The development of modern industry, therefore, cuts from under its feet the very foundation on which the bourgeoisie produces and appropriates products. What the bourgeoisie therefore produces, above all, are its own grave-diggers. Its fall and the victory of the proletariat are equally inevitable.

## Proletarians and Communists

In what relation do the Communists stand to the proletarians as a whole?

The Communists do not form a separate party opposed to other working class parties.

They have no interests separate and apart from those of the proletariat as a whole.

They do not set up any sectarian principles of their own, by which to shape and mould the proletarian movement.

The Communists are distinguished from the other working class parties by this only: 1. In the national struggles of the proletarians of the different countries, they point out and bring to the front the common interests of the entire proletariat, independently of all nationality. 2. In the various stages of development which the struggle of the working class against the bourgeoisie has to pass through, they always and everywhere represent the interests of the movement as a whole.

The Communists, therefore, are on the one hand, practically, the most advanced and resolute section of the working class parties of every country, that section which pushes forward all others; on the other hand, theoretically, they have over the great mass of the proletariat the advantage of clearly understanding the line of march, the conditions, and the ultimate general results of the proletarian movement.

The immediate aim of the Communists is the same as that of all the other proletarian parties: Formation of the proletariat into a class, overthrow of bourgeois supremacy, conquest of political power by the proletariat.

The theoretical conclusions of the Communists are in no way based on ideas or principles that have been invented, or discovered, by this or that would-be universal reformer.

They merely express, in general terms, actual relations springing from an existing class struggle, from a historical movement going on under our very eyes. The abolition of existing property relations is not at all a distinctive feature of Communism.

All property relations in the past have continually been subject to historical change consequent upon the change in historical conditions.

The French Revolution, for example, abolished feudal property in favour of bourgeois property.

The distinguishing feature of Communism is not the abolition of property generally, but the abolition of bourgeois property. But modern bourgeois private property is the final and most complete expression of the system of producing and appropriating products that is based on class antagonisms, on the exploitation of the many by the few.

In this sense, the theory of the Communists may be summed up in the single sentence: Abolition of private property.

We Communists have been reproached with the desire of abolishing the right of personally acquiring property as the fruit of a man's own labour, which property is alleged to be the groundwork of all personal freedom, activity and independence.

Hard-won, self-acquired, self-earned property! Do you mean the property of the petty artisan and of the small peasant, a form of property that preceded the bourgeois form? There is no need to abolish that; the development of industry has to a great extent already destroyed it, and is still destroying it daily.

Or do you mean modern bourgeois private property?

But does wage-labour create any property for the labourer? Not a bit. It creates capital, *i.e.*, that kind of property which exploits wage-labour, and which cannot increase except upon condition of begetting a new supply of wage-labour for fresh exploitation. Property, in its present form, is based on the antagonism of capital and wage-labour. Let us examine both sides of this antagonism.

To be a capitalist, is to have not only a purely personal, but a social *status* in production. Capital is a collective product, and only by the united action of many members, nay, in the last resort, only by the united action of all members of society, can it be set in motion.

Capital is therefore not a personal, it is a social, power.

When, therefore, capital is converted into common property, into the property of all members of society, personal property is not thereby transformed into social property. It is only the social character of the property that is changed. It loses its class character.

Let us now take wage-labour.

The average price of wage-labour is the minimum wage, *i.e.*, that quantum of the means of subsistence which is absolutely requisite to keep the labourer in bare existence as a labourer. What, therefore, the wage-labourer appropriates by means of his labour, merely suffices to prolong and reproduce a bare existence. We by no means intend to abolish this personal appropriation of the products of labour, an appropriation that is made for the maintenance and reproduction of human life, and that leaves no surplus wherewith to command the labour of others. All that we want to do away with is the miserable character of this appropriation, under which the labourer lives merely to increase capital, and is allowed to live only insofar as the interest of the ruling class requires it.

In bourgeois society, living labour is but a means to increase accumulated labour. In Communist society, accumulated labour is but a means to widen, to enrich, to promote the existence of the labourer.

In bourgeois society, therefore, the past dominates the present; in Communist society, the present dominates the past. In bourgeois society capital is independent and has individuality, while the living person is dependent and has no individuality.

And the abolition of this state of things is called by the bourgeois, abolition of individuality and freedom! And rightly so. The abolition of bourgeois individuality, bourgeois independence, and bourgeois freedom is undoubtedly aimed at.

By freedom is meant, under the present bourgeois conditions of production, free trade, free selling and buying.

But if selling and buying disappears, free selling and buying disappears also. This talk about free selling and buying, and all the other "brave words" of our bourgeoisie about freedom in general, have a meaning, if any, only in contrast with restricted selling and buying, with the fettered traders of the Middle Ages, but have no meaning when opposed to the Communist abolition of buying and selling, of the bourgeois condition of production, and of the bourgeoisie itself.

You are horrified at our intending to do away with private property. But in your existing society, private property is already done away with for nine-tenths of the population; its existence for the few is solely due to its non-existence in the hands of those nine-tenths. You reproach us, therefore, with intending to do away with a form of property, the necessary condition for whose existence is the non-existence of any property for the immense majority of society.

In a word, you reproach us with intending to do away with your property. Precisely so; that is just what we intend.

From the moment when labour can no longer be converted into capital, money, or rent, into a social power capable of being monopolised, *i.e.*, from the moment when individual property can no longer be transformed into bourgeois property, into capital, from that moment, you say, individuality vanishes.

You must, therefore, confess that by "individual" you mean no other person than the bourgeois, than the middle class owner of property. This person must, indeed, be swept out of the way, and made impossible.

Communism deprives no man of the power to appropriate the products of society; all that it does is to deprive him of the power to subjugate the labour of others by means of such appropriation.

It has been objected, that upon the abolition of private property all work will cease, and universal laziness will overtake us.

According to this, bourgeois society ought long ago to have gone to the dogs through sheer idleness; for those of its members who work, acquire nothing, and those who acquire anything, do not work. The whole of this objection is but another expression of the tautology: There can no longer be any wage-labour when there is no longer any capital.

All objections urged against the Communist mode of producing and appropriating material products, have, in the same way, been urged against the Communist modes of producing and appropriating intellectual products. Just as, to the bourgeois, the disappearance of class property is the disappearance of production itself, so the disappearance of class culture is to him identical with the disappearance of all culture.

That culture, the loss of which he laments, is, for the enormous majority, a mere training to act as a machine.

But don't wrangle with us so long as you apply, to our intended abolition of bourgeois property, the standard of your bourgeois notions of freedom, culture, law, etc. Your very ideas are but the outgrowth of the conditions of your bourgeois production and bourgeois property, just as your jurisprudence is but the will of your class made into a law for all, a will whose essential character and direction are determined by the economic conditions of existence of your class.

The selfish misconception that induces you to transform into eternal laws of nature and of reason, the social forms springing from your present mode of production and form of property—historical relations that rise and disappear in the progress of production—this misconception you share with every ruling class that has preceded you. What you see clearly in the case of ancient property, what you admit in the case of feudal property, you are of course forbidden to admit in the case of your own bourgeois form of property.

Abolition of the family! Even the most radical flare up at this infamous proposal of the Communists.

On what foundation is the present family, the bourgeois family, based? On capital, on private gain. In its completely developed form this family exists only among the bourgeoisie. But this state of things finds its complement in the practical absence of the family among the proletarians, and in public prostitution.

The bourgeois family will vanish as a matter of course when its complement vanishes, and both will vanish with the vanishing of capital.

Do you charge us with wanting to stop the exploitation of children by their parents? To this crime we plead guilty.

But, you will say, we destroy the most hallowed of relations, when we replace home education by social.

And your education! Is not that also social, and determined by the social conditions under which you educate, by the intervention of society, direct or indirect, by means of schools, etc.? The Communists have not invented the intervention of society in education; they do but seek to alter the character of that intervention, and to rescue education from the influence of the ruling class.

The bourgeois claptrap about the family and education, about the hallowed co-relation of parent and child, becomes all the more disgusting, the more, by the action of modern industry, all family ties among the proletarians are torn asunder, and their children transformed into simple articles of commerce and instruments of labour.

But you Communists would introduce community of women, screams the whole bourgeoisie in chorus.

The bourgeois sees in his wife a mere instrument of production. He hears that the instruments of production are to be exploited in common, and, naturally, can come to no other conclusion than that the lot of being common to all will likewise fall to the women.

He has not even a suspicion that the real point aimed at is to do away with the status of women as mere instruments of production.

For the rest, nothing is more ridiculous than the virtuous indignation of our bourgeois at the community of women which, they pretend, is to be openly and officially established by the Communists. The Communists have no need to introduce community of women; it has existed almost from time immemorial.

Our bourgeois, not content with having the wives and daughters of their proletarians at their disposal, not to speak of common prostitutes, take the greatest pleasure in seducing each other's wives.

Bourgeois marriage is in reality a system of wives in common and thus, at the most, what the Communists might possibly be reproached with is that they desire to introduce, in substitution for a hypocritically concealed, an openly legalised community of women. For the rest, it is self-evident, that the abolition of the present system of production must bring with it the abolition of the community of women springing from that system, *i.e.*, of prostitution both public and private.

The Communists are further reproached with desiring to abolish countries and nationality.

The workingmen have no country. We cannot take from them what they have not got. Since the proletariat must first of all acquire political supremacy, must rise to be the leading class of the nation, must constitute itself *the* nation, it is, so far, itself national, though not in the bourgeois sense of the word.

National differences and antagonisms between peoples are vanishing gradually from day to day, owing to the development of the bourgeoisie, to freedom of commerce, to the world market, to uniformity in the mode of production and in the conditions of life corresponding thereto.

The supremacy of the proletariat will cause them to vanish still faster. United action, of the leading civilised countries at least, is one of the first conditions for the emancipation of the proletariat.

In proportion as the exploitation of one individual by another is put an end to, the exploitation of one nation by another will also be put an end to. In proportion as the antagonism between classes within the nation vanishes, the hostility of one nation to another will come to an end.

The charges against Communism made from a religious, a philosophical, and, generally, from an ideological standpoint, are not deserving of serious examination.

Does it require deep intuition to comprehend that man's ideas, views, and conceptions, in one word, man's consciousness, changes with every change in the conditions of his material existence, in his social relations and in his social life?

What else does the history of ideas prove, than that intellectual production changes its character in proportion as material production is changed? The ruling ideas of each age have ever been the ideas of its ruling class.

When people speak of ideas that revolutionise society, they do but express the fact that within the old society the elements of a new one have been created, and that the dissolution of the old ideas keeps even pace with the dissolution of the old conditions of existence.

When the ancient world was in its last throes, the ancient religions were overcome by Christianity. When Christian ideas succumbed in the 18th century to rationalist ideas, feudal society fought its death-battle with the then revolutionary bourgeoisie. The ideas of religious liberty and freedom of conscience, merely gave expression to the sway of free competition within the domain of knowledge.

"Undoubtedly," it will be said, "religion, moral, philosophical and juridical ideas have been modified in the course of historical development. But religion, morality, philosophy, political science, and law, constantly survived this change.

"There are, besides, eternal truths, such as Freedom, Justice, etc., that are common to all states of society. But Communism abolishes eternal truths, it abolishes all religion, and all morality, instead of constituting them on a new basis; it therefore acts in contradiction to all past historical experience."

What does this accusation reduce itself to? The history of all past society has consisted in the development of class antagonisms, antagonisms that assumed different forms at different epochs.

But whatever form they may have taken, one fact is common to all past ages, *viz.*, the exploitation of one part of society by the other. No wonder, then, that the social consciousness of past ages, despite all the multiplicity and variety it displays, moves within certain common forms, or general ideas, which cannot completely vanish except with the total disappearance of class antagonisms.

The Communist revolution is the most radical rupture with traditional property relations; no wonder that its development involves the most radical rupture with traditional ideas.

But let us have done with the bourgeois objections to Communism.

We have seen above, that the first step in the revolution by the working class, is to raise the proletariat to the position of ruling class, to establish democracy.

The proletariat will use its political supremacy to wrest, by degrees, all capital from the bourgeoisie, to centralise all instruments of production in the hands of the state, *i.e.*, of the proletariat organised as the ruling class; and to increase the total of productive forces as rapidly as possible.

Of course, in the beginning, this cannot be effected except by means of despotic inroads on the rights of property, and on the conditions of bourgeois production; by means of measures, therefore, which appear economically insufficient and untenable, but which, in the course of the movement, outstrip themselves, necessitate further inroads upon the old social order, and are unavoidable as a means of entirely revolutionising the mode of production.

These measures will of course be different in different countries.

Nevertheless in the most advanced countries, the following will be pretty generally applicable.

1. Abolition of property in land and application of all rents of land to public purposes.
2. A heavy progressive or graduated income tax.
3. Abolition of all right of inheritance.
4. Confiscation of the property of all emigrants and rebels.
5. Centralisation of credit in the hands of the state, by means of a national bank with state capital and an exclusive monopoly.
6. Centralisation of the means of communication and transport in the hands of the state.
7. Extension of factories and instruments of production owned by the state; the bringing into cultivation of waste lands, and the improvement of the soil generally in accordance with a common plan.
8. Equal obligation of all to work. Establishment of industrial armies, especially for agriculture.
9. Combination of agriculture with manufacturing industries; gradual abolition of the distinction between town and country, by a more equable distribution of the population over the country.
10. Free education for all children in public schools. Abolition of child factory labour in its present form. Combination of education with industrial production, etc.

When, in the course of development, class distinctions have disappeared, and all production has been concentrated in the hands of a vast association of the whole nation, the public power will lose its political character. Political power, properly so called, is merely the organised power of one class for oppressing another. If the proletariat during its contest with the bourgeoisie is compelled, by the force of circumstances, to organise itself as a class; if, by means of a revolution, it makes itself the ruling class, and, as such sweeps away by force the old conditions of production, then it will, along with these conditions, have swept away the conditions for the existence of class antagonisms, and of classes generally, and will thereby have abolished its own supremacy as a class.

In place of the old bourgeois society, with its classes and class antagonisms, we shall have an association, in which the free development of each is the condition for the free development of all.

# Socialist and Communist Literature

## Reactionary Socialism

*Feudal Socialism* Owing to their historical position, it became the vocation of the aristocracies of France and England to write pamphlets against modern bourgeois society. In the French revolution of July, 1830, and in the English reform agitation, these aristocracies again succumbed to the hateful upstart. Thenceforth, a serious political struggle was altogether out of the question. A literary

battle alone remained possible. But even in the domain of literature the old cries of the restoration period had become impossible.

In order to arouse sympathy, the aristocracy was obliged to lose sight, apparently, of its own interests, and to formulate its indictment against the bourgeoisie in the interest of the exploited working class alone. Thus the aristocracy took its revenge by singing lampoons against its new master, and whispering in his ears sinister prophecies of coming catastrophe.

In this way arose Feudal Socialism: Half lamentation, half lampoon; half echo of the past, half menace of the future; at times, by its bitter, witty and incisive criticism, striking the bourgeoisie to the very heart's core, but always ludicrous in its effect through total incapacity to comprehend the march of modern history.

The aristocracy, in order to rally the people to them, waved the proletarian almsbag in front for a banner. But the people, as often as it joined them, saw on their hindquarters the old feudal coats of arms, and deserted with loud and irreverent laughter.

One section of the French Legitimists, and "Young England," exhibited this spectacle.

In pointing out that their mode of exploitation was different from that of the bourgeoisie, the feudalists forget that they exploited under circumstances and conditions that were quite different, and that are now antiquated. In showing that, under their rule, the modern proletariat never existed, they forget that the modern bourgeoisie is the necessary offspring of their own form of society.

For the rest, so little do they conceal the reactionary character of their criticism, that their chief accusation against the bourgeoisie amounts to this, that under the bourgeois regime a class is being developed, which is destined to cut up root and branch the old order of society.

What they upbraid the bourgeoisie with is not so much that it creates a proletariat, as that it creates a *revolutionary* proletariat.

In political practice, therefore, they join in all coercive measures against the working class; and in ordinary life, despite their high-falutin phrases, they stoop to pick up the golden apples dropped from the tree of industry, and to barter truth, love, and honour for traffic in wool, beetroot-sugar, and potato spirits.

As the parson has ever gone hand in hand with the landlord, so has Clerical Socialism with Feudal Socialism.

Nothing is easier than to give Christian asceticism a Socialist tinge. Has not Christianity declaimed against private property, against marriage, against the state? Has it not preached in the place of these, charity and poverty, celibacy and mortification of the flesh, monastic life and Mother Church? Christian Socialism is but the holy water with which the priest consecrates the heartburnings of the aristocrat.

*Petty Bourgeois Socialism*   The feudal aristocracy was not the only class that was ruined by the bourgeoisie, not the only class whose conditions of existence pined and perished in the atmosphere of modern bourgeois society. The mediaeval burgesses and the small peasant proprietors were the precursors of the modern bourgeoisie. In those countries which are but little developed, industrially and commercially, these two classes still vegetate side by side with the rising bourgeoisie.

In countries where modern civilisation has become fully developed, a new class of petty bourgeois has been formed, fluctuating between proletariat and bourgeoisie, and ever renewing itself as a supplementary part of bourgeois society. The individual members of this class, however, are being constantly hurled down into the proletariat by the action of competition, and, as modern industry develops, they even see the moment approaching when they will completely disappear as an independent section of modern society, to be replaced, in manufactures, agriculture and commerce, by overseers, bailiffs and shopmen.

In countries, like France, where the peasants constitute far more than half of the population, it was natural that writers who sided with the proletariat against the bourgeoisie, should use, in their criticism of the bourgeois regime, the standard of the peasant and petty bourgeois, and from the standpoint of these intermediate classes should take up the cudgels for the working class. Thus arose petty bourgeois Socialism. Sismondi was the head of this school, not only in France but also in England.

This school of Socialism dissected with great acuteness the contradictions in the conditions of modern production. It laid bare the hypocritical apologies of economists. It proved, incontrovertibly, the disastrous effects of machinery and division of labour; the concentration of capital and land in a few hands; overproduction and crises; it pointed out the inevitable ruin of the petty bourgeois and peasant, the misery of the proletariat, the anarchy in production, the crying inequalities in the distribution of wealth, the industrial war of extermination between nations, the dissolution of old moral bonds, of the old family relations, of the old nationalities.

In its positive aims, however, this form of Socialism aspires either to restoring the old means of production and of exchange, and with them the old property relations, and the old society, or to cramping the modern means of production and of exchange within the framework of the old property relations that have been, and were bound to be, exploded by those means. In either case, it is both reactionary and utopian.

Its last words are: Corporate guilds for manufacture; patriarchal relations in agriculture.

Ultimately, when stubborn historical facts had dispersed all intoxicating effects of self-deception, this form of Socialism ended in a miserable fit of the blues.

*German or "True" Socialism*   The Socialist and Communist literature of France, a literature that originated under the pressure of a bourgeoisie in power, and that was the expression of the struggle against this power, was introduced into Germany at a time when the bourgeoisie, in that country, had just begun its contest with feudal absolutism.

German philosophers, would-be philosophers, and men of letters eagerly seized on this literature, only forgetting that when these writings immigrated from France into Germany, French social conditions had not immigrated along with them. In contact with German social conditions, this French literature lost all its immediate practical significance, and assumed a purely literary aspect. Thus, to the German philosophers of the 18th century, the demands of the first French Revolution were nothing more than the demands of "Practical Reason" in general, and the utterance of the will of the revolutionary French bourgeoisie signified in their eyes the laws of pure will, of will as it was bound to be, of true human will generally.

The work of the German *literati* consisted solely in bringing the new French ideas into harmony with their ancient philosophical conscience, or rather, in annexing the French ideas without deserting their own philosophic point of view.

This annexation took place in the same way in which a foreign language is appropriated, namely by translation.

It is well known how the monks wrote silly lives of Catholic saints *over* the manuscripts on which the classical works of ancient heathendom had been written. The German *literati* reversed this process with the profane French literature. They wrote their philosophical nonsense beneath the French original. For instance, beneath the French criticism of the economic functions of money, they wrote "alienation of humanity," and beneath the French criticism of the bourgeois state, they wrote, "dethronement of the category of the general," and so forth.

The introduction of these philosophical phrases at the back of the French historical criticisms they dubbed "Philosophy of Action," "True Socialism," "German Science of Socialism," "Philosophical Foundation of Socialism," and so on.

The French Socialist and Communist literature was thus completely emasculated. And, since it ceased in the hands of the German to express the struggle of one class with the other, he felt conscious of having overcome "French one-sidedness" and of representing, not true requirements, but the requirements of truth; not the interests of the proletariat, but the interests of human nature, of man in general, who belongs to no class, has no reality, who exists only in the misty realm of philosophical phantasy.

This German Socialism, which took its school-boy task so seriously and solemnly, and extolled its poor stock-in-trade in such mountebank fashion, meanwhile gradually lost its pedantic innocence.

The fight of the German and especially of the Prussian bourgeoisie against feudal aristocracy and absolute monarchy, in other words, the liberal movement, became more earnest.

By this, the long-wished-for opportunity was offered to "True" Socialism of confronting the political movement with the Socialist demands, of hurling the traditional anathemas against liberalism, against representative government, against bourgeois competition, bourgeois freedom of the press, bourgeois legislation, bourgeois liberty and equality, and of preaching to the masses that they had nothing to gain, and everything to lose, by this bourgeois movement. German Socialism forgot, in the nick of time, that the French criticism, whose silly echo it was, presupposed the existence of modern bourgeois society, with its corresponding economic conditions of existence, and the political constitution adapted thereto, the very things whose attainment was the object of the pending struggle in Germany.

To the absolute governments, with their following of parsons, professors, country squires and officials, it served as a welcome scarecrow against the threatening bourgeoisie.

It was a sweet finish after the bitter pills of floggings and bullets, with which these same governments, just at that time, dosed the risings of the German working class.

While this "True" Socialism thus served the governments as a weapon for fighting the German bourgeoisie, it, at the same time, directly represented a reactionary interest, the interest of the German Philistines. In Germany the petty bourgeois class, a relic of the 16th century, and since then constantly cropping up again under various forms, is the real social basis of the existing state of things.

To preserve this class, is to preserve the existing state of things in Germany. The industrial and political supremacy of the bourgeoisie threatens it with certain destruction—on the one hand, from the concentration of capital; on the other, from the rise of a revolutionary proletariat. "True" Socialism appeared to kill these two birds with one stone. It spread like an epidemic.

The robe of speculative cobwebs, embroidered with flowers of rhetoric, steeped in the dew of sickly sentiment, this transcendental robe in which the German Socialists wrapped their sorry "eternal truths," all skin and bone, served to increase wonderfully the sale of their goods amongst such a public.

And on its part, German Socialism recognised, more and more, its own calling as the bombastic representative of the petty bourgeois Philistine.

It proclaimed the German nation to be the model nation, and the German petty Philistine to be the typical man. To every villainous meanness of this model man it gave a hidden, higher, socialistic interpretation, the exact contrary of his real character. It went to the extreme length of directly opposing the "brutally destructive" tendency of Communism, and of proclaiming its supreme and impartial contempt of all class struggles. With very few exceptions, all the so-called Socialist and Communist publications that now (1847) circulate in Germany belong to the domain of this foul and enervating literature.

## Conservative or Bourgeois Socialism

A part of the bourgeoisie is desirous of redressing social grievances, in order to secure the continued existence of bourgeois society.

To this section belong economists, philanthropists, humanitarians, improvers of the condition of the working class, organisers of charity, members of societies for the prevention of cruelty to animals, temperance fanatics, hole-and-corner reformers of every imaginable kind. This form of Socialism has, moreover, been worked out into complete systems.

We may cite Proudhon's *Philosophy of Poverty* as an example of this form.

The socialistic bourgeois want all the advantages of modern social conditions without the struggles and dangers necessarily resulting therefrom. They desire the existing state of society minus its revolutionary and disintegrating elements. They wish for a bourgeoisie without a proletariat. The bourgeoisie naturally conceives the world in which it is supreme to be the best; and bourgeois Socialism develops this comfortable conception into various more or less complete systems. In requiring the proletariat to carry out such a system, and thereby to march straightway into the social New Jerusalem, it but requires in reality, that the proletariat should remain within the bounds of existing society, but should cast away all its hateful ideas concerning the bourgeoisie.

A second and more practical, but less systematic, form of this Socialism sought to depreciate every revolutionary movement in the eyes of the working class, by showing that no mere political reform, but only a change in the material conditions of existence, in economic relations, could be of any advantage to them. By changes in the material conditions of existence, this form of Socialism, however, by no means understands abolition of the bourgeois relations of production, an abolition that can be effected only by a revolution, but administrative reforms, based on the continued existence of these relations; reforms, therefore, that in no respect affect the relations between capital and labour, but at the best, lessen the cost, and simplify the administrative work of bourgeois government.

Bourgeois Socialism attains adequate expression, when, and only when, it becomes a mere figure of speech.

Free trade; For the benefit of the working class. Protective duties: For the benefit of the working class. Prison reform: For the benefit of the working class. These are the last words and the only seriously meant words of bourgeois Socialism.

It is summed up in the phrase: the bourgeois are bourgeois—for the benefit of the working class.

## Critical-Utopian Socialism and Communism

We do not here refer to that literature which, in every great modern revolution, has always given voice to the demands of the proletariat, such as the writings of Babeuf and others.

The first direct attempts of the proletariat to attain its own ends—made in times of universal excitement, when feudal society was being overthrown—necessarily failed, owing to the then undeveloped state of the proletariat, as well as to the absence of the economic conditions for its emancipation, conditions that had yet to be produced, and could be produced by the impending bourgeois epoch alone. The revolutionary literature that accompanied these first movements of the proletariat had necessarily a reactionary character. It inculcated universal asceticism and social levelling in its crudest form.

The Socialist and Communist systems properly so called, those of St. Simon, Fourier, Owen and others, spring into existence in the early undeveloped period, described above, of the struggle between proletariat and bourgeoisie (see Section 1. Bourgeois and Proletarians).

The founders of these systems see, indeed, the class antagonisms, as well as the action of the decomposing elements in the prevailing form of society. But the proletariat, as yet in its infancy, offers to them the spectacle of a class without any historical initiative or any independent political movement.

Since the development of class antagonism keeps even pace with the development of industry, the economic situation, as such Socialists find it, does not as yet offer to them the material conditions for the emancipation of the proletariat. They therefore search after a new social science, after new social laws, that are to create these conditions.

Historical action is to yield to their personal inventive action; historically created conditions of emancipation to phantastic ones; and the gradual, spontaneous class organisation of the proletariat to an organisation of society specially contrived by these inventors. Future history resolves itself, in their eyes, into the propaganda and the practical carrying out of their social plans.

In the formulation of their plans they are conscious of caring chiefly for the interests of the working class, as being the most suffering class. Only from the point of view of being the most suffering class does the proletariat exist for them.

The undeveloped state of the class struggle, as well as their own surroundings, causes Socialists of this kind to consider themselves far superior to all class antagonisms. They want to improve the condition of every member of society, even that of the most favoured. Hence, they habitually appeal to society at large, without distinction of class; nay, by preference, to the ruling class. For how can people, when once they understand their system, fail to see in it the best possible plan of the best possible state of society?

Hence, they reject all political, and especially all revolutionary action; they wish to attain their ends by peaceful means, and endeavour, by small experiments, necessarily doomed to failure, and by the force of example, to pave the way for the new social gospel.

Such phantastic pictures of future society, painted at a time when the proletariat is still in a very undeveloped state and has but a phantastic conception of its own position, correspond with the first instinctive yearnings of that class for a general reconstruction of society.

But these Socialist and Communist writings contain also a critical element. They attack every principle of existing society. Hence they are full of the most valuable materials for the enlightenment of the working class. The practical measures proposed in them—such as the abolition of the distinction between town and country; abolition of the family, of private gain and of the wage-system; the proclamation of social harmony; the conversion of the functions of the state into a mere superintendence of production—all these proposals point solely to the disappearance of class antagonisms which were, at that time, only just cropping up, and which, in these publications, are recognised in their earliest, indistinct and undefined forms only. These proposals, therefore, are of a purely utopian character.

The significance of Critical-Utopian Socialism and Communism bears an inverse relation to historical development. In proportion as the modern class struggle develops and takes definite shape, this phantastic standing apart from the contest, these phantastic attacks on it, lose all practical value and all theoretical justification. Therefore, although the originators of these systems were, in many respects, revolutionary, their disciples have, in every case, formed mere reactionary sects. They hold fast by the original views of their masters, in opposition to the progressive historical development of the proletariat. They, therefore, endeavour, and that consistently, to deaden the class struggle and to reconcile the class antagonisms. They still dream of experimental realisation of their social utopias, of founding isolated *phalanstères,* of establishing "Home Colonies," or setting up a "Little Icaria"—pocket editions of the New Jerusalem—and to realise all these castles in the air, they are compelled to appeal to the feelings and purses of the bourgeois. By degrees they sink into the category of the reactionary conservative Socialists depicted above, differing from these only by more systematic pedantry, and by their fanatical and superstitious belief in the miraculous effects of their social science.

They, therefore, violently oppose all political action on the part of the working class; such action, according to them, can only result from blind unbelief in the new gospel.

The Owenites in England, and the Fourierists in France, respectively, oppose the Chartists and the *Réformistes.*

## Position of the Communists in Relation to the Various Existing Opposition Parties

Section 2 has made clear the relations of the Communists to the existing working class parties, such as the Chartists in England and the Agrarian Reformers in America.

The Communists fight for the attainment of the immediate aims, for the enforcement of the momentary interests of the working class; but in the movement of the present, they also represent and take care of the future of that movement. In France the Communists ally themselves with the Social-Democrats, against the conservative and radical bourgeoisie, reserving, however, the right to take up a critical position in regard to phrases and illusions traditionally handed down from the great Revolution.

In Switzerland they support the Radicals, without losing sight of the fact that this party consists of antagonistic elements, partly of Democratic Socialists, in the French sense, partly of radical bourgeois.

In Poland they support the party that insists on an agrarian revolution as the prime condition for national emancipation, that party which fomented the insurrection of Cracow in 1846.

In Germany they fight with the bourgeoisie whenever it acts in a revolutionary way, against the absolute monarchy, the feudal squirearchy, and the petty bourgeoisie.

But they never cease, for a single instant, to instil into the working class the clearest possible recognition of the hostile antagonism between bourgeoisie and proletariat, in order that the German workers may straightway use, as so many weapons against the bourgeoisie, the social and political conditions that the bourgeoisie must necessarily introduce along with its supremacy, and in order that, after the fall of the reactionary classes in Germany, the fight against the bourgeoisie itself may immediately begin.

The Communists turn their attention chiefly to Germany, because that country is on the eve of a bourgeois revolution that is bound to be carried out under more advanced conditions of European civilisation and with a much more developed proletariat than what existed in England in the 17th and in France in the 18th century, and because the bourgeois revolution in Germany will be but the prelude to an immediately following proletarian revolution.

In short, the Communists everywhere support every revolutionary movement against the existing social and political order of things.

In all these movements they bring to the front, as the leading question in each case, the property question, no matter what its degree of development at the time.

Finally, they labour everywhere for the union and agreement of the democratic parties of all countries.

The Communists disdain to conceal their views and aims. They openly declare that their ends can be attained only by the forcible overthrow of all existing social conditions. Let the ruling classes tremble at a Communist revolution. The proletarians have nothing to lose but their chains. They have a world to win.

Workingmen of all countries, unite!

# The Road to Serfdom

By Friedrich Hayek

## The Abandoned Road

A programme whose basic thesis is, not that the system of free enterprise for profit has failed in this generation, but that it has not yet been tried.

*F. D. Roosevelt.*

When the course of civilization takes an unexpected turn, when instead of the continuous progress which we have come to expect, we find ourselves threatened by evils associated by us with past ages of barbarism, we blame naturally anything but ourselves. Have we not all striven according to our best lights, and have not many of our finest minds incessantly worked to make this a better world? Have not all our efforts and hopes been directed towards greater freedom, justice, and prosperity? If the outcome is so different from our aims, if, instead of freedom and prosperity, bondage and misery stare us in the face, is it not clear that sinister forces must have foiled our intentions, that we are the victims of some evil power which must be conquered before we can resume the road to better things? However much we may differ when we name the culprit, whether it is the wicked capitalist or the vicious spirit of a particular nation, the stupidity of our elders, or a social system not yet, although we have struggled against it for half a century, fully overthrown—we all are, or at least were until recently, certain of one thing: that the leading ideas which during the last generation have become common to most people of goodwill and have determined the major changes in our social life cannot have been wrong. We are ready to accept almost any explanation of the present crisis of our civilization except one: that the present state of the world may be the result of genuine error on our own part, and that the pursuit of some of our most cherished ideals have apparently produced results utterly different from those which we expected.

While all our energies are directed to bringing this war to a victorious conclusion, it is sometimes difficult to remember that even before the war the values for which we are now fighting were threatened here and destroyed elsewhere. Though for the time being the different ideals are represented by hostile

353

nations fighting for their existence, we must not forget that this conflict has grown out of a struggle of ideas within what, not so long ago, was a common European civilization; and that the tendencies which have culminated in the creation of the totalitarian systems were not confined to the countries which have succumbed to them. Though the first task must now be to win the war, to win it will only gain us another opportunity to face the basic problems and to find a way of averting the fate which has overtaken kindred civilizations.

Now, it is somewhat difficult to think of Germany and Italy, or of Russia, not as different worlds, but as products of a development of thought in which we have shared; it is, at least so far as our enemies are concerned, easier and more comforting to think that they are entirely different from us and that what happened there cannot happen here. Yet, the history of these countries in the years before the rise of the totalitarian system showed few features with which we are not familiar. The external conflict is a result of a transformation of European thought in which others have moved so much faster as to bring them into irreconcilable conflict with our ideals, but which has not left us unaffected.

That a change of ideas, and the force of human will, have made the world what it is now, though men did not foresee the results, and that no spontaneous change in the facts obliged us thus to adapt our thought, is perhaps particularly difficult for the English to see, just because in this development the English have, fortunately for them, lagged behind most of the European peoples. We still think of the ideals which guide us and have guided us for the past generation, as ideals only to be realized in the future, and are not aware how far in the last twenty-five years they have already transformed, not only the world, but

also this country. We still believe that until quite recently we were governed by what are vaguely called nineteenth-century ideas or the principle of *laissez-faire*. Compared with some other countries, and from the point of view of those impatient to speed up the change, there may be some justification for such belief. But although till 1931 this country had followed only slowly on the path on which others had led, even by then we had moved so far that only those whose memory goes back to the years before the last war know what a liberal world has been like.

The crucial point of which people here are still so little aware is, however, not merely the magnitude of the changes which have taken place during the last generation, but the fact that they mean a complete change in the direction of the evolution of our ideas and social order. For at least twenty-five years before the spectre of totalitarianism became a real threat, we had progressively been moving away from the basic ideas on which European civilization has been built. That this movement on which we have entered with such high hopes and ambitions should have brought us face to face with the totalitarian horror has come as a profound shock to this generation, which still refuses to connect the two facts. Yet this development merely confirms the warnings of the fathers of the liberal philosophy which we still profess. We have progressively abandoned that freedom in economic affairs without which personal and political freedom has never existed in the past. Although we had been warned by some of the greatest political thinkers of the nineteenth century, by de Tocqueville and Lord Acton, that socialism means slavery, we have steadily moved in the direction of socialism. And now that we have seen a new form of slavery arise before our eyes, we have so completely forgotten the warning, that it scarcely occurs to us that the two things may be connected.

How sharp a break not only with the recent past but with the whole evolution of western civilization the modern trend towards socialism means, becomes clear if we consider it not merely against the background of the nineteenth century, but in a longer historical perspective. We are rapidly abandoning not the views merely of Cobden and Bright, of Adam Smith and Hume, or even of Locke and Milton, but one of the salient characteristics of western civilization as it has grown from the foundations laid by Christianity and the Greeks and Romans. Not merely nineteenth- and eighteenth-century liberalism, but the basic individualism inherited by us from Erasmus and Montaigne, from Cicero and Tacitus. Pericles and Thucydides is progressively relinquished.

The Nazi leader who described the National-Socialist revolution as a counter Renaissance spoke more truly than he probably knew. It was the decisive step in the destruction of that civilization which modern man had built up from the age of the Renaissance and which was above all an individualist civilization. Individualism has a bad name today and the term has come to be connected with egotism and selfishness. But the individualism of which we speak in contrast to socialism and all other forms of collectivism has no necessary connection with these. Only gradually in the course of this book shall we be able to make clear the contrast between the two opposing principles. But the essential features of that individualism which, from elements provided by Christianity and the philosophy of classical antiquity, was first fully developed during the Renaissance and has since grown and spread into what we know as western European civilization—the respect for the individual man *qua* man, that is

the recognition of his own views and tastes as supreme in his own sphere, however narrowly that may be circumscribed, and the belief that it is desirable that men should develop their own individual gifts and bents. "Freedom" and "liberty" are now words so worn with use and abuse that one must hesitate to employ them to express the ideals for which they stood during that period. Tolerance is, perhaps, the only word which still preserves the full meaning of the principle which during the whole of this period was in the ascendant and which only in recent times has again been in decline, to disappear completely with the rise of the totalitarian state.

The gradual transformation of a rigidly organized hierarchic system into one where men could at least attempt to shape their own life, where man gained the opportunity of knowing and choosing between different forms of life, is closely associated with the growth of commerce. From the commercial cities of Northern Italy the new view of life spread with commerce to the west and north, through France and the southwest of Germany to the Low Countries and the British Isles, taking firm root wherever there was no despotic political power to stifle it. In the Low Countries and Britain it for a long time enjoyed its fullest development and for the first time had an opportunity to grow freely and to become the foundation of the social and political life of these countries. And it was from there that in the late seventeenth and eighteenth centuries it again began to spread in a more fully developed form to the west and east, to the New World and the centre of the European continent where devastating wars and political oppression had largely submerged the earlier beginnings of a similar growth.

During the whole of this modern period of European history the general direction of social development was one of freeing the individual from the ties which had bound him to the customary or prescribed ways in the pursuit of his ordinary activities. The conscious realization that the spontaneous and uncontrolled efforts of individuals were capable of producing a complex order of economic activities could come only after this development had made some progress. The subsequent elaboration of a consistent argument in favor of economic freedom was the outcome of a free growth of economic activity which had been the undesigned and unforeseen byproducts of political freedom.

Perhaps the greatest result of the unchaining of individual energies was the marvellous growth of science which followed the march of individual liberty from Italy to England and beyond. That the inventive faculty of man had been no less in earlier periods is shown by the many highly ingenious automatic toys and other mechanical contrivances constructed while industrial technique still remained stationary, and by the development in some industries which, like mining or watchmaking, were not subject to restrictive controls. But the few attempts towards a more extended industrial use of mechanical inventions, some extraordinarily advanced, were promptly suppressed, and the desire for knowledge was stifled, so long as the dominant views were held to be binding for all: the beliefs of the great majority on what was right and proper were allowed to bar the way of the individual innovator. Only since industrial freedom opened the path to the free use of new knowledge, only since everything could be tried—if somebody could be found to back it at his own risk—and, it should be added, as often as not from outside the authorities officially entrusted with the cultivation of learning, has science made the great strides which in the last hundred and fifty years have changed the face of the world.

As is so often true, the nature of our civilization has been seen more clearly by its enemies than by most of its friends: "the perennial western malady, the revolt of the individual against the species," as that nineteenth-century totalitarian, Auguste Comte, has described it, was indeed the force which built our civilization. What the nineteenth century added to the individualism of the preceding period was merely to make all classes conscious of freedom, to develop systematically and continuously what had grown in a haphazard and patchy manner and to spread it from England and Holland over most of the European Continent.

The result of this growth surpassed all expectations. Wherever the barriers to the free exercise of human ingenuity were removed man became rapidly able to satisfy ever-widening ranges of desire. And while the rising standard soon led to the discovery of very dark spots in society, spots which men were no longer willing to tolerate, there was probably no class that did not substantially benefit from the general advance. We cannot do justice to this astonishing growth if we measure it by our present standards, which themselves result from this growth and now make many defects obvious. To appreciate what it meant to those who took part in it we must measure it by the hopes and wishes men held when it began: and there can be no doubt that its success surpassed man's wildest dreams, that by the beginning of the twentieth century the working man in the western world had reached a degree of material comfort, security, and personal independence which a hundred years before had seemed scarcely possible.

What in the future will probably appear the most significant and far-reaching effect of this success is the new sense of power over their own fate, the belief in the unbounded possibilities of improving their own lot, which the success already achieved created among men. With the success grew ambition—and man had every right to be ambitious. What had been an inspiring promise seemed no longer enough, the rate of progress far too slow; and the principles which had made this progress possible in the past came to be regarded more as obstacles to speedier progress, impatiently to be brushed away, than as the conditions for the preservation and development of what had already been achieved.

## The Great Utopia

What has always made the state a hell on earth has been precisely that man has tried to make it his heaven.
*F. Hoelderlin.*

That socialism has displaced liberalism as the doctrine held by the great majority of progressives does not simply mean that people had forgotten the warnings of the great liberal thinkers of the past about the consequences of collectivism. It has happened because they were persuaded of the very opposite of what these men had predicted. The extraordinary thing is that the same socialism that was not only early recognized as the gravest threat to freedom, but quite openly began as a reaction against the liberalism of the French Revolution, gained general acceptance under the flag of liberty. It is rarely remembered now that socialism in its beginnings was frankly authoritarian. The French writers who laid the foundations of modern socialism had no doubt that their ideas could be put into practice only by a strong dictatorial government. To them socialism meant an attempt to "terminate the revolution" by a deliberate reorganization of society on hierarchical lines, and the imposition of a coercive "spiritual power." Where freedom was concerned, the founders of socialism made no bones about their intentions. Freedom of thought they regarded as the root-evil of nineteenth-century society, and the first of modern planners, Saint-Simon even predicted that those who did not obey his proposed planning boards would be "treated as cattle."

Only under the influence of the strong democratic currents preceding the revolution of 1848 did socialism begin to ally itself with the forces of freedom. But it took the new "democratic socialism" a long time to live down the suspicions aroused by its antecedents. Nobody saw more clearly than de Tocqueville that democracy as an essentially individualist institution stood in an irreconcilable conflict with socialism:

Democracy extends the sphere of individual freedom |he said in 1848], socialism restricts it. Democracy attaches all possible value to each man; socialism makes each man a mere agent, a mere number. Democracy and socialism have nothing in common but one word: equality. But notice the difference: while democracy seeks equality in liberty, socialism seeks equality in restraint and servitude.

To allay these suspicions and to harness to its cart the strongest of all political motives, the craving for freedom, socialism began increasingly to make use of the promise of a "new freedom." The coming of socialism was to be the leap from the realm of necessity to the realm of freedom. It was to bring "economic freedom," without which the political freedom already gained was "not worth having." Only socialism was capable of effecting the consummation of the agelong struggle for freedom in which the attainment of political freedom was but a first step.

The subtle change in meaning to which the word freedom was subjected in order that this argument should sound plausible is important. To the great apostles of political freedom the word had meant freedom from coercion, freedom from the arbitrary power of other men, release from the ties which left the individual no choice but obedience to the orders of a superior to whom he was attached. The new freedom promised, however, was to be freedom from necessity, release from the compulsion of the circumstances which inevitably limit the range of choice of all of us, although for some very much more than for others. Before man could be truly free, the "despotism of physical want" had to be broken, the "restraints of the economic system" relaxed.

Freedom in this sense is, of course, merely another name for power or wealth. Yet, although the promises of this new freedom were often coupled with irresponsible promises of a great increase in material wealth in a socialist society, it was not from such an absolute conquest of the niggardliness of nature that economic freedom was expected. What the promise really amounted to was that the great existing disparities in the range of choice of different people were to disappear. The demand for the new freedom was thus only another name for the old demand for an equal distribution of wealth. But the new name gave the socialists another word in common with the liberals and they exploited it to the full. And although the word was used in a different sense by the two groups, few people noticed this and still fewer asked themselves whether the two kinds of freedom promised really could be combined.

There can be no doubt that the promise of greater freedom has become one of the most effective weapons of socialist propaganda and that the belief that socialism would bring freedom is genuine and sincere. But this would only heighten the tragedy if it should prove that what was promised to us as the Road to Freedom was in fact the High Road to Servitude. Unquestionably the promise of more freedom was responsible for luring more and more liberals along the socialist road, for blinding them to the conflict which exists between the basic principles of socialism and liberalism, and for often enabling socialists to usurp the very name of the old parly of freedom. Socialism was embraced by the greater part of the intelligentsia as the apparent heir of the liberal tradition: therefore it is not surprising that to them the idea should appear inconceivable of socialism leading to the opposite of liberty.

## Individualism and Collectivism

The socialists believe in two things which are absolutely different and perhaps even contradictory: freedom and organization.

*Elie Halévy.*

Before we can progress with our main problem, an obstacle has yet to be surmounted.

A confusion largely responsible for the way in which we are drifting into things which nobody wants must be cleared up.

This confusion concerns nothing less than the concept of socialism itself. It may mean, and is often used to describe, merely the ideals of social justice, greater equality and security which are the ultimate aims of socialism. But it means also the particular method by which most socialists hope to attain these ends and which many competent people regard as the only methods by which they can be fully and quickly attained. In this sense socialism means the abolition of private enterprise, of private ownership of the means of production, and the creation of a system of "planned economy" in which the entrepreneur working for profit is replaced by a central planning body.

There are many people who call themselves socialists although they care only about the first, who fervently believe in those ultimate aims of socialism but neither care nor understand how they can be achieved, and who are merely certain that they must be achieved, whatever the cost. But to nearly all those to whom socialism is not merely a hope but an object of practical politics, the characteristic methods of modern socialism are as essential as the ends themselves. Many people, on the other hand, who value the ultimate ends of socialism no less than the socialists, refuse to support socialism because of the dangers to other values they see in the methods proposed by the socialists. The dispute about socialism has thus become largely a dispute about means and not about ends—although the question whether the different ends of socialism can be simultaneously achieved is also involved.

This would be enough to create confusion. And the confusion has been further increased by the common practice of denying that those who repudiate the means value the ends.

But this is not all. The situation is still more complicated by the fact that the same means, the "economic planning" which is the prime instrument of socialist reform, can be used for many other purposes. We must centrally direct economic activity if we want to make the distribution of income conform to current ideas of social justice. "Planning," therefore, is wanted by all those who demand that "production for use" be substituted for production for profit. But such planning is no less indispensable if the distribution of incomes is to be regulated in a way which to us appears to be the opposite of just. Whether we should wish that more of the good things of this world should go to some racial élite, the Nordic men, or the members of a party or an aristocracy, the methods which we shall have to employ are the same as those which could ensure an equalitarian distribution.

It may, perhaps, seem unfair to use the term socialism to describe its methods rather than its aims, to use for a particular method a term which for many people stands for an ultimate ideal. It is probably preferable to describe the methods which can be used for a great variety of ends as collectivism and to regard socialism as a species of that genus. Yet, although to most socialists only one species of collectivism will represent true socialism, it must always be remembered that socialism is a species of collectivism and that therefore everything which is true of collectivism as such must apply also to socialism. Nearly all the points which are disputed between socialists and liberals concern the methods common to all forms of collectivism and not the particular ends for which socialists want to use them; and all the consequences with which we shall be concerned in this book follow from the methods of collectivism irrespective of the ends for which they are used. It must also not be forgotten that socialism is not only by far the most important species of collectivism or "planning"; but that it is socialism which has persuaded liberal-minded people to submit once more to that regimentation of economic life which they had overthrown because, in the words of Adam Smith, it puts governments in a position where "to support themselves they are obliged to be oppressive and tyrannical."

## The Constitution of Liberty

### The Decline of Socialism and The Rise of The Welfare State

Experience should teach us to be most on our guard to protect liberty when the Government's purposes are beneficent. Men born to freedom are naturally alert to repel invasion of their liberty by evil-minded rulers. The greatest dangers to liberty lurk in insidious encroachment by men of zeal, well meaning but without understanding.

*L. Brandeis.*

Efforts toward social reform, for something like a century, have been inspired mainly by the ideals of socialism—during part of this period even in countries like the United States which never has had a socialist party of importance. Over the course of these hundred years socialism captured a large part of the intellectual leaders and came to be widely regarded

as the ultimate goal toward which society was inevitably moving. This development reached its peak after the second World War, when Britain plunged into her socialist experiment. This seems to have marked the high tide of the socialist advance. Future historians will probably regard the period from the revolution of 1848 to about 1948 as the century of European socialism.

During this period socialism had a fairly precise meaning and a definite program. The common aim of all socialist movements was the nationalization of the "means of production, distribution, and exchange," so that all economic activity might be directed according to a comprehensive plan toward some ideal of social justice. The various socialist schools differed mainly in the political methods by which they intended to bring about the reorganization of society. Marxism and Fabianism differed in that the former was revolutionary and the latter gradualist; but their conceptions of the new society they hoped to create were basically the same. Socialism meant the common ownership of the means of production and their "employment for use, not for profit."

The great change that has occurred during the last decade is that socialism in this strict sense of a particular method of achieving social justice has collapsed. It has not merely lost its intellectual appeal; it has also been abandoned by the masses so unmistakably that socialist parties everywhere are searching for a new program that will insure the active support of their followers. They have not abandoned their ultimate aim, their ideal of social justice. But the methods by which they had hoped to achieve this and for which the name "socialism" had been coined have been discredited. No doubt the name will be transferred to whatever new program the existing socialist parties will adopt. But socialism in the old definite sense is now dead in the western world.

Though such a sweeping statement will still cause some surprise, a survey of the stream of disillusionist literature from socialist sources in all countries and the discussions inside (he socialist parties amply confirm it. To those who watch merely the developments inside a single country, the decline of socialism may still seem no more than a temporary setback, the reaction to political defeat. But the international character and the similarity of the developments in the different countries leave no doubt that it is more than that. If, fifteen years ago, doctrinaire socialism appeared as the main danger to liberty, today it would be tilting at windmills to direct one's argument against it. Most of the arguments that were directed at socialism proper can now be heard from within the socialist movements as arguments for a change of program.

Unlike socialism, the conception of the welfare state has no precise meaning. The phrase is sometimes used to describe any stale that "concerns" itself in any manner with problems other than those of the maintenance of law and order. But, though a few theorists have demanded that the activities of government should be limited to the maintenance of law and order, such a stand cannot be justified by the principle of liberty. Only the coercive measures of government need be strictly limited. We have already seen that there is undeniably a wide field for non-coercive activities of government and that there is a clear need for financing them by taxation.

Indeed, no government in modern times has ever confined itself to the "individualist minimum" which has occasionally been described, nor has such confinement of governmental activity been advocated by the "orthodox" classical economists. All modern governments have made provision for the indigent, unfortunate, and disabled and have concerned themselves with questions of health and the dissemination of knowledge. There is no reason why the volume of these pure service activities should not increase with the general growth of wealth. There are common needs that can be satisfied only by collective action and which can be thus provided for without restricting individual liberty. It can hardly be denied that, as we grow richer, that minimum of sustenance which the community has always provided for those not able to look after themselves, and which can be provided outside the market, will gradually rise, or that government may, usefully and without doing any harm, assist or even lead in such endeavors. There is little reason why the government should not also play some role, or even take the initiative, in such areas as social insurance and education, or temporarily subsidize certain experimental developments. Our problem here is not so much the aims as the methods of government action.

References are often made to those modest and innocent aims of governmental activity to show how unreasonable is any opposition to the welfare state as such. But, once the rigid position that government should not concern itself at all with such matters is abandoned—a position which is defensible but has little to do with freedom—the defenders of liberty commonly discover that the program of the welfare state comprises a great deal more that is represented as equally legitimate and unobjectionable. If, for instance, they admit that they have no objection to pure-food laws, this is taken to imply that they should not object to any government activity directed toward a desirable end. Those who attempt to delimit the functions of government in terms of aims rather than methods thus regularly find themselves in the position of having to oppose state action which appears to have only desirable consequences or of having to admit that they have no general rule on which to base their objections to measures which, though effective for particular purposes, would in their aggregate effect destroy a free society. Though the position that the state should have nothing to do with matters not related to the maintenance of law and order may seem logical so long as we think of the state solely as a coercive apparatus, we must recognize that, as a service agency, it may assist without harm in (he achievement of desirable aims which perhaps could not be achieved otherwise. The reason why many of the new welfare activities of government are a threat to freedom, then, is that, though they are presented as mere service activities, they really constitute an exercise of the coercive powers of government and rest on its claiming exclusive rights in certain fields.

The current situation has greatly altered the task of the defender of liberty and made it much more difficult. So long as the danger came from socialism of the frankly collectivist kind, it was possible to argue that the tenets of the socialists were simply false: that socialism would not achieve what the socialists wanted and that it would produce other consequences which they would not like. We cannot argue similarly against the welfare state, for (his term does not designate a definite system. What goes under that name is a conglomerate of so many diverse and even contradictory elements that, while some of them may make a free society more attractive, others are incompatible with it or may at least constitute potential threats to its existence.

We shall see that some of the aims of the welfare state can be realized without detriment to individual liberty, though not necessarily by the methods which seem the most obvious and are therefore most popular; that others can be similarly achieved to a certain extent, though only at a cost much greater than people imagine or would be willing to bear, or only slowly and gradually as wealth increases; and that, finally, there are others—and they are those particularly dear to the hearts of the socialists—that cannot be realized in a society that wants to preserve personal freedom.

There are all kinds of public amenities which it may be in the interest of all members of the community to provide by common effort, such as parks and museums, theaters and facilities for sports—though there are strong reasons why they should be provided by local rather than national authorities. There is then the important issue of security, of protection against risks common to all, where government can often either reduce these risks or assist people to provide against them. Here, however, an important distinction has to be drawn between two conceptions of security; a limited security which can be achieved for all and which is, therefore, no privilege, and absolute security, which in a free society cannot be achieved for all. The first of these is security against severe physical privation, the assurance of a given minimum of sustenance for all; and the second is the assurance of a given standard of life, which is determined by comparing the standard enjoyed by a person or a group with that of others. The distinction, then, is that between the security of an equal minimum income for all and the security of a particular income that a person is thought to deserve. The latter is closely related to the third main ambition that inspires the welfare state; the desire to use the powers of government to insure a more even or more just distribution of goods. Insofar as this means that the coercive powers of government are to be used to insure that particular people get particular things, it requires a kind of discrimination between, and an unequal treatment of, different people which is irreconcilable with a free society. This is the kind of welfare state that aims at "social justice" and becomes "primarily a redistributor of income." It is bound to lead back to socialism and its coercive and essentially arbitrary methods.

## Taxation

Those who advocated progressive taxation during the latter part of the nineteenth century generally stressed that their aim was only to achieve equality of sacrifice and not a redistribution of income; also they generally held that this aim could justify only a "moderate" degree of progression and that its "excessive" use (as in fifteenth-century Florence, where rates had been pushed up to 50 per cent) was, of course, to be condemned. Though all attempts to supply an objective standard for an appropriate rate of progression failed and though no answer was offered when it was objected that, once the principle was accepted, there would be no assignable limit beyond which progression might not be carried with equal justification, the discussion moved entirely in a context of contemplated rates which made any effect on the distribution of income appear negligible. The suggestion that rates would not stay within these limits was treated as a malicious distortion of the argument, betraying a reprehensible lack

of confidence in the wisdom of democratic government.

It was in Germany, then the leader in "social reform," that the advocates of progressive taxation first overcame the resistance and its modern evolution began. In 1891, Prussia introduced a progressive income tax rising from 0.67 to 4 per cent. In vain did Rudolf von Geist, the venerable leader of the then recently consummated movement for the *Rechtsstaat*, protest in the Diet that this meant the abandonment of the fundamental principle of equality before the law, "of the most sacred principle of equality," which provided the only barrier against encroachment on property. The very smallness of the burden involved in the new schemes made ineffective any attempt to oppose it as a matter of principle.

Though some other Continental countries soon followed Prussia, it took nearly twenty years for the movement to reach the great Anglo-Saxon powers. It was only in 1910 and 1913 that Great Britain and the United States adopted graduated income taxes rising to the then spectacular figures of 8½ and 7 per cent, respectively. Yet within thirty years these figures had risen to 97½ and 91 per cent.

Thus in the space of a single generation what nearly all the supporters of progressive taxation had for half a century asserted could not happen came to pass. This change in the absolute rates, of course, completely changed the character of the problem, making it different not merely in degree but in kind. All attempt to justify these rates on the basis of capacity to pay was, in consequence, soon abandoned, and the supporters reverted to the original, but long avoided, justification of progression as a means of bringing about a more just distribution of income. It has come to be generally accepted once more that the only ground on which a progressive scale of overall taxation can be defended is the desirability of changing the distribution of income and that this defense cannot be based on any scientific argument but must be recognized as a frankly political postulate, that is, as an attempt to impose upon society a pattern of distribution determined by majority decision.

An explanation of this development that is usually offered is that the great increase in public expenditure in the last forty years could not have been met without resort to steep progression, or at least that, without it, an intolerable burden would have had to be placed on the poor and that, once the necessity of relieving the poor was admitted, some degree of progression was inevitable. On examination, however, the explanation dissolves into pure myth. Not only is the revenue derived from the high rates levied on large incomes, particularly in the highest brackets, so small compared with the total revenue as to make hardly any difference to the burden borne by the rest; but for a long time after the introduction of progression it was not the poorest who benefited from it but entirely the better-off working class and the lower strata of the middle class who provided the largest number of voters. It would probably be true, on the other hand, to say that the illusion that by means of progressive taxation the burden can be shifted substantially onto the shoulders of the wealthy has been the chief reason why taxation has increased as fast as it has done and that, under the influence of this illusion, the masses have come to accept a much heavier load than they would have done otherwise. The only major result of the policy has been the severe limitation of the incomes that could be earned by the most successful and thereby gratification of the envy of the less-well-off.

# Law, Legislation and Liberty

## Construction and Evolution

There are two way of looking at the pattern of human activities which lead to very different conclusions concerning both its explanation and the possibilities of deliberately altering it. Of these, one is based on conceptions which are demonstrably false, yet are so pleasing to human vanity that they have gained great influence and are constantly employed even by people who know that they rest on a fiction, but believe that fiction to be innocuous. The other, although few people will question its basic contentions if they are stated abstractly, leads in some respects to conclusions so unwelcome that few are willing to follow it through to the end.

The first gives us a sense of unlimited power to realize our wishes, while the second leads to the insight that there are limitations to what we can deliberately bring about, and to the recognition that some of our present hopes are delusions. Yet the effect of allowing ourselves to be deluded by the first view has always been that man has actually limited the scope of what he can achieve. For it has always been the recognition of the limits of the possible which has enabled man to make full use of his powers.

The first view holds that human institutions will serve human purposes only if they have been deliberately designed for these purposes, often also that the fact that an institution exists is evidence of its having been created for a purpose, and always that we should so re-design society and its institutions that all our actions will be wholly guided by known purposes. To most people these propositions seem almost self-evident and to constitute an attitude alone worthy of a thinking being. Yet the belief underlying them, that we owe all beneficial institutions to design, and that only such design has made or can make them useful for our purposes, is largely false.

This view is rooted originally in a deeply ingrained propensity of primitive thought to interpret all regularity to be found in phenomena anthropomorphically, as the result of the design of a thinking mind. But just when man was well on the way to emancipating himself from this naive conception, it was revived by the support of a powerful philosophy with which the aim of freeing the human mind from false prejudices has become closely associated, and which became the dominant conception of the Age of Reason.

The other view, which has slowly and gradually advanced since antiquity but for a time was almost entirely overwhelmed by the more glamorous constructivist view, was that that orderliness of society which greatly increased the effectiveness of individual action was not due solely to institutions and practices which had been invented or designed for that purpose, but was largely due to a process described at first as 'growth' and later as 'evolution', a process in which practices which had first been adopted for other reasons, or even purely accidentally, were preserved because they enabled the group in which they had arisen to prevail over others. Since its first systematic development in the eighteenth century this view had to struggle not only against the anthropomorphism of primitive thinking but even more against the reinforcement these naive views had received from the new rationalist philosophy. It was indeed the challenge which this philosophy

provided that led to the explicit formulation of the evolutionary view.

## The Permanent Limitations of Our Factual Knowledge

The constructivist approach leads to false conclusions because man's actions are largely successful, not merely in the primitive stage but perhaps even more so in civilization, because they are adapted both to the particular facts which he knows and to a great many other facts he does not and cannot know. And this adaptation to the general circumstances that surround him is brought about by his observance of rules which he has not designed and often does not even know explicitly, although he is able to honour them in action. Or, to put this differently, our adaptation to our environment does not consist only, and perhaps not even chiefly, in an insight into the relations between cause and effect, but also in our actions being governed by rules adapted to the kind of world in which we live, that is, to circumstances which we are not aware of and which yet determine the pattern of our successful actions. ...

What we must ask the reader to keep constantly in mind throughout this book, then, is the fact of the necessary and irremediable ignorance on everyone's part of most of the particular facts which determine the actions of all the several members of human society. This may at first seem to be a fact so obvious and incontestable as hardly to deserve mention, and still less to require proof. Yet the result of not constantly stressing it is that it is only too readily forgotten. This is so mainly because it is a very inconvenient fact which makes both our attempts to explain and our attempts to influence intelligently the processes of society very much more difficult, and which places severe limits on what we can say or do about them. There exists therefore a great temptation, as a first approximation, to begin with the assumption that we know everything needed for full explanation or control. This provisional assumption is often treated as something of little consequence which can later be dropped without much effect on the conclusions. Yet this necessary ignorance of most of the particulars which enter the order of a Great Society is the source of the central problem of all social order and the false assumption by which it is provisionally put aside is mostly never explicitly abandoned but merely conveniently forgotten. The argument then proceeds as if that ignorance did not matter.

## The Concept of Order

The central concept around which the discussion of this book will turn is that of order, and particularly the distinction between two kinds of order which we will provisionally call 'made' and 'grown' orders. Order is an indispensable concept for the discussion of all complex phenomena, in which it must largely play the role the concept of law plays in the analysis of simpler phenomena. There is no adequate term other than 'order' by which we can describe it, although 'system', 'structure' or 'pattern' may occasionally serve instead. The term 'order' has, of course, a long history in the social sciences, but in recent times it has generally been avoided, largely because of the ambiguity of its meaning and its frequent association with authoritarian views. We cannot do without it, however, and shall have to guard against misinterpretation by sharply defining the general sense in which we shall employ it and then clearly distinguishing

between the two different ways in which such order can originate.

By 'order' we shall throughout describe *a state of affairs in which a multiplicity of elements of various kinds are so related to each other that we may learn from our acquaintance with some spatial or temporal part of the whole to form correct expectations concerning the rest, or at least expectations which have a good chance of proving correct.* It is clear that every society must in this sense possess an order and that such an order will often exist without having been deliberately created. As has been said by a distinguished social anthropologist, 'that there is some order, consistency and constancy in social life, is obvious. If there were not, none of us would be able to go about our affairs or satisfy our most elementary needs.'

Living as members of society and dependent for the satisfaction of most of our needs on various forms of co-operation with others, we depend for the effective pursuit of our aims clearly on the correspondence of the expectations concerning the actions of others on which our plans are based with what they will really do. This matching of the intentions and expectations that determine the actions of different individuals is the form in which order manifests itself in social life; and it will be the question of how such an order does come about that will be our immediate concern. The first answer to which our anthropomorphic habits of thought almost inevitably lead us is that it must be due to the design of some thinking mind. And because order has been generally interpreted as such a deliberate *arrangement* by somebody, the concept has become unpopular among most friends of liberty and has been favoured mainly by authoritarians. According to this interpretation order in society must rest on a relation of command and obedience, or a hierarchical structure of the whole of society in which the will of superiors, and ultimately of some single supreme authority, determines what each individual must do.

## The Fatal Conceit

### Was Socialism a Mistake?

The idea of Socialism is at once grandiose and simple. ... We may say, in fact, that it is one of the most ambitious creations of the human spirit,... so magnificent, so daring, that it has rightly aroused the greatest admiration. If we wish to save the world from barbarism we have to refute Socialism, but we cannot thrust it carelessly aside.

*Ludwig von Mises.*

This book argues that our civilization depends, not only for its origin but also for its preservation, on what can be precisely described only as the extended order of human cooperation, an order more commonly, if somewhat misleadingly, known as capitalism. To understand our civilization, one must appreciate that the extended order resulted not from human design or intention but spontaneously: it arose from unintentionally conforming to certain traditional and largely *moral* practices, many of which men tend to dislike, whose significance they usually fail to understand, whose validity they cannot prove, and which have nonetheless fairly rapidly spread by means of

an evolutionary selection—the comparative increase of population and wealth—of those groups that happened to follow them. The unwitting, reluctant, even painful adoption of these practices kept these groups together, increased their access to valuable information of all sorts, and enabled them to be 'fruitful, and multiply, and replenish the earth, and subdue it' (Genesis 1:28). This process is perhaps the least appreciated facet of human evolution.

Socialists take a different view of these matters. They not only differ in their conclusions, they see the facts differently. That socialists are wrong *about the facts* is crucial to my argument, as it will unfold in the pages that follow. I am prepared to admit that if socialist analyses of the operation of the existing economic order, and of possible alternatives, were factually correct, we might be obliged to ensure that the distribution of incomes conform to certain moral principles, and that this distribution might be possible only by giving a central authority the power to direct the use of available resources, and might presuppose the abolition of individual ownership of means of production. If it were for instance true that central direction of the means of production could effect a collective product of at least the same magnitude as that which we now produce, it would indeed prove a grave moral problem how this could be done justly. This, however, is not the position in which we find ourselves. For there is no known way other than by the distribution of products in a competitive market, to inform individuals in what direction their several efforts must aim so as to contribute as much as possible to the total product.

The main point of my argument is, then, that the conflict between, on one hand, advocates of the spontaneous extended human order created by a competitive market, and on the other hand those who demand a deliberate arrangement of human interaction by central authority based on collective command over available resources is due to a factual error by the latter about how knowledge of these resources is and can be generated and utilized. As a question of fact, this conflict must be settled by scientific study. Such study shows that, by following the spontaneously generated moral traditions underlying the competitive market order (traditions which do not satisfy the canons or norms of rationality embraced by most socialists), we generate and garner greater knowledge and wealth than could ever be obtained or utilized in a centrally-directed economy whose adherents claim to proceed strictly in accordance with 'reason'. Thus socialist aims and programmes are factually impossible to achieve or execute; and they also happen, into the bargain as it were, to be logically impossible.

This is why, contrary to what is often maintained, these matters are not merely ones of differing interests or value judgements. Indeed, the question of how men came to adopt certain values or norms, and what effect these had on the evolution of their civilization, is itself above all a factual one, one that lies at the heart of the present book. The demands of socialism are not moral conclusions derived from the traditions that formed the extended order that made civilization possible. They endeavor to overthrow these traditions by a rationally designed moral system whose appeal depends on the instinctual appeal of its promised consequences. They assume that, since people had been able to *generate* some system of rules coordinating their efforts, they must also be able to *design* an even better and more gratifying system. But if humankind owes its very existence to one particular rule-guided form of conduct of proven effectiveness, it simply does not have the option of choosing another merely for the sake of the apparent pleasantness of its immediately visible effects. The dispute between the market order and socialism is no less than a matter of survival. To follow socialist morality would destroy much of present humankind and impoverish much of the rest.

# Appendix

Appendix

# The Declaration of Independence

IN CONGRESS, July 4, 1776.

## The Unanimous Declaration of the Thirteen United States of America

When in the Course of human events, it becomes necessary for one people to dissolve the political bands which have connected them with another, and to assume among the powers of the earth, the separate and equal station to which the Laws of Nature and of Nature's God entitle them, a decent respect to the opinions of mankind requires that they should declare the causes which impel them to the separation.

We hold these truths to be self-evident, that all men are created equal, that they are endowed by their Creator with certain unalienable Rights, that among these are Life, Liberty and the pursuit of Happiness—That to secure these rights, Governments are instituted among Men, deriving their just powers from the consent of the governed,—That whenever any Form of Government becomes destructive of these ends, it is the Right of the People to alter or to abolish it, and to institute new Government, laying its foundation on such principles and organizing its powers in such form, as to them shall seem most likely to effect their Safety and Happiness. Prudence, indeed, will dictate that Governments long established should not be changed for light and transient causes; and accordingly all experience hath shewn, that mankind are more disposed to suffer, while evils are sufferable, than to right themselves by abolishing the forms to which they are accustomed. But when a long train of abuses and usurpations, pursuing invariably the same Object evinces a design to reduce them under absolute Despotism, it is their right, it is their duty, to throw off such Government, and to provide new Guards for their future security.— Such has been the patient sufferance of these Colonies; and such is now the necessity which constrains them to alter their former Systems of Government. The history of the present King of Great Britain is a history of repeated injuries and usurpations, all having in direct object the establishment of an absolute Tyranny over these States. To prove this, let Facts be submitted to a candid world.

He has refused his Assent to Laws, the most wholesome and necessary for the public good.

He has forbidden his Governors to pass Laws of immediate and pressing importance, unless suspended in their operation till his Assent should be obtained; and when so suspended, he has utterly neglected to attend to them.

He has refused to pass other Laws for the accommodation of large districts of people, unless those people would relinquish the right of Representation in the Legislature, a right inestimable to them and formidable to tyrants only.

He has called together legislative bodies at places unusual, uncomfortable, and distant from the depository of their public Records, for the sole purpose of fatiguing them into compliance with his measures.

He has dissolved Representative Houses repeatedly, for opposing with manly firmness his invasions on the rights of the people.

He has refused for a long time, after such dissolutions, to cause others to be elected; whereby the Legislative powers, incapable of Annihilation, have returned to the People at large for their exercise; the State remaining in the mean time exposed to all the dangers of invasion from without, and convulsions within.

He has endeavoured to prevent the population of these States; for that purpose obstructing the Laws for Naturalization of Foreigners; refusing to pass others to encourage their migrations hither, and raising the conditions of new Appropriations of Lands.

He has obstructed the Administration of Justice, by refusing his Assent to Laws for establishing Judiciary powers.

He has made Judges dependent on his Will alone, for the tenure of their offices, and the amount and payment of their salaries.

He has erected a multitude of New Offices, and sent hither swarms of Officers to harrass our people, and eat out their substance.

He has kept among us, in times of peace, Standing Armies without the Consent of our legislatures.

He has affected to render the Military independent of and superior to the Civil power.

He has combined with others to subject us to a jurisdiction foreign to our constitution, and unacknowledged by our laws; giving his Assent to their Acts of pretended Legislation:

For Quartering large bodies of armed troops among us:

For protecting them, by a mock Trial, from punishment for any Murders which they should commit on the Inhabitants of these States:

For cutting off our Trade with all parts of the world:

For imposing Taxes on us without our Consent: For depriving us in many cases, of the benefits of Trial by Jury:

For transporting us beyond Seas to be tried for pretended offences

For abolishing the free System of English Laws in a neighbouring Province, establishing therein an Arbitrary government, and enlarging its Boundaries so as to render it at once an example and fit instrument for introducing the same absolute rule into these Colonies:

For taking away our Charters, abolishing our most valuable Laws, and altering fundamentally the Forms of our Governments:

For suspending our own Legislatures, and declaring themselves invested with power to legislate for us in all cases whatsoever.

He has abdicated Government here, by declaring us out of his Protection and waging War against us.

He has plundered our seas, ravaged our Coasts, burnt our towns, and destroyed the lives of our people.

He is at this time transporting large Armies of foreign Mercenaries to compleat the works of death, desolation and tyranny, already begun with circumstances of Cruelty & perfidy scarcely paralleled in the most barbarous ages, and totally unworthy of the Head of a civilized nation.

He has constrained our fellow Citizens taken Captive on the high Seas to bear Arms against their Country, to become the executioners of their friends and Brethren, or to fall themselves by their Hands.

He has excited domestic insurrections amongst us, and has endeavoured to bring on the inhabitants of our frontiers, the merciless Indian Savages, whose known rule of warfare, is an undistinguished destruction of all ages, sexes and conditions.

In every stage of these Oppressions We have Petitioned for Redress in the most humble terms: Our repeated Petitions have been answered only by repeated injury. A Prince whose character is thus marked by every act which may define a Tyrant, is unfit to be the ruler of a free people. Nor have We been wanting in attentions to our British brethren. We have warned them from time to time of attempts by their legislature to extend an unwarrantable jurisdiction over us. We have reminded them of the circumstances of our emigration and settlement here. We have appealed to their native justice and magnanimity, and we have conjured them by the ties of our common kindred to disavow these usurpations, which, would inevitably interrupt our connections and correspondence. They too have been deaf to the voice of justice and of consanguinity. We must, therefore, acquiesce in the necessity, which denounces our Separation, and hold them, as we hold the rest of mankind, Enemies in War, in Peace Friends.

We, therefore, the Representatives of the united States of America, in General Congress, Assembled, appealing to the Supreme Judge of the world for the rectitude of our intentions, do, in the Name, and by Authority of the good People of these Colonies, solemnly publish and declare, That these United Colonies are, and of Right ought to be Free and Independent States; that they are Absolved from all Allegiance to the British Crown, and that all political connection between them and the State of Great Britain, is and ought to be totally dissolved; and that as Free and Independent States, they have full Power to levy War, conclude Peace, contract Alliances, establish Commerce, and to do all other Acts and Things which Independent States may of right do. And for the support of this Declaration, with a firm reliance on the protection of divine Providence, we mutually pledge to each other our Lives, our Fortunes and our sacred Honor.

*[The 56 signatures on the Declaration were arranged in six columns:]*

**Georgia:**
- Button Gwinnett
- Lyman Hall
- George Walton

**North Carolina:**
- William Hooper
- Joseph Hewes
- John Penn

**South Carolina:**
- Edward Rutledge
- Thomas Heyward, Jr.
- Thomas Lynch, Jr.
- Arthur Middleton

**\Massachusetts:**
- John Hancock

**Maryland:**
- Samuel Chase
- William Paca
- Thomas Stone
- Charles Carroll of Carrollton

**Virginia:**
- George Wythe
- Richard Henry Lee
- Thomas Jefferson
- Benjamin Harrison
- Thomas Nelson, Jr.
- Francis Lightfoot Lee
- Carter Braxton

**Pennsylvania:**
- Robert Morris
- Benjamin Rush
- Benjamin Franklin
- John Morton
- George Clymer
- James Smith
- George Taylor
- James Wilson
- George Ross

**Delaware:**
- Caesar Rodney
- George Read
- Thomas McKean

**New York:**
- William Floyd
- Philip Livingston
- Francis Lewis
- Lewis Morris

**New Jersey:**
- Richard
- Stockton
- John
- Witherspoon
- Francis
- Hopkinson
- John Hart
- Abraham Clark

**New Hampshire:**
- Josiah Bartlett
- William Whipple

**Massachusetts:**
- Samuel Adams
- John Adams
- Robert Treat
- Paine
- Elbridge Gerry

**Rhode Island:**
- Stephen
- Hopkins
- William Ellery
- **Connecticut:**
- Roger Sherman
- Samuel
- Huntington
- William Williams
- Oliver Wolcott

**New Hampshire:**
- Matthew
- Thornton

# Articles of Confederation

To all to whom these Presents shall come, we the undersigned Delegates of the States affixed to our Names send greeting.

Articles of Confederation and perpetual Union between the states of New Hampshire, Massachusetts-bay Rhode Island and Providence Plantations, Connecticut, New York, New Jersey, Pennsylvania, Delaware, Maryland, Virginia, North Carolina, South Carolina and Georgia.

## I.

The Stile of this Confederacy shall be **"The United States of America"**.

## II.

Each state retains its sovereignty, freedom, and independence, and every power,

jurisdiction, and right, which is not by this Confederation expressly delegated to the United States, in Congress assembled.

## III.

The said States hereby severally enter into a firm league of friendship with each other, for their common defense, the security of their liberties, and their mutual and general welfare, binding themselves to assist each other, against all force offered to, or attacks made upon them, or any of them, on account of religion, sovereignty, trade, or any other pretense whatever.

## IV.

The better to secure and perpetuate mutual friendship and intercourse among the people of the different States in this Union, the free inhabitants of each of these States, paupers, vagabonds, and fugitives from justice excepted, shall be entitled to all privileges and immunities of free citizens in the several States; and the people of each State shall free ingress and regress to and from any other State, and shall enjoy therein all the privileges of trade and commerce, subject to the same duties, impositions, and restrictions as the inhabitants thereof respectively, provided that such restrictions shall not extend so far as to prevent the removal of property imported into any State, to any other State, of which the owner is an inhabitant; provided also that no imposition, duties or restriction shall be laid by any State, on the property of the United States, or either of them.

If any person guilty of, or charged with, treason, felony, or other high misdemeanor in any State, shall flee from justice, and be found in any of the United States, he shall, upon demand of the Governor or executive power of the State from which he fled, be delivered up and removed to the State having jurisdiction of his offense.

Full faith and credit shall be given in each of these States to the records, acts, and judicial proceedings of the courts and magistrates of every other State.

in November, in every year, with a power reserved to each State to recall its delegates, or any of them, at any time within the year, and to send others in their stead for the remainder of the year.

No State shall be represented in Congress by less than two, nor more than seven members; and no person shall be capable of being a delegate for more than three years in any term of six years; nor shall any person, being a delegate, be capable of holding any office under the United States, for which he, or another for his benefit, receives any salary, fees or emolument of any kind.

Each State shall maintain its own delegates in a meeting of the States, and while they act as members of the committee of the States.

In determining questions in the United States in Congress assembled, each State shall have one vote.

Freedom of speech and debate in Congress shall not be impeached or questioned in any court or place out of Congress, and the members of Congress shall be protected in their persons from arrests or imprisonments, during the time of their going to and from, and attendence on Congress, except for treason, felony, or breach of the peace.

## V.

For the most convenient management of the general interests of the United States, delegates shall be annually appointed in such manner as the legislatures of each State shall direct, to meet in Congress on the first Monday

## VI.

No State, without the consent of the United States in Congress assembled, shall send any embassy to, or receive any embassy from, or enter into any conference, agreement, alliance or treaty with any King, Prince or State; nor shall any person holding any office of profit or trust under the United States, or any of them, accept any present, emolument, office or title of any kind whatever from any King, Prince or foreign State; nor shall the United States in Congress assembled, or any of them, grant any title of nobility.

No two or more States shall enter into any treaty, confederation or alliance whatever between them, without the consent of the United States in Congress assembled, specifying accurately the purposes for which the same is to be entered into, and how long it shall continue.

No State shall lay any imposts or duties, which may interfere with any stipulations in treaties, entered into by the United States in Congress assembled, with any King, Prince or State, in pursuance of any treaties already proposed by Congress, to the courts of France and Spain.

No vessel of war shall be kept up in time of peace by any State, except such number only, as shall be deemed necessary by the United States in Congress assembled, for the defense of such State, or its trade; nor shall any body of forces be kept up by any State in time of peace, except such number only, as in the judgement of the United States in Congress assembled, shall be deemed requisite to garrison the forts necessary for the defense of such State; but every State shall always keep up a well-regulated and disciplined militia, sufficiently armed and accoutered, and shall provide and constantly have ready for use, in public stores, a due number of filed pieces and tents, and a proper quantity of arms, ammunition and camp equipage.

No State shall engage in any war without the consent of the United States in Congress assembled, unless such State be actually invaded by enemies, or shall have received certain advice of a resolution being formed by some nation of Indians to invade such State,

and the danger is so imminent as not to admit of a delay till the United States in Congress assembled can be consulted; nor shall any State grant commissions to any ships or vessels of war, nor letters of marque or reprisal, except it be after a declaration of war by the United States in Congress assembled, and then only against the Kingdom or State and the subjects thereof, against which war has been so declared, and under such regulations as shall be established by the United States in Congress assembled, unless such State be infested by pirates, in which case vessels of war may be fitted out for that occasion, and kept so long as the danger shall continue, or until the United States in Congress assembled shall determine otherwise.

## VII.

When land forces are raised by any State for the common defense, all officers of or under the rank of colonel, shall be appointed by the legislature of each State respectively, by whom such forces shall be raised, or in such manner as such State shall direct, and all vacancies shall be filled up by the State which first made the appointment.

## VIII.

All charges of war, and all other expenses that shall be incurred for the common defense or general welfare, and allowed by the United

States in Congress assembled, shall be defrayed out of a common treasury, which shall be supplied by the several States in proportion to the value of all land within each State, granted or surveyed for any person, as such land and the buildings and improvements thereon shall be estimated according to such mode as the United States in Congress assembled, shall from time to time direct and appoint.

The taxes for paying that proportion shall be laid and levied by the authority and direction of the legislatures of the several States within the time agreed upon by the United States in Congress assembled.

## IX.

The United States in Congress assembled, shall have the sole and exclusive right and power of determining on peace and war, except in the cases mentioned in the sixth article—of sending and receiving ambassadors—entering into treaties and alliances, provided that no treaty of commerce shall be made whereby the legislative power of the respective States shall be restrained from imposing such imposts and duties on foreigners, as their own people are subjected to, or from prohibiting the exportation or importation of any species of goods or commodities whatsoever—of establishing rules for deciding in all cases, what captures on land or water shall be legal, and in what manner prizes taken by land or naval forces in the service of the United States shall be divided or appropriated—of granting letters of marque and reprisal in times of peace—appointing courts for the trial of piracies and felonies commited on the high seas and establishing

courts for receiving and determining finally appeals in all cases of captures, provided that no member of Congress shall be appointed a judge of any of the said courts.

The United States in Congress assembled shall also be the last resort on appeal in all disputes and differences now subsisting or that hereafter may arise between two or more States concerning boundary, jurisdiction or any other causes whatever; which authority shall always be exercised in the manner following. Whenever the legislative or executive authority or lawful agent of any State in controversy with another shall present a petition to Congress stating the matter in question and praying for a hearing, notice thereof shall be given by order of Congress to the legislative or executive authority of the other State in controversy, and a day assigned for the appearance of the parties by their lawful agents, who shall then be directed to appoint by joint consent, commissioners or judges to constitute a court for hearing and determining the matter in question: but if they cannot agree, Congress shall name three persons out of each of the United States, and from the list of such persons each party shall alternately strike out one, the petitioners beginning, until the number shall be reduced to thirteen; and from that number not less than seven, nor more than nine names as Congress shall direct, shall in the presence of Congress be drawn out by lot, and the persons whose names shall be so drawn or any five of them, shall be commissioners or judges, to hear and finally determine the controversy, so always as a major part of the judges who shall hear the cause shall agree in the determination: and if either party shall neglect to attend at the day appointed, without showing reasons, which Congress shall judge sufficient, or being present shall refuse to strike, the Congress shall proceed to nominate three persons out of each State, and the secretary of Congress shall strike in behalf of such party absent or refusing; and the judgement and sentence of the court to be appointed, in the manner before prescribed, shall be final and conclusive; and if any of the parties shall refuse to submit to the authority of such court, or to appear or defend their claim or cause, the court shall nevertheless proceed to pronounce sentence, or judgement, which shall in like manner be final and decisive, the judgement or sentence and other proceedings being in either case transmitted to Congress, and lodged among the acts of Congress for the security of the parties concerned: provided that every commissioner, before he sits in judgement, shall take an oath to be administered by one of the judges of the supreme or superior court of the State, where the cause shall be tried, 'well and truly to hear and determine the matter in question, according to the best of his judgement, without favor, affection or hope of reward': provided also, that no State shall be deprived of territory for the benefit of the United States.

All controversies concerning the private right of soil claimed under different grants of two or more States, whose jurisdictions as they may respect such lands, and the States which passed such grants are adjusted, the said grants or either of them being at the same time claimed to have originated antecedent to such settlement of jurisdiction, shall on the petition of either party to the Congress of the United States, be finally determined as near as may be in the same manner as is before presecribed for deciding disputes respecting territorial jurisdiction between different States.

The United States in Congress assembled shall also have the sole and exclusive right and power of regulating the alloy and value of coin struck by their own authority, or by that of the respective States—fixing the standards of weights and measures throughout the United States—regulating the trade and managing all affairs with the Indians, not members of any of the States, provided that the legislative right of any State within its own limits be not infringed or violated—establishing or regulating post offices from one State to another, throughout all the United States, and exacting such postage on the papers passing through the same as may be requisite to defray the expenses of the said office—appointing all officers of the land forces, in the service of the United States, excepting regimental officers—appointing all the officers of the naval forces, and commissioning all officers whatever in the service of the United States—making rules for the government and regulation of the said land and naval forces, and directing their operations.

The United States in Congress assembled shall have authority to appoint a committee, to sit in the recess of Congress, to be denominated 'A Committee of the States', and to consist of one delegate from each State; and to appoint such other committees and civil officers as may be necessary for managing the general affairs of the United States under their direction—to appoint one of their members to preside, provided that no person be allowed to serve in the office of president more than one year in any term of three years; to ascertain the necessary sums of money to be raised for the service of the United States, and to appropriate and apply the same for defraying the public expenses—to borrow money, or emit bills on the credit of the United States, transmitting every half-year to the respective States an account of the sums of money so borrowed or emitted—to build and equip a navy—to agree upon the number of land forces, and to make requisitions from each State for its quota, in proportion to the number of white inhabitants in such State; which requisition shall be binding, and thereupon the legislature of each State shall appoint the regimental officers, raise the men and cloath, arm and equip them in a solid-like manner, at the expense of the United States; and the officers and men so cloathed, armed and equipped shall march to the place appointed, and within the time agreed on by the United States in Congress assembled. But if the United States in Congress assembled shall, on consideration of circumstances judge proper that any State should not raise men, or should raise a smaller number of men than the quota thereof, such extra number shall be raised, officered, cloathed, armed and equipped in the same manner as the quota of each State, unless the legislature of such State shall judge that such extra number cannot be safely spread out in the same, in which case they shall raise, officer, cloath, arm and equip as many of such extra number as they judge can be safely spared. And the officers and men so cloathed, armed, and equipped, shall march to the place appointed, and within the time agreed on by the United States in Congress assembled.

The United States in Congress assembled shall never engage in a war, nor grant letters of marque or reprisal in time of peace, nor enter into any treaties or alliances, nor coin money, nor regulate the value thereof, nor ascertain the sums and expenses necessary for the defense and welfare of the United States, or any of them, nor emit bills, nor borrow money on the credit of the United States, nor appropriate money, nor agree upon the number of vessels of war, to be built or purchased, or the number of land or sea forces to be raised, nor appoint a commander in chief of the army or navy, unless nine States assent to the same: nor shall a question on any other point, except for adjourning from day to day be determined, unless by the votes of the majority of the United States in Congress assembled.

The Congress of the United States shall have power to adjourn to any time within the year, and to any place within the United States, so that no period of adjournment be for a longer duration than the space of six months, and shall publish the journal of their proceedings monthly, except such parts thereof relating to treaties, alliances or military operations, as in their judgement require secrecy; and the yeas and nays of the delegates of each State on any question shall be entered on the journal, when it is desired by any delegates of a State, or any of them, at his or their request shall be furnished with a transcript of the said journal, except such parts as are above excepted, to lay before the legislatures of the several States.

## X.

The Committee of the States, or any nine of them, shall be authorized to execute, in the recess of Congress, such of the powers of Congress as the United States in Congress assembled, by the consent of the nine States, shall from time to time think expedient to vest them with; provided that no power be delegated to the said Committee, for the exercise of which, by the Articles of Confederation, the voice of nine States in the Congress of the United States assembled be requisite.

## XI.

Canada acceding to this confederation, and adjoining in the measures of the United States, shall be admitted into, and entitled to all the advantages of this Union; but no other colony shall be admitted into the same, unless such admission be agreed to by nine States.

## XII.

All bills of credit emitted, monies borrowed, and debts contracted by, or under the authority of Congress, before the assembling of the United States, in pursuance of the present confederation, shall be deemed and considered as a charge against the United States, for payment and satisfaction whereof the said United States, and the public faith are hereby solemnly pleged.

## XIII.

Every State shall abide by the determination of the United States in Congress assembled, on all questions which by this confederation are submitted to them. And the Articles of this Confederation shall be inviolably observed by every State, and the Union shall be perpetual; nor shall any alteration at any time hereafter be made in any of them; unless such alteration be agreed to in a Congress of the United States, and be afterwards confirmed by the legislatures of every State.

And Whereas it hath pleased the Great Governor of the World to incline the hearts of the legislatures we respectively represent in Congress, to approve of, and to authorize us to ratify the said Articles of Confederation and perpetual Union. Know Ye that we the undersigned delegates, by virtue of the power and authority to us given for that purpose, do by these presents, in the name and in behalf of our respective constituents, fully and entirely ratify and confirm each and every of the said Articles of Confederation and perpetual Union, and all and singular the matters and things therein contained: And we do further solemnly plight and engage the faith of our respective constituents, that they shall abide by the determinations of the United States in Congress assembled, on all questions, which by the said Confederation are submitted to them. And that the Articles thereof shall be inviolably observed by the States we respectively represent, and that the Union shall be perpetual.

In Witness whereof we have hereunto set our hands in Congress. Done at Philadelphia in the State of Pennsylvania the ninth day of July in the Year of our Lord One Thousand Seven Hundred and Seventy-Eight, and in the Third Year of the independence of America.

Agreed to by Congress 15 November 1777 In force after ratification by Maryland, 1 March 1781

# U.S. Constitution

## Preamble

We the People of the United States, in Order to form a more perfect Union, establish Justice, insure domestic Tranquility, provide for the common defence, promote the general Welfare, and secure the Blessings of Liberty to ourselves and our Posterity, do ordain and establish this Constitution for the United States of America.

## Article I.—The Legislative Branch

### Section 1—The Legislature

All legislative Powers herein granted shall be vested in a Congress of the United States, which shall consist of a Senate and House of Representatives.

## Section 2—The House

The House of Representatives shall be composed of Members chosen every second Year by the People of the several States, and the Electors in each State shall have the Qualifications requisite for Electors of the most numerous Branch of the State Legislature.

No Person shall be a Representative who shall not have attained to the Age of twenty five Years, and been seven Years a Citizen of the United States, and who shall not, when elected, be an Inhabitant of that State in which he shall be chosen.

*(Representatives and direct Taxes shall be apportioned among the several States which may be included within this Union, according to their respective Numbers, which shall be determined by adding to the whole Number of free Persons, including those bound to Service for a Term of Years, and excluding Indians not taxed, three fifths of all other Persons.)* **(The previous sentence in parentheses was modified by the 14th Amendment, section 2.)** The actual Enumeration shall be made within three Years after the first Meeting of the Congress of the United States, and within every

subsequent Term of ten Years, in such Manner as they shall by Law direct. The Number of Representatives shall not exceed one for every thirty Thousand, but each State shall have at Least one Representative; and until such enumeration shall be made, the State of New Hampshire shall be entitled to chuse three, Massachusetts eight, Rhode Island and Providence Plantations one, Connecticut five, New York six, New Jersey four, Pennsylvania eight, Delaware one, Maryland six, Virginia ten, North Carolina five, South Carolina five and Georgia three.

When vacancies happen in the Representation from any State, the Executive Authority thereof shall issue Writs of Election to fill such Vacancies.

The House of Representatives shall chuse their Speaker and other Officers; and shall have the sole Power of Impeachment.

## Section 3—The Senate

The Senate of the United States shall be composed of two Senators from each State, *(chosen by the Legislature thereof,)* **(The preceding words in parentheses superseded by 17th Amendment, section 1.)** for six Years; and each Senator shall have one Vote.

Immediately after they shall be assembled in Consequence of the first Election, they shall be divided as equally as may be into three Classes. The Seats of the Senators of the first Class shall be vacated at the Expiration of the second Year, of the second Class at the Expiration of the fourth Year, and of the third Class at the Expiration of the sixth Year, so that one third may be chosen every second Year; *(and if Vacancies happen by Resignation, or otherwise, during the Recess of the Legislature of any State, the Executive thereof may make temporary Appointments until the next Meeting of the Legislature, which shall then fill such Vacancies.)* **(The preceding words in parentheses were superseded by the 17th Amendment, section 2.)**

No person shall be a Senator who shall not have attained to the Age of thirty Years, and been nine Years a Citizen of the United States, and who shall not, when elected, be an Inhabitant of that State for which he shall be chosen.

The Vice President of the United States shall be President of the Senate, but shall have no Vote, unless they be equally divided.

The Senate shall chuse their other Officers, and also a President pro tempore, in the absence of the Vice President, or when he shall exercise the Office of President of the United States.

The Senate shall have the sole Power to try all Impeachments. When sitting for that Purpose, they shall be on Oath or Affirmation. When the President of the United States is tried, the Chief Justice shall preside: And no Person shall be convicted without the Concurrence of two thirds of the Members present.

Judgment in Cases of Impeachment shall not extend further than to removal from Office, and disqualification to hold and enjoy any Office of honor, Trust or Profit under the United States: but the Party convicted shall nevertheless be liable and subject to Indictment, Trial, Judgment and Punishment, according to Law.

## Section 4—Elections, Meetings

The Times, Places and Manner of holding Elections for Senators and Representatives, shall be prescribed in each State by the

Legislature thereof; but the Congress may at any time by Law make or alter such Regulations, except as to the Place of Chusing Senators.

The Congress shall assemble at least once in every Year, and such Meeting shall *(be on the first Monday in December,)* **(The preceding words in parentheses were superseded by the 20th Amendment, section 2.)** unless they shall by Law appoint a different Day.

## Section 5—Membership, Rules, Journals, Adjournment

Each House shall be the Judge of the Elections, Returns and Qualifications of its own Members, and a Majority of each shall constitute a Quorum to do Business; but a smaller number may adjourn from day to day, and may be authorized to compel the Attendance of absent Members, in such Manner, and under such Penalties as each House may provide.

Each House may determine the Rules of its Proceedings, punish its Members for disorderly Behavior, and, with the Concurrence of two-thirds, expel a Member.

Each House shall keep a Journal of its Proceedings, and from time to time publish the same, excepting such Parts as may in their Judgment require Secrecy; and the Yeas and Nays of the Members of either House on any question shall, at the Desire of one fifth of those Present, be entered on the Journal.

Neither House, during the Session of Congress, shall, without the Consent of the other, adjourn for more than three days, nor to any other Place than that in which the two Houses shall be sitting.

## Section 6—Compensation

*(The Senators and Representatives shall receive a Compensation for their Services, to be ascertained by Law, and paid out of the Treasury of the United States.)* **(The preceding words in parentheses were modified by the 27th Amendment.)** They shall in all Cases, except Treason, Felony and Breach of the Peace, be privileged from Arrest during their Attendance at the Session of their respective Houses, and in going to and returning from the same; and for any Speech or Debate in either House, they shall not be questioned in any other Place.

No Senator or Representative shall, during the Time for which he was elected, be appointed to any civil Office under the Authority of the United States which shall have been created, or the Emoluments whereof shall have been increased during such time; and no Person holding any Office under the United States, shall be a Member of either House during his Continuance in Office.

## Section 7—Revenue Bills, Legislative Process, Presidential Veto

All bills for raising Revenue shall originate in the House of Representatives; but the Senate may propose or concur with Amendments as on other Bills.

Every Bill which shall have passed the House of Representatives and the Senate, shall, before it become a Law, be presented to the President of the United States; If he approve he shall sign it, but if not he shall return it, with his Objections to that House in which it shall have originated, who shall enter the Objections at large on their Journal, and proceed to reconsider it. If after such Reconsideration two thirds of that House shall agree to pass the Bill, it shall be sent, together with the Objections, to the other House, by which it shall likewise be reconsidered, and if approved by two thirds of that House, it shall become a Law. But in all such Cases the Votes of both Houses shall be determined by Yeas and Nays, and the Names of the Persons voting for and against the Bill shall be entered on the Journal of each House respectively. If any Bill shall not be returned by the President within ten Days (Sundays excepted) after it shall have been presented to him, the Same shall be a Law, in like Manner as if he had signed it, unless the Congress by their Adjournment prevent its Return, in which Case it shall not be a Law.

Every Order, Resolution, or Vote to which the Concurrence of the Senate and House of Representatives may be necessary (except on a question of Adjournment) shall be presented to the President of the United States; and before the Same shall take Effect, shall be approved by him, or being disapproved by him, shall be repassed by two thirds of the Senate and House of Representatives, according to the Rules and Limitations prescribed in the Case of a Bill.

## Section 8—Powers of Congress

The Congress shall have Power To lay and collect Taxes, Duties, Imposts and Excises, to pay the Debts and provide for the common Defence and general Welfare of the United States; but all Duties, Imposts and Excises shall be uniform throughout the United States;

To borrow money on the credit of the United States;

To regulate Commerce with foreign Nations, and among the several States, and with the Indian Tribes;

To establish an uniform Rule of Naturalization, and uniform Laws on the subject of Bankruptcies throughout the United States;

To coin Money, regulate the Value thereof, and of foreign Coin, and fix the Standard of Weights and Measures;

To provide for the Punishment of counterfeiting the Securities and current Coin of the United States;

To establish Post Offices and Post Roads;

To promote the Progress of Science and useful Arts, by securing for limited Times to Authors and Inventors the exclusive Right to their respective Writings and Discoveries;

To constitute Tribunals inferior to the supreme Court;

To define and punish Piracies and Felonies committed on the high Seas, and Offenses against the Law of Nations;

To declare War, grant Letters of Marque and Reprisal, and make Rules concerning Captures on Land and Water;

To raise and support Armies, but no Appropriation of Money to that Use shall be for a longer Term than two Years;

To provide and maintain a Navy;

To make Rules for the Government and Regulation of the land and naval Forces;

To provide for calling forth the Militia to execute the Laws of the Union, suppress Insurrections and repel Invasions;

To provide for organizing, arming, and disciplining the Militia, and for governing such Part of them as may be employed in the Service of the United States, reserving to the States respectively, the Appointment of the Officers, and the Authority of training the Militia according to the discipline prescribed by Congress;

To exercise exclusive Legislation in all Cases whatsoever, over such District (not exceeding ten Miles square) as may, by Cession of particular States, and the acceptance of Congress, become the Seat of the Government of the United States, and to exercise like Authority over all Places purchased by the Consent of the Legislature of the State in which the Same shall be, for the Erection of Forts, Magazines, Arsenals, dock-Yards, and other needful Buildings; And

To make all Laws which shall be necessary and proper for carrying into Execution the foregoing Powers, and all other Powers vested by this Constitution in the Government of the United States, or in any Department or Officer thereof.

## Section 9—Limits on Congress

The Migration or Importation of such Persons as any of the States now existing shall think proper to admit, shall not be prohibited by the Congress prior to the Year one thousand eight hundred and eight, but a tax or duty may be imposed on such Importation, not exceeding ten dollars for each Person.

The privilege of the Writ of Habeas Corpus shall not be suspended, unless when in Cases of Rebellion or Invasion the public Safety may require it.

No Bill of Attainder or ex post facto Law shall be passed.

*(No capitation, or other direct, Tax shall be laid, unless in Proportion to the Census or Enumeration herein before directed to be taken.)* **(Section in parentheses clarified by the 16th Amendment.)**

No Tax or Duty shall be laid on Articles exported from any State.

No Preference shall be given by any Regulation of Commerce or Revenue to the Ports of one State over those of another: nor

shall Vessels bound to, or from, one State, be obliged to enter, clear, or pay Duties in another.

No Money shall be drawn from the Treasury, but in Consequence of Appropriations made by Law; and a regular Statement and Account of the Receipts and Expenditures of all public Money shall be published from time to time.

No Title of Nobility shall be granted by the United States: And no Person holding any Office of Profit or Trust under them, shall, without the Consent of the Congress, accept of any present, Emolument, Office, or Title, of any kind whatever, from any King, Prince or foreign State.

## Section 10—Powers Prohibited of States

No State shall enter into any Treaty, Alliance, or Confederation; grant Letters of Marque and Reprisal; coin Money; emit Bills of Credit; make any Thing but gold and silver Coin a Tender in Payment of Debts; pass any Bill of Attainder, ex post facto Law, or Law impairing the Obligation of Contracts, or grant any Title of Nobility.

No State shall, without the Consent of the Congress, lay any Imposts or Duties on Imports or Exports, except what may be absolutely necessary for executing it's inspection Laws: and the net Produce of all Duties and Imposts, laid by any State on Imports or Exports, shall be for the Use of the Treasury of the United States; and all such Laws shall be subject to the Revision and Controul of the Congress.

No State shall, without the Consent of Congress, lay any duty of Tonnage, keep Troops, or Ships of War in time of Peace, enter into any Agreement or Compact with another State, or with a foreign Power, or engage in

War, unless actually invaded, or in such imminent Danger as will not admit of delay.

# Article II.—The Executive Branch

## Section 1—The President

The executive Power shall be vested in a President of the United States of America. He shall hold his Office during the Term of four Years, and, together with the Vice-President chosen for the same Term, be elected, as follows:

Each State shall appoint, in such Manner as the Legislature thereof may direct, a Number of Electors, equal to the whole Number of Senators and Representatives to which the State may be entitled in the Congress: but no Senator or Representative, or Person holding an Office of Trust or Profit under the United States, shall be appointed an Elector.

*(The Electors shall meet in their respective States, and vote by Ballot for two persons, of whom one at least shall not lie an Inhabitant of the same State with themselves. And they shall make a List of all the Persons voted for, and of the Number of Votes for each; which List they shall sign and certify, and transmit sealed to the Seat of the Government of the United States, directed to the President of the Senate. The President of the Senate shall, in the Presence of the Senate and House of Representatives, open all the Certificates, and the Votes shall then be counted. The Person having the greatest Number of Votes shall be the President, if such Number be a Majority of the whole Number of Electors appointed;*
*and if there be more than one who have such Majority, and have an equal Number of Votes, then the House of Representatives shall immediately chuse by Ballot one of them for President; and if no Person have a Majority, then from the five highest on the List the said House shall in like Manner chuse the President. But in chusing the President, the Votes shall be taken by States, the Representation from each State having one Vote; a quorum for this Purpose shall consist of a Member or Members from two-thirds of the States, and a Majority of all the States shall be necessary to a Choice. In every Case, after the Choice of the President, the Person having the greatest Number of Votes of the Electors shall be the Vice President. But if there should remain two or more who have equal Votes, the Senate shall chuse from them by Ballot the Vice-President.)* **(This clause in parentheses was superseded by the 12th Amendment.)**

The Congress may determine the Time of chusing the Electors, and the Day on which they shall give their Votes; which Day shall be the same throughout the United States.

No person except a natural born Citizen, or a Citizen of the United States, at the time of the Adoption of this Constitution, shall be eligible to the Office of President; neither shall any Person be eligible to that Office who shall not have attained to the Age of thirty-five Years, and been fourteen Years a Resident within the United States.

*(In Case of the Removal of the President from Office, or of his Death, Resignation, or Inability to discharge the Powers and Duties of the said Office, the same shall devolve on the Vice President, and the Congress may by Law provide for the Case of Removal, Death, Resignation or Inability, both of the President and Vice President, declaring what Officer shall then act as President, and such Officer shall act*

*accordingly, until the Disability be removed, or a President shall be elected.)* **(This clause in parentheses has been modified by the 20th and 25th Amendments.)**

The President shall, at stated Times, receive for his Services, a Compensation, which shall neither be increased nor diminished during the Period for which he shall have been elected, and he shall not receive within that Period any other Emolument from the United States, or any of them.

Before he enter on the Execution of his Office, he shall take the following Oath or Affirmation:

"I do solemnly swear (or affirm) that I will faithfully execute the Office of President of the United States, and will to the best of my Ability, preserve, protect and defend the Constitution of the United States."

## Section 2—Civilian Power over Military, Cabinet, Pardon Power, Appointments

The President shall be Commander in Chief of the Army and Navy of the United States, and of the Militia of the several States, when called into the actual Service of the United States; he may require the Opinion, in writing, of the principal Officer in each of the executive Departments, upon any subject relating to the Duties of their respective Offices, and he shall have Power to Grant Reprieves and Pardons for Offenses against the United States, except in Cases of Impeachment.

He shall have Power, by and with the Advice and Consent of the Senate, to make Treaties, provided two thirds of the Senators present concur; and he shall nominate, and by and with the Advice and Consent of the Senate, shall appoint Ambassadors, other public Ministers and Consuls, Judges of the supreme Court, and all other Officers of the United States, whose Appointments are not herein otherwise provided for, and which shall be established by Law: but the Congress may by Law vest the Appointment of such inferior Officers, as they think proper, in the President alone, in the Courts of Law, or in the Heads of Departments.

The President shall have Power to fill up all Vacancies that may happen during the Recess of the Senate, by granting Commissions which shall expire at the End of their next Session.

## Section 3—State of the Union, Convening Congress

He shall from time to time give to the Congress Information of the State of the Union, and recommend to their Consideration such Measures as he shall judge necessary and expedient; he may, on extraordinary Occasions, convene both Houses, or either of them, and in Case of Disagreement between them, with Respect to the Time of Adjournment, he may adjourn them to such Time as he shall think proper; he shall receive Ambassadors and other public Ministers; he shall take Care that the Laws be faithfully executed, and shall Commission all the Officers of the United States.

## Section 4—Disqualification

The President, Vice President and all civil Officers of the United States, shall be removed from Office on Impeachment for, and Conviction of, Treason, Bribery, or other high Crimes and Misdemeanors.

# Article III.—The Judicial Branch

## Section 1—Judicial Powers

The judicial Power of the United States, shall be vested in one supreme Court, and in such inferior Courts as the Congress may from time to time ordain and establish. The Judges, both of the supreme and inferior Courts, shall hold their Offices during good Behavior, and shall, at stated Times, receive for their Services a Compensation which shall not be diminished during their Continuance in Office.

## Section 2—Trial by Jury, Original Jurisdiction, Jury Trials

*(The judicial Power shall extend to all Cases, in Law and Equity, arising under this Constitution, the Laws of the United States, and Treaties made, or which shall be made, under their Authority; to all Cases affecting Ambassadors, other public Ministers and Consuls; to all Cases of admiralty and maritime Jurisdiction; to Controversies to which the United States shall be a Party; to Controversies between two or more States; between a State and Citizens of another State; between Citizens of different States; between Citizens of the same State claiming Lands under Grants of different States, and between a State, or the Citizens thereof, and foreign States, Citizens or Subjects.)* **(This section in parentheses is modified by the 11th Amendment.)**

In all Cases affecting Ambassadors, other public Ministers and Consuls, and those in which a State shall be Party, the supreme Court shall have original Jurisdiction. In all the other Cases before mentioned, the supreme Court shall have appellate Jurisdiction, both as to Law and Fact, with such Exceptions, and under such Regulations as the Congress shall make.

The Trial of all Crimes, except in Cases of Impeachment, shall be by Jury; and such Trial shall be held in the State where the said Crimes shall have been committed; but when not committed within any State, the Trial shall be at such Place or Places as the Congress may by Law have directed.

## Section 3—Treason

Treason against the United States, shall consist only in levying War against them, or in adhering to their Enemies, giving them Aid and Comfort. No Person shall be convicted of Treason unless on the Testimony of two Witnesses to the same overt Act, or on Confession in open Court.

The Congress shall have power to declare the Punishment of Treason, but no Attainder of Treason shall work Corruption of Blood, or Forfeiture except during the Life of the Person attainted.

# Article IV.—The States

## Section 1—Each State to Honor All Others

Full Faith and Credit shall be given in each State to the public Acts, Records, and judicial Proceedings of every other State. And the Congress may by general Laws prescribe the Manner in which such Acts, Records and

Proceedings shall be proved, and the Effect thereof.

## Section 2—State Citizens, Extradition

The Citizens of each State shall be entitled to all Privileges and Immunities of Citizens in the several States.

A Person charged in any State with Treason, Felony, or other Crime, who shall flee from Justice, and be found in another State, shall on demand of the executive Authority of the State from which he fled, be delivered up, to be removed to the State having Jurisdiction of the Crime.

*(No Person held to Service or Labour in one State, under the Laws thereof, escaping into another, shall, in Consequence of any Law or Regulation therein, be discharged from such Service or Labour, But shall be delivered up on Claim of the Party to whom such Service or Labour may be due.)* **(This clause in parentheses is superseded by the 13th Amendment.)**

## Section 3—New States

New States may be admitted by the Congress into this Union; but no new States shall be formed or erected within the Jurisdiction of any other State; nor any State be formed by the Junction of two or more States, or parts of States, without the Consent of the Legislatures of the States concerned as well as of the Congress.

The Congress shall have Power to dispose of and make all needful Rules and Regulations respecting the Territory or other Property belonging to the United States; and nothing in this Constitution shall be so construed as to

Prejudice any Claims of the United States, or of any particular State.

## Section 4—Republican Government

The United States shall guarantee to every State in this Union a Republican Form of Government, and shall protect each of them against Invasion; and on Application of the Legislature, or of the Executive (when the Legislature cannot be convened) against domestic Violence.

# Article V.—Amendment

The Congress, whenever two thirds of both Houses shall deem it necessary, shall propose Amendments to this Constitution, or, on the Application of the Legislatures of two thirds of the several States, shall call a Convention for proposing Amendments, which, in either Case, shall be valid to all Intents and Purposes, as part of this Constitution, when ratified by the Legislatures of three fourths of the several States, or by Conventions in three fourths thereof, as the one or the other Mode of Ratification may be proposed by the Congress; Provided that no Amendment which may be made prior to the Year One thousand eight hundred and eight shall in any Manner affect the first and fourth Clauses in the Ninth Section of the first Article; and that no State, without its Consent, shall be deprived of its equal Suffrage in the Senate.

## Article VI.—Debts, Supremacy, Oaths

All Debts contracted and Engagements entered into, before the Adoption of this Constitution, shall be as valid against the United States under this Constitution, as under the Confederation.

This Constitution, and the Laws of the United States which shall be made in Pursuance thereof; and all Treaties made, or which shall be made, under the Authority of the United States, shall be the supreme Law of the Land; and the Judges in every State shall be bound thereby, any Thing in the Constitution or Laws of any State to the Contrary notwithstanding.

The Senators and Representatives before mentioned, and the Members of the several State Legislatures, and all executive and judicial Officers, both of the United States and of the several States, shall be bound by Oath or Affirmation, to support this Constitution; but no religious Test shall ever be required as a Qualification to any Office or public Trust under the United States.

## Article VII.—Ratification

The Ratification of the Conventions of nine States, shall be sufficient for the Establishment of this Constitution between the States so ratifying the Same.

Done in Convention by the Unanimous Consent of the States present the Seventeenth Day of September in the Year of our Lord one thousand seven hundred and Eighty seven and of the Independence of the United States of America the Twelfth. In Witness whereof We have hereunto subscribed our Names.

Go Washington—President and deputy from Virginia

New Hampshire—John Langdon, Nicholas Gilman

Massachusetts—Nathaniel Gorham, Rufus King

Connecticut—Wm Saml Johnson, Roger Sherman

New York—Alexander Hamilton

New Jersey—Wil Livingston, David Brearley, Wm Paterson, Jona. Dayton

Pensylvania—B Franklin, Thomas Mifflin, Robt Morris, Geo. Clymer, Thos FitzSimons, Jared Ingersoll, James Wilson, Gouv Morris

Delaware—Geo. Read, Gunning Bedford jun, John Dickinson, Richard Bassett, Jaco. Broom

Maryland—James McHenry, Dan of St Tho Jenifer, Danl Carroll

Virginia—John Blair, James Madison Jr.

North Carolina—Wm Blount, Richd Dobbs Spaight, Hu Williamson

South Carolina—J. Rutledge, Charles Cotesworth Pinckney, Charles Pinckney, Pierce Butler

Georgia—William Few, Abr Baldwin

Attest: William Jackson, Secretary

## The Amendments

**The following are the Amendments to the Constitution. The first ten Amendments**

**collectively are commonly known as the Bill of Rights.**

## Amendment 1—Freedom of Religion, Press, Expression. Ratified 12/15/1791.

Congress shall make no law respecting an establishment of religion, or prohibiting the free exercise thereof; or abridging the freedom of speech, or of the press; or the right of the people peaceably to assemble, and to petition the Government for a redress of grievances.

## Amendment 2—Right to Bear Arms. Ratified 12/15/1791.

A well regulated Militia, being necessary to the security of a free State, the right of the people to keep and bear Arms, shall not be infringed.

## Amendment 3—Quartering of Soldiers. Ratified 12/15/1791.

No Soldier shall, in time of peace be quartered in any house, without the consent of the Owner, nor in time of war, but in a manner to be prescribed by law.

## Amendment 4—Search and Seizure. Ratified 12/15/1791.

The right of the people to be secure in their persons, houses, papers, and effects, against unreasonable searches and seizures, shall not be violated, and no Warrants shall issue, but upon probable cause, supported by Oath or affirmation, and particularly describing the place to be searched, and the persons or things to be seized.

## Amendment 5—Trial and Punishment, Compensation for Takings. Ratified 12/15/1791.

No person shall be held to answer for a capital, or otherwise infamous crime, unless on a presentment or indictment of a Grand Jury, except in cases arising in the land or naval forces, or in the Militia, when in actual service in time of War or public danger; nor shall any person be subject for the same offense to be twice put in jeopardy of life or limb; nor shall be compelled in any criminal case to be a witness against himself, nor be deprived of life, liberty, or property, without due process of law; nor shall private property be taken for public use, without just compensation.

## Amendment 6—Right to Speedy Trial, Confrontation of Witnesses. Ratified 12/15/1791.

In all criminal prosecutions, the accused shall enjoy the right to a speedy and public trial, by an impartial jury of the State and district wherein the crime shall have been committed, which district shall have been previously ascertained by law, and to be informed of the nature and cause of the accusation; to be confronted with the witnesses against him; to have compulsory process for obtaining witnesses in his favor, and to have the Assistance of Counsel for his defence.

## Amendment 7—Trial by Jury in Civil Cases. Ratified 12/15/1791.

In Suits at common law, where the value in controversy shall exceed twenty dollars, the right of trial by jury shall be preserved, and no fact tried by a jury, shall be otherwise reexamined in any Court of the United States, than according to the rules of the common law.

## Amendment 8—Cruel and Unusual Punishment. Ratified 12/15/1791.

Excessive bail shall not be required, nor excessive fines imposed, nor cruel and unusual punishments inflicted.

## Amendment 9—Construction of Constitution. Ratified 12/15/1791.

The enumeration in the Constitution, of certain rights, shall not be construed to deny or disparage others retained by the people.

## Amendment 10—Powers of the States and People. Ratified 12/15/1791.

The powers not delegated to the United States by the Constitution, nor prohibited by it to the States, are reserved to the States respectively, or to the people.

## Amendment 11—Judicial Limits. Ratified 2/7/1795.

The Judicial power of the United States shall not be construed to extend to any suit in law or equity, commenced or prosecuted against one of the United States by Citizens of another State, or by Citizens or Subjects of any Foreign State.

## Amendment 12—Choosing the President, Vice-President. Ratified 6/15/1804.

The Electors shall meet in their respective states, and vote by ballot for President and Vice-President, one of whom, at least, shall not be an inhabitant of the same state with themselves; they shall name in their ballots the person voted for as President, and in distinct ballots the person voted for as Vice-President, and they shall make distinct lists of all persons voted for as President, and of all persons voted for as Vice-President and of the number of votes for each, which lists they shall sign and certify, and transmit sealed to the seat of the government of the United States, directed to the President of the Senate;

The President of the Senate shall, in the presence of the Senate and House of Representatives, open all the certificates and the votes shall then be counted;

The person having the greatest Number of votes for President, shall be the President, if such number be a majority of the whole number of Electors appointed; and if no person have such majority, then from the persons having the highest numbers not exceeding three on the list of those voted for as President, the House of Representatives shall choose immediately, by ballot, the President. But in choosing the President, the votes shall be taken by states, the representation from each state having one vote; a quorum for this purpose shall consist of a member or members from two-thirds of the states, and a majority of all the states shall be necessary to a choice. And if the House of

Representatives shall not choose a President whenever the right of choice shall devolve upon them, before the fourth day of March next following, then the Vice-President shall act as President, as in the case of the death or other constitutional disability of the President.

The person having the greatest number of votes as Vice-President, shall be the Vice-President, if such number be a majority of the whole number of Electors appointed, and if no person have a majority, then from the two highest numbers on the list, the Senate shall choose the Vice-President; a quorum for the purpose shall consist of two-thirds of the whole number of Senators, and a majority of the whole number shall be necessary to a choice. But no person constitutionally ineligible to the office of President shall be eligible to that of Vice-President of the United States.

## Amendment 13—Slavery Abolished. Ratified 12/6/1865.

1. Neither slavery nor involuntary servitude, except as a punishment for crime whereof the party shall have been duly convicted, shall exist within the United States, or any place subject to their jurisdiction.
2. Congress shall have power to enforce this article by appropriate legislation.

## Amendment 14—Citizenship Rights. Ratified 7/9/1868.

1. All persons born or naturalized in the United States, and subject to the jurisdiction thereof, are citizens of the United States and of the State wherein they reside. No State shall make or enforce any law which shall abridge the privileges or immunities of citizens of the United States; nor shall any State deprive any person of life, liberty, or property, without due process of law; nor deny to any person within its jurisdiction the equal protection of the laws.
2. Representatives shall be apportioned among the several States according to their respective numbers, counting the whole number of persons in each State, excluding Indians not taxed. But when the right to vote at any election for the choice of electors for President and Vice-President of the United States, Representatives in Congress, the Executive and Judicial officers of a State, or the members of the Legislature thereof, is denied to any of the male inhabitants of such State, being twenty-one years of age, and citizens of the United States, or in any way abridged, except for participation in rebellion, or other crime, the basis of representation therein shall be reduced in the proportion which the number of such male citizens shall bear to the whole number of male citizens twenty-one years of age in such State.
3. No person shall be a Senator or Representative in Congress, or elector of President and Vice-President, or hold any office, civil or military, under the United States, or under any State, who, having previously taken an oath, as a member of Congress, or as an officer of the United States, or as a member of any State legislature, or as an executive or judicial officer of any State, to support the Constitution of the United States, shall have engaged in insurrection or rebellion against the same, or given aid or comfort to the enemies thereof. But Congress may by a

vote of two-thirds of each House, remove such disability.

4. The validity of the public debt of the United States, authorized by law, including debts incurred for payment of pensions and bounties for services in suppressing insurrection or rebellion, shall not be questioned. But neither the United States nor any State shall assume or pay any debt or obligation incurred in aid of insurrection or rebellion against the United States, or any claim for the loss or emancipation of any slave; but all such debts, obligations and claims shall be held illegal and void.

5. The Congress shall have power to enforce, by appropriate legislation, the provisions of this article.

## Amendment 15—Race No Bar to Vote. Ratified 2/3/1870.

1. The right of citizens of the United States to vote shall not be denied or abridged by the United States or by any State on account of race, color, or previous condition of servitude.

2. The Congress shall have power to enforce this article by appropriate legislation.

## Amendment 16—Status of Income Tax Clarified. Ratified 2/3/1913.

The Congress shall have power to lay and collect taxes on incomes, from whatever source derived, without apportionment among the several States, and without regard to any census or enumeration.

## Amendment 17—Senators Elected by Popular Vote. Ratified 4/8/1913.

The Senate of the United States shall be composed of two Senators from each State, elected by the people thereof, for six years; and each Senator shall have one vote. The electors in each State shall have the qualifications requisite for electors of the most numerous branch of the State legislatures.

When vacancies happen in the representation of any State in the Senate, the executive authority of such State shall issue writs of election to fill such vacancies: Provided, That the legislature of any State may empower the executive thereof to make temporary appointments until the people fill the vacancies by election as the legislature may direct.

This amendment shall not be so construed as to affect the election or term of any Senator chosen before it becomes valid as part of the Constitution.

## Amendment 18—Liquor Abolished. Ratified 1/16/1919. Repealed by Amendment 21, 12/5/1933.

1. After one year from the ratification of this article the manufacture, sale, or transportation of intoxicating liquors within, the importation thereof into, or the exportation thereof from the United States and all territory subject to the jurisdiction thereof for beverage purposes is hereby prohibited.

2. The Congress and the several States shall have concurrent power to enforce this article by appropriate legislation.

3. This article shall be inoperative unless it shall have been ratified as an amendment to the Constitution by the legislatures

of the several States, as provided in the Constitution, within seven years from the date of the submission hereof to the States by the Congress.

## Amendment 19—Women's Suffrage. Ratified 8/18/1920.

The right of citizens of the United States to vote shall not be denied or abridged by the United States or by any State on account of sex.

Congress shall have power to enforce this article by appropriate legislation.

## Amendment 20—Presidential, Congressional Terms. Ratified 1/23/1933.

1. The terms of the President and Vice President shall end at noon on the 20th day of January, and the terms of Senators and Representatives at noon on the 3d day of January, of the years in which such terms would have ended if this article had not been ratified; and the terms of their successors shall then begin.
2. The Congress shall assemble at least once in every year, and such meeting shall begin at noon on the 3d day of January, unless they shall by law appoint a different day.
3. If, at the time fixed for the beginning of the term of the President, the President elect shall have died, the Vice President elect shall become President. If a President shall not have been chosen before the time fixed for the beginning of his term, or if the President elect shall have failed to qualify, then the Vice President elect shall act as President until a President shall

have qualified; and the Congress may by law provide for the case wherein neither a President elect nor a Vice President elect shall have qualified, declaring who shall then act as President, or the manner in which one who is to act shall be selected, and such person shall act accordingly until a President or Vice President shall have qualified.

4. The Congress may by law provide for the case of the death of any of the persons from whom the House of Representatives may choose a President whenever the right of choice shall have devolved upon them, and for the case of the death of any of the persons from whom the Senate may choose a Vice President whenever the right of choice shall have devolved upon them.
5. Sections 1 and 2 shall take effect on the 15th day of October following the ratification of this article.
6. This article shall be inoperative unless it shall have been ratified as an amendment to the Constitution by the legislatures of three-fourths of the several States within seven years from the date of its submission.

## Amendment 21—Amendment 18 Repealed. Ratified 12/5/1933.

1. The eighteenth article of amendment to the Constitution of the United States is hereby repealed.
2. The transportation or importation into any State, Territory, or possession of the United States for delivery or use therein of intoxicating liquors, in violation of the laws thereof, is hereby prohibited.

3. The article shall be inoperative unless it shall have been ratified as an amendment to the Constitution by conventions in the several States, as provided in the Constitution, within seven years from the date of the submission hereof to the States by the Congress.

## Amendment 22—Presidential Term Limits. Ratified 2/27/1951.

1. No person shall be elected to the office of the President more than twice, and no person who has held the office of President, or acted as President, for more than two years of a term to which some other person was elected President shall be elected to the office of the President more than once. But this Article shall not apply to any person holding the office of President, when this Article was proposed by the Congress, and shall not prevent any person who may be holding the office of President, or acting as President, during the term within which this Article becomes operative from holding the office of President or acting as President during the remainder of such term.
2. This article shall be inoperative unless it shall have been ratified as an amendment to the Constitution by the legislatures of three-fourths of the several States within seven years from the date of its submission to the States by the Congress.

## Amendment 23—Presidential Vote for District of Columbia. Ratified 3/29/1961.

1. The District constituting the seat of Government of the United States shall appoint in such manner as the Congress may direct: A number of electors of President and Vice President equal to the whole number of Senators and Representatives in Congress to which the District would be entitled if it were a State, but in no event more than the least populous State; they shall be in addition to those appointed by the States, but they shall be considered, for the purposes of the election of President and Vice President, to be electors appointed by a State; and they shall meet in the District and perform such duties as provided by the twelfth article of amendment.
2. The Congress shall have power to enforce this article by appropriate legislation.

## Amendment 24—Poll Tax Barred. Ratified 1/23/1964.

1. The right of citizens of the United States to vote in any primary or other election for President or Vice President, for electors for President or Vice President, or for Senator or Representative in Congress, shall not be denied or abridged by the United States or any State by reason of failure to pay any poll tax or other tax.
2. The Congress shall have power to enforce this article by appropriate legislation.

## Amendment 25—Presidential Disability and Succession. Ratified 2/10/1967.

1. In case of the removal of the President from office or of his death or resignation, the Vice President shall become President.
2. Whenever there is a vacancy in the office of the Vice President, the President shall nominate a Vice President who shall take office upon confirmation by a majority vote of both Houses of Congress.
3. Whenever the President transmits to the President pro tempore of the Senate and the Speaker of the House of Representatives his written declaration that he is unable to discharge the powers and duties of his office, and until he transmits to them a written declaration to the contrary, such powers and duties shall be discharged by the Vice President as Acting President.
4. Whenever the Vice President and a majority of either the principal officers of the executive departments or of such other body as Congress may by law provide, transmit to the President pro tempore of the Senate and the Speaker of the House of Representatives their written declaration that the President is unable to discharge the powers and duties of his office, the Vice President shall immediately assume the powers and duties of the office as Acting President.

Thereafter, when the President transmits to the President pro tempore of the Senate and the Speaker of the House of Representatives his written declaration that no inability exists, he shall resume the powers and duties of his office unless the Vice President and a majority of either the principal officers of the executive department or of such other body as Congress may by law provide, transmit within four days to the President pro tempore of the Senate and the Speaker of the House of Representatives their written declaration that the President is unable to discharge the powers and duties of his office. Thereupon Congress shall decide the issue, assembling within forty eight hours for that purpose if not in session. If the Congress, within twenty one days after receipt of the latter written declaration, or, if Congress is not in session, within twenty one days after Congress is required to assemble, determines by two thirds vote of both Houses that the President is unable to discharge the powers and duties of his office, the Vice President shall continue to discharge the same as Acting President; otherwise, the President shall resume the powers and duties of his office.

## Amendment 26—Voting Age Set to 18 Years. Ratified 7/1/1971.

1. The right of citizens of the United States, who are eighteen years of age or older, to vote shall not be denied or abridged by the United States or by any State on account of age.
2. The Congress shall have power to enforce this article by appropriate legislation.

## Amendment 27—Limiting Congressional Pay Increases. Ratified 5/7/1992.

No law, varying the compensation for the services of the Senators and Representatives, shall take effect, until an election of Representatives shall have intervened.

# Acknowledgments

A work of this type is not one that is accomplished alone. First, to my colleagues Dr. Jim Roberts and Dr. Toni Marzotto (former and current chair of the Political Science Department at Towson University, respectively), for giving a graduate student an opportunity to teach a course almost ten years ago, thank you! To my colleagues in the TU POSC department, thank you for your kindness and professionalism. A special thank-you to my friends and mentors Dr. Allison McCartney and Dr. Michael Korzi; your dedication to service and academic scholarship is an inspiration to me.

To my friends, personal and political, I am humbled by your love, loyalty, and care. This book has occurred only because you have blessed me with your insight, intelligence, and honest questions of who we are as a nation, how we got here, and whether we can recover the greatness of America.

To my family: God has given me the greatest parents. My two brothers and I are blessed beyond imagining. My hope is that we fulfill the promise given to us by our parents, Pastor and Evangelist Tom and Winnie Campbell.

A big thank-you to all the people at Cognella Academic Publishing (Sarah, Jess, Chelsey, and others) for turning this dream into a reality. Your hard work, professionalism, and dedication to this project have been incredible. I look forward to more collaborations in the future.

# Credits

CPSIA information can be obtained
at www.ICGtesting.com
Printed in the USA
LVOW02s0522130116

470334LV00001B/1/P

9 781631 890